CRIMES OF THE CENTURIES

CRIMES OF THE CENTURIES

Notorious Crimes, Criminals, and Criminal Trials in American History

VOLUME 1: A–G

Steven Chermak and Frankie Y. Bailey
Editors

An Imprint of ABC-CLIO, LLC
Santa Barbara, California • Denver, Colorado

Library of Congress Cataloging-in-Publication Data

Crimes of the centuries : notorious crimes, criminals, and criminal trials in American history / Steven Chermak and Frankie Y. Bailey, editors.
     volumes cm
  Includes bibliographical references and index.
  ISBN 978-1-61069-593-0 (set : alk. paper) — ISBN 978-1-61069-594-7 (ebk)
1. Crime—United States—Case studies. 2. Criminals—United States—Case studies. 3. Trials—United States.   I. Chermak, Steven M.
  II. Bailey, Frankie Y.
  HV6783.C88 2016
  364.10973—dc23   2015022854

ISBN: 978-1-61069-593-0
EISBN: 978-1-61069-594-7

20 19 18 17 16   1 2 3 4 5

This book is also available on the World Wide Web as an eBook.
Visit www.abc-clio.com for details.

ABC-CLIO
An Imprint of ABC-CLIO, LLC

ABC-CLIO, LLC
130 Cremona Drive, P.O. Box 1911
Santa Barbara, California 93116-1911

This book is printed on acid-free paper ∞
Manufactured in the United States of America

Contents

Volume 1

Volume 2

Volume 3

Primary Documents

Preface

Crimes of the Centuries: Notorious Crimes, Criminals, and Criminal Trials in American History includes many of the major crimes that have occurred in the United States over the past 400 years. The entries are organized alphabetically across the three-volume set. Cases included were not chosen at random; we attempted to identify 500 of the most celebrated and well-known crime events that have occurred in the United States. We tried to choose a sample of crimes from many different historic eras, but it is not surprising that many of those selected occurred during the past 30 years. As media technology and social media have changed and expanded, it appears as though more and more cases have come to be defined as notorious or celebrated.

The purpose of this encyclopedia is to help secondary school students and general readers understand the most notorious and historically significant crimes, criminals, and criminal trials that have shaped America since its founding. Aside from the enormous popular appeal of the cases selected, the encyclopedia provides curricular benefits for students in Social Studies and English classes, in which students frequently write research papers on sensational and infamous crimes and trials in U.S. history, such as the Salem Witch Trials, Prohibition Era Gangsters, and Sacco and Vanzetti. This encyclopedia also supports the National Standard's curriculum mandate that students should be able to "describe historical and contemporary events and practices that illustrate the absence or breakdown of the rule of law."

The reader will notice that many contributors have included a "sidebar" to accompany his or her case. These sidebars provide additional or related information that will assist the reader in placing the case in context. Some examples of the sidebars include additional details about a specific aspect of a trial or case, a timeline of events, how a case was presented in the media or popular culture, or why a case raised interesting legal questions or caused notable social impacts.

With each entry, the contributors also provide a short list of books and articles related to the case. Since each entry is relatively short (about 1,200 words), contributors had to make tough choices about what information was critical to include in the description of the case, and, naturally, some elements of a case had to be excluded. The list of printed and electronic works offered in the bibliography for each entry will provide the opportunity for readers intrigued by the case to seek out additional information sources. In addition, each entry includes a short list of related entries that the reader might want to read for comparison.

Similarly, we include a general bibliography that provides additional books and materials related to many of these important cases. Readers will be able to examine these materials for additional context and a broader understanding of the impacts of these cases. We also include a list of general topics and related entries that will allow the reader to read multiple entries covering the same topic, such as serial killers, mass murderers, women killers, and terrorists. The introduction puts the broad topic of American crime into context for the reader, a chronology allows readers to easily trace cases across time, and a detailed subject index offers readers access to important information within entries.

Acknowledgments

We would like to first thank the contributors. As you might imagine, because of the number of entries that are included here, it was quite difficult managing the work flow. The contributors were extraordinarily helpful and understanding, and really made our job quite easy by turning in very strong first drafts. They were also very responsive to requests for changes and additional fact-finding. We are particularly appreciative of those contributors that we were able to count on for additional work as new entries became available and they were able to submit these contributions in a very short amount of time.

The staff at ABC-CLIO were just fantastic to work with and although it is difficult to mention all by name, we did want to specifically name a few. Thanks to Michael Millman for encouraging us to take on the project, supporting us, and being patient with our multiple requests for more information and clarification. We were assisted by two Development Editors on this project, and they were both terrific and very patient. Thanks to Stephen Gutierrez for his help at the beginning of the project and for John Wagner's help through the middle and end. Thanks to Barbara Patterson, our Project Coordinator, who also responded quickly—even when we continued to make the same request.

Introduction

How does a crime become notorious? Since the 19th century, when the "penny press" made newspapers available to urban working-class readers, crime and violence have been mainstays of news reporting. But even before the birth of the mass media, some crimes got people talking. Throughout history, what famous crimes have had in common is that the event, its aftermath, or the people involved in it capture public attention and the public imagination in some way. During four centuries of American history, the crimes that have become notorious have shared certain characteristics. Such characteristics are consistent with long-held notions of "newsworthiness." Serious crimes, such as murder, terrorism, and rape, dominate daily news offerings. Crimes that are extraordinary or unique—those least likely to occur—are mostly likely to get coverage in the news. It is not just the event itself that is important, but who is involved—demographics such as race, gender, age, and occupation all contribute to news interest in a crime story. There are other factors, such as historical timing; events tied to larger social, cultural, or political concerns; and events that test the effectiveness of the criminal justice system. Examining the social contexts in which these crimes have occurred provides us with windows into our past. This is important because these crimes have played an important role in shaping American perceptions of crime and justice.

The notoriety of certain crimes means that they enter the public consciousness. They may take on symbolic significance and be put to use in social, economic, and political debates. They are written about, discussed, and reworked into books, films, and songs. Past cases may even be used to make a statement about a current situation. For example, playwright Arthur Miller looked back at an unusual event that occurred in colonial New England and found an analogy for what was occurring in the United States in the 1950s. In 1692, Salem, Massachusetts, experienced what is now often described as "mass hysteria." The bizarre physical "afflictions" displayed by several adolescent girls and their accusations served as the catalyst for a witch-hunt conducted before magistrates in a court of law. Twenty people were convicted of witchcraft and executed. In his play, *The Crucible* (1953), Miller used the witch trials as an allegory for the 1950s congressional hearings intended to root out Communists and Communist sympathizers.

Miller was asserting that mass hysteria is not confined to one historical period. Fear and uncertainty in a changing world has led Americans to search for menacing "others" to blame for their own troubles and for societal woes. This is one of the themes that we will see being played out through the centuries in the cases and events in these volumes. In Salem in 1692, during the New York City Draft Riots of 1863, with the birth of the Ku Klux Klan in the post–Civil War South, during the "Red Scare" of the 1920s and blacklisting of the 1950s, and in the post-9/11 world, fear and hatred have been catalysts for a unique brand of

American conflict and violence that has challenged our democratic ideals.

These notorious crimes have been subjected to multiple interpretations. How such crimes are interpreted often changes over time, reflecting the increasing ability of certain groups to participate in the discussion. In the 20th century, feminist historians and social scientists looked back at the Salem witch trials through the lens of gender. The majority of the accused "witches" in Salem were women. These scholars view the trials as a display of male patriarchal power and misogyny. The trials also have been used to explore the intersections of race, class, and gender in colonial America. What did it mean that Tituba, the first woman to be accused, was a Native American slave from the West Indies who was owned by a minister? How this question has been answered during the intervening centuries has reflected evolving sensibilities.

Aside from their social meaning, some notorious crimes fascinate us because of their sensational nature. Since "Jack the Ripper" terrorized the residents of London's Whitechapel district in 1888, stories about serial killers have been in the news. In the modern era, the story of the intrepid police detective who draws on all the forensic resources available as he or she tracks a monstrous, but sometimes brilliant, human predator has become a popular plotline in books, movies, and TV crime shows. The visibility of the serial killer in the news and in entertainment perpetuates a situation in which the notoriety of individual perpetrators and the sensational claims made about a type of crime distort public perceptions. As frightening as they are, serial killers are not common. However, serial killers are much more likely than more typical criminals to become famous. Serial killers, because of the number of victims, their methods and abilities to evade capture, and their willingness to engage in bizarre behaviors (e.g., "Dracula" killers and cannibals), achieve even higher profiles.

But even with the distortions about these killers, their cases can be used to examine how society and the criminal justice system function. The victims chosen by serial killers are often those who are marginalized in society (e.g., prostitutes). Serial killers may continue to operate over a long period of time because their victims are not missed or their murders are given limited attention until a pattern emerges. The ability of some serial killers to operate under the radar has led to a discussion about the related "invisibility" of victims, such as homeless teenagers and women of color in poor communities. The response of law enforcement to these victims often becomes a part of how these cases are viewed and used in discussions about crime and justice.

If some cases become notorious because of the type of crime, other cases become notorious because of the people involved. People who are in the public spotlight, such as politicians, business tycoons, professional athletes, and Hollywood celebrities, are automatically newsworthy when they become the victim of a crime or an alleged offender. The entries in this book include a long line of public figures who achieve everlasting notoriety in the morgue or in the courtroom. These cases have particular fascination because of the opportunity the public has to see inside the exclusive worlds in which these people live. The wealth and privilege of these worlds may be equated with decadence. The people involved may be viewed with little empathy when they experience a downfall.

What many cases involving public figures illustrate is how perceptions of criminality may be grounded in beliefs about morality. Historically, social reformers have struggled to gain mainstream acceptance for their beliefs about moral or "good" behavior. These reformers have at various times turned their attention to the abolition of slavery, the reform of "fallen women" (prostitutes), temperance, child-saving, and a variety of activities aimed at "cleaning up" cities and improving the conditions of those who had found their way into the criminal justice system. The "moral crusades" of social reformers have often brought them into conflict with those who hold different views. The reformers themselves have sometimes achieved notoriety for their activities. Temperance crusader Carrie Nation became famous by smashing up saloons. Anthony Comstock, postal inspector and agent of the New York Society for the Suppression of Vice, appeared in several cases in these volumes as a zealous foe of "deviance" and "depravity."

But there are other cases involving public figures that are famous not because they were the focus of debates about morality but because the event shocked the nation. The assassination or attempted assassination of a president is a moment of crisis requiring a transition of leadership. A violent attack on any political or civic leader challenges the ideal of nonviolent discourse. As the entries about assassinations illustrate, a common aspect of these cases is the debate about whether the assassin or would-be assassin acted alone or was part of a larger conspiracy. The sanity of the known assassin often becomes a matter for debate in a courtroom and in the public sphere.

Questioning the sanity of the offender is a fairly common theme across categories of famous cases. In domestic homicides in which the offender kills an intimate partner, spouse, child, or other family member, the contradiction between expected care and nurturing and the lethal actions of the offender are stark. In the popular dichotomy, the offender must be "mad" or "evil." Cases involving women who kill their husbands or children are sensationalized because such homicides are at odds with gendered assumptions about women and violence. Cases involving husbands who kill become notorious when their wives are perceived as innocent and unsuspecting victims of duplicity and violence by men they loved and trusted. In the courtroom, the sanity of the domestic/family killer becomes the subject of expert testimony about whether the offender met the test of legal insanity at the time of the offense. Did he or she know the difference between right and wrong? Was he or she able to control his or her behavior?

In the United States, women are rarely sentenced to death and are much less likely to commit murder compared to men. The women who have been executed or who are presently on death row prompt discussion about gender bias (against men), chivalry (toward women), and the characteristics of those women who do end up being sentenced to death. In fact, the use of the death penalty in the case of women remains controversial. But this debate about executing women is part of a larger debate about the use of the death penalty in the United States.

Historically, opponents of the death penalty have questioned the morality of the sentence. In recent years, botched executions by lethal injection (supposed to be a more humane way of administering death) have spurred calls for a moratorium on executions in the United States. But the discovery that wrongful convictions have resulted in innocent men being on death row has been an even more powerful weapon for opponents of the death penalty. The use of DNA has allowed advocates to revisit the cases of some death row inmates who claim they are innocent. These cases are at the top of the hierarchy of cases taken on by those active in the "innocence movement." In law schools and journalism schools across the country and in nonprofit organizations, advocates reinvestigate the cases of prisoners who they believe were wrongfully convicted.

Challenges to errors in the criminal justice process have led to a number of landmark legal decisions by the U.S. Supreme Court. These decisions often revolve around the rights granted to citizens in the U.S. Constitution. Among these cases are those that have limited the powers of criminal justice authorities when investigating crimes, such as *Miranda v. Arizona* and *Mapp v. Ohio*. In a number

of the more famous cases, the Court attempted to define "citizen." For example, in the Dred Scott Decision (1857), after reviewing the history of Africans and their descendants in the United States, the Court declared slaves were not citizens and not entitled to the protections enjoyed by free people. In *Ex parte Crow Dog* (1883), the Court decided the federal government had no legal standing to intervene in a murder case involving a Native American victim and offender. Congress responded by enacting the Major Crimes Act (1885), which gave the federal government jurisdiction over felony offenses committed on reservations. The landmark legal cases decided by the Supreme Court reflect the tensions of the eras in which they are decided. In the 20th century, the Supreme Court moved steadily toward expanding due process protections to defendants.

At the same time, other cases in these volumes illustrate the ongoing challenge to repressive laws and policies. Cases such as Nat Turner's Rebellion (1831) or John Brown's raid on Harpers Ferry (1859) inspire difficult questions about the use of violence in a liberation struggle. Other cases raise questions about the tactics used by state and federal governments in responding to protestors and freedom fighters. For example, COINTELPRO, the counterintelligence program that existed in the Federal Bureau of Investigation (FBI) under J. Edgar Hoover, involved the surveillance of a long list of American citizens and the infiltration of organizations deemed subversive. The program was dismantled once it came to light, but the activities of the FBI played a crucial role in a number of the political cases of the 1960s.

But aside from the notorious cases that are remembered because of their importance in the political and social debates about their eras, there are other cases that are famous because they fit into recognized genres of crime storytelling. These are the stories of western outlaws and bank robberies and gangsters. These are the "bad men" and "good bad men" whose legends never die as they move from dime novels and true detective magazines into films and television. These are the "men with guns" found on the Western Frontier of the 19th century and in American cities during Prohibition. The challenge as we study their crimes is to distinguish myth from fact and understand who these men (and occasionally women) were and what they can tell us about crime and justice. Why do we make folk heroes of outlaws? What characteristics do they have that we value in American culture?

These volumes also include the cases of those less easily romanticized by the American mainstream. Mass murderers become notorious because of the number of people that they kill and the ruthless manner in which they go about carrying out their crime. Mass murderers who kill children have been especially reviled. But one troubling fact is that some mass murderers have been children who killed children. These school shootings have led to investigations in search of warning signals and policy changes. The mass murders carried out with guns have been incorporated into the debate about gun control.

Across categories, the cases in these volumes provide us with important information about the tensions, conflicts, and beliefs that define us. The durability of famous cases in the American consciousness tells us there is much we can learn by studying them.

Guide to Related Topics

Acquaintance Homicides

Bickford, Maria, Murder of (1845)

Bishop, Amy (1965–)

Fisher, Amy (1974)

Gunness, Belle (1859–c. 1908)

Jewett, Helen, Murder of (1836)

Judd, Winnie Ruth (1905–1998)

Kent, Bobby, Murder of (1993)

Klimek, Tillie (1876–1936)

Knox, Amanda, Murder Trials of (2009–2015)

Le, Annie, Murder of (2009)

Levin, Jennifer, Murder of (August 26, 1986)

Levy, Chandra, Disappearance of (2001–2002)

Manhattan Well (NY), Murder at (1800)

Mitchell, Alice (1872–1898)

Nowak, Lisa (1963–)

Quinn, Roseann, Murder of (1973)

Reinert, Susan, Murder of (June 22, 1979)

Rockefeller, Clark (1961–)

Sharer, Shanda, Murder of (1992)

Shelton, Lee (1865–1912) and Billy Lyons (1864–1895)

Todd, Crystal, Murder of (November 16, 1991)

White, Stanford, Murder of (1907–1908)

Zamora, Diane (1978–), and David Graham (1977–)

Arson/Fire

Cocoanut Grove Nightclub Fire (Boston) (1942)

Detroit Halloween Fires (1972–)

Gonzales, Julio (1954–)

Station Nightclub Fire (West Warwick, RI)
(February 20, 2003)

Triangle Shirtwaist Factory Fire (1911)

Assassinations

Cermak, Anton Joseph, Assassination of
(February 15, 1933)

Evers, Medgar, Assassination of (June 12, 1963)

Ford, Gerald, Assassination Attempts on (1975)

Fromme, Lynette "Squeaky" (1948–)

Garfield, James, Assassination of (July 2, 1881)

Hinckley, John, Jr. (1955–)

Kennedy, John F., Assassination of (November 22, 1963)

Kennedy, Robert F. "Bobby,"
Assassination of (1968)

King, Martin Luther, Jr., Assassination of (April 4, 1968)

Lincoln, Abraham, Assassination of (April 14, 1865)

Malcolm X, Assassination of (February 21, 1965)

McKinley, William, Assassination of (September 6, 1901)

Milk, Harvey, Assassination of (November 27, 1978)

Prendergast, Patrick Eugene (1868–1894)

Surratt, Mary (1823–1865)

Wallace, George, Attempted Assassination of
(May 15, 1972)

Bank Robbers

Cassidy, Butch (1866–1908)

Crime and Medicine

Hazzard, Linda (1867–1938)
Kevorkian, Jack (1928–2011)

Crime and Sports

Armstrong, Lance (1971–)
Baseball and Steroids (1980–)
Black Sox Scandal (1919)
Bryant, Kobe, Rape Accusation against (June 30, 2003)
Carruth, Rae (1974–)
Glen Ridge (NJ) Rape Case (March 1, 1989)
Muhammad Ali Draft Case (1964–1971)
Robinson, Jackie, Court-Martial of (1944)
Rose, Pete, Gambling Scandal (1989)
Sandusky, Gerald "Jerry" A. (1944–)
Simpson, O. J. (1947–)
Vick, Michael, Dogfighting Case (2007)

Crime and the Military

Abu Ghraib Prisoner Abuse Scandal (Iraq) (2003–2004)
Bales, Robert (1973–)
Brownsville (TX) Affair (August 13, 1906)
Massie, Thalia (1911–1963)
Mitchell, Billy, Court-Martial of (1925)
My Lai Massacre (March 16, 1968)
Wirz, Captain Henry (1823–1865)
Zamora, Diane (1978–), and David Graham (1977–)

Crimes against Humanity

Dakota Conflict Trials (1862)
Japanese American Internment Camps (1942–1945)
Peltier, Leonard (1944–)
Sand Creek (CO) Massacre (November 29, 1864)
Wounded Knee Incident (SD) (February 27–May 8, 1973)
Wounded Knee Massacre (SD) (December 29, 1890)

Death Penalty

Alcala, Rodney (1943–)
Allen, Wanda Jean (1959–2001)
Baker, Lena (1900–1945)
Bagwell, Dennis (1963–2005)
Barfield, Velma (1932–1984)
Becker, Lieutenant Charles (1870–1915)
Becker–Rosenthal Murder Trials (1912)
Buenoano, Judy (1943–1998)
Bundy, Ted (1946–1989)
Celia (a Slave), Murder Trial of (1855)
Cherry Hill Murder (Albany, NY) (May 7, 1827)

Cheshire (CT) Home Invasion Murders (2007)
Chessman, Caryl (1921–1960)
Chino Hills (CA) Murders (June 4, 1983)
Christian, Virginia (1895–1912)
Cole, Tiffany (1981–)
Coo, Eva (1889–1935)
Copeland, Ray (1914–1993), and Faye Copeland (1921–2003)
Crowley, Francis "Two Gun" (1912–1932)
Dyer, Mary Barrett, Execution of (1660)
Eubanks, Susan (1964–)
Gaskins, Donald "Pee Wee" (1933–1991)
Gilmore, Gary (1940–1977)
Graham, Barbara (1923–1955)
Hahn, Anna Marie (1906–1938)
Harp Boys (1770s–1800s)
Hill, Joe (1879–1915)
Judd, Winnie Ruth (1905–1998)
Lewis, Teresa (1969–2010)
Lonely Hearts Killers (1947–1949)
Lucas, Henry Lee (1936–2001)
Martinsville (VA) Seven (1949–1951)
Moore, Blanche Taylor (1933–)
Ocuish, Hannah (1774–1786)
Parker, Marian, Murder of (1927)
Pomeroy, Jesse (1859–1932)
Prendergast, Patrick Eugene (1868–1894)
Rosenberg, Julius and Ethel Rosenberg Espionage Case (1950–1953)
Ross, Michael Bruce (1961–2005)
Routier, Darlie Lynn (1970–)
Sacco, Ferdinando Nicola (1891–1927) and Bartolomeo Vanzetti (1888–1927)
Smith, Edgar (1934–)
Sonnier, Elmo Patrick (1951–1984)
Spooner, Bathsheba (1746–1778)
Starkweather, Charles, and Caril Ann Fugate, Murder Spree of (1957)
Tucker, Karla Faye (1959–1998)
Walters, Christina S. (1978–)
Wesson Family Massacre (2004)
Wuornos, Aileen (1956–2002)

Domestic/Family Homicides

Allen, Wanda Jean (1959–2001)
Bishop, Amy (1965–)
Borden, Lizzie (1860–1927)
Brando, Christian (1958–2008)

Ray Allen Gang (1974–1980)
Shakur, Sanyika (1963–)
St. Clair, Stephanie (1886–1969)
Tri-State Gang (1930s)
Walters, Christina S. (1978–)
Westies (1970s–1980s)

Hate Crimes
Amedure, Scott, Murder of (1995)
Brandon, Teena, Murder of (1993)
Byrd, James, Jr., Murder of (1998)
Chin, Vincent Jen, Murder of (1982)
Clementi, Tyler, Death of (2010)
Howard Beach Case (1986)
Shepard, Matthew, Murder of 1998)

Hijacking
Cooper, D. B., Airplane Hijacking (November 24, 1971)
Eastern Air Lines Hijacking (1970)
TWA Flight 800, Crash of (1996)
United Airlines Flight 553, Crash of
   (December 8, 1972)

Hoax
Smith, Susan (1971–)
Stuart, Charles (1959–1990)
Wilbanks, Jennifer, Disappearance of (2005)

Juveniles
Bosket, Willie (1962–)
Gates, Wyley (1969–)
Ocuish, Hannah (1774–1786)
Pomeroy, Jesse (1859–1932)
Sharer, Shanda, Murder of (1992)
Show, Laurie, Murder of (1991)
Tate, Lionel (1987–)

Kidnappings
Dugard, Jaycee, Kidnapping of (1991)
Getty, John Paul, III, Kidnapping of (1973)
Hearst, Patricia, Kidnapping of (1974)
Lindbergh Kidnapping Case (1932)
Mackle, Barbara Jane, Kidnapping of (1968)
O'Connell, John, Jr., Kidnapping of (1933)
Rockefeller, Clark (1961–)
Ross, Charley, Kidnapping of (1874)
Sinatra, Frank, Jr., Kidnapping of (1963)
Smart, Elizabeth, Kidnapping of (2002)

Labor Relations
B & O Railroad Strike (1877)
Haymarket Square Riot/Bombing (Chicago) (1886)
Haywood, William "Big Bill," Trial of (1907)
Hoffa, Jimmy, Disappearance of (July 30, 1975)
Molly Maguires
Pullman Strike (1894)
Silkwood, Karen, Death of (1974)

Landmark Legal Cases
Alien and Sedition Acts (1798)
Anthony, Susan B., Trial of (1873)
Cherokee Nation v. Georgia, Forced
   Removal of Indian Tribes (1831)
Dred Scott Decision (1857)
Ex parte Crow Dog (1883)
Ferguson v. City of Charleston (2001)
Loving v. Virginia (1967)
Mapp, Dollree, Case of (1961)
Miranda, Ernesto (1941–1976)
Plessy v. Ferguson (1896)
Rideout Marital Rape Case (1978)
Snyder v. Phelps (2011)
Scopes Monkey Trial (July 10–21, 1925)
Scottsboro Boys (1931)
Sheppard, Sam (1923–1970)
Shipp, Sheriff Joseph, Trial of (1909)
Skokie (IL) Case (1977–1978)
United States v. One Book Called Ulysses (1933)
Zenger, John Peter, Sedition Trial of (1735)

Liberation Struggles
Amistad Slave Ship Case (1839)
Attica Prison Riot (1971)
Black Liberation Army (BLA) (c. 1970–1981)
Boston Massacre (March 5, 1770)
Chicago Seven (1968)
Davis, Angela, Trial of (1972)
Fugitive Slave Laws (1793, 1850)
Harpers Ferry (VA), Raid on
   (October 17,1859)
Jackson, George, Death of (1971)
Mann Act (1910)
Mariel Boatlift (1980)
Molly Maguires
Nat Turner's Rebellion (1831)
New York Slave Conspiracy (1741)
Pratt, Geronimo (1947–2011)

Race and Ethnicity Controversies

Atlanta Race Riot (1906)

Branion, Dr. John (c. 1926–1990)

Brawley, Tawana (1972–)

Brownsville (TX) Affair (August 13, 1906)

Byrd, James, Jr., Murder of (1998)

Detroit Riot (1943)

Detroit Riot (1967)

East St. Louis Race Riot (1917) and Chicago Race Riot (1919)

Frank, Leo (1884–1915)

Franklin, Joseph Paul (1950–2013)

Hampton, Fred, Shooting of (December 3, 1969)

Harlem Riot (March 19–20, 1935)

Harlem Riot (August 1–2, 1943)

Hawkins, Yusef, Murder of (1989)

Howard Beach Case (1986)

Jena Six (Jena, LA) (2006)

King, Martin Luther, Jr., Assassination of (April 4, 1968)

King, Rodney, Beating of (1991)

Malcolm X, Assassination of (February 21, 1965)

Martin, Trayvon, Death of (February 26, 2012)

Martinsville (VA) Seven (1949–1951)

McDuffie, Arthur, Death of (1979)

Mississippi Burning Case (1964)

Neal, Claude, Lynching of (1934)

Omaha Two (1970)

Pratt, Geronimo (1947–2011)

Shipp, Sheriff Joseph, Trial of (1909)

16th Street Baptist Church Bombing (Birmingham, AL) (September 15, 1963)

Sleepy Lagoon Murder Case (Los Angeles) (1942)

Smith, Susan (1971–)

Stuart, Charles (1959–1990)

Sweet, Ossian (1895–1960)

Till, Emmett, Murder of (1955)

Zebra Murders (1972–1974)

Rape

Alcala, Rodney (1943–)

Bianchi, Kenneth (1951–) and Angelo Buono (1934–2002)

Big Dan Gang Rape Case (1983–1984)

Bryant, Kobe, Rape Accusation against (June 30, 2003)

Celia (a Slave), Murder Trial of (1855)

Central Park Jogger Case (1989)

Chessman, Caryl (1921–1960)

Dugard, Jaycee, Kidnapping of (1991)

Glen Ridge (NJ) Rape Case (March 1, 1989)

Goudeau, Mark (1964–)

Louima, Abner, Sexual Assault of (Brooklyn, NY) (1997)

Martinsville (VA) Seven (1949–1951)

Miranda, Ernesto (1941–1976)

Rideout Marital Rape Case (1978)

Sonnier, Elmo Patrick (1951–1984)

Smith, William Kennedy, Rape Case (1991)

Stephenson, David Curtiss

Steubenville (OH) Rape Case (August 12, 2012)

Worthington, Christa, Murder of (January 6, 2002)

Religion

Beecher, Henry Ward, Adultery Trial of (1875)

Carthage Conspiracy Trial (1844)

Catholic Priest Child Sex Abuse Scandal (1950s–2000s)

Frank, Leo (1884–1915)

Hall–Mills Murder Trial (1922–1926)

Hofmann, Mark William (1954–)

Hutchinson, Anne, Trial of (1637–1638)

McPherson, Aimee Semple (1890–1944)

O'Hair, Madalyn Murray, Disappearance of (1995)

School Crimes

Amish School Shootings (Lancaster County, PA) (October 2, 2006)

Bath (MI) School Massacre (1927)

Clementi, Tyler, Death of (2010)

Columbine High School Shootings (Littleton, CO) (April 20, 1999)

Dartmouth College Murders (January 27, 2001)

Florida A&M Hazing Death (November 19, 2011)

Gallaudet University Murders (2000–2001)

Harvard Medical College, Murder at (November 23, 1849)

Kent State Shootings (May 4, 1970)

Jackson State College (MS) Shootings (1970)

Jovin, Suzanne, Murder of (1998)

Lanza, Adam Peter (1992–2012)

Le, Annie, Murder of (2009)

Virginia Tech Massacre (April 16, 2007)

Weise, Jeffrey (1988–2005)

Serial Killers

Alcala, Rodney (1943–)

Armstrong, John Eric (1973–)

Ball, Joseph (1896–1938)

Barfield, Velma (1932–1984)

Berkowitz, David Richard (1953–)

Bianchi, Kenneth (1951–) and Angelo Buono (1934–2002)
Boston Strangler Murders (1962–1964)
Buenoano, Judy (1943–1998)
Bundy, Ted (1946–1989)
Carpenter, David (1930–)
Cleveland Torso Murders (1935–1938)
Copeland, Ray (1914–1993), and Faye Copeland (1921–2003)
Corona, Juan (1934–)
Cullen, Charles (1960–)
Cunanan, Andrew (1969–1997)
Dahmer, Jeffrey (1960–1994)
Edwards, Edward Wayne (1933–2011)
Fish, Albert (1870–1936)
Franklin, Joseph Paul (1950–2013)
Gacy, John Wayne (1942–1994)
Gaskins, Donald "Pee Wee" (1933–1991)
Gein, Ed (1906–1984)
Goudeau, Mark (1964–)
Gunness, Belle (1859–c. 1908)
Harp Boys (1770s–1800s)
Holmes, Dr. H.H. (1861–1896)
Hoyt, Waneta (1946–1998)
Jones, Genene (1950–)
Klimek, Tillie (1876–1936)
Lonely Hearts Killers (1947–1949)
Lucas, Henry Lee (1936–2001)
Puente, Dorothea (1929–2011)
Rader, Dennis (1945–)
Ramirez, Richard (1960–2013)
Reldan, Robert (1940–)
Ridgway, Gary Leon (1949–)
Ross, Michael Bruce (1961–2005)
Sherman, Lydia (1824–1878)
Sowell, Anthony (1959–)
Speck, Richard (1941–1991)
Toppan, Jane (1854–1938)
Watts, Carl "Coral" Eugene (1953–2007)
Zodiac Killer (1960s–)

Suicide
Foster, Vince, Death of (1993)
Heaven's Gate Mass Suicide (March 24–26, 1997)
Kevorkian, Jack (1928–2011)
Markoff, Philip (1986–2010)

Terrorism
Boston Marathon Bombings (April 15, 2013)

Kaczynski, Theodore John "Ted" (1942–)
Oklahoma City Bombing (April 19, 1995)
Rudolph, Eric (1966–)
September 11 Terrorist Attacks (2001)
World Trade Center Bombing (February 26, 1993)

Theft
Harris-Moore, Colton (1991–)
Isabella Stewart Gardner Museum Art Theft (1990)

Unsolved Cases
Black Dahlia Murder (1947)
Cleveland Torso Murders (1935–1938)
Cooper, D.B., Airplane Hijacking (November 24, 1971)
Grimes Sisters, Murder of (1956)
Jovin, Suzanne, Murder of (1998)
McElroy, Ken, Murder of (1981)
Oklahoma Girl Scout Killings (June 12, 1977)
Ramsey, JonBenét, Murder of (1996)
Reeves, George, Death of (1959)
Rogers, Mary, Murder of (1841)
Silkwood, Karen, Death of (1974)
Taylor, William Desmond, Murder of (1922)
Watson, Tina, Death of (2003)
Zodiac Killer (1960s–)

Victims and Vigilantes
Genovese, Catherine Susan "Kitty," Murder of (1964)
Goetz, Bernhard (1947–)

White-Collar Crimes
Abagnale, Frank, Jr. (1948–)
Bakker, Jim (1940–)
Boesky, Ivan, Insider Trading Scandal (1980s)
Enron Case (1985–2001)
Exxon Valdez Oil Spill (1989)
Helmsley, Leona (1920–2007)
Madoff, Bernard (1938–)
Mozilo, Angelo (1938–)
Ponzi, Charles (1882–1949)
Stewart, Martha, Insider Trading Case (2001–2004)

Women Killers
Allen, Wanda Jean (1959–2001)
Arias, Jodi (1980–)
Aron, Ruthann (1942–)
Baker, Lena (1900–1945)
Barfield, Velma (1932–1984)

Bishop, Amy (1965–)
Buenoano, Judy (1943–1998)
Bustamante, Alyssa (1994–)
Christian, Virginia (1895–1912)
Coo, Eva (1889–1935)
Crimmins, Alice, Murder Trials of (1968, 1971)
Eubanks, Susan (1964–)
Graham, Barbara (1923–1955)
Green, Debora (1951–)
Gunness, Belle (1859–c. 1908)
Hahn, Anna Marie (1906–1938)
Hughes, Francine (1947–)
Jones, Genene (1950–)
Judd, Winnie Ruth (1905–1998)
Klimek, Tillie (1876–1936)

Lewis, Teresa (1969–2010)
Longet, Claudine (1942–)
Moore, Blanche Taylor (1933–)
Ocuish, Hannah (1774–1786)
Puente, Dorothea (1929–2011)
Riggs, Christina (1971–2000)
Routier, Darlie Lynn (1970–)
Sherman, Lydia (1824–1878)
Smith, Susan (1971–)
Tinning, Marybeth (1942–)
Toppan, Jane (1854–1938)
Trueblood, Lydia (1892–1958)
Tucker, Karla Faye (1959–1998)
Wuornos, Aileen (1956–2002)
Yates, Andrea (1964–)

Chronology

1692–1693
A witch panic occurred in the Massachusetts Bay Colony where close to 200 people were accused of witchcraft. Nineteen of the accused were executed.

1770 (March 5)
The Boston Massacre, where British soldiers killed five and injured several others, occurred. This was a critical event leading to the American Revolutionary War.

1807 (September 1)
Aaron Burr, a former U.S. vice president, was acquitted of treason. He was charged with trying to annex parts of Louisiana and parts of Spanish territory in Mexico.

1865 (April 14)
President Abraham Lincoln was assassinated in Ford's Theater by John Wilkes Booth.

1865 (November 10)
Captain Henry Wirz was executed for war crimes. He was in charge of a Confederate prisoner-of-war camp called Camp Sumter. He was charged with crimes related to how prisoners were treated in the camp.

1868 (February 24)
The U.S. House of Representatives voted 126–47 to impeach President Andrew Johnson.

1872 (November 5)
Susan B. Anthony, women's suffragist and abolitionist, was put on trial for illegally casting a presidential ballot. She was later found guilty.

1874 (July 1)
Four-year-old Charley Ross was kidnapped outside of his home in Germantown Pennsylvania.

1881 (July 2)
President James Garfield was shot by Charles Guiteau. He died two months later.

1890 (December 29)
Hundreds of Native American men, women, and children were murdered at the Wounded Knee Massacre.

1893 (June 20)
Lizzie Borden was acquitted of murdering her father and stepmother with a hatchet.

1896 (May 7)
Dr. H. H. Holmes, one of the world's first known serial murderers, was executed by hanging.

1901 (September 14)
President William McKinley (1843–1901), the 25th president of the United States, died from gunshot wounds

sustained from assassin Leon Czolgosz on September 6. He was shot days earlier, but died from an infection caused by his wounds.

1902 (October 29)
Jane Toppan, a New England nurse who poisoned upward of a hundred of her patients, was arrested at the age of 45.

1917 (June 15)
Emma Goldman and Alexander Berkman were arrested under the newly created Espionage Act for their anarchist views. They were eventually convicted, served time in prison, and were deported after their release.

1920 (May 11)
Mob boss James Colosimo was murdered. The murder remains unsolved.

1920 (September 16)
A bomb was detonated in the financial district of New York City. Thirty-eight people were killed and almost 150 were injured in the blast. The perpetrators were never caught.

1927 (May 18)
Andrew Kehoe murdered his wife, destroyed his farm, and detonated bombs at a nearby school. Known as the Bath School Massacre, 45 people died and nearly 60 were injured in the attack.

1929 (February 14)
One of the most notorious Chicago Mob killings occurred when seven members of George "Bugs" Moran gang were murdered in what is referred to as the Saint Valentine's Day Massacre.

1932 (March 1)
Charles August Lindbergh, Jr., the 20-month-old son of the famous American aviator Charles August Lindbergh, was kidnapped and murdered.

1932 (November 7)
The Supreme Court issued its landmark ruling in *Powell v. Alabama*. The Court held that the convictions of the "Scottsboro Boys," seven African American males charged with rape, should be overturned because they were denied the assistance of legal counsel.

1933 (February 15)
Anton Cermak, the 44th mayor of Chicago, was killed by a bullet aimed at president-elect Franklin D. Roosevelt, in Miami, Florida.

1934 (May 23)
Bonnie Parker and Clyde Barrow's crime spree through the American Southwest ended as they were ambushed and killed.

1934 (July 22)
John Dillinger was killed by agents outside the Biograph Theater in Chicago, Illinois.

1942 (August 1)
The Sleepy Lagoon became a part of Los Angeles history, when a murder occurred on the Williams Ranch. The murder led to the Los Angeles Police Department arresting over 600 Mexican Americans and sparked the Zoot Suit Riot.

1947 (January 25)
Chicago crime boss Al Capone died.

1953 (June 19)
Julius and Ethel Rosenberg, convicted of selling secrets of the U.S. nuclear program to the Russians, were executed.

1954 (July 4)
Marilyn Sheppard was beat to death in her bedroom. Her husband, Sam Sheppard, was convicted of the murder. The U.S. Supreme Court, however, later overturned his conviction because of prejudicial pretrial publicity.

1955 (August 31)
Emmett Till's savagely beaten body was discovered in the Tallahatchie River in Mississippi. Roy Bryant and J. W. Milam stood trial for his murder, but were acquitted.

1961 (June 19)
The U.S. Supreme Court decided to overturn Dollree Mapp's conviction because her home was entered without a search warrant. This ruling by the Court extended the *exclusionary rule* used in federal court (throwing out evidence that does not conform to exact constitutional standards) to be applied in state courts.

1963 (June 12)
Medgar Evers, Mississippi's first field secretary for the National Association for the Advancement of Colored People (NAACP), was murdered in Jackson, Mississippi, by white supremacist Byron De La Beckwith.

1963 (November 22)
John F. Kennedy was shot and killed on November 22, 1963, in Dallas, Texas, while campaigning for the 1964

election. Lee Harvey Oswald, a 24-year-old former Marine, was identified as the lone assassin in his death.

1964 (June 21)
Three civil rights activists, Michael "Mickey" Schwerner, Andrew Goodman, and James Earl Chaney, were shot to death and buried at a dam site. The state's refusal to prosecute the suspects on murder charges and the Department of Justice's limited success in prosecuting them on civil rights charged led to a public outcry and legislative change.

1965 (February 21)
Civil rights leader Malcolm X was assassinated while speaking at the Audubon Ballroom in Manhattan. Three men, Talmadge Hayer, Norman 3X Butler, and Thomas 15X Johnston, were convicted of his murder.

1968 (April 4)
Dr. Martin Luther King, Jr., one of the great leaders of the civil rights movement, was assassinated outside his room at the Lorraine Hotel in Memphis, Tennessee, by James Earl Ray.

1968 (June 5)
Robert F. Kennedy, who had just won California's Democratic primary, was assassinated by Sirhan Sirhan at the Ambassador Hotel in Los Angeles, California.

1969 (August 8–10)
Four members of the Manson family murdered actress Sharon Tate and four others at the Los Angeles home of Tate and her husband, director Roman Polanski. They also murdered supermarket executive Leno LaBianca and his wife Rosemary in their Los Angeles home.

1970 (May 4)
War protestors at Kent State University in Ohio were fired upon by national guardsmen. Four students died and other students were wounded.

1971 (June 13)
The New York Times began publishing excerpts from a Department of Defense study of U.S. political and military involvement in Vietnam referred to as the "Pentagon Papers."

1971 (September 9)
One of the most notorious prison riots in the United States occurred at Attica Prison in Upstate New York. Thirty-nine inmates and guards were killed. Publicity of the riot helped bring attention to prison conditions.

1972 (August 4)
Arthur Bremer was found guilty of attempting to assassinate presidential candidate George Wallace and injuring several other people.

1973 (February 27–May 8)
The Wounded Knee Incident occurred amid intertribal turmoil at the Pine Ridge reservation. This turmoil ultimately involved the U.S. Marshals Service, the Federal Bureau of Investigation (FBI), and National Guard. At its conclusion, two Native Americans and FBI agents were killed, one U.S. Marshal was critically wounded, and civil rights activist Ray Robinson was missing.

1974 (August 8)
Richard Nixon resigned as U.S. president. His presidency started to unravel two years earlier after a break-in at the Democratic Party headquarters in the Watergate building. Journalists Bob Woodward and Carl Bernstein uncovered attempts to cover up the break-in and other illegal acts of his administration.

1975 (September)
Two separate assassination attempts were made upon President Gerald Ford. Neither attempt was successful and both were unique in that they were perpetrated by women with connections to radical antigovernment groups.

1977 (November 1)
Francine Hughes was found not guilty by reason of insanity in the burning death of her abusive husband. Her story was eventually made into a movie and the case contributed to developing a better understanding of battered women in the United States.

1978 (November 27)
Dan White murdered San Francisco mayor George Moscone and San Francisco Board supervisor Harvey Milk. Milk was the first openly gay man to hold public office in California at the time.

1980 (December 8)
Mark David Chapman murdered John Lennon.

1981 (March 30)
John Hinckley, Jr., attempted to assassinate President Ronald Reagan in Washington, D.C. as the president was leaving the Hilton Hotel. The president was not directly hit, though he was wounded when a bullet ricocheted off the presidential limousine and hit him in the chest. Press secretary

James Brady was shot in the head, and Thomas Delahanty, a D.C. Metropolitan police officer, and Timothy McCarthy, a Secret Service agent, also were wounded.

1981 (July 27)
Adam Walsh was kidnapped and murdered. This case led to significant changes in the criminal justice system and national response to missing children. Serial killer Ottis Tooke eventually confessed to his murder.

1989 (April 19)
Trisha Meili was attacked, raped, sodomized, and beaten in what came to be known as the "Central Park jogger case." Five black and Hispanic youth were wrongfully convicted of the crime.

1991 (July 22)
Jeffrey Dahmer, responsible for the murder and dismemberment of at least 17 young males, was arrested in Milwaukee, Wisconsin.

1993 (April 19)
The Federal Bureau of Investigation used military vehicles to insert tear gas into the Branch Davidian compound in Waco, Texas. Seventy-five men, women, and children died.

1995 (April 19)
Timothy McVeigh detonated a truck bomb in Oklahoma City, Oklahoma. The bombing killed 168 people and injured many more. The case impacted concern about domestic terrorists.

1996 (April 3)
Ted Kaczynski, better known as the Unabomber, was arrested at his secluded cabin in Montana. He sent 16 bombs through the mail, killing three people and injuring many others.

1998 (February 3)
Karla Faye Tucker was executed in the state of Texas.

1998 (October 12)
Matthew Shepard died from wounds he sustained in a brutal, hate crime attack. His murder became an important symbol of the antihate movement and the case led to positive social changes.

1999 (February 4)
Amadou Bailo Diallo, a 23-year-old immigrant from Guinea, was shot and killed by officers Kenneth Boss, Sean Carroll, Edward McMellin, and Richard Murphy from New York Police Department's (NYPD) Street Crimes Unit. The case contributed to a national discussion of police brutality and race relations.

1999 (April 20)
Eric Harris and Dylan Klebold attacked students and teachers at Columbine High School in Littleton, Colorado. Twelve students and one teacher were killed.

2001 (September 11th)
Nineteen terrorists affiliated with the al-Qaeda terrorist group hijacked and then flew two passenger airplanes into the World Trade Center towers in New York City, another airplane into the Pentagon, and a fourth plane, although targeted for a landmark in Washington, D.C., was brought down in a field in Pennsylvania. Nearly 3,000 people died.

2007 (April 16)
A gunman opened fire on the Virginia Tech Campus, killing 33 people and injuring many more.

2011 (January 8)
Jared Loughner opened fire outside a supermarket northwest of Tucson, Arizona. Six people were murdered and others were injured, including U.S. representative Gabrielle "Gabby" Giffords.

2011 (November 7)
Dr. Conrad Murray was found guilty of involuntary manslaughter of the death of pop icon Michael Jackson.

2012 (February 26)
Trayvon Martin was fatally shot by George Zimmermann, a watch program coordinator. Zimmerman was tried but acquitted of the shooting.

2012 (July 20, 2012)
A deadly mass shooting occurred at a movie theater in Aurora, Colorado, during a late night showing of the Batman film *The Dark Night Rises*. James Holmes killed 12 and injured 55 people in the attack.

2012 (December 14th)
Adam Peter Lanza entered Sandy Hook Elementary School in Newtown, Connecticut, and killed 20 first-grade students in two classrooms along with six educators. He also had killed his mother prior to arriving at the school.

2013 (April 15)

Two improvised explosive devices (IEDs) detonated within seconds of each other near the finish line of the 117th Boston Marathon in Massachusetts. Three individuals were killed and 264 others sustained injuries. Tamerlan and Dzhokhar Tsarnaev were identified as the primary suspects. Tamerlan was killed and Dzhokhar is in custody.

2015 (March 27)

The Italian Supreme Court overturned the guilty verdicts brought in previously against Amanda Knox and her Italian boyfriend Raffaelel Sollecito for the 2007 murder of Knox's roommate Meredith Kercher in Perugia, Italy. The decision finally put an end to the case.

A

Abagnale, Frank, Jr. (1948–)

Frank William Abagnale, Jr., is a security consultant and public speaker best known for his notorious crimes. Over the course of five years, when he was still a teenager, he passed millions of dollars in fraudulent checks across 26 countries. It was around this time that he also became known as a famous imposter, having assumed the identities of multiple individuals, including a pediatrician, an airline pilot, and an attorney. His criminal acts soon caught up with him, as he served time in prison in France, Sweden, and the United States. He was released early from prison while locked up in the United States under the condition that he would assist federal law enforcement agencies with their fraud prevention efforts. He has worked with the federal government as a security consultant and lecturer for over the past 30 years.

Born in Bronxville, New York, Frank W. Abagnale Jr. had a normal upbringing. Frank, along with his parents, Frank and Paulette Abagnale, and three siblings were a close-knit family. During his teen years, Frank's parents unexpectedly separated and later divorced. This incidence had a dramatic impact on his life. After the divorce, Frank decided to live with his father, whom he considered a role model. Around this time, Frank slowly started to associate himself with a group of adolescents who were committing minor crimes, such as thievery. After being arrested and put into a center with other juvenile delinquents, he stopped hanging with that group of juveniles.

Frank Jr. was an exceptionally intellectual person, which was evident as he was growing up. His crime spree did not end after his trip to the juvenile center. In fact, it was only the beginning. His new wave of crimes began after his father bought him a car and gave him a credit card. He came up with a scheme that cost his father thousands of dollars. It was believed that his father could not afford the money owed on the credit card and eventually caused his already plummeting stationary business to rapidly go downhill. Frank Jr. went back to live with his mother who then placed him in a school for boys to help correct his deviant behavior.

In 1964, at the age of 16, Frank Jr. left home to try to support himself. Like his father, Frank tried his hand working in the stationary business; however, that was not making him much money. With knowledge acquired over the years, he figured out how to exaggerate his age on his driver's license by 10 years and fabricate his educational background in hopes of finding a more lucrative job. Frank achieved success in finding better jobs, but his regular income barely surpassed his expenses. This is when he started writing fraudulent checks. As time progressed, he had written so many bad checks that he overdrew his account by thousands of dollars. It was at this time that he decided to go into hiding in hopes that he would not get caught and sent back to jail. In total, he cashed over $2 million in fraudulent checks in all the 50 U.S. states and a number of foreign countries.

Former impostor and con man, Frank Abagnale, Jr., is seen here in a December 16, 2002, photo taken at the upscale Four Seasons Hotel in Beverly Hills, California. After serving time in prison in his youth, Abagnale is now a security consultant. (AP Photo/ Lucy Nicholson)

His illegal behavior and deceptive actions did not conclude with writing fraudulent checks. Between the ages of 16 and 21, Frank Jr. illegally impersonated a number of different individuals. For instance, he believed that airline pilots were well respected, so he decided to impersonate a Pan American Airlines pilot. He counterfeited his own pilot's license and subsequently learned as much as he could about flying. This helped him to successfully impersonate a pilot so that he could fly free of charge around the country. As time progressed, the authorities started to catch on to what Frank Jr. was doing. Therefore, he decided to embrace another identity, namely that of a pediatrician. For nearly one year, he studied as much as he could about the medical profession, and he eventually was promoted to a medical resident supervisor. Moving forward, Frank Jr. would move from one profession to the next when he thought he was close to being caught.

After a few years of regularly switching jobs and duping banks for hundreds of thousands of dollars, Frank Jr. decided it was a good idea to lie low and live crime-free in Montpelier, France. His hiding did not last for long, however. He was apprehended in 1969 when a previous girlfriend recognized a public photo of him and reported him to the local police. At the time of his arrest, multiple countries were seeking his arrest and subsequent deportation. Frank Jr. first served a relatively short prison sentence in France, where he was confined in a crude cell with no amenities. It was here that he nearly died due to malnutrition and pneumonia caused by the inhumane living conditions. After six months in confinement, he was then extradited to Sweden to serve time for forgery at a low-security prison. He spent an additional six months behind bars before he was deported back to the United States to stand trial for multiple counts of forgery. After a lengthy trial, he was convicted and subsequently sentenced to 12 years in a federal prison in Petersburg, Virginia.

At the age of 26, after serving only five years of the original 12-year prison sentence, Frank Jr. was released on parole on the condition that he lend his knowledge and services without pay to the federal government. In particular, he agreed to help assist the Federal Bureau of Investigation (FBI) and other federal law enforcement agencies in their efforts to prevent fraud and other financial crimes. He works closely with the FBI as a security consultant and lecturer at their academy and field offices. He also has served a pivotal role in assisting with the investigation of crimes committed by individuals attempting to fraud the government.

Frank Jr. has been linked, in some form, to the FBI for more than three decades. While working with the FBI, he developed his own program, Abagnale and Associates, to help other financial institutions and agencies with their fraud prevention efforts. He has also assisted and lectured to countless other organizations, police agencies, and financial institutions around the world. To this day, close to 14,000 different companies and financial institutions use his fraud prevention programs. This lends credence to the notion that Frank Jr. is one of the most respected authorities on forgery and other financial crimes.

Over the years, Frank Jr. has also been widely depicted in film, theater, and the media. For instance, the life story and crimes of Frank Jr. served as the basis for the 2002 film *Catch Me If You Can*, starring Leonardo DiCaprio and Tom Hanks. This film was based on a book that Frank Jr. wrote years prior about his life and financial crimes. His life was the inspiration to a 2011 Broadway musical, also of the same name as the film.

JUSTIN N. CROWL

See also: Boesky, Ivan, Insider Trading Scandal (1980s); Stewart, Martha, Insider Trading Case (2001–2004)

Further Reading

Abagnale, Frank William, Jr. 2001. *The Art of the Steal.* New York: Broadway Books.

Abagnale, Frank William, Jr., and Stan Redding. 2000. *Catch Me if You Can.* New York: Broadway Books.

Edry, Sandy Lawrence. 2003. "Criminally Entertaining: The Imposter Behind Catch Me If You Can." *Biography* 7: 26.

Abbott, Jack Henry (1944–2002)

The case of Jack Henry Abbott is an important one that helped push the country toward harsher attitudes toward criminal offenders in the 1970s and 1980s. Furthermore, his involvement with the criminal justice system from an early age provided scholars with a particularly interesting case study of the effects of prison. Abbott was institutionalized from a young age, although a record of him being a violent youth is absent. Rather, maladjustment to state care in the absence of Abbott's biological parents is frequently blamed for his antisocial attitudes. He was first sent to federal prison for a property crime, but Abbott became violent once inside; he was found guilty of murder in prison and was able to escape. Despite this, his relationship with pen pal and esteemed author Norman Mailer (1923–2007) was instrumental in earning Abbott parole. Abbott was praised by Mailer for being a gifted writer—a talent that helped him publish a book containing letters that detailed aspects of prison life. Abbott's reflections on the penal system and prisons received critical acclaim. Once free, Abbott murdered another man in a disagreement, leading to criticisms of the parole system and Mailer himself (Worth 2002). He returned to prison in 1982 and was found dead in his cell in 2002. Though having spent the vast majority of his adult life in prison, Abbott is known both for the infamy of his acts, and his brief rise to literary stardom.

Abbott was born on January 21, 1944, in Oscoda, Michigan. Little is known of Abbott's parents and his childhood was marked by instability. He spent the vast majority of his rebellious early years under the charge of the state and foster parents (Farber 1981b). His formal education ceased in the sixth grade and from the age of nine on, Abbott reports being institutionalized in juvenile detention centers

for long periods of time (Abbott 1981). At age 12 he was sent to the Utah State Industrial School for Boys, where he spent all but 60 days until he turned 18. Needless to say, Abbott's childhood and adolescence was a far cry from a nurturing experience. Abbott wrote that his only crime as a juvenile was failing to adjust to foster care (Abbott 1981).

Upon Abbott's release from reform school as an adult he was free for six months. His attitude toward American society at this time was reportedly resentful. In his writings, Abbott reflected on the impact of having been raised by the state; he had little control over his life, had very few freedoms, and was subject to what he called arbitrary punishments (Abbott 1981). Abbott specifically notes that he, as a "state-raised convict," could not tolerate institutionalization; having spent so much of his adolescence in reform school, his conception of a free life was akin to the conditions in prison (Abbott 1981, 12).

Cashing fraudulent checks earned Abbott his first stay in a federal penitentiary in 1965; his sentence was for a maximum of five years. While serving this sentence, Abbott stabbed and killed a fellow inmate for which he was given a concurrent sentence of 3 to 20 years. Abbott was able to escape for a period of six weeks, during which he committed an armed robbery in Denver, Colorado. The escape and robbery earned Abbott an additional 19-year sentence. Abbot's prison record was marked by a slew of alleged violent attacks. Prison psychologists stated Abbott was "extremely angry," "capable of sudden violence," and had been paranoid and unsociable (Farber 1981b, 2). These types of reports were consistently given in the prison system during the years which Abbott was incarcerated.

During his long prison sentence, Abbott began corresponding with Norman Mailer, a Pulitzer Prize–winning novelist. Mailer noticed Abbott's passion and talent in his writings about prison. Mailer stated that Abbott's letters embodied "an intellectual, a radical, a potential leader, a man obsessed with a vision of more elevated human relations in a better world that revolution could forge" (Abbott 1981, xi). The underpinnings of Abbott's perspectives of the penal system and prisons were rooted in his self-education. Though he claims to never have stepped foot inside a prison school, Abbott was able to access books; of particular interest to Abbott were theoretical and philosophical works. As evident in his writings, Abbott was versed in critical philosophies of law and justice—he denounced the legitimate authority of the prison system, stating the prison strips prisoners of their rights in an attempt to suppress their rebellion (Abbott 1981).

Abbott also wrote at length about the ability of prison to change prisoners and guards alike. Described as particularly traumatic were his stays in solitary confinement involving black-out cells and starvation diets—conditions he described as having the ability to alter the very nature of stone itself (Abbott 1981). Abbott goes so far as to contrast the living quarters of animals in zoos with the prison cell, summarizing his position on prison and the conditions of confinement as inhumane.

Mailer helped Abbott gain a contract to publish these letters in *The Belly of The Beast*, which was released in June 1980, the same month that Abbott was released from prison. Mailer was instrumental in helping Abbott gain parole, admiring his ability to overcome the horrors of prison and becoming a good writer. In doing so he made Abbott somewhat famous, after appearing on Good Morning America and being interviewed by Rolling Stone.

After six weeks of freedom, Abbott stabbed and killed Richard Adan in a dispute in Manhattan (Wolffs 2014). In fact, the homicide occurred just one day before *The New York Times* gave his book a positive review. Though Abbott was identified as the killer immediately, he was not caught nor tried for the crime until January 1982 (Worth 2002).

The trial included Abbott's testimony about his life, from foster care to alleged prison abuses. Abbott was found guilty of manslaughter and sentenced to 15 years to life. Many viewed the verdict as too lenient. Some of the jury thought that Abbott was less accountable because Abbott's childhood and experiences in prison did not rehabilitate him but, rather, further damaged him (Montgomery 1982). In civil court, Richard Adan's widow, Ricci, was awarded $7.5 million in damages for wrongful death. The judgment garnered Ricci Adan the future royalties of Abbott's two books. Abbott failed to show remorse for the killing of Adan, partially blaming Adan for his death during the civil proceedings (Sullivan 1990). As of 1990, Abbott's works netted more than a quarter million dollars, which were subsequently seized by the New York State Crime Victims Board and the New York County Sheriff under the "Son of Sam" statute (Sullivan 1990).

On February 10, 2002, Abbott was found dead in his prison cell, hanging from a bed sheet and shoelace (Worth 2002). Though initially thought to be the act of another, it was determined that his death was suicide.

TYLER J. VAUGHAN

See also: Clutter Family Murders (1959); Gilmore, Gary (1940–1977); Shakur, Sanyika (1963–)

Further Reading

Abbott, Jack Henry. 1981. *In the Belly of the Beast: Letters from Prison.* New York: Vintage Books.

Farber, M.A. 1981a. "Killing Clouds Ex-Convict Writer's New Life." *The New York Times.* July 26. http://www.nytimes.com/1981/07/26/nyregion/killing-clouds-ex-convict-writer-s-new-life.html. Accessed April 13, 2015.

Farber, M.A. 1981b. "Freedom for Convict-Author: Complex and Conflicting Tale." *The New York Times.* August 17. http://www.nytimes.com/1981/08/17/nyregion/freedom-for-convict-author-complex-and-conflicting-tale.html. Accessed April 13, 2015.

Montgomery, Paul L. 1982. "Abbott Is Sentenced to 15 Years to Life in Slaying of Waiter." *The New York Times.* April 16. http://www.nytimes.com/1982/04/16/nyregion/abbott-is-sentenced-to-15-years-to-life-in-slaying-of-waiter.html. Accessed April 13, 2015.

Sullivan, Ronald. 1990. "Author is told to pay millions for '81 slaying." *The New York Times*, June 16. http://www.nytimes.com/1990/06/16/nyregion/author-is-told-to-pay-millions-for-81-slaying.html.

Wolffs, Claudia. 2014. "In the Belly of the Beast." *Time.* http://content.time.com/time/magazine/article/0,9171,949268,00.html. Accessed January 29, 2015.

Worth, Robert F. 2002. "Jailhouse Author Helped by Mailer Is Found Dead." *The New York Times.* February 11. http://www.nytimes.com/2002/02/11/nyregion/jailhouse-author-helped-by-mailer-is-found-dead.html. Accessed April 13, 2015.

Abu Ghraib Prisoner Abuse Scandal (Iraq) (2003–2004)

Early in the War in Iraq (2003–2011), a series of media reports and investigations illuminated a dark pattern of cruel, inhuman, and degrading detainee treatment inside Abu Ghraib prison. Military personnel committed various human rights violations, including the rape, torture, and killing of prisoners of war. Personnel had abused naked, hooded prisoners with trained dogs, urinated on individuals, and drove prisoners in a caravan with their genitals tied together by ropes. They had even redeployed torture methods that torturers had used during the Spanish Inquisition and the Stalin show trials while also creating new ones. For example, they subjected detainees to *strappado* hanging, whereby the subject was hung from the wrists with both hands tied behind his back to slowly dislocate his shoulders. Seventeen soldiers were removed from duty because of their role in the torture, and 11 were court-martialed and sent to military prison. The abuses raised important questions about responsibility and oversight during a time of war.

Abu Ghraib is located west of Baghdad in Iraq. During Saddam Hussein's (1937–2006) rule, he used the Abu Ghraib prison to incarcerate, torture, and execute thousands of political dissidents. After Hussein's regime fell during the Iraq invasion, the prison, which at the time had been deserted, was used for military purposes, including the incarceration of insurgents and common criminals.

In November 2003, the Associated Press published a report documenting numerous abuses at Abu Ghraib. That month, the Army's provost also reported that prison conditions in Iraq constituted a violation of the Geneva Conventions and were thus war crimes. The U.S. Department of Defense waited to begin the investigations of allegations until January 2004, but by April, officials were overwhelmed by a scandal. In April and May 2004, Seymour Hersh published articles, with photographs, in *The New Yorker*, detailing the abuses, and a televised *60 Minutes II* report aired the pictures. Various human rights watchdogs like Amnesty International and Human Rights Watch also documented abuses and torture.

In addition, Major General Anthony Taguba's report, the so-called Taguba report, provided photographic evidence of torture and abuse including numerous rapes of both male and female prisoners and the use of foreign objects such as phosphorescent tubes, truncheons, and broom sticks with which soldiers and translators sodomized them. International Red Cross inspectors reported prisoner abuse in their confidential report to the American authorities in February 2004. They documented various abuses including incommunicado detention, excessive use of solitary confinement and force, as well as serious injury and death. When the photographs and these reports were released, the world community was shocked. Torture and abusive treatment of detainees, even in circumstances of military conflict, violate various military codes, domestic and international legal conventions such as the Uniform Code of Military Justice, the 1994 U.S. Torture Statute, and the 1949 Geneva Conventions, among others.

Although President Bush and other senior officials condemned the abuses, there is a wealth of documentary materials that the abuses resulted from a series of high-level policy decisions and directives developed and implemented by senior Bush administration officials and high-ranking military commanders charged with waging the war against terrorism in Iraq and elsewhere. In 2002 and 2003, high-level Bush administration lawyers, Jay Bybee and John Yoo, deputy assistant attorney general in the Office of Legal Counsel, at the behest of William Haynes,

general counsel for the Department of Defense, wrote what would become known as the "Torture Memos." Yoo created the opinion that federal laws prohibiting torture do not apply to foreign detainees held abroad and that anyone prosecuted for following orders would be legally protected. Bybee, later appointed to the federal judiciary, created an idiosyncratic new definition of "torture" that was so narrow that abuse would have to be severe enough to cause organ failure and death for it to be considered torture.

These opinions would guide the Bush administration policy. The legal team authorized what it called "enhanced interrogation techniques," techniques that had already been prohibited by law as torture, to be used against foreign detainees. The legal team created a legally fictitious category called "enemy combatant" to designate these foreign detainees. A February 2002 Presidential Order declared that the administration would consider itself no longer constrained by Geneva Convention provisions prohibiting cruel and inhumane treatment and would use its very narrow and novel definition of torture as a guide.

While a small number of the low-level personnel believed to have committed crimes at Abu Ghraib have been prosecuted and punished, as of 2013, no high-ranking officials have been held criminally accountable. The U.S. Department of Defense removed 17 low-ranking soldiers and officers from duty. Between 2004 and 2006, 11 servicemen and women were charged with, and convicted of, dereliction of duty, maltreatment, aggravated assault and battery in military court, sentenced to military prison, and dishonorably discharged from military service. Nine individuals were imprisoned, though prison terms were typically very short, ranging from 90 days to 10 months. These included Private First Class Lynndie England and Specialist Charles Graner who featured prominently in some of the more infamous photographs.

In 2005, England and Graner were sentenced to military prison for 3 and 10 years, respectively. Graner's was the longest prison term in the Abu Ghraib scandal, lasting six-and-a-half years. Colonel Thomas Pappas received only nonjudicial punishment under the Uniform Code of Military Justice while Colonel Steven Jordan was acquitted of some charges and reprimanded for others.

Brigadier General Janis Karpinski was reprimanded for dereliction of duty and demoted to colonel in May 2005. She denied knowledge of any abuses and claimed that her superiors had authorized the interrogations and denied her access to them.

Intelligence agents and private contractors outside the military chain of command seem to have orchestrated some of the more deadly abuses. The U.S. Army determined that interrogators had killed a detainee named Manadel al-Jamadi by torturing him to death. But neither the Central Intelligence Agency (CIA) operative nor the private contractor was charged with murder. Indeed, as of 2015, no one has yet been tried and convicted for the homicides at Abu Ghraib.

In 2004, the U.S. Supreme Court ruled that a presidential administration cannot legally decide to disregard the Geneva Convention protections. On June 29, 2006, the Court reaffirmed its 2004 ruling in *Hamdan v. Rumsfeld, et al.*, in which it declared that foreign detainees are entitled to Geneva Convention and U.S. War Crimes Act of 1996 protections. In 2004, Secretary Rumsfeld testified before the U.S. Senate Armed Services Committee and conceded that he was fully accountable for the torture and abuses at Abu Ghraib. Yet he retained his post until his retirement and has not yet been criminally prosecuted.

Most Abu Ghraib abuse photographs have never been publicly released, though the whistleblower Web site WikiLeaks and the British newspaper *The Guardian* shared hundreds of thousands of documents and detailed uninvestigated abuse and torture cases even after the scandal waned. Amnesty International reported that untold thousands of detainees appear to have been tortured and abused, contradicting the official assertions that abuses were simply random, individual acts. Still, no American officials have been prosecuted, and it appears that they never will.

PAUL R. SCHUPP

See also: My Lai Massacre (March 16, 1968)

Further Reading

Hersh, Seymour M. 2004. *Chain of Command: The Road from 9/11 to Abu Ghraib.* New York: HarperCollins.

Rajiva, Lila. 2005. *The Language of Empire: Abu Ghraib and the American Media.* New York: Monthly Review Press.

Strassers, Steven. 2004. *The Abu Ghraib Investigations: The Official Reports of the Independent Panel and the Pentagon on the Shocking Prisoner Abuse in Iraq.* New York: Public Affairs.

Adams, Randall Dale (1948–2010)

On November 28, 1976, late on a Saturday night, Officer Robert W. Wood and his partner, Teresa Turko, stopped a car because only its parking lights were on. Officer Wood was shot by the driver and his partner fired several rounds at the car as it pulled away. Officer Turko caught only a brief glimpse of the driver (the only occupant of the vehicle) and could give no concrete description of him.

Earlier on the day of the shooting, Randall Dale Adams ran out of gas and walked to a service station where David Harris, who had an extensive criminal record, gave him a ride and subsequently spent the entire day with him. Harris was arrested in relation to the shooting because he had been bragging to friends that he had shot the officer in Dallas. However, Harris was never brought up on charges in connection with the murder. Following his arrest, Harris implicated the defendant.

The key prosecution witness, David Harris (aged 16 at the time of the offense), testified that he picked up the defendant in a stolen car and that they drove around during the day smoking marijuana and drinking. They then went to a drive-in movie. After the movie, they were stopped by the police. Harris was afraid he would be identified (he had stolen the car and a pistol, which was under the front seat), so he hid in the front seat. Harris stated that as the police officer approached the car, Adams retrieved the stolen gun from under the seat and shot Officer Wood. Several days after the murder, Harris boasted to friends that he had shot the police officer. In addition, Harris went on to commit a burglary and robbery, which he tried to blame on others. This evidence was never presented to the jury.

Randall Dale Adams testified on his own behalf. He relayed the same story as Harris with the exception that following the drive-in movie, he was taken back to his motel by 10 p.m. The defense claimed that Harris must have been alone in the car when he killed the officer and was trying to place the blame on Adams. Officer Turko also testified, after hypnosis (which was not revealed to the defense at trial), that she saw only one person in the stopped car and this time she was able to give a brief description of the driver as having a similar hairstyle as Adams.

As rebuttal witnesses, the state introduced Emily Miller, Robert Miller, and Michael Randell. The Millers testified that they drove past the police traffic stop and identified Adams as the only individual in the stopped car. Randell testified that he saw two people in the stopped car and that Adams was the driver. Following the trial, the defense learned that Emily Miller had made a previous statement describing the driver as a "Mexican or a very light skinned black." After learning this, the defense wanted to recall Miller but was told by the prosecution that she had returned home.

Convicted murderer Randall Dale Adams whose claim of innocence spawned the documentary *The Thin Blue Line*, in Eastham Unit prison in Texas. (Photo by Shelly Katz/Getty Images)

New evidence later surfaced that the Millers had not returned home but had moved to a different motel in Dallas, called the Alamo Plaza Motel. Additional evidence was uncovered that Emily Miller had told the prosecutor which motel they were moving to. Although the prosecutor denied knowledge of their whereabouts, a phone bill from the Alamo motel was included in his file, which indicated that he did know where the Millers were located and had lied at the trial when the defense tried to recall her.

Further testimony by Emily Miller at the writ hearing revealed that there was a $20,000 reward for any information that would help the police solve the Wood murder. She also stated that she testified falsely at trial when she claimed to identify Adams in a police lineup. In actuality, she had originally identified someone else as the killer and the police officer told her she had picked "the wrong person" and gave her "the applicant's number in the lineup." Additional evidence was uncovered that Randell had lied about his whereabouts on the night of the murder and, by lying, was attempting to cover up an affair (Adams et al., 1991). Further investigation revealed that Adams's

depiction of events regarding the timing of the drive-in movie was accurate.

In 1979, the Texas Court of Criminal Appeals affirmed Adams's conviction. However, in 1980, the Supreme Court overturned his death sentence because of a technical issue involving the death qualification of jurors. As a result, Adams's death sentence was reversed. Since the prosecutor knew that the case was not strong, he convinced the governor to commute Adams's sentence to life in prison (Adams et al., 1991).

The Innocence Project

The Innocence Project was founded by Barry Scheck and Peter Neufeld in 1992. Its purpose was to litigate and advocate to exonerate wrongfully criminally defendants. The widespread usage of DNA evidence has been critical evidence that has helped countless defendants. As of February 2014, there have been 143 capital exonerations nationwide since 1972 based on factual innocence (see www.deathpenalty-info.org). Additionally, the Innocence Project in New York has documented 312 postconviction DNA exonerations in capital and noncapital cases in the United States (see www.innocenceproject.org).

In 1985, Errol Morris came to Texas to make a documentary about James Grigson, also known as "Dr. Death." Grigson is a psychiatrist who has testified in death penalty cases and has assisted in sentencing many defendants, including Adams, to death (Kennedy, March 2, 1989). In the course of doing interviews for his project, Morris became convinced that Adams was innocent. Three years later his documentary titled *The Thin Blue Line* was released. During the course of Morris's research, the district attorney, Henry Wade, turned over his file about the case, which led to the discovery of exculpatory evidence. Morris located many witnesses and interviewed them for the movie. He located Harris and found that he had joined the military, had been convicted of several offenses, including capital murder, and spent much time incarcerated (Adams et al., 1991). Harris also confessed to the murder of Officer Wood. Finally, in 1989, the Texas Court of Criminal Appeals overturned Adams's conviction because of suppression of evidence by the prosecution and perjury of witnesses (Pasztor, March 1, 1989). After the reversal, the prosecution dismissed the charges against Adams due to a lack of evidence (Belli, October 7, 1989).

Adams was in prison for 12 years, including three years on death row, and in 1979, he came within three days of being executed (Adams, November 1998). After his release, he made public appearances to speak out against the death penalty and has spoken at Senate hearings on prosecutorial misconduct (Belli, October 7, 1989). Harris was executed on June 30, 2004, for an unrelated murder, which occurred during the course of a kidnapping. In the summer of 1997, Adams moved back to Texas to get married to a woman whose brother was on death row (Adams, November 1998). Adams never received any compensation for his wrongful conviction and he died of a brain tumor on October 30, 2010 (Martin, 2011).

TALIA ROITBERG HARMON

See also: Carter, Rubin "Hurricane" (1937–2014); Central Park Jogger Case (1989); Cotton, Ronald (1962–)

Further Reading

Adams, Randall Dale. 1998. Presentation at the National Conference on Wrongful Convictions and the Death Penalty, Chicago, Illinois, November.

Adams, Randall Dale, William Hoffer, and Marilyn Mona Hoffer. 1991. *Adams v. Texas.* New York: St. Martin's.

Adams v. State, 577 S.W.2d 717 (Tex.Crim.App. 1979).

Adams v. Texas, 448 U.S. 38, 100 S.Ct. 2521, 65 L.Ed. 2d 581 (1980).

Belli, Anne. 1989. "Adams Seeking Prison-Related Job." *Dallas Morning News.* October 7.

Ex Parte Adams, 768 S.W.2d 281 (Tex.Cr.App. 1989).

Harris v. Texas, Texas Court of Criminal Appeals, No.69,634 (September 13, 1989).

Kennedy, Michael, and Daniel Cerone. 1989. "Conviction Set Aside for 'Thin Blue Line' Character." *Los Angeles Times.* March 2.

Martin, Douglas. 2011. "Randall Adams, 61, Dies; Freed with Help of Film." *New York Times.* June 25.

Morris, Errol. 1988. *The Thin Blue Line* (unpublished synopsis of film).

Pasztor, David. 1989. "Adams' Murder Conviction Reversed." *Dallas Times Herald.* March 1.

Adler, "Polly" Pearl (1900–1962)

Madame "Polly" Pearl Adler, a Jewish Russian who migrated to the United States in the early 1900s, became known as the "madam of all madams," for rebranding the age-old yet illegal profession of prostitution. In addition to

this controversial label, her fame increased due to her association with popular members of the literary and theatrical world, such as Robert Benchley and Dorothy Parker; mobsters like Charles "Lucky" Luciano and Dutch Schultz; and politicians such as James Walker, the mayor of New York. She was also directly involved in two famous cases: the Seabury Commission Investigation in 1930 on Mayor James Walker and Lucky Luciano's Vice Royal trial in 1936. These two cases served as the watershed for political and legal issues within the United States in the early 1900s. Adler's story also offers a glimpse into the social issues of the time, including pursuit of the American Dream, melding of the criminal underworld and local government officials, and the effects of prohibition on both legitimate and illegitimate businesses.

Pearl Adler, the oldest of nine children of Gertrude Koval and Morris Adler, was born in Yanow, Russia, on April 16, 1900. The Adler family decided to migrate to the United States of America; however, Adler preceded them at the age of 12. Adler spent the first couple of years living with friends of her family and doing odd jobs while attending school. Her desire to embrace the culture and venture out on her own to make a living soon saw her moving to Brooklyn to work at one of the clothing factories. It was at one of these sweatshops that at age 17 that Adler became pregnant after being raped by her supervisor. With the aid of her roommate and other friends, Adler was able to get an abortion. Hoping to make a new start to her life, Adler moved to Manhattan, where she resumed working in the clothing industry, this time in a corset factory.

At age 20, Adler turned her misfortune into wealth and fame. Adler had an insatiable desire for the arts and entertainment and quickly made friends with many New York entertainers. Not long after, Adler's entry into what she would become known for seemed to have occurred quite coincidental. In an attempt to keep an affair discrete, one of her male acquaintances, also known for his involvement in bootlegging, paid Adler to keep an apartment, where he and his married lover would meet. Adler soon offered this place to others and quickly became known for these services. In 1922, Adler's first of multiple arrests to come throughout her career occurred, and she served one month in jail. The criminalization and concern for prostitution in the United States increased with the passage of the Mann Act in 1910. The practice of prostitution continued but, under less desirable conditions, as police surveillance increased, particularly in urban and working-class areas and the need for protection services and procurers rose. Returning to the one business that Adler seemed successful in, she decided to make her product appealing to the middle and upper class, by catering to clients who were both willing and able to pay a high price for the services offered. Adler's bordello heralded significant changes to the profession, through location and caliber of girls. Her girls were known not only for their beauty and youth but also for their impeccable health and social graces. Adler ensured that her girls got regular medical checkups and were free from any diseases. She took good care of her girls even unto their death and showed the stark contrast between herself and male pimps. In addition, the locations of her "houses" were in upper class areas such as Central Park and Madison Avenue and were exquisitely furnished.

Adler's house offered a revolutionary form of entertainment to this age-old business. There were numerous parties and dinners that were thrown on a regular basis; however, "Polly's house" was simply a place persons would meet to have drinks, write, or relax. Her houses were more like a club, which offered a wide gamut of entertainment, with the girls not generally at the forefront. The entertainment reflected the changing social climate as after World War I, changes in the music, with the introduction of jazz, scientific advances with the discovery of insulin and penicillin, and the progressive movement of women into the workforce, politics, and general freedom in dress and expression of their sexuality. With the legislation of Prohibition, the manufacturing and consumption of alcohol did not stop, but only moved underground. This period also saw an increase in spending as the economic boom in the United States was still evident.

Understanding the value of confidentiality, Adler provided her clients with ways to hide from the media and the public. The "Magnificent," Adler's most popular brothel, had secret pathways and rooms that bore little resemblance to a house of disrepute, attracting both public and underworld figures. Adler as the "Queen of Tarts" unlike many madams at the time, and held a unique position of being directly linked to a number of mobsters and corrupt politicians. Adler's deep involvement in crime through prostitution was compounded by her close acquaintance with two of the most notorious mobsters during the Prohibition period, Charles "Lucky" Luciano and Dutch Schultz, who interestingly were not fond of each other. This close association gave the impression that she knew more about the crimes associated with bootlegging, political and police corruption. However, Adler insisted that this was not the case, "my life depended on not being the recipient of confidences, even inadvertently. Only if I knew nothing and avoided hearing anything could I expect to survive" (Adler 1953, 212). This silence and loyalty to her clients and friends was evident was asked to testify before the Seabury Commission. The other case Adler was involved in was the trial against Lucky Luciano in 1936 where she was once again summoned to testify against Luciano. Although Luciano was convicted, she was able to discredit the state's key witness.

Adler's motivation to achieve the American Dream was seen in the pragmatic approach. There was a need for the type of entertainment she offered and it was evident from the wealth she attained. With the onset of the Great Depression, the taste in entertainment shifted. This shift, coupled with the regulation to prevent corruption within the police force and Adler's 17th arrest in 1944 brought Polly's House era to an end. Polly Adler moved to California in 1945, pursued her goal of education, graduating from high school at 50 years of age, pursuing college, and penning her autobiography before her death in 1962.

The United States, in the early 1900s, represented a time of industry and growth. The Progressive Era heralded rights for women as well as better labor conditions for children and a higher call for morality, hence the Prohibition laws and the criminalization of prostitution. However, the increase in corruption throughout the political and law enforcement agencies, the deeply embedded culture of alcohol use along with the heightened taste for extravagant entertainment, served to perpetuate crime in the United States. Adler's success was not only based on her natural business talent, but also her courage to capitalize on the social and political environment in which she operated.

Sharmaine Tapper

See also: Luciano, Charles "Lucky" (1897–1962); Schultz, Dutch (1901–1935)

Further Reading

Adler, Polly. 1953. *A House Is Not a Home*. New York: Rinehart and Company.

McNeil, Maggie. 2012. "The Honest Courtesan: Ladies of the Night." https://maggiemcneill.wordpress.com/2012/07/12/polly-adler/. Accessed April 4, 2015.

Millin, Ann. 2009. "Polly Adler." *Jewish Women: A Comprehensive Historical Encyclopedia*. March 1. Jewish Women's Archive. http://jwa.org/encyclopedia/article/adler-polly. Accessed April 13, 2015.

Poulsen, Ellen. 2010. "The 1936 Luciano Vice Trial: Material Witness." http://lucianotrial1936.com/pollyadler.html. Accessed April 4, 2015.

Alcala, Rodney (1943–)

Rodney James Alcala, who was born as Rodrigo Jacques Alcala-Buquor on August 23, 1943, in San Antonio, Texas, is a convicted American rapist and serial murderer. Like Ted Bundy, he was an excellent student, charming and popular, and he bludgeoned, raped, and strangled young woman and girls in the 1970s. He played with his victims by strangling them until they lost consciousness and waiting until they revived. He would repeat this process several times before killing them. He has been sentenced to death three times, but his sentence was overturned twice. He is also called the "Dating Game Killer" because of being a winning bachelor in the U.S. matchmaking TV show *The Dating Game* in 1978.

Alcala was born into a middle-class family, consisting of his maternal grandmother, father Raoul Alcala-Buquor, mother Anna Maria Gutierrez, one brother, and two sisters. When he was eight years old, the family moved to Mexico. There, his beloved grandmother died, and his father returned to the United States. At the age of 12, the family went to Los Angeles. In 1961, Alcala became a clerk in the army. According to intelligence measurements, he had a genius IQ. In 1962, the unexpected death of his father, despite having left the family, deeply saddened him. The following year, he went AWOL (i.e., absence without official leave) and was diagnosed with chronic, severe antisocial personality disorder. Upon his discharge from the army in 1964, Alcala enrolled at California State University. His

On January 7, 2013, convicted serial killer Rodney Alcala appeared in a New York courtroom to plead guilty to the murders of two young women in the 1970s. Sentenced to 25 years-to-life in New York, Alcala claims he wanted to return to California to appeal his death sentence there for five other murders. (AP Photo/David Handschuh)

excellent grades allowed him to join the University of California, Los Angeles, where he completed a Bachelor of Fine Arts in 1968.

The same year, he raped and tried to kill his first known victim, eight-year-old Tali Shapiro. A passerby noticed the girl in Alcala's car and called the police. When they arrived at Alcala's apartment, they at first thought that Tali was dead, but she recovered. Despite being on the FBI's most wanted list, Alcala could not be found. Calling himself John Berger, he was now studying film at New York University under Roman Polanski. He was a gifted student and professors liked him. In 1971, Alcala got his diploma and a job at an all-girl summer camp in New Hampshire, where two girls recognized him on a wanted poster. He was returned to Los Angeles, and charged with rape, kidnapping, assault, and attempted murder. Since Tali had moved to Mexico, Alcala was offered a plea agreement. He pled guilty to a lesser charge of child molestation in March 1972. He was sentenced to one year to life. Appearing rehabilitated, he was released on parole in August 1974.

Ten weeks later, he was caught providing marijuana to a 13-year-old. He pled guilty to felony possession of marijuana and returned to state prison from which he was released on parole in June 1977. Nine months later, he was found with marijuana and photographs of nude children and taken into custody for a few weeks. In June 1978, he was discharged from parole. Despite being a registered sex offender, Alcala was hired by *The Los Angeles Times* as a typesetter. On September 13, 1978, he was presented on *The Dating Game* as a photographer who enjoyed motorcycling and skydiving. Due to his charming and cheeky answers, he won the bachelorette's heart. However, she found him creepy and never went on a date with him.

The following year, Alcala raped a 15-year-old hitchhiker. Facing charges, he was released on bail, only to be arrested again for murdering 12-year-old Robin Samsoe, who disappeared in the Huntington Beach area. Her remains, scavenged by animals, were discovered more than 40 miles away. Based on a sketch by her best friend, Alcala could be identified. However, he claimed that he had not been to Huntington Beach since 1974. In his house, police found a receipt for a secret Seattle storage locker with hundreds of photos of young women and girls. Despite asking the public for help, many of them still have not been identified. Although no photos of Robin could be found, they discovered a photo of another young girl taken near Huntington Beach. Police also found a pair of earrings that Robin's mother identified as her own.

Alcala was convicted of first-degree murder and sentenced to death. However, the California State Supreme Court overturned the verdict, concluding that the trial court had committed a prejudicial error by admitting Alcala's prior offenses. In a retrial in 1986, Alcala was sentenced to death a second time, and again, the verdict was overturned by the 9th Circuit Court of Appeal due to multiple constitutional errors that had resulted in an unfair trial. Among those errors was the exclusion of a defense psychologist who would have testified that the main witness had been hypnotically influenced in her interviews with investigation officers.

Finally, DNA, blood, and fingerprint evidence allowed the prosecution of four capital murders in the Los Angeles area between 1977 and 1978. All women had been raped and strangled to death: 18-year-old Jill Barcomb, 27-year-old Georgia Wixted, 33-year-old Charlotte Lamb, as well as 21-year-old Jill Parenteau, whose case had been dismissed in 1981 due to discrediting the only witness. All of the victims were (partially) nude and revealing clear evidence of sexual assault, beating, and strangulation. Also, Lamb's DNA was on a pair of earrings found in his locker.

In 2010, Alcala was put on trial for murdering these women and Robin. Like Bundy, he was his own attorney. He focused on Robin and ignored the other cases. He questioned himself in the third person, and also cross-examined Robin's mother to show that she was lying. For example, he asked her why she had brought a pistol to one of his 1980 hearings, or if she possessed any photos showing Robin wearing those earrings from his locker. Alcala also presented a clip of his appearance on *The Dating Game*, and played part of Arlo Guthrie's 1967 song *Alice's Restaurant*. His strategy failed. The jury found him guilty in all five cases and recommended the death penalty.

He was later tried in Manhattan for killing two 23-year-old women. The first victim, Cornelia Crilley, was found raped, bitten, beaten, and strangled in her New York apartment in 1971. A bite mark on her body turned out to be identical with Alcala's impression. The second victim, Helen Hover, disappeared in 1977. Her strangled body was discovered about a year later north of New York City. Being unable to continue fighting his death sentence, Alcala quickly wanted to return to California and therefore pled guilty to both murders. In 2012, he was sentenced to at least 25 years in prison.

Based on the photos in his locker, he is suspected to also have killed 19-year-old Pamela Jean Lambson in 1977 in the San Francisco Bay area. Lambson was to meet an unidentified photographer and never returned. Although the case was reopened after more than 30 years, Alcala has not been charged due to insufficient genetic material. While speculations range between 50 and 130 murders, he has only confessed to the two New York murders. He is still on death row at San Quentin State Prison, fighting his sentence.

DANIELA RIBITSCH

See also: Bundy, Ted (1946–1989); Dahmer, Jeffrey (1960–1994); Ridgway, Gary Leon (1949–)

Further Reading

Alcala v. Superior Court, 43 Cal. 4th 1205, 185 P.3d 708, 78 Cal. Rptr. 3d 272 (2008). http://www.lexisnexis.com/us/lnacademic/. Accessed July 7, 2014.

"Convicted Killer Pleads Guilty to 2 New York Murders." 2012. *The New York Times*. December 15.

"Rodney Alcala: 'The Dating Game Killer' to Face New York Murder Charges." 2012. *The Huffington Post*. May 12.

Sands, Stella. 2011. *The Dating Game Killer. The True Story of a TV Dating Game Show, a Violent Sociopath, and a Series of Brutal Murders*. New York: St. Martin's Press.

Alien and Sedition Acts (1798)

In 1798, President John Adams's governing Federalists enacted four Alien and Sedition Acts to suppress Democratic-Republican (later called Republicans) political opposition. This would be the first time that federal authorities would legislatively criminalize political and immigrant groups for speech and writings that federal authorities viewed as being disloyal toward the federal government or seditious during a time of national crisis or foreign war. But it would not be the last.

The Federalists justified criminalizing opposition speech on the grounds that the new American Union and its federal government might fall into anarchy from internal dissention. The only way they could protect the United States from suffering this fate was through the Sedition Act trials, successfully prosecuting and convicting at least 26 individuals accused of seditious libel, a high misdemeanor punishable by fine and imprisonment.

Federalists narrowly won passage of a series of four laws in June and July 1798 to give Federalist-dominated federal government expansive powers to silence critics of Federalist officials and their government: the "Naturalization Act," the "Alien Friends Act," the "Alien Enemies Act," and the "Sedition Act. " The "Sedition Act"

would prove to be the most controversial and resulted in well-publicized criminal prosecutions. Most states already had their own sedition and libel acts, and it was not clear that the federal government had authority over common-law crimes. The new federal Sedition Act prohibited opposition to the operation of federal laws or officers, aiding insurrections or assembling unlawfully, or making defamatory statements about the federal government or the president.

The acts ignited the first serious debate about the U.S. Constitution's First Amendment free speech protections. The opposition Democratic-Republicans offered a broad and spirited defense that included assertions that state governments could nullify unconstitutional federal laws and even secede from the Union, as Confederate states would in the Civil War. They also questioned the appropriate role of the federal judiciary, this in response to the openly partisan conduct of the Federalist judges presiding over the sedition trials.

Secretary of State Thomas Pickering enforced the act by identifying seditious writers and having them prosecuted in the federal circuit courts. At least 26 people, mostly Democratic-Republican publishers, were prosecuted, and 10 convicted in U.S. federal courts for seditious libel under the Sedition Act between 1799 and 1801 for publishing false information or speaking critically against the federal authorities. The trials of Matthew Lyon, James Thompson Callender, and Thomas Cooper were the most publicized.

While running for reelection, Irish-born Vermont congressman Lyon wrote a letter to *The Vermont Journal* to defend himself from political attacks that the Adams administration had leveled against him. In another letter, Lyon criticized Adams and Congress and became the first person indicted for violating the Sedition Act. Despite his argument that the act was unconstitutional, Judge Samuel Chase instructed the jury that they were to disregard this defense. Upon conviction, Lyon was fined $1,000 and sentenced to four months imprisonment. He was to be brought up again on the same charges for his jailhouse writing, but he evaded prosecution by moving to Kentucky where he was elected to Congress in 1802.

Great Britain had expelled Scottish citizen James Thompson Callender for his seditious writings. In his book *The Prospect before Us*, he criticized the Adams administration as being oppressive and hypocritical. Callender was indicted while writing for *The Richmond Examiner* in Virginia. Judge Chase, openly hostile to Callender, regularly interrupted defense counsel, made it impossible to introduce evidence, and in lengthy jury instructions, condemned the defense's claim that juries could decide on constitutionality. Distressed, defense counsel argued that federal judicial discretion should be limited, and they resigned the case. Callender was found guilty, fined $200, and jailed for nine months.

In 1794, Great Britain also exiled English-born Thomas Cooper for supporting the French Revolution. He edited a paper in Pennsylvania in which he criticized Adams, claiming that the president had conspired to attack his character, a claim authorities deemed seditious libel. He represented himself and challenged the constitutionality of the Sedition Act as contrary to having a democratic electoral system. He also argued that his statements were true, and therefore lawful. As evidence, he attempted to call the president as a witness. But Judge Chase thwarted this defense and condemned Cooper's defense as being further seditious libel. Cooper was found guilty, fined $400, and jailed for six months.

There were many other cases that had invoked this act. For example, by 1798, Philadelphia-based *Aurora* was the nation's preeminent Democrat-Republican newspaper. Benjamin Bache, Benjamin Franklin's grandson, sometimes known as Lighting Rod Junior, edited *Aurora*. His writings had accused both George Washington's and Adams's administrations of financial improprieties. He even criticized Adams's physical appearance. But Federalist leaders became convinced that Democratic-Republicans were conspiring with French revolutionaries and resolved to prosecute Bache for seditious libel when he published a copy of a letter from French foreign minister Charles-Maurice de Talleyrand. Public outcry over his arrest was fierce, and the *Aurora*'s circulation and influence greatly increased. Bache died of yellow fever before his trial while incarcerated and William Duane became the *Aurora*'s editor. In 1799, a mob of Federalist loyalists physically beat him and his companions. Federalist officials responded by trying Duane for seditious riot in the state court. He was acquitted, but a month later he accused the Federalist administration of essentially being British puppets, and he claimed to have had evidence of this in Adams's own handwriting. They arrested him, but the case faltered because authorities feared that Duane would enter Adams's embarrassing letter into evidence and win acquittal anyway.

Democratic-Republicans leaked to him a Federalist bill that would establish a new procedure for resolving contested presidential elections via a closed-door tribunal. Duane was to testify before the U.S. Senate, but his would-be counsel deemed that the senators had already prejudged Duane guilty of sedition, making his appearance pointless and dangerous, so they refused to appear. He was charged with contempt of the Senate, but evaded the process server with the warrant for his arrest until after Congress had adjourned. When Vice President Jefferson became the president, all charges against Duane were dropped.

The Alien and Sedition trials' aftermath proved bitterly ironic for the powerful Federalists, who had seen their rule as synonymous with American unity. They sought to strengthen their rule against the Democratic-Republican opposition, its dissenting speech, and its anti-federalist immigrants who altogether represented an unnerving form of popular democracy. The Alien and Sedition Acts failed to quell any of these threats and permanently ruined the Federalists.

The acts became the key issue in the 1798 and 1800 elections. Public hatred of the acts was so strong that the "revolution of 1800" permanently swept away the Federalists, bringing Jefferson's new Republican Party into power at all governmental levels. The Sedition Act expired in 1801.

Those convicted were pardoned and compensated. But the acts and the sedition trials set an important national precedent. They demonstrated for the first time that federal authorities could, and would, successfully criminally prosecute political opposition speech, and that due process protections would falter under pressure.

PAUL R. SCHUPP

See also: Haymarket Square Riot/Bombing (Chicago) (1886); *Primary Documents*/Alien and Sedition Acts (1798)

Further Reading

Kittrie, Nicholas N. and Eldon D. Wedlock, Jr. 1998. *The Tree of Liberty: A Documentary History of Rebellion and Political Crime in America, Volume I*, revised edition. Baltimore, MD: The Johns Hopkins University Press.

Ragsdale, Bruce A. 2005. "The Sedition Act Trials." Washington, D.C.: Federal Judicial Center, Federal Judicial History Office. http://www.fjc.gov/history/docs/seditionacts.pdf. Accessed April 10, 2015.

Woody, Kaity. 2013. "Alien and Sedition Trials (1798): Selected Links &Bibliography." http://law2.umkc.edu/faculty/projects/ftrials/aliensedition/alienseditionlinks.html. Accessed April 10, 2015.

Allen, Clarence Ray. *See* Ray Allen Gang (1974–1980)

Allen, Wanda Jean (1959–2001)

Wanda Jean Allen was the first black woman since 1954 to be executed in the United States, and only the sixth woman to be executed in the country since the death penalty was reinstated in 1976. Convicted in 1988 of first-degree murder of her partner, Gloria Leathers, Allen died by lethal injection at the Oklahoma State Penitentiary on January 11, 2001. Controversy arose about moral issues and biases within the judicial system regarding Allen's mental competency, sexual orientation, race, and socioeconomic status (Goodwin 2003). Due to the financial limitations of Allen's family, some supporters believe she was not presented with the proper legal opportunity to defend herself. Officially diagnosed with mild mental retardation,

the media and her supporters criticized Allen's case and execution, believing that her mental status was a factor that should have been considered at her sentencing. Allen's case would later prove to be useful to anti-death penalty activist groups.

Born into a disadvantaged family, Wanda Jean Allen suffered from brain damage and mild mental retardation from an early age. In 1975, when she was 15, a doctor was officially consulted regarding Allen's mental capacity. Allen was given an IQ test in which she scored a 69, placing her in the upper limits of mental retardation. Although treatment and a neurological exam were prescribed to help her cope with more difficult conditions and stress, neither was ever conducted (Cohen 2001).

In 1982, Wanda Jean Allen was sentenced to four years in prison on a manslaughter conviction for having killed a close childhood friend and roommate, Dedra Pettus, with whom she had gotten into an intense argument. As the argument turned violent, Allen shot Pettus in the stomach. Allen professed in a 1981 confession that she accidentally

Wanda Jean Allen appears before the Oklahoma Clemency Board to spare her life during a clemency hearing in Lexington, Oklahoma, on December 15, 2000. Her clemency was denied, and Allen was executed in January 2001. (AP Photo/J. Pat Carter)

shot Pettus from approximately 30 feet away while attempting to shoot back at Pettus's boyfriend. Conversely, forensic evidence contradicted Allen's story. A police expert alleged that powder burns and contusions on Pettus's body showed that Allen had hit her with a pistol, before shooting her in the stomach at point-blank range. Despite the evidence, however, prosecutors cut a deal with Allen, and she received a four-year prison term in exchange for pleading guilty to manslaughter.

While in prison, Allen met Gloria J. Leathers, who was serving time for forgery and larceny charges. They eventually became involved in a romantic relationship. Some prosecutors say that they became intimate while still in prison, but Allen stated that it was not until after they had both been released that the relationship formed. Allen was released from prison in 1982. Upon Leathers's release, she moved in with Allen. They lived together on and off for three years, fighting frequently, some instances of which included physical violence. Police were called to their residence on multiple occasions, forcing Leathers to temporarily move out. In 1988, Leathers decided to leave Allen permanently due to their turbulent and unstable relationship.

In October 1988, Leathers and her mother, Ruby Wilson, drove to the Village Police Station to file a report against Allen, claiming that the couple had a spat over a welfare check and the ownership of some clothing. Unbeknownst to Leathers and Wilson, Allen followed the pair to the police station in the hope to dissuade Leathers from leaving her. As Leathers exited the car, Allen confronted Leathers with her hands underneath her sweatshirt. In the midst of the conversation, Allen pulled out a gun and shot Leathers in the stomach. Leathers was rushed to the hospital in critical care and died four days later.

For Allen's murder trial, her family hired Bob Carpenter, a practitioner with no experience in trying capital cases, to represent Allen. After the prosecution made it known that they would seek the death penalty, it was believed that Carpenter wanted to withdraw from the case. During the trial, Ruby Wilson testified that Allen shot her daughter after Leathers told Allen she would not be returning to their residence. Conversely, Allen told the court that she shot Leathers in self-defense. In December 1988, the state of Oklahoma charged Wanda Jean Allen with first-degree murder and sentenced her to death. During the trial, no introduction of evidence about Allen's poor childhood or her mental status was

made. Those who criticized this omission claim that this evidence may have compromised Allen's ability to control her violent behavior during her last argument with Leathers.

In 1994, an appeal was conducted based on the notion that Allen's original murder trial had omitted pieces of pertinent evidence that could have affected the penalty imposed by the court. Notably, during the appeal, evidence of Allen's mental capacity and her disadvantaged childhood did not help to overturn the imposed death sentence.

While on death row for 12 years at Mabel Bassett Correctional Center in Oklahoma, Wanda Jean Allen became a born-again Christian and renounced her lesbianism. After numerous appeals, Allen's request for clemency was denied. At the Oklahoma State Penitentiary in McAlester, Oklahoma, Allen was executed by lethal injection on January 11, 2001. Many relatives of both Dedra Pettus and Gloria Leathers were present at the time of the execution.

Wanda Jean Allen's mental status, sexuality, and race, among other characteristics in addition to her death sentence, brought widespread attention to her case—a case that would spark much controversy and serve as a valuable reference point to many death penalty abolitionists in years to come.

TAYTE OLMA

See also: Barfield, Velma (1932–1984); Riggs, Christina (1971–2000); Wuornos, Aileen (1956–2002); *Primary Documents/Wanda Jean Allen's Clemency Letter (January 3, 2001)*

Further Reading

Allen v. State. 871 P.2d 79 (1994). https://www.courtlistener.com/oklacrimapp/81gZ/allen-v-state/. Accessed April 13, 2015.

Cohen, Adam B. 2001. "Who Was Wanda Jean?" *The Advocate* 833 (March 13): 27–31.

The Execution of Wanda Jean. 2002. Directed by Liz Garbus. New York: Home Box Office Entertainment (2006 DVD).

"The Execution of Wanda Jean' Chronicles the First Black Woman Executed in U.S." 2002. *Los Angeles Sentinel*, B3.

Goodwin, Michele. 2003. "Gender, Race, and Mental Illness: The Case of Wanda Jean Allen." In Adrien K. Wing, ed. *Critical Race Feminism*. New York: New York University Press, pp. 228–37.

Philofsky, Rachel. 2008. "The Lives and Crimes of African-American Women on Death Row: A Case Study." *Crime, Law, and Social Control* 49: 289–302.

Steele, Bruce. 2002. "Love and Death: A New Documentary about the Last Months in the Life of Executed Lesbian Wanda Jean Allen Becomes a Wrenching Love Story." *The Advocate* 859 (March 19): 63.

Altamont Free Concert (Alameda County, CA) (December 6, 1969)

The Altamont Speedway Free Festival, which took place on December 6, 1969, was billed as the largest gathering of people in modern California history. Conceived of as the "Woodstock of the West," this outdoor free rock 'n' roll concert occurred less than four months after the glorified East Coast outdoor concert in upstate New York. Located at the Altamont Motor Speedway, an unincorporated area within Alameda County approximately 50 miles east of San Francisco, rock 'n' roll acts performing included Ike and Tina Turner, Santana, The Flying Burrito Brothers, Jefferson Airplane, Crosby, Stills, Nash and Young, and the Rolling Stones. The event—fueled by rampant drug and alcohol use, violence perpetrated by the hired security force of the outlaw motorcycle gang the Hells Angels, and extremely poor large-scale concert planning—is heralded by many as the beginning of the end of the 1960s counterculture. The event ended with four deaths including the stabbing/beating death of Meredith Hunter at the hands of a Hells Angel member and 800–850 other reported injuries. Much of the violence, including the Meredith Hunter stabbing, was captured on film within the music documentary *Gimme Shelter*, which was originally conceived of as a West Coast counterpart to the filming of the Woodstock music festival, filmed earlier in 1969 in upstate New York.

Altamont, as it is widely referred to, was originally conceived of by Jefferson Airplane members Jorma Kaukonen and Spencer Dryden, as well as members of the band The Grateful Dead as a free concert to be held in San Francisco's Golden Gate Park involving multiple acts, including the Rolling Stones. After numerous venue changes the event was switched to the Altamont Speedway 48 hours prior to the concert. Organization of the event on the barren plot of land, where the concert was held, did not include a sufficient amount of medical tents or portable toilets for a crowd of 300,000. In addition, the stage for the event was constructed at the bottom of a sloping hill and was only built one meter in height above the ground. The location and height of the stage coupled with an insufficient sound system resulted in the crowd pushing downhill toward the front of the stage along with the ability of the crowd to climb onto the stage.

The Hells Angels, who had previously served as security at other hippie events within San Francisco, were enlisted by the Rolling Stones, through contacts with the Grateful Dead as stage security for the event. Though contested by some individuals involved, the Rolling Stones management allegedly provided the Hells Angels with $500 in beer in return for their security services. According to Hells Angels members including Ralph "Sonny" Barger, chief of the Bay area Angels they were enlisted to sit on the front of the stage, drink beer provided by the Rolling Stones, listen to music, and keep the crowd back from the stage. In addition and in a show of force, the Angels rode their motorcycles through the crowd and parked them in front of the stage as a barrier between the crowd and the performers.

Rampant drug and alcohol use by members of the Hells Angels, as well as many of the estimated 300,000 concertgoers, was widely acknowledged through media reports, witness statements, and the documentary film of the event, *Gimme Shelter*. In addition to beer, Hells Angels members and concertgoers were knowingly and unknowingly ingesting large amounts of lysergic acid diethylamide (LSD) in paper tab form and through laced red wine freely provided by the "Hippie Mafia" from Laguna Beach. Added to this were reports of Hells Angels ingesting secobarbital (reds) and amphetamines (speed) chased with the LSD-laced red wine.

The mixture of poor venue planning, Hells Angels security, and high levels of intoxication fueled an event that was marred by four deaths and approximately 800–850 reported injuries. Deaths included the stabbing and beating death of an 18-year-old African American male, Meredith Hunter, by Alan Passaro, a member of the Hells Angels, two deaths resulted from an unidentified hit-and-run driver who drove through a camp site, and another death occurred from an individual who drowned in a drainage ditch. Injuries included multiple skull and facial fractures from Hells Angels striking concertgoers with sawed off pool cues and throwing full cans of beer into the crowd. Marty Balin, the lead singer of the band Jefferson Airplane, while interceding in a disturbance in front of the stage, was knocked unconscious after being punched by a member of the Hells Angels. Much of the violence, including the stabbing and beating death of Meredith Hunter, occurred near the front of stage and is captured within the documentary *Gimme Shelter*.

The documentary team of the Maysles brothers and their assisting cameramen, Stephen Lighthill, and future multiple Oscar winners Walter Murch and George Lucas captured the darkness of a drug-fueled mob riot and concert on film. Included within the film is a slow motion presentation of the stabbing and beating death of Meredith

Hunter as he brandished a pistol in front of the stage while the Rolling Stones played the song *Under My Thumb*. As Rolling Stones guitarist Keith Richards stated in his 2010 biography *Life*, "As the evening went dark and we went on stage, the atmosphere became very lurid and hairy." After Meredith Hunter's stabbing, Rolling Stones lead singer Mick Jagger pled with the audience to stop the violence and requested medical attention for victims, including Hunter. Meredith Hunter was pronounced dead at the scene and a later autopsy revealed deep stab wounds in his back and temple. Hells Angel Alan Passaro was eventually arrested and charged but later acquitted by a jury, which concluded he acted in self-defense because Hunter had brandished a gun. Even after the acquittal, the case remained open until 2004 when investigators dismissed an alternative theory that a second Hells Angel took part in the killing.

The Altamont Free Concert is considered by many to be the end of a counterculture, which was highlighted by the relative peace, love, and flower power of Woodstock and the West Coast Haight-Ashbury hippie movement. In the minds of many, the anarchy and violence of Altamont served as a bookend to the free-spirited peace of Woodstock and the beginning of tumultuous violent incidents including the almost concurrent and controversial deaths of Black Panther Party members Fred Hampton and Mark Clark on December 4, 1969, at the hands of the Chicago Police Department and the discovery of the Manson family murders in August 1969 in metropolitan Los Angeles, California.

JOHN WALSH

See also: Chicago Seven (1968); Hampton, Fred, Shooting of (December 3, 1969); Hells Angels Motorcycle Club; Manson, Charles (1934–)

Further Reading

Bangs, Lester, Reny Brown, John Burks, Sammy Egan, Michael Goodwin, Geoffrey Link, Greil Marcus, John Morthland, Eugene Schoenfeld, Patrick Thomas, and Langdon Winner. 1970. "The Rolling Stones Disaster at Altamont: Let It Bleed." *Rolling Stone*. January 21. http://www.rollingstone.com/music/news/the-rolling-stones-disaster-at-altamont-let-it-bleed-19700121. Accessed April 10, 2015.

Gimme Shelter. 1970. Directed by Albert Maysles, David Maysles, and Charlotte Zwerin (Criterion Video, 2001), DVD.

Gleason, Ralph. 1970. "Aquarius Wept." *Esquire*. August. http://www.esquire.com/features/Altamont-1969-aquarius-wept-0870. Accessed February 1, 2015.

Kirkpatrick, Rob. 2011. *1969: The Year Everything Changed*. New York: Skyhorse Publishing.

Richards, Keith. 2010. *Life*. New York: Little Brown.

Schou, Nicholas. 2011. *Orange Sunshine: The Brotherhood of Eternal Love and Its Quest to Spread Peace Love and Acid to the World*. New York: St. Martin's Press.

Sragow, Michael. 2000. "'Gimme Shelter': The True Story." *Salon*. August 10. http://www.salon.com/2000/08/10/gimme_shelter_2/. Accessed February 1, 2015.

Amber Alert. *See* Hagerman, Amber, Kidnapping and Murder of (1996)

Amedure, Scott, Murder of (1995)

Scott Bernard Amedure (1963–1995) is a murder victim who was fatally shot to death in 1995 after his brief appearance on *The Jenny Jones Show*, where he revealed his attraction to a male acquaintance, Jonathan Schmitz. Schmitz, the perpetrator, was found guilty of second-degree murder and sentenced to 25–50 years in prison with the possibility of parole after 20 years. The case created a media firestorm about the confrontational nature of talk shows, the limits of the First Amendment, and partly, an examination into the ethics of television. Companies involved in the production of the show were sued. Many executives and producers of talk shows were reportedly unaware of the content on many of these shows. Amedure's death forced many advertisers to stay away from talk shows until the scrutiny disappeared. The case led to further discussions on the merit of a *gay panic defense*, and the potential consequences for the criminal justice system if such a defense was sufficient to protect the defendant from criminal liability. At the time, discussion of homosexuality was rare and its presentation on television was the initial source of controversy.

Amedure was born in Pittsburgh, Pennsylvania, on January 26, 1963. He moved to Michigan with his family shortly after, and resided there until his death. He dropped out of high school, but later earned his GED, the high-school diploma equivalent. Amedure served in the military for about four years before returning to Michigan. As an openly gay man, he was invited by *The Jenny Jones Show* for a taping in 1995, where the show's topic was reportedly titled "Secret Admirers." At the time, Amedure lived in a mobile home and was a bartender, but unemployed.

Schmitz, who was born on July 18, 1970, reportedly had a documented history of mental illness. He was gainfully employed at Fox and Hounds Restaurant in Michigan, and lived in his own apartment. Although there are disputes about whether Schmitz was warned that his admirer might be a male, he was reportedly uncomfortable and embarrassed by Amedure's display of affection and statement of a sexual fantasy involving him. The episode featuring both Amedure and Schmitz was never aired live on television, but segments with Amedure proclaiming his affection for Schmitz was repeatedly shown on a number of different television stations. Despite reports that Amedure left Schmitz a suggestive note at his home after the show, there was no evidence that Amedure acted on his fantasy. The note, however, was sufficient to influence Schmitz's actions. He called 911 and reported that he killed Amedure.

In 1996, Schmitz was convicted of second-degree murder and the possession of a firearm in the commission of a felony and was sentenced to 25–50 years in prison with the possibility of parole after 20 years. Schmitz's legal team appealed the ruling, which was overturned in 1998 because of an error involving the selection of the jury. He was granted a retrial in 1999 where prosecutors were barred from seeking a first-degree murder conviction, while the defense was prohibited by Michigan's law from including the diminished capacity defense in a second-degree murder charge. Schmitz was found guilty of the same charge and his sentence was reinstated with credit given for the time already served.

The case gave rise to one of the most documented cases of the so-called gay panic defense (also known as the homosexual panic defense [HPD]), which is described as a state of temporary insanity as a result of unwanted sexual advances (Lee 2003, 68). This defense was considered controversial because as a form of psychosis, not much was known about it and the debate was far from settled. Schmitz reported claim of embarrassment and outrage by a secret gay admirer might have been reasonable and true, if he had expected his admirer to be a female. In part, because in 1995, heterosexual orientation was regarded as the norm in society, which supports a reasonable assumption that a secret admirer will be of the opposite sex (Lee 2003, 93–95). Given that he killed Amedure three days after the show, he was not in an immediate state of panic and had time to plan the killing.

Amedure's family sued *The Jenny Jones Show*, Telepictures, and Warner Brothers for negligence and the tactics that led to his death. In the case of Michigan's law, a jury's unanimity is not required in civil cases. The jury consisted of nine members—five women and four men, who voted 8-to-1 to hold Warner Brothers negligent. As such, Amedure's family was awarded over $25 million—$20 million for his death, $5 million for his pain and suffering, and $6,500 for funeral expenses. Based on the ruling, the show was responsible for his death because it deliberately created a contentious environment without regard to the potential consequences. It also suggests that journalists and media organizations should be mindful of their own responsibilities because failure to do so might result in both professional and financial repercussions. The decision forced other talk shows to screen guests more closely while many producers made a decision not to air any shows in the future that featured crushes of the same-sex.

Although Warner Brothers was found negligent, initial payment was not necessary until appeals were exhausted. At each stage of the appeal process, the company could continue its appeal until it reached the U.S. Supreme Court. However, in October 2002, the Michigan Court of Appeals in a 2-to-1 decision overturned the previous ruling by concluding that the show was not responsible for Amedure's death. The Michigan Supreme Court has declined to review the case.

The case was closely monitored by many different interest groups that had various opinions on who should be held responsible. Gay rights advocates argued that by shifting the blame to the talk show rather than Schmitz, accusers have fed homophobic ideas that preclude Schmitz from legal responsibilities for his criminal actions. Others suggested that the public should be able to decide which shows they wish to watch, given the success of other similar shows, such as *The Jerry Springer Show*, which have become successful in drawing in audiences. Some legal experts who were familiar with the case claimed that the case had set a precedent that may influence mass media in the future. The ruling from the criminal case suggests that any so-called temporary insanity as a result of unwanted homosexual advances was unfounded.

Marika Dawkins

See also: Judd, Winnie Ruth (1905–1998); Mineo, Sal, Murder of (1976); Schaeffer, Rebecca, Murder of (1989)

Further Reading

Barkin, Steve Michael. 2003. *American Television News: The Media Marketplace and the Public Interest.* Armonk, NY: M.E. Sharpe.

Biagi, Shirley. 2011. *Media/Impact: An Introduction to Mass Media, 2011 Update.* 9th ed. Boston: Wadsworth.

Bradsher, Keith. 1999. "Talk Show Ordered to Pay $25 Million After Killing." *The New York Times.* May 8. http://www.nytimes.com/1999/05/08/us/talk-show-ordered-to-pay-25-million-after-killing.html. Accessed April 13, 2015.

Carter, Bill. 1995. "Killing Poses Hard Questions about Talk TV." *The New York Times.* May 14. http://www.nytimes.com/1995/03/14/us/killing-poses-hard-questions-about-talk-tv.html?pagewanted=all&src=pm (Accessed April 26, 2014). Accessed April 13, 2015.

Carter, Bill. 1996. "Talk-Show Host Is to Testify in Trial." *The New York Times.* October 16. http://www.nytimes.com/1996/10/31/us/talk-show-host-is-to-testify-in-trial.html?pagewanted=all&src=pm. Accessed April 13, 2015.

Goodman, Walter. 1999. "Critic's Notebook; Curbing Jennys and Jerrys without Curbing Rights." *The New York Times.* May 12. http://www.nytimes.com/1999/05/13/arts/critic-s-notebook-curbing-jennys-and-jerrys-without-curbing-rights.html?src=pm. Accessed April 13, 2015.

Green, Michael. 1995. "TV's Fatal Attraction: A Surprise Meeting on Jenny Jones Ends in a Shocking Shotgun Murder." *People.* March 27. http://www.people.com/people/archive/article/0,,20105369,00.html. Accessed April 13, 2015.

James, Caryn. 1996. "From Talk to Murder, Via TV." *The New York Times.* October 29. http://www.nytimes.com/1996/10/29/arts/from-talk-to-murder-via-tv.html. Accessed April 13, 2015.

Lee, Cynthia. 2003. *Murder and the Reasonable Man: Passion and Fear in the Criminal Courtroom.* New York: New York University Press.

Sadler, Roger L. 2005. *Electronic Media Law.* Thousand Oaks, CA: Sage Publications.

American Gothic Killers. *See* Copeland, Ray (1914–1993) and Faye Copeland (1921–2003)

Ames, Aldrich Hazen (1941–)

Aldrich Hazen Ames was a Central Intelligence Agency (CIA) officer, who secretly volunteered to spy for the then-Soviet Union against the United States. His treachery led to the deaths of at least 10 men who secretly cooperated with the CIA and Federal Bureau of Investigation (FBI), providing sensitive information about Soviet operations and plans at the height of the Cold War (Duffy 1995). Ames spied against the United States for nine years, rendering ineffective many intelligence and counterintelligence operations targeting the Soviet Union. In 1994, the FBI arrested Ames. He was convicted of espionage and sentenced to life in prison without parole.

On April 16, 1985, Aldrich Hazen Ames visited the Soviet Embassy in Washington, D.C., not far from the White House (Maas 1995). While there, he provided secret CIA information to the KGB and volunteered to supply additional secret and top secret information in exchange for money (Wise 1995). At the time, Ames was employed by the CIA as the chief of the Counterintelligence Unit within the Soviet-East European (SE) Division (Weiner, Johnston, and Lewis 1995).

As chief of the Counterintelligence Unit, Ames was supposed to review the procedures for secretly communicating with the recruited Soviet officials, each of whom had—at great risk to themselves—agreed to secretly work for the United States (Grimes and Vertefeuille 2012); instead, he betrayed their identities to the KGB, which quietly rounded up the officers that Ames told them about. Most of the officers—at least 10—were executed with a bullet to the back of the head.

Not long after Ames visited the Soviet Embassy, the window into Soviet plans and intentions went dark, a potentially disastrous development at the height of the Cold War between the United States and the Union of Soviet Socialist Republics (USSR). Ames's wife, Rosario, was a former Colombian diplomat. He met her while stationed in Mexico where she was also assigned (Wise 1995). Prior to their wedding in August 1985, Ames became convinced that he would be unable to provide the kind of lifestyle he thought she wanted. He was also a heavy alcohol user. After he began secretly working for the Soviets, he told her about his spying and she assisted him.

The Year of the Spy

Ames volunteered to work for the KGB, the Soviet Union's foreign intelligence agency, in 1985, but 1985 became known as the Year of the Spy because several prominent espionage arrests occurred against the backdrop of the Cold War. These arrests included members of the John Walker family, including his brother Arthur, his son Michael, and Walker's friend Jerry Whitworth, who sold U.S. Navy secrets to the

Soviets. Ronald Pelton, a National Security Agency (NSA) employee, was arrested for selling details of a top secret eavesdropping operation to the KGB. Edward Lee Howard, a former CIA officer who sold secrets to the KGB, escaped arrest and prosecution by fleeing to the Soviet Union. Jonathan Jay Pollard was arrested for selling navy secrets to Israel, and Larry Wu-Tai Chin was arrested for selling State Department secrets to the Chinese. Sharon Scranage was a CIA secretary in Accra, Ghana, who was arrested for spying for Ghana.

The Soviets paid him for the information he provided. In all, after nine years, the Soviets paid him $2.7 million (Johnston 1994, 7B). In the Washington, D.C. area, Ames placed top secret and secret CIA documents in "dead drops," usually under bridges or in a pipe. A "dead drop" is a means of communication where the sender and the receiver never see each other, each visiting the "dead drop" at different times (Affidavit 1994). Typically, Ames would make a chalk mark at a "signal site," letting the KGB know that he planned to make a drop at a prearranged location. Later, he would fill the dead drop at the prearranged location. After some time had passed, a KGB officer would ensure he was not being followed by the FBI and would retrieve the documents. Later, the KGB would erase the chalk mark Ames had made earlier that day. Finally, Ames would revisit the signal site to make sure the chalk mark had been erased—the sign to him that his documents had been safely retrieved by the KGB (Wise 1995).

When Ames was working in Italy in the late 1980s and when he visited his wife's family in Bogota, Colombia, the KGB would spirit Ames into the local Soviet (and later, Russian) Embassy where they would accept the documents and debrief him.

When the CIA realized that secret information from recruitments-in-place and technical operations had dried up, they began to try to determine what had gone wrong. At the same time, the KGB was aware of the jeopardy in which they had placed Ames when they arrested the U.S. recruitments-in-place so suddenly (Cherkashin 2005); therefore, they initiated deception operations to mislead the mole hunters.

These CIA analysts worked together with FBI analysts and, over time, concluded that Ames should be the focus of investigation (Early 1997). In May 1993, the FBI opened an espionage investigation regarding Ames codenamed NIGHTMOVER (Major Case 43) (Wise 1995). Normally, a FBI squad has as many as 200 cases; a special ad hoc squad, MC-43, as it was known, was formed and had only one case: NIGHTMOVER.

MC-43, using the FBI's Special Surveillance Group (SSG), conducted physical surveillance of Ames, following him in airplanes, in cars, and on foot. SSG members are surveillance specialists, who are skilled in photography and disguises. A special agent accountant conducted an in-depth financial analysis, which demonstrated that Ames was living far above his means. Special agents and Spanish language specialists listened in on telephone calls placed by Ames and Rosario, who often spoke to her family in Bogota. They also listened to microphones that Squad MC-43 surreptitiously placed inside the Ames residence. Listening in on their conversations provided valuable information about Ames's plans. Electronic surveillance using wiretaps and microphones was authorized by a special court, which was established pursuant to the Foreign Intelligence Surveillance Act (FISA) (Affidavit 1994).

A big break in the case occurred in September 1993 when SSG members found a yellow "Post-it" note in Ames's trash. The 2-inch-by-2-inch note, which had been torn into nine pieces, made reference to a planned trip to Bogota, where Ames would meet his KGB handler (Wiser 1994).

Aftermath of Ames Case

The Intelligence community was subjected to intense scrutiny in the days and months following Aldrich Ames's arrest for the failure to identify him sooner and failures with respect to vetting. In addition, the espionage statute was later amended to add Supreme Court–mandated aggravating circumstances to its text, so that persons who commit crimes similar to Ames would be eligible for the death penalty. Finally, the Foreign Intelligence Surveillance Act was amended to authorize court-ordered physical searches.

FBI special agents secretly followed Ames during his next visit to Bogota where they photographed Ames and, separately, his KGB handler inside a shopping mall (Affidavit 1994). In addition, FBI special agents secretly searched Ames house one night when Ames, Rosario, and their son were away from home. The search was conducted pursuant to the power of the president and without a warrant, because the agents did not want to disclose the search to Ames, which would be required if a search warrant had been obtained.

In February 1994, when Ames's CIA assignment required him to travel to Russia, the FBI obtained warrants for his arrest on espionage charges, the arrest of his wife, and searches of his house and car (Wiser, 1994). Inside the house, the FBI found documents from his KGB handlers and other evidence. As part of a plea agreement, Rosario Ames pled guilty and was sentenced to 63 months in prison. Ames pled guilty, forfeited his assets, agreed to cooperate in the intelligence community damage assessment, and was sentenced to the maximum penalty available, life in prison without parole.

LESLIE G. WISER, JR.

See also: Arnold, Benedict (1741–1801); Burr, Aaron, Treason Trial of (1807); Hiss, Alger (1904–1996) and Whittaker Chambers (1901–1961); Rosenberg, Julius and Ethel Rosenberg Espionage Case (1950–1953)

Further Reading

Affidavit of FBI Supervisory Special Agent Leslie G. Wiser, Jr. in the matter of *United States v. Aldrich Hazen Ames et al.* before the United States District Court for the Eastern District of Virginia, February 21, 1994 (unpublished).

Cherkashin, Victor, and Gregory Feifer. 2005. *Spy Handler: Memoir of a KGB Officer.* New York: Basic Books.

Duffy, Brian. 1995. "The Cold War's Last Spy." *U.S. News & World Report* 118 (March 6): 48–63.

Early, Pete. 1997. *Confessions of a Spy: The Real Story of Aldrich Ames.* New York: G.P. Putnam's Sons.

Grimes, Sandra, and Jeanne Vertefeuille. 2012. *Circle of Treason: A CIA Account of Traitor Aldrich Ames and the Men He Betrayed.* Annapolis, MD: Naval Institute Press.

Johnston, David. 1994. "U.S. Shows List of Secrets Moscow Wanted to Obtain." *New York Times*, March 2.

Maas, Peter. 1995. *Killer Spy: The Inside Story of the FBI's Pursuit and Capture of Aldrich Ames, America's Deadliest Spy.* New York: Warner Books.

Weiner, Tim, David Johnston, and Neil A. Lewis. 1995. *Betrayal: The Story of Aldrich Ames, an American Spy.* New York: Random House.

Wise, David. 1995. *Nightmover: How Aldrich Ames Sold the CIA to the KGB for $4.6 Million.* New York: HarperCollins.

Amish School Shootings (Lancaster County, PA) (October 2, 2006)

On October 2, 2006, Charles Carl Roberts IV entered the one-room schoolhouse in the Old Order Amish community of Nickel Mines, located in Lancaster County, Pennsylvania. After excusing the male students and women who either were pregnant or had infants with them, Roberts took 10 girls between the ages of 6 and 13, hostage inside the schoolhouse. Responding law enforcement attempted to get Roberts to surrender, but to no avail. Just after 11:00 a.m., Roberts opened fire, shooting all 10 girls execution style. Roberts then committed suicide. Five of the girls who were shot survived, but the others were killed.

At approximately 10:25 a.m., as the children reentered the schoolhouse following recess, Roberts arrived at the building. Using the ruse of searching for a missing clevis pin, a piece of a fastener used in farming equipment, Roberts accessed the schoolhouse. When teacher Emma Mae Zook denied seeing the pin, Roberts exited to his vehicle, only to return moments later with a 9 mm handgun. He ordered the male students to help him unload his truck, which he had stocked with two other weapons (a 12-gauge shotgun and a 30 caliber bolt action rifle), ammunition for

Amish School Shooting gunman, Charles Carl Roberts IV, appears in this November 25, 2013, photo taken by his mother, Terri Roberts. When her son was forgiven by the Amish community, Roberts was comforted and then inspired to share her experience and message of hope with others. (AP Photo/Bradley C Bower)

the three firearms, lumber, chains, and tools, among other items. He also had a duffle bag with provisions including a change of clothes, toilet paper, candles, and flexible plastic ties.

As the boys helped Roberts unload his vehicle, Zook and her mother, who was visiting the schoolhouse that day, managed to escape and run to a nearby farm, where they called 911. The call was received around 10:36 a.m. Once the vehicle was unloaded, Roberts used the lumber to barricade the front door. He then ordered the 15 male students, one pregnant woman, and three parents with infant children to leave the schoolhouse. One of the younger female students, nine-year-old Emma Fisher, also escaped when she fled after her brother. Fisher did not speak English, so she did not understand Roberts's orders for all of the girls to line up in front of the chalkboard or be shot. The remaining 10 girls complied, and stood in a line with their backs to Roberts. He then bound them using the plastic ties.

At approximately 10:42 a.m., the first trooper arrived on scene. As they waited for reinforcement, the first responding officers attempted to make contact with Roberts over the public address system. A request was made for Roberts to throw his weapons out and surrender, but he declined and demanded that officers retreat. Additional troopers, emergency medical personnel, and members of the Amish community had all gathered outside of the schoolhouse over the next 18 minutes. Police dispatchers were able to establish contact with Roberts via telephone, and again asked him to release the children and surrender. He again refused, and ordered law enforcement back or he would start shooting the girls.

Just before 11:00 a.m., Roberts placed a second call to his wife. He had last seen her earlier that morning, as they walked their three children to the school bus stop near their home. They spoke only for a few moments as she drove back to their home from her prayer study group meeting, during which time Mrs. Roberts recounted that her husband sounded emotionally distressed and very disturbed as he confessed to molesting two young family members years earlier. As she arrived at the house, she found four separate suicide notes carefully laid on the kitchen table—one addressed to her, and one to each of the children. At 10:58 a.m., she called 911 and was connected with the state police to provide them with additional information about her husband.

Moments prior to the start of the shooting, two of the older students, sisters Marian and Barbara Fisher, aged 13 and 11, respectively, pled with Roberts to shoot them first, in the hopes that the remaining girls would be spared. The girls, along with their classmates, also conversed with one another, offering prayers and support for one another when they realized their fate. At approximately 11:07 a.m., Roberts opened fire, shooting each of the girls, some multiple times. As law enforcement immediately converged on the building, Roberts committed suicide with a gunshot to the head.

The Legacy of the Amish Schoolhouse Shooting

Following many mass shooting events, responses, particularly those toward the shooters, are punitive in nature. This, however, was not the case following the massacre at the Amish schoolhouse. Following the shootings, members of the Amish community rejected the idea of hate toward the shooter or the surviving members of his family. Within hours, in fact, some of the Amish reached out to Roberts's widow, Marie, and their three children. They offered both forgiveness of Roberts's actions and support for his family. Approximately 30 members of the Amish community attended Roberts's funeral, and his widow was one of the few outsiders invited to the funeral for one of the slain girls. Members of the Amish community also set up a charitable fund to help support Roberts's family left behind. Ultimately, despite the loss of life that day, it is the compassion and forgiveness of the Amish community that remains the legacy of October 2, 2006.

After two-and-a-half minutes, law enforcement was able to make entry into the building. Barbara Fisher and four other students—Rosanna King, age six; Rachel Ann Stoltzfus, age 8; Sarah Ann Stoltzfus, age 12; and Esther King, age 13—each were wounded in the attack but survived. Barbara's sister, Marian, and seven-year-old Naomi Rose Ebersol were pronounced dead at the scene. Anna Mae Stolzfus, age 12, was pronounced dead on arrival at Lancaster General Hospital on the day of the shooting. Two of the younger students—Lena Zook Miller, age eight, and Mary Liz Miller, age seven—died at other hospitals the next day.

Roberts was not a stranger to the Amish community. Though he lived in Georgetown in a neighboring township, Roberts worked as a milk truck driver who regularly delivered to several of the Amish farms, including families of several of the victims. Coworkers described Roberts's mood as changing over the prior few months, though rebounding to an upbeat and happy mood within the week prior to the shootings. Though a specific motive was not identified, it was speculated that Roberts was angry with God over the death of his daughter nine years earlier. She had died 20 minutes after birth, and the suicide notes indicated that Roberts had never gotten over this loss.

Nearly a week after the shooting, the West Nickel Mines School was demolished. As a tribute to the victims, the area was left as a quiet pasture to commemorate the lives of those lost in the event. A new schoolhouse was erected, and construction completed six months to the day after the shooting. Christened the New Hope School, the schoolhouse was set in another area of the community and was designed to bore no resemblance to the West Nickel Mines School. Despite suffering serious and, in some cases, debilitating injuries during the shooting, four of the five girls wounded returned to class at the New Hope School.

JACLYN SCHILDKRAUT

See also: Columbine High School Shootings (Littleton, CO) (April 20, 1999); Lanza, Adam Peter (1992–2012); Virginia Tech Massacre (April 16, 2007); Weise, Jeffrey (1988–2005)

Further Reading

Beiler, Jonas. 2009. *Think No Evil: Inside the Story of the Amish Schoolhouse Shooting … and Beyond.* New York: Howard Books.

Kraybill, Donald B., Steven M. Nolt, and David L. Weaver-Zercher. 2010. *Amish Grace: How Forgiveness Transcended Tragedy.* San Francisco, CA: Jossey-Bass.

Logue, James N. 2008. "Violent Death in American Schools in the 21st Century: Reflections Following the 2006 Amish School Shootings." *Journal of School Health* 78(1): 58–61.

Spicher-Kasdorf, Julia. 2007. "To Pasture: 'Amish Forgiveness,' Silence, and the West Nickel Mines School Shooting." *Cross Currents* 57(3): 328–347.

Amistad Slave Ship Case (1839)

The African revolt onboard the slave-ship *L'Amistad* and their subsequent legal struggle all the way up to the Supreme Court fascinated the American people, and placed slavery into a context that helped humanize the African slave as never before. The Africans' success in throwing off their own shackles, and overcoming their captors, also emboldened those who believed in militant action to end slavery. The revolt's leader, Cinque, became a "Black Spartacus" to the antislavery movement. John Brown was inspired by Cinque's "personal bravery." Newspapers in the north lionized the Amistad Africans. Plays, such as *The Long, Low, Black Schooner* made the Africans the central figures and heroes in a dramatic fashion. In a pamphlet about the Amistad, an author wrote that "Liberty is Heaven born, 'Twas man that made the slave." On the other hand, the Southern reaction was one of fear and betrayal. The Supreme Court had turned loose men who killed slaveholders; it was a tacit endorsement of a slave rebellion, the biggest fear of the Southern states. Nat Turner had led a slave revolt in Virginia just eight years prior wherein slaves killed roughly 60 whites. The Amistad rebellion and the Supreme Court's ruling was further evidence, to Southerners, that the federal government was turning against them.

The Amistad Africans were primarily of the Mende tribe, although roughly nine ethnic groups were represented. Most of them were farmers, craftsmen, and hunters. Warfare was a way of life in eastern Africa. All villages had a wall or palisade to keep livestock in and attacking raiders out. Mende towns had a "war village" at the center where weapons could be snatched up at a moment's notice to fight attackers. This warrior culture also practiced slavery; prisoners of war often became slaves. Slavery and warfare among Africans exploded due to the slave trade. Prisoners were not just domestic servants to the conqueror, but valuable commodities for trade.

The Amistad Africans were gathered at Fort Lomboko, and set aboard a ship bound for Havana, Cuba. The British had declared the slave trade illegal in 1807, but the demand for slaves was so high that slavers risked being attacked by British ships. The Mende made it to Havana, and were secretly put on board the *Amistad*. The 1,200-ton British man-of-war *Romney* had made port in Havana, and the slavers knew that if the British realized they were about to ship slaves out that they would be arrested. The *Amistad* made it out of Havana, headed for a second Cuban port.

Life on a slave ship was a harrowing experience for the captive. Beatings were common. Slaves were given just enough food to keep them alive. The ship's captain, Ferrer, was identified as especially cruel, as was the cook, Celestino. The Mende later told chroniclers about how Celestino would drink water in front of them as they sat in the heat without refreshment. Several of the slaves were flogged and then had salt rubbed into their wounds.

The common perception among whites of the day was that Africans were docile, subservient, and cowardly. This explains why slavers believed that beatings were the most effective way to control Africans on slave-ships. Celestino actually told Cinque' that the *Amistad* prisoners were going to be taken to an island nearby, cooked, and eaten. Celestino's intent was to pacify and terrorize the prisoners. It backfired.

An older Mende, Lubos, roused the prisoners under the deck. Lubos reminded the Mende that they were warriors who had not been conquered by fair means. Soon someone asked "[w]ho is for war?" Cinque' and three others snuck onto the upper deck under the cover of darkness. The four men picked up clubs and beat Celestino to death. More prisoners made their way to the deck. A sailor, Ruiz, told them to get back below the decks. Ruiz called to a sailor named Montes to kill some of the slaves, because Africans were "great cowards." The Africans then killed Captain Ferrer and two unnamed sailors. Two other sailors dove overboard in the fray. Antonio, Montes, and Ruiz were left alive, although Montes and Ruiz were battered.

The Mende did not know how to navigate the ship, so they chose to leave the remaining sailors alive. The sailors were ordered to take the ship to Africa. Instead, the sailors plotted a course for the Southern United States—slave territory. However, the ship wound up being captured by the U.S. Navy in Connecticut, and the mutineers were imprisoned on murder charges.

At this point, various parties began to claim the Amistad slaves as their property. Montes and Ruiz, the Spanish government (represented by the United States), and several "salvagers" claimed ownership of the Mende. Abolitionists quickly retained an attorney for the Mende's defense: Roger Sherman Baldwin. He proposed a bold defense. In essence, Baldwin argued that because the Mende were free men, they had the right to defend their freedom, with violence if necessary.

The court quickly ruled that there was no jurisdiction to hear murder charges, as the killings had taken place at open sea well away from U.S. territory. An expert witness, Dr. Richard Madden, testified that based on his interactions with the Mende that they were not born in Cuba or there prior to 1820, which would have legally made them slaves. Dr. Madden concluded that the Mende were from Africa itself. This made them, as a matter of law, free men taken in defiance of law banning the importation of slaves. Judge

Judson, the District Court judge, ruled that the Mende had been taken illegally, and ordered them returned to Africa. The ruling was appealed to the Supreme Court.

Arguing for the Mende, with Baldwin, was former president John Quincy Adams. Adams was opposed to slavery, and had been approached to argue the case before the Supreme Court. A person with Adams's importance and fame was needed for the case, because it had become abundantly clear that the sitting president, Martin Van Buren, wanted to turn the Mende over to Spain as to avoid any kind of friction with the Spanish crown. Adams agreed, despite his advanced age and the fact that he had not practiced law in roughly 30 years.

The Supreme Court affirmed the lower court's ruling 7–1, holding that the Mende had never been slaves, and therefore could not be sent back to Cuba or turned over to the Spanish. At least tacitly, this meant the Supreme Court had acknowledged the legitimacy of the Mende's rebellion aboard the *Amistad*, and their right to secure their liberty by violent means.

The *Amistad* incident achieved something extraordinary. As recently as 1838, riots against antislavery politicians and African Americans had taken place in the Northern United States. Yet the Mende were not hated; the Mende's public image was largely positive. Some scholars believe this is because the *Amistad* rebellion allowed Americans to see slavery in a more objective fashion than they had before. The Mende were all African, born on another continent, and pressed into slavery against their will. The slavers were Spanish. The situation was different from an African American born a slave owned by a fellow American. Whatever the reason, the *Amistad* incident strengthened the political power of antislavery forces, and helped pave the way for future abolitionists to finally put an end to the practice.

JOHN FRIEND

See also: Harpers Ferry (VA), Raid on (October 17, 1859); Nat Turner's Rebellion (1831); *Primary Documents/Amistad* Case: Arguments of Roger S. Baldwin before the U.S. Supreme Court (1841)

Further Reading

Jones, Howard. 1997. *Mutiny on the Amistad: The Saga of a Slave Revolt and Its Impact on American Abolition, Law, and Diplomacy.* New York: Oxford University Press.

Osagie, Iyunolu Folayan. 2000. *The Amistad Revolt: Memory, Slavery, and the Politics of Identity in the United States and Sierra Leone.* Athens: University of Georgia Press.

Rediker, Marcus. 2012. *The Amistad Rebellion: An Atlantic Odyssey of Slavery and Freedom.* New York: Viking.

Anastasia, Albert (1902–1957)

Albert Anastasia, born Umberto Anastasio in the Calabria region of Italy in 1902, was involved in violence and organized crime from a young age. He began his career as an assassin and worked his way up as an integral part of Murder, Inc. He was a close associate of Lucky Luciano and other famous mobsters of the era. He rose to power as a boss of the Mangano crime family, predecessors of the Gambino crime family, but was himself assassinated in the barbershop of the Park Sheraton Hotel in Manhattan at the age of 55 on October 25, 1957.

Albert "the Executioner" Anastasia was the eldest son of a railroad worker. He was born in the fishing village of Tropea in the Calabria region of Italy in 1902. He had eight brothers, though only his brother Anthony joined him in organized crime. He also had three sisters. He was working on a ship when he and his brother left the ship and entered the United States illegally, settling in Brooklyn and becoming active in the Longshoremen's Union and activities on the waterfront by 1919. He had committed his first homicide before he turned 20, of a fellow longshoreman by the name of Joe Torino in 1920. He was originally convicted and sent to Sing Sing, but after 18 months his conviction was overturned and he was released. A new trial was scheduled, but many witnesses disappeared or changed their story, as such, no new trial ever took place. Anastasia would only serve another brief term in prison for gun possession and a year for tax evasion, despite his long and violent career in organized crime.

Anastasia continued to work on the waterfront, mostly controlling local gambling and loan-sharking rackets and as a strike breaker. He gained a position of power in the Longshoremen's Union and made several alliances with established Mafiosi that led to his involvement in the Commission and Murder, Inc. after the Castellammarese War. Anastasia's taste for violence drew the attention of Charles "Lucky" Luciano. So much so, that Luciano chose Anastasia along with Meyer Lansky and Bugsy Siegel to be his assassination squad against mob bosses Giuseppe "Joe the Boss" Masseria and Salvatore Maranzano, the assassinations that resulted in Luciano's ascension to the boss of bosses and led to the conclusion of the Castellammarese War in 1931.

Anastasia's reward for his participation was control of Murder, Inc, the enforcement arm of Luciano's national crime syndicate, the Commission. Murder, Inc operated out of a candy shop in Brooklyn called Midnight Rose's. Anastasia developed a reputation for being a brutal and callous killer, often called the Lord High Executioner or the Mad Hatter, by both detractors and associates. In the early 1940s Murder Inc was disbanded after Abe Reles, one of its hit men was arrested and opted to cooperate with the prosecutor's office. While his information dissolved Murder Inc and led to the conviction of Louis "Lepke" Buchalter, Anastasia's closest associate in Murder, Inc., Anastasia avoided arrest. He swore out a contract on Reles that resulted in the former hit man's death. Reles, despite being under the protection of law enforcement, fell to his death from his hotel room.

Anastasia joined the U.S. military in 1942 and became a naturalized citizen. It is thought that he and his brother Anthony "Tough Tony" Anastasia were engaged in sabotage on the New York waterfront before the United States entered World War II. The purpose of this sabotage is thought to be related to a plan to convince the U.S. Navy that the mafia would be of great assistance in the coming war, partly in controlling the waterfront and partly in the conquest of Italy and that such assistance could be assured through their interaction with Luciano. This plan was partly conceived as a means to acquire a pardon for the imprisoned Luciano. Anastasia was stationed in Pennsylvania for two years and then relieved of duty.

By 1944, the Syndicate was no longer able to maintain control of the contract killing side of organized crime. Individual families reclaimed this prerogative from the floundering Murder, Inc., which never recovered from Reles's betrayal. Anastasia maintained close ties with Luciano and also Frank Costello, which angered the head of the Mangano crime family, Vincent Mangano, who was, at least in name, Anastasia's superior. He and Anastasia argued over a wide range of criminal activities and Anastasia's work with Luciano and Costello. Anastasia opted to end the argument permanently in 1951. Mangano disappeared and Anastasia took control of the Mangano crime family.

Costello backed Anastasia's bid for power and convinced the Syndicate that Anastasia's unauthorized assassination of Mangano was acceptable, as it was in self-defense. With Anastasia in control of the Mangano family, Costello gained a powerful ally against other families who were interested in Luciano's territory after Luciano was exiled to Italy after World War II. Despite the alliance, Anastasia caused a variety of problems for Costello, including his violent temper and tendency to order assassinations of non-mafia figures, an inclination that often brought too much attention to the activities of organized crime.

Anastasia had drawn the attention and ire of the U.S. government as well. In the 1950s, Anastasia's citizenship was revoked and attempts were made to deport him. He also faced tax evasion charges, though nothing stuck to Anastasia for long. The deportation hearing in 1953 for criminal activity resulted in no charges and Anastasia was permitted to stay in the United States. His tax evasion trial first resulted in a hung jury and the second trial ended in a plea bargain. Anastasia spent one year in prison for tax evasion. The key witnesses for the trial disappeared. While the government was attempting to remove Anastasia, there were also organized crime figures that were increasingly unhappy with his activities. Anastasia made an enemy of Vito Genovese, who was an enemy of Luciano and Costello. Unlike Luciano and Costello, Anastasia did not possess the same power and protection. He also ran afoul of Meyer Lansky when he attempted to gain a larger part of Lansky's gambling racket in Cuba.

Genovese successfully lobbied Anastasia's underboss, Carlo Gambino, and Gambino made a move on Anastasia. On October 25, 1957, Anastasia went to the barber shop in the Park Sheraton Hotel in Manhattan. Two masked men entered the barber shop and shot Anastasia. The murder remains unsolved. Anastasia's funeral was a quiet, private family affair. He was buried in Green-Wood Cemetery in Brooklyn. Carlo Gambino gained control of the Mangano crime family, which he then renamed after his own family. The Gambino crime family continues to operate today. Anastasia's mafia associates conspired with Gambino to arrange for Genovese's conviction for narcotics trafficking.

CLAIRISSA D. BREEN

See also: Costello, Frank (1891–1973); Genovese, Vito (1964); Murder, Incorporated; Schultz, Dutch (1901–1935)

Further Reading

Bell, Graham. 2010. *Murder, Inc.: The Mafia's Hit Men in New York City*. London: The History Press.

Elmaleh, Edmund. 2009. *The Canary Sang but Couldn't Fly: The Fatal Fall of Abe Reles, the Mobster Who Shattered Murder, Inc.'s Code of Silence*. New York: Union Square Press.

English, T.J. 2009. *Havana Nocturne: How the Mob Owned Cuba and Then Lost It to the Revolution*. New York: William Morrow Paperbacks.

Federal Bureau of Investigation (FBI). 2009. *The Albert Anastasia FBI Files*. Washington, D.C.: Federal Bureau of Investigation.

Anthony, Casey, Murder Trial of (May 24–July 5, 2011)

On July 5, 2011, millions of viewers tuned in to watch as the verdict in the Casey Anthony murder trial was handed down. Anthony stood trial for the murder of her two-year-old daughter, Caylee, in Orlando, Florida. She had pled not guilty to first-degree murder, and was facing the death penalty. After a six-week trial, during which approximately 400 pieces of evidence were presented and numerous witnesses testified, Anthony was found not guilty on charges of first-degree murder, aggravated child abuse, and aggravated manslaughter of a child. She was, however, convicted of four counts of providing false information to law enforcement, though two of these charges were overturned in a 2013 appeal.

Caylee Marie Anthony first disappeared on June 16, 2008, though the missing child was not reported to the authorities until a month later, on July 15. The report was filed by Caylee's grandparents, George and Cindy Anthony, who notified police that they had not seen the little girl in about 30 days, and that their daughter, Caylee's mother, Casey, had given them a number of different stories as to where Caylee was before finally telling them she hadn't seen her in nearly a month. During the 911 call, Cindy also reported that Casey's car, which recently had been impounded, smelled like there had been a dead body inside of it. A nationwide search ensued, but on December 11, 2008, the remains of Caylee Anthony were found in a garbage bag in a wooded swamp area just minutes from the family home.

During the search and investigation, a number of discrepancies were found in Casey's story. She had reported several times, including in her signed statement, that Caylee had been kidnapped by her nanny, Zenaida Fernandez-Gonzalez, also known as "Zanny." Casey even led police to an apartment she claimed to belong to the nanny, though would later confess that Zanny never existed, despite that she had told friends and family of her role as Caylee's nanny. Casey also claimed to work at Universal Studios, one of the local theme parks, where she had told her parents she worked for years. On July 16, 2008, as Casey and the authorities walked through the employee back lot of the park, she advised the authorities that she had not worked at the park in years, and was arrested for making false statements to police.

On October 14, 2008, after several stays in jail on various charges, Casey Anthony was indicted by a grand jury

Casey Anthony listens to testimony during the last day of hearings on a series of motions by the defense and the prosecution during her murder trial in Orlando, Florida, on March 3, 2011. Casey Anthony, accused of killing her two-year-old daughter, was found not guilty of the crime. (AP Photo/Red Huber)

on charges of first-degree murder, as well as aggravated child abuse, aggravated manslaughter of a child, and four counts of providing false information to the police, though charges of child neglect were dropped a week later. Casey was taken into custody and held without bail. She pled not guilty to all charges.

The murder trial of Casey Anthony began on May 24, 2011, in a crowded Orange County, Florida, courtroom. Judge Belvin Perry presided over the case, and the state was represented by Linda Drane Burdick and Jeff Ashton. The state hypothesized in their opening statement that Caylee's death was an attempt by Casey to free herself of parental responsibility. Casey's legal team was led by Jose Baez, who was assisted by several attorneys, including J.

Cheney Mason. While Baez acknowledged Caylee's death, he suggested that the child accidentally drowned in the family's swimming pool, and that Casey disposed of the body out of fear of her father, who the defense also claimed sexually abused Casey.

The case against Casey Anthony hinged on several key pieces of evidence. The prosecution, supported by evidence from the medical examiner, suggested that Caylee had been rendered unconscious, possibly with chloroform, by Casey, who then covered the child's nose and mouth with duct tape to suffocate her. Evidence presented indicated that an initial search of the Anthony family computer showed 84 searches related to chloroform, though this was later refuted when an error in the software was detected, revealing only one search, which, in cross-examination, Cindy Anthony revealed she had searched for the term relating to its uses in the 19th century.

The duct tape found on Caylee's remains also was admitted into evidence, as was a blanket found with the body that matched the bedding at the Anthony home. Reports from the earlier forensic examinations of the duct tape indicated that there had been residue from a heart-shaped sticker on the tape, also reviewed in UV testing, but when the tape was reexamined, the shape was no longer visible. It also was reported that there were no fingerprints found on the duct tape, though it was suggested that these could have deteriorated after such prolonged exposure to the elements.

The Other Casey Anthony Cases

In addition to the criminal murder trial for Caylee Anthony's death, Casey Anthony has also been the subject of several other suits. In September 2008, Zenaida Fernandez-Gonzalez—a.k.a. "Zanny" the nanny—sued Anthony for defamation of character, seeking punitive damages. Fernandez-Gonzalez testified during the deposition that she had lost her job, was evicted, and received numerous death threats as a result of Anthony's lies. The case is still pending. While awaiting trial for Caylee's murder, Anthony also stood trial for check fraud. Anthony admitted to stealing a checkbook from her friend, Amy Huizenga, and writing four checks, totaling approximately $650. She was sentenced to time served, but was ordered back to Florida after her July 2011 release to serve out her probation. Texas EquuSearch, a nonprofit group that assisted in the search for Caylee, sued Casey in July 2011 for fraud. The group claimed that they spent over $100,000 on the search, but that Anthony was liable because she knew the child already was dead.

Two other key pieces of evidence in the case were found in Casey's vehicle's trunk. The first, a strand of hair, was matched to Caylee using a sample from her hairbrush at the home. The strand of hair from the trunk, however, showed decomposition called "root-banding," where the hair forms a dark band close to the root upon death. Similarly, an air sample had been extracted from

the trunk and tested at the Oak Ridge National Laboratory for chemical compounds. The sample revealed compounds that were "consistent with a decompositional event," although there was no proof that it was the result of human decomposition. The laboratory's research group, headed by Dr. Arpad Vass, also testified there were traces of chloroform in the trunk, and two separate K-9 handlers testified that their dogs had alerted to decomposition, both in the trunk and also in the Anthony's backyard.

In addition to the vast amount of physical evidence in the case, the prosecution and the defense presented 59 and 47 witnesses, respectively. Among the witnesses were Casey's ex-boyfriend, Anthony Lazzaro, and several of her friends, each of whom testified about Casey's behavior in the month following Caylee's disappearance. A volunteer search worker named Krystal Holloway, who claimed to have had an affair with George Anthony, also was called by the defense, though Judge Perry advised jurors her testimony could not be used against Casey, but could be used to impeach testimony by her father. Casey Anthony never took the stand in her own defense.

Closing arguments lasted for two days, after which the jury began deliberations. The next day, they declared they had reached a verdict. Casey Anthony was acquitted on all charges related to homicide and abuse, but was found guilty of four counts of falsifying information to law enforcement. She was sentenced to four years and $4,000 in fines (one for each count), but with credit for time served, Casey Anthony was freed on July 17, 2011.

Jaclyn Schildkraut

See also: Gunness, Belle (1859–c. 1908); Hoyt, Waneta (1946–1998); Smith, Susan (1971–) ; Yates, Andrea (1964–)

Further Reading

Ashton, Jeff. 2012. *Imperfect Justice: Prosecuting Casey Anthony*. New York: HarperCollins.

Battaglia, Nicholas A. 2011. "The Casey Anthony Trial and Wrongful Exonerations: How 'Trial by Media' Cases Diminish Public Confidence in the Criminal Justice System." *Albany Law Review* 75: 1579–1613.

Gabriel, Richard. 2011. "American Justice or American Idol? Two Trials and Two Verdicts in the Casey Anthony Case." *The Jury Expert* 23(4): 1–7. http://tje.geistopolis.com/wp-content/uploads/TJEJuly2011CaseyAnthony.pdf. Accessed April 14, 2015.

Speegle, Clinton T. 2012. "The Socially Unpopular Verdict: A Post-Casey Anthony Analysis of the Need to Reform Juror Privacy Policy." *Cumberland Law Review* 43: 259–361.

Anthony, Susan B., Trial of (1873)

Women's suffragist and abolitionist, Susan B. Anthony (1820–1906), was put on trial for illegally casting a ballot on November 5, 1872, in the presidential election of Ulysses S. Grant. Anthony's decision to vote in the 1872 election was based on her protest against the lack of women's legal and suffrage rights and one that she hoped could be deemed legal due to the recent passage of the Fourteenth Amendment, which granted citizenship privileges to anyone born or naturalized in the United States. Susan B. Anthony was arrested on November 18 and on June 18, 1873, she was found guilty and sentenced to pay a fine of $100.

In 1872, the women's suffrage movement was looking grim. African American men and freed male slaves received the right to vote with the Fifteenth Amendment passed in 1869 and ratified in 1870. The women's suffragists had hoped that a version of that amendment would call for universal suffrage, including women, but their counterparts in the abolitionist movement considered women's suffrage too much of a polarizing issue and requested that the women put their hopes aside so as to not prevent the passage of the amendment.

Susan B. Anthony, considered by many to be one of the founders of the American women's suffrage movement with Elizabeth Cady Stanton, had been optimistic that the passage of the Fifteenth Amendment would result in an increase of interest in women's suffrage as well, but such interest was not forthcoming. At this time, women's rights, social, educational, political and legal were limited and the desire to vote was considered unfeminine. Women were not thought to have the appropriate mental faculties to vote. In 1872, Susan B. Anthony had been active in the women's suffrage movement for 20 years. She was 50 years old and had been campaigning ceaselessly, speaking anywhere she could and amassing a debt of $10,000 publishing her own women's rights newspaper, *The Revolution.*

She was rarely home, but had resolved in 1869 when the Fifteenth Amendment passed, that as soon as she was home for the requisite 30-day residency necessary to register to vote for an election in her home district, she would register and she would vote, hoping that she could either bring anyone who refused to allow her to do so into civil court and possibly receive a judgment that would further the cause. Her chance to put this idea into action came on November 1, 1872. Susan B. Anthony, her sisters, and 50 other women came to a voter's registration office at a local barber shop. Anthony demanded that they be allowed to register, citing the Fourteenth Amendment and their status as American citizens. She threatened legal action against the registrars. The supervisor of elections, Daniel Warner, allowed them to register, arguing that if they registered and it was wrong for them to do so, it would be on the women, rather than against the registrars.

With the appropriate registration, Susan B. Anthony prepared to vote in the upcoming presidential election. Meanwhile, the story reached the local press and a fierce debate raged as to whether or not women should vote, with most arguing that Anthony's belief that she could vote under the Fourteenth Amendment as a citizen was false, as citizenship did not guarantee suffrage. On November 5, 1872, Anthony and seven others went to the polls. The poll inspectors held a vote among themselves and decided 2-to-1 to accept her ballot.

Democratic poll watcher, Sylvester Lewis, filed a complaint against Anthony for illegal voting and it was acted upon by U.S. commissioner William C. Storrs who swore out a warrant against her on November 14, 1872, under the Enforcement Act, an act of Congress that allowed for illegal voting to carry a potential $500 fine or three years in prison. A U.S. deputy marshall came to Susan B. Anthony's residence on November 18 to place her under arrest. Fourteen women were arrested that day along with the voting inspectors who permitted them to vote.

Anthony's lawyer refused to enter a plea at the time of her arrest and a preliminary hearing was held on November 29. Arguments were made as to whether or not Anthony had knowingly violated the Enforcement Act, which required that the individual willingly and with full knowledge vote illegally. The hearing was adjourned until December. At the December hearing, the women were remanded to jail after they refused to post bail. Anthony had been hoping for this, as it would give her an option of seeking an appeal to the Supreme Court. However, despite refusing to pay bail twice, her attorney could not see her remaining in jail and paid the bail himself, closing off potential Supreme Court evaluation of the case. Anthony was indicted for illegal voting on January 24, 1873, and the trial would take place in May. Susan B. Anthony used the time between her indictment and trial to engage in a speaking tour to sway public opinion.

Susan B. Anthony's trial began on June 17, 1873, the delay a result of the prosecutor's and judge's opinions that her speaking tour had potentially prejudiced jurors in her favor and moving the trial from Monroe County to Ontario County. Recent Fourteenth Amendment cases that had been heard by the Supreme Court in the interim had not been favorable to women's rights and Anthony and her lawyer were concerned that the case was already stacked against her. At trial, Susan B. Anthony was not allowed to take the stand in her own defense, however, her attorney, Judge Henry R. Selden did call himself to the stand to testify in her defense and gave a three-hour closing argument laying out Anthony's position.

Bradwell v. Illinois

While the right to vote was the primary focus of women like Susan B. Anthony, others were attempting to use the Fourteenth Amendment to make greater in roads for women in education and the professions. The state of Illinois had a law prohibiting women from receiving a law license. In *Bradwell v. Illinois*, Myra Bradwell argued that she had the right to practice law under the Fourteenth Amendment. On December 18, 1872, Justice Bradley presented the majority opinion that the Fourteenth Amendment did not give women the right or opportunity to seek any employment, occupation, or profession outside of the home. Though she lost the case, the state of Illinois did grant Bradwell a license to practice 18 years later in 1890.

District Attorney Richard Crowley responded with a two-hour closing argument in rebuttal. After these statements, presiding Judge Ward Hunt read a statement prepared before the trial and declared that Anthony had knowingly and illegally voted and that the Fourteenth Amendment did not grant women's suffrage. He stated that her actions were illegal and charged the jury to find her guilty. Anthony was sentenced the next day on June 18, 1873, despite her attorney's motion for a new trial. Anthony was given an opportunity to speak before sentencing, however, while she spoke, Judge Hunt repeatedly interrupted her and demanded that she sit down and be silent. She was fined $100 and refused to pay. She demanded that she be imprisoned. Judge Hunt refused to do so to prevent her from being able to appeal his decision to a higher court.

Susan B. Anthony never paid her fine and petitions to Congress to remit the fine were ignored. No attempt to collect the fine was made. Susan B. Anthony died in 1906,

14 years before the ratification of the Nineteenth Amendment granting women's suffrage.

CLAIRISSA D. BREEN

See also: *Cherokee Nation v. Georgia*, Forced Removal of Indian Tribe (1831); *Plessy v. Ferguson* (1896); *Snyder v. Phelps* (2011)

Further Reading

An Account of the Proceedings on the Trial of Susan B. Anthony, on the Charge of Illegal Voting, at the Presidential Election in Nov., 1872, and on the Trial of Beverly W. Jones, Edwin T. Marsh and William B. Hall the Inspectors of Election by Whom Her Vote was Received. 1874. Rochester, NY: Daily Democrat and Chronicle Book Print.

Anthony, Susan B. 2003. *The Trial of Susan B Anthony.* Amherst, NY: Humanity Books.

Sherr, Lynn. 1996. *Failure Is Impossible.* New York: Time Books.

Arbuckle, Roscoe "Fatty," Murder Trials of (1921–1922)

The Roscoe "Fatty" Arbuckle Trials, a series of three trials in 1921–1922, constituted arguably Hollywood's first real scandal. Roscoe Arbuckle was a superstar of his time until he was accused of the murder of Virginia Rappe in 1921. The events surrounding his three trials ruined Arbuckle's career. This case received unprecedented media coverage, and marks the beginning of a trend to publicize all aspects of Hollywood star's lives.

On March 24, 1887, Roscoe Arbuckle (1887–1933) was born to William and Mary Arbuckle. His nickname was "Fatty," which often was mentioned in the title of his films. He was the "silent movies' king of slapstick" starring roles in over 150 films, directing 78 films, and had a million dollar contract with Paramount Pictures (Merritt 2013, 2). Arbuckle was truly a worldwide star.

Arbuckle's career was destroyed on September 5, 1921 (Sheerin 2011). He decided to throw a party on Labor Day weekend to celebrate his million dollar contract. He rented three rooms on the 12th floor of the San Francisco's St Francis Hotel. One of people in attendance of the party was Virginia Rappe (1891–1921) who was noted to be a struggling actress and model of the early 1920s.

Rappe came to the party accompanied by Bambina Delmont, a woman who had numerous run-ins with law enforcement. At some point during the night, Rappe and Arbuckle were alone in one of the rooms together and then there were screams from the aspiring actress. Party

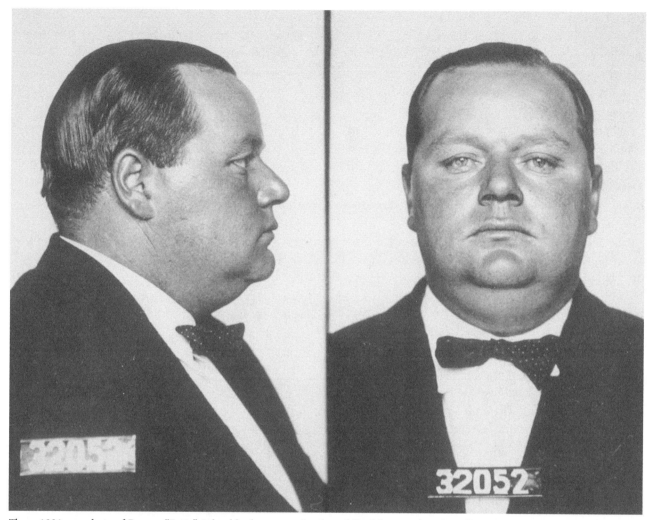

These 1921 mugshots of Roscoe "Fatty" Arbuckle document the downfall of the popular silent film actor, comedian, and director. By the time he was acquitted after a third trial for the rape and death of actress Virginia Rappe, Arbuckle's career and reputation had been destroyed. (University of California)

guests, including Delmont, rushed into the room. Despite Rappe being found fully clothed, she insisted that "he did this to me" (Sheerin 2011). Upon first examination by the Dr. Olav Kaarboe, her pain and hysteria was written off as being drunk from the free-flowing alcohol the party offered (Merritt 2013). Delmont, getting involved, told the doctor that Virginia Rappe was raped by Arbuckle, but no evidence of this assault existed. However, after developing a fever, she died in the hospital on September 9, 1921, of peritonitis (Sheerin 2011). Peritonitis is an inflammation in the tissue of the abdomen (MedlinePlus 2013). In Rappe's case this condition was caused by a ruptured bladder; the uncertainty as to the cause of her ruptured bladder is what truly launched her death into a spectacle.

Although there are conflicting accounts of what happened that night, one account was Arbuckle forced himself on Rappe, and because he was overweight, he ruptured her bladder leading to her untimely death only four days after the party. Arbuckle was brought in on charges of rape and manslaughter soon after.

From the beginning of the indictment process, this case received extraordinary media attention painting Arbuckle as a criminal with newspaper headings reading "Fatty Arbuckle Sought in Orgy Death" (PBS 2008). Furthermore, he was blacklisted in Hollywood and his films were censored. The public had condemned him. Arbuckle just wanted to get the trial over because of how it impacted his career and friendships. But there was not a quick resolution.

His first trial began November 14, 1921. The sequestered jury selected over four days consisted of five women and seven males; the attorneys were Gavin McNab, lead defense attorney, headed against assistant district attorney Milton

U'Ren (Merritt 2013, 198–202). Prosecutors called medical personnel who testified about the cause of death and the injuries sustained by Rappe such as William Ophuls and Dr. Shelby Strange, the nurse and doctor who treated Rappe, and Dr. Edward Castle. Prosecutors also called Zey Prevost and Alice Blake to provide eyewitness testimony. Delmont was never introduced as a witness because of her criminal history. The final piece of evidence from the state was the door from room 1219 that had the fingerprints of Rappe's hand being pressed to the door by Arbuckle, indicating that he might have prevented her exit. It was on this note that the state rested.

The defense focused on bringing in doctors and more importantly people that could speak to Rappe's character. Minnie Neighbors, Harry Barker, Florence Bates, and Philo McCullough all spoke of previous occasions where they have seen Rappe be pained and pulling at her clothes in public just like the night of the party. On November 28, 1921, Arbuckle took the stand. Arbuckle stuck to his story that he went to the bathroom and when he came out Rappe had fallen off the bed and onto the floor; he thought she was just drunk (Sheerin 2011).On December 2, 1921, the jury went into deliberations (Merritt 2013, 223). Two days later the jury came back 10-to-2 for acquittal, a hung jury, and a retrial was set for January 9, 1922 (226).

The second trial had a jury of 11 men and one woman that were yet again sequestered to stay away from media. However, the media had already affected most people due to the first trial. The same star witnesses appeared for District Attorney Brady as the first trial. However, Zey Prevost and Alice Blake changed their testimony now saying they did not remember that night as well. The same point of the fingerprints on the room 1219 door drove the state's case yet again. However, the defense added two fingerprint experts, Adolph Juel and Milton Carlson, to prove the fingerprints on the door could have been faked. The defense was so sure that it had disproved the state's case as the jury went into deliberations on February 1, 1922 (Merritt 2013, 252). However, this time the jury came back 10-to-2 for conviction and yet again the jury was declared hung.

The third trial began on March 16, 1922, and had a jury of four women and eight males (Merritt 2013, 259). The trial yet again followed the same line of questioning with doctors being critical for each side. Overall, the witnesses were the same as the first two trials with only slight variations. The jury needed only five minutes to finally reach a consensus: acquittal. The jury went further to say, "Acquittal is not enough for Roscoe Arbuckle. A grave injustice has been done" (Sheerin 2011, 267). It is now widely accepted that there was not any evidence tying Arbuckle to Rappe's death and the state clearly had no case.

While Arbuckle was not convicted of manslaughter, he was convicted of a violation of prohibition, the Volstead Act (Merritt 2013). This resulted in a fine of $500 in addition to $700,000 owed to his attorneys who represented him in the three trials. Furthermore, the media had already done irreversible damage to his career (PBS 2008). Arbuckle spent the rest of his life trying to get back into the movie business and on July 27, 1933, he finally received a contract with Warner Brothers. However, this contract was never fulfilled as he died later that year at the age of 46 from a heart attack (Sheerin 2011).

Kiersten Call

See also: Blake, Robert, Murder Trial of (2005); Monroe, Marilyn, Death of (1962); Simpson, O. J. (1947–)

Further Reading

MedlinePlus. 2013. "Peritonitis." http://www.nlm.nih.gov/medlineplus/ency/article/001335.htm. Accessed April 16, 2015.

Merritt, Greg. 2013. *Room 1219: The Life of Fatty Arbuckle, the Mysterious Death of Virginia Rappe, and the Scandal That Changed Hollywood.* Chicago: Chicago Review Press.

PBS. 2008. "Executed in Error: Perennial Thrillers: Murder, Mystery, Obsession." http://www.pbs.org/wnet/secrets/perennial-thrillers-murder-mystery-obsession/203/. Accessed April 16, 2015.

Sheerin, Jude. 2011. "'Fatty' Arbuckle and Hollywood's first scandal." BBC. http://www.bbc.co.uk/news/magazine-14640719. Accessed April 16, 2015.

Arch Murderess of Connecticut. *See* Sherman, Lydia (1824–1878)

Arias, Jodi (1980–)

Travis Alexander was brutally murdered in Mesa, Arizona, on June 4, 2008. His body was found in his shower with multiple stab wounds, a slit throat, and a gunshot wound to the head. Following a police investigation, his ex-girlfriend Jodi Arias became the prime suspect. After multiple denials and several different accounts of the events of the day in question, Arias claimed that Travis had been abusive in their relationship and she had killed him in self-defense.

She was charged and tried for his murder in early 2013, and was ultimately convicted of the crime of first-degree murder, punishable by death in Arizona.

The trial received a great deal of publicity and was televised in its entirety. Due to Arias's claim of having been a victim of domestic abuse, her relationship with Travis was put under a microscope during the course of the trial, leading to controversial disclosures of intimate exchanges between the two via text messages, as well as sexually suggestive pictures that were entered into evidence in an attempt to establish the nature of their relationship. After the conviction, Arias faced the penalty phase of a capital trial, where her sentence was to be decided by the jury. The jury was unable to reach a unanimous verdict and a second penalty phase had to be rescheduled. Some of the challenges faced in this trial were the selection of an impartial jury in the face of such publicity as well as the difficulties associated with determining a sentence in a capital trial.

Jodi Arias was born on July 9, 1980, in Salinas, California. She was a high school dropout who worked odd jobs while pursuing an interest in photography. Travis Alexander (1977–2008) was born in Riverside, California. He was taken in by his paternal grandmother following his father's death. She taught him and his siblings about Mormonism. He went on a two-year religious mission after high school and then moved to Mesa, Arizona, where there is a strong Mormon community. By the time he and Jodi met, Travis was a successful motivational speaker, salesman, and published author of a self-help book.

Jodi and Travis met at a work conference in Las Vegas in September 2006, and started a long-distance relationship. They e-mailed, called, and texted each other on a daily basis. Within a couple of months, Jodi had been baptized into the Mormon Church. A few months after that, in the summer of 2007, Jodi and Travis decided to end their romantic relationship, but continued to see each other as sexual partners. Following their breakup, Travis started seeing another woman. Jodi allegedly hacked into Travis's Facebook and e-mail accounts, slashed his tires and sent anonymous threatening e-mails to Travis's new girlfriend in response to this news. Despite Jodi's alarming behavior toward him and his new love interest, the evidence suggests they maintained the sexual relationship.

In early 2008 Jodi, who had moved to Mesa, decided to move to California and live with her grandparents. The relationship with Travis progressed along the same lines it had in the past. Travis continued dating other women within his church, and decided to go to Cancun with one of them. It is during this time that Jodi's grandparents' home was burglarized. Her grandfather's .25-caliber gun was among the items that were missing from the house, along with some money and a CD player.

Within a few days of the burglary, Jodi set out on a trip to Utah to meet a love interest of her own. On her way there, she stopped in Mesa to see Travis. A few days later, some of Travis's friends went to check on him after being unable to reach him for some time. Upon entering his home, they saw a trail of blood in the hallway leading to his bedroom. They found his dead body in the shower and called 911. One of Travis's friends immediately identified Jodi as a suspect.

When the police arrived, they noticed the bed looked like it had been tossed, and the linen was missing. They recovered fingerprints from the bathroom and collected blood and hair samples. Travis's camera was found in the washing machine, along with the bed linen and some of his clothing, including religious undergarments worn by people of the Mormon faith. Although the camera had been damaged, the memory card was intact and photographs of Jodi and Travis, recording the sexual encounter that took place on the day of his death, were recovered. There were also some blurry photos, seemingly taken by accident, of Travis's body covered in blood as well as random things like the bathroom ceiling and floor. This evidence, in addition to fingerprints and DNA, placed Jodi in Travis's home and implicated her in the murder.

During the investigation Jodi was interrogated several times, with her story changing with each interview. Initially, she denied any involvement in Travis's death and alleged she was nowhere near Mesa that day. Later her story evolved to admitting being in his home, but stating that some unknown intruders, whom she tried to fight off, had killed him. Eventually, she confessed to killing Travis, but said she could not remember the incident and did it because he had abused her.

During the trial, the defense argued that Travis had been violent and controlling in the relationship and he, not Jodi, had been the one to have trouble dealing with the breakup. On the day of the murder, they said, Travis attacked Jodi after becoming angry because she dropped his new camera. Experts testified that Jodi suffered from post-traumatic stress disorder (PTSD) and this diagnosis would explain her excessively violent reaction. They contended that when Travis went at her, Jodi took his gun and pointed it at him to keep him away. In the midst of the struggle the gun accidentally went off, killing Travis. Jodi claimed to have no memory of stabbing him or slitting his throat, something that could also be explained by PTSD.

On the other hand, prosecutors claimed Jodi planned out the murder. She staged the burglary at her grandparents' home so she could take the gun, rented a car, and set out to see Travis. While he showered, the prosecution said, Jodi stabbed him. Travis stepped out and struggled with her until she slit his throat in the corridor, where a large pool of blood had been found. She dragged him back to the bathroom where she shot him in the head after he was already dead.

During the trial, their intimate text messages, e-mails, and conversations were read in court. Jodi, who chose to testify on her own behalf, was asked many sexually explicit questions during her testimony. She was ultimately convicted. Because she was found to be eligible for the death penalty, the sentencing phase of the trial began immediately after her conviction. Jodi had initially said she would prefer death to life in prison, but recanted in front of the jury and made a case for why she should be given a sentence of life. The penalty phase ended with a hung jury. A second penalty phase resulted in another hung jury, which rules out the possibility of a death sentence. In April 2015 Jodi was sentenced by a judge to life without parole. She will serve her sentence in a maximum security prison in Arizona.

Eugenia Garcia-Dubus

See also: Baker, Lena (1900–1945); Fisher, Amy (1974–)

Further Reading

Lohr, David. 2012. "Jodi Arias Timeline: Key Dates in Case of California Woman Accused of Stabbing Ex-Boyfriend 27 Times (UPDATED)." *Huffington Post*. December 31. http://www.huffingtonpost.com/2012/12/31/jodi-arias-timeline_n_2387245.html. Accessed April 18, 2015.

Mesa Police Department. (2008). *Incident/Investigation Supplement Report: Case number 2008–1610844* by E. Flores.

Armstrong, John Eric (1973–)

It was around the first of the year 2000 when a man called the Dearborn Heights Police Department to report observing a dead body in the Rouge River. The corpse was that of Wendy Jordan, a known prostitute, and it was in an area of the river that was difficult to actually catch sight of. The man told police that he had fallen ill while taking a walk, and stopped to lean over the side of the bridge when he spotted the corpse. That man, John Eric Armstrong, a

husband and father of two, was about to become the focus of an investigation into the murders of five local prostitutes. His peculiar story led to intense questioning and surveillance by the police. The department began receiving tips from women (and one man posing as a woman) who were prostitutes and had been attacked by a man matching Armstrong's description. The attacker reportedly told each of them that he hated whores and prostitutes during the assaults. Police collected evidence from John Eric Armstrong and found that fibers on victim Wendy Jordan's body came from fabric in his jeep. Witnesses reported seeing him on the bridge before he placed himself there, and DNA analysis also confirmed that he had sex with Wendy Jordan before she died. Armstrong broke down when confronted with the evidence and confessed to the five Detroit-area murders. He unleashed a vicious story of killings in Thailand, Singapore, Japan, Korea, Israel, and other ports while he was a crewman on the USS *Nimitz*, the largest aircraft carrier in the world, but has not been charged with any of these murders. If his confessions are true, he would be among the most murderous serial killers of our time, and certainly the most international.

John Eric Armstrong discontinued using his first name at an early age to distance himself from his abusive (namesake) father, and was called Eric by his family and friends. He reportedly suffered a broken leg at the age of two after falling out of a window while being supervised by his father. When Armstrong was five years old, his younger brother died from sudden infant death syndrome, and his neglectful father left the family soon after. He reported being teased as a child because he was overweight. He claimed that his hatred of prostitutes began when a high-school girlfriend he adored shunned him for a different suitor who bombarded her with lavish gifts. Eric Armstrong associated the gift acceptance with prostitution, and the incident paved the way for his pursuit of infamy. Armstrong enlisted in the Navy shortly after graduating from high school. He worked as a serviceman aboard the USS *Nimitz* from 1993 through 1999, earning medals of good conduct and honorable service. He met his wife onboard the ship, marrying in 1998. Eric Armstrong left the Navy the following year, finding work at the airport as an aircraft refueler. The unassuming sailor who lived a seemingly quiet life with his family was about to be all over the headlines for his detailed claims of murdering prostitutes across the globe.

The bodies of three strangled prostitutes were found on April 10, 2000, in a secluded rail yard. They were Rose

Marie Felt (32), Kelly Hood (34), and Nicole Young (20, also known as Robbin Brown), and had been placed there at different times over the span of a month. The police suspected John Eric Armstrong since he reported finding Wendy Jordan's dead body earlier that year. They had also recently found Monica Johnson, another prostitute who was strangled and dumped barely alive along nearby Interstate 94. Investigators now knew they were dealing with a serial killer. And by the time of the rail yard discovery, they were focusing the investigation on Armstrong. Several prostitutes had identified him as their attacker in recent weeks, and evidence soon confirmed he had killed Wendy Jordan—the woman whose corpse he reported finding in the first place. John Eric Armstrong was arrested while it appeared that he was out hunting for his next victim near Detroit's southwest border, an area frequented by prostitutes. He was charged with five counts of first-degree murder and four counts of assault with intent to murder for crimes committed in the Detroit area. Though he recanted his confessions, the evidence was overwhelming. Armstrong was convicted of intently murdering Wendy Jordan after a two-week trial and sentenced to life in prison. He was also tried and convicted of the first-degree murder of Kelly Hood, receiving another life sentence. At that sentencing hearing, he pled guilty to the murders of Monica Johnson, Rose Marie Felt, and Nicole Young. The charges were reduced to second-degree murder for the plea, and John Eric Armstrong was sentenced to another 31 years to life in prison.

Investigators around the world were once trying to determine if any of Armstrong's other claims are true. Eric Armstrong admitted to as many as 30 murders around the world, beginning in 1992 in North Carolina. His confession began without delay once he was arrested. He detailed dates and particulars of several murders and assaults. Detectives found that he was supplying very intimate details about crimes that only the offender would know. During the confession, he shifted from composed to short-tempered to a sometimes sorrowful demeanor. Aside from the five women in Michigan, he has been proven to have two other victims, Linette Hillig (34) of Virginia and Lisa Fracassi (36) of Hawaii. Unfortunately, we probably won't ever know his true number of victims for several reasons. Many serial killers create elaborate stories and inflate the number of people they have killed for notoriety; the death of prostitutes often goes unnoticed or unreported; and Armstrong may believe that some of the victims he left for dead did not survive (when they actually did survive their

attacks). It is not expected that any authorities will pursue additional charges against Armstrong at this point.

NICOLE LAROSA

See also: Bundy, Ted (1946–1989); Dahmer, Jeffrey (1960–1994); Holmes, Dr. H. H. (1861–1896); Sowell, Anthony (1959–)

Further Reading

Cohen, Sharon. 2000. "Police Question Credibility of Ex-Sailor's Confession." *Los Angeles Times*. May 7.
Green, J. 2000. "A Killer on Land and Sea." *Newsweek* 135(17): 65.

Armstrong, Lance (1971–)

Lance Armstrong had an illustrious career as one of the most revered athletes in the world. Not only did he have a miraculous professional comeback after successfully fighting cancer, but he also excelled in one of the world's most difficult endurance cycling events—the Tour de France. In fact, Armstrong won the Tour de France an astonishing seven times after recovering from his bout with cancer. Furthermore, Armstrong profited millions of dollars from sponsorships throughout his career and founded the Livestrong Foundation to support people affected by cancer. Armstrong was viewed not only as an accomplished athlete but also as a beacon of hope to many suffering from life-threatening illnesses. However, everything changed in January 2013 when Armstrong, after years of feverishly denying any illegal activities in the sport of cycling, admitted the allegations of years of blood doping were true.

Armstrong's admission sent shockwaves across the world. Other cyclists had admitted to doping allegations in the past, however, none had such accomplished careers, continuously stated their innocence, and even utilized the legal system to counter the allegations. Armstrong routinely had his legal team file lawsuits and countersuits against individuals proclaiming he had doped during his career. Through these suits, Armstrong was awarded putative damages for libel and allowed to maintain his innocence. The entire process has presented the legal system with various challenges; namely, performing a retroactive removal of an athlete's accomplishments, professional status, and compensation from sponsors.

Armstrong's crime took place over several years (i.e., 1998–2005) and through various settings and events (e.g., le Tour de France, Olympic Games). In fact, blood doping in cycling was not a new crime at the time of Armstrong's doping. Cyclists were required to complete drug tests not only at the event in which they competed but also during the off-season in an attempt to catch cyclist attempting to benefit from blood doping in training. The performance enhancing substances and methods most notably under investigation are erythropoietin (EPO), corticosteroids, and blood transfusions. EPO is a synthetic version of the natural hormone that boosts red blood cell counts in the body. Corticosteroids ease inflammation and promote muscle recovery, and blood transfusions increase the overall number of red blood cells to give the athlete a performance boost.

Armstrong successfully ran what the United States Anti-Doping Agency (USADA) coined the "most sophisticated, professionalized and successful doping program that sport has ever seen" (USADA, 2012). Armstrong himself adamantly proclaimed that he has successfully passed approximately 600 drug tests in his cycling career. To further bolster his claim, Armstrong claims to have submitted to 24 unannounced drug tests by various antidoping authorities after he returned to cycling in the fall of 2008 until March 2009 without failing a single one. The methods in which Armstrong avoided detection included the aforementioned EPO, blood transfusions, corticosteroids, as well as other performance-enhancing measures.

Armstrong was not alone in his endeavors. In fact, he had a large contingent of people that helped him along the way. Former teammates reported engaging in blood doping with Armstrong, however, the most controversial figure is that of Michele Ferrari. Ferrari is a controversial athletic trainer linked to athlete doping. He received a ban from practicing medicine with cyclists by the Italian Cycling Federation for his participation in various doping cases. Furthermore, in a sworn affidavit submitted in conjunction to a lawsuit filed against Armstrong, a former therapist (Emma O'Reilly) testified that she witnessed Armstrong's principal investor, Thom Weisel, and Armstrong develop a backstory to explain the presence of a banned substance. They decided they would state Armstrong received the corticosteroids to treat saddle sores and it was unintentional. The men, allegedly, obtained a backdated prescription from team doctor Luis Garcia del Moral—Moral has since been banned from sports for his complicity in the cycling team's doping program.

The actions taken within the criminal justice system are composed of several lawsuits and investigations filed against Armstrong throughout his career. While there were many lawsuits and federal reports filed, the three most influential ones were conducted by SCA Promotions, federal prosecutors, and ultimately the USADA. In 2006 a French news report was released stating Armstrong admitted to a physician that he had received performance-enhancing drugs in his lifetime. Armstrong maintains that he was referring to steroids and EPO that he received during his normal postoperative treatment following his bout with cancer. Regardless, SCA Promotions, a promotion company that owed Armstrong a $5 million bonus following his 2005 Tour de France victory, attempted to withhold the bonus. Armstrong filed suit to receive the $5 million plus interest and attorneys' fees.

While the SCA Promotions case was based on testimony regarding Armstrong's alleged doping, no official investigation had taken place. This changed in 2010 when U.S. federal prosecutors officially followed allegations of Armstrong's alleged doping practices. The federal grand jury inquiry requested urine samples from the French antidoping agency. However, on February 2, 2012, after two years of investigating Armstrong, the federal prosecutors decided to officially drop their criminal investigation without any official charges.

Following the dismissal of federal charges, the USADA officially accused Armstrong of doping in June 2012. Armstrong issued a public statement again denying all doping allegations and was subsequently suspended from competition in all official cycling and triathlon events. This led to Armstrong filing a lawsuit to stop the USADA from issuing any sanctions against him, claiming the USADA was circumventing the due process of athletes by imposing sanctions without a finding of guilt. U.S. District Judge Sam Sparks ruled in favor of the USADA and the sanctions were imposed. The USADA went one step further and stripped Armstrong of all competition results from August 1998 to the present.

Ultimately, Armstrong did not contest the findings. He issued a statement that he would not fight the USADA because "there comes a point in every man's life when he has to say, 'Enough is enough'" (Macur 2012). Therefore, Armstrong forfeited all awards earned after August 1998. The UCI requested a decision from the USADA as to why the UCI should strip Armstrong of his titles—namely the seven Tour de France victories. On October 10, 2012, the USADA released a 200-page report that detailed the findings of their investigation. In this investigation were hundreds of supporting documents including statements from former teammates who witnessed Armstrong using performance-enhancing drugs. On October 22, Armstrong was officially stripped of all of his titles.

Upon the release of the USADA's and UCI's decisions, Armstrong maintained his innocence but decided not to fight the process. On January 13, 2013, Armstrong admitted on national television that he had participated in a large, doping scheme throughout his career. He admitted he had wrongfully attacked doubters through the legal system in an effort to protect himself. Following the admission, the International Olympic Committee stripped Armstrong of his bronze medal from the 2000 Sydney Games. Currently, several lawsuits are in motion attempting to recuperate money paid to Armstrong throughout his career. Notably, the Justice Department filed court documents in April 2013 to attempt to recover $17 million paid to Armstrong by the United States Postal Service (USPS) from 1998 to 2004. The basis of the lawsuit is Armstrong accepted contractual money while knowingly cheating in the process, thus he defrauded the USPS.

M. Hunter Martaindale

See also: Baseball and Steroids (1980–); Black Sox Scandal (1919); *Primary Documents*/House Bill Authorizing the President to Present a Gold Medal on Behalf of Congress to Lance Armstrong (2000)

Further Reading

Macur, Juliet. 2012. "Armstrong Drops Fight against Doping Charges." *The New York Times*. August 23.

USADA. 2012. "Reasoned Decision of the United States Anti-Doping Agency on Disqualification and Ineligibility." Colorado Springs, CO: USADA.

Arnold, Benedict (1741–1801)

Benedict Arnold, an American Revolutionary War general and hero who defected to the British, schemed for command of West Point in 1780 to surrender it to the British, thereby opening American forces to attack. The plot was exposed, and Arnold's name became synonymous with "traitor" in American culture.

Arnold, born in Norwich, Connecticut, in 1741, descended from an original settler of Rhode Island. The name Benedict was a family tradition; his father, grandfather, and great-grandfather (a Rhode Island governor) all shared the name. In the 1730s, Arnold's father left Rhode Island for Norwich and married wealthy widow Hannah Waterman King, becoming an affluent merchant and local official. Of the couple's many children, only Benedict and his sister, Hannah, reached adulthood. Arnold, whose education was disrupted by his father's declining fortunes and

alcoholism, secured an apprenticeship with his mother's kinsman, Daniel Lathrop, who ran an apothecary. In the 1750s, Arnold enlisted to fight the French on three occasions. He deserted during his third enlistment to visit his dying mother.

After his father's death in 1762, Arnold moved to New Haven, becoming a pharmacist and bookseller under Lathrop's patronage. Arnold soon established himself as a merchant, engaging in lucrative overseas trading ventures, sometimes commanding his own ships. While in Honduras, Arnold fought a duel with a British sea-captain who called him a "damn Yankee." Arnold's sister helped manage his businesses, even after he married Margaret Mansfield, the sheriff's daughter. The Sugar Act (1764) and Stamp Act (1765) curtailed colonial mercantile activity. Consequently, Arnold, a leader in Connecticut's anti-British movement, joined the Sons of Liberty, a secret society.

Although he would soon become infamous as a traitor and spy, Benedict Arnold at first served the revolutionary cause with considerable skill, especially during the American invasion of Canada in 1775–1776. After his failed plot to surrender West Point to the British, Benedict escaped behind enemy lines. (Library of Congress)

He pursued his mercantile activities illegally, becoming a prosperous smuggler.

In 1775, the battle of Lexington ignited the fight for American independence. Arnold and his Connecticut militiamen marched to Massachusetts. He proposed the capture of Ticonderoga on the New York–Canadian frontier to the Massachusetts Committee of Safety. The same scheme to protect New England from invasion had been entertained in Connecticut; Ethan Allen's expedition was already en route. Arnold and Allen ultimately became joint commanders of the successful expedition; afterward, Allen minimized Arnold's role. Arnold then raided Fort Saint-Jean. Connecticut and Massachusetts squabbled over responsibility for supporting efforts at Ticonderoga. Arnold resigned. Upon his return to New Haven, he learned of his wife's death.

Congress authorized an invasion of Canada. Arnold proposed to General George Washington an expedition to Quebec City. With Aaron Burr among his aids, Arnold began an arduous trek through Maine. His depleted forces reached Quebec in November 1775. Richard Montgomery and his men arrived from Montreal as reinforcements. During the expedition, the wounded Arnold was promoted to brigadier-general. He maintained a siege of Quebec until early 1776, when he took command of Montreal. Reinforced British forces soon expelled American troops from Canada. Retreating to New York, Arnold battled the British fleet near Valcour Island in October to delay the British advance up Lake Champlain. His defense forced the British to retire to Montreal and postpone their offensive on Ticonderoga. Arnold, however, became subject to impropriety charges. The charges, eventually dismissed, revealed a developing anti-Arnold faction comprised of jealous military figures and politicians wary of his influence.

In February 1777, Congress appointed five new major-generals, passing over Arnold, the senior brigadier. Two months later, British forces invaded Connecticut, destroying Danbury's military stores. Arnold, then at New Haven, organized a militia response with David Wooster and Gold Silliman. He and his men rushed to Danbury's defense, fighting the British in nearby Ridgefield. During the battle, Arnold had two horses shot from under him; Wooster was mortally wounded. The British, driven to their ships, barely escaped. Arnold subsequently went to Philadelphia to inquire about his rank. His actions at Ridgefield prompted Congress to promote him to major-general, but his seniority was not restored.

On Washington's prodding, Arnold joined the northern army. He led operations to relieve Fort Stanwix and distinguished himself in both battles of Saratoga in late 1777. General Horatio Gates removed Arnold from field command after the first battle after Arnold criticized his leadership. At the second battle, Arnold nevertheless rushed the field and broke through the British lines, forcing a British retreat. Arnold received a severe leg wound, but refused an amputation. Congress then restored his military seniority.

While recovering, Arnold took command of Philadelphia. There, he met and married in 1779 Margaret "Peggy" Shippen, a member of a wealthy Loyalist family. Arnold lived extravagantly, came into debt, and quarreled with politician Joseph Reed, whose charges against Arnold prompted a congressional investigation. Due to Reed's persistence, the matter eventually went to a court-martial, which in 1780 cleared Arnold of all but two minor charges but decreed that he receive Washington's reprimand.

In 1779, Arnold initiated defection overtures to the British. News reached Major John André, Arnold's wife's former paramour, now the British spy chief. Difficulty with Congress over pay, reimbursements, and perceived slights to his loyalty, frustrated Arnold. The American government's financial and military situation also seemed dire. General Clinton authorized André's talks with Arnold. The two, sometimes involving Peggy, corresponded secretly. Arnold provided the British with troop locations and strengths. Clinton, seeking control of the Hudson Valley to crush the northern army, wanted information about West Point. By the fall, negotiations stalled. Patriot mobs began threatening Loyalist families, putting Arnold and his in-laws in danger.

Benedict Arnold Monuments

Despite his reputation as a traitor, monuments to his bravery exist throughout the United States. There is an unnamed memorial on the Saratoga battlefield. Further, the Saratoga victory monument has four niches, three of which are occupied with generals' names; an empty fourth niche remains for Arnold. At the U.S. Military Academy at West Point, plaques commemorate every American Revolutionary War general; an unnamed plaque commemorates Arnold. Other markers exist in Massachusetts, Maine, and New York. Shock at Arnold's betrayal and admiration for André's bravery facing death ironically made André a New York hero. A monument to him exists in Tarrytown near the tree marking his point of capture. Folklore holds that the area around "André's tree," featured in Washington Irving's Legend of Sleepy Hollow, is haunted by his ghost.

In 1780, Philip Schuyler, Washington's confident, approached Arnold about commanding West Point. Arnold, enticing the British with these developments, reopened defection negotiations. In June, Arnold inspected West Point, sending the British a report and information about Washington's forces. In August, Arnold assumed West Point's command; the British agreed to pay him £20,000 upon West Point's surrender. Arnold began weakening the fort's defenses and military strength.

After a failed meeting attempt, Arnold and André met in New York on September 21 at a local spy's house. American forces fired upon the *Vulture*, the ship intended to retrieve André. Now forced to return by land, Arnold gave André West Point's plans and passes to get through American lines. On September 23, André was captured near Tarrytown. His incriminating papers were sent to Washington. Arnold, receiving news of André's capture, left in haste and sought refuge on the *Vulture*. He wrote Washington a letter successfully requesting Peggy's safe passage to her family. An American military tribunal tried André; he was hanged in Tappan on October 2. That month, newspapers published Arnold's open letter explaining his actions.

Since the plot failed, the British only appointed Arnold a brigadier general and reduced his compensation for defecting. In 1781, he led an expedition to Virginia. He subsequently attacked New London and Groton, Connecticut, before Washington's victory at Yorktown effectively ended the war.

In 1782, he moved to London, where he received mixed acceptance. He later moved to New Brunswick, Canada, and resumed a merchant's life. During the French Revolution, he was imprisoned in the French Caribbean on suspicion as a British spy. He escaped, helped organize militias on British-held Caribbean islands, and received as a reward a land-grant in Upper Canada. He returned to London in 1791 and died there in 1801. He allegedly asked for his American army uniform, saying, "May God forgive me for ever having put on another." Although buried at St. Mary's

Church, his remains were accidentally relocated decades later to an unmarked mass grave during renovations.

ERIC MARTONE

See also: Burr, Aaron, Treason Trial of (1807); *Primary Documents*/Benedict Arnold's "Letter to the Inhabitants of America" (1780)

Further Reading

Harr, John Ensor. 1999. *Dark Eagle: A Novel of Benedict Arnold and the American Revolution.* New York: Viking.

Martin, James. 2000. *Benedict Arnold, Revolutionary Hero: An American Warrior Reconsidered.* New York: New York University Press.

Randall, Willard Sterne. 1990. *Benedict Arnold: Patriot and Traitor.* New York: Quill/William Morrow.

Aron, Ruthann (1942–)

Ruthann Aron attempted to have two people killed, one of whom was her husband, and then pleaded not guilty by reason of insanity. Ruthann claimed she was entrapped by police. This case was of national interest because the defendant was a successful professional woman who plotted to have multiple people, who crossed her, murdered and highlights concerns about police entrapment and the rare successful use of an insanity plea.

Ruthann Greenzweig was born on October 24, 1942, in Brooklyn, New York, to David and Frieda Greenzweig. Ruthann also has a younger brother, Neil. David moved the family to Fallsburg, New York when Ruthann was a child, where he owned and operated a diner. From a young age, Ruthann was a hard worker and it showed in her grades, along with the work she put in at the family diner. She eventually graduated in the top of her class, received a bachelor's degree in microbiology and a master's degree in education. During her time in college, she met and married Barry Aron.

The Aron's marriage was troubled from early on. Barry had an affair but despite the problems, the couple had two children. The struggles continued, specifically financial, as Barry worked his way through medical school. Once Barry graduated and got a job, Ruthann went back to school and earned a law degree. She was admitted to the Maryland bar in 1980, with a focus on zoning and land use. By 1983, she was putting all of her efforts into real estate development. With Barry's medical practice and Ruthann's real estate projects the money struggles seemed to be over, but the couple spent an estimated $2 million on legal bills for suits filed against Ruthann for business deals that had gone bad. One of the lawsuits was filed by a lawyer named Arthur G. Kahn, who would later become the target of Ruthann's anger.

Ruthann changed careers again when she entered the world of politics. She served as president of the West Montgomery County Citizen's Association for a brief period and was then elected into a position on the Montgomery County Planning Board in 1992. Ruthann then decided to run for the U.S. Senate in 1994. She was running as a Republican, and had to defeat William E. Brock III in the primary. The battle for the nomination was brutal.

Ruthann was doing well with her campaign until her father was murdered in August 1994. She halted her campaign and returned to Fallsburg for the funeral. Once the services were over, she returned to the campaign trail and used her father's death to support her position for a tougher stance on crime. She also began to attack Brock during media events, interrupting him and calling him a liar. Brock didn't like the way Ruthann was sabotaging his campaign. In September 1994, he started telling his audiences that Ruthann had been convicted of fraud. These statements implied that she had a criminal record, but was not accurate because civil lawsuits (like the ones filed against Ruthann) do not involve criminal records. The damage was already done and Ruthann lost to Brock in the primary.

Ruthann filed a slander suit against him. The trial began in 1996 and lawyers from the previous lawsuits against her testified, including Arthur G. Kahn. Arthur's testimony was crucial and led to a defeat for Ruthann. On a technicality, Ruthann was granted a new trial against Brock in May 1997 but the new trial would never take place.

In June 1997, Ruthann ran into William H. Mossburg Jr. Mossburg was a familiar face to Ruthann because he had several run-ins with the county government that Ruthann knew about from her time spent on the Planning Board. They had a meeting for lunch and Ruthann told Mossburg that she wanted to have someone eliminated. Mossburg told Ruthann that he would think about helping her and get back to her. He instead contacted the FBI, who ignored him. Mossburg then contacted deputy state attorney Robert Dean, who informed the Montgomery County Police Department. The police met with Mossburg to question him. After determining that Mossburg was being truthful, they asked him to be an informant. Mossburg agreed to wear a wire and have more meetings with Ruthann. Mossburg and Ruthann met again on June 4, 1997. In this

conversation, Ruthann did not openly ask to have someone killed, but there was enough for investigators to believe something was going on.

The next meeting was on June 7, 1997. Mossburg told her that he knew of someone who could help her and gave her the phone number of Detective Terry Ryan, an undercover police officer. Ruthann and Terry talked over the phone and Terry agreed to kill someone for $10,000. Ruthann told Terry the name of his target: Arthur Kahn. She wanted him dead so that he could not testify against her in the new trial. After several more conversations, Ruthann added another person she wanted killed for an additional $10,000: Barry Aron.

At Terry's request, Ruthann left an envelope with $500 at the front desk of a hotel. Terry paged Ruthann, who had gone to play golf, to ask if she was sure she wanted the murders carried out. When she said yes, investigators moved in. Ruthann was arrested walking back to her car after the phone call with Terry. She was charged with two counts of solicitation to murder.

Ruthann chose to plead insanity, which is difficult to prove. Her attorneys Barry Helfand, Erik D. Bolong, and Judy Catterton argued that Ruthann was mentally ill and was not accountable for her criminal behavior. Ruthann had psychiatric evaluations in two different facilities and ended up with several diagnoses. Despite her mental illnesses, doctors believed that she was aware of her actions while she was planning the murders.

The trial was presided over by Judge Paul A. McGuckian and the prosecution was headed by deputy state's attorney I. Matthew Campbell. Opening arguments began on February 26, 1998. Ruthann's defense claimed that she had been sexually abused by her father, which was the cause of her vulnerable mental state. They also claimed that she had a brain injury known as a temporal lobe encephalopathy, which is thought to affect impulse control. Finally, the defense also stated that the police had entrapped her by making her take the plan further than she would have gone with it on her own. After 15 days of testimony from mental health experts, Barry Aron, and Frieda Singer (Ruthann's mother who took on her maiden name after divorcing Ruthann's father), the jury began deliberating. The deliberations ended with a hung jury and a mistrial.

A new trial began in July 1998. Surprisingly, on July 31, 1998, Ruthann decided to plead no contest. She was sentenced to three years in county jail and was eventually released on probation in 2001. While she was in jail, Barry divorced her. She moved to New York City to be closer to her son, but he was tragically killed in the events of September 11, 2001. As of today, Ruthann's whereabouts are unknown.

Angela M. Collins

See also: Barfield, Velma (1932–1984); Fish, Albert (1870–1936); Hinckley, John, Jr. (1955–); Lennon, John, Murder of (December 8, 1980); Moore, Blanche Taylor (1933–)

Further Reading

"Aron's Murder-for-Hire Case." 1998. *Washington Post*. http://www.washingtonpost.com/wp-srv/local/longterm/aron/caseindex.htm.

Bell, Rachel. n.d. "Ruthann Aron: A Deadly Campaign." In *Crime Library: Criminal Minds and Methods*. http://www.crimelibrary.com/criminal_mind/psychology/ruthann_aron/1_index.html. Accessed March 7, 2015.

Duggan, Paul and Manuel Perez-Rivas. 1997. "Aron Grew to Be a Political Scrapper. *Washington Post*. June 15. http://www.washingtonpost.com/wp-srv/local/longterm/aron/stories/aronprofile.htm.

Politics and Murder. 2009. In *Law & Ordinance*. http://lawandordnance.com/Politics-and-Murder.html. Accessed March 7, 2015.

Shaver, Katherine. 1998. "Aron Gets Three Years in Murder Plot." *Washington Post*. November 23. http://www.washingtonpost.com/wp-srv/local/longterm/aron/aron.htm. Accessed March 7, 2015.

Vick, Karl. 1997. "Aron Released From Mental Hospital." *Washington Post*. November 6. http://www.washingtonpost.com/wp-srv/local/longterm/aron/home.htm. Accessed March 7, 2015.

Ashley, John (1888–1924) and His Gang (Florida Everglades)

John Ashley, commonly known as the King of the Everglades, began his criminal career at the age of 18. With the murder of an animal trapper, John Ashley would begin his notorious life of crime that would ultimately lead to his demise. John Ashley was the leader of a gang that controlled much of the Florida Everglades. Throughout the gang's reign, the group committed a range of crimes from robbing banks and trains to rum-running. However, Ashley's legacy would end after a long feud with Sheriff Baker of Palm Beach County on Sebastian Bridge. Ashley died under suspicious circumstances. Specifically, there is evidence that Sheriff Baker or one of this deputies took the law into their own hands and killed him.

John Ashley came from a family of bootleggers located in the Florida Everglades. While little is recorded about

Ashley's childhood, history shows a mention of him in 1911 after a fur trapper was murdered. Desoto Tiger was a known leader of the Seminole Nation in Florida, where he caught and sold animal furs. One day his body was found near Fort Lauderdale, Florida, shortly after he had been in contact with Ashley. Ashley had also recently sold several otter hides in Miami for a large sum of money, which were believed to have belonged to Tiger (Stuart 1928). Sheriff George Baker sent two deputies to arrest Ashley at his home. Instead of returning to the jail with Ashley, the deputies had a message for Baker from Ashley: "Tell him not to send any more chicken-hearted men or they might get hurt" (Procyk 2012). From this point in time, a long dispute between Baker and Ashley would ensue. Ashley fled from Florida for several years and did not return until 1914. When he returned he turned himself in, but later escaped custody. The battle between Baker and Ashley would only get worse at this point, as the feud grew to include Baker's son, Robert Baker.

In 1915, John Ashley would form a gang that would go on to commit several crimes. One particularly well-known crime was the robbery of Stuart bank. During this robbery a gang member, Kid Lowe, shot Ashley in the eye. Ashley required medical attention from the injury, which resulted in his capture for the murder of Desoto Tiger and the robbery of Stuart Bank. Ashley attempted multiple escapes, but none were successful. His brother, Bob Ashley, decided to go to Dade County and attempt to free his brother. On June 2, Bob showed up at Sheriff Hendrickson's home where he shot and killed the sheriff at point-blank range. Bob Ashley was seen by Hendrickson's wife grabbing a pistol off her husband before fleeing on foot. As police chased Ashley, Officer John Riblet caught up to him and a shootout began between the two. Both men eventually died (Wilbanks 1998).

After the death of Bob Ashley, John was convicted for a bank robbery and was sentenced to a 17-and-half-year prison term; the court ultimately dropped the case against Ashley for the murder of Tiger. While Ashley was in jail, the gang continued to commit more crimes under the lead of Handford Mobley and Roy Matthews. Many of the crimes involved rum-running from the Bahamas (Sonne 2007). Eventually, John Ashley escaped from prison and rejoined the gang. At this point Prohibition was established, thus the gang continued illicit activities involving obtaining and selling alcohol.

After another robbery of the Stuart Bank in 1924, Sheriff Robert Baker unsuccessfully pursued the gang in a 265-mile manhunt. A while later, Ashley and his gang robbed another bank, but this time Ashley left a witness a bullet, asking him to give it to Sheriff Baker (Procyk 2012). In an attempt to capture Ashley, Sheriff Baker and a group of officers surrounded the camp where the gang was hiding out. While the officers were attempting to ambush the gang, a dog barked, alarming Ashley, causing a firefight. John's father, Joe Ashley, was shot and killed while his girlfriend, Laura Upthegrove, was also shot. Her screams caused a temporary ceasefire, at which time John escaped. Several officers were also killed in the gunfire, including Baker's cousin Fred. Following this incident, Baker found and destroyed all of Ashley's hideouts in the Everglades and fervently pursued Ashley. The feud between Baker and Ashley was coming to a close (McGoun 1998).

In November 1924, Sheriff Baker finally had Ashley. Through an informant, believed to possibly be an angry girlfriend (though unconfirmed), Baker found out when and where Ashley and his gang would be driving. It turns out they would be crossing a bridge over the Sebastian river, so Baker put a chain with a lantern across the bridge and had the officers hide. Ashley stopped when he saw the chain, at which point the deputies ambushed the gang; by the end of the night, all four men in the gang would be dead (Stuart 1928).

It is still unknown today what truly happened on the Sebastian Bridge where John Ashley and his gang members died. The most known story comes from Ada Williams (1997) who claimed that she was told the true story by one of the deputies. According to this story, while the four men were being detained, Ashley dropped his hands while making a forward movement, causing an officer to react with lethal force. Other stories claim that the four pulled guns on the officers, causing a firefight that resulted in the death of the four gang members (McGoun 1998). In the end, the coroner confirmed that the deaths were justifiable and that the officers acted in accordance with their duties (Procyk 2012). While there may be no proof of what happened, Ashley was dead and the era of his gang ended.

The ambiguous and vague circumstances of John Ashley's death have led historians to question whether or not the death was "frontier justice." Sheriff Baker had been after John Ashley for 15 years and had many reasons to want to ensure Ashley's criminal career was truly over. After many heinous crimes and escapes, Ashley was a constant threat to the public. The Baker family also had personal reasons to extract revenge against Ashley. While there is

no evidence that Baker intended to kill Ashley that night of November 1, 1924, it is certainly one of many possibilities.

KATHLEEN FREY

See also: Billy the Kid (1859–1881); Ray Allen Gang (1974–1980)

Further Reading

Brown, Elizabeth. 1972. "Frontier Justice: Wayne County 1796–1836." *The American Journal of Legal History*: 126–153.

McGoun, William. 1998. *Southeast Florida Pioneers: The Palm and Treasure Coasts.* Sarasota, FL: Pineapple Press.

Procyk, Richard. 2012. The Ashley Gang and Frontier Justice. *History of Town Jupiter.* http://www.jupiter.fl.us/Document Center/View/2032. Accessed April 19, 2015.

Sonne, Warren. 2007. "The Ashley Gang: What Really Happened." *Indian River Magazine.* Fort Pierce, FL: Indian River Store.

Stuart, Hix Cook. 1928. *The Notorious Ashley Gang: A Saga of the King and Queen of the Everglades.* Port St. Lucie, FL: St. Lucie Printing Company.

Wilbanks, William. 1998. *Forgotten Heroes: Police Officers Killed in Early Florida, 1840–1925.* Paducah, KY: Turner Publishing Co.

Williams, Ada Coats. 1997. *Florida's Ashley Gang.* Florida Classics Library. Fort Pierce, FL: Indian River Store.

Atlanta Child Killer. *See* Williams, Wayne (1958–)

Atlanta Race Riot (1906)

The Atlanta Race Riot of 1906 spanned four days and highlighted growing racial tensions in the expanding city of Atlanta, Georgia. From September 22, 1906, to September 24, 1906, white mobs attacked local African Americans and their businesses. The mob attacks were in response to a series of newspaper reports that claimed African American men had, on four separate occasions, assaulted white women. These newspaper reports were never substantiated; they were fraught with inflammatory and sensationalistic language and were all intended to ignite fear and revenge among Atlanta's white population. Soon after the newspaper articles were published, thousands of white men and boys gathered in downtown Atlanta and began targeting African American–run businesses and neighborhoods. In the end, a reported 24 to 40 African Americans and two white Americans had been killed. The riot death toll is suspected to be substantially higher but fear of retribution from the white community kept many African American families from reporting the death of a loved one. Therefore, an accurate death toll is difficult to determine.

The race riots were a response to growing discontent amongst Atlanta's white population. During the time preceding the riots, Atlanta had become a growing hub for the regional economy, making it one of the most desirable cities to live in, in the southern United States. From 1880 to 1900, the city's population nearly doubled in size from 89,000 people to over 150,000 people. Many of these newly arrived people were African Americans. The rapid population expansion put a serious strain on the city's public services. It also increased job competition, heightened class distinctions, and contributed to a growing discontent between Atlanta whites and African Americans. City leaders responded to the growing population by instituting restrictionist policies aimed at oppressing the expanding working class. These policies had mixed results and brought about public fear of social intermingling of races, propelling the expansion of Jim Crow segregation, particularly in neighborhoods and on public transit. In spite of this, African Americans were becoming increasingly socially mobile, with Atlanta seeing both a development, and subsequent expansion in, the African American upper class.

Paralleling the upper class expansion was the changing political climate in the United States more broadly. Reconstruction (1867–1876) had given African American men the right to vote, which, for the first time, allowed them to be active in the Atlanta political arena. African American participation in local politics brought about intense fear among local politicians particularly Hoke Smith (1855–1931) and Clark Howell (1863–1936), the gubernatorial candidates for Atlanta's 1906 governor's race. These two candidates were particularly visible examples of political fear as both were involved in local newspaper outlets (Hoke was the former publisher of *The Atlanta Journal* and Clark was the current editor of *The Atlanta Constitution*). Smith inflamed racial tensions by publicly insisting that African Americans needed to maintain positions of inferiority relative to whites in Atlanta. Smith argued that African Americans receiving the right to vote bought about desires for them to be both socially and economically equal, which made it difficult for Atlanta's white population to maintain social order. Howell, like Smith, agreed that African Americans needed to remain in relative separation from whites within the social structure. He also argued that Hoke had cooperated with African American

political leaders and could not be counted on to advance the cause of white supremacy.

In addition to increasing political participation among African Americans, the group had also started growing local businesses, challenging established white business owner revenue, and establishing client bases from the growing African American populous. This growth led to the development of extensive social networks and the movement of African American elites out of poor, crime-ridden neighborhoods and into more affluent neighborhoods. The physical separation led to a concentration of both poverty and crime in certain areas, particularly areas with saloons. As these areas experienced a rise in crime, the public fear of victimization by African Americans became more pronounced. No crime of victimization elicited more condemnation or fear than that of the sexual victimization of white women by African American men.

On September 22, 1906, this fear was capitalized on by local newspapers that reported four separate incidents of African American men assaulting white women. Although the claims were never substantiated, shortly after the reports surfaced, thousands of white men and children gathered in downtown Atlanta in protest. The then Mayor James Woodward (1845–1923) attempted to calm the crowd but failed. The mob stormed through Atlanta neighborhoods assaulting hundreds of African Americans on streets and in streetcars. The crowd openly vandalized African American businesses, in some cases, killing store owners and their customers. On the first day of rioting, the militia was summoned and streetcars service was suspended. Despite these disruptions, the mob maintained its attacks against Africans Americans. The rioting continued into the early morning of September 23 until a heavy rainfall eventually dispersed the crowd. That same day, local newspapers reported that the militia had taken control of Atlanta and because of the rioting African Americans were no longer an issue for Atlanta's whites. The police and the militia patrolled the streets and guarded white property. These patrols did little to dissuade African American fears of assault. African Americans began acquiring weapons to protect themselves against a potential mob resurgence. And, as African Americans had predicted, white vigilante groups stormed into African American neighborhoods, again assaulting and killing innocent African Americans.

On September 24, 1906, a group of heavily armed African Americans traveled to the nearby town of Brownsville to meet privately regarding the riots. The Fulton County police got wind of the gathering and launched a raid on

Brownsville. The group of African Americans and the police exchanged gunfire, resulting in the death of a police officer. In response, three separate militia groups descended on Brownsville, seizing weapons and arresting nearly 250 African Americans. On the final day of rioting, city officials, local business owners, faith leaders, and the press publicly pled with rioters to end the violence. After the violence subsided, an estimated 25 to 40 African Americans and two white Americans had been killed. The number of victims was much greater than the officials records showed. Families, fearful that they would be assaulted or killed, failed to report the death of loved ones. In addition, city officials did not want to report the actual number of people killed because it would further damage Atlanta's already tainted reputation.

In an attempt to maintain civil order and ensure that another race riot would not occur both African American and white leaders in Atlanta began to meet. This marked the beginning of interracial cooperation within Atlanta. These meetings were meant to discuss the issues that contributed to the riot in hopes that another riot would never occur. Although the riot had an enormous impact on Atlanta's residents, over time the riot was minimized and forgotten, eventually being overlooked in official histories of the city. Only recently has the Atlanta race riot been revisited as a seminal event in U.S. history.

LAURA A. SILLER

See also: Detroit Riot (1943); Detroit Riot (1967); East St. Louis Race Riot (1917) and Chicago Race Riot (1919); Los Angeles Riots (1992)

Further Reading

Mixon, Gregory. 1997. "Good Negro—Bad Negro: The Dynamics of Race and Class in Atlanta during the Era of the 1906 Riot." *The Georgia Historical Quarterly* 81:593–621.

Mixon, Gregory. 2005. *The Atlanta Riot: Race, Class, and Violence in a New South City.* Gainesville: University Press of Florida.

Attica Prison Riot (1971)

On September 9, 1971, one of bloodiest and most notorious prison riots and hostage crisis in American history broke out in a maximum security men's prison located 35 miles from Buffalo, New York. The Attica prison riot, hostage standoff, and subsequent violent retaking of the prison by state authorities dramatized how racial conflicts, civil rights debates, and law-order-order attitudes of the era came together inside America's overcrowded prisons. New York State governor Nelson Rockefeller ordered law enforcement to retake the prison because of the fear that the hostages had been brutalized and killed. Before the crisis would end 39 men were killed.

The riot began spontaneously after breakfast on September 9 as a guard disciplined two prisoners for a minor infraction. An estimated 1,100 of Attica's 2,225 prisoners rioted, breaking through a gate into the central area known as Times Square. They gained access to the cellblocks occupied D Yard, surrounded by 35-foot walls and gun towers. The rioters did beat one correctional officer, William Quinn, and threw him out of a second-story window as the riot broke out on September 9. He later died in the hospital. But only three other prisoners were killed prior to the attempt to retake the prison.

Once the prison was under control of the inmates, they quickly organized themselves and assumed responsibility for maintaining order within the facility. Despite the racial tensions precipitating the riot and the prominent role that black prisoners played in it, the riot became a remarkably democratic, pan-racial rebellion. Prisoners elected leaders of different races and ethnicities who were responsible for establishing and enforcing prison rules as well as drawing up a list of grievances.

The prisoners desired to publicize their grievances over a host of prison conditions and negotiate with authorities to achieve reforms. A committee of observers was established to oversee the hostage negotiations. This committee included politicians such as Republican state senator John Dunne, journalists such as *The New York Times*' Tom Wicker, and notable civil rights activists William Kuntzler and Black Panther Party figure Bobby Seale. Prisoners, armed with clubs and knives, held 39 hostages whom they had bound and blindfolded and they prohibited anyone from harming them as long as negotiations continued.

They protested against racial discrimination at the prison. In the years immediately before the riot, Attica's population changed from nearly all-white to disproportionately black. Fifty-four percent of the prisoner population was black and urban while the staff was all white and predominantly rural. Worse, the guards were openly hostile toward minority prisoners. The prisoners also demanded an end to dangerous overcrowding. The facility, built in the 1930s, was antiquated and chronically overcrowded. As a result, it was hard to safely secure and the conditions were unhygienic. Official practices such as limiting showers to once weekly

A September 10, 1971, photo of inmates of Attica Correctional Facility (Attica, New York) during their occupation of the prison yard after their takeover of the facility. They are negotiating with Corrections Commissioner Russell Oswald, lower left, about the conditions of their surrender. (AP Photo)

and supplying prisoners with just one roll of toilet paper a month worsened poor health conditions. Prisoners also argued that the conditions were in violation of their constitutional rights. They wanted less censorship of their mail, greater religious liberty, and expanded phone access.

Oswald himself would represent the state in the hostage negotiations. Authorities agreed to 28 of 33 inmate demands. But there were some to which they would not. For instance, prisoners demanded that the prisoners be granted amnesty for crimes that had occurred during the initial rebellion. As well, they demanded that authorities repatriate to a "non-imperialist" nation for those who desired to leave the United States and find safe haven in a foreign country. Neither authorities nor rebels would concede ground on these demands and negotiations came to an impasse.

Both Oswald and the rebels wanted Governor Rockefeller to come to Attica and participate in negotiations. He steadfastly refused. It is not clear if his having done so would have made any difference, and many surmised that he was largely unwilling to do so because he planned to run for U.S. president and did not wish to appear weak toward convicted felons.

Rockefeller ordered 300 correctional officers, 587 state police troopers, and 300 other area sheriffs and deputies to retake the prison. Although this would essentially be a military operation, there was never any unified command structure for the state's troops. Worse, racial prejudice and anger at rumors of hostage maltreatment pervaded their mood, setting the stage for what would be a chaotic and vengeful assault on the prison. The retaking of Attica was bloody. On September 13, state troops dropped tear gas canisters into the prisoner-controlled yard and began spraying the yard with gunfire, killing both prisoners and hostages.

The aftermath was barbaric and vengeful. Officers denied wounded and injured prisoners medical treatment, condemning some of them to death. Officers brutalized prisoners by forcing them to strip naked and run a gauntlet of nightsticks and ordering them to crawl naked over broken glass.

Authorities may have feared that prisoners were planning to kill hostages, encouraging Rockefeller to order the prison's retaking, and government troops may have believed that rioters had already committed atrocities against hostages, thus increasing their rage. Indeed, false news reports had crossed the nation, claiming that rioters had slit hostages' throats and castrated one prisoner. Newspapers all across the country, including *The New York Times* and *Los Angeles Times*, carried the story on the front page. But it appeared afterward that officials had initiated these stories. Independent autopsies later proved that these reports were false. All 10 of the dead hostages had been shot by police during the prison's retaking. Still, the impact of the initial throat-slashing reports was long-lived and exacerbated the riot's controversial aftermath.

There was a cover-up regarding various aspects of the siege, which prompted the creation of a special commission and resulted in a wave of prison riots in other parts of the country. Although there seemed to be a willingness to investigate prisoners who may have committed crimes during the crisis, there did not appear to be the same enthusiasm to investigate government agents who may have done so. Sixty prisoners were criminally indicted and eight were convicted for crimes associated with the riot. Yet only one law enforcement officer was charged, and that was the minor charge of reckless endangerment. Authorities eventually dropped that case.

Shortly after the Attica investigations, prisoners and their families filed a class-action lawsuit seeking compensation for over 1,200 prisoners for those killed and injured during the violent aftermath. In 2000, it was finally settled when a judge ordered New York State to pay $12 million.

Advocates for the prisoners, hostages, and their survivors hope that the state will open a closed treasure trove of investigatory material into the Attica riot. The New York State Special Commission on Attica produced boxes of material that remain at the New York State Archives. Yet these boxes remain sealed, unavailable to the public. In 2013, the New York State attorney general said that he would request the release of these materials, giving hope that survivors and historians may be able to learn even more about one of America's most notorious prison riots.

PAUL R. SCHUPP

See also: Haymarket Square Riot/Bombing (Chicago) (1886); Los Angeles Riots (1992)

Further Reading

Useem, Bert, and Peter Kimbal. 1991. *States of Siege: U.S. Prison Riots 1971–1986*. New York: Oxford University Press.

Wicker, Tom. 2011. *A Time to Die: The Attica Prison Revolt*. Chicago: Haymarket Books.

Aurora (CO) Movie Theater Shooting (July 20, 2012)

On July 20, 2012, a deadly mass shooting occurred at a movie theater in Aurora, Colorado, during a late night showing of the Batman film *The Dark Knight Rises*. A lone gunman calmly walked into the packed movie theater, detonated two tear gas grenades, and fired dozens of shots from multiple firearms at moviegoers. Panic and fear permeated throughout the theater as soon as the first shots rang out. A large number of people ran to the exits to escape the chaos, while others protected their loved ones and provided them with comfort. A total of 12 people were killed in the deadly attack, including a six-year-old girl, while 58 others were injured. The shooting initiated a swift, vigorous law enforcement response that resulted in the arrest of the gunman within minutes of the attack. It also prompted a vast social response and fundamental political changes.

The deadly shooting occurred at the Century Aurora 16 Multiplex movie theater operated by Cinemark, located at a shopping mall in Aurora, Colorado. The shooter, James Eagan Holmes, who was born on December 13, 1987, entered the movie theater building with a ticket to the film screening that he purchased online weeks prior. He walked to theater #9 and sat down in the front row. After about 20 minutes or so, he exited the building through an emergency door. It was at this point that he proceeded to his vehicle, changed into military-type protective clothing, and retrieved multiple guns and tear gas canisters. He then reentered the building through the same door he exited, wearing all black clothing, a helmet, a vest, and other tactical gear. Many of the moviegoers, at least initially, were not troubled by the sight of Holmes. Some people thought that he was dressed up for the film, while others believed that he was part of a publicity stunt orchestrated by management. The threat, therefore, was not readily apparent in the eyes of those in attendance.

Upon reentering the building, Holmes tossed two tear gas canisters into the theater, thereby initiating a state of mass panic and confusion among persons in the audience. He then opened fire after the canisters exploded, using multiple firearms in the process. He first fired numerous shots at random from a tactical shotgun, hitting several people. Dozens of rounds from a semiautomatic rifle were then fired. The firearm malfunctioned soon thereafter, so Holmes then grabbed a 40-caliber handgun and continued firing into the audience. Gunfire filled the air, forcing the moviegoers to do everything possible to avoid being hit. The shooting rampage lasted for over five minutes. A total of 82 people were killed or injured in the attack, making it one of the worst mass shootings on American soil in the modern era.

Law enforcement officers were dispatched to the scene after multiple calls to 911 were made. The police response was rapid, having arrived within minutes after the initial calls were received. Holmes was apprehended without incident while standing next to his vehicle, which was parked behind the movie theater building. It was at this time when Holmes informed police that he bobby-trapped his residence with multiple explosives. The police initiated a prompt response upon hearing this information. The buildings that surrounded Holmes's apartment were first evacuated to ensure the safety and welfare of occupants. The following day, a number of homemade grenades and other explosive devices were disarmed from Holmes's residence.

Following the shooting, the police retrieved multiple guns from the crime scene and his apartment. It quickly became apparent that Holmes devoted substantial time and effort in planning the deadly attack. About two months before the shooting, Holmes bought a pistol at a local sporting goods store. Over the next five weeks, he purchased three additional firearms, including a shotgun, a semiautomatic rifle, and another pistol. He also bought over 6,000 rounds of ammunition along with two magazine holders, an assault vest, and a knife from the Internet (Healy 2012). All of these items were obtained lawfully through various stores and online Web sites.

Directly after being taken into custody, Holmes was incarcerated at a county detention center. His involvement in the judicial process began just three days after the shooting, particularly at the initial appearance. At this stage, Holmes was provided with a public defender by the court. His court-appointed attorney was unable to secure his pretrial release, as bail was denied by the presiding judge. Throughout the hearing, Holmes appeared perplexed and disoriented, further fueling widespread speculation that he was a mentally disturbed individual. Approximately one week after the hearing, initial formal charges against Holmes were filed by prosecutors. These charges included 24 counts of first-degree murder, 116 counts of attempted murder, possession of explosive devices, and inciting violence (Riccardi and Banda 2012). Holmes was charged with two counts of murder for each person who was killed and two counts of attempted murder for each person who was injured. As the case moved forward, the state filed motions to bring an additional 24 counts of attempted murder against Holmes, thereby bringing the total to 166 felony charges that stem from the mass shooting.

Holmes offered to plead guilty in exchange for leniency, namely avoiding the death penalty. The prosecutor rejected this offer and instead announced that he would seek the death penalty for the crimes in question. Upon hearing this news, and with guidance of his attorneys, Holmes later entered a plea of not guilty by reason of insanity. A short time later, in August 2013, Holmes was taken to a mental health institute for detailed evaluation of his mental state and cognitive abilities. He was extensively evaluated and released approximately two weeks later.

Holmes' trial was scheduled to begin October 2014, but it was delayed several months when his attorneys asked for and were granted a continuance. After three months of jury selection, the trial officially began April 2015. After a near three-month trial and over 12 hours of deliberation, Holmes was convicted on all charges, including 24 counts of first-degree murder, 140 counts of attempted first-degree murder, one count of possessing explosives, and a sentence enhancement of a crime of violence. For these crimes, Holmes was sentenced to life in prison with no possibility of parole.

The deadly shooting prompted a number of social, political, and legal responses. Following the shooting, an entire nation came together in tribute to the victims. People from around the world offered support, condolences, and monetary donations in remembrance of victims of the tragedy. Political leaders extended their thoughts and words of encouragement as a path was charted forward. Numerous celebrities took the time to visit victims and their families.

The shooting also raised questions about tighter gun control laws and the sale of firearms. Immediately following the deadly attack, calls for greater restrictions on guns were immense and wide-ranging. People were outraged how one person, James Holmes, could purchase so many firearms and high-capacity magazines with relative ease. It is these types of tragic events that will continue to fuel gun control debates for the foreseeable future.

JUSTIN N. CROWL

See also: Amish School Shootings (Lancaster County, PA) (October 2, 2006); Bath (MI) School Massacre (1927); Columbine High School Shootings (Littleton, CO) (April 20, 1999); Lanza, Adam Peter (1992–2012); Virginia Tech Massacre (April 16, 2007)

Further Reading

Adelmann, Bob. 2012. "Update on the Batman Shooter: From Obscurity to Infamy." *New American* 28: 18–21.

Associated Press. 2012. "30 Hospitalized in Colo. Mass Shooting". *CBS News.* July 21. http://www.cbsnews.com/8301-201_162-57477132/30-hospitalized-in-colo-mass-shooting/. Accessed April 13, 2015.

Brown, Jennifer. 2012. "12 Shot Dead, 58 Wounded in Aurora Movie Theater during Batman Premier." *The Denver Post.* July 21. http://www.denverpost.com/news/ci_21124893/12-shot-dead-58-wounded-aurora-movie-theater. Accessed April 13, 2015.

Healy, Jack. 2012. "Suspect Bought Large Stockpile of Rounds Online." *The New York Times.* July 22. http://www.nytimes.com/2012/07/23/us/online-ammunition-sales-highlighted-by-aurora-shootings.html?pagewanted=all&_r=0. Accessed April 13, 2015.

Riccardi, Nicholas, and P. Solomon Banda. 2012. "Colo. Suspect Charges: Murder, Attempted Murder." http://bigstory.ap.org/article/colorado-shooting-suspect-faces-formal-charges. Accessed April 13, 2015.

Welsh, Teresa. 2012. "Should the Colorado Theater Shooting Spur More Gun Control?" *U.S. News and World Report.* July 20. http://www.usnews.com/opinion/articles/2012/07/20/should-the-colorado-theater-shooting-spur-more-gun-control. Accessed April 13, 2015.

B

B & O Railroad Strike (1877)

Charles Carroll, the last living signer of the Declaration of Independence, presided over the laying of the first stone in the grand opening ceremony of the Baltimore and Ohio Railroad (B & O Railroad) on July 4, 1828, making it one of the oldest railroads in the United States. As it grew, the B & O gained the distinction of being America's first common carrier, the first Class I railroad in the country, and the first to offer scheduled freight and passenger service to the general public. By 1877, the B & O Railroad stretched from New York to Illinois and employed thousands of workers. B & O workers also had the distinction of being the first workers to begin the Great Railroad Strike of 1877 when they stopped the trains in Camden Junction near Baltimore, Maryland, and Martinsburg, West Virginia, in July 1877.

At the end of the Civil War, railroads were the second largest employer in the country just behind agriculture, and between 1866 and 1873, railroads laid 35,000 miles of new track from the East to West Coast. Since railroads required large amounts of capital investment involving huge financial risks, speculators poured mountains of money into them, which caused bloated growth and overexpansion.

The Panic of 1873 especially shook the foundations of the railroads and the stagnant economy, coupled with an enormous surplus in railroad capacity, pitted the major railroads in a cutthroat struggle for survival. Each railroad slashed its rates to win passenger and freight traffic while passenger rates fell by one-half and freight rates by two-thirds among some competing routes.

The Great Railroad Strike of 1877 began in July 1877 at Camden Junction near Baltimore, Maryland, when brakemen and firemen refused to work. For the second time in a year, the B&O Railroad had instituted a wage cut and a cut in the number of workdays, an action that motivated the trainmen in Martinsburg, West Virginia, to strike work on July 14 and freeze the entire yard, preventing the railroad from hiring replacement workers. The situation worsened when railroad officials petitioned West Virginia governor Henry M. Mathews to send in the state militia. The arrival of the soldiers strengthened the determination of the strikers to stand firm, and on July 16, 1877, a confrontation between a soldier and a striker provoked gunfire in the Martinsburg rail yard, beginning the Great Railroad Strike of 1877.

On July 20, 1877, the B & O Railroad asked the Maryland governor to send in the National Guard to end protest in the Cumberland rail junction in Maryland after violence between protestors and troops brought about the death of 10 young men. Word of the events in Martinsburg and Maryland spread to the Pennsylvania Railroad in Pittsburgh where the railroad had already inflamed workers by cutting jobs and pay and instituting double headers where one train crew performed the work of two. People divided themselves into factions even before the strike

During the Great Railroad Strike of 1877, railroad workers tried to halt the movement of trains. The Roundhouse in Pittsburgh, Pennsylvania, was set on fire. (Library of Congress)

began. Newspaper headlines in *The Baltimore Sun* and *Brooklyn Eagle* tagged the strikers rabble and rioters. Publications like *The Annals of the Great Strikes in the United States*, published in 1877, insinuated that the strikers were not railroad strikers at all, but internationalists and communists. People supporting the strike saw it as a revolt of working men against low wages that did not correspond with food, clothing, and rent prices.

Worker passion and desperation stimulated unions to expand and in June 1877, Robert Ammons of Pittsburgh founded the Trainmen's Union. Breaking from tradition, the Trainmen's Union worked to organize its members across job titles. The common goals of the union included resisting the Pennsylvania Railroad's tactic of using single crews for double work shifts and lobbying to restore wages and improve working conditions.

The increasingly loud and large demonstrations and unity among workers alarmed Pennsylvania Railroad president Thomas Scott, and Pittsburgh division superintendent Robert Pitcairn, and their supporters. A strike spreading from a small B & O station in Martinsburg, West Virginia, to the Pennsylvania Railroad, a major link in the Transcontinental Railroad system would spell disaster to railroads across the country. President Scott and his allies demanded military protection of railroad property and Scott called upon President Rutherford B. Hayes, his political ally, for help. President Hayes ordered the strikers to disperse within 24 hours, but they did not disperse. Hurrying back to Pennsylvania from Wyoming, Pennsylvania governor John Hartranft called in the National Guard. The Pennsylvania National Guard sent 600 troops to Pittsburgh, and in the struggle on July 21 and 22, 1877, between the guardsmen and strikers, 20 people, including women and children, were killed.

Moving as relentlessly as a runaway locomotive, the Great Railroad Strike continued to spread across the

United States. Within days, 100,000 workers were on strike, with many more unemployed on the picket lines in support. In Maryland, Pennsylvania, and Illinois especially, workers halted the nation's rail traffic with a literal and figurative screech of locomotive brakes. In Chicago, armed policemen killed 30 protesters and then the strike moved across the South, where crossing racial lines, white and black workers from Texas to Kentucky to Tennessee fought together for a better life. The strike spread to other industries including textile factories and shipyards as workers joined together in their common search for economic justice.

The Great Railroad Strike hit St. Louis last, and less violently than other states, but events in St. Louis underscored a fact of life that would be true of American labor issues into the 21st century—labor issues involve more than money or working conditions. They are a complicated dynamic of power relations and class structure, issues that cause continuing hostility in American workplaces.

Finally, influenced at least partially by Pennsylvania Railroad president Thomas Scott who had helped decide the election of 1876 in his favor, President Rutherford B. Hayes called out federal troops to end the strike, sending the message that the federal government had chosen corporations over workers who had legitimate grievances. The Great Railroad Strike of 1877 ended after 45 days, with 100 people dead, 1,000 people in jail, 100,000 workers on strike, and half of the freight on the nation's 75,000 miles of track halted at the height of the strike.

The Great Railroad Strike of 1877 focused national attention on labor and its problems. Strike historian Robert Bruce wrote that the strikes taught many people empathy for the hardships of other workers and led to congressional regulation of railroads. Political and corporate officials blamed the strike on what they called a communist revolution, and used the fear of foreign ideologies to justify the violent suppression of worker agitation. The railroads made some concessions to the strikers, but working conditions remained basically the same as before the strike. The strike motivated unions such as the American Federation of Labor and the Knights of Labor to grow and encouraged workers to create new unions. Many workers emerged from the strike with new confidence in themselves and the power of the strike which they carried into the 21st century.

KATHY WARNES

See also: Pullman Strike (1894)

Further Reading

Barnard, Harry. 2005. *Rutherford Hayes and His America.* Newtown, CT: American Political Biography Press.

Bruce, Robert V. 1989 [1957]. *1877: Year of Violence.* Reprint ed. New York: Ivan R. Dee.

Salvatore, Nick. 1980. "Railroad Workers and the Great Strike of 1877." *Labor History* 21: 522–45.

Stover, John F. 1987. *History of the Baltimore and Ohio Railroad.* West Lafayette, IN: Purdue University Press.

Stowell, David O. 1999. *Streets, Railroads, and the Great Strike of 1877.* Historical Studies of Urban America. Chicago: University of Chicago Press.

Bagwell, Dennis (1963–2005)

Many criminal justice scholars would argue that the life of Dennis Wayne Bagwell shows the progression of a serious criminal career path. He had an extensive criminal record, including multiple attempted and completed murders. While on parole in 1995 for an attempted capital murder, Bagwell committed five more murders. He allegedly committed the senseless multiple killings of family members to finance his drug addiction, and much of the evidence in two of the murder cases was corroborated by Bagwell's then girlfriend, Victoria Wolford. The trials were lengthy but the juries reached verdicts in both guilt and sentencing phases within a few hours. While incarcerated and awaiting execution, Bagwell filed numerous unsuccessful appeals to fight the death sentence to both Texas State Appeals Court and Texas Federal District Appeals Court, claiming violations of the Fifth, Sixth, and Fourteenth Amendments of the Constitution. In 2005, he was executed for the horrific murders of his mother and three other female family members.

On September 20, 1995, Ronald Boone found the bodies of Dennis Bagwell's mother and Boone's wife, Leona Boone, 47, Libby Best, 24 (half-sister), Reba Best, 4 (Libby's daughter), and Tassy Boone, 14 (granddaughter of Ronald Boone). Ronald Boone was coming home from work and found Leona and Tassy beaten and strangled, with their necks broken by the violent force. Tassy had also been sexually assaulted. Libby had been shot in the head twice while Reba's skull had been crushed with a hammer and a metal exercise bar. A few weeks before the murder, Bagwell had lived in his trailer on his mother's property. According to testimony, Bagwell had gone to his mother to borrow money, but when she refused, he killed her, Libby, Reba, and Tassy. Bagwell was arrested for the murders and indicted for capital murder on November 21, 1995. In Texas, murder of more than one person during the same criminal transaction is a capital offense, and thus means eligibility for the death penalty (Texas Penal Code §19.03a7).

During the trial, Bagwell was required to wear nonvisible leg restraints because he had previously threatened law enforcement personnel and was assessed as dangerous. During the guilt phase of the trial, the prosecution presented several witnesses. Among them was Bagwell's girlfriend, Victoria Wolford, who testified against him. Wolford explained that she had been with Bagwell during the murders. Additionally, she had led investigators to different locations where Bagwell had disposed of evidence, resulting in recovered evidence presented at the trial. Given his troubled past, Bagwell did not testify because his attorneys believed doing so would hurt their defense. After both sides had presented their cases, the jury deliberated for three hours before they returned a guilty verdict. During the sentencing phase, the prosecution emphasized his long criminal record, parole records, and violent behaviors during past incarcerations and present pretrial detention. The defense brought witnesses, such as Bagwell's ex-wife and a former parole officer, who pled for a life sentence. The jury deliberations lasted for four hours. The jury was unanimous that Bagwell should be sentenced to death (*Bagwell v. Dretke* 2004).

Bagwell's situation was further complicated because he was charged with another murder while incarcerated for the multiple murders. On September 5, 1995, before the murder of Bagwell's mother, George Barry, a janitor at a local bar in Seguin, Texas, was found murdered. Bagwell was later found to be linked to the murder. During the trial in 1997, Bagwell's girlfriend, Victoria Wolford, testified yet again after being offered immunity against prosecution. Bagwell had allegedly looked for a bar employee to buy marijuana from. When he was unable to find him, he decided to rob and viciously kill Barry for drug money. The next day Bagwell and Wolford left Seguin for San Antonio, Texas. In their shared room, police officers had found an empty money bag similar to those used at the bar, which implicated Bagwell in the crime. Finger and palm prints were also found in the bar. The defense presented no witnesses, and Bagwell was convicted of capital murder and was sentenced to life in prison. The state waived the death penalty because he had already been sentenced to death for the other murders. Bagwell appealed the conviction, suggesting that the evidence did not corroborate the testimony by Wolford. The appeals court, however, determined that the finger and palm prints on the crime scene were strong enough evidence to overrule and affirm the conviction (*Bagwell v. State* 1997).

Bagwell filed several additional appeals regarding his capital sentence to different levels of courts. He appealed the conviction and the sentence to the Texas Court of Criminal Appeals (*Bagwell v. State* 1999). Shortly before his execution, Bagwell filed motions for authorization to file both petitions of writ of habeas corpus and stay of execution. He claimed that his counsel forced him not to testify during the trial, thereby violating his Fifth and Fourteenth Amendment rights. Bagwell further argued that the trial court did not ask whether he had waived his right to testify, which violates the Sixth Amendment. The problem is that these issues had not been raised in the initial federal petition. Bagwell's initial intentions were not to show his innocence but that his state of mind had changed after the death of his mother. However, in the decision of the appeal, it was argued that there was strong evidence against Bagwell and that the counsel had been right in warning him against testifying in court because of his extensive and violent criminal record. It did not help his case that while in prison, he made violent threats, committed disciplinary violations, and refused psychiatric treatment. Therefore, his requests were denied (*IN RE: Dennis Bagwell* 2005).

Bagwell's final meal consisted of a beef steak, medium rare with A1 Sauce, three fried chicken breast, three fried chicken thighs, BBQ ribs, a large order of french fries, a large order of onion rings, a pound of fried bacon, a dozen scrambled eggs with onions, fried tatters with onions, sliced tomatoes, a salad with ranch dressing, two hamburgers with everything, peach pie or cobbler, ketchup, salt and pepper, milk and coffee, and ice tea with real sugar. Bagwell's last statement before his execution on February, 17, 2005, was "Yes sir, can you hear me? To you Irene, Thank You. I love you all. All right Warden, I'm ready" (Texas Department of Criminal Justice Offender Information, 2014).

CATRIN ANDERSSON

See also: Luetgert, Adolph (1845–1899); Peterson, Laci, Murder of (2002–2004); Rader, Dennis (1945–)

Further Reading

Carson, David. 2005. "Dennis Bagwell." Texas Execution Information Center, February 18. http://www.txexecutions.org/reports/339.asp. Accessed February 10, 2015.

Clark Prosecutor's Office. 2014. "Dennis Wayne Bagwell." http://www.clarkprosecutor.org/html/death/US/bagwell949.htm. Accessed February, 10, 2015.

Dennis Bagwell v. Dretke, 2004 372 F 3d 748.

Dennis Bagwell v. State of Texas, 1997 956 S.W.2d 709.

IN RE: Dennis Bagwell, Movant, 2005 401F 3d 312.

Texas Department of Criminal Justice. 2014. "Dennis Bagwell." https://www.tdcj.state.tx.us/death_row/dr_info/bagwell dennislast.html. Accessed February 10, 2014.

Baker, Lena (1900–1945)

In 1944, Lena Baker was an African American housemaid and former prostitute who was convicted of killing her employer, Earnest B. Knight (Liddell 2009; Peace 2011; Phillips 2005). Knight was a white mill owner who had hired Baker to care for him after he suffered a broken leg. At some time during Baker's employment with Knight, they began having a sexual relationship. There is some argument regarding the consent of the relationship, with Baker claiming that the intimacy between her and Knight started after the latter raped her (Liddell 2009). Although it may seem peculiar that Baker would continue to have intimate relations with Knight after being sexually victimized, Baker claimed that Knight supplied her with alcohol and additional income, which was crucial for her, a mother of three, to survive (Liddell 2009). Baker also claimed that the Knight's behavior became increasingly violent, to the point that she had no choice but to shoot Knight because he had held her captive and tried to attack her. Baker was convicted of capital murder and executed on March 5, 1945. She was the only woman ever executed in the state of Georgia (Phillips 2005).

Lena Baker was raised in poverty in a former slave cabin in Randolph County, Georgia. During her teenage years, she and her mother moved to a house on Morgan Street in Cuthbert, Georgia (Phillips 2005). Soon after, Baker had her first confrontation with the law. Baker and a neighbor were arrested and convicted for "running a lewd house," and Baker was sentenced to 10 months of hard labor on a state farm (Peace 2011). After she was released Baker fought to live a legitimate lifestyle. She moved back in with her mother and became a housekeeper. Baker later had three children and continued living with her mother up until the time of her arrest (Liddell 2009; Peace 2011).

Ernest B. Knight was a mill owner who was known for severe alcoholism and vulgar language, and he was known for always carrying a gun (Liddell 2009). After Knight injured his leg, his son, Edward C. Knight, went to Baker's mother to request that she care for the elder Knight.

Baker's mother declined, so Knight's son asked Lena to be Ernest's caretaker (Liddell 2009; Phillips 2005). Lena obliged because she did not have any income, so working for Ernest was better than not working at all. Within a few weeks of working for Ernest, Baker claimed that Knight approached her while she was doing dishes, began groping her, and ultimately raped her. The next day, Lena returned to find a bottle of gin and a $10 bill left on an end table. She contemplated whether or not she should accept the items, knowing that she was symbolically condoning Knight's inappropriate behavior. She chose to take the items, perhaps because she balanced the weight of income versus the trauma she had just experienced (Liddell 2009).

After the initial rape, Baker continued to work for and participate in a sexual relationship with Ernest Knight. The day that Knight died, Baker claimed that she had decided not to return. Knight came to her home and threatened to cause enough commotion that it would wake her mother and children (Liddell 2009). Baker stated that she complied because she did not want Knight to disturb her family. Although Baker described several occasions in which Knight had held her captive, this particular day ended differently (Liddell 2009). Once again, Baker was locked in the mill, but when Knight returned from church, he told her that if she did not cooperate with his demands, he would kill her. She reportedly told him, "then I guess you'll have to do it." At this point, the couple scuffled, and Baker was able to obtain Knight's gun. Baker shot Knight directly above his left ear, killing him instantly (Liddell 2009). Knight was dead, and Baker had to figure out how to handle the situation.

After killing Knight, Baker went to a nearby neighbor's house to get help. The neighbor was the county coroner, J. A. Cox. Cox told Baker to report the murder to the police. Once the police arrived, Baker was arrested and later charged with capital murder (Liddell 2009; Peace 2011). The trial was only a few hours long, with reports that the judge stated that he preferred quick litigation because he planned on being done with the case "in time for dinner" (Liddell 2009). Further, the jury consisted of 12 white males who deliberated over Baker's fate for less than 30 minutes (Liddell 2009; Phillips 2005). Baker was convicted of capital murder and sentenced to death by electrocution. Accounts of the trial suggest that the most aggravating factor in the case was the fact that Baker was an African American, while Knight was a white male. These accounts suggest that had this race–offender relationship not existed, Baker would likely have been charged with manslaughter instead of capital murder (Liddell 2009).

Interestingly, a similar case was tried the next day with the exception that the offender and victim were both white males. This offender was charged with manslaughter (Peace 2005).

As Baker awaited execution, her lawyer, W. L. Ferguson, filed an appeal on her behalf. However, soon after, Ferguson dropped Baker as a client (Phillips 2005). Governor Ellis Arnali granted Baker a 60-day reprieve so that the Board of Pardons could review the case, but the board denied Baker clemency in January 1945. Baker was transferred to Reidsville State Prison and executed in less than two months after being sentenced (Phillips 2005). Baker's final words were, "What I done, I did in self-defense, or I would have been killed myself. Where I was I could not overcome it. God has forgiven me. I have nothing against anyone. I picked cotton for Mr. Pritchett, and he has been good to me. I am ready to go. I am one in the number. I am ready to meet my God. I have a very strong conscience" (Liddell 2009, 33).

Because the whites of Cuthbert, Georgia, refused to permit Lena Baker's body to be buried in her hometown, she was buried in an unmarked grave outside the churchyard where she was raised (Liddell 2009). Out of fear of retribution, most of her family left Georgia and moved north. For decades, the story of Lena Baker's life disappeared until historical injustices of the South were explored. Once informed, Lena's family joined together and placed a tombstone on her grave. In 2003, Lena's great nephew, Roosevelt Curry, requested a pardon from the Parole Board. In 2005, Lena Baker was awarded a full and unconditional pardon, with commentators supporting earlier arguments that the charge of capital murder should have been downgraded to manslaughter (Liddell 2009).

The case of Lena Baker is an illustration of the presence of racial discrimination within the criminal justice system. Although African Americans were no longer slaves, public and official perceptions of blacks remained negative. As a result, Lena Baker and other African Americans were subjected to penalties that were more severe than those experienced by their white counterparts.

MONICA E. SUMMERS

See also: Atlanta Race Riot (1906); Little, Joan, Murder Trial of (1975)

Further Reading
Liddell, Janice L. 2009. *Who Will Sing for Lena?* Burlington, MA: JAC Publishing & Promotions.
Peace, Stephen. 2011. *Lena Baker: A Quick Case of Murder*. Seattle, WA: Amazon Digital Services.
Phillips, Lena. 2005. "Lena Baker Case." http://www.georgiaencyclopedia.org/articles/history-archaeology/lena-baker-case. Accessed April 13, 2015.

Bakker, Jim (1940–)

Televangelist and former minister James (Jim) Orsen Bakker was born on January 2, 1940. In the 1980s, Bakker and his then-wife, Tammy Faye Bakker (married from 1961 to 1992; Tammy Faye passed away in 2007), hosted a nationally syndicated television show, *The PTL* ("Praise the Lord" or "People That Love") *Club*. The Bakkers were well known nationally for their charismatic and persuasive ministry, offering tearful and emotional orations. At the peak of success, their TV show was watched by more than 13 million people internationally, their fund-raising efforts brought in over a hundred million dollars a year, and the enterprise employed more than 2,000 people. However, their prosperity came to a crashing halt as criminal fraud charges and a sexual scandal led to the collapse of Bakker's reign as one of the most recognized televangelists of the 1980s.

In 1966, the Bakkers worked at Pat Robertson's Christian Broadcasting Network and were instrumental in the success of *The 700 Club* in the late 1960s. In the early 1970s, the Bakkers hosted a local TV show in Charlotte, North Carolina, and developed the PTL Television Network, a 24-hour worldwide Christian cable television network. *The Jim and Tammy Show* was a major success and the Bakkers asked viewers to support the PTL ministry. In the early 1980s, along with running the PTL ministry, the Bakkers established Heritage USA, a 2,300-acre religious resort, conference center, and theme park, just south of Charlotte, in Fort Mills, South Carolina. The Bakkers implored viewers and supporters to help raise the $25 million needed to build Heritage USA. Heritage Park would grow to include hotels, shopping centers, TV studios, a satellite broadcast center, and even a water park.

The Charlotte Observer investigated PTL's fund-raising efforts in the mid-1980s. The investigation, led by reporter Charles Shepard (who later was awarded a Pulitzer for his investigative journalism efforts related to PTL), uncovered major fraudulent activity from 1984 to 1987. The newspaper reported that Jim Bakker and his associates oversold thousands of "lifetime memberships" and "exclusive partnerships" to Heritage USA, which included a three-night

Ordered to undergo psychiatric evaluation when he failed to appear in court on August 31, 1989, televangelist Jim Bakker (center) is escorted by U.S. Marshals from his attorney's office in Charlotte, North Carolina, to a waiting car. (AP Photo/Chuck Burton)

annual visit to the resort for life. Bakker asked 25,000 people to contribute $1,000 but sold thousands more partnerships than could be satisfied. In less than four years, over $150 million poured into PTL's coffers. Bakker was accused of diverting donations for construction of Heritage USA into PTL's operating expenses and his own pockets.

Interestingly, the mid-1980s investigation was preceded by a 1979 *Charlotte Observer* investigation that examined PTL's fund-raising efforts for international missionary work with the investigation, leading to suggestions that the money was not spent overseas but used internally. The Federal Communications Commission (FCC) launched an investigation from 1979 to 1982 but no charges were filed. An Internal Revenue Service (IRS) probe led to findings of inaccurate accounting but the Justice Department did not investigate further.

On March 19, 1987, Bakker resigned from PTL due to his involvement in a sex scandal. He and another minister were accused of drugging and raping his 21-year-old church secretary, Jessica Hahn. He admitted to a sexual relationship with Hahn but said it was consensual. The sexual scandal was quickly overshadowed by allegations of financial fraud.

A 16-month federal grand jury probe led to his indictment on 8 counts of mail fraud, 15 counts of wire fraud, and 1 count of conspiracy in 1988. Tammy Faye Bakker was not charged. A five-week trial commenced on August 28, 1989, in Charlotte, North Carolina. When the trial began, Bakker was 49 years old and PTL, once a multimillion dollar enterprise, was in the midst of bankruptcy proceedings. The prosecution showed that Bakker overwhelmingly oversold the "lifetime partnerships." The prosecution presented evidence that Bakker spent close to $4 million of PTL contributions on luxury houses, cars, jewelry, and vacations and collected hundreds of thousands of dollars in bonuses. Jurors were shown videos of Bakker's opulent lifestyle, including a video tour created by James Taggart, Bakker's then-interior designer (Taggart was sentenced to 17 years in prison and fined $500,000 a week prior for tax evasion while employed at PTL). The video tour highlighted the Bakker family luxury suites and a voice description of Bakker's gold-plated bathroom fixtures. Another witness testified that Bakker paid him $96,000 for a music career marketing plan for Bakker's daughter, Tammy Sue. Records presented at trial showed that Bakker spent over half a million dollars on music equipment for his home. At the trial, a witness also testified that Bakker approved a $265,000 payoff to Jessica Hahn for keeping quiet about the sexual scandal. The prosecution interspersed witnesses who donated money to Bakker and attempted to stay at Heritage USA as per the "lifetime partnership" agreement but were never granted access.

The trial was widely covered by the national media with frequent reports of Bakker's mental breakdowns that led to the suspension of the trial and a psychiatric evaluation. On August 31, 1989, the judge ordered the trial suspended and Bakker committed for psychiatric testing. Bakker's psychiatrist testified that Bakker was found in his attorney's office cowering in a fetal position under a couch, allegedly suffering from hallucinations. On September 6, 1989, Bakker was deemed competent when another psychiatrist testified that he suffered a panic attack but was not mentally ill. Tammy Faye and many of their devoted followers led frequent prayer vigils and encouraged devotees to continue to send money to support Bakker. On the stand, Jim Bakker, often in tears, stated that the money was donated to the ministry and denied that he defrauded his followers, blaming other ministers for the accounting mismanagement.

A jury of six men and six women deliberated for only 10 hours. On October 5, 1989, Bakker was found guilty on all 24 counts and U.S. District Court Judge Robert Potter sentenced Bakker to 45 years in prison along with a $500,000 fine. In 1991, the Fifth Circuit of Appeals upheld his conviction on the fraud and conspiracy charges but voided his sentence and fine. In 1992, his sentence was reduced to eight years and he was not required to pay restitution. Bakker was paroled in 1994 after serving approximately five years of his sentence. His wife, Tammy Faye, divorced Bakker while he was serving his sentence. In 1996, Jim Bakker published his side of the story in his book *I Was Wrong*.

Close to 165,000 people sued Bakker in civil courts. In 2003, a federal judge ordered a Charlotte law firm to distribute $6.54 to each of the 165,000 people defrauded by Bakker as part of a $1.2 million settlement. Today, Jim Bakker and his second-wife cohost *The Jim Bakker Show* from their Morningside residential and retail complex south of Branson, Missouri. On his website, Bakker sells emergency and survivalist packages and products in preparation for the end of the world.

MELISSA L. JARRELL

See also: Catholic Priest Child Sex Abuse Scandal (1950s–2000s); Clinton, Bill, Impeachment Trial of (1999); Enron Case (1985–2001)

Further Reading

Albert, James. 1999. *Jim Bakker: Miscarriage of Justice?* Peru, IL: Open Court.

Bakker, Jim, and Ken Abraham. 1996. *I Was Wrong*. Nashville, TN: Thomas Nelson.

Shepard, Charles E. 1989. *Forgiven: The Rise and Fall of Jim Bakker and the PTL Ministry*. New York: Atlantic Monthly Press.

Bales, Robert (1973–)

On the night of March 11, 2012, Sergeant Robert Bales left the U.S. military base in the Panjwai district of Afghanistan. He walked into two neighboring villages and fatally shot 16 Afghan citizens, 9 of whom were children. His rampage is known as the Kandahar massacre and has been described as "one of the worst war crimes in the Iraq and Afghanistan conflicts" (Dao 2012). The United States and Afghanistan were equally shocked and saddened by the tragedy. The U.S. Military led investigations, conducted an Article 32 Hearing, and the case was tried in military court. Bales pled guilty to the murders and on August 23, 2013, he was sentenced to life imprisonment without possibility of parole. Bales's rampage intensified the existing hostility between the United States and Afghanistan. In the days following the massacre, several "Death to America" protests erupted in and around the villages that Bales targeted. However, the Department of Defense is now investigating the effects of stress and warfare on the mental health of soldiers (Department of Defense 2012). As this inquiry is pursued, new treatments and preventative measures may emerge to help soldiers cope with combat.

Robert Bales was born on January 30, 1973, in Norwood, Ohio. He was the youngest of five boys and sources say that his family was pleasant and well liked (Dao 2012). Bales has been described as a social and busy teenager who was gregarious, extraverted, and had leadership qualities. Bales attended the College of Mount Saint Joseph from 1992 to 1993 and then transferred to Ohio State University. He studied economics there from 1993 to 1996, but left without earning a degree. In the following years Bales held several investment and financial jobs.

In November 2001, Bales enlisted in the U.S. Army. Friends say that he was inspired to join the Armed Forces after the terrorist attacks of September 11, 2001. Bales was a member of the 2nd Battalion, 3rd Infantry Regiment, 3rd Stryker Brigade Combat Team, 2nd Infantry Division. During his time in the military, Bales received combative training levels one and two and sniper training. Throughout his entire service, Bales was stationed out of Joint Base Lewis-McChord in Washington State. Bales was deployed to Iraq three times and his final tour was of Afghanistan in 2012.

During his first three tours of Iraq, Bales was injured twice. On his second tour of Iraq in 2012 Bales lost a part of his foot in battle. In 2012 he suffered a brain injury but was cleared for combat and was deployed to Afghanistan later that year (Dao 2012).

Robert Bales had an existing criminal history prior to the atrocities he committed in the Kandahar massacre. In 2002 after enlisting, Bales was convicted of assault. He was sentenced to 20 hours of anger management treatment and paid a fine. In 2008 Bales was involved in a car accident. Conflicting narratives surround the cause of the crash; Bales claims he fell asleep at the wheel, while others report smelling alcohol on him and seeing him run from the car. Additionally, Bales was accused of investment fraud by an elderly couple from Ohio. The couple claims that Bales never paid the $1.5 million they are owed (Sewell and Wagner 2012).

Despite his few brushes with the law, Bales was described as a dedicated and excellent soldier. Those he served with describe him as one of the best soldiers they've ever worked with (Dao 2012). He had earned the rank of army staff sergeant and received multiple awards for his service. Former friends and soldiers he served with were astonished to learn that Bales was responsible for the massive tragedy in Kandahar (Dao 2012).

On his fourth tour to Afghanistan, Bales was stationed in the Panjwai district of the Kandahar Province, a notoriously poor and dangerous region of Afghanistan known for Taliban activity. In the middle of the night on March 11, 2012, Bales left his military base. He walked into a two neighboring villages and shot, stabbed, and set fire to several innocent civilians. In the end, 16 died. Eleven of the victims belonged to the same family and nine were children. Witnesses recount that Bales walked into the village with a bright light on his helmet and did not say a word or cease firing when victims screamed and pleaded for mercy. Following the massacre, Bales retuned to the base where several other soldiers saw him in blood-stained clothes. He was apprehended later that morning and transported to Kuwait and then the most secure military facility in Fort Leavenworth, Kansas, to await investigations and trial.

Two soldiers admitted to drinking with Bales on the night of his rampage. It is prohibited for soldiers to drink on the base and those individuals are facing disciplinary sanctions. One soldier's account holds that Bales returned to the base came to reload his ammunition before terrorizing the second village.

When asked why he committed such violence, Bales offered no explanation. In the sentencing hearing he sat stoically and expressed no remorse. There are several competing perspectives that speculate as to what caused Bales's actions. Bales's defense attorney, John Henry Browne, claimed that Bales may have suffered posttraumatic stress disorder (PTSD) as a result of almost 10 years on active duty and a brain injury. The military prosecutor claimed that Bales was having marital and financial problems as well as issues with alcohol, which triggered his violence. Records indicate that Bales has no history of mental illness, but he did admit to using anabolic steroids, which made him irritable. Those who knew him personally as a soldier or friend insist that Bales must have snapped under the pressures of the war, because unprovoked violence was not characteristic of Bales (Dao 2012).

Because Bales was enlisted in the army, the U.S. military had jurisdiction over the case. They conducted an Article 32 investigation hearing and Bales was court-martialed. On May 29, 2013, Bales pled guilty to the 16 counts of murder, six assault charges, and attempted murder. Doing so removed the possibility of incurring a death sentence. A sentencing hearing was held to determine whether Bales would be sentenced to life imprisonment with or without the possibility of parole. Seven Afghani villagers came to testify at the sentencing hearing and several others retold their accounts over video message In August 2013, Bales was sentenced to life imprisonment without the possibility of parole and is incarcerated at the military prison in Fort Leavenworth, Kansas. Bales was demoted to the lowest possible rank and dishonorably discharged from the military.

NICOLE E. FRISCH

See also: Abu Ghraib Prisoner Abuse Scandal (Iraq) (2003–2004); Hasan, Nidal Malik (1970–); My Lai Massacre (March 16, 1968)

Further Reading

Dao, James. 2012. "At Home, Asking How 'Our Bobby' Became War Crime Suspect." *The New York Times.* March 18. http://www.nytimes.com/2012/03/19/us/sgt-robert-bales-from-small-town-ohio-to-afghanistan.html?pagewanted=all&_r=0. Accessed December 12, 2014.

Department of Defense. 2012. "DOD News Briefing with George Little and Capt. Kirby from the Pentagon." http://www.defense.gov/transcripts/transcript.aspx?transcriptid=4997. Accessed December 12, 2014.

Sewell, Dan, and Daniel Wagner. 2012. "Afghanistan Suspect Had Shaky Business Dealings." *The Associated Press.* March 21. http://www.businessweek.com/ap/2012-03/D9TL0Q880.htm. Accessed December 11, 2014.

Ball, Joseph (1896–1938)

Joseph (Joe) Ball, known as "The Alligator Man" and "The Butcher of Elmendorf," became famous for murdering women and allegedly feeding their bodies to alligators. Ball is believed to have killed at least 20 women in southern Texas. However, much is still unknown about Ball, as it is difficult to separate fact from folklore.

Born in 1896 in Elmendorf, Texas, Joe Ball was one of eight children born to Frank and Elizabeth Ball. After the United States entered World War I, Ball enlisted and served in the army for two years. He was honorably discharged and returned home to Elmendorf. After Prohibition, Ball opened a saloon called the Sociable Inn. To draw in more business, Ball dug a hole behind the saloon and filled the pit with live alligators. On Saturday evenings, he would make a show out of feeding live animals to the alligators.

In 1934, Ball met Minnie Gotthardt. The two began a relationship and started running the tavern together. However, after three years together, Ball began seeing one of his waitresses, Dolores Goodwin. Shortly after that, Ball started another relationship with another waitress, Hazel Brown.

Gotthardt disappeared in the summer of 1937, shortly after Ball began his relationship with Brown. Ball claimed Gotthardt had left town after giving birth to another man's baby. A few months later, Goodwin and Ball married. Ball reportedly confided in Goodwin that Gotthardt had not run off, but rather Ball had killed her. Goodwin did not believe Ball. However, in 1938, both Goodwin and Brown also disappeared.

Gotthardt's family pressured police to continue looking into Ball regarding the disappearances. Additionally, in mid-1938, another family came forward reporting Julia Turner as missing. She had worked part-time at Ball's tavern. Ball claimed Turner had personal problems she had left to take care of. Police had no evidence tying Ball to her disappearance. Within a few months, two more of Ball's employees went missing. Ball was consistently questioned with regard to the disappearances. However, there was never any evidence connecting him to the missing girls.

On September 23, 1938, a neighbor of Ball's came forward with a shocking claim. He claimed he saw Ball cutting up pieces of a human body and feeding it to his alligators. Another man came forward and claimed that a barrel inside Ball's sister's barn smelled as if something was dead inside. The barrel was gone by the time the police went to investigate; however, Ball's sister agreed with the man's claims.

Police went to Ball's tavern and informed him they were taking him to San Antonio for questioning. At that point, Ball took a .45 caliber revolver out of his cash register, pointed it at his heart, and pulled the trigger. The shot was fatal.

After Ball's death, police investigated the tavern. They found rotting flesh in the alligator pond. Additionally, they found an axe covered in human hair and blood. In the tavern they found a scrapbook filled with photos of dozens of women, who were all considered potential victims.

Police questioned a close friend of Ball's, Clifton Wheeler. Wheeler admitted he had knowledge that Ball killed Hazel Brown because she was planning on leaving him for another man. Wheeler even led police to Brown's body. Upon additional questioning, Wheeler told police about the death of Minnie Gotthardt. Ball had supposedly killed her because she was pregnant and Ball did not want that to get in the way of his relationship with Dolores Goodwin. Wheeler again led police to the body.

Not all of Ball's supposed victims, however, were killed. Police located Dolores Goodwin alive in California. She had apparently left Texas to start a new life. Another one of Ball's assumed victims was later found alive in Arizona. Additionally, the rotting flesh found in the alligator pond was not human. It is still unknown whether Ball actually fed any of his victims to his alligators.

It also still remains unknown how many women Joe Ball killed. Dolores Goodwin claims his only victims were Minnie Gotthardt and Hazel Brown. However, Ball has become somewhat of a legend in southern Texas, with some reports claiming he killed over 20 women.

CAITLIN B. HENRIKSEN

See also: Bundy, Ted (1946–1989); Dahmer, Jeffrey (1960–1994); Fish, Albert (1870–1936)

Further Reading

"Joe Ball" Murderpedia, the Encyclopedia of Murderers. http://murderpedia.org/male.B/b/ball-joseph.htm. Accessed April 13, 2015.

Montaldo, Charles. 2014. "Joe Ball and His Alligator Pond." Joe Ball and His Alligator Pond. August 15. http://crime.about.com/od/serial/p/joeball.htm. Accessed April 13, 2015.

Barfield, Velma (1932–1984)

Velma Barfield murdered at least five individuals. Her weapon of choice was clear, liquid ant or roach poison. Barfield's victims suffered severe stomach pains and vomiting before dying. Barfield claims that she murdered to hide the fact that she was stealing money from her victims to support her prescription painkiller addiction. Some scholars argue that Barfield was a coldblooded psychopath who was unable to take responsibility for her actions or feel any remorse (Vronsky 2007, 186). Barfield was only convicted for one murder and received the death penalty. She was executed in November 1984 and her case raised issues about the appropriateness of the death penalty for women.

Velma Barfield was born on October 23, 1932, in rural South Carolina. She grew up in a strictly Christian household. In school, Barfield was described as hostile and having a bad temper when she did not get her way. In 1949 at the age of 17, Barfield dropped out of high school and married Thomas Burke. The couple had two children, Ronnie and Kim. The family was religious and accounts describe Velma as a responsible, loving mother when the children were young. Unfortunately, things changed for the worse when Barfield had a hysterectomy and developed back pains (Vronsky 2007, 196). She was prescribed painkillers and became heavily addicted to prescription pills. For the

Convicted murderer, Velma Barfield awaited her execution on North Carolina's death row. Here she is shown during the taping of an October 1984 interview. (AP Photo)

rest of her life she would repeatedly overdose and forge checks to support her addiction.

In 1969 Barfield's first husband died and there is controversy as to whether or not she was responsible. He died from smoke inhalation during a house fire and she vehemently denied having killed him for most of her life. However, one source claims that in her final days Barfield admitted to her son that on the night of the fire she left Burke alone and asleep with a lit cigarette on the mattress and locked the bedroom door (Vronsky 2007, 198). The fire department reportedly had to break down the bedroom door to get to Burke.

After her first husband died, Velma remarried a man named Jennings Barfield. A few months after the two were wed, Jennings Barfield died of heart failure. Velma always denied killing her second husband; however, when she was charged with murder and authorities began investigating her past, Jennings's body was exhumed and traces of arsenic were recovered from the corpse (Office of the Clark County Prosecuting Attorney, n.d.).

After the death of Jennings Barfield, Velma moved back in with her mother. In her book, *Woman on Death*

Row, Barfield confesses that she always hated her mother because she was bossy and selfish. Later in life Barfield admitted resenting and blaming her mother for being complacent in the sexual and physical abuse she suffered from her father (Barfield 1985, 31–33). In 1974 Barfield's mother was sent to the hospital for severe stomach pains and vomiting. She was diagnosed with gastroenteritis and given medicine to help her recover. A few days later she was back in the hospital, again for severe stomach pains, and died two hours after being admitted. Barfield admitted to poisoning her mother but insisted that she never meant to kill her. She claimed that she took out a loan in her mother's name and was unable to pay it off. When her mother received notices from the bank and became suspicious, Barfield said that she poisoned her mother only to make her sick long enough to gather money to pay the loan off (Vronsky 2007, 208).

After her mother died, Barfield moved in with her daughter Kim and her husband Dennis. In 1975 Barfield was incarcerated for six months in North Carolina Correctional Center for Women in Raleigh for cashing fraudulent checks. Barfield had already been serving a suspended sentence for forging a prescription, and when she was caught cashing false checks, she was sentenced to six months in jail (Vronsky 2007, 209–211). Barfield served four months of this sentence and was let out on probation. Eleven days after her release, Barfield overdosed on painkillers, which she paid for with fraudulent checks. To avoid further incarceration, Barfield convinced her daughter to pay off the bad checks.

In November 1975, shortly after being incarcerated, Barfield was hired to take care of an elderly couple, Montgomery and Dollie Edwards. While caring for them, Barfield started dating their nephew, Stuart Taylor, a tobacco farmer. In January 1977 Montgomery Edwards died and in February 1977 Dollie Edwards died of severe stomach pains. Barfield would later admit to poisoning Dollie Edwards because she resembled her mother. Barfield admitted she could not stand being micromanaged by her while trying to care for her (Vronsky 2007, 212).

Taylor and Barfield continued dating after the deaths of his aunt and uncle. Barfield remembers Taylor as an alcoholic and angry drunk. The two fought viciously when he was informed that she had spent time incarcerated for forging checks. To support her painkiller habit, Barfield forged two of Taylor's checks. He discovered the first one and was furious (Barfield 1985, 89). Barfield claims that when she became desperate to fill her prescriptions, she forged a second check. She then decided to poison Taylor's beer to make him sick so he would not notice the fraudulent transaction.

When Taylor began experiencing intense stomach pains and frequent vomiting, Barfield waited two full days before taking him to the hospital. Taylor was given medicine for gastroenteritis at the hospital but died the next day. The medical examiner was perplexed with Taylor's death and performed an autopsy. The results revealed that Taylor died of poisoning triggered by massive arsenic ingestion.

Female Serial Killers

Violence and murder are traditionally thought of as crimes with male offenders, many people fail to realize that women kill, too. In fact, on average the male serial killer operates without being caught for four years and the female serial killer continues murdering for an average of eight years without detection. Females target family members, intimates, and people they know more often than males do and rarely victimize strangers. Like males, female serial killers are motivated by a multitude of different factors. Some kill in pursuit of financial or material gain, others aid a partner or kill under the direction of a leader. Some mothers murder their children in order to receive sympathy and other female serial killers are driven by power and vengeance.

After Taylor died, local police received a frantic phone call from a woman claiming that Barfield murdered Taylor and also murdered her own mother. The call came from Barfield's sister and the autopsy results later confirmed her assertions (Vronsky 2007, 188–189). The call pointed police in Barfield's direction and once agencies began sharing information, it quickly became clear that Barfield was responsible for several deaths. Her first two husbands died and several elderly people she cared for and her mother had died from gastroenteritis.

The time's "deadliest" district attorney Joe Freeman Britt prosecuted Barfield (Vronsky 2007, 217). Britt ended his career with 22 capital convictions. He charged Barfield with only the murder of Stuart Taylor and the jury returned a death sentence in December 1978. Barfield took the stand in her own defense but this quickly backfired when she became hostile and corrected Britt about the details of her crime in the cross-examination. Barfield appealed the sentence several times, claiming to have become a born-again Christian. Governor Jim Hunt refused to grant clemency (Barfield 1985, 150). Barfield was executed on November 2, 1984, by lethal injection. She was the first woman to be executed after the death penalty was reinstated in the 1976 *Gregg* decision (Vronsky 2007, 217).

NICOLE E. FRISCH

See also: Buenoano, Judy (1943–1998); Eubanks, Susan (1964–); Moore, Blanche Taylor (1933–); Puente, Dorothea (1929–2011); Tucker, Karla Faye (1959–1998); Wuornos, Aileen (1956–2002)

Further Reading

Barfield, Velma. 1985. *Woman on Death Row*. Nashville, TN: Oliver-Nelson Books.

Office of the Clark County Prosecuting Attorney. "Velma Barfield #29." http://www.clarkprosecutor.org/html/death/US/barfield 029.htm. Accessed February 5, 2015.

Vronsky, Peter. 2007. *Female Serial Killers: How and Why Women Become Monsters*. New York: The Berkley Publishing Group.

Barker, Kate "Ma" (1873–1935)

Kate "Ma" Barker was called the matriarch of the Barker–Karpis gang, which engaged in several kidnappings, robberies, and murders throughout the United States between 1931 and 1935. Barker's four sons all had lengthy criminal records, and at least two of her sons, Arthur "Doc" Barker and Fred Barker, were noted members of the Barker–Karpis gang. Ma Barker's son Fred brought her with him wherever he moved, and while it is unlikely that she actively engaged in criminal activity, she was aware of and benefitted from her sons' illegal activities. The Federal Bureau of Investigation (FBI) at the time claimed that Ma Barker was the mastermind behind the Barker–Karpis gang, but many years later the FBI admitted that these claims were exaggerated. The FBI especially felt the need to accuse Ma Barker of heinous criminal deviousness after she died at the age of 60 in a shootout. Ma Barker herself likely participated in returning fire during the shootout, but this is the only recorded mention of her actively involved in any of her sons' criminal pursuits.

Arizona Donnie Clark was born on October 8, 1873, in Ash Grove, Missouri, to a poor family of Scottish and Irish ancestry. She would grow up to adopt the name "Kate" and later marry George Barker, a tenant farmer. The couple had four sons—Herman, Lloyd ("Red"), Arthur ("Doc"), and Fred.

The adult Ma Barker was as poor as she had been as a child. None of her sons made it past the eighth grade, and from the time they entered their teenage years until their deaths, the four Barker boys engaged in a spree of thefts, kidnappings, bank robberies, and murders that stretched throughout the early 20th century and all over the United States.

Ma Barker was fiercely protective of her sons and forbade anyone from disciplining their bad behavior. This caused enough tension between her and her husband that the couple eventually divorced. George Barker left Ma Barker to open a gas station in Joplin, Missouri.

In 1921, 25-year-old Doc Barker robbed a safe at a construction site with two other men, and killed a night watchman who had surprised them. The next year, Doc Barker was found guilty of the murder and sentenced to life in prison. At the same time, Red Barker was convicted of mail robbery and sentenced to 25 years in Leavenworth.

In 1927, Herman Barker robbed a safe in an ice-making plant outside Wichita, Kansas. After the robbery, he and his accomplices were pulled over by two police officers, and Herman Barker killed one of the police officers before speeding away and crashing the car. Unable to escape the wreckage, Herman Barker pulled out his gun and killed himself. At that time Ma Barker was living in Tulsa, Oklahoma, in a tiny hovel, waiting for her remaining sons to come back to her.

One son did come back. In 1931, her youngest son Fred Barker was paroled from Kansas's Lansing Prison, and he brought home his jailhouse friend, Alvin Karpis. Together, the two men formed the Barker-Karpis gang. Ma Barker permitted the men to use her shack in Tulsa as a hideout, and when they decided it was time to leave, Karpis and Fred Barker brought Ma Barker to live with them wherever they went. That October Ma Barker, along with her boyfriend Arthur Dunlop and her son Fred, rented a farm in Thayer, Missouri. They had to leave quickly that December, though, because the men killed a sheriff the day after robbing a clothing store, and the little family moved to St. Paul, Minnesota.

The year of 1932 was somewhat idyllic for Ma Barker, even though she was constantly moving into different apartments. She did enjoy not having to work, being able to shop, going to the movies, listening to the radio, and walking her bulldog. On March 29, 1932, Karpis and Fred Barker robbed the Northwestern National Bank in Minneapolis, Minnesota, and got away with more than a quarter of a million dollars. That September, Doc Barker was paroled from his murder sentence, and both Barker boys pitched in to rob the Third Northwestern National Bank in Minneapolis.

The only interruption to Ma Barker's idyll was when her paramour, Arthur Dunlop, while under the influence of alcohol, gave a neighbor too much information about the Barker-Karpis gang. He was killed for his sins. His killer is still unknown, but it is generally agreed that the hit was committed to protect the Barker-Karpis gang, and by extension, Ma Barker.

On January 17, 1934, Edward Bremer, the grown son of wealthy businessman Adolph Bremer, was kidnapped. The kidnappers demanded $200,000 in ransom money, and ordered the Bremers to put an ad in *The Minneapolis Tribune*, which read "We are ready, Alice." Later it would be revealed that one of Ma Barker's nicknames was "Mother Alice." Three weeks later, the Bremers finally broke down, paid the ransom, and got their son back. The FBI, determined to find the kidnappers, started to close in on the Barker-Karpis gang, and Karpis and the Barkers could feel it.

Ma Barker's sons moved her one last time into 13250 East Highway C-25 in Ocklawaha, Florida, right on Lake Weir. On January 8, 1935, Doc Barker was arrested in Chicago, and the FBI found a map in his apartment on which he had marked the location of the Florida hideout where Ma and Fred Barker were living. At 6:00 a.m. on January 16, 1935, FBI agents surrounded the house on Lake Weir. From the front yard, Agent Earl Connelley called out to the house's inhabitants. Ma Barker opened the door, and when Connelley requested to speak to Fred, she asked who it was that wanted him, before shutting the door again. Agents again called out to Ma and Fred Barker, asking them to come out quietly. At 7:15 a.m., the agents threw tear gas canisters at the windows—and then the shooting began.

The Barkers fired at the federal agents with Thompson machine guns, and the agents returned fire with rifles, shotguns, and machine guns. Fred ran from window to window with his machine gun, and Ma Barker also added to the firefight with her own machine gun. Occasional lulls in the shooting heard agents persisting in calling out to the Barkers to lay down their arms and come out peacefully. By 11:30 a.m., the shooting finally came to an end. Handyman Willie Woodberry was talked into going into the house to ascertain whether the Barkers were dead. Woodberry found Ma Barker curled up under a bedroom window with her slippers on the floor near her. Fred Barker was also killed.

The life and death of Kate "Ma" Barker would go on to inspire several books, movies, and music. Long after the events of January 16, 1935, took place, the FBI eventually admitted that they had exaggerated the importance of Ma Barker to the Barker-Karpis gang. The FBI at the time insisted that she was the mastermind of the fierce crew, but in truth she was simply the nagging, overprotective mother to four uncontrollable boys. The shootout would become famous as the longest firefight in FBI history.

Erin Copland

See also: Barker–Karpis Gang (1931–1936); Capone, Al (1899–1947); Dillinger, John (1903–1934); Gillis, Lester Joseph "Baby Face Nelson" (1908–1934); St. Valentine's Day Massacre (February 14, 1929)

Further Reading

A&E Television Networks Bio. 2014. "Arizona Donnie Barker." http://www.biography.com/people/ma-barker-14515515#a-violent-death. Accessed April 13, 2015.

MacCabee, Paul. 1995. *John Dillinger Slept Here.* St. Paul, MN: Minnesota Historical Society Press.

Mahoney, Tim. 2013. *Secret Partners: Big Tom Brown and the Barker Gang.* St. Paul, MN: Minnesota Historical Society Press.

Shanklin, Mary. 2012. "Ma Barker's Shot-Up Hide-out for Sale." *The Orlando Sentinel.* August 17. http://articles.orlandosentinel.com/2012-08-17/business/os-ma-barker-house-20120817_1_ma-barker-barker-karpis-carson-bradford. Accessed April 13, 2015.

Vanderborg, Carey. 2012. "Kate 'Ma' Barker, Mother of 1930s Gangster Fred 'Doc' Barker, Home for Sale." *The International Business Times.* August 22. http://www.ibtimes.com/kate-ma-barker-mother-1930s-gangster-fred-doc-barker-home-sale-florida-house-still-riddled-original. Accessed April 13, 2015.

Barker–Karpis Gang (1931–1936)

The Barker–Karpis gang was a group of criminals who terrorized the Midwest during the Great Depression. The core members, Alvin Karpis, Fred Barker, and Doc Barker, completed several bank robberies and kidnappings, making them one of the country's most notorious criminals of the 1930s. The Barker–Karpis gang is not as well known as the Dillinger gang of the same era, but several sources say that Karpis and the Barker brothers were more brutal than any other criminals of their time. The men were known for carrying large machine guns. When faced with possible arrest and surrounded by police, it was not uncommon for the gang members to shoot their way out without any regard for who or how many people they were hurting in the process. The gang has been linked to between 5 and 15 murders. The Barker–Karpis gang was also famous for their involvement in the kidnapping of William Hamm, son of the founder of Hamm's Beer, in June 1933, and the kidnapping of Edward Bremer Jr. in January 1934. Both cases were high profile and received media attention. With law enforcement quickly encroaching on their operation, the gang members were in hiding or on the run for the majority of 1934 and 1935. The gang unraveled when Doc Barker was arrested in January 1935 and a few days later his brother Fred and mother Kate were killed in a shoot-out at Fred's cottage in Florida. Shortly after on May 1, 1936, Alvin Karpis was arrested in New Orleans, Louisiana.

Alvin Karpis and Fred Barker established connections while both served time in Kansas State Penitentiary. In 1931 they completed their sentences and were released. Together, Karpis and Barker began robbing banks (Karpis 1971). In 1932, Fred's brother Doc was released from prison and began aiding in the bank robberies. These three men comprised the heart of the Barker–Karpis gang; while they worked with several other criminals, these three were involved with every decision and every operation. From 1931 to 1934 the gang completed several successful bank robberies in multiple states. Their tactic was to constantly switch locations and use aliases to avoid detection. Ironically, the men were easily identifiable, Karpis was 5'10" and

lanky while the two Barker brothers were quite short. Their appearance easily connected them to several robberies. However, Karpis was a man of incessant planning. He was detail oriented and thoughtfully devised intricate plans for the group to successfully avoid apprehension.

After committing several successful bank robberies, the gang changed tactics and completed two high-profile kidnappings. In June 1933 the gang targeted the Hamm's Beer family. The gang held William Hamm hostage until a ransom of $100,000 was paid. A few months later in January 1934 the gang kidnapped Edward Bremer Jr. from St. Paul, Minnesota, in the middle of the day. Bremer was held captive until February 1934 when the family paid a $200,000 ransom. The Bremer case was particularly sensational because the Bremer family was friendly with President Franklin Roosevelt. It appeared that the gang was growing bolder, moving from bank robberies to kidnappings to kidnappings in broad daylight. The president put the pressure on law enforcement to apprehend the men responsible. This tension would ultimately lead to the group's demise.

The Federal Bureau of Investigation (FBI) hunted the gang tirelessly before they were successful. On January 8,

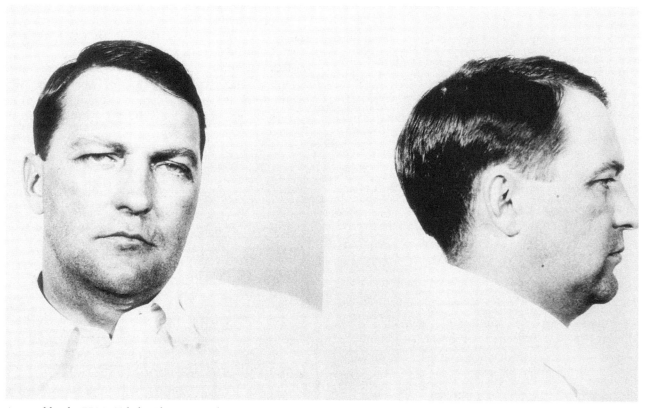

Arrested by the FBI in Toledo, Ohio, on April 30, 1936, Harry Campbell, a leading member of the Barker-Karpis gang, was brought to St. Paul. He is shown here on May 12, 1936. (AP Photo)

1935, Doc Barker was arrested leaving his apartment. He was charged with the two kidnappings and sentenced to a long prison term at Alcatraz. Doc was completely stoic throughout several lengthy interrogations (Kudisch 2014). He never revealed the location of other gang members or where he kept his weapons. In 1939, Doc attempted to escape from Alcatraz. He successfully made it out of the building but was shot and killed by correction officers on the premise.

A few days after Doc was apprehended, on January 16, 1935, Fred and Kate Barker were killed in an FBI shootout at their cottage in Florida. Interestingly there is controversy over the role of Kate Barker, the mother of Fred and Doc, in the gang's criminal actions. Shortly after the arrests were made, the media speculated that Kate was the true mastermind behind the group and that her sons executed her methodically planned crimes. Others suggested that she was extremely abusive and the abuse resulted in her criminal sons. In his book, Karpis does not mention Kate as a conspirator (Karpis 1971). It is unclear from the available evidence what her role, if any, was in the gang's crimes.

After Doc, Fred, and several other associates of the Barker–Karpis gang were in custody, the police and FBI focused their efforts on apprehending Karpis. On November 28, 1934, Alvin Karpis was declared the FBI's number one public enemy (Burrough 2009). His picture was plastered all over the country and every law enforcement agency both local and federal were looking to bring him down. Even with the full force of the FBI looking for him he still committed several risky crimes and was highly involved in the criminal underworld. The FBI came very close to catching Karpis in January 1935 in Atlantic City. The FBI had located an apartment that Karpis was renting under a fake name. They planned an entire sting operation but Karpis and an associate Harry Campbell shot their way out with machine guns and managed to escape to a car and drive away (Karpis 1971).

Later, while on the run, Karpis, new accomplice Fred Hunter, and three others successfully robbed a train carrying U.S. mail in Ohio. This event received a great deal of attention and heightened the pressure to capture Karpis. Karpis and his associate Fred Hunter were finally caught on May 1, 1936, while leaving a rental apartment in New Orleans (Kudisch 2014). Karpis was sentenced to imprisonment in Alcatraz Maximum Security Prison where he was housed until 1969 when he was paroled. Alvin Karpis died of natural causes in 1979 (Burrough 2009).

The arrest of Alvin Karpis, the last member of the Barker–Karpis gang, was a great victory for law enforcement and the FBI. The gang's crimes had made national headlines and the country was eager to see law enforcement succeed in bringing the men to justice. This was a particularly prominent victory for the FBI because J. Edgar Hoover began professionalizing the FBI in the early 1930s. His goal was to create an honest agency of competent investigators. The success of the agency in bringing down the Barker–Karpis gang, and Hoovers role in their demise, shifted public attention from the failures of law enforcement to its victories. Hoover was even deemed the nation's number one public hero. The apprehension of the Barker–Karpis gang members became a symbol of the legitimacy of the FBI and their ability to track, capture, and punish big-name criminals who evaded other law enforcement agencies for several years.

Nicole E. Frisch

See also: Barker, Kate "Ma" (1873–1935); Billy the Kid (1859–1881); Capone, Al (1899–1947); Dillinger, John (1903–1934); Kelly, George "Machine Gun" (1895–1954)

Further Reading

Alcatraz History. "Alvin Karpis." Ocean View Publishing Company. http://www.alcatrazhistory.com/karpis.htm. Accessed April 13, 2015.

Burrough, Bryan. 2009. *Public Enemies*. New York: Penguin.

Federal Bureau of Investigation. Barker/Karpis Gang. FBI Records: The Vault. http://vault.fbi.gov/barker-karpis-gang. Accessed April 14, 2015.

Karpis, Alvin, with Bill Trent. 1971. *The Alvin Karpis Story*. New York: Coward, McCann & Geoghegan.

Kudisch, Richard. "Alvin Karpis: Pursuit of the Last Public Enemy." TruTv Crime Library. http://web.archive.org/web/20140116210240/http://www.trutv.com/library/crime/gangsters_outlaws/outlaws/karpis/1.html. Accessed April 13, 2015.

Barrow, Clyde. *See* Parker, Bonnie (1910–1934) and Clyde Barrow (1909–1934)

Baseball and Steroids (1980–)

Playing professional baseball is a demanding physical task for one's body due to the lengthy season and demand to perform at such a high level for a prolonged amount of time. Historically, to meet these demands, some players have turned to performance-enhancing drugs (PEDs). It is thought that players turn to such substances to increase performance, prolong their careers, and land larger contracts. Other reasons for using PEDs include rehabbing from injury quicker and overcoming the demands of constant travel during the season that limits strength and conditioning routines.

The use of PEDs has evolved over time and has presented itself in professional baseball for decades. Major League Baseball (MLB) has adopted an antidrug policy, which it continues to refine in an attempt to eradicate the use of PEDs and other banned substances. However, from the late 1980s through the late 2000s, increased offensive production led MLB officials and fans to be skeptical. Further investigation resulted in the involvement of the federal justice system and U.S. Congress, resulting in indictments and convictions of players and others associated with MLB that had connections to the use and/or distribution of PEDs.

By past players' own admissions, the use of PEDs in professional baseball can be traced as far back as 1889. Early forms of PEDs consisted of testosterone extracted from animals and amphetamines used to improve memory, physical strength, speed, stamina, and endurance. The use of PEDs received little resistance from MLB officials, which resulted in the use of such drugs for much of the 1970s and 1980s. Although there is no defined timeframe for the "steroid era" in MLB, it typically refers to the period of time beginning in the late 1980s and lasting through the late 2000s. This period of time was categorized by the emergence of new types of PEDs such as anabolic steroids and human growth hormone (HGH).

Steroids and other PEDs were labeled as banned substances by MLB in 1991. MLB commissioner Francis "Fay" T. Vincent addressed the issue of PEDs by delivering a memorandum to all teams, in which he stated "The possession, sale or use of any illegal drug or controlled substances by Major League players and personnel is strictly prohibited" (Epstein 2009). Many players and front office officials found that even after the memorandum from the commissioner, there was very little, if any, enforcement of illegal drugs and performance-enhancing substances policies. In the mid-1990s, an offensive surge dominated MLB, which reached its pinnacle in 1998 with the homerun race between Mark McGwire and Sammy Sosa. The offensive performance of MLB players continued into the early 2000s with Barry Bonds breaking McGwire's homerun

record in 2001. Additionally, many MLB players experienced record-breaking offensive statistics during this time.

In 2001, MLB implemented a random drug testing program for all minor league players; however, major league players could not be tested without probable cause. Less than a year later, a Senate subcommittee urged MLB commissioner Bud Selig and director of the Players Association (PA), Don Fehr, to adopt a drug testing program for major league players. Although a number of PEDs had been banned by MLB since 1991, it was not until 2003 that testing of major league players was implemented. A joint agreement by MLB and the PA allowed for random testing in an effort to gauge the use of PEDs in baseball. This initial testing program was anonymous and carried no punishments for players found to be in violation of the antidrug policy.

In 2002, the Bay Area Laboratory Co-operative (BALCO), owned by Victor Conte, was discovered by federal authorities to be producing steroids and other PEDs that could not be detected by current drug tests. MLB players Barry Bonds and Jason Giambi were among the high-profile athletes connected to the BALCO investigation. In total, 10 MLB players were called to testify before a grand jury hearing testimony in the BALCO case. It was reported by media outlets that Giambi admitted to using a variety of steroids, whereas Bonds stated he was given substances by his trainer Greg Anderson, but never believed them to be steroids. Conte and Anderson arranged a plea bargain and received four and three months in jail, respectively, for distributing steroids and money laundering. Bonds was later indicted and charged with perjury and obstruction of justice for his 2003 grand jury testimony. Barry Bonds was found guilty of obstruction of justice and was sentenced to house arrest for 30 days along with two years' probation and 250 hours of community service.

Prior to the 2005 MLB season, the House Committee on Government Oversight and Reform began hearings on steroid use in baseball. The committee stated that "Major League Baseball has failed in its responsibility to stop the use of performance enhancing drugs and was encouraging their use among young athletes" (Newman 2005). Several high-profile players including Mark McGwire, Sammy Sosa, and Jose Canseco were called to testify before the committee. Later that year, MLB and the PA strengthened the drug testing policy by imposing harsher penalties for players found to be in violation and making the names of those players testing positive public. The new penalties included a 50-game suspension for first-time violators, a

100-game suspension for second-time violators, and lifetime banishment from MLB for third-time violators.

In 2006, Selig requested that George Mitchell, a former U.S. senator, investigate the use of PEDs in MLB. Upon completion of his investigation, a 409-page report was released that listed 89 current or former MLB players that Mitchell claimed had used steroids or other illegal substances. Brian McNamee, Roger Clemens's trainer, and Kirk Radomski, a former bat boy for the New York Mets, were among the individuals who provided substantial evidence to Mitchell during his investigation. In 2008, Clemens and McNamee were called before Congress to testify on Clemens's alleged steroid use detailed in the "Mitchell Report." Clemens denied ever using steroids or any other PEDs, while McNamee provided evidence and testimony to indicate otherwise. A grand jury later indicted Clemens for obstruction of Congress, making false statements, and perjury, for which Clemens was found not guilty.

The scandal surrounding baseball and steroids continued in 2009 when *Sports Illustrated* reported that star player Alex Rodriguez had tested positive for steroids and other PEDs in 2003. Rodriguez admitted to using banned substances from 2001 to 2003, but denied using them at any other time in his career. Other high-profile players such as Miguel Tejada (convicted of making false statements to congressional investigators) and Manny Ramirez (received a 50-game suspension) were also associated with the use of PEDs. Rodriguez's name was again connected to steroids in 2013 when reports of his association with Biogenesis of America, an antiaging clinic that had been discovered for selling PEDs and growth hormones, surfaced. In total, 13 players were suspended in connection with the Biogenesis, including notable players Rodriguez (211 games), Ryan Braun (65 games), and Nelson Cruz (50 games). In 2013, MLB and the PA again strengthened the drug testing program by adding in season testing for HGH.

JOSEPH M. McKENNA

See also: Armstrong, Lance (1971–); Black Sox Scandal (1919)

Further Reading

Canseco, Jose. 2005. *Juiced: Wild Times, Rampant 'Roids, Smash Hits & How Baseball Got Big.* New York: Harper Collins Publishers.

Canseco, Jose. 2008. *Vindicated: Big Names, Big Liars, and the Battle to Save Baseball.* New York: High Traffic Media, LLC.

Epstein, David. 2009. "The Rules, the Law, the Reality: A Primer on Baseball's Steroid Policy through the Years." *Sports Illustrated.* February 16. http://si.com/vault/article/magazine/MAG1151761/index.htm. Accessed January 6, 2015.

Fainaru-Wada, Mark, and Lance Williams. 2006. *Game of Shadows: Barry Bonds, BALCO, and the Steroids Scandal that Rocked Professional Sports.* New York: Gotham Books.

Newman, Maria. 2005. "Congress Opens Hearings on Steroid Use in Baseball." *The New York Times,* March 18. http://www.nytimes.com/learning/teachers/featured_articles/20050318friday.html. Accessed January 6, 2015.

Baseline Killer/Baseline Rapist. *See* Goudeau, Mark (1964–)

Bath (MI) School Massacre (1927)

The Bath school massacre is the deadliest school killing in U.S. history and occurred in 1927 within the town of Bath, Michigan. On May 18, 1927, a farmer by the name of Andrew Kehoe (1872–1927) murdered his wife, destroyed his entire farm, and detonated multiple bombs under a school, killing a total of 45 individuals and injuring 58 others. Among the deadliest school attacks within the United States, the number of lives lost during the Bath school massacre was 32 more than the lives lost in the 1999 Columbine High School shootings in Columbine, Colorado, 13 more than the lives lost in the 2007 VA Tech Massacre in Blacksburg, Virginia, and 19 more than the lives lost in the 2012 Sandy Hook Elementary School shootings in Newtown, Connecticut. While the initial impact of the Bath school massacre was overshadowed by headlines regarding Charles Lindbergh's transatlantic flight (Johnston 1999), it continues to be the deadliest school killing and one of the most devastating acts of domestic terrorism within the United States (Parker 1992).

Kehoe was born seven years after the Civil War. When Kehoe was young his mother passed away and his father remarried a younger woman, whom also later died after accidently setting herself on fire from the oil stove. Kehoe had tried to save his stepmother by throwing a bucket of water on her, but unfortunately since the fire was oil based, it spread the flames rather than subdued them, which ultimately resulted in her death. After studying electrical engineering at Michigan State College and years of working as an electrician, he married his wife Ellen "Nellie" Price in 1912 at the age of 40.

When he was 55 years old, Kehoe implemented a series of bombings on May 18, 1927, which targeted his farm and Bath Consolidated School. Experts believe that Kehoe was an adamant tax protester, who blamed rising property taxes, specifically in regards to the district's plan to build a new school, for his personal financial problems (Bernstein 2009; Ellsworth 1927). Kehoe was the treasurer of Bath Consolidated School board for several years until losing a reelection in 1926. Shortly after the reelection, Kehoe was notified that foreclosure proceedings would occur against his farm property and all of his assets, including the farm equipment and farm animals. Upon receiving news of his failed reelection, foreclosure, and his ailing wife who was diagnosed with terminal tuberculosis, Kehoe spent the next 12 months preparing to destroy his farm and detonate bombs under the Bath Consolidated School located in Bath, Michigan.

From approximately June 1926 to May 1927, Kehoe spent his days planning for the destructive revenge of the Bath Consolidated School community (Ellsworth 1927). Over the course of the year, Kehoe stopped maintenance on his farm and focused his time and effort on destroying his own farm property. Kehoe had consciously cut all of his wire fences around the farm, destroyed the bark on young trees to kill them, and cut his grapevine plants before placing them back on their stumps to hide the damage he had inflicted. Significant time was also spent at his part-time electrician job at Bath Consolidated School, where he constructed and wired an elaborate system of detonation devices underneath the school buildings.

On the morning of May 18, 1927, Kehoe detonated his explosive networks to destroy his house and farm property so that there was nothing left for the tax collectors, followed by the destruction of the Bath Consolidated School. Detonation of both Kehoe's property and the school occurred almost simultaneously at approximately 8:45 a.m. Kehoe's wife Nellie had also been killed on their farm property sometime between the evening of May 16, 1927, and the morning of May 18, 1927, prior to the complete destruction of the property (State of Michigan 1927, 349). After setting fire to his own property and rigging his own truck with explosive devices, Kehoe proceeded to drive to Bath Consolidated School and demanded that the school superintendent come forward, who was already assisting with the recovery efforts of the initial bombings at the school. As the superintendent came forward, Kehoe detonated the explosives within his truck, instantly killing himself, the superintendent, and several others.

During the recovery efforts after the school explosions, rescuers determined that there was an additional 504 pounds of pyrotol and dynamite located under the south wing of the school building (State of Michigan 1927, 338, 349). Only the north wing of the school building had been destroyed from the detonation of explosive devices. State police, investigators, and the coroner concluded that the pyrotol and dynamite found underneath the south wing of the school failed to detonate because the batteries used were too weak to set off the explosive material. On May 19, 1927, state police investigated the fires at the Kehoe farm and that is when they discovered the charred body of Kehoe's wife. A wooden sign was also found wired to Kehoe's farm fence, which provided Kehoe's last message to his community, "Criminals are made, not born" (State of Michigan 1927, 106, 345). A "Coroner's Inquest" followed Kehoe's actions, where six community leaders were assigned as a jury to investigate the death of the school's superintendent. After more than 50 individuals testified on behalf of Kehoe's actions, the janitor and the school board employees were exonerated of charges for failing to prevent the massacre by recognizing Kehoe's prior suspicious behavior (Bernstein 2009; Ellsworth 1927; State of Michigan 1927).

Shortly after the Bath school massacre, Michigan's governor Fred Green announced the creation of the Bath Relief Fund where citizens could donate money to assist the Bath community, and Senator James Couzens provided money to build a new school. Not only did government officials offer aid to the Bath community, but so did the children within the state of Michigan by donating their pennies to pay for a statue of a young girl holding a cat. Today the statute holds a plaque that reads, "This bronze statue was sculpted by University of Michigan Professor Carlton W. Angell in memory of the victims of the Bath School Disaster of May 18, 1927. School children throughout Michigan contributed pennies to fund this lasting memorial" (Heath et al. 2007, 212).

ALLISON MCDOWELL-SMITH

See also: Columbine High School Shootings (Littleton, CO) (April 20, 1999); Lanza, Adam Peter (1992–2012); Virginia Tech Massacre (April 16, 2007); *Primary Documents*/Bath School Massacre: Inquest Testimony (1927)

Further Reading

Bauerle, Ronald. 2000–2007. "The Bath School Disaster". http://freepages.history.rootsweb.ancestry.com/~bauerle/disaster.htm. Accessed April 13, 2015.

Bernstein, Arnie. 2009. *Bath Massacre: America's First School Bombing*. Ann Arbor, MI: University of Michigan Press.

Ellsworth, M. J. 1927. *The Bath School Disaster*. Personal Memoirs. Bath, Michigan.

Heath, Melissa, Katherine Ryan, Brenda Dean, and Rebecca Bingham. 2007. "History of School Safety and Psychological First Aid for Children." *Brief Treatment and Crisis Intervention* 7(3): 206–223.

Johnston, Robert. 1999. "Events Stir Memories of Dark Day at Mich. School." *Education Week* 18(34): 16.

Parker, Grant. 1992. *Mayday: History of a Village Holocaust.* New York: Liberty Press.

"School Dynamiter First Slew Wife." 1927. *New York Times.* http://freepages.history.rootsweb.ancestry.com/~bauerle/nyt520.txt. Accessed April 13, 2015.

State of Michigan. 1927. "Transcript of the May 23–25, 1927 Clinton County, Michigan Coroner's Inquest." Edited by James L. Daggy. http://daggy.name/tbsd/cinquest.htm#DfnPyrotol. Accessed April 13, 2015.

BBC Consolidated of North America. *See* Hunt, Joe (1959–)

Beck, Martha. *See* Lonely Hearts Killers (1947–1949)

Becker, Lieutenant Charles (1870–1915)

On July 15, 1912, "Bald" Jack Rose held a meeting at Bridgey Webber's poker club in New York City to explain that fellow gambler, Herman Rosenthal, was losing control and needed to be put back into line. The plan was to scare Rosenthal who had just provided District Attorney Charles Whitman a signed testimony claiming a police lieutenant became his partner, later betrayed him and set up a false raid of his club. Shortly after seeing his third story published in the early morning edition on July 16, Rosenthal was called outside the Hotel Metropole on the north side of 43rd Street. Once on the sidewalk, Rosenthal was shot twice in the chest and twice in the head. What had been initially planned as a beating had quickly turned into murder. Within days, Whitman and the press named the prime suspect as the named police lieutenant involved in gambling graft—Charles Becker. Consequently, Becker

would be the first policeman in history to receive the death penalty for murder.

Charles Becker was born, July 26, 1870, as the youngest of 10 children on a farm outside Callicoon Center in Sullivan County, New York. He arrived in New York City at the age of 20, just two years after his brother, John, left to join the New York City Police Department (NYPD). Becker worked briefly as a clerk at a furniture store, a baker's assistant, and a bouncer. Combined with his brother's influence, Becker raised the $300 "fee" to pay the Police Commission and secured a spot with the NYPD in November 1893. By February 1894, he was officially in uniform.

Becker was of German descent, Republican, stood at 6'2", and was 200 pounds of muscle. While different from the predominantly short and stocky Irish American Democratic police force, Becker quickly learned the ways of the force. His early posts were considered prestigious and atypical for new officers. His first assignment was in the

Charles Becker (1870–1915) with his wife in 1914. A lieutenant in the New York City Police Department, Becker was convicted of the murder of gambler Herman Rosenthal. Becker was executed at Sing Sing prison in July 1915. (Library of Congress)

Second Precinct in which he served with the "Dock Rats," a special squad assigned to the harbor wharfs. In spring 1895, he was transferred to the Tenderloin (a.k.a. Satan's Circus), which was considered the most lucrative beat due to the high concentration of gambling halls, drinking dens, and brothels. Within weeks he had earned the plainclothes detail and quickly learned to control the locals with his nightstick and keep a steady stream of arrests. It was also here that Becker would become involved in graft, taking cash from prostitutes and vice operators.

In 1906, Deputy Police Commissioner Rhinelander Waldo chose Becker to investigate Inspector Max Schmittberger, who oversaw the Tenderloin. During this time, Becker helped conduct a series of raids that exposed vice and corruption. He was rewarded with a promotion to sergeant in 1907. In 1911, he was promoted to lieutenant and named to head a special squad whose focus was on gangs and later gambling. During one of his raids, he met Jacob Rosenzweig (a.k.a. Jack Rose). Rose offered to be an informant in exchange for protection and Becker agreed.

A similar partnership was formed between Becker and Herman Rosenthal, with Rose acting as Becker's graft collector. Through the anonymous snitching of Bridgey Webber, pressure was put on Becker to investigate Rosenthal's club. Although Becker warned Rosenthal of the raid on April 17, 1912, Rosenthal was resentful and financially strapped, so he decided to turn to the media. *New York World* reporter Herbert Swope published two affidavits written by Rosenthal on July 13 and 14, with the second naming Becker as his partner. Becker announced that afternoon he would sue for libel and District Attorney Whitman was not yet impressed. Fearing for his life, Rosenthal promised to obtain witnesses to corroborate his story and Whitman agreed to meet with him Monday morning, July 15, 1912. However, Rosenthal would be murdered just five hours later.

The initial targets of the murder investigation included Rose, Harry Vallon, and Sam Schepps. Also questioned was Webber. On July 18, Rose went to police headquarters for questioning but stated he did not believe Becker was involved in the shooting. During this time, Becker was removed from heading the strong-arm squad and later moved to desk duty as he was being investigated for false raids. Vallon turned himself into the police on July 23 and initially confirmed with Rose and Webber that Becker had nothing to do with the murder. William Shapiro, a driver, stated he saw Rose, Schepps, Vallon, and another man he couldn't make out meeting after the murder. Shapiro's

testimony brought fright upon the three men in custody, and when they were called in to Whitman's personal headquarters, they were ready to make the deal that would seal Becker's fate.

On August 6, Rose would testify that Becker ordered him to have Rosenthal killed for causing trouble for the police. Rose stated that he hired the four gunmen—Lefty Louis, Whitey Lewis, Dago Frank, and Gyp the Blood—to assemble at Webber's before heading to the Metropole. Both Webber and Vallon backed up Rose during the grand jury. For the testimony to be believable, Whitman needed a corroborator who was not an accomplice. Schepp served this purpose and was also granted immunity along with the other three.

On October 7, jury selection began for Becker's first trial. Along with the false testimony provided, Judge John Goff was blatantly in favor of the prosecution and often interjected to diminish the defense. Becker's key witness, Big Jack Zelig, was also gunned down three days before trial started. Therefore, on October 24, a jury found Becker guilty of murder in the first degree and on October 30, Judge Goff sentenced him to death on December 9, 1912. The four gunmen were also tried, convicted, and finally executed in April 1914, while Rose, Vallon, and Webber were released.

In 1914, the Court of Appeals granted Becker a new trial based on the unbelievable testimony provided and the prejudice of Judge Goff. His second trial began on May 6, 1914. Whitman's key witness in this trial was James Marshall, who claimed to have seen Becker meet with Rose in Harlem and thus confirming Vallon's initial testimony. Marshall would later confess that he was paid by Whitman to provide this false testimony. This time the jury only took an hour and a half to deliberate—Becker was found guilty again. After further unsuccessful appeals, Becker's wife, Helen, tried to get Whitman, who was now the governor, to pardon him. However, Whitman was not willing to pardon a man he fought veraciously to convict.

On July 30, 1915, at 5:42 a.m., Becker was placed into the electric chair at Sing Sing. He was the largest prisoner ever put to death and he had to be shocked three times over the course of nine minutes before he was pronounced dead. It would later be described as "the clumsiest execution in the history of Sing Sing" (Dash, 2007).

SHELLEY S. HYLAND

See also: Knapp Commission, New York City Police Corruption Investigation (1971); McDuffie, Arthur, Death of (1979); Serpico, Frank (1936–)

Further Reading

Dash, Mike. 2007. *Satan's Circus: Murder, Vice, Police Corruption, and New York's Trial of the Century*. New York: Crown Publishers.

Delmar, Vina. 1968. *The Becker Scandal: A Time Remembered*. New York: Harcourt, Brace & World, Inc.

Keefe, Rose. 2008. *The Starker*. Nashville, TN: Cumberland House Publishing, Inc.

Klein, Henry. 1927. *Sacrificed: The Story of Police Lieutenant Charles Becker*. New York: Isaac Goldman Company.

Logan, Andy. 1970. *Against the Evidence: The Becker–Rosenthal Affair*. New York: McCall Publishing Company.

Becker–Rosenthal Murder Trials (1912)

During the early part of the 20th century, New York was a city teeming with gambling and corruption. Nothing exemplifies this more than the Becker–Rosenthal trials. Charles Becker was a corrupt police officer who, in 1912, organized the homicide of known gambler Herman Rosenthal, who had been his partner in an illegal gambling operation. Becker was the first American policeman and only New York police officer (to date) to be sentenced to death for murder. This was the first time the use of a getaway car was recorded. The trial also encouraged New York and other cities to crack down on corruption. Becker was put to death in the electric chair at Sing Sing in 1915. The publicity of the trial highlighted the corruption rampant in New York at the time and encouraged large cities to crack down on crime.

Charles Becker, born in 1870, was the son of German immigrants. Becker became a police officer with the New York City Police Department in 1893. This was a time of heavy corruption in New York. Charles Becker became actively involved in the New York City crime world despite his position with the police department. Problems began for Becker in 1896 when he had his first major disciplinary hearing. Becker had made headlines for supposedly killing a burglar attempting to make a getaway. He was celebrated as a hero for two days until the victim was identified by his family as an innocent bystander. Becker was suspended for one month after a disciplinary trial. Becker made headlines again when he arrested Dora Clark for prostitution. He claimed to have caught her in the act, when in actuality, Clark was spending the evening with author Stephen Crane, who was not paying for her company. Despite these disciplinary problems, in 1911 Becker was promoted to lieutenant and aide to New York Police commissioner Rhinelander Waldo by the newly elected mayor, William Gaynor. Becker was also put in charge of a special squad in charge of cracking down on crime. Becker quickly turned his squad into his personal strong arm squad. While the squad did do some good, most of the work they did was for Becker's clandestine activities. Becker used his squad to shut down some of the less profitable gambling establishments while collecting payoffs from the more profitable ones.

Charles Becker met gambler Herman Rosenthal on New Year's eve 1911. Herman "Beansie" Rosenthal was friends with Big Tim Sullivan, who was running gambling in the Tenderloin area, the name for the red light district. In February 1912, Sullivan gave Rosenthal permission to open a gambling establishment in the Tenderloin area, near Times Square. Rosenthal borrowed $1,500 from Becker and agreed to give Becker 20 percent of the profits. In March, Rosenthal opened The Hesper Club. A short time later, tension arose between the two. Since Becker was receiving 20 percent of profits, Rosenthal felt he was exempt from police payoffs. Becker ordered his squad to raid and shut down Rosenthal's operation. In retaliation, Rosenthal went to District Attorney Charles S. Whitman, as well as reporter Herbert Swope from the newspaper *New York World*, and shared all the information he knew of Becker's criminal operations. Whitman summoned a grand jury to bring criminal charges against Lieutenant Becker for his criminal operations. Enraged, Becker ordered his men to kill Rosenthal. A group of Becker's deputies, led by a man named Jacob Rosenzweig, commonly known as Bald Jack Rose, approached Rosenthal outside Cafe Metropole and shot him to death on July 21, 1912. Rosenthal was 38 years old. District attorney Whitman was able to trace the getaway car back to Rose. At first, Rose refused to talk, until he realized Becker would not come to his rescue. Rose then told police everything about Becker's involvement with Rosenthal's murder and later testified against Becker at his trial.

On October 7, 1912, Charles Becker's first trial began with Judge John W. Goff presiding. Goff had a reputation for zero-tolerance for corruption and was known to be one of the toughest judges in New York City, giving District Attorney Whitman and assistant prosecutor Frank Moss an advantage. The prosecution called Jack Rose, Louis "Bridgey" Webber, Harry Vallon, and Sam Schepps, four of the men involved in execution of the murder to testify against

Becker. Becker's defense attorneys, John F. McIntyre, Lloyd B. Stryker, and George W. Whiteside, knew winning the trial would be near-impossible. Additionally, Judge Goff continually cut off McIntyre during cross-examinations and denied motions for more time. McIntyre began to lay the ground work for an appeal based on a New York law that a defendant could not be convicted solely on the testimony of accomplices. Becker was found guilty on October 30, 1912, for the murder of Herman Rosenthal.

As McIntyre predicted, the Court of Appeals overturned the conviction and ordered a new trial citing Goff for "gross misconduct" and stating Whitman's witnesses, the primary forces behind the conviction, were "dangerous and degenerate." On May 2, 1914, Becker's second trial began. This trial was presided by Judge Samuel Seabury with prosecutor Charles S. Whitman and defense attorneys W. Bourke Cockran, John Johnstone, and Martin Manton. In this trial, Whitman focused less on Becker's accomplices and more on James Marshall, a young black man who had been on Becker's pay role as an informant and was present when Becker gave the order to kill Rosenthal. Since Marshall did not take part in the murder, Whitman believed the Court of Appeals would be less likely to overturn the conviction a second time. Defense Attorney Manton tried to convince the jury that Marshall could not be trusted due to the color of his skin and his history as a police informant "who betrays others for pay."

Trial as a Stepping Stone

While Becker was busy appealing his conviction, prosecutor Charles S. Whitman capitalized on his victory by running for governor and winning the election on November 3, 1914, becoming New York's 41st governor. His primary focus was reformation of state finances which he did by reorganizing state departments and thoroughly investigating the salaries of civil service workers. In 1916, Whitman was also elected chairman of the Republican National Convention. He served two terms as governor of New York before being defeated by Democrat Alfred E. Smith of Tammany Hall in the 1918 election.

On May 22, 1914, Charles Becker was once again found guilty of murder after only one hour and 50 minutes of deliberation. Judge Seabury sentenced former lieutenant Becker to death by the electric chair. From prison, Becker

accused Marshall of perjury. His claims were substantiated in 1915 when Marshall was arrested for spouse abuse in Philadelphia. Two reporters witnessed Marshall's wife at the police station stating her husband was guilty of telling lies about a policeman in New York. At first Marshall agreed with his wife's claim then retracted his original retraction, standing by what he had testified in the court room. Manton, Becker's defense attorney from the second trial, filed a 540-page brief with the court of appeals, but Becker's conviction was upheld.

The appeals process delayed his execution for a year but the conviction was ultimately upheld. On July 21, 1915, Charles Becker released a lengthy apology not only for his dealings with Jack Rose and involvement in Herman Rosenthal's murder, but for all of his criminal activities. Despite this apology, on July 30, 1915, Charles Becker was the first American policeman to be sentenced to death for murder. He was put to death in the electric chair at Sing Sing. The publicity of the Becker trial highlighted urban corruption and the efforts of people such as Charles Whitman to combat it.

COURTNEY D'ALLURA

See also: King, Rodney, Beating of (1991); Knapp Commission, New York City Police Corruption Investigation (1971); Los Angeles Riots (1992); Serpico, Frank (1936–)

Further Reading

Christiansen, Stephen G. 1994. *Great American Trials: From Salem Witchcraft to Rodney King.* Edited by Edward W. Knappman. Detroit: Visible Ink.
Cohen, Stanley. 2006. The *Execution of Officer Becker: The Murder of a Gambler, The Trial of a Cop, and the Birth of Organized Crime.* New York: Carroll & Graf Publishers.
Logan, Andy. 1970. *Against the Evidence: The Becker–Rosenthal Trial.* New York: The McCall Publishing Company.

Beecher, Henry Ward, Adultery Trial of (1875)

In media sensationalism, the adultery trial of Reverend Henry Ward Beecher between January and July 1875 resembles the 20th-century Sam Sheppard or O. J. Simpson trials without the murders and equals the most dramatic of 21st-century soap operas. In historical and legal interpretations the Beecher trial reflects the profound changes that America and American culture experienced after the Civil War. Although the jury empaneled in Brooklyn could not agree—three voted Reverend Beecher guilty and nine considered him not guilty—the trial featured religious and women's suffrage conflicts, moral issues including adultery, rape, betrayal, and legal issues like perjury.

One of the best-known ministers in the United States, the Reverend Beecher represented a schism between the conservative and liberal components of his Congregationalist church, preaching a gospel of a loving, benevolent God instead of emphasizing the stern Calvinist God of his father, the Reverend Lyman Beecher, and generations of New England Puritans. The Reverend Beecher's unorthodox preaching had become so popular that his sermons regularly filled the 3,000-seat Plymouth Church and the ferries from Manhattan to Brooklyn were called "Beecher Boats."

The Reverend Beecher stood unique in areas other than his biblical interpretation. He passionately embraced antislavery, staging mock slave actions during his services at Plymouth Church and raising funds to buy freedom for Southern slaves. During the civil war in Kansas, he led the campaign to ship rifles and supplies to antislavery settlers and opponents claimed that Sharpe's carbines were shipped in boxes labeled as Bibles. Sharpe's carbines were ever afterward known as "Beecher's Bibles." During the Civil War, Reverend Beecher toured Britain, eloquently speaking for the Union cause and decreasing British support for the South. He also developed a lucrative side career writing for newspapers and lecturing.

After a five-year engagement, the Reverend Beecher married Eunice Bullard in 1837, but rumor had it that their marriage was unhappy because of his long absences from home, the deaths of four of their eight children, and his wife's alleged nagging.

Rumors of affairs with other women circulated around the Beecher marriage as early as their newly wed days in his pastorate in Indiana and they did not cease when they moved to Plymouth Church in Brooklyn. In 1858, *The Brooklyn Eagle* published a story charging that he had been involved with another church member. The wife of his editor Henry Bowen confessed on her deathbed to an affair with Reverend Beecher, and several members of his inner circle reported an affair with Edna Dean Proctor, an author who collaborated with him on a book of his sermons.

In 1872, women's rights advocate Victoria Woodhull first drew public notice to Reverend Henry Ward Beecher's close relationship with the Tiltons when she published an article accusing him of adultery. Theodore Tilton told Elizabeth Cady Stanton about his wife's confession, and she in turn told the story to Victoria Woodhull and Isabella Beecher Hooker, Reverend Beecher's sister. On November 2, 1872, Victoria Woodhull published a story called "The Beecher-Tilton Scandal Case," in her paper *Woodhull and Claflin's Weekly*, containing detailed descriptions of the affair.

Beginning in 1870, Elizabeth Tilton confirmed and afterward several times denied an affair with the Reverend Henry Ward Beecher. The press began to publish stories about the affair, including letters from Theodore Tilton.

Reverend Henry Ward Beecher's close and longtime friend Theodore Tilton finally brought suit against him for "criminal conversation"—adultery—with his wife Elizabeth and the trial, which began in Brooklyn's Courthouse on January 11, 1875, lasted for 112 days. Evidence for and against the Reverend Beecher flooded the courtroom. While Reverend Beecher and Theodore Tilton presented lengthy testimony, the court permitted Elizabeth to give only one statement, which the judge read aloud.

Paradoxically, as the chief accuser, Elizabeth had originated the charges and presented and recanted her testimony several times, but she was confined to a statement that someone else read and conflicting statements after the trial. Elizabeth Tilton proved to be an unreliable witness, presenting contradictory accounts of the story before, during, and after the trial and changing her version of Reverend Beecher's guilt or innocence. Third-party witnesses including Theodore Tilton's mother-in-law, Elizabeth Cady Stanton, and Susan B. Anthony testified as well as Victoria Woodhull and Henry C. Bowen who claimed that Beecher had also had an affair with his wife.

After six months of testimony from over one hundred witnesses, the evidence was not conclusive, the testimonies presented were contradictory, and the jury could not reach a verdict. It was impossible to pinpoint whether or not Elizabeth Tilton and the Reverend Henry Ward Beecher had conducted a physical or emotional affair or both.

The court had exonerated the Reverend Beecher, but his credibility diminished in some areas in the court of public opinion. The Reverend Beecher remained as minister at Plymouth Church and continued his public life with lectures and speaking engagements. Elizabeth and Theodore Tilton were divorced and both of them as well as others were excommunicated from Plymouth Church. The scandal made it impossible for Theodore Tilton to earn a living in the United States, so he eventually moved to Paris.

KATHY WARNES

See also: Bakker, Jim (1940–); Harpers Ferry (VA), Raid on (October 17, 1859)

Further Reading

Applegate, Debby. 2007. *The Most Famous Man in America: The Biography of Henry Ward Beecher.* New York: Image.

"The Beecher Trial: A Review of the Evidence." 1875. *New York Times.* July 3. https://play.google.com/books/reader?id=7JX T8wt7wSIC&printsec=frontcover&output=reader&authus er=0&hl=en&pg=GBS.PA2. Accessed April 20, 2015.

Fox, Richard Wightman. 1999. *Trials of Intimacy: Love and Loss in the Beecher-Tilton Scandal.* Chicago: University of Chicago Press.

Frisken, Amanda. 2004. *Victoria Woodhull's Sexual Revolution: Political Theater and the Popular Press in Nineteenth-Century.* Philadelphia, PA: University of Pennsylvania Press.

Gedge, Karin E. 2003. *Without Benefit of Clergy: Women and the Pastoral Relationship in Nineteenth-Century American Culture.* Religion in America Series. New York: Oxford University Press.

Goldsmith, Barbara. 1999. *Other Powers: the Age of Suffrage, Spiritualism, and the Scandalous Victoria Woodhull.* New York: Harper Perennial.

Korobkin, Laura Hanft. 1995. "The Maintenance of Mutual Confidence: Sentimental Strategies at the Adultery Trial of Henry Ward Beecher." *Yale Journal of Law & the Humanities* 7 (1). http://digitalcommons.law.yale.edu/yjlh/vol7/iss1/2. Accessed April 20, 2015.

Sherwin, Richard K. 2000. *When Law Goes Pop: The Vanishing Line between Law and Popular Culture.* Chicago: University of Chicago Press.

Waller, Altina L. 1982. *Reverend Beecher and Mrs. Tilton: Sex and Class in Victorian America.* Amherst, MA: University of Massachusetts Press.

Berkman, Alexander. *See* Goldman, Emma, and Alexander Berkman, Trial of (1917)

Berkowitz, David Richard (1953–)

David Richard Berkowitz, known as Son of Sam, was one of the most notorious serial killers in U.S. history. During 1976 and 1977 he terrorized New York by killing six people and wounding seven. His crimes were often targeted at young women with long, dark hair. The crimes sparked outrage, panic, and fear in the city. He was caught after an investigation of a parking ticket written near the scene of one of his murder victims. He was arrested outside of his apartment and commented that he was planning

on killing again that evening. He claimed that his neighbor's dog was possessed and was telling him to kill. Berkowitz pled guilty and was sentenced to 365 years in prison. Several books and movies have been made based on the case, and there was speculation that Berkowitz would have been paid handsomely for the rights to his story. This sparked New York (and other states) to pass laws that prevented criminals from profiting from their crimes.

Berkowitz was born on June 1, 1953, and grew up in the Bronx. He was adopted as a child, and his mother later died in 1967 when he was a teenager. Berkowitz had a very difficult time with getting over this, was not very successful with women, and was known as a loner. After graduating from high school, Berkowitz served in the army for three years. After leaving military service, he moved back to New York and started a job at the postal service.

His attacks occurred over a 13-month period in 1976 and 1977 in New York City that resulted in the deaths of six people and injuries to seven other people. On July 29, 1976, Donna Lauria, 19, and Jody Valenti, 19, were sitting

David Berkowitz, the serial killer known as "Son of Sam," at a New York police station. (AP Photo)

in Valenti's car when they were approached and shot by Berkowitz. Lauria was killed at the scene and Valenti was injured. On October 23, he killed a young couple that was in a parked car in Queens. The next month, on November 27, he shot two teenage girls in Queens. It was on January 30, 1977, that he shot another couple. In March that year, he shot a college student who was walking home from the subway in Queens. On April 17, 1977, he shot a couple in the Bronx. On June 26, 1977, he shot a couple sitting in a car and the following month shot another couple, killing the woman and wounding the man.

Berkowitz primarily targeted women with long, dark hair, which caused some women to bleach their hair. Berkowitz was originally referred to in tabloids as being the ".44 caliber killer." This nickname was changed when Berkowitz left a note behind after the April 17, 1977, shooting and referred to himself as the "Son of Sam." He began to leave letters behind at crime scenes, some of which were addressed to a reporter. These letters increased the hysteria and panic that was occurring throughout the city. The city began to live in fear and it sparked what New York City has referred to as the largest manhunt in the city's history. The search for the killer was called Operation Omega and included hundreds of officers and detectives.

Berkowitz was caught when a woman had observed officers ticketing a car that was parked too close to a hydrant and was located near the scene of his last murder. Police traced the car back to his address on August 10, 1977. Officers arrived at Berkowitz's apartment and saw in his car a clearly visible semiautomatic rifle on the seat, and a note written in a similar nature to those written by the Son of Sam. Berkowitz was arrested as he exited his apartment and when arrested he asked why it took so long to catch him and he told officers that he had plans to attack again that night. Upon arrest, Berkowitz had a journal with him that detailed more than 300 fires that he had set.

After he was arrested and interviewed, Berkowitz claimed that his neighbor who was named Sam Carr had a Labrador retriever that was possessed. He had written letters to his neighbor and his wife about the dog and its barking and had weeks previously shot the dog, but it had survived. He claimed that this retriever was possessed by a demon that lived 6,000 years ago and had commanded him to kill. Berkowitz claimed that his nickname was tied to this dog. Berkowitz would later tell a Federal Bureau of Investigation (FBI) veteran when interviewed that he had made up the demon dog story to try to convince authorities when caught that he was insane. He claimed that he

really did the killings because of the resentment he felt toward his mother as well as his inability to establish relationships with women. Berkowitz has also claimed that he did not commit all the killings and rather that he was a member of a cult and was too afraid to speak out about who had committed some of the murders.

Psychologists found Berkowitz fit to stand trial but that would not be necessary since Berkowitz decided to plead guilty. He was sentenced to 365 years in prison. Berkowitz is now serving time in a prison in New York, has converted to Christianity, and spends his time as a jailhouse pastor. He has been up for parole several times and has refused to go to the hearings and told authorities that he does not deserve to be released.

David Abrahamsen authored a book *Confessions of Sam*, which was published in 1985, based on 50 hours of interviews with Berkowtiz, his friends, family members, and others. There have also been several other books published about the case (see Further Reading). Spike Lee produced a movie about the killings in 1999 called *Summer of Sam* and another blockbuster movie was released in 2001 called *Summer of Terror: The Real Son of Sam Story*.

The publicity caused by this case prompted courts and authorities to question the notion of criminals profiting from their notoriety. After speculation of several offers from publishers for Berkowitz to tell his story, New York enacted a law to prevent criminals from profiting from their notoriety. The law made the state able to seize money that criminals made from books, movies, and paid interviews. The law was challenged in court and ruled unconstitutional by the Supreme Court. In 2001, New York adopted a new and similar law referred to as the "Son of Sam" law, which requires that victims be notified if a convicted criminal is to receive $10,000 or more from anything. This law also extends the time that victims can sue the criminal in civil court.

Sarah Fitzgerald

See also: Dahmer, Jeffrey (1960–1994); Manson, Charles (1934–); Rader, Dennis (1945–); Zodiac Killer (1960s–); *Primary Documents*/Son of Sam Case: U.S. Supreme Court Decision in *Simon & Schuster v. Members of the New York State Crime Victims Board* (1991)

Further Reading

Abrahamsen, David. 1985. *Confessions of Son of Sam*. New York: Columbia University Press.

Carpozi, George. 1977. *Son of Sam: The .44-Caliber Killer*. n.p.: Manor Books.

"The Prodigal 'Son' Returns: An Assessment of Current 'Son of Sam' Laws and the Reality of the Online Murderabilia

Marketplace." 2004–2005. *Rutgers Computer & Technical Law Journal* 31: 430.

Terry, Maury. 1999. *The Ultimate Evil: The Truth about the Cult Murders: Son of Sam and Beyond*. New York: Barnes & Noble Incorporated.

Bianchi, Kenneth (1951–) and Angelo Buono (1934–2002)

The case of the Hillside Strangler was unique for two reasons. First, the public was led to believe that the perpetrators were police officers. The Hillside Stranger would pretend to be a police officer and Los Angeles police was worried that an officer was behind the rapes and murders of these women. Second, this case exposed an unexpected partnership: two cousins were responsible for the crimes rather than a single man. The murder victims varied in type; therefore, women were afraid to leave their house or drive alone at night. At least 13 women lost their lives during the killing spree of the Hillside Stranglers.

On October 13, 1977, the nude body of Yolanda Washington (19), a prostitute working on Hollywood Boulevard in Los Angeles, was found on a hillside close to the Ventura freeway. A second victim, Judy Miller (15), was found in a flowerbed in Glendale, California, nude with indication of ligature marks around her neck, ankles, and wrists. Sexual assault was confirmed. Miller was a drug user and runaway who occasionally engaged in prostitution. For a moment, police suspected a prostitute serial killer was on the loose. On November 6, 1977 a third body, identified as Lissa Katsin (20), was found in Glendale. Kastin was not a prostitute or drug user like the previous two victims. Similar to Washington and Miller, her body lay nude, found on a golf course.

An examination of Judy Miller's body changed the entire focus of the case. During her autopsy, it was revealed two men had sexually assaulted her as two different secretions were found. One male involved was identified as a nonsecretor, meaning the antigen characteristics pertaining to his blood group are not secreted into body fluids. At this point, police thought they were dealing with two killers, not one. Absence of clothing and other evidence indicated these three victims were killed elsewhere then dumped in specific sites. Two more bodies, Jill Barcomb (18) and Kathleen Robertson (17), were found on November 10 and November 17, respectively. Both women were part of the prostitute scene on Hollywood Boulevard, similar to Yolanda Washington.

The possible connection of knowing the killers was questioned when the bodies of Dolores Cepeda (12) and Sonja Johnson (14) were discovered on November 20, 1977, in Elysian Park. Within a few hours of discovering the two girls another body, that of student Kristina Wechler (20), was found in Hollywood Park. On November 23, the body of Jane King was found near an off-ramp on the Golden State freeway in Los Feliz. It appeared she had been raped and was suffocated. On November 29, 1977, Lauren Wagner (18), a college student, was found dead on the hills of Glendale. These last five victims were not only sexually assaulted, but tortured and mutilated as well. At this point, the assumption was the murders were linked. Most of the bodies were found nude; signs of being gagged, bound, and handcuffed were evident; these women were raped by two individuals, and their bodies were dumped off of roads or highways, usually at hillsides above Hollywood.

On December 16, the body of 17-year-old prostitute Kimberly Martin was found in Echo Park on a hillside. She worked as a call girl to avoid any run-ins with the Hillside Strangler as news of the murders began to surface through media outlets. Police investigated the apartment she was dispatched to on December 15, 1977, and found evidence of a break in, yet the apartment was vacant. The last known victim in California was Cindy Hudspeth (20), a student and waitress found on February 17, 1978. A report of a car halfway down the cliff off the Angeles Crest Highway led to the raped, sodomized, and naked body in the vehicle's trunk. Conversely as quick as these murders began to come to light, they ceased.

It was not until January 1979 where the case of the Hillside Stranglers began to surface again. Two university students in Bellingham, Washington, Karen Mandic (22) and Diane Wilder (22), were found strangled in the back of a car—their bodies indicated sexual assault had occurred. These murders became the break in the case police needed. Karen's boyfriend told police the women were hired by a man from a local security company to house-sit for two hours while he disconnected the alarm for repairs. Even though Karen was told by the man no one could know about the job, Karen told her boyfriend and included the man's name, Kenneth Bianchi.

Bianchi was called in for questioning, where he denied knowing the women. After gathering physical evidence from the Bellingham house and Bianchi's apartment, police had little doubt this man committed the crime. The police chief in Bellingham was a former Los Angeles police officer, and knew a great deal about the case as one of the victims was a friend's daughter. Moreover, something triggered his attention to the murders of these two women in which the similarities to the Hillside victims were striking. After questioning Kelli, Bianchi's girlfriend, the chief found she met Bianchi in Los Angeles 18 months ago and after having their child, she moved home to Bellingham where Bianchi followed in May 1978. This was three months after the Hillside Strangler murders stopped. The police chief called the Los Angeles police department and connections began to come together. The chief found Kelli and Bianchi lived at the building where victim Kimberly Martin was sent the night she was murdered. Kelli also stated they did not own a home phone and Bianchi would make calls from a pay phone in the Glendale library, the same phone used to contact Kimberly. In addition, Bianchi first lived on Garfield Avenue when Kelli met him, a location where two other Hillside victims were last seen before their murders. The evidence piled against Bianchi; thus he was charged with the Hillside Strangler murders and the Bellingham murders.

Bianchi confessed to the murders and implicated his cousin, Angelo Buono, as the second Hillside Strangler. Bianchi described how he and Buono used fake police badges to abduct women. After the abduction, women were taken to Buono's house in Glendale for torture, sexual assault, and murder. Bianchi made a deal with lawyers to escape the death penalty if he pled guilty to seven counts of murder and provided evidence that Buono was the second strangler. After a short time of having too little evidence, Buono was finally charged and found guilty of nine murders. Buono's trial began on November 16, 1981, and lasted for two years. He was sentenced to life imprisonment without the possibility of parole. Bianchi was sent back to Washington to serve 27 years before eligibility of parole.

STACIE MERKEN

See also: Boston Strangler Murders (1962–1964); Bundy, Ted (1946–1989); Rader, Dennis (1945–); Ramirez, Richard (1960–2013); Washington Area, D.C., Area Snipers (October 2–24, 2002)

Further Reading

Greig, Charlotte. 2006. *Evil Serial Killers: In the Minds of Monsters.* New York: Arcturus Publishing Limited.

Innes, Brian. 2006. *Serial Killers: The Stories of History's Most Evil Murderers.* London: Quercus Publishing, Plc.

Lane, Brian, and Wilfred Gregg. 1995. *The Encyclopedia of Serial Killers.* New York: The Berkley Publishing Group.

Newton, Michael. 2000. *The Encyclopedia of Serial Killers: A Study of the Chilling Criminal Phenomenon, from the "Angels of Death" to the "Zodiac Killer."* New York: Checkmark Books.

Vronsky, Peter. 2004. *Serial Killers: The Method and Madness of Monsters.* New York: Berkley Books.

Bickford, Maria, Murder of (1845)

The murder of Maria Bickford set precedence as being the first documented case to use the sleepwalking defense. The accused murderer, Albert Tirrell, was acquitted of murdering his lover, Maria, after his lawyer successfully argued that he had committed the murder in his sleep. This case set a legal precedent, which has since been used in some of the most famous murder trials to date. As of 2005, approximately 68 cases worldwide have used the sleepwalking defense (Smith-Spark 2005). In recent years, the case for automatism, legally known as performing an action without conscious thought, has been scrutinized by academics and the legal system regarding its legitimacy. The debate over the use of the sleepwalking defense is an area that continues to be discussed, including its origins in the murder of Maria Bickford.

Maria Bickford was born in 1824 in Bath, Maine, as Mary Ann Dunn. When she was 16 years old, her family moved to Bangor, Maine, where she met her husband James Bickford, a local shoemaker. She and her husband lived comfortably but modestly in Bangor for the first three years of their marriage (1939). In 1842, friends of the couple convinced the young bride, who had never been out of Maine, to take a vacation to Boston with them. With the agreement of her husband, Maria accompanied her friends to Boston, quickly becoming dazzled by the brilliance of the city. Maria returned home after her trip, informing her husband that she wanted to move to Boston. Her husband refused but agreed to allow Maria to continue to visit the city. Months later, Maria met a young man who lived in the Boston boarding house where she would stay. According to her husband, Maria and the young man started an affair that led Maria to leave Maine and move permanently to Boston with her new lover. Within weeks, the affair was over, and Maria was left alone and penniless. Maria turned to prostitution in a local brothel to pay her mounting bills. There she had a regular client named Albert J. Tirrell.

The son of a prominent shoe manufacturer, Tirrell was born and raised in Boston. Tirrell married young and had a child by the time he met Maria Bickford. Tirrell was a known adulterer and had been known to have many illicit affairs during his marriage. Tirrell and Bickford fell madly in love and were soon inseparable. In 1844, Tirrell's father passed away, leaving him approximately $8,000, which for the time was a substantial inheritance. Tirrell used the money to begin traveling with Maria, only staying at the most lavish of hotels. Both Maria and Tirrell carried on their affair in public, even declaring that they were husband and wife. However, both were still married to their respective partners. Tirrell purchased elegant gowns and made Maria the talk of the town, including renting a house for the two to live in under Maria's name. Although Tirrell and Maria lived together as husband and wife, Maria continued to work at the brothel, a point of contention between the couple.

By 1845, Tirrell's inheritance was running out. Maria also began writing her estranged husband reporting to him that Tirrell had become physically abusive. Finally in the summer of 1845, after a final altercation with Maria, Tirrell broke up with his lover, leaving her to return to the boarding house where they had met. Weeks after ending the affair, Tirrell was arrested for adultery and "lascivious cohabitation" in connection with his affair with Maria.

With Tirrell in jail, Maria continued her life as a prostitute. In October 1845, Tirrell was released from jail and immediately sought out Maria. On October 26, Tirrell arrived at the boarding house. The owners of the house later reported that that evening they heard Maria and Tirrell fighting in her room. Tirrell stayed the night and all was quiet until 5 a.m. the following morning. The owners of the boardinghouse, Joel Lawrence and his wife, reported hearing a loud scream come from Maria's room followed by a loud "thud." Seconds later, they heard footsteps rushing down the stairs and someone exit the building. Deciding to check on Maria, the couple and a fellow boarder went to her room. When they entered the room, Maria was found on the bed with her throat cut "from ear to ear." Part of her hair and face was burned as though someone had attempted to set the body on fire. There was blood covering the walls near the body and a bloody razor, later identified as the murder weapon, which was found at the end of the bed. It was later noted that throughout the room it appeared little fires had been started as though to cover up evidence of the murder. In the room, clothing was found to contain the initials of M.A.B, Maria A. Bickford, and A.J.T., Albert J. Tirrell.

Another Sleepwalking Defense

The sleepwalking defense was used more recent in the case of Kenneth Parks. Parks was 23 at the time of the event, and lived in Toronto, Canada with his wife and daughter. On May 23, 1987, Parks had fallen asleep in his living room watching TV. In a later testimony, it was revealed that Parks, in his sleep, had driven his car to his in-laws' house, approximately 10 minutes away. Once there, Parks repeatedly stabbed his mother-in-law and father-in-law. As a result of her injuries, his mother-in-law died but his father-in-law survived the attack. After extensive testing by top sleep experts, it was found that Parks had a brain abnormality, causing him to suffer from parasomnia, a sleep disorder known to cause sleepwalking. It was concluded that he was most likely sleepwalking during the attack. Parks was acquitted of the murder and attempted murder charges on May 25, 1988.

Tirrell, whose footsteps were heard as he ran out of the house, had borrowed a horse from a nearby stable and rode to Canada. Tirrell had initially stated to those who knew him that he had gotten into some trouble and was seeking the advice of his father-in-law. Later, Tirrell's wife received a letter postmarked from Canada stating he had booked passage on a ship bound for Liverpool, England. However, the ship had problems and returned to port in New York. Tirrell immediately booked passage for another ship that would send him to Louisiana. Unbeknownst to Tirrell, the authorities found record of his trip and were ready for his arrival in Louisiana on December 5 to transport him back to Boston for the trial.

Tirrell and his family hired one of most respected lawyers of the time, Rufus Choate (1799–1859). Before the trial, Choate began discrediting Maria. By the time that Tirrell made it to court the popular opinion was that Tirrell was the real victim, by being seduced by a heartless prostitute. Throughout the trial, Choate argued that the evidence was circumstantial and that the strongest evidence, the testimony of the Lawrences, was all fabricated. Choate implied that Joel Lawrence was attempting to frame Tirrell. Finally, Choate presented his winning explanation that Tirrell had a history of sleepwalking and becoming violent during these episodes. Choate even had one of Tirrell's cousins testify that a sleepwalking Tirrell had attacked him not a month before the murder. On March 27, 1846, Choate gave his closing arguments speaking for over six hours. The following day the jury deliberated for two hours before reaching a not guilty verdict. Although he got off for murder, Tirrell still had to stand trial for arson and adultery. While he was able to get off for the arson using his sleepwalking defense, he did not get off for the adultery and had to serve three years of hard labor. This case has been memorialized as the first case to ever get an accused murderer acquitted with the sleepwalking defense.

SAMANTHA TOALE

See also: Adler, "Polly" Pearl (1900–1962); Fleiss, Heidi (1965–); Jewett, Helen, Murder of (1836)

Further Reading

Cohen, Daniel A. 1990. "The Murder of Maria Bickford: Fashion, Passion, and the Birth of a Consumer Culture." *American Studies* 31(2): 5–30.

Cohen, Daniel A. 1993. *Pillars of Salt, Monuments of Grace: New England Crime Literature and the Origins of American Popular Culture, 1674–1860.* New York: Oxford University Press.

Hobson, Barbara Meil, 1987. *Uneasy Virtue: The Politics of Prostitution and the American Reform Tradition.* New York: Basic Books.

Smith-Spark, Laura. 2005. "How Sleepwalking Can Lead to Murder." *BBC News.* March 18. http://news.bbc.co.uk/2/hi/uk_news/4362081.stm. Accessed January 20, 2015.

Wilheim, Robert. 2011. "The Sleepwalking Defense. Murder by Gaslight." January 15. http://www.murderbygaslight.com/2011/01/sleepwalking-defense.html. Accessed April 20, 2015.

Big Dan Gang Rape Case (1983–1984)

The rape of Cheryl Araujo (1961–1986) openly in front of bar patrons at Big Dan's sparked national attention about victim blaming, the role of bystanders, media coverage of rape victims, and relations of immigrants in small communities. The victim in this case was accused of being a slut, a prostitute, and wanting the rape to occur. The public blamed her for the rape because they saw her actions—being in the bar after dark and drinking—as her being responsible, which raised public dialogue about victim's role in rape cases. Bar patrons stood by and watched as the rape occurred and did nothing—indeed some also encouraged it to occur. The media attention and coverage of this case led to congressional hearings about the role of the media in coverage of rape, specifically how to navigate between due process and victims' rights and the First Amendment right of press to have access to criminal proceedings. Additionally, questions about racism and an inability to get a fair trial were raised because the suspects were Portuguese immigrants.

On March 6, 1983, in New Bedford, Massachusetts, Cheryl Araujo was raped in Big Dan's Tavern by six men as others watched. She had stopped at the tavern to buy cigarettes and had a drink with a woman there, as well as spoke with a couple of guys at the tavern. She attempted to leave after her friend had left, but she was grabbed by her collar and dragged across the floor, hitting her head and other body parts on bar furniture. Six men then raped her. Araujo stated that as she was being raped she could hear other patrons cheering the rapists on, but no one came to her rescue. Finally, when one of the rapists began talking to a friend, Araujo got free and ran into the street. Half naked, she flagged down a truck with three college men. The men viewed her battered body and got her help.

Four men were arrested for rape: David Silva, John Cordeiro, Joseph Vieira, and Victor Raposo. Jose Medeiros and Virgilio Medeiros were charged with joint enterprise for encouraging the rapists. Cordeiro confessed to police that he and Raposo held Araujo's legs and he was drunk, but acknowledged that his drunken state was not an excuse for his actions. A bartender testified that Vieira and Silva removed Araujo's pants, Raposo and Cordeiro forced sex on Araujo and the Medeiros cheered on the others with chants of "do it" (Cullen-DuPont 2002). The other bystander said that he had saw Araujo earlier and she was flirting with men and needed to go home, introducing the victim-blaming element to this case.

The trial took place from February 21 to March 23, 1984. There were two separate juries in an effort to minimize the effect of the publicity of the case and the effect that some defendants would incriminate others. There were six jurors on each jury and four alternates. The four defendants charged with rape were split into groups of two, Silvia and Vieira and Raposo and Cordeiro. Araujo took the stand in her own defense for 15 hours in total and described in harrowing details the rape to the court, and that her rape lasted 90 minutes. Detectives described the rapists as "sharks at a feeding frenzy" and described that the patrons around "cheered as though they were at a baseball game" (Vespa 1984). Defense attorneys battered Araujo by questioning her character. They painted her as a slut; someone that enjoyed what happened to her. They painted the defendants as individuals that were being vilified due to their Portuguese heritage.

On March 17, 1984, Daniel Silva and Joseph Vieira were found guilty of Ajauro's rape and the reactions to the verdicts were mixed, with many members of the Portuguese community feeling as though the men were vilified. On March 22, 1984, five days after the conviction of Silvia and Vieira, John Cordeiro and Victor Raposo were found guilty of aggravated rape. Again, there was an outcry in the New Bedford community about the men being sentenced for their immigrant status. Women's rights activists marched in support of the victim while others protested the convictions of the men. Those who were convicted were sentenced to 6 to 12 years each. The judge made it clear to state the men were not getting a lighter sentence because of victim characteristics such as style of dress and entrance into the bar. All appeals were rejected, but not one served over six and one half years, and all were released. Tragically in 1986, Araujo died in a car accident at the age of 25.

The Big Dan rape case elicited strong reactions from the Portuguese community in New Bedford and the nation as a whole. Initially, many viewed Araujo as a victim and believed she deserved justice. As the trial unfolded on national television, as well as radio and talk shows the tides seemed to change. Araujo's face was never seen on camera, due to previous legislation on the issue of sexual violence cases, but news outlets like CNN broadcasted her name. The way the case played out had many implications for the small community and Araujo, as well as future victims of sexual violence.

Congressional hearings held discussed how to stem the tide of victim blaming and protect individuals in the future from having to endure the shame and hurt associated with this type of crime. Not since *Chandler v. Florida* (1981) had the issue been reviewed by the Supreme Court, and the precedence set forth by Chandler was that it is the discretion of judges to allow cameras in courtrooms for child abuse and sexual violence cases. Many congressional discussions post Big Dan proposed having these types of proceedings be closed unless there was an overriding interest to open them, in an effort to shield victims like Araujo from the public; however, legislation on the issue is slippery in conjunction with first amendment rights of the press. The 1994 Violence Against Women Act enacted a federal rape shield law to protect the identity of rape victims, and many media outlets as a courtesy do not disclose the name of alleged rape victims.

KEIONDRA GRACE

See also: Central Park Jogger Case (1989); Genovese, Catherine Susan "Kitty," Murder of (1964)

Further Reading
Bayles, Fred. 1984. "Big Dan's Rape Trial to Start." *Times-News.* February 4.
Congressional Hearing. 1985. *Impact of Media Coverage of Rape Trials: Hearing before the Subcommittee on Criminal Law of the Committee on the Judiciary, United States Senate, Ninety-Eighth Congress, Second Session, April 24, 1984.* (J-98–112). Washington, D.C.: U.S. Government Printing Office.
Cullen-DuPont, Kathryn. 2002. "New Bedford Rape Trial: 1984." *Great American Trials.* Encyclopedia.com.
Vespa, Mary. 1984. "No Town Without Pity, a Divided New Bedford Seeks Justice in a Brutal Gang Rape Case." *People.* March 12. http://www.people.com/people/article/0,,20087332,00.html. Accessed April 13, 2015.
Winokoor, Charles. 2009. "Frank O'Boy Speaks Out on Big Dan's Rape Case." *Taunton Daily Gazette.* May 28.

"Billionaire Boys' Club." *See* Hunt, Joe (1959–)

Billy the Kid (1859–1881)

The story of Billy the Kid is one that spans across the southwestern United States during a time when cattle barons and rustlers waged a war for control of the local cattle economy. Billy the Kid, originally known as William H. McCarthy Jr. and later William H. Bonney, would become a major participant in the Lincoln County War (February–July 1878) in the New Mexico Territory during 1878. Billy the Kid was drawn into the Lincoln County War after his boss John Tunstall was murdered by rival cattle merchants in an attempt to seize control of the local cattle trade (Jacobsen 1994). What ensued in the aftermath of Tunstall's murder was the formation of the Regulators, a gang in which Billy the Kid would later lead. During Billy the Kid's time with the Regulators he would be credited with 21 murders, including two jail guards. The Regulators began as deputized law men who were tasked with bringing in those responsible for Tunstall's murder, but would later be hunted by the law as renegades and vigilantes. Pat Garrett (1850–1908) was elected as sheriff of Lincoln County in 1880 and sought out the Regulators to bring them to justice. Garrett would eventually kill Billy the Kid in 1881 in what is often described as an execution-style murder.

Billy the Kid arrived in the New Mexico Territory in 1877 after living a life as a cattle and horse thief in Arizona. His exploits caught the attention of local authorities in Arizona, forcing Billy to leave for New Mexico. After working on various ranches, Billy was hired by John Tunstall as a ranch hand and cattle guard in 1877. It was during this time that the Lincoln County War began between the existing cattle barons of the time, Murphy and Dolan, and the newly established cattle merchant John Tunstall. The feud between the competing cattle merchants would not only fuel the Lincoln County War, but also create Billy's gang the Regulators (Jacobsen 1994). In February 1878, Tunstall was murdered by Murphy and Dolan's men while driving several horses toward Lincoln (Nolan 1965). Riding with the men who murdered Tunstall was the sheriff of Lincoln County William Brady (1829–1878). Sheriff Brady was a supporter of Murphy and Dolan and actively participated in their crimes to control the cattle trade of New Mexico.

Portrait of Billy the Kid taken around 1880. Billy the Kid was one of the most celebrated figures of the Old West. (Library of Congress)

Although the murder of Tunstall was staged to appear as a justifiable homicide, evidence at the scene indicated that Tunstall attempted to flee his attackers before being gunned down. Tunstall's business partner, an attorney, McSween (1843–1878) attempted to utilize legal channels to resolve the case against Murphy and Dolan's men. Arrest warrants were obtained for Tunstall's murderers through the local justice of the peace and Tunstall's men were deputized as the Regulators who were tasked with bringing them to justice. The Regulators quickly captured two of the perpetrators in March 1878 and while transporting the men back to Lincoln they were shot and killed, along with a Regulator suspected of being a traitor, for attempting to flee. In response to the Regulators intervention, then governor Samuel Axtell (1819–1891) acknowledged the Regulators as outlaws who had no legal authority. Now labeled as outlaws, the Regulators continued to serve warrants on those who had participated in Tunstall's demise despite being hunted by the law themselves (Utley 1991).

While attempting to exact revenge on Sheriff Brady for his role in Tunstall's murder, Billy and the Regulators killed Sheriff Brady in the center of Lincoln. The U.S. Calvary, with the aid of Dolan, surrounded the Regulators in Lincoln in April 1878. The Regulators responded by firing upon the soldiers and Dolan in what would increase pressure to capture them. The Regulators were eventually trapped by the soldiers and Dolan's men in McSween's house in Lincoln. Here, McSween died, but the rest of the Regulators escaped and went on the run.

A new governor, Lew Wallace (1827–1905), was appointed for New Mexico in the fall of 1878. In an effort to bring an end to any lingering conflicts in the wake of the Lincoln County War, Wallace offered amnesty deals to those who were involved in the war, but not already indicted. Billy agreed to speak with Wallace in person and traveled from Texas in hiding back to Lincoln for the meeting. Wallace and Billy agreed to amnesty in exchange for him testifying in front of a grand jury. Billy's testimony resulted in the arrest and indictment of Dolan for his role in the Lincoln County War. Nonetheless, Billy was not set free as had been agreed upon with Wallace but he was able to escape with fellow Regulator O'Folliard. The remaining Regulators would spend the next 18–20 months on the run from posses organized by Wallace.

The Regulators would narrowly escape capture at least once during this time on the run. After Pat Garrett was elected sheriff of the Lincoln County in 1880 he set off to bring Billy to justice. Garrett and his men would eventually capture Billy after surrounding the remaining Regulators as they slept. In December 1880 Billy was officially captured by Garrett and transported to Santa Fe, New Mexico. By April 1881, Wallace had refused to help Billy and a trial was held wherein Billy was found guilty of killing Sheriff Brady. Billy was then sentenced to death by hanging. Billy was then transferred to Lincoln to await his death sentence. Despite the sentence and incarceration, Billy was able to escape custody after killing two jail guards (Utley 1991). Again on the run, Billy was being tracked by Sheriff Garrett. Garrett and a couple of his officers eventually tracked Billy back to Fort Sumner in July 1881. While questioning Billy's friends, Sheriff Garrett killed Billy after he mistakenly walked in during the interrogation.

Sheriff Garrett shot Billy unexpectedly in what is often a disputed account of events. What is not in dispute though is that Billy did not fight back and was killed by surprise once Sheriff Garrett noticed who had entered the room. The end result of Billy's criminal exploits was his death at the hands of Sheriff Garrett and the conclusion of the Lincoln County War and the reign of the Regulators throughout the New Mexico Territory. A pardon for Billy was considered by New Mexico governor Richardson in 2010 in response to Governor Wallace's original promise, but Governor Richardson did not find sufficient evidence to grant such a pardon. Billy the Kid, although having been attributed to as many as 21 murders, was convicted of the murder of Sheriff Brady and was killed by Sheriff Garrett after escaping his own death sentence in 1881 (Tuska 1986).

DUSTIN EICKE

See also: Cassidy, Butch (1866–1908); James, Jesse (1847–1882); *Primary Documents*/Description of Billy the Kid: Federal Writers' Project Interview of Berta Ballard Manning (1937)

Further Reading

Garrett, Pat F., and Ash Upson. 2009. *The Authentic Life of Billy, the Kid*. Waiheke Island, New Zealand: Floating Press.

Jacobsen, Joel. 1994. *Such Men as Billy the Kid: The Lincoln County War Reconsidered*. Lincoln: University of Nebraska Press.

Nolan, Frederick. 1965. *The Life and Death of John Henry Tunstall*. Santa Fe, NM: Sunstone Press.

Tuska, Jon. 1986. *Billy the Kid, a Handbook*. Lincoln: University of Nebraska Press.

Utley, Robert Marshall. 1987. *High Noon in Lincoln: Violence on the Western Frontier*. Albuquerque: University of New Mexico Press.

Utley, Robert Marshall. 1991. *Billy the Kid: A Short and Violent Life*. Lincoln: University of Nebraska Press.

Birdman of Alcatraz. *See* Stroud, Robert ("Birdman of Alcatraz") (1890–1963)

Bishop, Amy (1965–)

A former professor of the University of Alabama in Huntsville, Amy Bishop gained notoriety after shooting six colleagues during a routine faculty meeting on the afternoon of February 12, 2010. The catalyst for her actions was a denial of tenure in March 2009 and the subsequent rejection of her appeal. The attention given to this incident caused increased examination into Bishop's previous encounters with the law. Most notably, in 1986, at the age of 21, Bishop shot her 18-year-old brother, Seth. Ruled an accident at the time, further investigation into the event in 2010 led to Bishop being charged with the first-degree murder of her brother. Additionally, in 1993, investigators suspected both Bishop and her husband, James Anderson, in a case involving a package, containing two pipe bombs that failed to explode, sent to Bishop's supervisor at the time. In 2002, Bishop assaulted a woman in an International House of Pancakes in an altercation over a booster seat. During the trial in Alabama, Bishop pled guilty and is now serving a sentence of life-without-parole. Due to this outcome, the Norfolk district attorney in Massachusetts decided not to pursue a case against Bishop for the murder of her brother in 1986. Amy Bishop's actions raised a number of issues, including the pressures professors face when vying for a tenure position, Bishop's sanity, the potential police cover-up at the time of her brother's shooting, and whether there existed a pattern of violent behavior that should have been identified and acted upon prior to Bishop murdering her colleagues.

On the afternoon of February 12, 2010, the biology department at the University of Alabama in Huntsville met for a routine faculty meeting in Room 369 of the Shelby Center for Science and Technology. A little before 4 p.m. CST, Amy Bishop rose from her seat by the door and methodically began shooting her colleagues, beginning with those closest to her, with a 9mm Ruger.

Bishop killed Gopi K. Podila, the chairman of the biology department, Maria Ragland Davis, and Adriel D. Johnson, Sr., both associate professors of biology. Joseph G. Leahy, an associate professor of biology, and Stephanie Monticciolo, the biology department staff assistant, were both shot in the head, but survived the considerable damage caused by their wounds. Luis Rogelio Cruz-Vera, an assistant professor of biology, suffered less extensive injuries from a bullet to the chest and was released from the hospital after one night.

Debra Moriarty, dean of the Graduate School and biochemistry professor, acted by first ducking under the table and then crawling toward Bishop, trying to grab her legs, while pleading with Bishop to think about the impact of her actions. Bishop sidestepped her and Moriarty partially crept into the hallway. At this point, Bishop turned the gun on Moriarty and attempted to shoot her, but the gun jammed. Moriarty maneuvered herself back into the room and shut the door. The other uninjured people helped block the door and two people called 911.

Bishop next went into a ladies room and disposed of the gun and her bloodied coat in a trash can before heading into a lab class and asking to borrow a student's phone. She used it to call her husband and ask him to pick her up, saying she was finished for the day, though police arrested Bishop before she left campus.

On the surface, Bishop's actions seemed inexplicable, given her roles as a wife, mother of four, and respected neurobiologist. However, her denial of tenure in March 2009 triggered resentment toward her colleagues in the biology department at the University of Alabama in Huntsville. With her appeal also rejected, Bishop was teaching her last term at the university in the spring semester of 2010, per school policy. The faculty meeting on February 12, 2010, primarily focused on events and scheduling relevant to the upcoming fall term, after Bishop's contract expired.

Attaining tenure involves a grueling process that puts a great deal of pressure on aspiring professors. However, closer examination of Bishop's life revealed multiple incidents of violent behavior. The first dated back to 1986 when 21-year-old Bishop shot and killed her 18-year-old brother, Seth, in their childhood home in Braintree, Massachusetts. She then fled the house and police apprehended her outside of an auto dealership. At the time, the police report concluded that it was a case of accidental death and Bishop was released to her parents within 24 hours.

The 2010 shooting in Huntsville caused Massachusetts officials to reexamine this case in more depth, as discrepancies in police procedure, various people's recollections of what happened, evidence, and police reports came to light. A formal inquest led to Bishop indicted in Massachusetts on the charge of first-degree murder of her brother.

In 1993, police investigated Bishop and her husband, James Anderson, as suspects in a case involving two pipe bombs that failed to explode. These were sent to Dr. Paul Rosenberg, a neurobiologist working at Harvard Medical School and Children's Hospital in Boston, also Bishop's postdoctoral supervisor at the time. However, the police brought no charges against Bishop or Anderson and the case remains unsolved.

Bishop faced charges of misdemeanor assault and disorderly conduct in Peabody, Massachusetts, in 2002, following an altercation with another customer at an International House of Pancakes. A woman requested the last available booster seat just before Bishop asked for one, prompting Bishop to hurl obscenities at the woman before punching her in the head when the manager asked her to leave for creating a disturbance.

Initially, Bishop pled not guilty to the one charge of capital murder and three counts of attempted murder for the mass shooting that occurred at the university. Her lawyer intended to use an insanity defense. According to an Alabama mandatory sentencing law, if found guilty of capital murder, Bishop faced either the death penalty or life in prison without parole. During the course of the trial, the defense agreed to change Bishop's plea to guilty if the prosecution agreed to forego pursuing the death penalty. The prosecution agreed and on September 24, 2012, Amy Bishop was sentenced to life in prison without the possibility of parole. As a result of this, the Norfolk district attorney in Massachusetts filed a *nolle prosequi*, effectively stopping the prosecution of Bishop for her brother's murder, but allowing prosecutors the option of reviving the first-degree murder charge against her at a later date, if so desired.

KATE MELODY BURMON

See also: Dartmouth College Murders (January 27, 2001); Jovin, Suzanne, Murder of (1998); Le, Annie, Murder of (2009); Schwartz, Robert, Murder of (December 8, 2001)

Further Reading

Keefe, Patrick Radden. 2013. "A Loaded Gun: A Mass Shooter's Tragic Past." *New Yorker*, February 11.

Black Dahlia Murder (1947)

The case of the Black Dahlia murder is of great importance for various reasons. First, it remains unsolved to this day. The individual(s) who killed Elizabeth Short have never been brought to justice. Second, the way in which Elizabeth was killed was grotesque in nature. This was not a simple strangulation, stabbing, or shooting. Her body was dismembered, cut in half with pieces of flesh missing, and a smile cut on her face. The position in which she lay was bizarre to the human eye; almost like a broken marionette. After over 300 initial suspects and more than a dozen confessions, no one was officially charged with the Black Dahlia murder. Several theories have spawned since the late 1940s as to who would have done this and why. This case remains as one of the most complex and notorious murders in the U.S. history.

In the morning of January 15, 1947, Betty Bersinger was walking her young girl on Norton Avenue and noticed something peculiar in the grass of the Leimert Park neighborhood in Los Angeles. After realizing it was a human body, she contacted the police. The announcement over the police radio attracted news reporters who often listened for lead stories. Among the first at the crime scene was Will Fowler and Felix Paegel, a reporter and photographer for *The Los Angeles Examiner*. The scene was atypical for a murder. The young woman was cut in half, with organs almost fully intact, her right breast missing. Her body was positioned in a way that her top half was above and left of the lower portion with her blood drained, also indicating her murder occurred elsewhere.

Newspaper photographs appeared the next day in which the victim 22-year-old Elizabeth Short from Massachusetts was identified. According to friends and acquaintances, Elizabeth was an aspiring actress, working some time as a waitress, moving around a lot, and always in need of money. She dated many men and at one point was engaged in 1945 to Matt Gordon Jr., a major in the Air Force who was killed the same year in a plane crash. Witnesses stated shortly before her murder, she seemed terrified of something, possibly someone. Robert "Red" Manley, thought to be the last person who saw her alive, drove her to the Biltmore hotel and told investigators she had a very jealous Italian boyfriend. A woman Elizabeth had stayed with mentioned the same information. A police reporter working for *The Herald Express* found Elizabeth was given the nickname "Black Dahlia" at a Long Beach soda fountain which she frequented for her constant wearing of black clothes and jet black hair.

Police decided not to reveal full details of Short's body in hopes of identifying the killer with knowledge of information yet to be disclosed to public. After six months of active investigation, the case began to slow down. Such reasons for this decrease in activity included possible corruption and cover-ups as well as lack of convincing evidence. One idea was certain: whoever killed Elizabeth had some type of surgical training to not only bisect the body, but drain the blood while leaving organs intact.

George Hodel, a physician in the 1940s, was the main suspect in the Black Dahlia murder. Hodel was married three times, had several affairs, and fathered 11 children in total. He lived in Hollywood and was friends with film director John Huston and the famous artist Man Ray. His friendship and appreciation of Man Ray's artwork struck a chord with investigators. Pieces such as *Coat Stand* (1920), *White and Black* (1929), and *La jumelle* (1939) are similar to the way in which Elizabeth Short's body was found. In addition, his famous gatherings were attended by many in the film industry with bizarre behavior and intoxication. Witnesses such as Lillian Lenorak who may have had any information on Elizabeth Short's connection were harmed or died mysteriously. Hodel admitted to drugging Lenorak after she identified Short in photographs kept in a photo album of his children, girlfriends, and other women. After a scandal consisting of alleged incest with 14-year-old daughter Tamar Hodel, the Los Angeles district attorney's office was interested enough in George to plant audio surveillance in his home from February 18 to March 27, 1950, but he was never officially charged with Elizabeth Short's murder. Much later, son Steve Hodel became convinced his father murdered Short after George's death in 1999. Working as a Los Angeles police detective, Steve investigated his father's life, finding a history of violence and other possible murders of women, including his secretary Ruth Spaulding who died of a suspicious drug overdose in 1945. Transcripts from the recordings were released when Steve's book *Black Dahlia Avenger* was first published in 2003. Certain words stated by George made many, including son Steve, believe he was the killer; however, there was never enough evidence to conclude that he was the murderer.

There remain other possible suspects. After repressed memories surfaced, Janice Knowlton in the 1980s and 1990s claimed her father George Knowlton murdered Elizabeth Short. The memories began to surface and Janice could recall younger women who were sexually assaulted and killed by her father. Janice also stated her father lived close to where Elizabeth Short attended high school in Massachusetts. A known pedophile, Janice believes George and Elizabeth may have crossed paths before she headed to California. Janice attributed Elizabeth's bizarre behavior and dating of several men to possible sexual abuse as a young teen by George. She even recalls one afternoon coming home to finding her dad in bed with a dark-haired young woman. Janice wondered whether that young woman was Elizabeth. According to Janice, George moved his family out to Westminster, California, in Orange County. In July 1946, Gertrude Landon told her husband she was off to mail some letters but never returned—her body was found within five miles of places where George would frequent. Janice has small memories of the body of a woman in her undergarments, and recalls seeing a picture of her father taken hours after Gertrude disappeared with apparent scratches on his arms. Later repressed memories of encounters with Elizabeth began to surface. Janice would visit Elizabeth with her father and Short would also watch Janice from time to time. According to Janice's repressed memories, Elizabeth was picked up by George at the Biltmore hotel, brought back to his garage area where she was sick with a fever and hemorrhaging. Apparently, Elizabeth had a miscarriage that night and Janice was told to take care of her. As she began to feel better a day or two later, Elizabeth was ready to go back to Los Angeles and get a film career started. George was angry she wanted to leave and the remainder of details by Janice showed that George killed Elizabeth Short. Police have rejected Janice's story and most argue George Hodel was the murderer; however, the case is still considered a mystery to this day.

STACIE MERKEN

See also: Levy, Chandra, Disappearance of (2001–2002); Monroe, Marilyn, Death of (1962); Moxley, Martha, Murder of (October 30, 1975); Peterson, Laci, Murder of (2002–2004); Show, Laurie, Murder of (1991)

Further Reading

Ellroy, James. 1987. *The Black Dahlia*. New York: Mysterious Press.

Gilmore, John. 1994. *Severed: The True Story of the Black Dahlia Murder*. Los Angeles: Amok Books.

Knowlton, Janice, and Michael Newton. 1995. *Daddy Was the Black Dahlia Killer*. New York: Pocket Books.

Nelson, Mark, and Sarah Hudson Bayliss. 2006. *Exquisite Corpse: Surrealism and the Black Dahlia Murder*. New York: Bulfinch Press.

Wolfe, Donald. H. 2005. *The Black Dahlia Files: The Mob, the Mogul, and the Murder That Transfixed Los Angeles*. New York: Regan.

Black Liberation Army (BLA) (c. 1970–1981)

The Black Liberation Army (BLA) was an American black nationalist organization that embraced urban guerrilla warfare as a means to achieve "national black self-determination" (BLA, n.d.). While the origins of the BLA are somewhat unclear, the organization had ties to the Black Panther Party (BPP) and the Revolutionary Action Movement (RAM). In their quest for the liberation of black Americans, the BLA carried out a series of domestic terrorism offenses.

One explanation for the formation of the BLA is that Eldridge Cleaver (1935–1998), a member of the BPP, was expelled from the party after a falling-out with the BPP cofounder Huey P. Newton (1942–1989) in 1971. Another likely but related explanation is that the BLA grew from the RAM group the Black Guards. According to accounts by Assata Shakur (b. 1947) and Geronimo ji Jaga (1947–2011), who were members of both the BPP and the BLA, the BLA was comprised of a variety of organizations operating out of many cities.

The BLA embraced a Marxist political philosophy. In an undated political statement, the BLA argued that American capitalism was based on exploitive relationships that created and supported "racist domination and subjugation" (BLA, n.d.). The group called for a violent revolution that would abolish the capitalist system that subjugates those who were not part of the American bourgeoisie. Because of their distaste for the economic system, they promoted the principles of being "anti-capitalist, anti-imperialist, anti-racist and anti-sexist," and advocated for replacing the capitalist economy with a socialist institution (BLA, n.d., ii).

The BLA used violence, in the form of urban guerilla warfare, to further their goals. Considered a domestic terrorist organization, the BLA is known to be responsible for 20 deaths, though more are suspected. As the BPP began to splinter, five members later identified as being members of the BLA shot and killed Sgt. Frank Von Colln (1927–1970) in Philadelphia on August 29, 1970. Two months later, on October 22, 1970, the BLA bombed a San Francisco church during the funeral of a police officer who had been killed during a bank robbery.

After breaking from the BPP in 1971, the BLA quickly began committing additional violent acts, particularly against police officers. On May 19, 1971, two members of the BLA shot officers Thomas Curry and Nicholas Binetti outside of the New York district attorney's apartment. Two days later, between three and five members of the BLA shot and killed two other New York Police Department (NYPD) officers, Joseph Piagentini and Waverly Jones.

The violence continued throughout the 1970s. The BLA claimed responsibility for the October 29, 1971, shooting of San Francisco police officer John Victor Young. On

November 3, 1971, two members of the BLA shot and killed Atlanta Police Department officer James Greene. NYPD officers Gregory Foster and Rocco Laurie were shot by members of the BLA on January 27, 1972. In St. Louis, Missouri, BLA members shot and wounded St. Louis police officer Richard Archambault. Later, on July 31, 1972, five members of the BLA hijacked a Detroit-to-Miami Delta Air Lines flight, received a $1 million ransom, and escaped to Paris, France. On January 25, 1973, members of the BLA shot at and wounded Carlo and Vincent Imperato, who were patrolling in Brooklyn, New York. Officers Michael O'Reilly and Roy Pollina were wounded by gunfire in Queens, New York, on January 28, 1973.

Perhaps the most notorious of the BLA's exploits is a shoot-out that occurred between members of the BLA and New Jersey State Troopers on May 2, 1973. The shoot-out was the result of a traffic stop for a broken tail light. Several passengers, who were members of the BLA, opened fired on the State Troopers. Assata Shakur, also known as JoAnne Chesimard, was accused of killing Trooper Werner Foerster. She is also accused of wounding State Trooper James Harper. Shakur was indicted for, and convicted of, the murder of Foerster and seven related felonies. In 1979, she escaped from prison and eventually fled to Cuba. She is classified as a domestic terrorist by the Federal Bureau of Investigation (FBI) and in 2013, was the first woman added to the FBI's most wanted terrorist list.

By the mid-1970s, the BLA's momentum began to slow down. The "underground" nature of the BLA created a political isolation, and the incarceration of many members left gaps in the group. The BLA began connecting with other organizations, such as the New Republic of Afrika (RNA). However, the extreme leftist movement was dying down, and the BLA was unable to renew its membership. The BLA's last high-profile act of violence occurred in 1981, when members of the BLA robbed a Brinks armored truck.

CHERIE M. CARTER

See also: Chicago Seven (1968); Evers, Medgar, Assassination of (June 12, 1963); King, Martin Luther, Jr., Assassination of (April 4, 1968)

Further Reading

Black Liberation Army. n.d. "Message to the Black Movement: A Political Statement from the Black Underground." http://archive.lib.msu.edu/DMC/AmRad/messageblackmovement.pdf. Accessed October 15, 2014.

Rosenau, William. 2013. "'Our Backs Are against the Wall': The Black Liberation Army and Domestic Terrorism in 1970s America." *Studies in Conflict & Terrorism* 36(2): 176–192. http://www.tandfonline.com/doi/pdf/10.1080/1057610x.2013.747074. Accessed October 15, 2014.

Stanford, Maxwell C. 1986. "Revolutionary Action Movement (RAM): A Case Study of an Urban Revolution Movement in Western Capitalist Society." MA Thesis, Atlanta University. http://www.ulib.csuohio.edu/research/portals/blackpower/stanford.pdf. Accessed October 15, 2014.

Umoja, Akinyele Omowale. 1999. "Repression Breeds Resistance: The Black Liberation Army and the Radical Legacy of the Black Panther Party." *New Political Science* 21(2): 131–155. http://web.a.ebscohost.com/ehost/pdfviewer/pdfviewer?vid=2&sid=b3d15dcc-3e15-458e-bafd-7d39966e9ae1%40sessionmgr4004&hid=4214. Accessed October 15, 2014.

Black Sox Scandal (1919)

One of the most infamous scandals in sports history occurred when eight members of the Chicago White Sox conspired with gamblers to fix the 1919 World Series. The players would become collectively known as the "Black Sox" and their involvement in the scandal would lead to their criminal indictment by a grand jury on various charges of defrauding the public and injuring the business of baseball. Although all were legally innocent, the eight players received a lifetime ban from professional baseball. Much debate still exists about the exact events that led up to the indictments and trial. The attempts to cover up the scandal make it difficult to determine what actually took place in the fall of 1919. While some have described the criminal trial as "superficial" and "farcical" (Carney 2006, 148), the scandal and accompanying lifetime bans of the players have had a lasting effect on a number of American institutions including professional baseball, the media, and popular culture. The significance of the scandal, then, is that it continues to serve as a reference point for almost every major corrupt act that has taken place since (Nathan 2003).

The idea for fixing the 1919 World Series is often credited to Arnold "Chick" Gandil (1888–1979), the team's first baseman. It is said that Gandil met with professional gambler Joseph Sullivan and came up with a proposal where the team would throw the series for $80,000. The result of this meeting led Gandil to try and recruit other team members and Sullivan to obtain the funding for the players' payment. On September 21, 1919, Gandil held a meeting in New York to try and recruit seven other players: Eddie Cicotte (1884–1969), the team's star pitcher who had previously agreed to help Gandil; George "Buck" Weaver (1890–1956); Fred McMullin (1891–1952); Charles "Swede" Risberg (1894–1975); Oscar "Happy" Felsch (1891–1964); Claude "Lefty" Williams (1893–1955); and "Shoeless" Joe Jackson (1887–1951). In attempting to recruit the players, Gandil used the team's dislike of White Sox owner Charles Comiskey's (1859–1931) practices of controlling players' contracts and underpaying them for their services. The result of the meeting had the majority of the players agreeing in principle to participating in the fix (Linder 2010).

On September 26, 1919, Sullivan attempted to come up with the money by contacting Arnold Rothstein (1882–1928), a prominent figure in America's underworld. Rothstein agreed to fund $40,000 to the players up front and the remaining $40,000 after they lost the series. It should be noted that another set of gamblers "Sleepy" Bill Burns (1880–1953) and Bill Maharg had also approached Rothstein with a proposal to fix the series after they met with Cicotte who told them of the plan. Although Rothstein declined their proposal, Burns and Maharg would play significant roles during the criminal trial. While it would seem that the fix had been set, a number of double crosses between the two sets of gamblers and the players occurred, making the actual events of the scandal a matter of debate (Asinof 1963; Carney 2006; Linder 2010). What is known is that the White Sox lost the series to the Cincinnati Reds and seven of the eight players received money. Furthermore, the major gamblers involved were also said to have won significant amounts of money by betting on the series.

Right after the World Series, it appeared that everyone involved would get away with the scandal. However, Ban Johnson (1865–1931), a powerful executive in baseball, convinced Judge Charles McDonald (1864–1951) to form a grand jury in Cook County, Illinois, almost a year later. The grand jury convened on September 22, 1920. Eventually, Cicotte ended up confessing and signed a waiver, allowing his statements to be admissible in any subsequent legal proceedings. After being implicated by Cicotte, Jackson and Williams voluntarily went before the grand jury to confess and sign waivers (Carney 2006). The evidence also began to implicate Sullivan, Rothstein, Burns, and Rothstein's associate Abe Attell. Rothstein volunteered to testify before the grand jury and said that Attell and Burns had unknowingly used his name to start the proceedings that led to the fix (Asinof 1963). The grand jury cleared Rothstein of any involvement. The eight players and Attell, Burns, and Sullivan ended up being indicted (formally charged) with conspiring to defraud the public and conspiring to injure the business of Comiskey, among other things (Linder 2010).

Although indictments had been handed down, it was unknown if a trial would take place. This type of case had not really ever been brought to criminal court before (Carney 2006). Furthermore, merely conspiring to fix baseball games was not a crime, and so establishing the burden of proof (the standard needed to convict someone of a crime) for convicting on charges of defrauding the public and Comiskey was questionable. In addition, the signed confessions of Cicotte, Jackson, and Williams mysteriously disappeared. Many believed that the disappearance of the papers was due in part to Rothstein and Comiskey. Getting rid of the confessions would further distance Rothstein from the scandal as the players had implicated him in the fix. It would also allow the players to refute their statements, giving Comiskey hope that his players' current suspensions from baseball would be lifted.

After two weeks of jury selection, the trial, the *People of the State of Illinois v. Edward V. Cicotte, et al.* began on July 18, 1921. The prosecution made a strong case with their witness, Burns who received immunity for his testimony. Burns recounted his involvement with the players and the other gamblers. The prosecution also benefited from the fact that copies of Cicotte, Jackson, and Williams's confessions were in existence even though the signed originals were missing. The defense focused on Comiskey's wealth, claiming that his business could not have been injured. The defense also benefited from the fact that there was virtually no hard evidence against the players. The presiding judge even noted that he would not be able to let a conviction stand against Weaver or Felsch (Carney 2006).

On August 2, 1921, the players and gamblers were acquitted of all charges. Despite their acquittal, the newly appointed commissioner of baseball, Judge Kenesaw Mountain Landis (1866–1944), placed a lifetime ban on the players the day after the trial had ended to ensure that baseball's image would remain clean and to show that it would no longer allow corruption to occur (Carney 2006). None of them would ever play professional baseball again, and none of them have ever been reinstated.

JASON R. INGRAM

See also: Baseball and Steroids (1980–); Rose, Pete, Gambling Scandal (1989); *Primary Documents*/Black Sox Scandal of 1919: Senate Resolution Calling for Honoring of the Baseball Accomplishments of "Shoeless Joe" Jackson (October 27, 2005)

Further Reading

Asinof, Eliot. 1963. *Eight Men Out: The Black Sox and the 1919 World Series.* New York: Henry Holt and Company.

Carney, Gene. 2006. *Burying the Black Sox: How Baseball's Cover-up of the 1919 World Series Fix Almost Succeeded.* Washington, D.C.: Potomac Books.

Ingram, Jason R. 2007. "The Black-Sox Scandal: More than a Story of Eight Men Out." In S. Chermak and Frankie Bailey, eds. *Crimes & Trials of the Century.* Westport, CT: Greenwood Press, pp. 1–18.

Linder, Douglas O. 2010. "The Black Sox Trial: An Account." http://law2.umkc.edu/faculty/projects/ftrials/blacksox/blacksoxaccount.html. Accessed April 14, 2015.

Nathan, Daniel A. 2003. *Saying It's So: A Cultural History of the Black Sox Scandal.* Chicago: University of Illinois Press.

Black Widow. *See* Buenoano, Judy (1943–1998)

An illustration of Edward Teach, "Blackbeard, the Pirate," from an 18th-century manuscript. (Jupiterimages)

Blackbeard the Pirate (Edward Teach) (d. 1718)

Even outside of North Carolina, where he was killed by a Royal Navy lieutenant, people shudder when they hear the name "Blackbeard the Pirate." Ordinary people reading about him and historians writing about him have portrayed him as evil, vicious, and the worst pirate of all time. Edward Teach would be pleased at this appraisal of his character.

Blackbeard the Pirate, or Edward Teach, was an English pirate notorious for his forays against shipping in the West Indies, the Spanish Main, and the coast of North Carolina. His life story is interwoven with legend and fact, much like the history of piracy. His real name was Edward Teach, or Thatch, or various other phonetic spellings such as Thach or Thache. Unusual for mariners in his time, he was intelligent and literate. He was centuries ahead of his time in understanding the importance of image, reputation, and psychological warfare. He was a skillful manager of ships and men, but his human weaknesses like greed and lust for adventure and women brought about his downfall.

Little is known of his early life, but it is thought that he was born in Bristol, England. Teach was born into an intelligent, respectable, and well-to-do family, and it's probable that he abandoned his real name and used an alias to protect his family (Lee 1974). He could read and write because he corresponded with merchants, and at the time of his death on November 22, 1718, he had letters from the chief justice and secretary of the Province of North Carolina, Tobias Knight, in his pocket. He seemed to be equally at ease with ruffians and governors (1974, 4).

Edward Teach revealed through historical documents may not have been politically ambitious, but he lived in a politically ambitious country, which may have influenced his turn toward piracy. The English, anxious for England to become master of the seas, encouraged piracy. England endowed privateering and piracy with a high level of legitimacy, and this helped usher in the Golden Age of Piracy, roughly from 1680 to 1730.

Captain Charles Johnson documented that Blackbeard sailed for some time out of Jamaica on privateer ships during Queen Anne's War and that "he had often distinguished himself for his uncommon boldness and personal courage" (Johnson 1724, 45). Blackbeard went to the West Indies during the War of the Spanish Succession. Active in privateering, he turned pirate at the war's end in 1713. Although his first recorded act of piracy took place in 1716, he might have started earlier, further blurring the line between privateer and pirate. Eventually, Teach found a berth on a merchantman, deserted in the Caribbean, and made his way to New Providence, where he met and made friends with Captain Benjamin Hornigold. Hornigold enjoyed a reputation as the most fierce and talented privateer, and the Brethren of the Coast esteemed him highly. As a young hand aboard Hornigold's pirate ship, Blackbeard demonstrated a marksman's eye, an affinity for dirty infighting and, according to Captain Johnson, a thirst for blood rivaling any other pirate of the time. Hornigold made Blackbeard his protégé.

Blackbeard continued to learn piracy, studying the art and craft of weapons with increasing interest. Most pirates' weapons of choice were pistols, knives, cutlasses, boarding axes, and pikes. Their flintlock pistols, fitted with hooks for attaching to the belt or to a broad leather sling across the chest, were of large caliber and accurate only at a comparatively short distance. They could fire only one shot at a time, and there was always the chance of a misfire because of an incorrectly placed flint or damp primary powder. To make sure he or she had continuing firepower, a pirate had to carry several braces of pistols while attacking an enemy. Blackbeard was said to have carried 12 pistols (Whipple 1957, 47–49).

Edward Teach christened himself Blackbeard for the spectacular beard that he had discovered he could grow with no extra work. Effortlessly, he had grown "a matted, greasy, mass of jet-black hair, which covered nearly all of his face and hung down to his chest." His bushy and bristly eyebrows added to the forbidding countenance he was constructing. Tall, robust, and broad-shouldered with a hard-muscled strength, Blackbeard was an imposing physical presence (Whipple 1957, 46).

In 1717, Blackbeard commanded a sloop and cruised in company with another vessel under Captain Benjamin Hornigold. In November that year, off the island of St. Vincent, the two pirate sloops closed on a large French merchantman, the *Concorde*, and captured it. Blackbeard took it as his own flagship, refitted it as a 40-gun warship and renamed it the *Queen Anne's Revenge*.

Blackbeard's signature victory came when the *Queen Anne's Revenge* encountered the British 30-gun man-of-war HMS *Scarborough*, which the English Crown had sent out to deal with him. Rather than run from the warship with his faster vessel, Blackbeard decided to battle the British man-of-war. He prided himself on never having run away from a battle. The *Queen Anne's Revenge* and HMS *Scarborough* began a running duel that lasted for hours, and the British warship was definitively losing the fight to

the skillful pirate crew. The British captain realized that he was losing the battle and began to withdraw. Blackbeard allowed him to withdraw, since he saw no purpose in continuing to attack a warship that would not have the kind of cargo that the pirates wanted. Blackbeard's reputation grew dramatically after this battle. A pirate who could defeat a British man-of-war deserved respect.

Aboard his own vessel, Blackbeard was a savvy leader who kept his men from voting him down or throwing him overboard by capturing so many rich prizes that they were left too happy to disagree with him. Ashore, he was loud and sometimes arrogant, but open-handed and good-hearted. His fellow pirate captains respected and sometimes feared him.

In May 1718, Blackbeard's fleet appeared at Charleston, South Carolina, with a force of 400 pirates and six vessels. They stopped every vessel entering and leaving the harbor for the next week and plundered the cargo and the belongings of the passengers. Blackbeard sent a landing party ashore. The landing party returned to the *Queen Anne's Revenge* with many high-ranking citizens as prisoners, hoping they would be useful. Blackbeard sent one of the hostages and two of his crew to deliver a ransom note in which he stated that he was holding the citizens for medical supplies, and threatening to kill them all if he did not get what he wanted. Several days later, he received his medical trunk and, true to his word, he released all the prisoners without loss of life. Historians speculate that Blackbeard must have been ill to take this drastic action. No one knows how many of his crew were ill, but the numbers must have been great enough for him to risk a confrontation with a city by taking some of its most illustrious citizens hostage. He continued to plunder vessels, and almost 10 were looted before Charleston acted on the problem.

At this point in his career, Blackbeard decided to retire from pirating and take advantage of pardons that were being given to other pirates. Blackbeard and his men collected their pardons, and Blackbeard soon settled in Bath Town, where he lived from 1716 to 1718. However, by mid-1718, pirate life had tempted Blackbeard out of retirement, and he was once again pirating, although at times he tried to cover it up.

Leaders from North Carolina, upset that the governor would do nothing about Blackbeard, addressed a list of complaints to the lieutenant governor of Virginia, Colonel Alexander S. Spotswood, who in turn referred the matter to Captains George Gordon and Ellis Brand of the HMS *Pearl* and the HMS *Lyme*, two British frigates stationed in the James River. When Lieutenant Governor Spotswood told the captains about the problem, they informed the governor that their large men-of-war would not be able to maneuver through the inlet and engage Blackbeard in among the shoals of the sound. They would, however, provide the men if the governor could find some shallow-draft sloops. Lieutenant Governor Spotswood used his own money to lease two sloops, *Ranger* and *Jane*, for the job, and they were fitted out and manned from the frigate. Robert Maynard, first lieutenant of the *Pearl*, was selected to lead the two ships for the hunt while Captain Brand of HMS *Lyme* would lead the ground forces.

Ocracoke Inlet was Blackbeard's favorite anchorage. The two sloops set out for Blackbeard's hideout at Ocracoke Island and arrived late on November 21, 1718. The next morning, November 22, 1718, the battle began. The two leased sloops were unarmed, so they had to fight only with small guns and swords. *Ranger* was essentially knocked out from a lethal broadside shot from *Adventure*, so Maynard moved in alone with *Jane*. *Jane* managed to damage *Adventure* enough to slow her down, and Maynard ordered most of his crew below decks to bluff Blackbeard into thinking the crew had been killed. His bluff worked, and when the two ships drew alongside each other, Blackbeard and several of his crew boarded *Jane*.

At this time, Maynard's armed and waiting crew surfaced from below deck, and a raging hand-to-hand battle ensued. Soon Maynard and Blackbeard were fighting each other in a duel of naval officer versus pirate. After Blackbeard wounded Maynard's fingers with a cutlass blow, Maynard moved back and shot him, but this did not stop Blackbeard. Several other *Jane* crewmen fought Blackbeard before his numerous wounds eventually overcame him. It has been stated in lore that Blackbeard was decapitated with a sword-blow to the back of the head during the fighting rather than having his head removed after his death. Maynard himself later commented that Blackbeard fell with at least five gunshot wounds and at least 20 sword wounds.

KATHY WARNES

Further Reading

Johnson, Capt. C. 1724. *A General History of the Robberies and Murders of the Most Notorious Pirates.* London.

Lee, R.E. 1974. *Blackbeard the Pirate: A Reappraisal of His Life and Times.* Winston-Salem, NC: John F. Blair.

Pendered, N. C. 1975. *Blackbeard, the Fiercest Pirate of All.* Kill Devil Hills, NC: Times Printing Co.

Whipple, A. B. C. 1957. *Pirates: Rascals of the Spanish Main.* New York: Doubleday & Co.

Blake, Robert, Murder Trial of (2005)

The world was shocked when Robert Blake, a well-known actor, was arrested and charged in connection with the murder of his wife, Bonnie Lee Bakley, in 2002. The prosecution painted a picture of a man who was desperate to get out of an unhappy marriage and saw murder as the only answer. The defense claimed that Blake was an innocent victim who was being charged due to circumstantial evidence and that a lack of forensic evidence would prove Blake's innocence. On March 16, 2005, Blake was found innocent of all charges against him. A civil suit was brought against Blake by Bakley's children, which resulted in Blake being held liable for Bakley's death. Blake was ordered to pay Bakley's children $30 million. Due to rising debt, Blake filed for bankruptcy in 2006. Since the trial, Blake maintains his innocence and hopes to continue his acting career. He has appeared on television shows, such as *Dr. Phil*, and recently wrote a book.

Robert Blake was born Michael James Vincenzo Gubitosi on September 18, 1933, in Nutley, New Jersey. His father, Giacomo Gubitosi, and mother, Elizabeth Cafone, moved the family to Los Angeles, California, in 1938. Soon after the move, Blake began working with his siblings as movie extras. According to Blake, acting was a great experience for him because it allowed him to escape an unhappy and abusive childhood.

Blake began his acting career as Mickey Gubitosi in the film *Bridal Suite* (1939). He then began appearing in *Our Gang* shorts that became known as *The Little Rascals* under his real name. Between 1939 and 1942, Blake appeared in over 40 shorts. In 1942 he acquired the name Bobby Blake and continued his childhood career with films such as *Andy Hardy's Double Life* (1942), *The Big Noise* (1944), *Humoresque* (1946), and *The Treasure of the Sierra Madre* (1948).

Blake joined the army in 1950, but continued acting. While Blake was away, his father committed suicide. According to Blake, the death of his father had a tremendous impact on him. Blake was first billed as Robert Blake in 1956. Over the next 20 years, Blake appeared in approximately 20 films. Blake is best known for playing the role of Tony Baretta in the television series *Baretta*, which ran from 1975 to 1978. Blake continued to act throughout the 1980s and 1990s, mostly in television roles.

Blake married his first wife, Sondra Kerr, in 1961. The couple had two children, Noah and Delinah, but they got divorced in 1983. Blake met Bonnie Lee Bakley in 1999. Bakley became pregnant soon after meeting Blake. The paternity of the child was in question, however, because Bakley was also dating Christian Brando, son of Marlon Brando, during her relationship with Blake. Bakley told both men that they were the father of the child. Blake took a paternity test to determine if he was the father of the child, initially named Christian Shannon Brando. When it was determined that Blake was the father, the child was renamed Rose Blake. Bakley and Blake married in 2000. This would be Blake's second marriage and Bakley's 10th.

On May 4, 2001, Bakley and Blake went out for dinner at an Italian restaurant in Hollywood. While walking out to the car, Blake returned to the restaurant to retrieve a handgun that he had left behind. Blake said he was carrying a handgun because Bakley believed that she was being stalked. When Blake returned to his car, he found Bakley shot twice in the head while sitting in the passenger seat of the car. The window of the car was rolled down on the passenger side. The murder weapon was a semiautomatic pistol that was found in a dumpster a few yards away from the parked car.

Blake was arrested on April 18, 2002, in connection with his wife's murder. Blake's bodyguard, Earle Caldwell, was also arrested on related charges. On April 22, 2002, Blake was charged with one count of murder, two counts of soliciting murder, and one count of murder conspiracy. Caldwell was charged with a single count of murder conspiracy. Both Blake and Caldwell pled not guilty to all charges. The prosecution had two men willing to testify against Blake, Ronald Hambleton and Gary McLarty, who would both testify that Blake tried to hire them to kill his wife.

Bail was initially denied for Blake and he spent approximately one year in jail prior to the trial. He was finally granted bail on March 13, 2003, and placed on house arrest. On October 31, 2003, a judge dismissed the conspiracy charge against Blake during a pretrial hearing. Blake's trial began on December 20, 2004. The prosecution argued that Blake intentionally murdered Bakley because he was unhappy in the marriage. The defense claimed that Blake was innocent and that there was no forensic evidence linking him to the murder.

Throughout the trial, Blake had a total of four different lawyers. Two lawyers quit due to Blake's insistence on conducting television interviews prior to his trial and a third was dismissed after citing "irreconcilable differences" with his client. Blake's fourth lawyer, Gerald Schwartzbach, assisted him throughout the remainder of his trial.

The prosecution rested its case on February 14, 2005. The defense attempted to prove that Blake was innocent by calling into question the testimony of Hambleton and McLarty due to their criminal records and histories of drug use. Also, there was a lack of forensic evidence tying Blake to the crime scene. No gunshot residue was found on Blake's hands and his fingerprints were not on the murder weapon. Blake chose not to testify during the trial, but maintained his innocence in interviews. The defense rested on February 23, 2005, and the jury was left to deliberate on March 4, 2005. On March 16, 2005, a jury of seven men and four women found Blake not guilty of all charges.

Bakley's three children from previous relationships filed a civil suit against Blake shortly after the criminal trial ended. On November 18, 2005, a jury found Blake civilly liable for the death of Bakley. He was ordered to pay $30 million to Bakley's children. On February 3, 2006, Blake filed for bankruptcy. Blake's lawyer filed an appeal for the civil case; however, an appellate court upheld the decision.

Blake remains in California and reports that he hopes to return to acting to help pay his bills. On April 9, 2010, the state of California filed a tax lien against Blake for over $1 million in unpaid back taxes. Blake has been interviewed on television shows such as *Dr. Phil, Tavis Smiley,* and *Piers Morgan Tonight* and maintains his innocence. In 2011, Blake wrote a book called *Tales of a Rascal: What I Did for Love.* He also facilitates a personal website, which contains his life story, details about his book, as well as original poetry that he has written.

Darla D. Darno

See also: Anthony, Casey, Murder Trial of (May 24–July 5, 2011); Knox, Amanda, Murder Trials of (2009–2015); Simpson, O. J. (1947–)

Further Reading
"Blake Found Not Guilty of Wife's Killing." 2005. CNN. www.cnn.com/2005/LAW/03/16/blake.case. Accessed April 22, 2015.
Blake, Robert. 2011. *Tales of a Rascal: What I Did for Love.* n.p.: Black Rainbow Publications.
Dr. Phil Show. 2012. "Robert Blake Revealed: The Man behind the Murder Headlines." *Dr. Phil* video, 49. September 20. http://drphil.com/shows/show/1869/. Accessed April 22, 2015.

Bobbed Haired Bandit. *See* Cooney, Celia (1904–1992)

Boesky, Ivan, Insider Trading Scandal (1980s)

Ivan Boesky was a major figure in the 1980s insider trading scandals in the United States. Insider trading involves trading stocks based on information that has not been made public. Buying before good corporate news is announced, or selling before bad news becomes public, enables an inside trader to obtain stocks at a lower price (before the good news becomes public) or unload them at a higher price (before the bad news causes the stock price to fall). Boesky primarily obtained inside information concerning future mergers and acquisitions. He got this information from the lawyers and financiers working on these buyouts, and he used this information to buy the stock of companies at a low price before a merger was announced. Through insider trading, Boesky made a great deal of money. Boesky was eventually turned in by one of the people providing inside information to him. He served a short jail term; however, he did retain most of his ill-gotten gains. He also fingered Michael Milken, who developed the practice of using junk bonds to raid corporations. The prosecution of Milken, Boesky, and others for insider trading ended an era of corruption and merger activity on Wall Street.

Boesky grew up in a middle-class neighborhood in Detroit. His father, an immigrant from Russia, owned a chain of restaurants called The Brass Rail. Ivan began working as well as skirting the law early in life. While still in school, he worked selling ice cream from a truck and was frequently picked up by the police for violating the curfew on his work permit (Stewart 1991, 34).

Boesky attended several Michigan colleges, but never graduated. He then enrolled at the Detroit College of Law (now the Michigan State University College of Law), which did not require a college degree for admission. After dropping out twice, he received his law degree in 1964 and became a partner in his father's restaurant chain (Stewart 1991, 35).

In 1962 Boesky married Seema Silberstein. Her father, a wealthy Detroit real estate developer, bought the couple an expensive Park Avenue apartment in Manhattan so that Boesky could pursue his dream of making a fortune on Wall Street through arbitrage trading.

Arbitrage involves buying and selling in different places, attempting to make money on price differences. If a barrel of oil sells for $100 in Mexico and $101 in Canada, I can make money purchasing oil in Mexico and reselling it in Canada—if I am quicker than other traders. When many people seek to make money this way, it equalizes prices in the two countries; so speed is essential.

Boesky, unfortunately, was not a good arbitrageur. He was fired from his job at Kalb Voorhis when he lost $20,000 on a single trade. At Edward & Hanley, a small brokerage firm with only $1 million in capital, Boesky ran the arbitrage department and took positions that could lead to $2 million losses. His risky investment strategies forced the firm land in bankruptcy in 1975 (Stewart 1991, 36).

With $700,000 in seed money from his wife's family, Boesky started his own firm, Ivan F. Boesky & Co., in 1975. Still unable to make money through arbitrage, Boesky began trading based on inside information he received from Martin Siegel, an investment banker at Kidder, Peabody, and a merger and acquisition star on Wall Street (Bruck 1988, 101). Boesky and Siegel played tennis together and discussed business on a regular basis. Siegel gave Boesky ideas about investment strategies involving mergers and acquisitions. Boesky used these suggestions when making investment decisions. At some point Boesky let Siegel know that he was willing to pay for inside information on upcoming mergers.

Siegel thought that passing information to Boesky was risk-free since he (Siegel) was not doing the trading and because he thought Boesky was too smart to do anything that would attract the attention of securities regulators. In addition, since Boesky did so much trading, Siegel thought it would be impossible to prove that he was trading on inside information in a few instances.

The practice of insider trading is illegal in the United States and most other developed countries. It is thought to be unfair to let someone profit from knowledge that they possess and is not public yet. For example, if senior executives knew their firm was in financial or legal trouble, they could sell any stock they hold in their own firm before this knowledge becomes public. As a result, they would not lose money because they had inside information and were able to trade on it.

Trading on inside information about upcoming merger and acquisition activity enabled Boesky to become so wealthy that he made to the Forbes list of the 400 wealthiest Americans. Boesky made $65 million in 1984 when Chevron bought Gulf and Texaco bought Getty Oil. He made $50 million in 1985 when Philip Morris bought General Foods. In today's dollars these numbers would be more than twice as large.

Siegel, however, did not realize that many other people were also passing inside information to Boesky. Junk bond traders, in particular, regularly provided Boesky with inside information for a percentage of his profits. Junk bonds (low-quality, high-interest bonds) financed numerous mergers and acquisitions during the 1970s and 1980s. Through issuing these bonds, one firm borrowed money and then used that money to buy the stock of a rival it sought to acquire.

Boesky paid Dennis Levine, managing director of Drexel Burnham Lambert, for inside information about the coming merger between Nabisco and R. J. Reynolds (Frantz 1987, 155). Levine was arrested for insider trading in May 1986. He then pled guilty to get a reduced sentence, and turned informant, fingering Boesky and others (Stewart 1991, 265–268).

Boesky realized that he was in trouble and bargained with the SEC (the Securities and Exchange Commission, which is the U.S. agency responsible for regulating and monitoring U.S. stock markets) for a lighter sentence. He pled guilty to insider trading on November 14, 1986, and agreed to pay a $100 million fine; however, he was able to retain most of his ill-gotten wealth. In an ironic twist, the SEC let Boesky sell $440 million of his stock holdings before the public knew of his settlement.

Boesky was wired, leading to 14 individuals charged with securities violations, including Michael Milken, who pioneered the practice of using junk bonds to finance corporate takeovers. The prosecution of Boesky and Milken ended the 1980s merger mania that destroyed many companies. These firms were bought out with junk bonds. When they were unable to make the interest payments required, many firms went under.

In April 1987 Boesky pled guilty in a criminal court to making false statements to the SEC (Bruck 1988, 322). He was never convicted of insider trading, even though he made large amounts of money by this means. He was sentenced to three years in prison, and served 22 months before being released for good behavior.

While Boesky never made a great deal of money legitimately, he did have a great impact on popular culture. Gordon Gekko in the 1987 movie *Wall Street* is based on Boesky, especially the famous "greed is good" speech. In a commencement address at the University of California at Berkeley, Boesky said "Greed is all right…. I think it is healthy. You can be greedy and still feel good about yourself" (Stewart 1991, 223). At that point, the students burst into applause.

STEVEN PRESSMAN

See also: Enron Case (1985–2001); Madoff, Bernard (1938–); Ponzi, Charles (1882–1949); Stewart, Martha, Insider Trading Case (2001–2004)

Further Reading

Alpert, William. 1987. "Judgement Day: Ivan Boesky Draws Three Year Jail Term." *Barron's* December 21: 24–25.

Bruck, Connie. 1988. *The Predator's Ball.* New York: Simon & Schuster.

Frantz, Douglas.1987. *Levine & Co. Wall Street's Insider Trading Scandal.* New York: Harry Holt.

Stewart, James.1991. *Den of Thieves.* New York: Simon & Schuster.

Bonnie and Clyde. *See* Parker, Bonnie (1910–1934) and Clyde Barrow (1909–1934)

Booth, John Wilkes. *See* Lincoln, Abraham, Assassination of (April 14, 1865)

Borden, Lizzie (1860–1927)

Lizzie Borden, an upper-class white female, was accused of murdering her father and stepmother with a hatchet. Lizzie is one of the most well-known female criminals. Not only did she change societal thinking in terms of the "ideal" criminal, but the gruesomeness and unusualness of the case itself led to the creation of a popular children's skipping rope rhyme: "Lizzie Borden had an axe, gave her mother forty whacks, when she'd seen what she had done, she gave her father forty one." Although this rhyme is not entirely accurate to the accounts of the Borden murders, it is widely known and speaks to the significance of this case.

Defendant Lizzie Borden stood trial for the August 1892 axe murders of her father and stepmother in Fall River, Massachusetts. Borden was a respectable spinster, the younger daughter of a wealthy businessman. (Chaiba Media)

Lizzie Andrew Borden was born in Fall River, Massachusetts, to Andrew and Sarah (née Morse) Borden. She had two older sisters, Emma Lenora Borden (b. 1851) and Alice Borden (b. 1856), but Alice died at the age of two. On March 26, 1893, her mother died of uterine congestion and Lizzie's father then married Abby Gray on June 6, 1865. With the death of their mother, Emma became very protective of Lizzie. In 1889, the Borden family hired 23-year-old Bridget Sullivan as their domestic maid.

Lizzie's relationship with her father and stepmother was unstable. This was aggravated in 1890, when the Borden family moved closer to Andrew's work and tensions within the Borden household increased. For example, Lizzie stopped calling Abby "mother" and began referring to her as "Mrs. Borden." This acrimony only increased when Lizzie's father and stepmother suspected her of being behind a burglary of their house. A few months before the murder, Andrew killed a group of pigeons that made a home in their backyard, and to which

Lizzie was quite attached. Although his motives were unknown, he had brought the decapitated birds, with their heads, into the house. This incident disturbed Lizzie and Emma so much that they left their father's house at the end of July 1892, but Lizzie returned home in less than a month. Soon after she arrived, her stepmother complained of nausea and stomach cramps, going so far as to see a physician. According to the physician's record (Dr. Seabury Bowen), Abby believed that she had been poisoned.

On August 4, 1982, Andrew Borden left to run errands, Bridget Sullivan was resting in her room, and Abby went to tidy up a guest bedroom. It was there that she was struck 19 times with a hatchet, causing her skull to cave in. When he returned home from work, Lizzie informed Andrew that Abby had gone to town. Minutes later, Andrew was struck with a hatchet 10 times while he was lying on the sofa.

Cesare Lombroso and the Female Offender

During the 19th century, criminals were viewed as atavistic creatures, as expressed by Cesare Lombroso's theoretical work. Lombroso, through studying the skulls and physical features of criminals, suggested that criminals were evolutionary throwbacks. In his book *The Female Offender*, Lombroso stated that female offenders were criminal because of their inferiority to men, thus causing them to be vengeful, morally lacking, jealous, and predisposed to cruelty. He also believed that females were more ferocious in their crimes than males. Through Lombroso's studies, criminals were viewed as abnormal individuals, who lacked education, and belonged to the poorer socioeconomic classes.

Lizzie was the primary suspect because of the hatred between the stepmother and Lizzie, and she stood to inherit her father's possession. She was arrested and held in Taunton, Massachusetts, until her preliminary trial on August 25, 1892, and was declared "probably guilty" on September 1 by Judge Josiah Blaisdell. On November 15, the grand jury began investigating, and Lizzie was indicted for the murders of Andrew and Abby Borden on

December 2, 1892. The trial, located in New Bedford, Massachusetts, began June 5, 1893. Lizzie's case was presented to three judges, whom ruled that the prosecution could not submit Lizzie's contradicting testimony into evidence, and a jury consisting of 12 men. The prosecuting attorneys (District Attorney Hosea Knowlton and District Attorney Thomas Moody), who rested their case on June 14, argued that Lizzie had both motive and opportunity to commit the murder. The defense team (Andrew Jennings and Melvin Adams), led by ex-governor George Robinson, portrayed Lizzie as a loving individual. He said she had a close relationship with her father and stepmother. On June 20, after approximately 90 minutes of deliberation, Lizzie was acquitted because the prosecution's evidence was circumstantial and Lizzie had not been found with blood on her at the time of the murders.

After her acquittal, Lizzie and her sister moved back into the Borden household. Lizzie received upwards of 200 letters a day, consisting of death threats and marriage proposals. In fact, a Lizzie Borden Fan Club was created in New Bedford. The sisters later moved and withdrew from society. In 1897, Lizzie was accused of shoplifting two paintings from a company in Providence, Rhode Island, which weakened her already questionable reputation and increased her level of isolation. In 1905, Emma, without any explanation, left the residence which she and Lizzie had shared with one another. Neither sister spoke to one another again. On June 1, 1927, Lizzie died from gall bladder operation complications, while Emma died nine days later in Newmarket, New Hampshire.

Lizzie was not a typical criminal suspect. She was an upper class, educated, white female. Although Lizzie was found not guilty by the court, the public was shocked that a woman could be accused of such heinous acts. Not only did the Lizzie Borden trial cause society to consider a different criminal typology, but it also caused society to consider women as having the potential to become violent, which impacted the criminological ideals of the late 18th and early 19th centuries. With the case having such an impact on the criminal justice system, there was a large amount of media coverage of the case, which was unusual for the time period. Such a large amount of media coverage caused society to become exceedingly interested in the case of Lizzie Borden. Due to this, an enormous amount of books and stories have been written about the case. As noted earlier, a children's skipping rope rhyme was even created based on the case, thus demonstrating how significant of a cultural impact the Lizzie Borden case has had on society.

Samantha M. Gavin

See also: Barfield, Velma (1932–1984); Starkweather, Charles, and Caril Ann Fugate, Murder Spree of (1957); *Primary Documents*/Newspaper Account of the Arrest of Lizzie Borden (August 11, 1892)

Further Reading

Kent, David. 1992. *40 Whacks: New Evidence in the Life and Legend of Lizzie Borden*. Dublin, NH: Yankee Publishing, Inc.

Linder, Douglas. 2004. "The Trial of Lizzie Borden." http://law2.umkc.edu/faculty/projects/ftrials/lizzieborden/borden home.html. Accessed April 14, 2015.

Lombroso, Cesare, and Guglielmo Ferro. 1895. *The Female Offender*. New York: D. Appleton and Company.

Rafter, Nicole H. 2009. *The Origins of Criminology: A Reader*. New York: Routledge.

Robertson, Cara W. 1996. "Representing "Miss Lizzie": Cultural Convictions in the Trial of Lizzie Borden." *Yale Journal of Law & the Humanities* 8 (2): 351–416.

Bosket, Willie (1962–)

Once regarded as the most dangerous man in the New York prison system, Willie Bosket engaged in a series of violent criminal acts as a juvenile offender that served as a catalyst for treating children as adults in criminal cases. Convicted of two murders and an attempted murder, a New York family court sentenced 15-year-old Bosket to a maximum term of five years, a sentence that spawned public outrage. Motivated by Bosket's case, the New York State Legislature passed the Juvenile Offender Act of 1978, becoming the first state to authorize trying juveniles as adults. While Bosket could not be sentenced under the new law because it took effect after his conviction, 100 days following his release from incarceration, police arrested Bosket for assault and attempted robbery. Bosket returned to prison, where subsequent attacks earned him three life sentences. Bosket remains incarcerated and is not eligible for parole until 2062.

Willie James Bosket was born on December 9, 1962, to a self-described broken home (Behar 1989). Willie never knew his father, Butch Bosket, who spent much of his life behind bars. Willie completed the third grade before behavior problems kept him out of the public school system. By age nine, his mother sent him to reform school fearing that she could no longer control his behavior. By 15, Willie claimed to have committed more than 2,000 crimes

(Eligon 2008). It was at age 15 that Bosket committed his most notorious crimes.

After stealing $380 from a sleeping passenger on a New York City subway train, Willie purchased a .22 caliber gun from the man who was, at the time, living with Willie's mother. With the gun strapped to his leg, Willie set out to rob someone on the subway (Butterfield 1995). On Sunday, March 19, 1975, Willie found himself with a solitary passenger, Noel Perez, on the number 3 train. Willie stalked 44-year-old Perez, who awoke as Willie drew close. Bosket pulled his weapon and shot the man in the right eye. When Perez screamed, Willie fired another round into his victim's temple. Bosket pulled $15 from the man's pockets, and stole jewelry that he later pawned for $20.

The police had no motive for the murder, and with no witnesses, Willie felt invincible (Ramsland 2009). Four days later, Willie set out with his cousin, Herman Spates, to rob again. The boys found Anthony Lamorte, a railway worker. Lamorte carried a CB radio the boys believed would fetch $100. When Lamorte ordered the boys out of the rail yard, Willie challenged the man. Lamorte alighted from a rail car and closed within 20 feet before Willie opened fire. Shot in the back, Lamorte survived, but police were unable to identify the culprits (Butterfield 1995).

Bosket engaged in two violent robberies over the next two nights—kicking one man down the stairs of a train platform, and shooting another in the hip—before committing his next murder. Just three days after shooting Lamorte, Bosket climbed aboard the uptown train where he found Moises Perez. Bosket demanded the man's money. Moises replied that he didn't have any. Bosket shot Perez, who slumped over in a pool of blood. Bosket rifled through the dying man's pockets and took $2. He threw Perez's wallet in the trash and made his way home, allegedly laughing about the ordeal (Butterfield 1995).

Detective Martin Davin investigated the killings as speculation grew that New York City might be dealing with a serial killer (Ramsland 2009). Combing over police records, Davin turned up Willie Bosket's name. He had been stopped in connection with the previous subway attacks, but released when the victims failed to identify him. Davin brought in Willie's cousin, Herman, who had participated in three of the attacks. Herman quickly turned on Willie.

The district attorney, Robert Silbering, prosecuted Bosket's case, but since Willie was a juvenile, even one with an extensive record, there wasn't much the court could do. Bosket pled guilty on two counts of murder and one count of attempted murder. Judge Edith Miller sentenced Willie

to a maximum sentence of five years—at 21, Willie Bosket would be free.

Crime Runs in the Family

The Bosket family men were no strangers to crime and violence. Willie's grandfather, James Bosket, had a history of abuse and cruelty. As a young married man, James beat his wife and he once fired a gun at her, but missed. James abandoned his family and moved to New Jersey where he was arrested and sentenced to jail for engaging in a string of armed robberies. Carrying on his father's legacy, James's son, Butch Bosket, learned at an early age to embrace a code of violence and toughness. After gaining a reputation as a hustler, Butch became known as the toughest boy on the streets. When he was 14, Butch was sent to live with his recently released father, who consistently abused and beat him. Following in his father's footsteps, Butch became involved in crime and was eventually arrested for armed robbery. After he was released from jail, Butch married a young woman and they were soon expecting a baby boy, Willie. However, Butch never got the chance to witness his son's birth, as he was arrested and sentenced to life in prison for violently attacking and killing a pawnshop owner and bystander. Butch Bosket died years later in a shoot-out with police.

The sentence created public uproar and caught the attention of Governor Hugh Carey, who had previously been opposed to prosecuting juveniles as adults. Outraged by Bosket's sentence, Governor Carey threw his support behind the Juvenile Offender Act of 1978, which provided for prosecuting kids 13 or older as adults for the crime of murder. The law passed and was the first of its kind in the United States. That would not matter for Willie Bosket, however. Since he had committed his crimes prior to the passage of the Juvenile Offender Act, he was not subject to the law's provisions.

Released at 21, Willie enrolled in community college and met a woman who he engaged to marry. But an altercation with a man in Bosket's apartment complex led to another arrest. While in court, Willie began a fight with three guards, which led to a felony assault conviction.

Willie had also tried, unsuccessfully, to escape the Goshen jail facility—his second felony conviction. The judge sentenced him to seven years and 30 days, the maximum sentence. Angry about the sentence, Bosket lashed out at the system, gaining a third felony conviction for arson and assault. Because it was his third felony, the judge sentenced Willie to life in prison. Nothing, it seems, could modify Willie's behavior. A short time later he stabbed a guard with a homemade knife, just missing the man's heart. For that, Bosket earned a second life sentence, followed by a third a few months later for bashing another guard over the head.

Willie Bosket's behavior worsened, earning him the infamous distinction of "most dangerous man" in the New York prison system (Butterfield 1995). Bosket's jailers placed him inside a specially constructed cell and to this day, keep him in isolation. The guards do not speak to Willie, he has no access to television, radio, or newspapers, and he remains shackled on the rare occasions he leaves his cage. Willie Bosket will not be eligible for parole until 2062, so he will likely die behind bars. Nonetheless, his legacy is a permanently changed juvenile justice system.

CHRISTOPHER SHIELDS

Further Reading

Behar, Richard. 1989. "I Won't Kill, I'll Just Maim." *New York Times.* http://content.time.com/time/magazine/article/0,9171,957805,00.html. Accessed April 14, 2015.

Butterfield, Fox. 1995. *All God's Children: The Bosket Family and the American Tradition of Violence.* New York: Alfred A. Knopf.

Eligon, John. 2008. "Two Decades in Solitary." *New York Times.* http://www.nytimes.com/2008/09/23/nyregion/23inmate.html?pagewanted=all&_r=0. Accessed April 14, 2015.

Ramsland, Katherine. 2009. "Willie Bosket," True TV, Crime Library Criminal Minds and Methods. http://web.archive.org/web/20121210112216/http://www.trutv.com/library/crime/notorious_murders/young/bosket/1.html. Accessed April 14, 2015.

Boston Marathon Bombings (April 15, 2013)

On Monday April 15, 2013, two improvised explosive devices (IEDs) detonated within seconds of each other at the 117th Boston Marathon in Massachusetts. Three individuals were killed and 264 others sustained injuries. The impact on the criminal justice system was significant as it called for the cooperation of multiple law enforcement agencies and officers. In addition, the overflow of information and 24/7 news coverage led to widespread criticism following the reporting of incorrect information and false rumors on social media. This ultimately impacted the way law enforcement handled investigative procedures, such as the decision to release images of the suspects to the public. A four-day manhunt led to the identification of Tamerlan and Dzhokhar Tsarnaev as the primary suspects responsible for the bombings, as well as the alleged murder of a campus police officer at the Massachusetts Institute of Technology (MIT). On April 19, four days after the bombings, Tamerlan was killed and Dzhokhar was captured and taken into custody. He was indicted on 30 federal charges, including the use of a weapon of mass destruction.

Approximately 23,000 runners and 500,000 spectators were participating in the 2013 Boston Marathon when the first of two IEDs detonated at 2:49 p.m. in front of Marathon Sports near the finish line. Twelve seconds later, and approximately 200 yards away, a second IED detonated in front of Forum Restaurant. Both devices had been concealed inside dark backpacks and placed on the ground near low metal barriers separating spectators from the marathon course. Forensic evidence revealed that the bombs were constructed from pressure cookers filled with ball bearings and nails. As a result, three people were killed and 264 others injured. At least 16 of those injured needed amputations (Federal Emergency Management Agency 2013).

A significant number of highly trained medical personnel were already stationed near the finish line and were therefore able to offer immediate assistance to victims in the aftermath of the explosions. The National Guard and Boston Police Department were also on site and able to quickly secure and clear the area. The Federal Bureau of Investigation (FBI) became the lead investigative agency, coordinating with over 30 other federal, state, and local law enforcement agencies and more than 1,000 law enforcement officers (Federal Bureau of Investigation 2013). Utilizing surveillance footage from local businesses, as well as the thousands of pictures provided by the public, law enforcement believed they had accurate depictions of the suspects by Wednesday morning, less than 48 hours after the bombings.

On Thursday, April 18, the FBI released photographs and a surveillance video of two suspects in the bombings. The decision to release the images was most likely a result of the media incorrectly reporting that suspects were in custody (Leonard et al. 2014). The identities of the two suspects were not known to law enforcement at the time, but were later identified as Tamerlan and Dzhokhar Tsarnaev, ethnic Chechen brothers living in Cambridge, Massachusetts.

Hours after releasing images of the two suspects, MIT officer Sean Collier was shot and killed while sitting in his patrol car in Cambridge. The suspects allegedly approached his vehicle and shot him multiple times in an attempt to steal his firearm (Leonard et al. 2014). Shortly thereafter, the suspects carjacked a SUV, kidnapping the driver. The driver was able to escape and contact authorities, who soon located the stolen vehicle in Watertown, Massachusetts. After coming into contact with the suspects, law enforcement came under fire, leading to a mass shootout. According to authorities, Tamerlan was shot multiple times before Dzhokhar drove off in the stolen SUV, running over Tamerlan in the process (*United States v. Dzhokhar Tsarnaev* 2013). Tamerlan was pronounced dead early Friday morning and an autopsy confirmed that he suffered from gunshot wounds and blunt trauma to his head and torso (Bidgood 2013).

Following the shootout in Watertown, an 18-hour manhunt ensued and a shelter-in-place order was issued for parts of Boston and surrounding neighborhoods. Shortly after the shelter-in-place order was lifted Friday evening, a Watertown resident found the second suspect hiding in his dry-docked boat in the backyard of his property. After being forced out by flash-bangs, Dzhokhar was taken into custody and transported to a local hospital for medical care. On Friday, April 19, at 9:32 p.m., law enforcement confirmed that the second suspect in the bombings was in custody (Leonard et al. 2014).

The Impact of Social Media on the Investigation

A key criticism in the aftermath of the bombings focused on media reporting errors and rumors circulating on social media. This impacted law enforcement's response to the high-profile event and the way the investigation was handled (e.g., releasing images of the suspects to the public). The day of the bombings, *The New York Post* reported that law enforcement sources confirmed a Saudi Arabian male was under guard at a local hospital and was being treated as a suspect, even though law enforcement denied the reports. Several other news outlets also mistakenly reported that an arrest had been made or that a suspect was in custody. In addition, photographs of "suspicious" individuals circulated social media sites, claiming that the FBI was looking for them in connection with the bombings. Once the FBI released official images of the bombing suspects, it was made clear that no other images were credible.

Tamerlan and Dzhokhar Tsarnaev immigrated to the United States after their Chechen family fled the Caucasus region of Russia in 2002. Tamerlan, 26 at the time of his death, was married to a U.S. citizen and was a lawful permanent resident living in Cambridge, Massachusetts. Dzhokhar, 19, was a naturalized U.S. citizen and a student at the University of Massachusetts Dartmouth (Volpp 2014).

According to law enforcement, the suspects were most likely motivated by extremist Islamic beliefs. Reports suggest that Tamerlan had become radicalized over time (Globe Staff 2013). Law enforcement confiscated computers from the suspects and reportedly discovered content advocating violent jihad. Additionally, they found an electronic copy of *Inspire Magazine*, a publication by al-Qaeda affiliates, detailing how to build pressure-cooker bombs. Furthermore, Dzhokhar had allegedly written extremist messages inside the boat he had been hiding in prior to his capture. In the messages, Dzhokhar claimed responsibility for the bombings and justified them as retribution for the innocent killing of Muslims (*United States v. Dzhokhar Tsarnaev* 2013).

Law enforcement was criticized when the public became aware that the FBI had previously carried out an assessment of Tamerlan. In 2011, the Russian government had contacted the FBI requesting more information about him, citing they had reason to believe he had been radicalized and was preparing to travel overseas. However, after conducting interviews with Tamerlan and his family, the FBI found no evidence to suggest a terrorist agenda (Office of the Director of National Intelligence 2014).

On April 22, 2013, Dzhokhar Tsarnaev was indicted on 30 federal charges, including the use of a weapon of mass destruction and the murder of MIT officer Sean Collier. On May 15, 2015, Tsarnaev was sentenced to death. His trial began in January 2015 in Boston, and he was found guilty on all 30 counts in the indictment on April 8, 2015.

Courtney D. Hopkins

See also: Hasan, Nidal Malik (1970–); Oklahoma City Bombing (April 19, 1995); September 11 Terrorist Attacks (2001); *Primary Documents*/Boston Marathon Bombing: House Resolution Commending Heroism of Slain MIT Police Officer Sean Collier (April 23, 2013)

Further Reading

Bidgood, Jess. 2013. "Autopsy Says Boston Bombing Suspect Died of Gunshot Wounds and Blunt Trauma." *The New York Times*. May 4. http://www.nytimes.com/2013/05/05/us/autopsy-says-boston-bombing-suspect-died-of-gunshot-wounds-and-blunt-trauma.html?_r=1&. Accessed November 13, 2014.

Federal Bureau of Investigation. 2013. "Updates on Investigation into Multiple Explosions in Boston." http://www.fbi.gov/news/updates-on-investigation-into-multiple-explosions-in-boston. Accessed April 13, 2015.

Federal Emergency Management Agency. 2013. *Boston Marathon Bombings: Hospital Readiness and Response.* Washington, D.C.: United States Department of Homeland Security. https://www.hsdl.org/?view&did=744165. Accessed April 9, 2015.

Globe Staff. 2013. "The Fall of the House of Tsarnaev." *The Boston Globe*. December 15. http://www.bostonglobe.com/metro/2013/12/15/the-fall-house-tsarnaev/lg5Q3XqtbOO-QR1ZCWgB1sK/story.html. Accessed April 9, 2015.

Helman, Scott, and Jenna Russell. 2014. *Long Mile Home: Boston Under Attack, the City's Courageous Recovery, and the Epic Hunt for Justice.* New York: Dutton.

Leonard, Herman B., Christine M. Cole, Arnold M. Howitt, and Philip B. Heymann. 2014. "Why Was Boston Strong? Lessons from the Boston Marathon Bombing." Harvard Kennedy School. April. http://www.hks.harvard.edu/content/download/67366/1242274/version/1/file/WhyWasBostonStrong.pdf. Accessed April 9, 2015.

Office of the Director of National Intelligence. 2014. *Unclassified Summary of Information Handling and Sharing Prior to the April 15, 2013 Boston Marathon Bombings.* April 10. http://www.dni.gov/files/documents/ICIG_Forum_Boston_Marathon_Bombings_Review_-_Unclassified_Summary.pdf. Accessed April 9, 2015.

United States v. Dzhokhar Tsarnaev. 2013. United States District Court. 13CR10200. June 27. http://www.justice.gov/usao/ma/news/2013/June/Indictment1.pdf. Accessed April 9, 2015.

Volpp, Leti. 2014. "The Boston Bombers." *Fordham Law Review* 82 (5): 2209–2220. http://ir.lawnet.fordham.edu/cgi/viewcontent.cgi?article=4983&context=flr. Accessed April 9, 2015.

Boston Massacre (March 5, 1770)

There were several key events that played a role in the lead up to the American Revolutionary War. One of the most notable events was the Boston Massacre. The events that unfolded the evening of March 5, 1770, as well as the subsequent criminal trials were influential in America's fight for independence. However, one must understand the events that led up to this fateful date in American history as well as the actual event itself. In 1767, the Townshend Acts began taxing colonists as a means of funding governor and judicial salaries. However, the colonists did not welcome the Townshend Acts. In fact, the colonies took official stance against the acts by petitioning King George III to repeal the acts. The crown responded by sending military support to Boston. On October 1, 1768, British troops began moving in to Boston. The colonists did not take kindly to the influx of British troops. The troops were housed in private homes and public buildings. Furthermore, British troops would take extra jobs around Boston; thus, Bostonians were housing and providing additional income to the British troops. The colonists were not accepting this intrusion quietly; rather, the Bostonians would attempt to incite the troops by yelling insults at them as they passed. The increase of anger toward the British Crown's taxation, and the increase in British troop presence, created an unabated tension between the colonists and the British troops. This helped lead to the events of March 5, 1770.

March 5 was not unlike others; British soldiers stood on guard throughout Boston. On King Street, wigmaker apprentice Edward Garrick shouted at British captain Goldfinch that he had not paid his debt to Garrick's master. This was merely a tactic to incite an argument. Captain Goldfinch had paid his debt and simply ignored Mr. Garrick. However, Private White, another British soldier, took offense to the colonist antagonizing his superior officer. Private White and Mr. Garrick spat insults at each other. Ultimately, Private White left his assigned position and hit Mr. Garrick in the head with his musket. The colonists noted this action and a crowd began to form around Private White. As the evening progressed the crowd began to grow to approximately 50 colonists. The church bells rang out to warn the citizens of a fire. This tactic was utilized to draw a larger crowd. The crowd was becoming rambunctious and began challenging Private White to fire his weapon. It was at this point that Private White began to seek assistance. Captain Preston dispatched one noncommissioned officer and six privates to join Private White at his post. The soldiers included Corporal Wemms and Privates Montgomery, Carroll, McCauley, Warren, and Kilroy.

Upon arrival, Captain Preston had his men load their muskets. The crowd was now estimated to be over 300. As Captain Preston yelled at the crowd to disperse they continued to taunt the soldiers. The Bostonians would yell, "fire," at the troops and throw snowballs at them. These tactics were used to tempt the soldiers to open fire so the colonists could legally react. At one point, Private Montgomery was struck by a thrown object and fell to the ground. Testimony states that he gathered himself and yelled, "Damn you, fire!" before discharging his rifle into the crowd (Zobel 1970, 197). Captain Preston did not give him the command to fire his weapon. A local innkeeper swung his club and contacted Montgomery in the arm. He then attempted to hit Captain Preston in the head, but, instead, struck him in the arm as well.

There was a pause in the action; however, it is not clear if the pause was a few mere seconds or minutes. Following the pause, the soldiers, without an order from Captain Preston, opened fire into the crowd. The shots struck 11 citizens in total. The crowds quickly moved from the point of attack and continued to grow in size in the adjacent streets. Captain Preston called in a large portion of the British soldiers to man defensive positions. The governor, Thomas Hutchinson, fought through the crowd and made his way onto a balcony overlooking the scene. He was able to restore order after promising a fair inquiry into the shootings would be made. Five men were killed. These include Samuel Gray, James Caldwell, Crispus Attucks, Samuel Maverick, and Patrick Carr.

Governor Hutchinson kept his promise and immediately began investigating the events of the evening. The next morning, Captain Preston and the soldiers had been arrested. Tensions between the Bostonians and the remaining British troops remained high. In fact, Governor Hutchinson held meetings with his council and the commanding officer of the British troops. During these meetings it was decided that they should remove the troops from the city. Governor Hutchinson, realizing Boston was too agitated for a fair trial, utilized this period to delay the trials for several months. Governor Hutchinson was adamant that the soldiers receive a fair trial. There was a lot at stake. If the soldiers did not receive a fair trial the British loyalists or colonists could retaliate depending on which side perceived the trial to be unfair. To this extent, the governor sought counsel that would fairly represent the troops. Eventually, John Adams, Josiah Quincy II,

Sampson Blowers, and Paul Revere agreed to represent the troops, while Samuel Quincy and Robert Paine handled the prosecution. The first trial did not begin until October 24, 1770—10 months after the incident occurred. The first trial was only for Captain Preston. The jury acquitted him after finding he did not order the troops to fire their weapons.

Who Was Crispus Attucks?

Crispus Attucks was an important figure in the Boston Massacre. However, little is known about his life outside of the events surrounding the massacre. Mr. Attucks was half Native American and half African descent. It is unclear whether he was a slave or free man; however, historians believe that Bostonians accepted him. Mr. Attucks was the first man shot at the Boston Massacre and is referred to as the first martyr of the American Revolution. He is considered one of the most important figures in African American history, not for what he did for his own race but what he did for all oppressed people.

The second trial began on November 27, 1770. To keep the trial fair, John Adams instructed the jury to ignore that their defendants were British troops. Rather, the jurors should decide if the soldiers were endangered by the mob of Bostonians. If they were truly endangered they had the right to fight back and were innocent. However, if the soldiers' lives were never endangered they were guilty of manslaughter. The jury ultimately agreed with John Adams. Six of the soldiers were acquitted after only two and half hours of deliberation. However, two soldiers were found guilty of manslaughter. The jury found them guilty because of the substantial evidence showing they fired directly into the crowd. The jury opined that they believed the soldiers felt threatened by the mob, but they should have delayed firing into the crowd.

Four civilians were also tried for their actions that night. However, there were no strong witnesses so the prosecution did not press the case. All four civilians were acquitted of their crimes that evening. Overall, the Boston Massacre Trials quietly came to an end. The events that occurred on March 5, 1770, were fundamental to the American Revolution. Patriots, including John Adams, believed the foundation of independence from British rule was established with the Boston Massacre. This event turned colonial opinion against King George III. While the Boston Massacre did not ignite the American Revolution by itself, it is believed by various scholars to have started the divisive relationship between the British Parliament and American colonies.

M. HUNTER MARTAINDALE

See also: Arnold, Benedict (1741–1801); Burr, Aaron, Treason Trial of (1807); Haymarket Square Riot/Bombing (Chicago) (1886)

Further Reading

Neyland, James. 1995. *Crispus Attucks: Patriot.* Los Angeles: Holloway House Publishing.

Zobel, Hiller B. 1970. *Boston Massacre.* New York: W.W. Norton & Company.

Boston Strangler Murders (1962–1964)

The Boston Strangler Murders influenced the way we label individuals in the criminal justice system. For decades many identified Albert DeSalvo as the Boston Strangler; however, new technology providing DNA analysis paved the way for reevaluating circumstantial evidence. DeSalvo's confession and acknowledgment of detailed facts while confined in a Boston State Hospital led to what appeared as an open-and-shut case. At the time women were frightened, yet trust of strangers such as the workman to enter one's home was commonplace. While the case still remains open today, most have accepted DeSalvo as the Boston Strangler. Recent funding from the National Institute of Justice's "cold case" examinations to the Boston Police Department may finally close the case. DNA from Mary Sullivan, the last victim of the Boston Strangler, initially did not match DeSalvo; however, through this new program of testing Y-STR's (male Y chromosomes on short-tandem repeats), Boston officials claimed the match implicated DeSalvo in Sullivan's murder. Moreover, the match excluded 99.9 percent of the male population. While this provides answers to Sullivan's killer, the question still remains as to whether DeSalvo was in fact the Boston Strangler (Bulman 2014).

The months of June 1962 through January 1964 created a wave of panic in the Boston community. Starting with the murder of Anna Slesers, strangled in her apartment, a continuation of sexual assaults and murders on

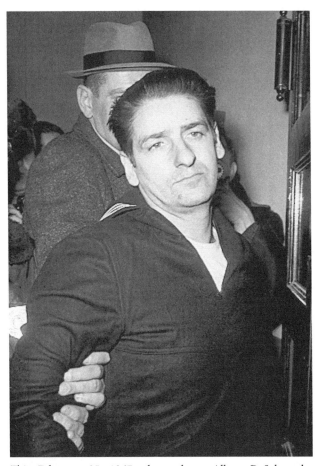

This February 25, 1967, photo shows Albert DeSalvo, the self-confessed serial killer, minutes after his capture in Boston. Claiming to be the "Boston Strangler," DeSalvo confessed to the murders officially attributed to the killer. (AP Photo)

five other elderly women caused police to assume a serial sexual sadist was on the loose. After the body of Helen Blake was found, police began to question all known sex offenders and males aged 18 to 40 released from mental institutions between 1960 and 1962. After investigations and lie-detector tests failed to match any of the men questioned, police issued a statement to all women, specifically lone residents to keep all windows and apartment doors locked, to report any suspicious men seen in the area, and to not allow any strangers into their residence. For three weeks, there were no identifying patterns of similar murder and police hoped the sexual assault and murder on Boston women was ending. However, on August 21, 1962, the body of Ida Irga was found with the same modus operandi as the other women: Sexually assaulted, strangled, her body left half-naked, spread out as if posing for a magazine photo with stockings (in other cases pantyhose or a pillowcase), tied around her neck. This moment solidified the initial thought of the Boston police—a serial killer was at work. By the end of August 1962, a sixth victim was found. Jane Sullivan had been dead for over a week when police discovered her body. It was determined Ms. Sullivan died one day after Ms. Irga. The deaths of both Ida Irga and Jane Sullivan in such close proximity showed an increase in the killer's desire to hunt.

It was not until the murder of Sophie Clark, a 20-year-old black student in December 1962, where the killer seemed to deviate from his pattern. Older women were no longer the only target and the man, identified as the "Boston Strangler," was expanding his range of victims. Following Ms. Clark, 23-year-old Patricia Bissette was also murdered in a similar fashion on December 31, 1962. The deaths of five other women aged 19 to 69 through January 1964, the failure of the Boston police to find the Boston Strangler, and an angry public caused the attorney general to take over the case. He assembled a task force to work throughout 1964. A break in the case occurred on October 27 when Albert DeSalvo, a handyman, was identified by a woman who was sexually assaulted in her apartment. During 1958 through 1960 the police received many reports of an individual nicknamed "The Measuring Man," a fake modeling agent who selected young women to take measurements and then seduced these women. During an arrest in 1960, DeSalvo admitted to being "The Measuring Man," but served only 10 months in prison and was out on parole. Reports from surrounding states also identified DeSalvo as the "Green Man" rapist nicknamed as such because the rapist wore green work clothes while committing his sexual assaults. DeSalvo was sentenced to a mental institution in Bridgewater, Massachusetts, in 1965. At the time, police had not identified DeSalvo as "The Boston Strangler;" however, a conversation with another inmate in Bridgewater revealed a major breakthrough in the Strangler case. George Nassar heard about the $100,000 reward for anyone able to provide information pertaining to the Strangler. He contacted his attorney, F. Lee Bailey about conversations with DeSalvo, which caused Bailey to interview and record DeSalvo and turn the tapes over to the police and attorney general. While DeSalvo was known as a narcissistic braggart, many including assistant attorney general John Bottomly believed "The Boston Strangler's" identity was now known. The taped conversations allegedly provided detailed information about the murders that only the killer could have known.

After the prosecution argued DeSalvo was sane enough to serve trial for crime committed while out on the streets (armed robbery, theft, sexual crimes, and breaking and entering), a conviction and sentence of life imprisonment was imposed. DeSalvo was never convicted for "The Boston Strangler" murders, nor was he officially declared "The Boston Strangler."

For decades the name Albert DeSalvo and "The Boston Strangler" were synonymous with one another. After his murder in Walpole State Prison in 1973, many believed "The Boston Strangler" had died. In 2001, however, new questions arose about the identity of the Strangler. Mary Sullivan, a 19-year-old and last known victim, was exhumed, with DNA analysis conducted by forensic scientists at George Washington University. Tests of stains from Ms. Sullivan's underwear indicated that they did not match her or DeSalvo's DNA. This led to the conclusion that someone else was responsible for her murder. A new examination of Sullivan's DNA against DeSalvo's nephews' found contradictory evidence. Testing the male Y chromosome against STRs (short-tandem repeats) on DNA patterns found a match so strong it excluded 99.9 percent of males in the population. With these results, the Boston Police Department exhumed DeSalvo's body in July 2013 to confirm the findings. Using DNA from a femur bone and three teeth provided all the evidence needed: the odds of another male committing this crime were 1 in 220 billion! Overall, "The Boston Strangler" murders are considered unsolved today but now we may be one step closer to solving this 50-plus year mystery (Bulman 2014).

STACIE MERKEN

See also: Bianchi, Kenneth (1951–) and Angelo Buono (1934–2002); Bundy, Ted (1946–1989); Rader, Dennis (1945–); Ramirez, Richard (1960–2013)

Further Reading

Bulman, Philip. 2014. *Solving Cold Case with DNA: The Boston Strangler Case.* Washington, D.C.: National Institute of Justice.

Foran, David, and James E. Starrs. 2004. "In Search of the Boston Strangler: Genetic Evidence from the Exhumation of Mary Sullivan." *Medicine, Science, and the Law* 44 (1): 47–54.

Greig, Charlotte. 2006. *Evil Serial Killers: In the Minds of Monsters.* New York: Arcturus Publishing Limited.

Innes, Brian. 2006. *Serial Killers: The Stories of History's Most Evil Murderers.* London: Quercus Publishing, plc.

Lane, Brian, and Wilfred Gregg. 1995. *The Encyclopedia of Serial Killers.* New York: The Berkley Publishing Group.

Vronksy, Peter. 2004. *Serial Killers: The Method and Madness of Monsters.* New York: Berkley Books.

Boy Fiend. *See* Pomeroy, Jesse (1859–1932)

Brando, Christian (1958–2008)

Christian Brando was the eldest child of legendary Hollywood actor Marlon Brando Jr. and actress Anna Kashfi. The marriage ended in divorce and the relationship between Christian's parents quickly deteriorated. After years of arguments, Marlon Brando was awarded sole custody of Christian Brando after Kashfi kidnapped Christian. In his teen years, Christian began abusing drugs and alcohol, dropped out of high school, and ran away to Washington to live with friends. Marlon Brando fully supported his son's decision and purchased a small cabin for Christian. Christian divided his time between his cabin in Washington and his father's house in Beverly Hills. On the evening of May 16, 1990, Christian's half-sister Cheyenne Brando confided in him that her boyfriend Dag Drollet had been physically abusive in their relationship. Later in the evening, Drollet was killed at Marlon Brando's residence after an altercation occurred between Drollet and Christian. Christian was charged with murder, but eventually pleaded guilty to voluntary manslaughter. Christian was sentenced to 10 years in prison but only served 5 years.

Christian Devi Brando was born on May 11, 1958. Brando was born in Los Angeles, California, to Hollywood acting legend Marlon Brando Jr. and actress Anna Kashfi. Christian Brando was the oldest of the 16 identified children of Marlon Brando. Anna Kashfi became pregnant with Brando's child in 1957, and in 1958 Marlon Brando and Anna Kashfi were married. However, the marriage quickly deteriorated and ended in divorce in 1959. Brando and Kashfi engaged in a prolonged and hostile custody battle over Christian. In 1972, Kashfi kidnapped Christian from school and drove him to Baja California, Mexico. Brando hired a group of private investigators, who found Christian living in a tent and suffering from bronchial pneumonia. This incident coupled with Kashfi's abuse of alcohol and drugs helped Brando gain sole custody of Christian (Biography 2015). However, the prolonged and hostile custody battle between Marlon Brando and Anna Kashfi had a major effect on the psychological well-being of Christian (Gribben 2007, 1).

As a teenager, Christian began drinking and using drugs, and he dropped out of high school. While Christian appeared in two small film roles as a child, he was not interested in following in his father's famous footsteps. Christian was also not interested in being in the spotlight that came with being the child of Marlon Brando. Christian Brando ran away to Washington to live with family friends. While in Washington, Christian developed an interest in artistic welding and was later supported in his endeavor by his father who bought him a cabin to practice his art (Biography, 2015). Christian split his time between his cabin in Washington and his father's home in Beverly Hills. Christian also returned to acting, appearing in four films and four made-for-TV productions between 1980 and 1990 (IMDB 2015).

On May 16, 1990, Christian Brando had dinner with his half-sister Cheyenne Brando at Musso & Frank Grill in Los Angeles, California. It was at this dinner that Cheyenne confided in Christian that her boyfriend of four years, Dag Drollet, had been physically abusive to her (McDougal and Murphy 2002, 178). Cheyenne Brando was eight months pregnant at the time and concerned about the well-being of her child. Christian had only just met Drollet a few hours prior to the dinner. But around 11:00 p.m., Christian Brando confronted Drollet about the abuse claims. The confrontation happened in the den of Marlon Brando's residence in Beverly Hills, California. In an attempt to scare Drollet, Brando brandished a .45-caliber firearm. However, the incident quickly escalated and Drollet was fatally shot (Gribben 2007, 6).

Christian Brando was immediately arrested and was charged with first-degree murder on May 18, 1990. Prosecutors felt that Cheyenne was a crucial component to prove that the murder was premeditated, however, Cheyenne refused to testify and fled back to Tahiti. On June 26, she gave birth to a son Tuki Brando (Ellis and Ellis 2005, 231). After the birth of her son, Cheyenne attempted suicide twice, and was hospitalized at the request of Marlon Brando for drug detoxification in a psychiatric hospital (Gribben 2007, 8). On December 22, 1990, Cheyenne was declared "mentally disabled" by a French judge and was deemed unable to testify in her brother's trial. After several attempts, a judge eventually stopped all efforts by the prosecution to get her to return (Ellis and Ellis 2005, 232). A taped confession from Christian Brando was ruled inadmissible because Brando was not fully advised of his Miranda rights in that he could have an attorney provided for him, if he could not afford one (Ellis and Ellis 2005, 232).

Initially, Brando claimed that his intention was only to scare Drollet and that the scuffle that ensued accidentally caused the firearm to go off. However, forensics revealed that Drollet died from a gunshot wound to the back of the head and not to the face (Ellis and Ellis 2005, 231). Furthermore, the paramedics on the scene told investigators that the den did not display signs of a struggle and that Drollet was found holding his tobacco pouch in one hand and the television remote in the other (Gribben 2007, 8). The prosecutors felt that without Cheyenne and the confession, they could not prove the death was premeditated. Prosecutors then presented Brando and his lawyer Robert Shapiro with a plea deal (Ellis and Ellis 2005, 232).

On January 5, 1991, Christian Brando pleaded guilty to voluntary manslaughter; however, this guilty plea did not include a sentencing guarantee (Ellis and Ellis 2005, 232). Three months after the guilty plea, Christian's sentencing hearing was held. During the sentencing hearing, prosecutors pushed for the maximum 16-year penalty. Marlon Brando took to the stand and pushed for a lesser sentence citing his failure as a parent in contributing to Christian's development. Judge Robert Thomas decided to split the difference and on March 1, 1991, sentenced Brando to a 10-year term of imprisonment (Gribben 2007, 10). Under the sentencing laws at the time, with good behavior and time served, Brando could be released in four years. Christian Brando served his time at the California Men's Colony at San Luis Obispo. During his incarceration, Cheyenne Brando committed suicide by hanging herself after losing custody of her child (Ellis and Ellis 2005, 235). Brando was released from prison in 1995 and returned to Washington.

Christian Brando was later suspected in the murder of Bonnie Lee Bakley—the wife of actor Robert Blake (1933–) (Thurber 2008). During the murder trial, Blake and his defense attorneys claimed that Brando murdered Bakley after learning that he was the father of her child, but a DNA test proved Blake to be the father (King 2001, 35). Brando was called to testify during the civil proceedings, but was held in contempt of court for refusing to testify by invoking his Fifth Amendment rights (Thurber 2008). Christian Brando died of pneumonia on January 26, 2008; he had just recently settled a lawsuit from his second wife claiming spousal abuse (Thurber 2008).

JOSEPH JOHN PASHEA, JR.

See also: Blake, Robert; Murder Trial of (2005); Crane, Bob, Murder of (1978); O'Connell, John, Jr., Kidnapping of (1933)

Further Reading

"Christian Brando." The Biography.com. http://www.biography.com/people/christian-brando-235819/. Accessed January 15 2015.

"Christian Brando." Internet Movie Database.com. http://www.imdb.com/name/nm0113598/. Accessed January 10, 2015.

"Christian Brando." 2008. *The Daily Telegraph*, January 28. http://www.telegraph.co.uk/news/worldnews/1576832/Christian-Brando.html. Accessed April 9, 2015.

Dawson, Nick. 2010. "Marlon Brando's Son Kidnapped: March 20, 1972." http://www.focusfeatures.com/article/marlon_brando_s_son_kidnapped. Accessed January 15, 2015

Ellis, Chris, and Julie Ellis. 2005. "The Mulholland Murder—Christian Brando." In *The Mammoth Book of Celebrity Murders*. New York: Carroll & Graf Publishers, pp. 223–241.

Gribben, Mark. 2007. "Christian Brando—A Hollywood Tragedy." Crimelibrary.com. http://web.archive.org/web/20110728063801/http://www.trutv.com/library/crime/notorious_murders/family/christian_brando/1.html. Accessed January 15, 2015.

King, Gary C. 2001. *Murder in Hollywood: The Secret Life and Mysterious Death of Bonny Lee Bakley*. New York: St. Martin's Press.

McDougal, Dennis, and Mary Murphy. 2002. *Blood Cold: Fame, Sex and Murder in Hollywood*. New York: New American Library.

Thurber, Jon. 2008. "Son of Acting Legend Was Guilty of Killing His Half-Sister's Lover." *Los Angeles Times*, January 27. http://articles.latimes.com/2008/jan/27/local/me-brando27. Accessed April 9, 2015.

Brandon, Teena, Murder of (1993)

Teena Brandon (1972–1993) was a young woman who was beaten and raped for being transgender. She was born female but presented herself as a man and wanted to become male. She was assaulted and murdered for being transgender by two men, Marvin Thomas (Tom) Nissen and John Lotter. Nissen and Lotter were convicted of Teena's murder, and were also charged with the deaths of Lisa Lambert and Philip DeVine, who were with Teena at the time of her death. Nissen was sentenced to life in prison and Lotter received the death penalty. This case highlights concerns about how society and law enforcement treat transgendered victims.

Teena Brandon was born in Lincoln, Nebraska, on December 12, 1972. Teena was attracted to women, but did not consider herself a lesbian. Teena wanted to have a sex change operation to become a man. She portrayed herself as a man, using names like Brandon or Billy. Teena was known to be deceitful and had multiple encounters with the police.

Teena moved to Humboldt, Nebraska, where she met and started a relationship with Lana Tisdel. Along with Lana, Teena made friends with several others including Tom Nissen, John Lotter, and Phillip DeVine. It did not take long for Teena to get into trouble by forging checks for money. Teena was arrested for forgery on December 15, 1993. When Lana arrived for a visit, she found her boyfriend in the women's side of the prison. Upon release on December 22, 1993, Teena and Lana returned to Nissen's house, who had offered Teena a place to stay.

On December 24, 1993, Teena, Lana, Nissen, and Lotter were at Nissen's house for a party. Nissen and Lotter had been drinking and forced Teena to reveal her gender. They pulled Teena's pants down and made Lana look at Teena. Shortly after this event, Lana went home and left Teena alone with Nissen and Lotter. Still drunk, Nissen and Lotter beat Teena, put her in a car, and drove her to a secluded spot. They raped Teena and continued to beat her. When it was over, Nissen warned Teena not to tell anyone. Teena found Lana and told her what happened. Lana encouraged Teena to report the rape, which Teena did.

Sheriff Charles B. Laux questioned Teena about the events of the reported crime. He asked many questions that did not have anything to do with the assault. He did not understand Teena's sexuality and pressed her for answers about her gender identity. The questions made Teena stop answering. At the end of the questioning, Teena signed a complaint to file charges against Nissen and Lotter. Nissen and Lotter, however, were not immediately questioned and evidence later showed that Sheriff Laux warned the two men about the complaint Teena had filed against them. On December 28, 1993, the two men were questioned by the police about the assault. After the interview, they decided to murder Teena.

Nissen and Lotter spent several days trying to find Teena to murder her. They waited outside of the police station on December 30, 1993, because they knew Teena had a follow-up interview. Teena did not enter the building when she spotted the men, which kept Nissen and Lotter from carrying out the murder plot. Nissen and Lotter continued drinking throughout the day and eventually discovered Teena's location. She was staying with another friend named Lisa Lambert.

When Nissen and Lotter entered Lisa's home, it appeared empty. However, Lisa, Lisa's eight-month-old son, Teena, and another one of their friends, Philip DeVine,

were in the home. Nissen and Lotter kicked in a bedroom door and found Lisa in bed. When they pressed her for information, she denied Teena was there, but the men found Teena hiding in some blankets. In later statements, Nissen says that he was distracted by the crying baby and did not mean to shoot Teena. Teena was shot and then stabbed in the stomach. Nissen and Lotter also killed Lisa and Philip to leave no witnesses. The baby was not hurt.

Nissen and Lotter were almost immediately arrested for the murders. The trial for Nissen began on February 21, 1995, and ended on March 3, 1995. Nissen was found guilty of first-degree murder for the deaths of Teena Brandon, Lisa Lambert, and Philip DeVine. Nissen's sentence was deferred until Lotter was tried. He used this time to his advantage to make a deal with the prosecutor. Nissen agreed to testify against Lotter in exchange for a sentence of three terms of life imprisonment instead of the death penalty.

The trial for Lotter began on May 15, 1995, and ended on May 25, 1995. Lotter was also convicted of first-degree murder for the deaths of Teena Brandon, Lisa Lambert, and Philip DeVine. Along with the murder convictions, Lotter was also found guilty of three counts of using a deadly weapon and one count of burglary. Lotter received the death penalty.

Sheriff Laux was also held partially responsible for warning Nissen and Lotter. Teena's mother, JoAnn Brandon, sued Sheriff Laux and Richardson County for the wrongful death of Teena. The Nebraska Supreme Court reinstated the case after it was dismissed in a lower court. The court found that Sheriff Laux had failed to protect Teena which may have led to her murder. The Brandon family was awarded $17,000. In 2001, the Nebraska Supreme Court reversed the reductions in the award, and the Brandon family received a total award of $80,000.

Lotter appealed his death sentence. He applied for an appeal in 2001 for deoxyribonucleic acid (DNA) testing on the gloves Nissen wore during the murders. The defense attorney argued that it would show that Nissen was the shooter, not Lotter. The appeal was denied because the judge stated that it might show blood was there, but no tests would be able to show how the blood got on the gloves.

In June 2003, Lotter took his appeal to the Nebraska Supreme Court. This time, the defense attorney argued that Nissen confessed his role in the murders to a cellmate and that cellmate was not allowed to testify at Lotter's trial. DNA testing was also requested by Lotter's attorney again. The appeal was again denied.

Nissen released a statement on September 19, 2007, stating that Lotter was not the shooter. Nissen claimed that he was the one who shot and killed Teena Brandon, Lisa Lambert, and Philip DeVine. Lotter filed another appeal with the Nebraska Supreme Court on September 4, 2009, using Nissen's statement that he lied during Lotter's trial in a final attempt to get his death sentence overturned. The Nebraska Supreme Court ruled that Lotter had failed to provide evidence that his constitutional rights were violated. After an appeal to the Eighth U.S. Circuit Court of Appeals in 2011, Lotter petitioned the U.S. Supreme Court. In 2012, the Supreme Court declined to review his case.

ANGELA M. COLLINS

See also: Shepard, Matthew, Murder of (1998)

Further Reading

Blanco, J.I. "Brandon Teena Murder Trial: 1995—The Rape and Murder, the Trials, Gender Issues." *Law Library—American Law and Legal Information.* http://law.jrank.org/pages/3684/Brandon-Teena-Murder-Trial-1995.html. Accessed April 14, 2015.

Blanco, J.I. "John L. Lotter." *Murderpedia.* http://murderpedia.org/male.L/l/lotter-john.htm. Accessed April 14, 2015.

"Teena Brandon, an American Tragedy." *Friedman Law Offices.* http://www.friedmanlaw.com/Articles/Teena-Brandon-An-American-Tragedy.shtml. Accessed April 14, 2015.

Branion, Dr. John (c. 1926–1990)

Branion was a prominent African American physician during the civil rights movement. He was educated at the University of Lausanne in Switzerland during a time when discrimination was widely practiced and accepted in America. His father was a prominent criminal defense attorney in Chicago and acted as the deputy public defender in Cook County, the first African American man to do so. His brother-in-law was also a successful attorney and his wife, Donna, came from one of the wealthiest black families in Chicago. The couple had two children, a daughter and a son.

Branion was well known for his activism within the civil rights movement, walking with Dr. Martin Luther King, Jr. during his visits to Chicago, tending to injured Black Panthers and other activists. Such activism at the time put him on a list of "undesirables" by the U.S. Department of Justice. Unfortunately for Branion, it was not his activism that he was remembered for, but for the mysterious death of his wife.

At 11:30 a.m. on December 22, 1967, Dr. John Branion rode off in his car from the Ida Mae Scott Hospital on Chicago's South Side. After picking up his son from nursery school, he arrived at his home and found his wife, Donna, lying on the utility room floor. She had been shot several times. He did not check the body for signs of life but immediately summoned police help. A neighbor, Dr. Helen Payne, examined the body to confirm death.

There was no sign of forced entry and Donna had not been sexually assaulted. Robbery did not appear to be a motive. Donna did not have any known enemies, nor was money an issue for the family and Branion did not stand to inherit anything in the case of his wife's death. Police initially recovered three bullets and four cartridge casings. The fourth bullet would eventually be found during autopsy. Two of the slugs were under the body and one was near it. The type of shell casing was typical of German-made Geco ammunition. The shell casings were believed to be from a .38 gun and police asked Branion if he had any guns in the home capable of firing this type of bullet. Branion was an avid gun collector and gave them a Luger pistol. Police were able to determine the gun had not recently been fired. Branion denied having any other weapons in the house. Firearms experts would later determine based on the rifling pattern, the only weapon capable of killing Donna Branion was a Walther PPK. Police asked Branion to submit to a lie detector test, which his lawyer advised against. He did ask police to perform a nitrate test, which would have shown if there was any gun powder residue on Branion. Police claimed to not have the resources for such a test.

Detectives were perplexed by the lack of motive for the killing. Police became suspicious when Dr. Branion left only a few days later for a Colorado Christmas ski vacation. This was compounded by his behavior at the crime scene when he stated he did not check his wife's body because it looked clear to him that she was dead and confusing the words lividity and cyanosis.

After returning from his vacation, on January 22, 1968, Detective Michael Boyle returned to Branion's home with a search warrant. Inside a cabinet, locked on the day of the murder, he discovered a brochure for a Walther PPK, an extra clip and a manufacturer's target all bearing the same serial number. He also found two boxes of Geco .38 caliber ammunition. One box was full, the other missing four shells. Police tracked the original purchase of this gun to James Hooks, a friend of Branion, who claimed to have given a Walther to him as a birthday gift the year before.

The gun itself was never found. While Branion originally said nothing was stolen from the apartment, his statement changed upon the discovery of the ammunition of Walther PPK materials to say that it must have been taken by the intruders who killed his wife. Shortly thereafter, Branion was arrested for murder. The state later argued that the most likely motive was Branion wanting to be rid of his wife so that he could establish a more prominent relationship with his mistress.

The state put forth the idea that sometime between when Branion left the hospital and before he picked up his son at nursery school, he killed his wife. Detective Boyle and another officer conducted a number of tests to establish Branion's timeline. They covered the journey of 2.8 miles in a minimum of six minutes and a maximum of 12 minutes, just enough time, according to the prosecution, for Branion to commit the murder, pick up his son, and create an alibi. The police, however, did not account for any heavy traffic on the days right before Christmas, nor did they account for the speed at which Branion moved when getting out of the car, searching for his son, and then getting back into the car with his son. They did not consider whether Branion would knowingly walk into his home with his young son, who would see his dead mother. With entirely circumstantial evidence, the prosecution went forth, with an entirely white jury, save one. After eight hours of deliberation, Branion was found guilty on May 28, 1968.

Branion appealed to have the verdict nullified by the judge on the case, Reginald Holzer, who stated he would take the motion under advisement. It is important to note that Judge Holzer was later convicted of corruption, extortion, and racketeering charges. In the case of Branion, an affidavit signed by a person connected to the case stated Nelson Brown (brother of Donna Branion) would pay $20,000 to have Holzer overturn Branion's case, with $10,000 being paid up front, and the rest when Branion was freed. Shortly after this, Branion was freed on $5,000 bail. When the prosecutor heard rumors of this deal, he threatened to expose it. Holzer could not overturn the verdict but with the release on bail, it gave Branion enough time to flee the country.

Branion fled to Africa where he stayed, in Uganda, until 1983. He was apprehended and returned to the United States to begin his 20- to 30-year sentence. In 1990, after seven years in prison, Branion was released on health grounds and died one month later of a brain tumor and heart ailment. During the time he was incarcerated, advocates continually attempted to reopen his case. Many of the

witnesses who could have confirmed his alibi were never brought to the stand. Branion also never testified. The pathologist additionally stated that Donna Branion was murdered slowly. Bruising on Donna Branion's neck indicated a rope or cord being used, the bruising taking at least 15 minutes to form and would not have formed after her death. Even the prosecutor, Patrick Tuite, later admitted he had doubts, citing that maybe Branion had hired someone. Branion defended his innocence to the end of his life.

SHERRY SILLER

See also: Carter, Rubin "Hurricane" (1937–2014); MacDonald, Jeffrey (1943–); Sweet, Ossian (1895–1960)

Further Reading

Evans, Colin. "John Marshall Branion Trial: 1968—Imperfect Alibi, Illicit Love, On the Run." http://law.jrank.org/pages/3172/John-Marshall-Branion-Trial-1968.html. Accessed April 13 2015.

Miner, Michael. 1989. "Can Tabloid TV Save Her Man?" *Chicago Reader.* http://www.chicagoreader.com/chicago/can-tabloid-tv-save-her-man-foreign-assignment/Content?oid=874758. Accessed April 14, 2015.

Sanders, Charles L. 1984. "A Man on the Run." *Ebony* (July): 112–119.

Tuohy, James, and Rob Warden. 1989. *Greylord.* New York: G.P. Putnam's Sons.

Brasco, Donnie. *See* Pistone, Joseph D. (1939–)

Brawley, Tawana (1972–)

Tawana Brawley, a young African American woman, made national headlines for allegedly fabricating a racial attack where she was victimized by six white adult men, three of whom had ties to local law enforcement agencies. Brawley's case received widespread attention because of the cruel state in which Brawley's body was found and allegedly attacked, in addition, racial slurs that were marked on Brawley's body created concern and tension among civil rights activists and the public alike. Brawley's support team, attorneys Alton Maddox, Vernon Mason, and Reverend Al Sharpton, claimed prosecutors were not able to represent Brawley accurately and expressed suspicion that the state may arrange to protect the men rather than

Brawley. A list of demands was presented to Attorney General Robert Abrams to gain cooperation from Brawley. Brawley's inability to cooperate with prosecutors resulted in suspicion and ultimately the grand jury concluded that Brawley fabricated the entire story. Brawley continues to confirm her story is truthful. One of the accused men,

Assistant District Attorney Steven A. Pagones, successfully filed a defamation case against Brawley, Maddox, Mason, and Sharpton. The Brawley case is a commonly known reference regarding racial matters in the legal system.

On November 28, 1987, at age 15, Tawana Brawley was found in Wappingers Falls, New York, curled inside a plastic

Teenager Tawana Brawley, left, accompanied by her adviser, the Reverend Al Sharpton, right, at a rally and protest near The Omni, site of the Democratic National Convention in Atlanta, Georgia, on July 20, 1988. In a case that drew national attention, Brawley alleged she had been kidnapped and raped by white men. (AP Photo/Neil Brake)

bag. Brawley had been beaten, she was covered in feces, her hair was chopped off, and the slurs "KKK" and "Nigger" were written on her torso using a black charcoal-like substance. Brawley told her family and law enforcement officials that she was abducted and raped by six white men, one of whom wore a police badge. Although reluctant to speak to law enforcement officials, Brawley gave a detailed account to her aunt and her mother, Glenda Brawley. According to Brawley, a man approached her with a badge on the afternoon of November 24, 1987, she assumed the man to be a police officer who asked her to get into a dark green vehicle with another man inside, at which point Brawley was struck and taken to a wooded area where she was sodomized by a total of six white men for the next four days (Iverem 1987).

Soon after, law enforcement agencies expressed concern with the truthfulness of Brawley's allegations, while antiracism agencies, including the National Association for the Advancement of Colored People (NAACP), cautioned the possibility of law enforcement covering up the incident, due to alleged police involvement in the attack. Community residents became racially divided, with some African American residents acknowledging issues of violent racism in the area, and some white residents questioning the truthfulness of the allegation (Iverem 1988a). On the other hand, some black and white residents joined in protest against the violent acts (Iverem 1988a). Racial tensions were particularly straining because of other instances, allegedly involving the KKK, in the area during the same time as the alleged attack on Brawley (Iverem 1988b). The Brawley case received national recognition as well, with well-known figures like Bill Cosby and Ed Lewis, publisher of *Essence* magazine, showing their support at news conferences as well as jointly offering a $25,000 reward for information on the attack on Brawley. Reverend Al Sharpton also played a major role in supporting Brawley's case.

Under the legal representation of Alton H. Maddox Jr., known for his work in the Howard Beach racial assault case, and Attorney Vernon Mason, Brawley refused to appear before a grand jury. Brawley demanded that Governor Cuomo designate a special prosecutor to handle the case. On January 26, 1988, Cuomo ordered Attorney General Robert Abrams as the special prosecutor who designated the case to John M. Ryan, who at the time was the chief of the criminal prosecutions bureau. Brawley's attorneys stated that the case involved elements that have plagued the African American community for decades, and thus were angered and suspicious of Ryan's appointment, because he

had no prior experience in civil rights cases. To ensure a fair trial, one that would not work to benefit the alleged law enforcement officials involved in the attack, Maddox and Mason developed strict criteria be met for Brawley to testify. The Brawley family and lawyers refused to work with Abrams and his team without these strict demands being met. Brawley's prolonged denial to cooperate and idealistic demands led to suspicion in Brawley's claims and weakened the case (Shipp 1988a). Cuomo also grew tired of waiting for cooperation and became publicly strict on not accommodating Brawley's requests. Despite this, Brawley supporters continued to protest and call for justice. In March 1988, Maddox announced at a news conference that Assistant District Attorney Steven A. Pagones was one of the six men responsible for the attack on Brawley and called for Pagones's immediate arrest, Maddox ensured that Brawley would not testify until Pagones was arrested. Maddox and Mason also accused a states trooper as well as a police officer of being involved in the attack. Neither attorney shared evidence with prosecutors, however. The police officer committed suicide shortly after the accusations. Glenda Brawley, Tawana's mother, also refused to testify and was held in contempt of court for failing to testify, Mrs. Brawley sought sanctuary in a church to avoid arrest.

Without the testimony of the Brawley family, the grand jury continued to observe evidence of over 100 testimonies and recorded over 1,000 pages of testimony (Blumenthal 1988). After seven months of compiling evidence, the grand jury found that Brawley had fabricated her story. According to investigators, Brawley intentionally hid from her family for four days and then wrote the racial slurs on herself, creating an appearance that she had been attacked; it was determined that no evidence supported a crime was committed against Brawley (Shipp 1988b). It was suggested that Brawley feared punishment from her stepfather, Ralph King, for staying away from home, and thus was motivated to fabricate the entire story (McFadden 1988). Brawley publicly denied these claims and pled that Mr. Abrams allow her to tell her story to an impartial jury and allow Brawley to speak to a team who will help her (Shipp 1988b). Furthermore, Steven A. Pagones sued Maddox, Mason, and Sharpton for defamation of character; he was eventually awarded $345,000 in 1998. Pagones successfully sued Brawley as well and was rewarded $185,000. Recently, in 2013, Brawley began having her wages garnished to go toward payment to Pagones.

Brawley's case continues to be regarded as a racial injustice in the legal system by many civil rights activists and Brawley's supporters. Brawley continues to maintain the truthfulness of her story.

Kayla Martensen

See also: Howard Beach Case (1986); King, Rodney, Beating of (1991); Ku Klux Klan (1866–); Los Angeles Riots (1992); Martin, Trayvon, Death of (February 26, 2012)

Further Reading

Barron, James. 1988. "Abrams Officer to Investigate Attack on Black Teen-Ager." *New York Times.* January 27.

Blumenthal, Ralph. 1988. "A 2-Month Extension Is Approved For Grand Jury in Brawley Case." *New York Times.* August 10.

Iverem, Esther. 1987. "Bias Cases Fuel Anger of Blacks." *New York Times.* December 14.

Iverem, Esther. 1988a. "Attack Puts Quiet Hudson Area in Civil-Rights Fight." *New York Times.* January 28.

Iverem, Esther. 1988b. "Questions Persist in Dutchess Assault." *New York Times.* February 4.

McFadden, Robert. 1988. "Advisers Assailed: Abrams Files Complaint—Inquiry Could Lead to Disbarments Grand Jury Says Brawley Story Fabricated, Clears Officials and Proposes Laws." *New York Times.* October 7.

Shipp, E.R. 1988a. "Actions of Brawley Lawyers Raise Troubling Questions: Role of Lawyers Leading to Troubling Questions." *New York Times.* February 23.

Shipp, E. R. 1988b. "Brawley Rejects Evidence Cited to Grand Jury Says She Is 'Not a Liar' in Account of Assault." *New York Times.* September 29.

Bremer, Arthur. *See* Wallace, George, Attempted Assassination of (May 15, 1972)

Brown, H. Rap (1943–)

H. Rap Brown was a conspicuous and controversial figure during the Black Power Movement of the late 1960s. Brown was a member of the Student Non-Violent Coordinating Committee (SNCC) and also a member of the Black Panther Party and had multiple encounters with law enforcement. He came to symbolize a more combative black youth that emerged in the latter part of the decade. SNCC rejected their philosophy of nonviolence in 1966, and Brown was noted for observing that "Violence is American as cherry pie" (Kennicott and Page 1971, 325–334). Some observers have speculated that Brown's early career as a

radical civil rights activist made him the target of FBI's Counter Intelligence Program (COINTELPRO), a series of covert FBI operations under the directive of J. Edgar Hoover with the sole purpose of infiltrating and neutralizing political groups. H. Rap Brown, now known as Jamil Abdullah al-Amin, is currently serving a life sentence without parole in ADX Florence supermax prison in Colorado for shooting two Georgia police officers in 2000. The event resulted in a four-day manhunt for Al-Amin, which led to his capture and arrest in White Hall, Alabama. Al-Amin pleaded not guilty and did not provide testimony during his trial. On March 9, 2002, he was convicted of 13 criminal charges and sentenced to life in prison without parole.

Hubert Gerold Brown was born October 4, 1943, in Baton Rouge, Louisiana, to Eddie and Thelma Brown. He received the nickname "Rap" in his youth because of his remarkable verbal skills and success at "the Dozens," a game of quick-witted insults between two participants, usually in front of a crowd. Brown found good use for his verbal aptitude when he succeeded Stokely Carmichael in 1967 as chairman of the SNCC, initially a nonviolent civil rights group that organized protests, voter registrations, and sit-ins at racially segregated white establishments during the civil rights movement. After 1966, SNCC had adopted a more militant stance, using the slogan "Black Power." Racial tensions ran high after African Americans had rebelled against police brutality in cities such as Newark, New Jersey, Detroit, and Los Angeles. When violence broke out after Brown gave a speech in Cambridge, Maryland, in 1967, he was accused of inciting a riot. Police fired into the crowd, and Brown's forehead was grazed. Several hours later, after Brown had departed to seek medical attention, Pine Street Elementary School burned to the ground with Brown's words still resonating with the public. "Black folks built America. If America don't come around, we going to burn it down, brother. We are going to burn it down if we don't get our share of it" (Kennicott and Page 1971, 325–334).

Brown turned himself in to the Federal Bureau of Investigation (FBI) on July 26, 1967, was charged with inciting a riot, and was later released on $10,000 bail. On August 14, 1967, Brown violated the Federal Firearms Act when he carried a rifle across state lines while visiting family. A judge ordered Brown to stay in the lower Manhattan area of New York and restricted travel unless permitted by the court. Brown was arrested on February 20, 1968, for violating the terms of his bond after traveling to California to meet with his attorneys. He also spoke at a Black Panther rally and was elected to the position of minister of justice.

Brown's attorneys demanded his release, but his bail was set at $100,000 and later reduced to $30,000 on April 19, 1968.

In August 1968, Brown returned to New York City from New Orleans where his trial was held, and while waiting for his appeal of a maximum five-year sentence and a $2,000 fine, he published his autobiography, *Die Nigger Die*. Brown's trial was to be held in Bel Air, Maryland; however, on March 9, 1970, SNCC members Ralph Featherstone and William Payne died in a car explosion on their way to the courthouse. Speculation abounded about a possible assassination attempt of Brown, who was thought to be riding in the car. The trial was rescheduled after a bomb was detonated in the courthouse the following night. Brown did not report to the trial, and in May 1970, he made to the FBI's 10 most wanted list. He evaded police detection until 1971 where he and several men were involved in a shootout with police and charged with the attempted robbery of a New York City bar. Brown served five years in Attica Prison, converted to Islam, and changed his name to Jamil Abdullah Al-Amin. Upon his release, Al-Amin went on the annual *Hajj*, a pilgrimage to Mecca, and one of the five pillars of the Muslim faith. He returned and opened a store and mosque in Atlanta, Georgia.

Al-Amin became a community activist in Atlanta, but a routine stop on May 31, 1999, set in motion a series of events that led to the life imprisonment of Al-Amin. A Cobb County police officer pulled Al-Amin over for driving a stolen vehicle. Upon searching Al-Amin, the officer discovered a badge in Al-Amin's possession, so he was charged with impersonating an officer and driving a stolen vehicle. He missed his court date on January 28, 2000. On March 16, 2000, sheriff deputy Ricky Kinchen and Aldranon English went to arrest Al-Amin. While driving from Al-Amin's property, the two officers, suspecting Al-Amin to be the driver, stopped a black vehicle headed toward the house. A gun fight ensued, and sheriff deputy Ricky Kinchen died from multiple shots while Aldranon English was wounded. Before Kinchen died, he stated that his assailant, who fled the scene, was wounded in the gun fight. English identified Al-Amin as the shooter from mug shots, and a four-day manhunt for Al-Amin ensued. Al-Amin was apprehended in White Hall, Alabama, and stayed in Montgomery jail for over a month before being sent to Cobb County to stand trial for the shootings of Kinchen and English.

Al-Amin's murder trial began on January 7, 2002, and the prosecution provided eyewitness testimony from deputy sheriff English that Al-Amin was his shooter, that Al-Amin was wearing a bulletproof vest at the time of his arrest, and that the automatic pistol and rifle found in the woods near the location of Al-Amin's capture matched the casing found at the crime scene. The defense questioned the accuracy of English's testimony, his ability to identify his shooter after being temporarily blinded by pepper spray that exploded from the assailant's bullet, and picking out his shooter in a series of photos while under the effects of 4 milligrams of morphine hours after the event. They also argued the lack of physical evidence linking Al-Amin to the crime, Al-Amin's fingerprints were not found on the casings or weapons, the bulletproof vest he wore at the time of his capture had no damage, and Al-Amin had no wounds despite both officers Kinchen and English affirming that they shot the assailant. After a six-day trial, the jury comprised of nine blacks, two whites, and one Hispanic deliberated for less than five hours, and came back with a guilty verdict, and a sentence of life in prison without parole. The same day it was revealed by a trial court that Al-Amin's initial traffic stop back in May 1999 violated his Fourth Amendment right prohibiting unreasonable search and seizure.

TERRANCE WINGATE AND JESSICA JAMES

See also: Attica Prison Riot (1971); House Un-American Activities Committee (HUAC) (1938–1975); Malcolm X, Assassination of (February 21, 1965); Pratt, Geronimo (1947–2011); *Primary Documents*/Excerpts from a Speech of H. Rap Brown Delivered at a "Free Huey" Rally (February 1968)

Further Reading

Brown, H. Rap. 1969. *Die Nigger Die!* New York: Dial.

Kennicott, Patrick C. and Wayne Page. 1971. "H. Rap Brown: The Cambridge Incident." *Quarterly Journal of Speech* 57: 325–334.

Siddiqui, Obaid H. 2012. "Rap Sheet: H. Rap Brown, Civil Rights Revolutionary—Cop Killer/FBI Target?" *The Journal of Pan African Studies* 5: 133–152.

Brown, John. *See* Harpers Ferry (VA), Raid on (October 17, 1859)

Brownsville (TX) Affair (August 13, 1906)

The Brownsville affair (also known as the Brownsville raid) was a racial incident that occurred after several shootings that occurred in Brownsville, Texas, around midnight on August 13, 1906. The shootings resulted in the death of a white bartender and the wounding of a Hispanic police lieutenant. The townspeople accused members of the U.S. Army 25th Infantry Regiment for the attacks. The 25th Infantry Regiment was a unit of Buffalo Soldiers stationed at Fort Brown near the town of Brownsville, and the events that followed the shootings arose out of racial tension between the black soldiers and the white citizens. Although the county court reviewed evidence against 12 enlisted soldiers and found no basis for indictment, President Theodore Roosevelt ordered an additional investigation be conducted by the U.S. Army inspector general. The investigation efforts assumed that the soldiers were guilty from the beginning and only focused on obtaining supporting evidence from other members of the regiment. Although not a single soldier presented testimony that they were involved in or knew anything about the shootings and any evidence that suggested that the soldiers had been involved was discredited, President Roosevelt ordered the dishonorable discharge of all 167 soldiers of the 25th Infantry Regiment. This decision was the largest summary dismissal in the history of the U.S. Army. Further, the decision cost the soldiers their pensions and made them ineligible to work in the civil service thereafter. In 1972, President Richard Nixon exonerated the discharged troops. The government granted pardons and entered honorable discharges in all of the men's records. The only surviving member of the battalion, Dorsie Willis, was given his $25,000 pension. He was not awarded retroactive compensation.

In 1906, when the Brownsville affair occurred, the state of Texas had legal segregation. Prior to the arrival of the Buffalo Soldiers that made up Companies A, B, and C of the 25th Infantry Regiment, only white soldiers had been stationed at Fort Brown, and the residents of Brownsville expressed resentment when the news that they would be replaced by a battalion of black soldiers was announced several months prior to the changeover. Some residents of Brownsville stated that the black soldiers would not stay long or that the town would get rid of them quick. Upon arrival, the black soldiers experienced severe discrimination by the white residents. However, the soldiers were largely able to avoid the white residents as five-sixths of the population of the town was Hispanic. As a result, the soldiers were able to frequent establishments kept by Hispanics rather than by whites. There was no indication that the soldiers resented the arrangement, and the few altercations that occurred between the black servicemen and the white residents amounted to minor incidents.

On August 12, 1906, an attack on a white woman was reported in the town. Although there was no evidence that either the woman had actually been attacked or that the alleged attacker was a soldier from Fort Brown, a frenzy come over the townspeople. For the protection of the troops, the commanding officer, after consulting with the mayor of the town, declared an early curfew the following night. On the night of August 13, 1906, gunshots broke out in the town. In response to the sound of gunfire, the sentinel on duty at the fort went between barracks B and C and fired three times into the air as a warning. In response to the call to arms, the soldiers from Companies B and D formed outside their barracks while the firing in town continued. Company C formed 5 to 10 minutes later because the noncommissioned officer in charge of their weapons refused to unlock the weapons racks without a direct order. Once the third company had formed, all three companies remained within the fort without firing a single shot.

Following the shootings in town and the deaths of the bartender and the police lieutenant, the residents of Brownsville presumed the guilt of the soldiers without identifying any specific assailants. Despite the commanding officer's testimony that the men had all been accounted for in their barracks that night, the townspeople continued to assert the soldiers' guilt. Shortly thereafter, the mayor of the town came to the fort with spent shells, cartridges, and clips that were the type used by the soldiers. Based on this evidence, the all-white military officers concluded that some of their men must have been involved in the attacks. Although forensic analysis indicated that the shells could not have been fired by the soldiers stationed at the fort that night, the army inquiry proceeded without the slightest consideration that the soldiers may have been innocent. The military inquiry then followed.

When the soldiers insisted that they had no idea who had committed the crimes, the army's inspector general recommended that they be dishonorably discharged for their conspiracy of silence. Despite the fact that six of the soldiers stationed there had been previously awarded the Congressional Medal of Honor and others had served over 20 years in the army, President Roosevelt dishonorably discharged all of the black troops stationed in Fort Brown that night. Due in part to the upcoming 1906 congressional elections and the fact that the black community largely supported the Republicans, Roosevelt withheld news of the discharge until after the election. When the news became public, many individuals, both black and white, were outraged. Black organizations, including the Constitution League and the National Association of Colored Women, spoke out against the dismissals.

Several later investigations attempted to resolve the matter. The U.S. Senate Military Affairs Committee investigated the incident from 1907 to 1908. Their investigation supported Roosevelt's determination; however, several senators submitted a minority report supporting the soldiers' innocence. Further, another group of four Republican senators submitted an additional minority report, indicating that there was no conclusive evidence of guilt in the matter. In 1909, the Committee on Military Affairs recommended that the dismissals be reversed, the records of the soldiers corrected, and the men reenlisted. Later that year, a military court of inquiry considered whether the discharged soldiers should be allowed to reenlist. In 1910, the court recommended 14 men for reenlistment.

ANNE LI KRINGEN

See also: Carter, Rubin "Hurricane" (1937–2014); Central Park Jogger Case (1989); Cotton, Ronald (1962–)

Further Reading

Christian, Garna L. 1989. "The Brownsville Raid's 168th Man: The Court-Martial of Corporal Knowles." *Southwestern Historical Quarterly* 93 (1): 45–59.

Foraker, Joseph B. 1908. "A Review of Testimony in the Brownsville Investigation." *The North American Review* 187: 550–558.

Lane, Anne, J. 1971. *The Brownsville Affair: National Crisis and Black Reaction.* Port Washington, NY: Kennikat Press.

Weaver, John. 1970. *The Brownsville Raid.* College Station: Texas A & M University Press.

Bruce, Lenny, Obscenity Trial of (1964)

The First Amendment in the Bill of Rights entitles Americans to the right of free speech—speech that today includes obscenities. However, it was not always the case that individuals could freely discuss matters, especially when the material was obscene. Lenny Bruce was a comedian who pushed the boundaries of free speech to levels never heard before. He used offensive language and made jokes on crude and risqué topics, causing backlash from certain spectators and public officials. During this time period, it was not common to broach these topics in a public forum; however, Lenny Bruce found that his stand-up excelled in

this area. Despite multiple arrests and a large trial, Lenny Bruce pushed for his right to free speech and paved the way for future comedians to joke on any topic (Linder 2003).

Lenny Bruce (1925–1966), born Leonard Schneider, grew up in a small suburb on Long Island, New York. He spent his childhood working on a farm and eventually enlisted in the military during World War II. During his time in the navy, Bruce performed comedy shows for his shipmates. In one particular show he dressed in drag and was dishonorably discharged for belief that he was homosexual. He eventually returned to New York City to make a life as a comedian. With the mentorship of comedians like Joe Ancis, Lenny Bruce found a life in comedy (Bruce 1965).

Bruce met his wife Honey Harlowe, who was working as a stripper in Baltimore, Maryland. His first big run-in with the law was while raising money to support Honey so she could retire from stripping. Bruce impersonated a priest and raised money for a foundation that supported a leper colony. However, Bruce kept a large amount of the

American comedian Lenny Bruce pushed the boundaries of the First Amendment with his comedy and writings. Although he was arrested and later convicted of obscenity, he would be posthumously pardoned for the charges. (Photo by Hulton Archive/Getty Images)

donated money for himself. While raising money, Bruce was arrested for panhandling, so he and Honey moved to Pittsburgh. It was in Pittsburgh, at a performance at Carnegie Melon, where Lenny Bruce really left his mark on the comic world. His performance on the night of April 9, 1959, was determined to be "the greatest performance of his career" (Goldman and Schiller 1974). Unfortunately, Bruce's comedy did not appeal to everyone. His use of race, religion, sex, and other less lewd topics provoked certain groups from speaking out against him. On multiple occasions, police showed up to his shows to record what was being said for evidence. On several different occasions, Bruce was arrested after a show for his use of obscene material.

Two years after his groundbreaking performance, Bruce found himself living in California. Here, Bruce was arrested for obscenity. Although he was acquitted, the arrest led to red flags for police and other groups to monitor Bruce's performances. A year later, Bruce was arrested in Los Angeles, and only two months after that in Chicago for more obscenity charges. The Chicago jury found Bruce guilty; however, the Illinois Supreme Court overruled the decision in violation of his First Amendment right to free speech. All the time these trials were going on, Bruce was also facing drug charges as he became more of an addict. In 1963, California ordered Bruce to a rehabilitation stint. After a final obscenity charge in California in 1964, Bruce returned to New York (Linder 2003).

The biggest trial in Bruce's career came about in 1964 in New York. The Café Au Go Go trial would ultimately lead to the demise of Lenny Bruce. New York State Penal Code 1140-A "prohibited obscene, indecent, immoral, and impure dram, play, exhibition, and entertainment … which would tend to the corruption of the morals of youth and others" (Linder 2003). In March 1964, Bruce was performing weekly at Café Au Go Go, entertaining approximately 350 a night. Unfortunately, on March 31, a New York City inspector, Herbert Ruhe, was in attendance. Ruhe submitted a report to the district attorney's office, citing the obscene material, controversial topics, and crude language used during the performance. At a later show, several officers attended and transcribed the skits. Bruce was indicted under Penal Code 1140-A, despite protests by many famous artists (Linder 2003).

The trial was an arduous process for Bruce that ultimately resulted in his untimely death. Bruce hired a chief First Amendment attorney, Ephraim London, as his defense attorney. John Murtagh was the presiding judge, along with two other judges instead of a jury. The prosecutor, District Attorney Frank Hogan, focused the trial on the dirty words, Bruce's so-called attempts to elicit sexual arousal with words, and his obscene gestures. The defense brought in several expert witnesses to explain how these accusations were not valid. The most influential witness was Dorothy Kilgallen, a newspaper columnist, who argued that Bruce's work was very important social commentary that she did not need to agree with to respect and admire it. Other witnesses for the defense included a minister, professors, and psychiatrists who argued that Bruce's material was not inappropriate, but satirical and indicative of society and that it did not elicit sexual responses. The trial was temporarily delayed when Bruce was hospitalized, during which time Bruce read several legal books and learned as much about the law as he could. When the trial itself ended, it was almost 100 days later when the judges came to a verdict (Collins and Skover 2002).

During the 99-day interval between the trial and the verdict, Bruce fired his lawyer and wrote several letters to Judge Murtagh explaining that the words used in his performance were almost all in the dictionary, and therefore his vocabulary cannot be so problematic. He also pled with the judges to view his performance once so that they themselves can see it first hand as opposed to hearing fragments of the act in testimony. Unfortunately for Bruce, he and the club owner were each found guilty and Bruce was sentenced to four months in a workhouse; only one judge dissented. He appealed his case to a higher court but during the process overdosed on morphine and died on August 3, 1966. The stress of the legal troubles and the court case pushed Bruce's drug addiction by ending his career as a comedian and forcing him into poverty (Collins and Skover 2002). In 2003, Governor George Pataki of New York pardoned Lenny Bruce in an effort to show support for First Amendment rights (Linder 2003).

The trial of Lenny Bruce may not have ended favorably for Bruce, but his case significantly influenced public discussions about free speech. Without Lenny Bruce, many comedians would not have pushed the boundaries of free speech to broach topics, like religion, sex, race, and obscenity, in general. George Carlin was greatly influenced by Lenny Bruce and moved into a world of comedy after listening to many of Bruce's acts, eventually resulting in the famous *seven dirty words* skit (Carlin 2009). Today comedians enjoy the freedom to openly use obscenity and discuss suggestive material, thanks to Lenny Bruce and his legacy.

KATHLEEN FREY

See also: Chicago Seven (1968); Muhammad Ali Draft Case (1964–1971); *Snyder v. Phelps* (2011)

Further Reading

Bruce, Lenny. 1965. *How to Talk Dirty and Influence People.* New York: Playboy Publishing.

Carlin, George. 2009. "My Comedian Here." *PBS*, January 12. http://www.pbs.org/wnet/makeemlaugh/episodes/my-comedian-hero/george-carlin/88/. Accessed April 20, 2015.

Collins, Ronald, and David Skover. 2002. *The Trials of Lenny Bruce: The Fall and Rise of an American Icon.* Indianapolis, IN: Sourcebooks Inc.

Goldman, Albert, and Lawrence Schiller. 1974. *Ladies and Gentlemen: Lenny Bruce!!* New York: Penguin Books.

Linder, Doug. 2003. "The Trials of Lenny Bruce." http://law2.umkc.edu/faculty/projects/ftrials/bruce/bruceaccount.html. Accessed April 20, 2015.

Bryant, Kobe, Rape Accusation against (June 30, 2003)

Kobe Bryant (1978–) began his career as a National Basketball Association (NBA) player in 1996. Bryant married his wife Vanessa in 2001 and in January 2003, they had their first child. That same year, on July 1, 2003, he was accused of raping a 19-year-old woman in a hotel room in Colorado. A warrant was eventually issued for his arrest and Bryant surrendered, but was quickly released. Bryant pled not guilty to his felony charge of sexual assault. Prior to the trial, the woman said she was unwilling to testify against Bryant, which caused all charges to be dropped. Eventually a civil suit was filed and both parties settled. As of 2015, Bryant remains active in the NBA.

On June 30, 2003, Kobe Bryant, a Los Angeles Lakers basketball player, checked into the Lodge and Spa at Cordillera in Edwards, Colorado. A 19-year-old employee gave Bryant a tour of the grounds. When she showed him to his room, she was invited in. She obliged and it was during this visit that they engaged in sexual activity. According to reports, Bryant viewed their sexual encounter as consensual. The woman, however, viewed it as rape. The woman went to the police the following day to report the rape and also had a sexual assault exam performed. The results came back showing that her injuries were consistent with sexual assault.

On July 4, 2003, Eagle County Sheriff Joe Hoy issued a warrant for Bryant's arrest. Bryant, back in Los Angeles, flew to Eagle, Colorado, to surrender. Bryant was immediately released on a $25,000 bond. A few days later, the story was all over the news outlets. Bryant maintained his innocence. He did admit to having an adulterous sexual encounter with the female, but implied that it was consensual. On July 18, 2003, formal charges were filed against Bryant. He was charged with one count of felony sexual assault. He soon gave a statement following the charges regarding the accusations with his wife by his side. Reports suggest that he was emotional upon admitting his sexual encounter with the woman, but again suggested that the encounter was consensual.

In May 2004, a preliminary hearing to determine if the case would go to trial took place. Detective Doug Winters told the court room about the events that the woman shared with him through interviews. He described in detail how the woman had told him that she was asked by Bryant to return to his room and snuck past his security guards by taking a back stairwell. Once she had met up with Bryant, they took a tour of the property and continued to converse after the tour in his room. He eventually asked her to join him in the hot tub and she declined. Upon attempting to leave, the two embraced in a hug and kissed. This, she admitted, was consensual; however, the following events were suggested to be forced. After the embrace, the woman again attempted, to leave. It was at that time when she alleged that Bryant grabbed her by her neck, lifted her skirt, and raped her. Winters continued by adding in some emotional aspect by alluding to the fear the woman had of being choked. He also claimed that the woman said "no" to Bryant at least twice, but was ignored both times. Some articles report that the woman also claimed that Bryant aggressively asked if she was going to tell anybody.

Aside from the testimony about the events, Winters continued by referring to the events that followed the alleged rape. Winters told the court that the woman returned to her shift until it ended. It was when she was back that she told her friend and Bellhop, Bobby Pietrack, that Bryant had raped her. He claimed that she appeared upset and followed her home to make sure she arrived safely. The following day she went and reported the rape to the police and also had a sexual assault exam performed.

The results of the exam confirmed that the woman had injuries consistent with sexual assault. She also had a small bruise on her jaw. The defense took this opportunity to question Winter about his familiarity with the medical terms noted on the exam results. They were quick to point out that he was not a medical expert. They also posed the question of the injuries being consistent with a person who had engaged sexual activity with more than one man in the days surrounding the alleged rape. The reason behind such a statement was due to the finding of semen and pubic hair on the woman's underwear that did not match Bryant's DNA. This was an action taken in attempt to attack the credibility of the woman. Along with bringing up sexual promiscuity, the defense also questioned her mental stability, discussing medication and past suicide attempts. However, the attempt to discredit the woman did not prove successful and a date was set for the trial. However, the trial never took place because the woman was unwilling to testify.

Bryant's Apology

According to the Associated Press (2004) on ESPN's website, this is the apology statement made by Bryant after the charges against him were dropped:

First, I want to apologize directly to the young woman involved in this incident. I want to apologize to her for my behavior that night and for the consequences she has suffered in the past year. Although this year has been incredibly difficult for me personally, I can only imagine the pain she has had to endure. I also want to apologize to her parents and family members, and to my family and friends and supporters, and to the citizens of Eagle, Colo.

I also want to make it clear that I do not question the motives of this young woman. No money has been paid to this woman. She has agreed that this statement will not be used against me in the civil case. Although I truly believe this encounter between us was consensual, I recognize now that she did not and does not view this incident the same way I did. After months of reviewing discovery, listening to her attorney, and even her testimony in person, I now understand how she feels that she did not consent to this encounter.

I issue this statement today fully aware that while one part of this case ends today, another remains. I understand that the civil case against me will go forward. That part of this case will be decided by and between the parties directly involved in the incident and will no longer be a financial or emotional drain on the citizens of the state of Colorado. (p. 1)

An important point to include concerning an event that surrounded the rape accusation is that the woman's name was released. This was done in court by the defense. It was also released on a radio show. Eventually the woman's personal information, including her address and phone number, began to be circulated around the Internet. This, of course, infuriated Victim Rights Advocates, but more importantly put her in danger. Soon after the release of her information, and before the trial, she began to receive hate mail and even death threats.

While the criminal trial never happened and all criminal charges against Bryant were dropped, the woman did file a civil suit. Both parties settled. However, the settlement was kept private and not disclosed to the public. After the charges were dropped, but prior to the civil suit, Bryant released a statement apologizing to the woman and others, including the community where the alleged rape took place. He also discussed how he viewed the act as consensual, but can now see that she did not. While Bryant continued to play basketball throughout every phase of the accusation, he did lose several endorsements. Eventually, he regained most of them and also won a few basketball awards, such as the NBA's Most Valuable Player in 2008.

MELISSA J. TETZLAFF-BEMILLER

See also: Glen Ridge (NJ) Rape Case (March 1, 1989); Simpson, O. J. (1947–); Smith, William Kennedy, Rape Case (1991)

Further Reading

Associated Press. 2004. "Kobe Bryant's Apology." ESPN: NBA. September 2. http://sports.espn.go.com/nba/news/story?id=1872928. Accessed February 27, 2015.

Associated Press. 2004. "Kobe Pleads Not Guilty in Rape Case." Fox News. May 11. http://www.foxnews.com/story/2004/05/11/kobe-pleads-not-guilty-in-rape-case/. Accessed February 27, 2015.

Colby, J., C. McKinley, R. Cosby, C. Donaldson-Evans, and the Associated Press. 2003. "Detective Details Alleged Rape in Kobe Hearing." Fox News. October 10. http://www.foxnews.com/story/2003/10/10/detective-details-alleged-rape-in-kobe-hearing/. Accessed February 24, 2015.

Gittrich, G., and C. Siemaszko. 2003. "Brutal Rape Tale Kobe Accuser: He Grabbed Me and Bent Me over a Chair." *New York Daily News*. October 10. http://www.nydailynews.com/archives/news/brutal-rape-tale-kobe-accuser-grabbed-bent-chair-article-1.527408. Accessed February 24, 2015.

BTK Killer. *See* Rader, Dennis (1945–)

Buchalter, Louis "Lepke" (1897–1944)

Louis "Lepke" Buchalter is one of the most well-known mobsters in American history. The first to use labor unions for racketeering purposes, Lepke was the head of murder for hire group, Murder, Inc. in the 1930s. Born in the Lower East Side Manhattan neighborhood in February 1897 to a Jewish family, his mother called him "Lepkeleh," a Yiddish nickname meaning "Little Louis," which stuck with him for the rest of his life.

Buchalter's father died when he was only 12. After his father's death, seeing his mother struggle to provide for her family, Buchalter dropped out of school and joined a street gang. The gang was known for robbing street carts of food and other merchandise. Eventually he earned a reputation as a good leader and organizer within the gang; having become so adept at stealing from these pushcarts, he left the gang to form his own. It was during one of these robberies that he met lifelong friend and criminal Jacob "Garrah" Shapiro. In 1915 he was caught and arrested by police; however, the police took pity on him after taking note of his impoverishment from his appearance alone and his young age and did not prosecute him. Later that year, Buchalter was sent to live with his uncle in Bridgeport, Connecticut, in an effort to curb his behavior. The move had no such effect and Buchalter was arrested in February 1916, on charges of burglary and sent to the Cheshire Reformatory for juvenile offenders until July 12, 1917. Shortly after his release, he returned to New York.

Buchalter was again arrested shortly after his return. On September 28, 1917, he was sentenced to 18 months in Sing Sing in Ossinning, New York, on a grand larceny conviction. He was released in January 1919 only to be arrested and convicted again for attempted burglary and sentenced to 30 months in January 1920. After his release in March 1922, he vowed to never again be caught and sent to prison again.

When Buchalter was released, Prohibition was in its early stages and he recognized the demand for illegal liquor as a much better venture than small-time burglaries. In New York, he went straight to the top of the food chain for a job: Arnold Rothstein. He helped Rothstein ship liquor across the East Coast, establishing himself as a prominent bootlegger in Rothstein's circle. Rothstein also became a mentor and father figure to Buchalter; a conservative man who eschewed any kind of spotlight or flamboyancy, he taught Buchalter the importance of anonymity and remaining inconspicuous. As a result, Buchalter soon left the bootlegging business for garments and unions.

In the 1920s, textiles in New York held a large chunk of the job market. By 1925, the slums of lower Manhattan were giving away to reform, and labor unions were making strides in factories. Class warfare broke out between management and labor workers. Long hours, poor wages, and

Louis "Lepke" Buchalter, center, handcuffed to J. Edgar Hoover, left, with another man on the right, at the entrance to courthouse in New York on November 30, 1939. Buchalter was a well-known mobster and head of the murder-for-hire group, Murder, Inc. (Library of Congress)

little fundamental rights heightened tensions to a breaking point that frequently turned bloody in the garment industry. These fights were what brought forth Buchalter's idea that one could control both labor and management. Buchalter and Shapiro together joined a street gang run by Jewish gangster, Jacob "Little Augie" Orgen who was well known for his violence and racketeering within the labor unions. Orgen's entire organization consisted of approximately 150 men, who would be "rented out" to violently shake up labor disputes. Orgen was not particular about who rented his services; only his price list mattered. Buchalter and Shapiro both believed they could do a better job running the organization than Orgen and on October 16, 1927, Orgen was shot and killed in a drive-by shooting by Buchalter and Shapiro.

With the death of Orgen, Buchalter and Shapiro were at the top of the New York labor rackets. Buchalter inherited all of Orgen's Jewish crime family. Buchalter believed the key to the future was in dominating the labor unions and there was virtually no competition compared to the other illegal empires of the time: bootlegging, gambling, and prostitution. Buchalter started with one of the biggest unions in New York, Amalgamated Clothing Workers of America, consisting of over 50,000 workers. He began by focusing on the smallest, but most powerful part of the union: the truckers. Through intimidation, attacks with acid bombs and beatings, the truckers eventually succumbed to the demands of Lepke Buchalter. The truckers would give Buchalter a percentage cut, and Buchalter would have them delivering to more locations than permitted by their union. It meant more money for both parties. For union members who failed to acknowledge Buchalter, enforcers would be sent out. By then, Buchalter's gang grew to over 500 members. Penalties for not meeting Buchalter's demands were steep. If a manufacturer did not meet Buchalter's monetary demands, he might burn down their building as a message to others, pour acid on fabric, or sabotage machinery. By 1929, at the age of 32, Lepke Buchalter was a millionaire.

After Buchalter completed his control of the textile industry, he set his sights on taking over the bakery unions. He followed the same strategy, using murder and extortion and soon, his racketeering business was booming. He used some of the money he earned stealing and murdering Jewish workers to fund his brothers, sister, and mother. He put one of his brothers through dental school and donated a considerable amount to Jewish synagogues. He also moved into an exclusive high-rise on the Upper West Side and

began a relationship with Betty Wasserman. They married in 1931, and Buchalter took her son under his wing as his own.

In the early 1930s, Buchalter's activities drew the attention of federal prosecutor Thomas E. Dewey. He was constantly watched and he believed his phones were being tapped. In an effort to rid himself of any witnesses to his multiple crimes, he hired a friend, Mandy Weiss, and a loosely organized group of violent enforcers and hit men from a variety of Jewish and Italian gangs to kill every witness who might speak against him. Over a three-year period, over 50 people died. The media dubbed this group Murder, Inc. These activities only furthered the scrutiny against Buchalter and in 1937 he and Shapiro went underground to avoid arrest. Buchalter continued to issue orders for the deaths of anyone he believed to be a threat. A manhunt carried on for two years and a reward of $25,000 for information leading to Buchalter's arrest.

On a tip from one of his mafia contacts, Buchalter was told if he turned himself in, the Federal Bureau of Investigation (FBI) would consider leniency. He agreed and on August 24, 1939, turned himself over to the FBI. Unfortunately, this was a lie and Buchalter was tried and convicted on federal narcotics trafficking charges. He was tried in New York State for labor extortion and convicted. On April 5, 1940, Buchalter was sentenced to 30 years to life in state prison. On May 9, 1941, Buchalter was also tried in New York for four murders. Corroborating evidence was given by fellow mobster Abe Reles, who turned state's evidence. After only four hours of deliberation, the jury found Buchalter guilty and on December 2, 1941, sentenced him to death. On March 4, 1944, Louis Buchalter was executed via electric chair in Sing Sing prison.

SHERRY SILLER

See also: Anastasia, Albert (1902–1957); Luciano, Charles "Lucky" (1897–1962); Murder, Incorporated; Schultz, Dutch (1901–1935)

Further Reading

Green, D. 2013. "This Day in Jewish History / Murderer and Racketeer Louis "Lepke" Buchalter Gets the Chair." Haaretz.com. March 4. http://www.haaretz.com/news/features/this-day-in-jewish-history/this-day-in-jewish-history-murderer-and-racketeer-louis-lepke-buchalter-gets-the-chair.premium-1.507082. Accessed April 14, 2015.

Tarkington, J. 2013. Louis "Lepke" Buchalter. YouTube.com. http://www.youtube.com/watch?v=dum503O3I64. Accessed April 14, 2015.

Buddhist Temple Massacre (Maricopa County, AZ) (1991)

On August 10, 1991, at approximately 8:00 a.m. an individual delivering food to the residents of the Wat Promkunaram Buddhist temple, west of Phoenix, Arizona, discovered six monks, one nun, and two acolytes dead. They were arranged in a circle with bullet wounds to the back of their heads. The number of bullet wounds varied from one to three, and there were other wounds on the individual's arms to cause law enforcement to suspect other foul play (Ramsland 2008). The oldest victim was nun Foy Sripanpiaserf (71) and the youngest was Matthew Miller, a 16-year-old sophomore who was training to be a monk (Time Series Wire 1991). It was determined that all individuals were killed in an execution style and were forced to remain in a circle during the murder of their fellow victims.

Jonathan Doody leaves Maricopa County Superior Court. Doody, convicted of killing nine people, including six monks, during a robbery at a Buddhist temple in metro Phoenix, was sentenced to 249 years in prison. (AP Photo/The Arizona Republic)

When law enforcement came on the scene they took note that some items were missing in two smaller rooms, but the main room was left alone. Cameras, jewelry, and $2,790 were missing (*Los Angeles Times* 1994). However, the large golden Buddha was left untouched in the main hall. There was also significant vandalism and a large number of shell casings from a 20-gauge shot gun and a .22 caliber weapon mixed between .22 longs and .22 shorts. It was determined that this was also a botched burglary.

Because the victims were foreigners, the crime was also a potential international issue and so the Federal Bureau of Investigation (FBI) was involved. Some considered the possibility that this was an organized crime, hit related or had a potential drug involvement; however, none of the victims had a criminal record or had significant connection to known organized crime syndicates.

On September 10, 1991, the police received a call from Tucson Psychiatric Institute from a man who called himself Michael McGraw, stating that he had additional information about the crime (Ramsland 2008). The police later detained Michael McGraw, age 24, due to the mysterious phone call they had received. When questioned, McGraw stated that he was not involved with the crime. However, after interrogation he implicated himself and four other men: Mark Felix Nunez, Leo Valdez Bruce, Dante Parker, and Victor Sarate. This group of men were all young adults with mixed experience with illicit activities. Two of the individuals had significant criminal records.

All were submitted to heavy interrogation sessions, and all of them confessed to the crime of murdering the nine residents of the Buddhist Temple. Some of the confessions pointed out details of the crime that had not been published or released to the public yet.

However, there were many discrepancies in the group's stories and confessions. Two of the individuals were exonerated due to video tape. For Michael McGraw, the video evidence showed him at work during the time of the crime. For Victor Zarate, another video showed him in Tucson at 8:30 a.m. on September 8, 2014. Victor Zarate was later released.

McGraw was still detained despite the evidence, and with Zarate gone, the group of men were called the Tucson Four. All would recant their confessions explaining that before their interrogation they were placed in rooms with photos of the crime committed.

Michael McGraw would later describe his experience during the interrogation to the media. He explained that his interrogation was 44 hours, and he was denied food, rest, and the use of a restroom. He described how the police forced him to urinate into soda cans instead of leaving the interrogation room. He also explained that he was interrogated by 30 law enforcement officers and was denied a lawyer.

While this investigation was taking place, an officer of the special investigation at Luke Airforce found a .22 caliber rifle in Roland Caratachea's, age 17, car. Behind his vehicle was his friend Johnathan Doody, age 17 (*Los Angeles Times* 1994) driving another vehicle. The officer took note because it seemed the Caratachea was trying to hide his weapon from plain view. The next day he saw both boys driving in one car and the rifle gone.

On October 24, 1991, the Arizona Department of Public Safety Ballistics finished analysis of the weapon taken from Caratachea and it matched the .22 caliber shells found at the temple on August 10, 1991. With this evidence the task force searched Johnathan Doody's apartment that he shared with his friend Alessandro "Alex" Garcia and Doody's parent's residents. They found the 20 gauge Stevens shot gun in Doody and Garcia's apartment, and found military paraphernalia, weapons, masks, gloves, and camouflage pants. Doody's younger brother, David, was involved with the temple as well (Ramsland 2008).

With these new suspects, the task force believed that these boys had a connection to the Tucson Four and pursued further investigation to connect the individuals to each other. The Tucson Four were to stay in jail until hair fibers from the scene of the crime were analyzed. They were finally released on November 11, 1991 (Ramsland 2008). Doody and Garcia did say they worked with others in committing the crime, but their testimony proved that they had never met the Tuscon Four. To avoid the death penalty in the Buddhist Temple Massacre case, Garcia pled guilty and testified against Doody.

In his confession, he explained what had happened on August 9, 1991. David Doody had told Garcia about the gold sculpture of Buddha in the temple and about how the monks had around $2,000 dollars hidden in the temple. The two boys planned for two months. They two bought additional military gear over the planning period.

That night they went to the temple around 10:00 p.m. They proceeded to tell the residents to get to the floor and then at gun point arranged them into a circle. While one boy held the nine at gun point, the other would search for valuable objects and partake in vandalism. Later the nun would come in and she was forced to join the circle with the men. Garcia testified that it was Doody who decided to shoot the priests to prevent witnesses.

The Tucson Four

The Tucson Four became suspects when one of them, a mental patient, had called in for a confession. As discussed all men were revealed later as innocent, but all had broken down under interrogation. They were released after three months of incarceration. Mark Felix Nunez, Leo Valdez Bruce, and Dante Parker later filed wrongful arrest civil suits against the sheriff's office. They all accepted the $2.8 million out-of-court settlement offered by Maricopa County. Victor Zarate never did confess to any of the crimes. However, he was still taken to jail.

Doody went to trial in May 1993 and was convicted for the nine murders with additional criminal counts on July 12, 1993. He was sentenced to 281 years in prison and Garcia was sentenced to 271 years in prison (Ramsland 2008). The judge later explained that he did not use the death penalty because he was unsure if it was Garcia or Doody who did the actual killings. In 1991 it was still permissible to sentence youth to the death penalty.

In 2011, Doody had his confession thrown out when the appeals court investigated the coercive tactics used against him. The found that he did not receive adequate Miranda rights before his interrogation, and as a child did not have proper protection during his investigation (lawyer, parents, and so on) (*Doody vs. Ryan* 2011). After the confession was thrown out, he was given a new trial but it ended in a jury deadlock. He was tried again on March 14, 2014, and the jury found him guilty again and sentenced him to 239 years in prison (Kiefer 2014).

ELIZABETH BUSH

See also: Duperrault Family Slayings (November 12, 1961); Gilley Family Murders (April 26, 1984); Heaven's Gate Mass Suicide (March 24–26, 1997); Hudson, Jennifer, Family Murders (October 24, 2008); Wesson Family Massacre (2004)

Further Reading

Johnathan Andrew Doody v. Charles L. Ryan. 2011. Megan Savage, Attorney General of the State Arizona. United State Court of Appeals for the Ninth Circuit. May 4.

Kiefer, Michael. 2014. "Guilty Verdict Reached in Buddhist Temple Massacre." *USA Today. The Arizona Republic.* January 23. Azcentral.com. Accessed April 9, 2015.

Martinez, Shandra, Todd Natenberg, Frederick Bermudez, David Cannella, Christine Keith, Pamela Manson, and Randy Collier. 1991. "9 Found Slain in Valley Temple." The Arizona Republic. August 11. Azcentral.com. Accessed April 9, 2015.

Ramsland, Katherine. 2008. "Buddhist Temple Massacre." http://web.archive.org/web/20121210115401/http://www.trutv.com/library/crime/criminal_mind/forensics/buddhist_temple/index.html.

Times Wire Services. 1994. "Teen-Ager Gets Life in Arizona Temple Murders." *Los Angeles Times.* February 12. http://articles.latimes.com/1994-02-12/news/mn-21916_1_buddhist-temple.

Buenoano, Judy (1943–1998)

Known as the "Black Widow," Judy Buenoano is one of only 14 women who have been executed in the United States since capital punishment was reinstated in 1976. She was the first woman executed in Florida in 150 years, and the first woman to die in the electric chair in over 40 years. She is one of the very small number of female serial killers. Actual execution of female offenders is also quite rare, which is why Judy's story was covered heavily by the media and spurred several books. The cases against Buenoano began in 1983 with a failed murder attempt of her then-boyfriend, John Gentry. An investigation revealed a $500,000 life insurance policy that Gentry was unaware of and the apparent motive for his attempted murder. Judy Buenoano had received at least $240,000 over the previous decade for the deaths of her first husband, her oldest son, and a common-law husband. She had also collected on home insurance policies after at least two separate house fires during that time. Judy was tried for each case, and received the death penalty for one of the murders. A prosecutor in one of the cases dubbed Judy the "Black Widow" because she sustained her materialistic lifestyle through profiting from the deaths of her mates and her son.

Judy (born Judias Welty), like many killers, experienced a tough childhood. Her mother died of an illness when Judy was four years old, and she later claimed to have been beaten, starved, and forced to work long hours on the farm by her father and stepmother. She reportedly served two months in prison at the age of 14 for physically attacking her father, stepmother, and two stepbrothers. Judy chose to live at a reform school after her release rather than return home to her abusive family. She gave birth to her first son, Michael, in 1961. His biological father is unknown. Judy married a sergeant in the U.S. Air Force, James Goodyear,

in 1962. James adopted Michael, and the family was soon complete with the births of James Jr. and Kimberly in 1966 and 1967. Judy opened a child care center in Orlando in 1968. James Goodyear Sr. served a tour of duty in Vietnam, but began suffering from an unidentified illness just three months after his return home in 1971. He died shortly after being admitted to the U.S. Naval Hospital, and Judy cashed in on his three life insurance policies. Judy also suffered a house fire at the end of that year, receiving another $90,000 in insurance money.

Judy soon moved on and relocated to Pensacola to be with Bobby Joe Morris in 1972. Her new life seemed to be going well, except for the disruptions from her oldest son, Michael, who was problematic at school. Michael entered a residential foster care facility for a time until 1977, when the family decided to follow Morris to Chicago. Before leaving Pensacola, however, Judy experienced another house fire and received another insurance payout. Shortly after the move, Morris was admitted to the hospital with mysterious symptoms. He was discharged after a couple of weeks, but returned within two days after collapsing at home. Morris died in January 1978, and Judy collected on his life insurance policies. Bobby Joe Morris's family suspected that Judy was involved in his death, and that it wasn't her first murder. Morris allegedly confessed on his deathbed to his part in killing another man with Judy in 1974, when the couple was visiting Morris's family in Alabama. After Morris's death, Judy moved back to Pensacola and legally changed her last name and that of her children to Buenoano, the Spanish equivalent to Goodyear (as an apparent homage to her first husband). Judy's oldest son, Michael, joined the army in 1979. He soon began experiencing unexplained symptoms, including paraplegia. His limbs weakened, leaving him unable to walk or use his hands. He was given heavy, metal leg braces and discharged into the care of his mother. In May 1980, Judy took Michael and her younger son, James, canoeing on the East River. The canoe overturned, and only Judy and James were able to escape. Michael was weighed down by his heavy braces and drowned. The police accepted Judy's version of events, but army investigators were suspicious. Judy received a payout from Michael's military life insurance policy and two other policies she had taken out on his life.

Judy soon opened her own beauty salon and met her next boyfriend, businessman John Gentry. She misrepresented herself as a former nurse and lied about other credentials. They were soon engaged and Judy hastily convinced Gentry that they should take out life insurance policies on one another, later increasing the value of his policy secretly. Gentry began experiencing mild side effects after taking what Judy provided and told him was vitamin capsules. In June 1983, Judy announced she was pregnant and suggested John Gentry go out to buy some celebratory champagne. When he started his car, a bomb exploded. Gentry was seriously injured, but able to provide information to investigators from his hospital bed within a few days. Gentry found out that Judy had lied to him about her medical qualifications and being pregnant, and had been attempting to poison him with arsenic in the capsules she had been passing along as vitamins. Judy was linked to the attempted murder of Gentry through dynamite, wire, and tape found in her home, as well as other evidence. She was arrested for attempted murder, and the investigation into the numerous insurance payouts and suspicious deaths surrounding her commenced.

Judy bailed out, but was arrested again in January 1984 and charged with murdering her son, Michael. The bodies of Bobby Joe Morris and James Goodyear were exhumed in February and March that year, respectively, revealing traces of arsenic. Arsenic was also found in Michael's remains, and suspected to be the cause of his incapacitating illness. Judy was tried separately for each of the murders and the attempted murder. She was found guilty of murdering her son, and sentenced to 25 years to life without parole. Judy was also found guilty of murdering her first husband, James Goodyear, and sentenced to death by electrocution. She was sentenced in 1985 to 12 years for the attempted murder of John Gentry. Judy was also convicted of several counts of grand theft. Prosecutors in Colorado decided not to pursue the case against Judy for the murder of Bobby Joe Morris since she was already on death row in Florida. She was suspected in the 1974 death of an unnamed man and the 1980 death of another one of her boyfriends, Gerald Dossett. Dossett's body was exhumed around the same time as the others, but no charges were ever made in that case. Judy Buenoano spent 13 years awaiting execution, allegedly discovering religion and always maintaining her innocence. She became a part of history on March 30, 1998, when she was the first woman executed in Florida since 1848.

NICOLE LAROSA

See also: Eubanks, Susan (1964–); Tucker, Karla Faye (1959–1998); Wuornos, Aileen (1956–2002)

Further Reading

Anderson, C., and S. McGehee. 1991. *Bodies of Evidence*. Secaucus, NJ: St. Martin's Paperback.

Bulger, James Joseph "Whitey," Jr. (1929–)

James Joseph Bulger was born September 3, 1929, in Dorchester, Massachusetts, which is part of South Boston. He was known in his neighborhood as a troublemaker even as a youth. He started his life of crime pretty early on and spent some time in a juvenile facility. Upon release, he continued to commit crimes and eventually was sentenced to 25 years in prison for bank robberies. He was paroled after only nine years and upon returning to Boston became part of an organized crime group. Simultaneously to moving up the ranks in the Winter Hill Gang, Bulger also became an informant for the Federal Bureau of Investigation (FBI). While helping the FBI and being somewhat protected, Bulger essentially ruled the organized crime scene in Boston. Eventually, he was dropped as an informant and a case was developed against him. Bulger was tipped off and fled Boston remaining on the run for 16 years. He was caught and arrested in 2011. In 2013, he was found guilty and sentenced to two life sentences and five years.

Bulger was born to James Joseph Bulger Sr. and Jane Veronica "Jean" McCarthy and was the oldest of six children. He received his infamous nickname, Whitey, as a child because of his natural light, almost white, blonde hair. Ironically, despite this nickname being infamous, several have indicated that he actually detests it. Bulger had a reputation as a troublemaker even as a child. He ran rampant through the streets of Southie, a part of South Boston. He even joined the circus for a few weeks as a teenager. While initially his mischief and mayhem involved fights, car chases, and other minor crime, it eventually escalated to that of a more serious nature. His first run-in with the police happened when he was only 14 years old for stealing. He later would spend five years in a juvenile reformatory. When released, Bulger joined the Air Force. His youthful criminal career did not end and he was arrested for assault and for being absent without leave (AWOL). He was honorably discharged in 1952.

Upon returning to Boston, he continued to advance his criminal career and in 1956 was sentenced to 25 years in federal prison for a string of bank robberies. He served nine years in multiple prisons including Atlanta, Alcatraz, and Leavenworth, before being paroled. He again returned to Boston and became involved with organized crime. By the early 1970s, Bulger had teamed up with Stephen Joseph Flemmi (June 9, 1935–present). While they started as associates to organized crime, Bulger eventually became the leader of the Winter Hill Gang. Upon initially joining the gang, he built a reputation of violence and moved rapidly through the ranks. It is said that he even sanctioned killings of many prominent figures in the area. The Winter Hill Gang was known for fixing horse races by paying jockeys to throw them. Eventually the race fixing became known to police and one of the gang's members agreed to a plea bargain where he would testify against the Winter Hill Gang and during testimony released the names of Howie Winter (March 17, 1929–present)—the then leader of the Winter Hill Gang, James Bulger, and Stephen Flemmi. Bulger and Flemmi were eventually not indicted for the crime due to connections with the FBI. It was after Howie Winter, former leader of the Winter Hill Gang, was indicted and found guilty in 1979 for fixing the races that Bulger assumed the position of leader.

Bulger's relationship with the FBI began back in 1975. There tends to be some debate on why Bulger agreed to become an informant with the FBI. One suggestion is that he was convinced by Special Agent John Connolly to become an informant. Connolly grew up in the same neighborhood as Bulger and even had a few run-ins with him when they were young. Another suggestion is that his friend and associate, Flemmi, had been working as an informant for years, some suggesting since 1965, and had betrayed Bulger. This left Bulger with the option of joining the FBI or go back to prison. Regardless of how he became an informant, he helped the FBI immensely when it came to taking down a mafia family. While helping the FBI, he essentially built up the Winter Hill gang and created a very powerful and rich organization. It seemingly was a good tradeoff: Bulger supplied information to the FBI and they, in turn, essentially protected him from being taken down. During the years as an informant, Bulger supplied information on several associates that led to arrests. He also helped with the take down of the Italian American Patriarca crime family. After the arrest of their boss, Gennaro Angiulo, and his associates, the Patriarcas fell apart and Bulger and Flemmi were able to take control of organized crime in Boston. It was during his time as an informant that Bulger's crime escalated. He was now in control and he and his gang took part in extortion, loansharking, truck hijackings, firearms trafficking, drug trafficking, and murder to name a few.

Unfortunately for Bulger and Flemmi, the union ended in the early 1990s when Connolly retired. The FBI dropped them as informants and began looking into their criminal activities. By 1995 the FBI had collected enough evidence to arrest them both. However, Bulger was tipped off prior to the arrest and fled the area. He had prepared for such a day and had set up safe deposit boxes containing cash and passports in many locations across the globe. Bulger was on the run trying to escape imprisonment for 16 years. Prior to his capture, he was added to the FBI's 10 most wanted list in 2000 and a $2 million reward for information leading to his capture was offered. In fact, he moved up the list to the second most wanted, only behind Osama bin Laden. He appeared on America's most wanted 16 times. A task force was developed and a media campaign was launched in an attempt to capture Bulger. Bulger was finally arrested on June 22, 2011, in Santa Monica, California. He and his girlfriend, Catherine Greig, had supposedly been living in the same apartment for 13 years. A tip from a neighbor led to his arrest. He was charged with murder, conspiracy to commit murder, extortion, narcotics distribution, and money-laundering.

Bulger was arraigned in a federal court on July 6, 2011. He pled not guilty to 48 charges including 19 counts of murder, extortion, money-laundering, obstruction of justice, perjury, narcotics distribution, and weapon violations. Bulger's trial began in June 2013 and lasted two months. The jury consisting of eight men and four women found Bulger guilty on 31 counts including federal racketeering, extortion, conspiracy, and 11 of the 19 murders. He was found not guilty of seven murders and the jury was unable to reach a verdict on one murder. Bulger, at the age of 83, was sentenced to two consecutive life sentences plus five years in prison on November 13, 2013. As of September 2014, he was in a federal prison in Florida.

Melissa J. Tetzlaff-Bemiller

See also: Gigante, Vincent "the Chin" (1928–2005); Gotti, John (1940–2002); Gravano, Salvatore "Sammy the Bull" (1945–)

Further Reading

Globe Spotlight Team. 1998. "Whitey & The FBI: Parts 1–5." http://www.bostonglobe.com/metro/1998/07/19/agent-mobster-forge-pact-old-southie-ties/Omh1bi12NTIr4FgaeWT78M/story.html. Accessed February 15, 2015.

"Whitey Bulger." Biography.com. http://www.biography.com/people/whitey-bulger--328770. Accessed February 15, 2015.

"Whitey Bulger Special Reports". Boston.com. http://www.boston.com/news/specials/whitey/. Accessed February 15, 2015.

Bumpurs, Eleanor, Shooting of (1984)

A white New York City policeman fatally shot Eleanor Bumpurs (1918–1984), a black senior citizen who was also mentally ill, in October 1984. The Bronx district attorney prosecuted the case and after some legal gymnastics, the courts finally acquitted the policeman. The Eleanor Bumpurs case still resonates because it is disturbing and disputed on many levels.

The undisputed facts about Eleanor Bumpurs include the fact that she was African American, 5 feet 8 inches tall, and overweight—some accounts say she weighed 275 pounds and other accounts say 300 pounds. The 66-year-old senior citizen suffered from arthritis and diabetes, and according to the New York City Housing Commission, the New York City Police, her neighbors, and even her children, she had been mentally ill for years. Eleanor Bumpurs lived in the Sedgwick Houses, 1551 University Avenue West 174th Street in the Highbridge section of the Bronx. There is also no argument that she had failed to pay her monthly rent of $89.44 for five months, and that more than one source said that Eleanor Bumpurs believed that government agents were coming through her walls to capture her.

The disputed facts revolve around the events of Monday, October 29, 1984, when city marshals knocked on Eleanor Bumpurs's door, apartment 4A, at 9:00 a.m. They had come to evict her from public housing and hospitalize her for what a city hired psychiatrist termed psychosis. Eleanor Bumpurs answered the knocks on her bolted door with screamed threats to pour lye on the heads of anyone who dared enter her apartment or continue to bother her. According to a New York Times story dated October 30, 1984, when emergency police officers arrived at apartment 4A, at 9:00 a.m., they broke down the door, entered her apartment, and found Eleanor Bumpers naked and hysterical in a room of the size of a closet. Lunging at them with a 10-inch butcher knife, she first attacked Officer George Adams and then turned to Officer John Elter. Officer Stephen Sullivan fired two shots, first shooting off her hand and then hitting her in the chest with his 12-gauge shotgun.

The grieving daughters of Eleanor Bumpurs and others were outraged that six police officers had restrained and killed an elderly woman over rent payments, and the incident caused a public outcry, especially since Eleanor Bumpurs was black, a senior citizen, mentally ill, and the policemen were white. Journalists wrote stories questioning police procedures, weapon-carrying practices, and fact that two shots had been fired at Eleanor Bumpurs. People also questioned the competency and complicity of the New York Human Resources Administration, although Eleanor's daughters had ignored several Human Resources Administration letters.

New York mayor Ed Koch said that her death "must distress every citizen," and he appointed a committee to question police procedures. Democratic congressman John Conyers Jr. of Michigan soon joined the New York mayor in investigating the Eleanor Bumpurs incident. The congressman's congressional subcommittee concluded in its report that racism appeared to be a major factor in New York police–community relations. Mayor Koch labeled the Conyers report one sided and unfair and The New York Daily News countered that New York had "one of the toughest police codes of conduct in the nation."

A Bronx grand jury convened to investigate Officer Stephen Sullivan's actions. Bronx district attorney Mario Merola prosecuted the case. After the grand jury indicted him on charges of second-degree manslaughter on January 30, 1985, about 5,000 police officers marched in protest. Officer Sullivan pled not guilty and on April 12, 1985, Judge Vincent A. Vitale of the New York State Supreme Court dismissed the indictment. He ruled that under the New York State Penal Code the evidence was legally insufficient to support the charged offense or any lesser included offense and that Officer Sullivan had conformed with the guidelines and procedures outlined in the New York Police Department's Emergency Service Unit Manual.

In a turn on appeal, the New York Court of Appeals reinstated Officer Sullivan's second-degree manslaughter indictment by a 6–1 vote. The lone dissenter, Chief Justice Sol Wachtler, argued that that evidence warranted more serious charges. Waving his right to a jury trial, Officer Stephen Sullivan opted for a bench trial before a judge only, basing his defense on the premise that he shot to protect a fallen comrade who was in the path of Eleanor Bumpurs's kitchen knife. The prosecution contended that the second fatal shot that Officer Sullivan fired at Eleanor Bumpurs was unnecessary because his first shot had shattered her hand and made it impossible for her to continue to wield the butcher knife she had been using to fight the police officers.

Officer Sullivan's trial opened on January 12, 1987. The verdict hinged on whether or not Officer Sullivan had used excessive force, especially in firing two shots at Eleanor Bumpurs. The police officers who had gone to her apartment with him testified that the first shot had not immobilized Eleanor Bumpurs when it hit her hand, so she still posed a threat to the police. Two doctors also testified that Eleanor Bumpurs could have continued to slash at the officers with her knife even after her hand had been injured by the first shotgun blast. Contradicting their testimony, the emergency room doctor who had treated Eleanor Bumpurs immediately after the shooting reiterated his grand jury testimony that the first shot left her hand a "bloody stump."

After a six-week trial, Judge Fred W. Eggert acquitted Office Stephen Sullivan of both the manslaughter and criminal negligence charges in a Bronx courtroom while over two hundred people protested the verdict and the fact that the small courtroom excluded some people from the trial. On August 4, 1987, federal prosecutors declined to investigate the Eleanor Bumpurs case. The U.S. attorney in Manhattan at the time, Rudy Giuliana, said that he found nothing indicating that the case had not been tried fairly and competently and that he saw no evidence that the policemen had used excessive force.

The New York City Department of Human Services eventually demoted two supervisors for failing to seek an emergency rent grant for Eleanor Bumpurs and for not providing her with psychiatric aid. The Bumpurs family eventually filed a civil suit against New York City suing for $10 million in damages. In March 1990, the city of New York agreed to pay $200,000 to the Eleanor Bumpurs estate, ending the legal actions resulting from her death. The New York Police Department revised its guidelines to stipulate that a senior officer be present before police can confront an emotionally disturbed person. The New York police also started to carry less lethal weapons, including Tasers.

KATHY WARNES

See also: Diallo, Amadou, Shooting of (1999); Hampton, Fred, Shooting of (December 3, 1969); King, Rodney, Beating of (1991); McDuffie, Arthur, Death of (1979)

Further Reading

Abel, Roger L. 2006. *The Black Shields.* n.p.: Authorhouse.

"The Bumpurs Case Endures." 1987. *New York Times.* February 27.

"The Eleanor Bumpurs Case." 1984. *New York Magazine.* December 17.

Hacker, Andrew. 2003. *Two Nations: Black and White, Separate, Hostile, Unequal.* New York: Scribner.

Hudson, Edward. 1987. "Ex-Officer Describes Key Moment at the Scene of the Bumpurs Shooting." *New York Times.* January 21.

"New York City Agrees to Pay Heirs in Bumpurs Case." 1991. *New York Times.* March 29.

Prial, Frank. 1987a. "Judge Acquits Sullivan in Shotgun Slaying of Bumpers." *New York Times.* February 27.

Prial, Frank. 1987b. "Officer Tells of Two Shots at Bumpurs." *New York Times.* February 6.

Raab, Selwyn. 1984. "Autopsy Finds that Bumpurs Was Hit By Two Blasts." *New York Times.* November 27.

Raab, Selwyn. 1985. "State Judge Dismisses Indictment of Officer in the Bumpurs Killing." *New York Times.* April 13.

Bundy, Ted (1946–1989)

Ted Bundy was one of America's most infamous, notorious, and active serial murderers. He carried out killings in Washington, California, Oregon, Utah, Florida, and Colorado during the 1970s. He escaped from prison twice. His victims were young, intelligent Caucasian women with long hair parted in the middle. Some of them he knew from his classes. He knocked them down, violently assaulted and sexually abused them, and strangled them. Shortly before his execution, he told his lawyer about having killed between 40 and 50 women. The precise number will never be known. As he was exceptionally organized, some of his crime scenes have never been located either. His motives have remained unclear as well. Also, the day of his first killing is unknown. According to his lawyer, before his execution, Bundy indicated that it happened in 1972. However, his first confirmed murder is Linda Healy, a student at the University of Washington who vanished in 1974. His last victim was 12-year-old Kimberley Leach. Bundy was already in custody when her body was discovered in an abandoned hog shed.

Ted Bundy was born Theodore Robert Cowell in Burlington, Vermont, on November 24, 1946, in a home for unwed mothers. Although his mother claimed an affair with a war veteran, people believed the baby to be by her own abusive father. Bundy spent the first few years of his life in Philadelphia, Pennsylvania, believing his maternal grandparents to be his parents and his mother to be his older sister. In 1950, they moved to Tacoma, Washington, to live with other relatives. A year later, his mother married Johnny Culpepper Bundy, who officially adopted Ted. Bundy was an intelligent and popular student. However, in junior high school he became quiet and less confident. He would spend his time reading pulp detective magazines and tales about victims of sexual violence. After high school, he got in trouble with the juvenile court for burglary and shoplifting. At the University of Washington in Seattle, where Bundy enrolled, he met the woman whom he considered to be the love of his life. When she broke up with him, he went to Vermont, where he learned the truth about his mother. He returned to school and graduated with honors in psychology. His ex-girlfriend was impressed

Informed of his indictment by the Leon County, Florida, grand jury, serial Ted Bundy mugs for the media. Bundy was indicted on two counts of first-degree murder, three counts of attempted murder, and two counts of burglary in the Chi Omega sorority house. (AP Photo)

with the new Bundy and agreed to marry him. However, in January 1974, he unexpectedly ended the engagement and young women began vanishing in Washington State. In fall, Bundy enrolled in law school at the University of Utah in Salt Lake City, where he brutally raped and killed several women.

As Bundy spread his "hunting ground" to other states, connecting these crimes was challenging for law enforcement. He had a gift of adapting his appearance to his surroundings similar to a chameleon. Witnesses found it hard to recognize him in photos as he looked so different in each photo, and even in person his different expressions were confusing. But all of the witnesses described him as a man who wore a cast on his arm or on his leg and used this disability as a way to lure women into his VW Beetle, asking them to help him load items into his car. His girlfriend responded to the public profile that the police had issued

and reported Bundy to the Salt Lake City police. However, he was quickly released.

Bundy was finally arrested when pulled over for a traffic violation. He claimed he had seen a movie and had got lost on the way home. When Bundy gave the officer the wrong movie title, a second officer was called. They searched Bundy's trunk and found a pair of handcuffs, a pantyhose mask, torn strips of sheets, ropes, and an ice pick. The officers thought they had caught a burglar and took Bundy's fingerprints. He was sent home expecting charges for the possession of burglary tools. However, when Salt Lake City detectives heard about a VW Beetle and handcuffs during a weekly police meeting, they connected him to more serious crimes. Later, Carol DaRonch, who had managed to escape, identified him. He was then charged with attempted kidnapping and sentenced to prison. Soon after, based on evidence of phone bills, hair samples, credit card slips, gas receipts, and witnesses, he was moved to Aspen to stand trial for murdering Caryn Campbell. He escaped by jumping out of a window from the second floor of the courthouse but was recaptured after a week. A few months later he again escaped through the steel ceiling of his prison cell. He flew to Chicago and then moved down to Florida, where he got a room near Florida State University. He assaulted four sisters of the university's Chi Omega sorority in one night, killing two of them. In a house nearby, he abused another woman but failed to kill her.

It was unusual for Bundy, who was particularly cautious, to assault five women in one night and to leave them at the crime scene. He had probably realized that he was unable to stop killing and that he would get caught again. On February 15, 1978, he was arrested in Pensacola, Florida, for driving a stolen car, and, despite using a false name, was identified that same day.

When Bundy was on trial for the murders of the sorority sisters, he was his own defense attorney. In this televised trial, he appeared confident and eloquent and occasionally became quite aggressive. He insisted on his innocence, but one of the dead women had Bundy's bite marks on her legs, bottom, and one of her nipples. These bite marks were the main evidence that led to his conviction for the murders.

During these legal proceedings in Florida, Carole Boone, with whom he had worked at the Washington State Department of Emergency Services in 1974, became his steady girlfriend and he later married her. She claimed that Bundy was the father of a girl to whom she gave birth in 1981.

In the subsequent search for motives behind Bundy's crimes, family members in Philadelphia described him as an embittered racist who beat women and abused animals. His aunt recalled that when she was 15 and he was three, he woke her by throwing several carving knives in her bed. Bundy himself put the blame on the violent pornography he had seen. He also blamed his grandfather, describing him as anti-Semitic and racist, torturing animals and beating his wife. In Bundy's mind, guilt was an unhealthy illusion that controlled people. He felt sorry for people who felt guilty and he did not.

During his time on death row, he ambitiously fought his sentence, gave interviews, and offered to help create a profile of the Green River Killer, believing he was the only person with a Ph.D. in serial murder. But on January 24, 1989, he was executed in the electric chair.

DANIELA RIBITSCH

See also: Dahmer, Jeffrey (1960–1994); Gacy, John Wayne (1942–1994); Ridgway, Gary Leon (1949–)

Further Reading

Keppel, Robert D., with William J. Birnes. 1995. *The Riverman. Ted Bundy and I Hunt for the Green River Killer.* New York: Pocket Books.

Michaud, Stephen G., and Hugh Aynesworth. 1999. *The Only Living Witness. The True Story of Serial Sex Killer Ted Bundy.* Irving, TX: Authorlink.

Rule, Ann. 2008. *The Stranger beside Me.* New York: Pocket Books.

Vronsky, Peter. 2004. *Serial Killers. The Method and Madness of Monsters.* New York: Berkley Books.

Buono, Angelo. *See* Bianchi, Kenneth (1951–)and Angelo Buono (1934–2002)

Burns, Robert Elliot (1892–1955)

Notorious for his involvement in the abolition of the chain gang system in 1945, Robert Burns fought the Georgia prison system for 13 years before finally receiving a pardon from Georgia governor Ellis Arnall. The conflict began in 1922 when Burns was given a 6- to 10-year sentence of hard labor in Atlanta, Georgia, for robbery. Exposed to inhumane conditions in the chain gang system, Burns fled from the Campbell County chain gang on June 21, 1922, and successfully evaded prison officials for eight years. Burns was eventually caught and extradited back to Georgia in 1929, where he was placed back in the chain gang system. Again Burns escaped from the system, becoming motivated to write his story, *I Am a Fugitive from a Georgia Chain Gang*. Published in 1931, this provided the public with a firsthand account of the corruption and brutality the prisoners in the Georgia chain gain system endured. The publicity was nationwide, generating a shift in public opinion against chain gangs. When he gained support of New Jersey governor Arthur Harry Moore, Burns fought his second extradition in December 1932. As a result of the extradition hearings against Burns, an examination of the Georgia penal system resulted in the repeal of the chain gang system in 1945.

Robert Elliot Burns was born in Queens, New York, on May 10, 1892. His younger brother, Vincent J. Burns, was a lifelong supporter of Robert. At age 25, Burns was a successful business accountant when the United States entered World War I in 1917, and he enlisted and fought for the next year. When the veteran returned, Burns suffered from shellshock, leading into his lifestyle as a homeless wanderer. In 1922, while jumping on freight trains to look for work, he was held at gunpoint and coerced into participating in a robbery in Atlanta. Hoping that the judge would be understanding of the circumstances, Burns pleaded guilty only to receive a 6- to 10-year sentence of hard labor in a chain gang. Approximately 140 chain gang camps existed in Georgia as a result of the states' approval for prisons to use offenders for public service projects as a source of revenue.

Burns was first sent to the Fulton County chain gang, a strict camp where at the end of each workday a few men from the chain gang were identified by guards and taken to be beaten with a leather strap. In June 1922, after being transferred to a more relaxed camp, Burns escaped from the Campbell County chain gang. A fugitive of the state, Burns fled to Chicago where he lived as a successful businessman and the editor of *Greater Chicago Magazine*. By March 1929, Burns, a married man, was seeking a divorce to be with another woman. This provoked his first wife to write the Georgia prison officials, notifying them of his location. On May 22, 1929, two Chicago detectives served an arrest warrant from Georgia for the extradition of Burns.

In the fight against his extradition, Burns's brother Vincent and many of his influential friends quickly publicized his case nationwide while Burns told the gruesome tales of being in the Georgia chain gang system. These actions allowed him to gain public support but also aggravate the already-angry Georgia state officials. Prison officials from Georgia went to Chicago to make a deal with Burns, agreeing that if he dropped his fight against extradition that he would not be sent to serve in another chain gang and that he would be released within 90 days. Since Burns knew of his fame among the public, he was sure that Georgia would not go back on their deal.

Deceived, Burns arrived in Atlanta, Georgia, on June 24, 1929, where he was sent back to the Campbell County chain gang from which he had first escaped. For five weeks Burns worked a job in the warden's office. However, once media and local attention died down, Burns returned to the chain gang. He was then transferred to Troup County Stockade, the camp most notorious for its brutality. After two months in the Georgia prison system, Burns's first hearing before the Prison Commission was held, and he was denied release.

On September 3, 1930, Burns escaped from the Georgia chain gang camp again. Fleeing to Newark, New Jersey, where his brother, Vincent, and his widowed mother lived, Burns finally decided to tell the full truth about Georgia's corrupt system. Mainly with the support of Vincent, in early 1931 Burns wrote a short story, *I Am a Fugitive from a Georgia Chain Gang,* for the *True Detective Magazine.* His story gained millions of fans and was such a big success that Burns had Vincent rewrite the story in book form. Published by the Vanguard Press in 1932, Warner Brothers quickly bought film rights and made Burns a technical advisor. By the spring of 1932, Burns was in Hollywood, but with so much publicity from the book alone, Georgia officials were offering a reward for Burns's capture. Warner Brothers had provided protection for Burns, but after two weeks he left, still fearing that he was to be extradited to Georgia at any time. Warner Brothers released the movie, *I Am a Fugitive from a Chain Gang*, in Atlanta, Georgia, on November 11, 1932.

As a result, Georgia officials were furious. Tracking Burns to Newark, New Jersey, they insistently tried to get New Jersey officials to serve an arrest warrant for extradition. For a short time Vincent used his political ties to keep Burns from going back to Georgia. However, as Burns continued to flaunt his freedom in front of the media, Vincent's connections in the Newark Police Department finally had the last straw with his publicity. On December 14, 1932, Burns was arrested and sent to the Essex County Jail in Newark. At the hearing, Georgia was represented by Troup County warden Harold Hardy and police chief R.B. Carter; Burns was represented by attorney Charles Handler.

The findings of the hearing was the extradition was denied after Burns's attorney produced a copy of a check, proving that Burns reimbursed Georgia for his previous extradition costs and served a sentence of 400 days compared to the deal of only 90. With the proof of the agreement made between Burns and Georgia in 1929 in a letter from the Chicago judge who oversaw the deal, Governor Moore was convinced that Burns had served more than his sentence. In 1945, Burns was pardoned by newly elected Georgia governor Ellis Arnall. With the public's responsiveness to Burns's book and the movie, the chain gang system was eliminated through the prison reform led by Governor Arnall.

CHELSEY R. BELL

See also: Abu Ghraib Prisoner Abuse Scandal (Iraq) (2003–2004); Attica Prison Riot (1971); Wirz, Captain Henry (1823–1865)

Further Reading

Burns, Robert. E. 1997. *I Am a Fugitive from a Georgia Chain Gang!* Athens: University of Georgia Press.

New Jersey History's Mysteries. 2013. "The Man Who Broke a Thousand Chains." http://www.njhm.com/burns.htm. Accessed April 14, 2015.

Burr, Aaron. *See* Burr, Aaron, Treason Trial of (1807); Burr–Hamilton Duel (July 11, 1804)

Burr, Aaron, Treason Trial of (1807)

The early 1800s was quite the dramatic times for Aaron Burr. Burr had become a U.S. vice president, shot and killed a Founding Father, conspired to establish an independent republic, and put on trial for treason. The 1804 duel with Alexander Hamilton had already made Aaron Burr infamous, and the Burr Conspiracy and subsequent treason trial added to Burr's infamy. Acknowledged by historians and scholars as one of the most significant criminal trials in American history, the Burr Treason Trial was important for several reasons. First, the legal proceedings lasted seven months and featured some of the nation's best lawyers. Second, it placed President Thomas Jefferson, Chief Justice John Marshall, and former vice president Aaron Burr against each other. In addition, the rights of criminal defendants, America's definition of treason, and the significance of separation of powers in the Constitution were all scrutinized in the trial.

The election of 1800 (the first national election with political parties) had Thomas Jefferson and Aaron Burr tied in the electoral college voting for the presidency. Hamilton lobbied Congress behind the scenes to vote against Burr in the runoff election and Jefferson went on to win the U.S. presidency. Burr had to settle for vice presidency. In 1804, Burr lost a bid for governor of New York. Hamilton had also lobbied against Burr's New York gubernatorial attempt. Burr and Hamilton had long been political rivals, and bothered by defeat and angered by Hamilton's relentless criticisms, Burr challenged Hamilton to a duel. On the early morning of July 11, 1804, Hamilton and Burr met in Weehawken, New Jersey, to settle their long-standing feud. When the duel was over, Hamilton would die after being shot by Burr, and Burr's political hopes in the East would also die. However, Burr saw hope and looked to the West for a chance at a second political life.

After his term as vice president ended (March 4, 1805), financially ruined, indicted for Hamilton's murder, and virtually an exile from New York state, Burr set out on a river voyage that would construct a web of cohorts that would forever be connected to the alleged Burr Conspiracy. In early May 1805, Burr visited Harman Blennerhassett on an island Blennerhassett owned in the Ohio River. It is not known what Burr and Blennerhassett discussed but this visit would link Blennerhassett with the Burr Conspiracy. Continuing down the Ohio River, and stopping in Cincinnati, Burr visited with a close friend, former Ohio senator Jonathan Dayton, who would later be indicted with Burr for treason. Burr then traveled to Nashville, Tennessee, where Burr stayed as the guest of General Andrew Jackson. After resuming his river voyage, Burr met with U.S. general James Wilkinson, who was the governor of Louisiana Territory and suspected of being an agent of Spain. Wilkinson was an interesting personality who had formerly been the head of a group in the Western states that favored a separation of the Western states from the Eastern states. Although historians are not certain on Burr's exact motives, speculation was Burr planned to either separate the Western states from the Union or seize territories in Spanish Florida, Texas, and Mexico to form an independent Union. Wilkinson supplied Burr with a barge, a sergeant, 10 armed men, and other traveling supplies. In 1806, Burr led the small armed group toward New Orleans, prompting immediate scrutiny by U.S. authorities.

Shortly, General Wilkinson for unclear reasons had decided to abandon the conspiracy and turned against Burr. In early October, an encrypted letter sent by Burr reached Wilkinson in New Orleans. Wilkinson decoded the letter and was determined to end Burr's plans. Wilkinson sent messages to President Jefferson detailing Burr's treasonous plot. On January 22, 1807, President Jefferson decreed Burr guilty of treason to Congress and to the public without a grand jury indictment or the benefit of a trial. Once more information regarding Burr's activities were known, and a warrant for his arrest was issued. On February 19, 1807, Burr was arrested, taken to Fort Stoddart for two weeks, and then sent to Richmond, Virginia, to be tried in a U.S. Circuit Court.

United States v. Aaron Burr was of national significance for both then and future America because surrounding it was constitutional implications such as individuals' right to due process, the definition of treason, and the objectivity of the national judiciary from partisan politics. Another question this case addressed was should the president of the United States have to appear in court when a judge requires him to be a witness?

On May 22, 1807, the Burr Treason Trial opened and Chief Justice John Marshall and Virginia district judge Cyrus Griffin presided over the court. Burr's council represented some of the best legal minds of the times, which included Luther Martin, Benjamin Botts, Edmund Randolph, John Wickham, Charles Lee, and also Burr himself cross-examined most of the prosecution's witnesses. The U.S. team of prosecutors included Alexander McCrae, George Hay, Caesar Rodney, and William Wirt. Prior to trial opening, during grand jury hearings Burr requested the court to subpoena President Jefferson so that Burr could view the evidence the prosecution would use against him. Chief Justice Marshall, in assuring due process throughout the proceedings, found himself ruling in opposition to President Jefferson who insisted on protection of presidential privilege. Marshall's ruling established precedence that not even the president is above the law.

The dramatic confrontations that were in abundance during the trial had significant results. Among the results and arguably most important to the U.S. citizen was the interpretation of due process as it is applied during the course of the criminal justice process. Although Burr had become a very unpopular character and charged as a traitor to the nation, Chief Justice Marshall applied the principles of equal protection and a well-ordered court process that is exemplified in the Fifth and Sixth Amendments to the Constitution.

Another major legal issue the Burr trial considered was whether England's common-law or America's constitutional definition of treason would be applied in the case. Due to the British abuse of common law, the Founding Founders feared a tyrannical government. They wrote into the Constitution: "Treason against the United States shall consist only in levying war against them, or in adhering to their enemies, giving them aid and comfort. No person shall be convicted of treason unless on the testimony of two witnesses to the same overt act, or on confession in open court" (Art. III, Sect. 3). Chief Justice Marshall's accepted the defense's argument that the application of the U.S. Constitution's definition of treason is

to be used in American courts for both legal and ethical reasons.

Although President Jefferson publicly insisted on Burr's guilt, on September 1, 1807, Burr was acquitted on the charges of treason. Chief Justice Marshall stated that although Burr had conspired against the United States, he was not guilty of treason because he had not been proven to have involved in an "overt act," as the Constitution requires. However, despite Burr's acquittal, he was a disgraced man and condemned by the public. Burr sailed to Europe where he lived for several years before returning to New York, where he resumed practicing law.

MICHAEL JOHNSON

See also: Arnold, Benedict (1741–1801); Burr–Hamilton Duel (July 11, 1804); *Primary Documents*/The Treason Trial of Aaron Burr: Prosecutor William Wirt's Speech to the Jury (1807)

Further Reading

Burton, H. H. 1951. "Justice the Guardian of Liberty: John Marshall at the Trial of Aaron Burr." *American Bar Association Journal* 735–788.

Hobson, F., Charles. 2006. *The Aaron Burr Treason Trial*. Federal Trials and Great Debates in United States History. Washington, DC: Federal Judicial Center.

Melton, B. F. 2001. *Aaron Burr: Conspiracy to Treason*. New York: John Wiley & Sons.

Rorabaugh, W. J. 1995. "The Political Duel in the Early Republic: *Burr v. Hamilton.*" *Journal of the Early Republic*: 1–23.

Burr–Hamilton Duel (July 11, 1804)

On the bright sunny morning of July 11, 1804, Alexander Hamilton and Aaron Burr stood on a small neck of land in Weehawken, New Jersey, their dueling pistols trained on each other. Hamilton and Burr stood on a ledge measuring about 11 paces wide and 20 paces long and 20 feet above the Hudson River on the Palisades not far from Captain James Deas's mansion. Long since eroded away, the ledge supported 18 documented duels and an unknown number of undocumented contests between 1798 and 1845.

In 1800, the two rival lawyers had worked together to acquit accused murdered Levi Weeks in a sensational New York City trial, but for the most part their relationship featured bitter rivalry and hatred. By 1804, Alexander Hamilton and Aaron Burr had also woven themselves into the political fabric of fledgling America. Federalist Alexander Hamilton had served the new U.S. government in various capacities including George Washington's secretary of the treasury In 1791, Aaron Burr won a U.S. Senate seat from Philip Schuyler, Alexander Hamilton's father-in-law. Treasury Secretary Hamilton fumed over the loss of an ally to support his policies. In 1800, Democrat-Republican Aaron Burr published a pamphlet highly critical of John Adams that Hamilton had written, which embarrassed Hamilton and widened rifts in the Federalist party. In the congressionally decided election of 1800, Aaron Burr and Thomas Jefferson were tied in electoral college balloting, and Hamilton lobbied Congress to decide the election for Jefferson with Burr as vice president.

The 1804 New York governor's race cocked the already politically loaded dueling pistols. Aaron Burr abandoned the Republicans and to run as an independent, believing that a victory would restore his power. Hamilton tried to persuade New York Federalists not to support Burr and his efforts contributed to the victory of Republican candidate Morgan Lewis. Then, at a dinner party in 1804, New York Republican Dr. Charles D. Cooper attended a dinner party and listened to Alexander Hamilton make an eloquent speech against Burr. Later Dr. Cooper wrote a letter to Hamilton's father-in-law Philip Schuyler, objecting to Hamilton's speech and the *Albany Register* published the letter.

With one eye fastened on his political career, Aaron Burr challenged Alexander Hamilton to a duel, which shoved Hamilton squarely in the crosshairs of a decision. If he admitted to using intemperate language about Burr, he would be deemed dishonorable, but if he refused Burr's challenge, he would also be judged dishonorable. His political career would end either way.

In the early morning hours of July 11, 1804, the two adversaries took separate boats to the Heights of Weehawken in New Jersey. To hide the evidence of a duel, the pistols were carried in a portmanteau and the rowers stood with their backs to the dueling men so they would not see any pistols.

According to the account of historian Joseph Ellis, Burr and his seconds and rowers arrived at the dueling site about half past six and began to clear underbrush from the dueling site. Hamilton and his second and Dr. David Hosack arrived a few minutes before seven, and Judge Nathaniel Pendleton, Hamilton's second, won the casting of lots for position and started the duel. Burr had challenged Hamilton, so Hamilton had the choice of both weapons and position, and Hamilton chose the upstream or north side position.

The two political and personal enemies fired their .56 caliber pistols at each other—smoothbore flint lock pistols, typical of American dueling weapons between 1750 and 1850. Alexander Hamilton symbolically chose the same pair of Wogdon dueling pistols, which his brother-in-law had used to shoot the button off Aaron Burr's coat five years earlier. Later officials discovered that Hamilton's pistols had been fitted with a hair trigger that allowed him an exceptionally accurate aim, a trigger so sensitive that a premature touch would have fired the pistol. Aaron Burr had the reputation of being a poor shot, but his steady aim showed his firm resolve.

Accounts of what happened at the duel differ. Some narratives report that Hamilton intentionally did not fire at Burr and others contend that he fired too soon. Historian Andrew Burstein noted Hamilton's dueling pistols with the larger barrel and secret hair trigger, stating that Hamilton gave himself an unfair advantage in the duel, but he lost anyway.

Historian Joseph Ellis surmises that Hamilton fired first and intentionally, but he aimed to miss Burr, sending his bullet into the tree above and behind where Burr stood. He did not withhold or waste his shot, honoring a pledge he had made before the duel. Burr did not know about the pledge and when the bullet from Hamilton's gun whizzed past him and thudded to the tree behind him, the principles of the Code Duello justified Burr in firing at Hamilton to kill.

Aaron Burr fired at Alexander Hamilton and hit him in the lower abdomen above his right hip. The musket ball ricocheted off Hamilton's second or third false rib and fractured it, causing much damage to his liver, diaphragm, and other internal organs and finally lodging in his lumbar vertebra. In his account Judge Pendleton said that Hamilton immediately collapsed and dropped his pistol while Burr moved toward him in seeming remorse before his second hustled him away.

Alexander Hamilton was paralyzed from the waist down, but still alive and his friends brought him to the home of his friend William Bayard on the Manhattan shore. Slowly bleeding to death internally like his son Philip had done, Hamilton died at 2:00 p.m. on the afternoon of July 12, 1804. He was buried in the Trinity Churchyard Cemetery in Manhattan. His friend Gouverneur Morris read the eulogy at his funeral and established a private fund to support his widow Elizabeth and their seven children.

Duels in American History

By 1804, dueling had become as woven into the fabric of American life as slavery and like slavery continued to grow. Despite the efforts of states, especially Northern states including New York, to outlaw both dueling and slavery, both grew in popularity over the next 30 years. In the South, influenced by the Code Duello and the Code of Chivalry, combatants chose dueling to defend their honor or even murder a rival without fear of prosecution. Both Hamilton and Burr had been involved in past duels, with Hamilton acting as principal in at least 10 shot less duels and acting as a second in at least two duels. Ironically Hamilton's son Philip was killed in a duel with George I. Eacker on November 23, 1801. In his letters, Aaron Burr claimed to have had two previous disputes about honor with Alexander Hamilton, while Hamilton contended they had just one previous honor incident.

Burr was indicted for murder and acquitted in New York and a grand jury in Bergen County, New Jersey, indicted Aaron Burr for murder in November 1804, but the New Jersey Supreme Court dismissed the indictment. Burr sought refuge with his daughter in South Carolina, but he soon returned to Washington D.C. to serve out his term as vice president. The death of Alexander Hamilton and the political backlash from the duel ended Aaron Burr's political career, and Hamilton's death also further weakened the Federalist Party, already weak from the defeat of John Adams in the 1800 presidential election.

Aaron Burr went West and became involved in a plan to establish a separate country from the Louisiana Territory. He was arrested and tried for treason, but acquitted of all charges. His reputation suffered further damage and he spent many years in Europe, finally returning to New York City in 1812. He continued to practice law and spent the rest of his life in obscurity.

KATHY WARNES

See also: Arnold, Benedict (1741–1801); Burr, Aaron, Treason Trial of (1807)

Further Reading

Chernow, Ron. 2005. *Alexander Hamilton*. New York: Penguin Books.

Ellis, Joseph. 2002. *Founding Brothers: The Revolutionary Generation*. New York: Vintage Books.

Elkins, Stanley, and Eric McKitrick. 1993. *The Age of Federalism*. New York: Oxford University Press.

Frisch, Morton J. 1991. *Alexander Hamilton and the Political Order*. Lanham, MD: University Press of America.

Isenberg, Nancy. 2008. *Fallen Founder: The Life of Aaron Burr*. New York: Penguin Books.

Stewart, David O. 2011. *American Emperor: Aaron Burr's Challenge to Jefferson's America*. New York: Simon & Schuster.

Bustamante, Alyssa (1994–)

Alyssa Dailen Bustamante was a 15-year-old girl convicted of killing her nine-year-old neighbor, Elizabeth Olten. On the evening of October 21, 2009, Olten was walking home from a friend's house when she was led into the woods, killed, and buried in a shallow grave. Two days later,

In 2009, 15-year-old Alyssa Bustamante was charged with the murder of nine-year-old Elizabeth Olten. In this photo from January 30, 2014, Bustamante appears at a hearing in Cole County Circuit Court to determine whether to set aside her plea to second-degree murder because of a later Supreme Court ruling regarding life sentences for juveniles. (AP Photo/Julie Smith)

police would discover her body with help of Bustamante. Bustamante stated she wanted to know how it felt to kill someone. She was subsequently arrested and charged with first-degree murder. Tried as an adult, prosecutors showed evidence of premeditation and depravity. After two years of court appearances including multiple motions, evaluations, and continuations, Bustamante pled guilty to the lesser charge of second-degree murder and armed criminal action on January 10, 2012. Less than a month later, at the age of 18, she was sentenced to life in prison plus 30 years with a chance of parole. Bustamante is one of thousands of individuals serving a life sentence for a crime committed as a juvenile.

Bustamante was born on January 28, 1994. Due to her mother being a drug addict and her father a convicted felon serving time in a Missouri prison, she lived with her grandparents and younger siblings in St. Martins, Missouri, from the age of seven. Bustamante suffered from depression and had a history of suicide attempts beginning at a young age. At the age of 11, her suicide attempts involved cutting herself and attempting to overdose on pain medications. She attended both inpatient and outpatient mental health treatment. While struggling with psychiatric problems, Bustamante spent most of her early teen years attending Jefferson City Schools, enjoying social media websites while describing her hobbies as cutting and killing people, and playing pranks on her younger brothers, such as encouraging them to electrocute themselves while she videotaped the incident.

On October 16, 2009, a Friday off from school, Bustamante spent the day digging two graves in the woods near her home. Police have speculated Bustamante originally intended to kill her twin younger brothers, but seized the opportunity when she saw Olten. Less than a week later, nine-year-old Elizabeth Olten went missing on her way home from a friend's house. When Olten did not return home from a friend's house, her mother reported her missing and a search ensued. Tracking her cell phone signal, the search party, including volunteers, local police, and the FBI, began searching a wooded area between the two homes. Over the next 48 hours the search party continued to look for Olten while tips came in leading the police to a suspect. An anonymous letter received by the police stated Bustamante may have been involved with the girl's disappearance. Bustamante was subsequently questioned about the disappearance of Olten. Two days later Bustamante led the police to a shallow grave in a wooded area where she buried the girl and covered her in leaves. The same area had

been searched by the police in the two days following the girl's disappearance. Though the global positioning system (GPS) had traced Olten's cell phone to the area, her body and the phone were buried and unable to be retrieved until Bustamante led police to the area.

Following the recovery of Olten's body, Bustamante admitted to strangling, stabbing, and cutting Olten's throat and wrists. A diary and muddy clothing were seized from Bustamante's bedroom. The diary revealed that after the killing, Bustamante wrote about enjoying the murder and attending a youth dance at her church the same night. This information would later be referenced in court. Additionally, Bustamante's boyfriend was questioned, but no claims against him being involved could be substantiated.

After Bustamante's arrest, she was formally charged with first-degree murder and armed criminal action. It was decided she would be charged as an adult. During her jail stay, Bustamante attempted suicide and was moved to the Hawthorn Children's Psychiatric Hospital. The judge then ordered a four-day psychological evaluation at the Fulton State Hospital.

Despite giving a full confession to police, Bustamante originally entered a plea of not guilty. The next two years consisted of multiple pretrial hearing and motions. Then on January 10, 2012, Bustamante subsequently pled guilty to second-degree murder and armed criminal action. Both charges could have resulted in a sentence of life in prison. During the sentencing hearing, Bustamante was required to describe her actions on the night of the crime. Bustamante again admitted to strangling, stabbing, and slitting the throat of Olten.

Defense attorneys referenced journal entries of Bustamante in asking for leniency. The journal entries described her suicidal and homicidal ideations. They attempted to argue that her life circumstances, mental illness, and use of Prozac predisposed her to violence. On the other hand, the prosecution asked for a life sentence plus 71 years to account for the years Olten lost. They presented evidence of premeditation in stating that Bustemante had dug two graves several days prior to the murder. They also stated that on the night of the murder, Bustamante sent her younger sister to lure Olten outside by asking her to play. All of these facts, the prosecution stated, pointed to calculation and premeditation on the part of Bustamante. Furthermore, prosecutors presented journal entries where Bustamante described the thrill of killing Olten. These were used to show her genuine disregard for the sanctity of human life.

Juvenile Waiver to Adult Court

A juvenile waiver, also called a certification or transfer, is an option available in juvenile court for eligible offenders to be transferred from a juvenile court to an adult court for trial and sentencing. In most states, if a juvenile is charged with a felony, the prosecutor or judge may opt to transfer the juvenile to adult court. In other states, the transfer may be mandatory for certain crimes, such as murder. Furthermore, an offender as young as 14 may be eligible for a transfer, such was the case for Alyssa Bustamante. Missouri, for example, provides for a discretionary judicial waiver, which allowed for the judge in Bustamante's case to transfer the charges to adult court. Since the implementation of these laws in the early 1980s, the number of youth convicted and incarcerated for felonies has increased while juvenile delinquency as a whole has decreased.

On February 8, 2012, Judge Patricia Joyce chose to sentence Bustamante to life in prison for the murder plus 30 years for armed criminal action. The sentences are to be served consecutively with a chance of parole. Since the conviction, Bustamante has been residing at the Women's Eastern Reception, Diagnostic and Correctional Center in Vandalia, Missouri.

In late 2013, Bustamante sought to appeal her life sentence. She cited the Supreme Court's recent decision in *Miller v. Alabama* as a justification for overturning her guilty plea resulting in a life sentence. Bustamante stated, had her attorneys at trial informed her of the impending court case, she would not have taken the plea deal for a life sentence knowing the facts of the *Miller* case. Her former attorneys stated they had informed her of the impending court case, but Bustamante chose to go forward with the plea deal at the time. In March 2014, Jude Joyce denied Bustamante's appeal to overturn her guilty plea. She was returned to the Women's Eastern Reception, Diagnostic and Correctional Center to serve the remainder of her sentence.

ALESA LILES

See also: Anthony, Casey, Murder Trial of (May 24–July 5, 2011); Ramsey, JonBenét, Murder of (1996); Tate, Lionel (1987–)

Further Reading

Associated Press. 2014. "Missouri Judge Denies Teen Killer's Appeal for New Trial." *CBS News.* March 11. http://www .cbsnews.com/news/missouri-judge-denies-teen-killer-alyssa-bustamantes-appeal-for-a-new-trial/. Accessed April 10, 2015.

Crimesider Staff. 2012. "Alyssa Bustamante Called Killing 9-year-old 'Enjoyable.' Then Went to Church." February 6. http://www.cbsnews.com/news/alyssa-bustamante-called-killing9-year-old-enjoyable-then-went-to-church/. Accessed April 10, 2015.

Newcomb, Alyssa. 2012. "Teen Thrill Killer Alyssa Bustamante Could Get Paroled Some Day." *ABC News.* February 8. http://abcnews.go.com/US/thrill-killer-alyssa-bustamante parole-day/story?id=15538798. Accessed April 10, 2015.

Staff Reporter. 2012. "Alyssa Bustamante: 5 Things to Know About the Teen Killer." *International Business Times.* February 7. http://www.ibtimes.com/alyssa-bustamante-5-things-know-about-teen-killer-406944. Accessed April 10, 2015.

Byrd, James, Jr., Murder of (1998)

The 1998 dragging murder of James Byrd Jr. (1949–1998) in Jasper, Texas, is considered one of the most horrific racially motivated crimes committed in the United States since the civil rights movement and has had significant effects on existing state and federal hate crime laws. In 2001, Governor Rick Perry signed the James Byrd, Jr. Hate Crimes Act into Texas law. Previous hate crime laws did not specify protected groups and were rarely enforced. The new law clarified that suspects who target victims because of their race, religion, color, sex, disability, sexual preference, age, or national origin may receive harsher penalties. Eight years later, a federal law bearing Byrd's name was also passed. The Matthew Shepard and James Byrd, Jr. Hate Crimes Prevention Act was signed into law by President Obama on October 28, 2009, as an expansion of the 1969 United States federal hate crime law. The current federal law now includes crimes motivated by a victim's actual or perceived race, color, religion, or national origin, as well as a victim's actual or perceived gender, sexual orientation, gender identity, or disability. The new law removed the requirement that victims must be participating in federally protected activities (e.g., voting) at the time that the crime was committed for it to be considered a hate crime. It also required the Federal Bureau of Investigation (FBI) to gather data on hate crimes based on gender and gender identity. Lastly, the federal law gave the FBI power to investigate hate crimes overlooked by local authorities.

Sometime after midnight on June 7, 1998, James Byrd began his walk home from a night of drinking at a house party in Jasper, Texas. Besides the fact that Byrd had been drinking, he was also not driving due to a history of seizures and other medical issues (Levin and McDevitt 2002, 9). On his way to his small apartment, the 49-year-old black man was approached by three white males in a gray pick-up truck. This may have been no cause for concern on a typical evening seeing as how Jasper is a small, racially mixed community with over 40 percent of its population being African American (King 2001, 13). However, it is likely it did not take long for Byrd to realize that he was in trouble once he accepted a ride from the inebriated group of men.

The three men who picked Byrd up that late evening were Lawrence Russell Brewer, John William (Bill) King, and Shawn Allen Berry. Each was a high-school dropout who had only participated in small-time criminal offenses up to that point. King and Brewer had met while incarcerated. They reportedly joined a Ku Klux Klan prison gang called the Confederate Knights of America for the purposes of protection while being locked up. The two men soon began having discussions about creating their own hate group. They eventually settled on the name Texas Rebel Soldiers and thereafter created a constitution and membership applications. They would soon partake in an act of violence that would capture substantial attention for their newly developed white supremacist group.

When Brewer, King, and Berry picked up Byrd, they knew that this was the moment they had been waiting for to gain attention for their group. So instead of driving him to his home, they continued on to a wooded area east of Jasper. At around 3 a.m. on a dark country road they pulled Byrd out of their truck. He was thrown onto the ground where the suspects then stomped on him and proceeded to spray-paint his face black. The three white supremacists continued to beat Byrd before tying him to the back of their truck using a heavy logging chain wrapped around his ankles. Byrd, while alive and conscious, was dragged a little over two miles down a dirt road that eventually turned into rough pavement. During this time, Byrd had managed to keep his head and shoulders from hitting the pavement by rocking his body back and forth. When he was discovered later that morning, police noticed that portions of his body, including his elbows and heels, had been ground to the bone in this effort to stay alive (Levin and McDevitt 2002, 10). Ultimately, the fatal moment came when Byrd's body hit the edge of a concrete culvert decapitating him and ripping off his right arm and shoulder. The three men then drove to an old black cemetery where they dropped off the remains of Byrd's body before returning home to sleep.

Police apprehended King, Brewer, and Berry soon after the incident due to evidence linking them to the crime scene. Law enforcement officials were convinced that Byrd's death was a hate crime based on several factors of the crime. The location of where they left the remaining part of Byrd's body, racist tattoos found on the offenders, and the white supremacist literature found during the investigation were some of the indicators that this crime was racially motivated. During this time, however, this crime could not be tried under federal hate crime laws because only racially motivated crimes that occurred while violating federally protected activities (e.g., voting, serving on a jury, attending public school) could be charged as hate crimes.

Despite not being able to convict the suspects under existing hate crime laws, prosecutors sought the death penalty for the brutal killing. The jury only deliberated for a little over two hours to reach a verdict in King's case. As a sympathetic gesture, the jury chose its only black member to read the verdict to a packed courtroom, which marked the end of the week-long trial. Aside from being convicted of murder, the jury also considered the dragging of Byrd to be an act of kidnapping as he was alive during the incident. Consequently, under Texas law John King was eligible to receive the death penalty. On February 25, 1999, John King was sentenced to death and remains on death row with appeals still pending. Lawrence Brewer was also charged with capital murder and received the death penalty. On September 21, 2001, Brewer was executed by lethal injection in the state of Texas. Shawn Berry had agreed to testify against his friends and received a life sentence, which he is currently serving in a Texas prison.

Kayla Gruenewald

See also: Brandon, Teena, Murder of (1993); Neal, Claude, Lynching of (1934); Shepard, Matthew, Murder of (1998)

Further Reading

King, Joyce. 2001. *Hate Crime: The Story of a Dragging in Jasper, Texas.* New York: Anchor Books.

Levin, Jack, and Jack McDevitt. 2002. *Hate Crimes Revisited: America's War on Those Who Are Different.* Boulder, CO: Westview Press.

Petersen, Jennifer. 2011. *Murder, the Media, and the Politics of Public Feelings: Remembering Matthew Shepard and James Byrd Jr.* Bloomington: Indiana University Press.

C

Capone, Al (1899–1947)

Al Capone, a Prohibition-era Chicago crime boss, is arguably the most famous mobster in American history. Born Alphonse (Alphonsus) Gabriel Capone in 1899 in Brooklyn, New York, to immigrants from Campania, Italy, he was expelled from school as a teenager and quickly became involved in crime. Part of a large family, some of his brothers and cousins also turned toward crime, although his brother, Jimmy, became a federal agent. After stints with junior local gangs, Capone joined the Five Points gang, becoming mobster Frankie Yale's protégé. Yale's headquarters was the Harvard Inn, a Coney Island saloon. While working there, Capone insulted a woman; her brother, Frank Gallucio, attacked Capone with a knife, leaving three scars on the left side of the latter's face. Capone later refrained from having his left profile photographed, occasionally claiming the scars were war wounds. The press later dubbed him "Scarface," a nickname he resented; he preferred "Snorky," a contemporary term for a sharp dresser.

In 1918, Capone married Mary ("Mae") Coughlin after she had their son, Albert Francis ("Sonny"). After murdering a rival White Hand gangster, Capone went to Chicago to avoid retaliation. He worked under his and Yale's former Five Points mentor, Johnny Torrio. Torrio had left for Chicago years earlier to resolve difficulties "Big Jim" Colosimo, Torrio's relative by marriage, was having with Black Hand extortionists. Afterward Torrio stayed on, running Colosimo's criminal operations. In 1919, they opened a brothel at 2222 South Wabash known as Four Deuces. Upon reaching Chicago, Capone began working there as a bartender and bouncer. Meanwhile, Colosimo's restaurant, a popular nightspot, attracted prominent visitors and celebrities.

Torrio recognized the bootlegging business' potential after Prohibition banned manufacturing, distributing, and selling alcoholic beverages in 1920. Colosimo, however, opposed moving into bootlegging. Torrio, turning against Colosimo, arranged for Yale's assistance with Colosimo's 1920 murder. Torrio and Capone assumed control, increasingly consolidating their position within Chicago's underworld. During nearby Cicero's corrupt town council elections in 1924, Capone's candidate won, but his brother, Frank, died following a shootout with the police. After Capone's puppet-mayor called for his removal from town, Capone famously bashed him down the steps of the town hall.

Torrio and Capone vied primarily with the Sicilian Genna crime family and Joe Aiello, and Dion O'Banion's north side gang. O'Banion sold Torrio shares of the Sieben Brewery after learning that authorities were about to raid it. Afterward, Torrio was arrested. His organization retaliated by murdering O'Banion in 1924. The murder, likely carried out by John Scalise and Albert Anselmi (brutal defectors to Capone's organization from the Gennas), launched an intense gang war. In 1925, Torrio was wounded in an attack. He retired to Italy, leaving Capone in charge.

Capone's "Outfit," as his organization was known, generated substantial wealth (over $100 million annually)

Mugshot of Al Capone, one of the most celebrated Prohibition era Chicago crime bosses. Capone's organized crime group generated incredible income through intimidation, bribery, corruption, and murder. He was eventually convicted of income tax evasion. (Library of Congress)

through bootlegging, but also gambling, prostitution, racketeering, and other crimes. Capone developed a vast international network to illegally produce and transport alcoholic beverages to his Chicago speakeasies. With his wealth, Capone increased control of local authorities, including Mayor "Big Bill" Thompson, through bribes and kickbacks. Among Capone's chief advisors and political "greasers" was Jake Guzik, a south side criminal allied to the Outfit. Capone, indulging in custom suits, expensive jewelry, and cigars, made the luxurious Lexington Hotel his headquarters. He acquired a mansion retreat on Palm Island, Florida, in 1928. In stark contrast to the earlier Italian American mob bosses who operated in the shadows, Capone attracted wide media attention, becoming a celebrity.

Capone's rivals, especially those in Chicago's north side, led by Hymie Weiss and George "Bugs" Moran, attempted to usurp Capone's dominance. In 1926, Capone was ambushed while dining at the Hawthorne Hotel restaurant, which was riddled with bullets. Capone's bodyguard, Frank

Rio, pulled him to safety but several bystanders were injured. Capone unsuccessfully sought a truce. He increased his security and developed secret safe havens. The north side gang, increasingly brazen, hijacked the Outfit's trucks supplying alcoholic beverages, murdered Capone's allies (such as the recent presidents of the Unione Siciliana, a former philanthropic society that had assumed criminal trappings), and made assassination attempts on Capone's enforcer Jack McGurn.

Capone, making substantial charitable donations, had cultivated a "Robin Hood" media image that was tarnished following the "St. Valentine's Day Massacre." The event's details, and Capone's exact involvement, are debated. Nevertheless, gunmen, some posing as law enforcement, murdered seven north side gangsters in a garage on February 14, 1929. Gruesome murder scene photos shocked the public and intensified federal authorities' efforts against Capone. In 1930, corrupt reporter Jake Lingle's widely witnessed murder received extensive media coverage, making Chicago appear dangerous because of criminals like Capone.

In 1929, Bureau of Prohibition agent Eliot Ness began investigating Capone's activities, hoping to convict him of Prohibition violations. Around that time, Treasury Department agent Frank Wilson began investigating Capone for income tax violations. Federal authorities, perceiving Wilson's approach more likely to result in a conviction, indicted Capone in 1931. Capone's attorneys unsuccessfully sought a settlement. Meanwhile, authorities uncovered Capone's efforts to compromise potential jurors.

Capone, convicted of five counts of tax evasion and failing to file returns, received an 11-year sentence, the longest tax evasion sentence then ever given. He also received fines and property liens. His appeal attempts were unsuccessful. Capone's underworld influence declined rapidly after his imprisonment and Prohibition's repeal in 1933. His right-hand man, Frank Nitti, took over the Outfit. Capone, sent to an Atlanta prison in 1932, arranged for special privileges. He was eventually transferred in 1934 to Alcatraz, a newly built prison on an island off San Francisco. After his 1939 release from prison, Capone retired to his Florida mansion. Suffering from advanced stages of neurosyphilis, contracted in his youth, he died in 1947 after a stroke.

Capone's infamy has made him an enduring American pop cultural icon. The stereotypical accent, mannerisms, and dress (suit and fedora) of a "gangster" parody Capone's. Capone has been included as a character in countless works of fiction, including Mario Puzo's *The Godfather*. Capone has also been featured in comics and served as inspiration for detective Dick Tracy's nemesis, "Big Boy" Caprice, and the gangster dummy, Scarface, used by Batman's foe, the Ventriloquist. He has inspired various cinematic and television adaptations and characters from the 1930s to the present. For example, Capone's life, the basis for the Armitage Trail novel, *Scarface* (1929), inspired the classic 1932 film and 1983 remake of the same name starring Al Pacino. Some notable actors to play Capone include Rod Steiger (*Al Capone*, 1959), Ben Gazzara (*Capone*, 1975), Robert De Niro (*Untouchables*, 1986), William Forsythe (*The Untouchables*, 1993–94), and Stephen Graham (*Boardwalk Empire*, 2010–14). He has also been featured in numerous pop songs by such diverse musical artists as Prince Buster, Paper Lace, Prodigy, Queen, Megadeth, Violent Femmes, and Michael Jackson.

In 1986, Geraldo Rivera hosted a highly rated live television special on the opening of a secret vault belonging to Capone; hyped as holding telling contents, it infamously contained only meaningless debris.

Eric Martone

See also: Colosimo, James "Big Jim," Mob Murder of (May 11, 1920); O'Banion, Dion, Mob Murder of (November 10, 1924); Nitti, Frank "the Enforcer" (1888–1943); St. Valentine's Day Massacre (February 14, 1929)

Further Reading
Iorizzo, Luciano. 2003. *Al Capone: A Biography*. Westport, CT: Greenwood Press.
Kobler, John. 2003. *Capone: The Life and World of Al Capone*. Reprint ed. New York: Da Capo Press.
Schoenberg, Robert. 1992. *Mr. Capone: The Real—and Complete—Story of Al Capone*. New York: William Morrow.

Carpenter, David (1930–)

David Joseph Carpenter, also known as the "trailside killer," is an American serial killer who stalked, raped, and killed women on hiking trails in Marin and Santa Cruz Counties, California. Between 1979 and 1981, he murdered at least seven women and one man. Although he has never confessed to these crimes, he has been convicted of seven counts of first-degree murder as well as three counts of rape, and has been sentenced to death twice. For a while, he was also believed to be the Zodiac killer. He is the oldest inmate on death row at San Quentin Prison in California and one of the oldest in the United States.

Carpenter was born on May 6, 1930, in San Francisco, California. As a child to abusive parents, he tortured animals, wetted his bed, and developed a severe stutter that would accompany him throughout his life. In 1947, he began his stint as a sex offender, and before his final arrest in 1981, he was convicted of rape, a federal assault with a deadly weapon charge, robbery, and kidnapping. He married in 1955 and fathered three children. In the 1960s, he became a suspect in the Zodiac killings, but was cleared by DNA and handwriting analysis.

In August 1979, he killed 44-year-old Edda Kane with a single gunshot in the back of the head. She was found in a kneeling position and facedown in Mount Tamalpais Park in Marin County. In October 1979, the body of 23-year-old Mary Francis Bennett, who had been stabbed multiple times, was found. However, it took until February 2010 to identify the killer, when San Francisco police announced the match of a DNA sample with Carpenter. In December 1979, Carpenter's 17-year-old acquaintance Anna Kelly Menjivar disappeared. Her body was found in 1981. In March 1980, he stabbed 23-year-old Barbara Schwartz, who was also found dead in a kneeling position.

In October the same year, Carpenter raped 26-year-old Anne Alderson and shot her in the head. Unlike the other victims, she was dressed and not kneeling. The public was frightened by the trailside killer, and the press speculated that he could actually be the Zodiac killer, who had been inactive since 1969. However, unlike the Zodiac killer, the trailside killer did not communicate with police or leave any messages behind.

Investigators found a likely suspect in Mark McDermand, who had killed his invalid mother and schizophrenic brother in their cabin on Mount Tamalpais. But then the killings resumed. In November 1980, 25-year-old Shauna May was found shot in a shallow grave on trails at Point Reyes National Seashore in Marin County next to a decomposed body that turned out to be 22-year-old Diana O'Connell, who had been missing for a month and had been shot during a rape attempt. The same day, 19-year-old Richard Stowers and his 18-year-old fiancée Cynthia Moreland were found murdered with their faces down in the woods. Investigators determined that they had been murdered the same October weekend as Anne Alderson.

With the discovery of four bodies in one day, communities were outraged, and pressure on authorities grew. The Federal Bureau of Investigation (FBI) got involved. The only link between the murders were the bullets used to murder the victims. Based on case histories of similar murder cases, police created a profile of a tall, thin, white man with black hair who was good-looking, charming, and between 20 and 25 years of age. Flyers with a sketch of him were distributed, and warnings were put up in state parks, while undercover agents walked the trails. Authorities wanted to catch the killer by immediately shutting down all roads leading from the park in Marin County as soon as the next attack was reported.

However, the next attack in March 1981 occurred in Santa Cruz County, and although police arrived within minutes, the murderer escaped. In Henry Cowell Redwoods State Park, 20-year-old Ellen Marie Hansen was threatened to be raped. When she protested, the trailside killer shot her. He also shot her boyfriend Steven Haertle, who survived and provided investigators with a description of the perpetrator that did not resemble the sketch. He described a large man between 50 and 60 years of age with broad shoulders, glasses, a moustache, crooked, yellow teeth, and thinning hair. At first, police thought that Haertle and Hansen had become victims of a copycat and thus a second perpetrator. But when it turned out that the bullets had come from the gun of earlier shootings,

police realized that the charming first suspect did not exist.

In May the same year, 20-year-old Heather Scaggs asked her coworker Carpenter for a ride. When she did not return, her boyfriend called police who questioned Carpenter. As he looked very similar to the new sketch of the trailside killer, police kept him under surveillance. A background check revealed that he had previously been convicted for assault and rape. Although no weapon could be found, a single bullet was retrieved from his car. A few days later, Scaggs's naked, raped, and decomposing body was found at Big Basin State Park near Santa Cruz. Haertle was brought in for a lineup and immediately recognized the perpetrator. In exchange for a lighter sentence, a suspect facing charges helped police retrieve Carpenter's gun from which the bullets had been fired.

Carpenter committed his crimes in local areas where he was comfortable. They were secluded, heavily wooded, and accessible by foot. Unlike John Wayne Gacy or Ted Bundy, he was asocial and did not charm his victims with conversations due to his speech impediment. Most victims were unknown to him and ranged in ages and appearance. Overseeing trails from a mountain vantage point, he especially targeted women for his sexual needs. The only way he could control his victims was through a blitz-style attack by shooting his victims in the back of the head in execution style or by stabbing them multiple times.

In October 1983, Carpenter went on trial in Los Angeles. In July 1984, he was convicted of first-degree murder for the murders of Hansen and Scaggs, and the attempted murder of Haertle. He was sentenced to death. A second trial opened in San Diego in January 1988. During the trial, Carpenter took the stand. From time to time he stuttered and showed some anger, but otherwise appeared calm and prepared. Although he gave detailed descriptions of activities during the time of the murders, prosecutors could prove his alibis were lies. In May, he was convicted of the murders of Alderson, O'Connell, May, Moreland, and Stowers, and the jury recommended the death penalty.

Carpenter appealed, claiming that prosecutors had twisted his alibis. It was also discovered that the jury forewoman, Barbara Durham, had lied under oath by concealing her knowledge regarding his convictions of the Santa Cruz murders in Los Angeles in 1984. In 1995, the California Supreme Court refused to give Carpenter a new trial, arguing that the trial and the penalty had been fair because Durham's knowledge had not unduly biased others. In 1997, the state Supreme Court upheld both death sentences. Still claiming his innocence, Carpenter has continued to appeal on every level of the judicial system, but he remains on death row.

DANIELA RIBITSCH

See also: Bundy, Ted (1946–1989); Gacy, John Wayne (1942–1994); Zodiac Killer (1960s–)

Further Reading

Graysmith, Robert. 1990. *The Sleeping Lady. The Trailside Murders above the Golden Gate.* New York: Dutton.

People v. Carpenter, 15 Cal.4th 312 (1997). Accessed November 19, 2014. http://law.justia.com/cases/california/supreme-court/4th/15/312.html. Accessed April 14, 2015.

"'Trailside Killer' Merits New Trial due to Juror Misconduct, Judge Says." 1989. *Los Angeles Times.* June 15.

Woodard, Boston. 2013. "A Deeper Look inside David Carpenter's Life." *San Quentin News.* July. http://sanquentinnews.files.wordpress.com/2011/06/san-quentin-news-july-2013.pdf. Accessed April 14, 2015.

Carruth, Rae (1974–)

Rae Carruth, a former wide receiver in the National Football League (NFL), murdered his girlfriend, Cherica Adams, who was pregnant with their child. Carruth is in the custody of North Carolina Department of Corrections, after being convicted of conspiracy to commit murder and two other felony charges related to the incident. He was the first active NFL player to be charged with first-degree murder.

Carruth was born Rae Lamar Wiggins, in Sacramento, California, January 20, 1974. His biological parents divorced while Carruth was a child; Carruth's surname comes from his stepfather Samuel Carruth. After her second marriage ended in divorce, Carruth's mother, Theodry, raised him alone in the rough neighborhood of Oak Park in Sacramento. Carruth was a student at Valley High School in Sacramento, and his talents earned a scholarship to the University of Colorado where he enjoyed success on the football field. He was the second player at the University of Colorado to gain 1,000 or more receiving yards in two consecutive seasons. He also shared the record for most touchdown catches in a season (Michaelis 1995). In his senior season he was named a first-team All-American in college football.

In college, Carruth's personal life was characterized by strong desires for fame. His success in college football elicited praise from coaches, local reporters, and teammates.

One coach remarked that Carruth would eventually be placed among the other elite receivers in history of the University of Colorado. Carruth, who was also an English major, yearned for a big stage on which to tell his stories, whether through writing screenplays or directing of films. As a student at the University of Colorado, Carruth's grades earned him a spot on the All-Division Academic team, an honorary designation rewarding football players in the Big-12 for their performance in the classroom. What was apparent was Carruth's desire to be perceived as one of the best, whether in football or in Hollywood film.

In addition to football and writing, Carruth had the ability to charm women. *Sports Illustrated* writer Michael Bamberger reported that Carruth would often date multiple women at the same time. Carruth fathered a child during his relationship with Michelle Wright in his freshman year in college; Wright was a friend from Sacramento. Later, Carruth would be ordered to pay child support for his son Raelondo. By that time, Carruth had begun dating other women.

Carruth entered the NFL draft in 1997, and was chosen in the first round by the Carolina Panthers. His professional career started with success; he led all NFL rookies in receiving yards and catches. Injuries, however, hampered his sophomore season and his involvement in Cherica Adams's murder all but put out the light on his NFL career.

Carruth, Michael Kennedy, and William Watkins were implicated in the conspiracy, which ultimately caused Adams's death. On November 16, 1999, Carruth and Adams departed Carruth's home, en route to Adams's home in separate vehicles. Carruth stopped his vehicle in front of Adams's on Rae Road at which time his accomplices drove alongside Adams's black BMW, and fired upon her. Kennedy was driving the vehicle, which carried Watkins, the shooter. Adams was hit four times, and Carruth, Kennedy, and Watkins fled. Remarkably, Adams was able to call for help on her cell phone. On December 14, 1999, after being shot in the neck, chest, and abdomen and undergoing an emergency Cesarean section to save her 10-week premature son Chancellor, Cherica Adams died.

Nearly three weeks before her death, police arrested Carruth, charging him with conspiracy to commit murder. After posting bail in the amount of $3 million Carruth fled, though a court order was issued that mandated Carruth's return if Adams or the baby passed. After Carruth fled North Carolina to Tennessee, federal agents arrested him after discovering him in the trunk of a car on December 15, 1999; his conspiracy charge had been changed to first-degree murder.

Relying on cell phone records, police connected Michael Kennedy and William Watkins to Carruth. In the course of the investigation they discovered that Watkins had been hired by Carruth to work on his car and the pair was then introduced to Kennedy. Both Carruth's accomplices had records of violence, weapon possession, and larceny. In the phone records police found that Carruth had called his accomplices that night and likely coordinated the attack by cell phone.

Investigators also looked into Carruth's relationship with Adams, piecing together accounts from teammates, former girlfriends, and family. Adams's financial problems had led her to take a job as a dancer at The Diamond Club, a topless bar that catered to professional athletes in Charlotte. After meeting Carruth, the pair began dating and in the spring of 1999, Adams discovered she was pregnant. The pregnancy came at a time when Carruth's football career was hampered by injury, and uncertainty about his financial future worried him. Carruth was still making child support payments, and was nearing the end of his NFL contract.

At trial, friends of Adams testified that Carruth had asked her to get an abortion, and that after another injury on the field Carruth's behavior toward the baby changed. He attended prenatal care appointments with Adams up until that point. Unsure of whether he would continue playing in the NFL because of injury, investigators used Carruth's pattern of behavior to develop their case—the eventual cost of Adams's pregnancy being Carruth's motivation for the attack. Carruth's other financial mishaps included lost money on a car-title pyramid scheme and a real estate deal gone bad, which resulted in a lawsuit.

Watkins asserted that Carruth offered to pay him $5,000 to assault and cause Adams to have a miscarriage. An alternate theory presented by Carruth's defense was that after backing out of an agreement to loan Kennedy money to purchase drugs from Watkins, the pair became angry and shot Adams. Statements made by Watkins, including "It was Rae's fault. If he had just given us the money, none of this would have happened," was the basis for this defense (McKinley 2000, D4). Carruth was eventually convicted of conspiracy to commit murder, avoiding the possibility of a death penalty. He was sentenced January 23, 2001, to a minimum of 18 years and 11 months. Carruth's accomplice Watkins pled guilty to second-degree murder, and was sentenced to a minimum of 40 years and five months.

TYLER J. VAUGHAN

See also: Blake, Robert, Murder Trial of (2005); Simpson, O. J. (1947–)

Further Reading

Bamberger, M. 1999. "First-Degree Tragedy." *Sports Illustrated* 95(25), December 27.

Freeman, M. 2001. "Conspiracy of Murder Conviction for Carruth." *The New York Times.* January 20, D1.

McKinley, J. M. 1999. "The Athlete Accused: Beneath the Smiles a Tangled Relationship." *The New York Times.* December 21, D1, D2.

McKinley, J. M. 2000. "The Capital Case against Carruth." *The New York Times.* November 7, D1, D4.

Michaelis, V. 1995. "Carruth's Big Future Is in Script." *The Denver Post.* November 10, D1.

Carter, Rubin "Hurricane" (1937–2014)

In 1966, Rubin Carter was convicted of the murder of three white patrons of a New Jersey establishment. Carter, an African American, middleweight boxing phenom, and John Artis, received life sentences for the murders. In many subsequent appeals, both men maintained their innocence, alleging racial prejudice, prosecutorial misconduct, and violations of their rights to due process and fair trial. Nearly two decades later, both convictions were overturned by a U.S. District Court. In granting the controversial writ of habeas corpus, Judge H. Lee Sarokin wrote in the opinion of the court, "… the need for review is amply demonstrated by this matter. […] The need to combat crime should never be utilized to justify an erosion of our fundamental guarantees" (*Carter v. Rafferty*, 621 F. Supp. 533 1985, 27).

In the early morning hours of June 17, 1966, two African American males entered the Lafayette Bar & Grill in Patterson, New Jersey. The men, armed with a shotgun and a .32 caliber revolver, opened fire on the bartender and several patrons. Two men, including the bartender and one patron, were killed. Another female patron died one month later from wounds suffered in the attack, and a fourth suffered a wound to the head that left her partially blind (*Carter v. Rafferty* 1985). Across the street, Alfred Bello was acting as lookout for Arthur Bradley as he robbed a nearby building. Bello heard gunshots and walked toward the bar. Bello and Bradley would both later testify they saw the shooters exiting the bar and fleeing the scene in a white car. Bello then entered the bar and, despite the carnage before him, proceeded to steal $62 from the cash register before calling the police. Across town, Carter and Artis were leaving a local hangout known as the Nite Spot with their friend John Royster. Not long after leaving in Carter's white Dodge, they were pulled over by police who were looking for the getaway vehicle described by Bello. They were only briefly detained, however, as the police were on the lookout for a vehicle with two occupants, not three (Hirsch 2000).

Artis, who was driving Carter's car, then dropped Royster off and continued to drive around town. At approximately 3 a.m., the pair was pulled over again, and instructed to follow the officers to the scene of the crime. Patricia Valentine, who lived upstairs from the bar, informed police that saw Carter's white Polara driving away after being awakened by the gunshots. In her statement to police, however, she reported that she was unable to get a good look at the shooters, and could only describe them as "negroes." From there, Carter and Artis were placed in a police wagon, which transported them first to the police station, and then shortly thereafter to a local hospital. At the hospital, the men were presented to Hazel Tanis, a female victim of the attack who would later succumb to her injuries, and William Marins, the only survivor of the shooting. Neither was able to identify the men as their attackers. Carter and Artis were then taken back to the police station. At the station, Bello, Bradley, and Valentine were asked if they recognized Carter and Artis as the assailants, to which all responded that they did not. Sixteen hours, two passed polygraphs, and several rounds of interrogations later, both men were released without charges. Poised to fight for the middle-weight championship, Carter continued to pursue his boxing career for the next few months. His aspirations were brought to an end, however, on October 14, 1966. Acting on statements signed that morning by Bello and Bradley that identified Carter and Artis as the shooters, police arrested both men and charged them with murder (Hirsch 2000; *Current Biography* 2000).

At their first trial, the defense produced several witnesses who placed Carter and Artis at the nightclub at the time of the murders. Bello and Bradley, however, both testified in front of the all-white jury that they saw the men exiting the Lafayette Bar and Grill that night (*State v. Carter*, 54 N.J. 436, 255 A.2d 746 1969). Despite the conflicting accounts, the circumstantial nature of the remaining evidence, and the lack of motive offered by the prosecution, the jury returned guilty verdicts for both men and they were sentenced to life in prison (Hirsch 2000).

In 1974, Carter filed a motion for a new trial after Bello and Bradley both publicly recanted their testimonies. Carter again filed for a new trial in early 1975 after it was discovered that the prosecution had withheld evidence indicating that, in return for their cooperation, the two key witnesses had both been promised leniency in regard to their own legal problems. Both motions were denied by the same judge who had presided over the 1967 trial, Samuel Larner. Larner found that the recantations were unreliable and that the withheld evidence was immaterial to the disposition of the original case (*State v. Carter*, 345 A.2d 808 1974; *State v. Carter*, 347 A.2d 383 1975). Carter appealed these decisions to the New Jersey Supreme Court in 1976. In reviewing the facts set forth in the motion, the court overturned the convictions and ordered a new trial (*State v. Carter*, 69 N.J. 420 1976). The court based this decision on grounds that the defendants' constitutional right to a fair trial had been violated when the prosecution withheld potentially exculpatory evidence, a legal precedent established in *Brady v. Maryland* (373 U.S. 83 1963).

Another Viewpoint

To this day, there are those who object to the release of Rubin Carter. These individuals argue that sensational media coverage swayed public opinion and ultimately led the courts to a misinformed decision in overturning the convictions. To learn more of the "other side" of this story, visit http://www.graphicwitness .com/carter/.

Shortly before the new trial, Bello was subjected to a polygraph. The results of the test indicated that Bello's recantation was truthful and that he had indeed falsified his original testimony. Despite requests made by the defense, the prosecution would not surrender the results prior to trial. At trial, Bello reverted to his original testimony. Not willing to rely on this testimony alone, the prosecution additionally argued that the murders were racially motivated, spurred by the killing of a local black man shortly before the bar shootings. In their second trial in 1976, Carter and Artis were again found guilty of the murders (Hirsch 2000; *Current Biography* 2000).

Carter remained in prison until 1985, when a U.S. District Court granted his petition for a writ of habeas corpus, a legal remedy that allows a federal court to review the findings of a state court, and overturned his conviction. The District Court ruled that the state violated Carter's constitutional rights by withholding the results of the polygraph and introducing racial revenge as a motive (*Carter v. Rafferty* 1985). The state filed two subsequent appeals to this decision, which were denied. All charges were officially dropped in 1988.

Carter went on to become a prominent speaker and advocate for the wrongfully accused. He lived in Toronto, where he was the executive director of the Association in Defense of the Wrongly Convicted. Carter also served on the board of directors for the Southern Center for Human Rights in Atlanta and the Alliance for Prison Justice in Boston (Hirsch 2000). Carter died on April 20, 2014.

Jacob M. Laan

See also: Adams, Randall Dale (1948–2010); Central Park Jogger Case (1989); Cotton, Ronald (1962–)

Further Reading

Carter, Rubin. 1974. *The Sixteenth Round: From Number 1 Contender to #45472*. New York: Viking Press.

"Carter, Rubin." 2000. *Current Biography: Biography Reference Bank*. New York: H.W. Wilson.

Carter, Rubin. 2011. *Eye of the Hurricane: My Path from Darkness to Freedom*. Chicago: Lawrence Hill.

Hirsch, James S. 2000. *Hurricane: The Miraculous Journey of Rubin Carter*. New York: Houghton Mifflin Company.

Wice, Paul B. 2000. *Rubin "Hurricane" Carter and the American Justice System*. Piscataway, NJ: Rutgers University Press.

Carthage Conspiracy Trial (1844)

On June 27, 1844, in Carthage, Illinois, a mob of over two hundred men stormed the local jailhouse. Prisoners Joseph Smith and his brother, Hyrum, were shot and killed (Oaks and Hill 1979). Two other prisoners, John Taylor and Willard Richards, were injured, along with three intruders. The rioting group mainly targeted Joseph Smith, prophet and founder of the Church of Jesus Christ of Latter-day Saints, due to hostility toward the growing religion.

Between 1830 and 1840, Hancock County, Illinois, had grown considerably from a population of approximately 500 to 10,000 (Oaks and Hill 1979). The population consisted of diverse individuals: Southerners from Virginia and Kentucky and Northerners from north and central Illinois. These two groups were able to put aside differences for the common goal to make Carthage, Illinois, a prosperous community. The Mormon group was an intricate part of this growth, making their historical mark in the area starting in 1839.

Joseph Smith, a farmer from New York, found a record of ancient people who had believed Jesus Christ visited them. Through divine intervention, Smith translated this document, that later became known as *The Book of Mormon* (Oaks and Hill 1979). With this document, he stated that God appeared to him and instructed him to organize a church, with himself as prophet. There were many intolerant outsiders as the religion grew, which caused the group to migrate to Kirtland, Ohio, then Independence, Missouri, then to the final settlement of Commerce, Illinois, in 1839. Smith renamed Commerce Nauvoo, which became a primarily Mormon area by 1843. Most individuals in the surrounding areas of Hancock County were initially tolerant of the Mormons, mainly due to the economic benefits.

In a short period of time, the state of Illinois allowed Smith to establish an official state militia unit in Nauvoo, called the Nauvoo Legion, along with a criminal justice

Joseph Smith, founder of the Church of Jesus Christ of Latter-day Saints. Smith moved across the country, attracting followers and promoting Mormonism. After settling in Illinois, he was arrested and then killed by a mob while in jail. (Library of Congress)

system. Also, in political elections, the Mormons voted as a unit, and often gained political control. Due to the rise of Mormons' economic and political power, disagreements arose in other areas of Hancock County, specifically in Warsaw and Carthage. In 1841, Thomas C. Sharp organized an anti-Mormon party in Warsaw and published his own newspaper called *The Warsaw Signal* (Linder 2010). He often attacked Smith's power and influence, speculated over acquisition of Mormon land, and questioned the force of the Nauvoo Legion. Along with the dissention, a scandal occurred within the Mormon group in Nauvoo during the summer of 1842 (Hill 2004). John C. Bennett, a member of the Mormon Church, was excommunicated due to soliciting female favors, outside the institutional guidelines of plural marriage (Hill 2004). Bennett countered by declaring that Smith himself was practicing polygamy. Due to this, polygamy within the Mormon Church became a statewide political issue, especially because it occurred during an election year.

During the election for governor, Joseph Duncan, the Whig candidate, took a stance against Mormonism and polygamy, hoping to garner more votes due to the controversy that had arisen. Thomas Ford, the Democratic candidate, garnered most of the Mormon votes, and won the election (Huntress 1969). However, when Ford took office, things began to cool between him and the Mormons. Many threats of civil war had been issued between Mormons and non-Mormons. Ford attempted to be the neutral force, trying to dissipate any issues between the two groups. He was soon unable to control the dissenters due to William Law, a former Mormon, and the publication of the *Nauvoo Expositor* (Hill 2004).

In the spring of 1844, Law began to hold meetings with other dissenters to discuss their outrage about the practice of polygamy and Smith's power in Nauvoo. On June 7, 1844, Law and his associates published the first and only edition of the *Nauvoo Expositor*, attacking Smith and other Mormon Church officials (Linder 2010). On June 10, 1844, Smith deemed the *Nauvoo Expositor* a public nuisance and called for immediate termination of the paper and destruction of the press. This action was legal under the Nauvoo Charter, which were laws set by the first mayor of Nauvoo that gave the city its independence. That evening, Mormon followers destroyed the press, which caused outrage among non-Mormons in Carthage (Linder 2010). Leading forces of non-Mormon called for rioting charges to be brought against Smith.

Due to the threats of an imminent attack, Ford ordered Smith to be brought out on charges in Carthage. On June 25, Smith and his brother voluntarily submitted to arrest on charges of rioting, with a second charge of treason added after they were detained (Linder 2010). The brothers were held without bail pending a trial scheduled for June 29, 1844 (Linder 2010).

Persecution of the LDS Church

The Mormon Church has been largely persecuted throughout history. In the early onset of the religion during their brief settlement in New York, land was stolen from the church and constitutional values were not upheld in their regard. These events sparked the movement that eventually caused the church to settle at Nauvoo. There has been much controversy surrounding the assassination of Joseph Smith, with speculation that government officials were negligent in protecting Smith during his incarceration, having knowledge of an imminent attack. Despite the hardships, after the Smith trial and further movement of the church, it has since continued to grow and flourish. The LDS Church (the current recognized abbreviation) is currently one of the largest and most successful religious groups in America. The organization has approximately 6.3 million members in the United States and approximately 15 million members worldwide, and publishes works in 177 languages.

The brothers did not make it to their trial date, as a mob shot and killed both men. The Carthage militia did not apprehend any members of the mob when the crime occurred, as many of the militiamen were members of the mob, known as the Carthage Greys. There were mixed feelings about the crime among Hancock residents. The residents of Nauvoo called for calm and encouraged non-retaliation. Sharp published in the *Warsaw Signal* that he believed the killings were regrettable, but justified. The decision to bring charges against the murderers of the Smith brothers came about after Hancock County office elections in 1844. Newly elected sheriff minor Deming recognized that many were involved in the murders, but vowed to only prosecute those largely responsible.

Many of the men being implicated in the murders managed to flee to Missouri before being caught. The investigation indicted nine men, but only five faced trial: Levi Williams, Thomas Sharp, Mark Aldrich, Jacob Davis, and William Grover. The trial began on May 21, 1845 (Linder 2010). The prosecution had a difficult time at trial, due to intimidation tactics that caused many Mormons to be fearful of testifying. Two of their star witnesses, William Daniels and Benjamin Brackenbury, were deemed to be not credible. Another major issue for the prosecution was the defense motion to have the jurors chosen by a new court appointed panel instead of the Mormon-dominated commissioners (Linder 2010). Due to this motion, only 4 of the 96 men on the panel were Mormons.

The defense called only 16 witnesses. The only evidence presented were the bullets, which were used by the Warsaw militia guns. The defendants never testified during trial, and no witnesses were called to provide alibis on their behalf. The jury deliberated for only two hours and acquitted all five men of the charges. The trial somehow managed to bring a sense of peace to both sides, with Mormons concluding that guilt is not often found in what they believed to be, a martyr situation (Doctrine and Covenants, Section 135). Less than a year following the trial, Brigham Young, the new leader of the church, began moving the Mormon followers West, into Mexico, into what would eventually be the state of Utah along the Wasatch Front.

SHAVONNE ARTHURS

See also: Bakker, Jim (1940–); McPherson, Aimee Semple (1890–1944)

Further Reading

The Church of Jesus Christ of Latter-Day Saints. The Doctrine and Covenants, Section 135. https://www.lds.org/scriptures/dc-testament/dc/135?lang=eng.

Hill, Marvin S. 2004. "Carthage Conspiracy Reconsidered: A Second Look at the Murder of Joseph and Hyrum Smith." *Journal of the Illinois State Historical Society* 97: 107–134.

Huntress, Keith. 1969. "Governor Thomas Ford and the Murders of Joseph Smith." *A Journal of Mormon Thought* 4: 41–52.

Linder, Douglas O. 2010. "The Carthage Conspiracy Trial: An Account." http://law2.umkc.edu/faculty/projects/ftrials/carthage/carthageaccount.html. Accessed April 14, 2015.

Oaks, Dallin H., and Marvin S. Hill. 1979. *Carthage Conspiracy: The Trial of the Accused Assassins of Joseph Smith.* Campaign: University of Illinois Press.

Cassidy, Butch (1866–1908)

The entertainment industry continually features television shows and cinematic movies on real-life criminals and the lawmen that tracked them. One such famous criminal is Butch Cassidy. Cassidy's real name was Robert Leroy Parker. However, the alias of Butch Cassidy is ever cemented in history. Cassidy, and his gang, committed several crimes (such as bank and train robberies) across the United States and even in South America. The allure of Cassidy is further perpetuated by the mystery surrounding his death, but Butch Cassidy will always be known as a famous bank and train robber that alluded law enforcement in the United States and abroad.

Evading Capture

Robbers Roost, located in Utah, and the Hole-in-the-Wall, located in Wyoming, are famous locations utilized by bandits to hide from law enforcement. These locations are both natural formations that provided protection and cover. Butch Cassidy and his gang would frequent these locations until the pressure from lawmen subsided. Generally, following a robbery, the Wild Bunch gang would ride in different directions to evade capture. Some members of the gang would go to one hidden location while others would go to another. The men had predetermined locations for them to reunite in order to complete the next robbery.

Butch Cassidy was raised in Utah and was the oldest of 13 children. Cassidy left his family's ranch while still in his early teens. It was at this point that he began to work for a cattle rustler and stole horses. Cassidy's first bank robbery occurred on June 24, 1889. Cassidy, along with three accomplices, robbed the San Miguel Valley Bank for approximately $21,000. The men then fled to a remote hideout in Utah known as Robbers Roost for safety. Cassidy did not serve jail time for this offense; however, he was arrested for stealing horses in Wyoming. He served 18 months of a two-year sentence after promising the governor that he would not offend in the state of Wyoming again. During this same time period Cassidy became romantically involved with Ann Bassett. Ann Basset was the daughter of a local rancher and would later play a significant role in Cassidy's life.

It was after this prison sentence that the legend of Butch Cassidy began to really grow. Cassidy began to associate with several other criminals (i.e., Elzy Lay, Harvey Logan, Ben Kilpatrick, Harry Tracy, Will Carver, Laura Bullion, and George Curry). These criminals, and Cassidy, formed the notorious gang known as the Wild Bunch. The Wild Bunch was responsible for several robberies. During a three-year period (i.e., summer 1896 through summer 1899) the Wild Bunch gang robbed a bank, ambushed men carrying money for a payroll, and robbed a Union Pacific Railroad. Between these robberies the men again found sanctuary at Robbers Roost and another location called the Hole-in-the-Wall. It was also during this period of time that the famous Butch Cassidy and the Sundance Kid partnership began. Cassidy recruited the Sundance Kid—whose real name was Harry Longabaugh—shortly after the first bank robbery performed by the Wild Bunch in 1986. Cassidy and the Sundance Kid performed the longest string of successful train and bank robberies in American history.

The Wild Bunch gang was involved in a several shootouts with lawmen even though they boasted to make every attempt to abstain from killing people. It was during these shootouts that members of the Wild Bunch gang killed upward of six lawmen. However, as before, to help avoid capture, the gang would split up and head to various hideouts, such as the Robber's Roost or the Hole-in-the-Wall before the next robbery was to take place. Beginning in the early fall of 1900, the robberies performed by Butch Cassidy and the Wild Bunch began to grow in terms of monetary value. For instance, in September 1990 Cassidy, the Sundance Kid, and Bill Carver robbed the First National Bank of Winnemucca of over $32,000. Shortly thereafter, Cassidy took part in a train robbery that netted over $60,000 in stolen cash.

While the robberies made Butch Cassidy infamous as an outlaw, his next move cemented Cassidy in American history. Within two months of the $60,000 train-robbery, Cassidy and the Sundance Kid departed the United States for Buenos Aires, Argentina. Eventually, Cassidy purchased a ranch in Argentina near the Andes Mountains with the Sundance Kid and their female companions. Four years after they moved there, in 1905, two English-speaking bandits robbed an Argentine Bank. Though it was never confirmed, it is believed that the bandits were Cassidy and the Sundance Kid.

Butch Cassidy's death begins with a robbery of a mine's payroll by two masked American robbers in Bolivia on November 3, 1908. The two robbers, believed to be Cassidy and the Sundance Kid, took the pack-mule to the boarding house. The owner became suspicious of his guests and notified the local military unit of his suspicions *via telegraph*. Three days later, on November 6, the military, police chief, and mayor arrived at location and surrounded the building. Once one of the soldiers approached the building the robbers opened fire. This action killed one soldier and wounded another. Afterward a gunfight commenced and lasted for hours. At approximately 2 a.m. the gunfire stopped. It was during this time that the soldiers heard a man screaming and then a single gunshot followed shortly by another single gunshot. The next morning, November 7, the locals found

two dead bodies inside the building. Both bodies were riddled with bullet wounds. The police suspected that one man was unable to continue so his partner ended his misery before committing suicide. These two bodies were unidentified and supposedly buried in a small, local cemetery. However, modern-day researchers have attempted, and failed, to find the remains to determine if these gentlemen were in fact the notorious Butch Cassidy and the Sundance Kid.

Following the supposed death of Butch Cassidy, there have been numerous claims by relatives that he did not die. Rather, these individuals claim that Butch Cassidy made appearances at family reunions and impromptu encounters. Some people state that he lived as long as 1945. However, the locations discussed as to where he lived varied from Nevada to Spokane, Washington. The life of Butch Cassidy has culminated in a rather extensive pop culture icon. His story as a bank, and eventually train robber, who evaded the lawmen by hiding in various bandit locations and eventually fled the country for South America is ripe for cinema and popular culture. Furthermore, the mystery surrounding his potential, but not proven, death in Bolivia in 1908 makes for cinematograph freedom. Therefore, there are several movies that chronicle Butch Cassidy's life. For example, in 1969 *Butch Cassidy and the Sundance Kid* depicted the life of Cassidy. The movie starred Paul Newman, Robert Redford, and Katharine Ross. The film was the top grossing film of the year with over $100 million in the box office. Furthermore, the film won four Academy Awards among many others.

M. Hunter Martaindale

See also: Billy the Kid (1859–1881); Dillinger, John (1903–1934)

Further Reading

Phillips, William T. 1986. *The Bandit Invincible: The Story of the Outlaw Butch Cassidy*. Salt Lake City: J. Willard Marriott Library, University of Utah.

Catholic Priest Child Sex Abuse Scandal (1950s–2000s)

The Catholic Priest Child Sex Abuse Scandal refers to allegations, investigations, and trials of sexual abuse of children committed by clergymen of the Roman Catholic Church. The worldwide scandal revealed sexual abuse of children by priests and coordinated efforts within the church hierarchy to cover up allegations of misconduct. Victims included both boys and girls ranging from ages 11 to 14, with some children being as young as three years old. The accusations initially garnered publicity in the late 1980s along with national awareness of sexual abuse and spanned several decades as witnesses surfaced years after abuse occurred. Charges were brought against members of the clergy who did not report accusations of abuse. The Catholic Church also relocated priests who were accused of sexual misconduct to various other parishes around the world rather than immediate dismissal that resulted in continued abuse. The allegations brought against the church was widely covered in the media with significant attention in the United States (Pew Research Center 2002) Canada, and Ireland, though cases were reported globally, including in the United Kingdom, Mexico, Belgium, France, Germany, Argentina, Austria, New Zealand, the Philippines, Australia and Tanzania. The cases indicate patterns of long-term abuse and deliberate cover-up of reports. Academic researchers and diocesan authorities note the silence surrounding sexual abuse by clergy makes it difficult to measure the scope of the allegations even today (John Jay Report 2004).

The United States and Ireland have conducted nationwide enquiries into allegations surrounding clerical sexual abuse of nonconsenting minors while Australia, New Zealand, and Canada have prosecuted perpetrators as well. The United States maintains the highest number of reported cases, followed by Ireland. As a result, the U.S. Conference of Catholic Bishops (USCCB) commissioned and funded a study popularly known as the John Jay Report (The Nature and Scope of the Problem of Sexual Abuse of Minors by Catholic Priests and Deacons in the United States 2004). The study examined the extent of sexual abuse of minors by Catholic priests, collected information about alleged abusers including official church status, age, number of victims, and legal responses, as well as characteristics of alleged victims, nature of relationship with abuser and the time frame which allegations were reported. Church officials have argued that sensational media coverage in the United States has been excessively disproportionate and detrimental to the Catholic Church. The Pew Research Center (2010) notes that in the early 2000s coverage was focused on the United States and by 2010 it had shifted to Europe.

Surveys completed by the Roman Catholic dioceses indicated 10,667 allegations against 4,392 priests accused of sexual abuse of minors between 1950 and 2002. Around 81 percent of the victims were male. Of those who alleged abuse, 17 percent also had siblings that were victims. More than half of the minors were between the ages of 11 and 14.

It is estimated that 2,000 very young children were victimized, which included 22 percent of victims younger than age 10. Of 9,281 victim surveys regarding an investigation, 6,696 (72 percent) of the cases were carried out with 4,570 (80 percent) of allegations substantiated. Of the 4,392 priests that were accused (about 4 percent of the total 109,694 priests that are in active ministry), 59 percent had one charge against them, and up to 3 percent (149 priests) had 10 or more allegations, accounting for 2,960 victims (27 percent of overall accusations). Thirty-eight percent of abuse allegations occurred within a one-year period. Forty-one percent of the priests were the subject of more than one case of abuse. Abuse claims were substantiated for 1,872 priests who were younger than the age of 35 at the time of the first incident of abuse. Reported abuse was classified into more than 20 categories including touching, disrobing, and forced sexual acts. While annual reports of sexual abuse continue to surface, the incidents of reports increased during the 1960s and 1970s for males aged 11 to 17. Reports decreased between the 1980s and 1990s. One in four child abuse allegations were made within 10 years of the incident and half were made between 10 and 30 years after the incident. Reports were made up to 30 years after the initial abuse and continue to surface today.

Financial settlements involving over 375 cases with 1,551 victims resulted in payments totaling $2.6 billion by 2012 (Childress 2014). Eight Catholic dioceses have subsequently declared bankruptcy due to child sex abuse cases between 2001 and 2011, while at least six dioceses have obtained bankruptcy protection. In addition to lawsuits, accused priests were forced to resign, defrocked, and crimes that fell within statutes of limitations resulted in imprisonment for some. Elderly priests who could not lose standing due to canon law live under restriction in monitored retreat homes. The legal system and media have largely focused on the unreported allegations for investigation and prosecution. As a result dioceses directed offending priests to seek psychiatric treatment, with the John Jay Report indicating that 40 percent of the accused perpetrators participated in counseling programs (that were later found to be insufficient). Catholic bishops were criticized for relocating offending priests to other parishes after abuse counseling as they were able to maintain contact with children.

There was also insufficient accountability within the church hierarchy, along with inability to grasp the seriousness of the issue, misguided willingness to forgive, emphasis on avoiding a scandal, and use of unqualified treatment centers that fostered the problem. The lack of procedural reporting within the church also encouraged the Charter for the Protection of Children and Young People to require background checks for church employees, maintain a safe environment for children, promote reconciliation efforts with victims, prompted response to allegations, including a zero tolerance of abusers policy (permanent removal from ministry), and cooperation with civil law enforcement. The U.S. National Review Board requires dioceses faced with allegations to alert authorities, conduct investigations, and remove accusers.

Global responses included a 2011 case lodged with the International Criminal Court stating that the pope (Benedict XVI), dean of the College of Cardinals, and various other high-ranking Vatican officials had committed a crime against humanity through abetting and covering up sexual assault of children by priests. The Vatican argued that this was a misuse of the international judiciary system. In 2014, the United Nations Committee on the Rights of the Child issued a report stating that the pope and the Roman Catholic Church had not done enough to protect children and recommended removal of all known or suspected child molesters.

ANEESA A. BABOOLAL

See also: Heaven's Gate Mass Suicide (March 24–26, 1997); McMartin Preschool Trial (1983–1990)

Further Reading

Childress, Sarah. 2014. "What's the State of the Church's Child Abuse Crisis?" *PBS Frontline*, February 25. http://www.pbs.org/wgbh/pages/frontline/religion/secrets-of-the-vatican/whats-the-state-of-the-churchs-child-abuse-crisis/. Accessed November 1, 2014.

D'Antonio, M. 2013. *Mortal Sins: Sex, Crime, and the Era of Catholic Scandal*. New York: Thomas Dunne Books, St. Thomas Press.

John Jay College of Criminal Justice. The City University of New York. 2004. "The Nature and Scope of the Problem of Sexual Abuse of Minors by Catholic Priests and Deacons in the United States." http://www.usccb.org/issues-and-action/child-and-youth-protection/upload/The-Nature-and-Scope-of-Sexual-Abuse-of-Minors-by-Catholic-Priests-and-Deacons-in-the-United-States-1950-2002.pdf. Accessed November 1, 2014.

Pew Research Center. 2010. "The Pope Meets the Press: Media Coverage of the Clergy Abuse Scandal." http://www.pewforum.org/2010/06/11/the-pope-meets-the-press-media-coverage-of-the-clergy-abuse-scandal/. Accessed November 1, 2014.

Plante, T.G. 2004. *Sin against the Innocents: Sexual Abuse by Priests and the Role of the Catholic Church*. Westport, CT: Praeger.

Celia (a Slave), Murder Trial of (1855)

The story of Celia, a slave who lived in Missouri from roughly 1850 to her execution in 1855, is another chapter in America's tortured past with slavery. Celia was a victim of constant sexual exploitation at the hands of her master from the age of 14. This was a not uncommon symptom of slavery—sexual exploitation of female slaves by male slaveowners. It was considered an extremely shameful practice in slave-owning society, but little was ever done to put an end to the practice. Slaves were considered property. This created major problems for a female slave attempting to end sexual abuse of a master. After all, a piece of property cannot be raped. This was yet another legal issue that the practice of slavery created. Almost exclusively, however, the legal system of the United States would dehumanize slaves, rendering them nearly defenseless in a court of law. Celia was no exception.

The codes and laws surrounding slavery are often confusing, contradictory, and illogical. But one theme is generally true: slaves were a form of property, often characterized as "chattel." Chattel is a legal term for personal property that is "movable." However, some states characterized slaves as a form of "real" property. "Real" property is a legal term that generally applies to land. Some states, such as Kentucky, characterized slaves as real property for inheritance purposes, that is, slaves would pass through a will to the person who inherited the land they worked.

Regardless of the proper legal designation, slaves were afforded very few protections by the law. Instructive on this point is the case of *State v. Mann*, 2. Dev. 263 (N.C. 1829). In that case, a female slave, Lydia, was shot and wounded by Mann when she tried to escape a lashing. A local jury imposed a $5 fine on Mann. The North Carolina Supreme Court overturned the verdict, saying "the power of the master must be absolute, to render the submission of the slave perfect." *Id.* This is the world Celia would be born into.

Robert Newsom, who would eventually purchase Celia, moved to Missouri from Virginia sometime in 1822. Newsom would gradually rise from being a simple farmer, on a small piece of land, to a well-known and prosperous landowner in Callaway County, Missouri. By 1850, he also owned five slaves; four fully grown men and a five-year-old boy. Later that year, he added a fifth: 14-year-old Celia.

Nearly nothing is known of Celia's life before her appearance on the Newsom farm. She was purchased from a neighboring county, and appeared to have some training as a cook. Like most slaves, there is no record of her family, her place or date of birth, nor anything of the sort.

Furthermore, the purchase of so young a female slave was questionable, given the fact that she would not have added to the productivity of the farm. It would soon become apparent why Newsom had purchased Celia. He wanted a replacement for his recently deceased wife.

Immediately upon their return to the Newsom farm, Newsom raped Celia for the first time. This matter, had it been discovered, would have likely subjected Newsom to considerable scorn from his neighbors. But Newsom owned an 800-acre farm and had complete access and control over his property; no one was in a position to intervene. Abolitionists frequently charged slave-owning society with allowing the frequent rape of female slaves. History has borne out this claim, as female slaves who later recorded their experiences made prominent mention of the ever-present threat of rape or sexual assault.

The rapes would continue over the next five years. Celia would have two children by Newsom. Eventually, Celia began a relationship with a male slave, George. Celia became pregnant again. George told Celia that he could not bear to share her with her master, who considered Celia his sexual property. Sometime on or around June 23, 1855, Celia told Newsom that she would not submit to his advances anymore. She told him that if he tried to force himself on her again, she would defend herself. Newsom did not care.

On June 23, 1855, at roughly 10 p.m., Newsom went to find Celia. He went to Celia's cabin. Celia walked into a corner of her cabin, and grabbed a large stick. She struck Newsom twice, the second blow killing him. She then burned his body in her fireplace.

Celia was not able to hide what she had done. The investigation immediately centered on George. The fact that on June 24, 1855, investigators were already interrogating George is a very strong indication that Newsom's family was aware of the sordid affair. George pointed the finger at Celia. Celia confessed to killing Newsom, and explained the circumstances surrounding his death.

At trial, Celia's attorneys argued a simple theory: that Celia was allowed to protect herself from rape, even from her master. Missouri law specifically made forcible intercourse illegal; the defense argued that Newsom ran afoul of this law by forcing himself on Celia. This would have entitled her to defend herself with violence. While many in slave-owning society did not approve of masters raping their slaves this argument poised a grave threat to a master's control over his slaves. The prosecution would argue that while it was illegal to rape a free woman, no such provision was made in the law regarding a slaveowner and his property. In other words, a slaveowner could rape his own slave legally.

The argument came down to jury instructions. The defense argued that the judge should include a self-defense instruction. The prosecution argued a self-defense instruction was improper. Judge William Hall agreed with the prosecution. The jury found Celia guilty, and she was sentenced to be hung.

What should strike the reader, as has struck those who study the law, is the tragic situation that presented slaves accused of crimes, such as Celia. Celia was a piece of property, who could not defend herself from her master forcing himself upon her sexually. However, Celia was considered a person capable of committing a murder. Put another way, the law refused to protect Celia from rape no more than the law would have protected Newsom from taking a hammer to his own furniture. Celia, like all slaves, was at the mercy of her master. But once Celia killed Newsom, the law considered her a person capable of murder, but not a person who could defend herself. Celia could not win.

It was these sorts of barbarous and illogical situations that fueled abolitionists. Celia's fate was sealed only six years before the outbreak of the American Civil War, and would be cited by some of those who supported Abraham Lincoln as yet another link in the chain of America's sordid history with human bondage.

John Friend

See also: *Amistad* Slave Ship Case (1839); Dred Scott Decision (1857); Fugitive Slave Laws (1793, 1850); *Primary Documents/* Account of the Confession and Execution of Celia, a Slave Who Murdered Her Master (1856)

Further Reading

Delombard, Jeannine Marie. 2007. *Slavery on Trial: Law, Abolitionism, and Print Culture*. Chapel Hill: The University of North Carolina Press.

Fehrenbacher, Don E. 1979. *The Dred Scott Case: Its Significance in American Law and Politics*. Oxford: Oxford University Press.

Hall, Kermit L., Paul Finkelman, Paul, and James W. Ely, Jr. 2005. *American Legal History: Cases and Materials*. Oxford: Oxford University Press.

McLaurin, Melton. 1991. *Celia, A Slave*. Athens: University of Georgia Press.

Tibbs, Donald F., and Tyron P. Woods, Tyron. 2008. "The Jena Six and Black Punishment: Law and Raw Life in the Domain of Nonexistence." *Seattle Journal for Social Justice* 7(1): 235.

Central Park Jogger Case (1989)

The Central Park Jogger case has become symbolic of issues in the criminal justice system. When the crime occurred, the case represented the racial tension and urban decay present in New York City and fueled discussions of race relations, racial profiling, and crime policies. Response to the case led to harsher penalties in the justice system and shaped the perception of high-profile cases to follow, such as the Yusef Hawkins murder in Bensonhurst later the same summer (Chancer 2005). The crime became important to criminological examinations of the impact of race in society, the media, and the justice system. After the Central Park Five were exonerated, the case became a focal point in the context of wrongful convictions, prompting further looks into juvenile vulnerability to interrogation, questionable interrogation tactics, the influence of media on verdicts, and causes of wrongful conviction (Kassin et al. 2010). As reported by Sean Gardiner in his July 7, 2014, *Wall Street Journal* article, the settlement of the Central Park Five's civil rights lawsuit is also impacting other New York City wrongful conviction suits as a new standard for settlement requests.

On the night of April 19, 1989, Trisha Meili, a 28-year-old white woman known only as "the Central Park jogger" in media coverage of the case, went jogging in Central Park. During her run, Meili was attacked, raped, sodomized, and beaten in what came to be known as the "Central Park jogger case." Her skull was fractured, her left eye socket was shattered, and she lost over 75 percent of her blood before she was discovered several hours later, comatose and hypothermic. The same evening, a group of 40–50 teenagers had been reported committing random physical assaults and attempting to rob various joggers, cyclists, and pedestrians in Central Park. When Meili was discovered, the crime was linked to the assaults committed by the youth that night. Five black and Hispanic youth—Raymond Santana, Kevin Richardson, Antron McCray, Yusef Salaam, and Korey Wise—were among those arrested on suspicion of being involved in the park assaults and jogger attack.

The interrogations of Richardson, Santana, McCray, Salaam, and Wise each lasted between 14 and 30 hours (Sullivan 1992). All five suspects confessed to participating in the attack, though each minimized his personal involvement in the crime. Four of the five suspects confessed on videotape; Salaam refused to confess on videotape. All five recanted their statements prior to trial and claimed police coercion. The police admitted to lying about evidence implicating the boys, such as telling Salaam his fingerprints had been found on the victim's clothing. The suspects and their relatives also alleged the police said they could return home if they cooperated, but the police denied making promises of leniency.

The trials relied upon the disputed confessions, as no other evidence implicated the suspects, known collectively as "the Central Park Five." The DNA, which failed to match the defendants, implicated an unknown male (Burns 2011). Elizabeth Lederer, the lead prosecutor, argued the results meant a sixth perpetrator had escaped capture. McCray, Salaam, and Santana were tried together and convicted of rape, assault, riot, and robbery on August 18, 1990. Judge Thomas Galligan sentenced each to 3 to 10 years for the assault on Meili and another 3 to 10 years for the assault on John Loughlin, another jogger attacked that night. Richardson and Wise were tried together and convicted on December 11, 1990. Richardson was convicted of attempted murder, rape, and sodomy. Wise was convicted of assault, sexual abuse, and riot but acquitted of rape and attempted murder. Richardson received a sentence of 3 to 10 years for each charge; Wise, tried as an adult, received 8 to 26 years. Wise ultimately served about 13 years in prison; the remaining four each served about seven years.

At the time of the crime, New York City was facing financial crisis, racial conflict, and a rapidly rising crime rate. Extensive media coverage framed the case as a prime example of wild inner city youth destroying society (Chancer 2005). Using sensationalistic terms such as "wilding" and "wolf pack," mainstream coverage depicted the Central Park Five in animalistic and dehumanizing terms. This coverage fed fear of the black community and perceptions of rampant black crime (Burns 2011). Local leaders in the African American community pointed to the rhetoric and the quick prosecution of the five defendants as reflective of widespread institutional racism. The case also fed political discourse, with many politicians and community leaders calling for harsher criminal justice penalties. Donald Trump spent $85,000 on full-page ads in four New York City newspapers, advocating for the reinstatement of the death penalty, and Republican mayoral candidate Rudolph Giuliani used a tough on crime platform to win the 1993 mayoral election (after a narrow loss in 1989) against Mayor David Dinkins.

The Central Park Five maintained their innocence during and after their incarcerations. With support from The Innocence Project, they contested their convictions. Progress finally occurred when Matias Reyes, a convicted rapist and murder serving a 33-1/3 year to life sentence, confessed in January 2002 to the Central Park jogger attack. A reinvestigation by the Manhattan District Attorney's office led by Nancy Ryan and Peter Casolaro found the DNA from the crime scene matched Reyes and the confessions of the five were inconsistent with each other and contradicted the case evidence (Burns 2011). No other evidence linked the five to the crime, and Reyes maintained he had committed the crime alone. On December 5, 2002, District Attorney Robert Morgenthau joined the motion to vacate the convictions of the Central Park Five. Judge Charles Tejada of the New York State Supreme Court vacated the convictions on December 19, 2002. The New York Police Department opposed the decision and released their own report maintaining the Central Park Five had likely participated in the crime with Reyes.

The Victim's Recovery

Trisha Meili was an investment banker at Salomon Brothers at the time of the Central Park jogger attack. After 12 days in a coma and a few months in physical therapy, Meili began running again despite still-present balance issues. Meili returned to work eight months after the attack. Meili left Salomon Brothers in 1998 and began working with nonprofit groups and speaking to survivors of sexual assault and traumatic brain injuries. Meili released her memoir in 2003, revealing her identity as the Central Park jogger, and still works as an inspirational speaker today.

Meili survived but sustained permanent brain damage, vision loss, and memory loss for the attack. Trisha Meili revealed her identity in 2003 when she released her memoir, *I Am the Central Park Jogger: A Story of Hope and Possibility.* Meili now acts as an inspirational speaker, using her experiences to help other survivors of trauma. The same year Meili came forward, the Central Park Five filed a $250 million civil rights lawsuit against the city of New York, alleging malicious prosecution, false arrest, and racial discrimination. The administration of Mayor Michael Bloomberg contested the claims, maintaining the city had acted appropriately throughout the case. In contrast, Bill de Blasio promised during his 2013 mayoral campaign to quickly settle the decade-long lawsuit upon his election. Bill de Blasio won the election, and, as reported by Sean Gardiner in his June 26, 2014, *Wall Street Journal* article, New York City Comptroller Scott Stringer approved a settlement of the lawsuit on June 26, 2014. On September 5, 2014, Magistrate Judge Ronald Ellis approved the $41 million settlement, which will pay the Central Park Five approximately $1 million for each year of their wrongful imprisonments. The city of New York denied any wrongdoing in the settlement agreement.

JENNIFER T. PERILLO

See also: Carter, Rubin "Hurricane" (1937–2014); Hawkins, Yusef, Murder of (1989); Jena Six (Jena, LA) (2006); Mississippi Burning Case (1964)

Further Reading

Burns, S. 2011. *The Central Park Five: A Chronicle of City Wilding.* New York: Knopf.

Chancer, Lynn. S. 2005. *High-Profile Crimes: When Legal Cases Become Social Issues.* Chicago: University of Chicago Press.

Kassin, Saul M., Steven A. Drizin, Thomas Grisso, Gisli H. Gudjonsson, Richard A. Leo, and Allison D. Redlich. 2010. "Police-Induced Confessions: Risk Factors and Recommendations." *Law and Human Behavior* 34: 3–38.

Meili, Trisha. 2004. *I Am The Central Park Jogger: A Story of Hope and Possibility.* New York: Scribner.

Smith, Chris. 2002. "Central Park Revisited." *New York Magazine.* October 21. http://nymag.com/nymetro/news/crimelaw/features/n_7836/. Accessed April 9, 2015.

Sullivan, Timothy. 1992. *Unequal Verdicts: The Central Park Jogger Trials.* New York: Simon & Schuster.

Cermak, Anton Joseph, Assassination of (February 15, 1933)

Anton Cermak, the 44th mayor of Chicago, was killed by a bullet aimed at president-elect Franklin D. Roosevelt (FDR), after FDR spoke at Bayfront Park, Miami, Florida, on February 15, 1933. Cermak nearly recovered from his lung wounds, only to die of ulcerative colitis at Jackson Park Memorial Hospital in Miami, on March 6.

The gunman who inflicted those wounds, Giuseppe Zangara, also shot four other people, one of whom died as a result. An alert and courageous bystander, Lillian Cross, deflected Zangara's arm with her purse, preventing further casualties. FDR escaped unharmed. Zangara, age 32, Italian by birth, U.S. citizen since 1923, bricklayer from Patterson, New Jersey, was promptly caught, arrested, jailed, tried, convicted of both murders, and of two failed murder attempts, sentenced to 80 years, then capital punishment, put in a "death cell," and electrocuted on March 20, two weeks after Anton Cermak died. He told Dade County judge Uly Thompson that he was not afraid to die, and his last words prior to the execution were "pusha da button!"

Those are facts. But the murder also created its own myths. Zangara is still viewed as an ignorant immigrant, anarchist, socialist, madman. He may have been all of these things, but he was also plagued by horrible stomach pain, which made his words and actions seem exaggerated if not insane. Neither orator nor scholar, he urged class warfare as the best (or only) solution to poverty and oppression,

On February 15, 1933, while appearing with President Franklin D. Roosevelt in Miami, Florida, Chicago mayor Anton Joseph Cermak was shot by assassin Giuseppe Zangara. He died on March 6, 1933. (Bettmann/Corbis)

yet he insisted that he held no grudges against the rich themselves, including Roosevelt. Zangara was eccentric, but not crazy or uneducated, and far from stupid. Today, he is known to posterity only for killing the "wrong" leader.

As for Cermak, his own life was the stuff of urban legends, most of which arose thanks to accidental death. Born in Bohemia (then part of the Austro-Hungarian empire, now Czech Republic), he came to the United States as a babe, grew up in a saloon, which he took over when he came of age. Thus he opposed Prohibition for personal reasons. Climbing the political ladder for 30 years, defeated in a Senate bid, he became mayor in 1931, defeating "Big Bill" Thompson. In the two years that Cermak served as mayor, he did something no one else had ever accomplished: he created (and consolidated) the patronage system still known as "the machine," which made it impossible to do anything in and around Chicago without mayoral approval. That system later elected both Mayors Daley, and their heirs.

Yet Cermak is not a household word, except in Chicago, where they named a street after him (22nd) following his death. So the question is, what was Cermak doing in Miami

on the night he was shot, evidently by mistake? Officially, the answer is that he had come to ask the president-elect for financial help, to pay the salaries and back pay of Chicago school teachers, who were working without contract or compensation for over a year. Unofficially, who knows? Cermak presided over the Democratic National Convention in 1932, held at Chicago Stadium, at which FDR was nominated for president. But Cermak didn't support FDR then, and only reluctantly thereafter. So he may have gone South to mend fences, and make his amends. Conversely, FDR owed Cermak (and Jacob "Jake" Arvey, who represented the 24th Ward on Chicago's West Side, where Cermak lived) for its staggering turnout: Alderman Arvey, whom everyone called the boss, dialed up the patronage machine, newly installed by Cermak, to give Roosevelt the highest percentage of votes (99.5 percent) of any precinct in the country, a record for a national election (versus Herbert Hoover) that still stands.

Speech over, Cermak crossed from one side of the park road to another, hoping to catch Roosevelt before he drove away with his entourage, to shake his hand, be seen by the crowd, noticed by the press, and then asked to pose with Roosevelt for photos and newsreels. Then the shots rang. What was said immediately before or after that moment, no one knows. What we do know (courtesy of Cermak's pals, who accompanied him to Florida and as loyal Aldermen, found ways to knight *the* boss) is that a day later, Cermak told FDR, "I'm glad it was me [who got shot] and not you." He may not have said it—or muttered just the opposite sentiment, under his breath. But the newspapers recorded it, and printed the legend.

Was Mayor Cermak's Murder Really an Accident?

Cermak's legacy as ruthless politician convinced many crime buffs and political pros (along with some historians) that his murder was no fluke, that (i) Cermak wanted to "centralize" corruption (organized crime) just as he had already done with patronage, thus insuring his "cut" (15 percent of proceeds from gambling, narcotics, vice), while posing as a "mob reformer" and (ii) Cermak allegedly had Frank Nitti (Capone's successor as head of the Outfit) shot and beaten by the police [detectives], just to show Nitti who was the boss. The speculation is that Zangara was hired to avenge or retaliate for Nitti's (nearly fatal) beating, to send Cermak a "message." The old rumors persist, in one form or another, devoid of any evidence. If you believe (against all the available data) that Zangara meant to kill Cermak, you must assume either that he acted on his own or that he was a hired killer. A hired killer would not (in all likelihood) use a .32 caliber pistol, fire it from a few feet away, in the midst of a crowd, where he was certain to be apprehended. The bullets perforated Cermak's chest, but such theories are full of holes. Zangara had no motive to kill Cermak: never dwelt on that, even in court. Those who still maintain that Zangara did not kill Cermak unintentionally face unbearable burdens of proof. But every urban legend has its reasons.

There is a comical aspect to this tragic spectacle. Giuseppe Zangara was so short, he had to stand on a chair to see his target—when he tried out a series of chairs during the speech, to test his aim and determine his range; he annoyed several spectators who wanted to see and hear FDR, thereby calling attention to himself, and also (inadvertently) placing himself at a bad angle, further from FDR than he wanted to be. The unpremeditated quarrels alone may have saved FDR's life, compelling Zangara to move to a less desirable (and hotly contested) outdoor seat, while he fumed at those around him, who refused to budge or yield to this uncouth fellow.

Zangara was obnoxious, befuddled, absent-minded: a rude, crude "nut," not a cautious, cold-blooded, circumspect killer. Mayor Cermak was in the way: an obstacle, not a goal. He interfered with Zangara, by chance. Zangara killed him, also by chance. No design—only a deadly collision.

While Zangara didn't think much about how or even whether to kill FDR, he did pay close attention to FDR's words, as citizens did then and students of that epoch do now, for declarations of policy and signs of renewed hope. Roosevelt coined the term "New Deal" in his acceptance speech at Chicago Stadium [Nomination Address, July 2, 1932], in Mayor Cermak's presence. For Zangara, it was a raw deal—continuous bondage, disguised as freedom. He saw no prospect of reconciling workers with owners, or overcoming the gap between labor and management, and sought none. Class struggle (and economic warfare between rich and poor) was both justified and inevitable. His political theories suffered from his lack of fluency in English, but they were coherent—and they were political. He made his ideas, his ideals, and his sense of betrayal (by those entrusted with living up to the principles of democracy) quite clear, and unmistakable. He was embittered, utterly and totally disillusioned for reasons that had nothing to do with the Windy City, but everything to do with the gap between ideal American myth and reality.

DENNIS ROHATYN

See also: McKinley, William, Assassination of (September 6, 1901); Nitti, Frank "the Enforcer" (1888–1943); Wallace, George, Attempted Assassination of (May 15, 1972)

Further Reading

Beito, David. 1989. *Taxpayers in Revolt: Tax Resistance during the Great Depression*. Chapel Hill: University of North Carolina Press.

Gottfried, Alex. 1962. *Boss Cermak of Chicago*. Seattle: University of Washington Press.

Gumbel, Andrew. 2005. *Steal This Vote: Dirty Elections and the Rotten History of Democracy in America*. New York: Nation Books.

Neal, Steven. 2004. *Happy Days Are Here Again: The 1932 Democratic Convention, the Emergence of FDR—and How America Was Changed Forever*. New York: HarperCollins.

Picchi, Blaise. 1998. *The Five Weeks of Giuseppe Zangara: The Man Who Would Assassinate FDR*. Chicago: Academy Chicago Publishers.

Ritchie, Donald A. 2007. *Electing FDR: The New Deal Campaign of 1932*. American Presidential Elections. Lawrence: University Press of Kansas.

Smith, Jean Edward. 2007. *FDR*. New York: Random House.

Chambers, Robert. *See* Levin, Jennifer, Murder of (August 26, 1986)

Chambers, Whittaker. *See* Hiss, Alger (1904–1996) and Whittaker Chambers (1901–1961)

Champion, Robert. *See* Florida A&M Hazing Death (November 19, 2011)

Chapman, Mark David. *See* Lennon, John, Murder of (December 8, 1980)

Chappaquiddick Incident (July 18–19, 1969)

In mid-July 1969, a young politician's dream of one day becoming president of the United States was severely damaged. Senator Ted Kennedy of Massachusetts, the younger brother of the late president John F. Kennedy and the late New York senator Robert F. Kennedy, drove his car over the side of the road into Poucha Pond on Chappaquiddick Island, Massachusetts. He had been attending a memorial celebration dedicated to his brother, when he left with Mary Jo Kopechne. When the car crashed into the water, Mary Jo Kopechne died. After Kennedy escaped and was safe on land, he traveled back to his hotel until the next morning. When he reported the accident some 10 hours after the crash, the police were already in the process of conducting an investigation because a fisherman had spotted the car. The case went to a grand jury in 1970, but Kennedy was never indicted for murder. His driver's license was suspended for leaving the accident scene, but this was nothing compared to the effect it had on his reputation and his presidential ambitions.

On July 18, 1969, Ted Kennedy hosted a reunion of six women who had worked together on his late brother Robert's 1968 presidential campaign. These young women were known as the "Boiler Room Girls." This gathering was held on Chappaquiddick Island off the coast of Martha's Vineyard in Massachusetts. Along with the Boiler Room Girls, Ted Kennedy and many other guests were also present. One of these young women at the party was Mary Jo Kopechne, a 28-year-old Boiler Room Girl.

Around 11 p.m., Ted Kennedy was ready to leave and asked his driver for the keys to the car. When Kopechne heard of his intentions to leave she asked him if he could give her a ride to the hotel. The two of them left together and Kopechne left her purse at the party without telling anyone where she was going. Kennedy proceeded to drive down Dyke Road, the opposite direction of the ferry. They came to the Dyke Bridge, which did not have any guardrails for protection. The road produced a slight curve and Kennedy lost control and went over the side.

The car flipped over and quickly started filling up with water. Kennedy was able to free himself to get to the surface. He claims to have attempted to rescue Kopechne from the sinking car, but was unable to rescue her. He was utterly exhausted, but eventually sought help for Kopechne.

Joseph Gargan and Paul Markham came back to the scene of the crime with Kennedy to help save Mary Jo Kopechne. They made several more attempts to rescue her, but again they could not free her from the car. The two went back to the party and did not call the police, because they thought that Kennedy was about to do so himself. Instead Kennedy claims to have swum back across the channel instead of taking the ferry. When he arrived back at his hotel he was so utterly exhausted that he went to sleep without ever contacting the authorities. In the morning he spoke to Gargan and Markham again and told them that he had yet to contact the police. Around 10 a.m., Kennedy finally contacted the authorities and informed them of the accident in Poucha Pond. However, the authorities were already on the scene around 9:15 a.m. after receiving a call from a fisherman. Kopechne's body was finally pulled out of the water.

In the days following the accident, Ted Kennedy attended Kopechne's funeral that was held at St. Vincent's Roman Catholic Church in Plymouth, Pennsylvania. About a week after the incident, Kennedy pled guilty to fleeing the scene after the accident had occurred. He was sentenced to two months in prison, but this sentence was suspended because of his age and reputation. On the day he was sentenced, he delivered a speech on national television describing the accident to the nation. He stated that the events have become cloudy in his memory, but that he was positive he did make an effort to try and save Kopechne's life from the sinking car. Kennedy also stated that he was debating on resigning from the Senate, following this accident and his actions.

There were additional efforts to search for the truth about what happened, including an inquest and grand jury hearing. For example, several conclusions were made at an inquest presided over by Judge James Boyle, including that Kennedy was negligent in the operation of his vehicle and that this negligence caused the death of Kopechne. Although the inquest result with this conclusion, Kennedy was not charged for this negligence. At a grand jury hearing in April 1970, the district attorney who attended the inquest told them that there was not enough evidence to indict Kennedy.

While Ted Kennedy was able to escape serious legal consequences from his decisions and actions on that night in July, his reputation was tarnished. The incident was an important reason why Kennedy never secured the presidency. With the memory of Chappaquiddick still fresh, Kennedy announced his decision not to seek the president in 1976, and when he did run in 1980, he lost in the Democratic primary to President Jimmy Carter. However, while Ted Kennedy was never president of the United States, he was elected to the Senate seven more times. In 1970, only one year after the incident, he won reelection to his Massachusetts Senate seat, securing over 62 percent of the vote. He died in August 2009.

RACHEL CSUTOROS

See also: Kennedy, John F., Assassination of (November 22, 1963); Kennedy, Robert F. "Bobby," Assassination of (1968); Smith, William Kennedy, Rape Case (1991)

Further Reading

Burns, James M. 1976. *Edward Kennedy and the Camelot Legacy*. New York: W.W. Norton & Company

Goss, Jennifer L. "Ted Kennedy and the Chappaquiddick Accident." 20th Century History. http://history1900s.about.com/od/1960s/a/Chappaquiddick.htm. Accessed April 17, 2015.

Hastings, H. Don. 1969. *The Ted Kennedy Episode*. Dallas: Reliable Press.

Jones, Richard E. 1979. *The Chappaquiddick Inquest: The Complete Transcript of the Inquest into the Death of Mary Jo Kopechne*. Pittsford, NY: Lynn Publications.

United Press International. 1969. "Chappaquiddick—Audio—1969—UPI.com." UPI.com. http://www.upi.com/Archives/Audio/Events-of-1969/Chappaquiddick/. Accessed April 17, 2015.

Cherokee Nation v. Georgia, Forced Removal of Indian Tribes (1831)

Several forces mitigated against the Cherokee Indians, part of the Five Civilized Tribes, in their battle to preserve their ancestral lands, their ancient customs, and their sovereignty as a nation against the relentless punches of the United States expanding westward in the 1830s. Forces working against the Cherokee included the Indian policies of U.S. presidents, the state of Georgia, land and gold hungry settlers, and divisions among the Cherokee themselves. Tensions about the division of powers between the federal and state governments, and slavery and antislavery factions factored into the situation as well, land and slaves being essential for cotton-growing and plantations. These ingredients combined to create an 1831 U.S. Supreme Court landmark case, *The Cherokee Nation v. The State of Georgia*.

The Cherokee had lived in Georgia for centuries and throughout their contact with Europeans and European culture struggled for a balance in adopting European customs while preserving their own nation and culture. They developed economically healthy towns, farms, mills, and animal herds patterned after the European lifestyle. In 1821, Sequoyah wrote a syllabary for the Cherokee language, and the tribe published a newspaper called *The Phoenix* in the Cherokee language. The Five Civilized Tribes also adapted the white man's practice of slavery into their cultures. Many Cherokee used black slaves as a bridge to white society and relied on them as English interpreters and translators.

By 1827, the Cherokee had adopted a written constitution modeled on the U.S. Constitution, set up their elected legislature, executive structure and court system, and named New Echota, Georgia, as the capitol of the Cherokee Nation. Relying on previous federal treaties that declared them sovereign and legally capable of ceding their lands, the Cherokee tried to use this status to save the remaining lands.

Surviving numerous unequal treaties and land cessions, the Cherokee Nation fought to save their Georgia lands. In 1802, the state of Georgia had signed an agreement with the federal government, promising to give its western lands to the government in exchange for the government extinguishing Indian land titles within Georgia. In 1820, Georgia pressured the federal government to remove the Cherokee from Georgia lands and in 1826 and 1827, the Georgia state legislature passed resolutions declaring state sovereignty over Cherokee lands. In 1828, the Georgia legislature passed a law annexing Cherokee lands and assuming jurisdiction over the Cherokee Nation, and nullifying any laws under the Cherokee constitution. Essentially, the law relegated the Cherokee to the status of tenants living on state land. More of hundreds of new settlers and miners encroached on Cherokee lands during the 1829 Georgia Gold Rush, which the Cherokee called the "great intrusion."

In resisting pressure from the state of Georgia to relinquish their lands and move, the Cherokee were also opposing the traditional Indian policies of the U.S. government. U.S. presidents from George Washington to James Monroe viewed the Cherokee with paternalistic vision, but treated them as a sovereign nation. President James Monroe and his administration established Indian policies that the U.S. government would follow for the next two centuries. President Monroe advocated giving a fee simple land title to Indians who wanted to own it, allowing the government and non-Indians to acquire "surplus" lands. He instructed his secretary of war John C. Calhoun to create the first plans for Indian removal and by 1824 he presented Congress with a plan for Indian removal, creating lands in the Arkansas and Indian Territory west of the Mississippi River for them to settle in exchange for their Georgia lands. The Senate passed the measure, but the Georgia delegation in the House of Representatives nullified it. Following the precedents of the U.S. Constitution and earlier presidents, President Monroe treated Indian tribes as sovereign nations and he often met with Indian delegations in Washington, D.C.

President John Quincy Adams adopted the Calhoun–Monroe policy, resolving to relocate the Indians without force, but again Georgia intervened, prompting President Adams to negotiate a treaty with the Indians in favor of Georgia's acquisition of Cherokee lands.

Andrew Jackson from the fledgling Democratic Party became president of the United States in 1829, and although he didn't originate Indian removal policy, he aggressively implemented it. President Jackson turned away from the policies of his predecessors of treating different Indian groups as separate nations, resolving to move all Indian tribes east of the Mississippi River to Indian Territory west of the Mississippi River. In his annual address to Congress in 1829, he stated that the United States did not support Cherokee sovereignty and ordered the Indians to move. After a fierce debate, Congress passed the Indian Removal Bill and President Jackson signed it into law on June 30, 1830.

In June 1830, Cherokee chief John Ross led a delegation of Cherokee to Washington, D.C., to defend Cherokee rights at the Supreme Court. Senators Daniel Webster and Theodore Frelinghuysen convinced Chief Ross to name William Wirt, the attorney general in the Monroe and Adams administrations, as their representative to present an injunction that claimed that Georgia's state legislature had created laws that erased the Cherokee as a political society. Attorney Wirt argued that the Cherokee Nation was a foreign nation under the definition of the U.S. Constitution and law, and he asked the Supreme Court to void all of the Georgia laws that extended over Cherokee lands.

He argued that the Georgia laws violated the U.S. Constitution, U.S.–Cherokee treaties, and U.S. intercourse laws.

The state of Georgia argued that the Cherokee Nation could not sue as a "foreign" nation because they did not have a constitution or a strong central government. The Supreme Court heard the case, but declined to rule on the merits, determining that the Constitution framers considered the Indian Tribes more as "domestic dependent nations" than foreign nations so the Cherokee Nation did not have the standing to sue as a "foreign" nation. Chief Justice John Marshall wrote that "the majority is of the opinion that an Indian tribe or nation within the United States is not a foreign state in the sense of the Constitution, and cannot maintain an action in the courts of the United States."

Associate Justice Smith Thompson wrote a dissenting opinion upholding the Cherokee Nation claims and in 1832 in *Worcester v. Georgia,* the Supreme Court ruled that Georgia could not impose laws in Cherokee territory because only the national government had authority in Indian matters.

These Supreme Court rulings did not spare the Cherokee people from removal to the Indian Territory in 1838 and 1839 or the United States from fighting a civil war over the issues of slavery and states' rights versus the federal government.

Kathy Warnes

See also: *Ex parte Crow Dog* (1883); Wounded Knee Incident (SD) (February 27–May 8, 1973); Wounded Knee Massacre (SD) (December 29, 1890); *Primary Documents/Cherokee Nation v. Georgia:* "Circular of the New-York Committee in Aid of the Cherokee Nation" (1832)

Further Reading
Conley, Robert J. 2008. *The Cherokee Nation: A History.* Albuquerque: University of New Mexico Press.
Hicks, Brian. 2011. *Toward the Setting Sun: John Ross, the Cherokees and the Trail of Tears.* New York: Atlantic Monthly Press.
Perdu, Theda, Michael Green, and Colin Colloway. 2008. *The Cherokee Nation and the Trail of Tears.* Penguin Library of American Indian History. Reprint ed. New York: Penguin Books.
Prucha, Francis Paul. 1986. *The Great Father: The United States Government and the American Indians.* Abridged edition. Lincoln: University of Nebraska Press.
Smith, Daniel Blake. 2011. *An American Betrayal: Cherokee Patriots and the Trail of Tears.* New York: Henry Holt and Co.
Wilkins, Thurman. 1989. *Cherokee Tragedy: The Ridge Family and the Decimation of a People.* The Civilization of the American Indian Series. 2nd ed. Norman: University of Oklahoma Press.

Cherry Hill Murder (Albany, NY) (May 7, 1827)

On May 7, 1827, in Albany, New York, an infamous murder occurred at Cherry Hill that resulted in two murder trials. The crime was centered on Elsie Lansing Whipple, her husband, John Whipple, and her lover, Jesse Strang. The allure of Cherry Hill is still wildly popular, with tours of the mansion continuously expanding to date (Morrow 2013).

Cherry Hill is a large yellow mansion in Albany that was built in 1787 for the wealthy Phillip Van Rensselaer. Phillip's son, Phillip P. Van Rensselaer, and his wife, Catherine, were also initial residents on the south side of the house. Later, a southwest room was rented to Elsie Lansing, niece of Catherine, her husband, John Whipple, and their son, Abraham Whipple. Elsie's father was Abraham A. Lansing, a successful businessman and brother-in-law of Catherine Van Rensselaer. John Whipple was a successful businessman, and was able to grow Elsie's inheritance into a large fortune (Schuyler 2012).

Jesse Strang resided in one of the basement rooms as a workman for the house under the alias of Joseph Orton. Jesse had a wife and four children who resided in Fishkill, New York. He was in crippling debt with his wife and children before abandoning them. He faked his own death, created an alias, and moved to Albany to reinvent himself.

Jesse and Elsie developed an affair through the time they spent together at Cherry Hill. Elsie no longer wanted to be with John, but did not want to lose her inheritance. Under New York State property laws, it was mandated for Elsie to put her inheritance in her husband's name (Jones 1980). If Elsie were to divorce John, she would lose her fortune. Jesse did not have money, so they needed access to Elsie's fortune to forge a life together. Elsie needed to devise a plan to be able to leave John while maintaining her inheritance.

Elsie decided killing John was her best option. Jesse and Elsie wrote many letters back and forth to each other in an attempt to devise a proper plan of action. Initially, Elsie poisoned John, which was an unsuccessful murder attempt. After the failed attempt, Elsie gave Jesse money to purchase a shotgun. At 9:15 p.m. on the evening of May 7, 1827, Jesse went to the top of the garage that was connected to the Cherry Hill house. From the garage, Jesse shot John through a window on the second floor of the house.

Days later, Jesse was arrested for the murder of John Whipple. Elsie was arrested approximately two weeks after Jesse, and admitted to having an affair with John, but not to her involvement in the murder. On June 14, 1827, Jesse confessed to the murder, his affair with Elsie, and her involvement in the murder (Jones 1980). Jesse's trial started on June 25, in which he was convicted of murder and sentenced to a public hanging. Elsie's trial began on June 30, in which she was acquitted of all charges. It was rumored that Elsie's class ranking in the community largely attributed to her acquittal (Schuyler 2012).

On August 24, Jesse's execution was carried out (Jones 1980). The hanging took place at the current day spot of The Egg on Eagle Street (Schuyler 2012). Jesse's ghost has been rumored to haunt the spot ever since. Approximately 30,000 to 40,000 individuals came to witness the hanging. Something went awry during the hanging, and it took Jesse over a half hour to pass. Due to this, Jesse's hanging was the last hanging to occur in Albany (Schuyler 2012).

After Jesse's execution, Elsie moved to New Brunswick, New Jersey, and married a man named Nathaniel Freeman. When Freeman died, Elsie moved to Onondaga, New York, where she later died in 1832 (Jones 1980). John Whipple was initially buried at the State Street Burial Grounds, and then was reburied at a North Ridge lot that was purchased by his son. Abraham Whipple and his wife, Hannah, are also buried in the spot.

The Cherry Hill house continued to be under Van Rensselaer family ownership for five generations. Emily Rankin, the last of the Cherry Hill descendants, donated the house and its contents to the people of New York. The Cherry Hill mansion opened as a museum in 1964, one year after Emily's death.

The murder at Cherry Hill brought many issues to light for the time period, including social class and other ethical dilemmas (Pasko 2008). Historians continue to be transfixed on the complete story of what happened at Cherry Hill, as a lot of details can only be speculated, especially the degree of Elsie's involvement in the murder. The story and contemplated details are discussed during current tours of the mansion. The Cherry Hill tour group also puts together a special murder mystery tour during Halloween each year (Pasko 2008). Presently, the mansion continues to be open for weekly regular tours.

Shavonne Arthurs

See also: Barfield, Velma (1932–1984); Borden, Lizzie (1860–1927); Longet, Claudine (1942–)

Further Reading

Jones, Louis Clark. 1980. *Murder at Cherry Hill: The Strang-Whipple Case, 1827*. Cherry Hill, NJ: Cherry Hill Publishing.

Morrow, Ann. 2013. "The Haunting of Cherry Hill House." *Metroland.* October 31. http://metroland.net/2013/10/31/the-haunting-of-cherry-hill-house/.

Pasko, Jessica. 2008. "The Cherry Hill Murder Tour." *All Over Albany.* September 26.

Schuyler Blog. 2012. "Murders, Hangings, and Hauntings in Albany." http://albanycvb.blogspot.com/2012/10/murders-hangings-and-hauntings-in-albany.html. Accessed April 14, 2015.

Cheshire (CT) Home Invasion Murders (2007)

The Cheshire Home Invasion Murders involved the murder of a mother and her two daughters in their Cheshire, Connecticut, home on July 23, 2007. The Petit family was subjected to home invasion, felony theft, sexual assaults, arson, murder, and restraint over the course of seven hours during July 22, 2007, to July 23, 2007, by perpetrators Steven Hayes (1963–) and Joshua Komisarjevsky (1980–). This case received substantial media attention and *The Hartford Courant* claims that is "possibly the most widely publicized crime in the state's history" (Kauffman 2010, 1). The perpetrators were both found guilty of 16 and 17 charges, respectively, including murder and were ultimately sentenced to death in 2011 and 2012.

On the afternoon of July 22, 2007, Jennifer Hawke-Petit (48 years old) and her daughter Michaela Petit (11 years old) were shopping at a local grocery store in Cheshire, Connecticut, with the intention of bringing supper home for their family, which also included daughter Hayley Petit (17 years old) and father William Petit. It was at the grocery store where Komisarjevsky targeted the Petit family and followed them to their Cheshire home. According to Hayes's testimony, the plan was to invade the Petit's home after dark and to leave the scene with the Petit family bound but unharmed. However, this was not the ultimate outcome of Cheshire home invasion.

Hayes and Komisarjevsky entered the Petit's home in the early hours of July 23, 2007, where they found William Petit asleep on the couch. Komisarjevsky used a baseball bat he had found in their front yard and struck William Petit in the head before restraining him in the basement at gunpoint. Hayes and Komisarjevsky then continued to restrain each member of the Petit family in their respective rooms. Upon restraining all members of the Petit family, the perpetrators determined that they were not satisfied with the items they had obtained within the home and realized that a bankbook showed an outstanding balance of funds, between $20,000 and $30,000 (Gardner 2010).

Later on in the morning of July 23, 2007, Hayes was captured on gas station surveillance video, filling up two cans of gasoline totaling $10. Upon returning the gas cans to the Petit's home, Hayes brought Jennifer Hawke-Petit to the bank when it opened to withdraw $15,000 from her credit line (Gardner 2010). While Jennifer Hawke-Petit was at the bank withdrawing the money, she informed the bank teller of her situation and claimed that the perpetrators were nice and only wanted money. As Jennifer Hawke-Petit left the bank and got into a vehicle with Hayes, the bank manager called 911 to inform them of the urgent nature of the events that were transpiring. The Cheshire Police Department spent approximately 30 minutes to assess the *urgent* situation and to set up a vehicle perimeter.

While the police were still trying to assess the situation, the crimes within the Petit home greatly intensified as Komisarjevsky sexually assaulted Michaela Petit and Hayes raped Jennifer Hawke-Petit. While Hayes was raping Jennifer Hawke-Petit, Komisarjevsky had realized that William Petit had escaped. Upon receiving this news, Jennifer Hawke-Petit was strangled, the daughters were tied to their beds with pillowcases over their heads, and all three were doused with gasoline. The perpetrators ignited a fire and fled the scene in the Petit's family car. During this time, William Petit had managed to get to a neighbor's home to call for help, but unfortunately it was too late, as both of his daughters had died from smoke inhalation and his wife had died from the initial strangling by Hayes. Police surveillance identified the perpetrators fleeing and they were apprehended and arrested one block away from the Petit house. Upon apprehension, both perpetrators attempted to place the blame of the escalated aggravated crimes on each other. However, Hayes was found guilty on 16 out of 17 counts related to the Petit home invasion on October 5, 2010 (Griffin and Kovner 2010). On December 2, 2010, Hayes was formally sentenced to death by lethal injection. Komisarjevsky was found guilty on all 17 counts related to the Petit home invasion on October 13, 2011. On January 27, 2012, Komisarjevsky was formally sentenced to death by lethal injection.

Explanations for the Slow Response Time?

Police departments are extraordinarily efficient and because of technology can respond to crime scenes in a matter of minutes for most cases. The police, however, did not respond quickly to the Petit home. Upon receiving the 911 call regarding a hostage situation, it took the Cheshire Police Department ("Department") approximately 30 minutes to arrive on scene. A patrol vehicle was ordered not to approach the house, while a hostage negotiator was turned away. The Department maintains that the house was already set ablaze when they arrived on scene, yet neighbors recall seeing police and Special Weapons and Tactics (SWAT) members surrounding the house approximately 15–25 minutes beforehand, with screams coming from within the house and a critically wounded man escaping from the basement yelling for immediate help from the neighbors. A HBO documentary titled "The Cheshire Murders," focuses on the Cheshire home invasion, including the response of the Department, which refused to be interviewed for the documentary and has yet to provide any explanation or investigation regarding their actions of July 23, 2007.

The implications of the Cheshire home invasion murders have been evident within Connecticut society, ranging from the jurors who participated in the actual trials of the perpetrators, to the surrounding communities, and to the state correctional system. For the first time in Connecticut's history, the Connecticut state judicial branch offered posttraumatic stress assistance to jurors who participated in the triple-murder trials based on the disturbing images and "grisly testimony" (Beach 2010). There continues to be controversy over whether or not the Cheshire police responded in an appropriate time frame and manner, as it was stated it took over 30 minutes for the police to take action and there were unconfirmed reports that screams were coming from the Petit household during this timeframe. Further, there has been great debate regarding the application of the death penalty on the perpetrators of this case. In 2009, Connecticut governor Jodi Rell refused to sign legislation abolishing the state's death penalty and cited the Cheshire home invasion murders as a clear

example in support of her reasoning. Yet on April 25, 2012, current Connecticut governor Dan Malloy signed a bill into law, which would repeal capital punishment for future cases (leaving past death sentences in place) (Lender 2013).

ALLISON McDOWELL-SMITH

See also: Clutter Family Murders (1959); Duperrault Family Slayings (November 12, 1961); Wesson Family Massacre (2004)

Further Reading

Beach, Randall. 2010. "Conn. Judicial Branch Offers Hayes Jurors Post-Trauma Assistance." *New Haven Register*. November 10. http://www.nhregister.com/general-news/20101110/conn-judicial-branch-offers-hayes-jurors-post-trauma-assistance-2. Accessed February 1, 2015.

Gardner, David. 2010. "'Things Got Out of Control': Chilling Confession of Connecticut Massacre 'Killer.'" *The Daily Mail*. September 23. http://www.dailymail.co.uk/news/article-1314418/Steven-Hayes-Chilling-confession-Connecticut-massacre-killer.html. Accessed February 1, 2015.

Griffin, Alaine, and Josh Kovner. 2010. "Jury Finds Steven Hayes Guilty, Now Must Decide if He Lives or Dies." *The Hartford Courant*. October 6. http://www.courant.com/community/cheshire/cheshire-home-invasion/hc-petit-cheshire-home-invasion-verdict,0,2650867.story?page=1. Accessed February 1, 2015.

Kauffman, Matthew. 2010. "Fair Trial Seen Likely for Other Cheshire Defendant." *The Hartford Courant*. November 9. http://articles.courant.com/2010-11-09/news/hc-komisarjevsky-fair-trial-1110-20101109_1_murder-trial-impartial-jury-prospective-panelist. Accessed February 1, 2015.

Lender, Tina. 2013. "Timeline: Deadly Cheshire Home Invasion." *The Hartford Courant*. July 16. http://www.courant.com/news/connecticut/hc-petit-cheshire-home-invasion-timeline,0,3135848.htmlstory. Accessed February 1, 2015.

Chessman, Caryl (1921–1960)

Caryl Chessman, also known as the Red Light Bandit, spent most of his adult life behind bars. After a brief period on parole in California, he was 27 when he was arrested and charged with robbery, kidnapping, and rape. The Red Light Bandit was said to follow people in their cars to secluded areas and then proceed to flash a red light, tricking them into thinking they were being followed by a police officer. After they stopped, the Red Light Bandit would wait for the victim to open their window or get out of the car, at which point he would trick them into thinking he was a police officer before robbing and raping them. Chessman was convicted on 17 counts of robbery, kidnapping, and rape in July 1948 and was sentenced to death. Controversy surrounding Chessman's conviction and death sentence stemmed from the application of the death penalty at the time. At the time, any crime involving kidnapping could be considered a capital offense. Moving the victims this short distance qualified as kidnapping, combined with robbery and bodily harm qualified Chessman for the death penalty. Chessman's case was the center of international attention in the movement to ban capital punishment. After losing numerous appeals, Chessman was executed at San Quentin Prison on May 2, 1960.

Chessman was a repeat offender with a lengthy criminal record at the time of his arrest, having spent most of his adult life in prison. In 1948, Chessman was out on parole when he was arrested and charged as the Red Light Bandit. The Red Light Bandit was a nickname given to a

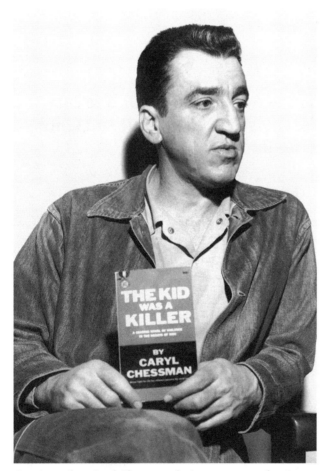

Convict-author Caryl Chessman during a news conference on April 30, 1960, a few days before his execution on May 2, 1960. Chessman holds *The Kid Was a Killer*, a book he wrote while on death row. (AP Photo)

serial rapist who would lure unsuspecting victims out of their vehicles by flashing a red light making them believe he was a police officer. Upon exiting their vehicle or rolling down their window, the Red Light Bandit would rob them and in several cases sexually assault the victims. At the time of his arrest, Chessman was subject to California's version of the "Little Lindbergh Law" passed in 1933. In response to the Lindbergh kidnapping and public demand to enforce more severe penalties on kidnappers, amended death statutes allowed for the death penalty in kidnapping cases. California's law allowed for the death penalty in any case involving kidnapping with bodily harm. Chessman was accused of dragging two of his victims a short distance from their cars before raping them, which the court determined sufficient to constitute kidnapping, making him eligible for the death penalty. During trial, Chessman acted as his own attorney and repeatedly argued his innocence despite being unable to provide substantiating evidence. While he initially signed a confession, he later recanted saying that the confession was the result of police brutality and that the Los Angeles Police Department (LAPD) had beat it out of him. Some of the evidence was questionable and may have indicated that more than one person was acting as the Bandit; however, two women testified against Chessman stating that he had robbed and sexually assaulted them. When prosecutors were able to successfully argue the kidnapping charges of moving the women a short distance from their cars, Chessman was eligible for life in prison or the death penalty.

Chessman's self-representation also did not help his cause as his attitude was often perceived as arrogant. Additionally, when the original court stenographer died early on during the trial, they were replaced with a relative of the prosecutor who made indiscriminate changes to the record, which became a point of contention upon appeal. Ultimately, there was enough evidence for a jury to determine that one of the kidnapping counts included bodily harm of the victim and when they did not recommend mercy, Chessman automatically received the death penalty. In October 1948, Chessman was convicted as the Red Light Bandit for the kidnapping and rape of Mary Alice Meza.

Chessman spent 12 years on death row during which time he became a household name in the movement to ban the death penalty. His story generated support as he continued to argue both his innocence and rehabilitation from his previous life of crime. While incarcerated, Chessman wrote several books including an autobiography, *Cell 2455 Death Row*, in which he described his own prison experience, demonstrating his intellectual ability as well as his rehabilitated persona. He used the books to bring public awareness to his case as well as the current state of the death penalty in the United States. Chessman's writing of multiple books while incarcerated was impressive in that his movements were restricted and he had to work to keep his writing hidden from prison administrators all the way up until his execution. Despite his literary abilities and presentation as a new man, even his lawyer, George T. Davis, believed that he was often perceived as arrogant and hard-headed, resulting in the media often presenting him as a monster. He also believed, however, that the exposure of the case in the media had drawn political attention to the issue of capital punishment.

While on death row, Chessman argued his innocence, filing dozens of appeals and avoiding execution on eight separate occasions. The foundation for his appeals was based on the improper conduct in the original trial. Chessman later argued his appeals were hampered by incomplete and incorrect transcripts of the original trial. While he achieved some success when the California Supreme Court ordered a complete review of the transcripts or release of Chessman, the review concluded the transcripts were substantially accurate. California repealed their Little Lindbergh Law in the mid-1950s and commuted the death sentences of many offenders who had been convicted under the law to life in prison. Governor Brown was unable to commute Chessman's sentence despite granting a previous stay of execution as California's Constitution required the commutation's of two-time felon's death sentences be ratified by the state Supreme Court. After the Supreme Court voted no by a 4–3 vote and exhausting last-minute habeas corpus appeals, Chessman was executed on May 2, 1960. His execution was carried out in the gas chamber of San Quentin. After the gas had been released, but before Chessman had died, the warden received a call from a U.S. district judge's secretary who misdialed the prison on a first attempt and was calling with a ninth stay of execution. The warden informed the caller that the execution had already begun and that attempts to stop the execution would be dangerous for those carrying out the execution. While witness testimony impacted his conviction, many believe that the greatest detriment to Chessman's case was his self-representation at his original trial. He has been mentioned in a variety of pop-culture references from song lyrics to television movies. Chessman's legacy was his death sentence and execution not for murder, but for rape and kidnapping

carried out even after such policies were modified during his incarceration.

BROOKE MILLER

See also: Abbott, Jack Henry (1944–2002); Gilmore, Gary (1940–1977); Shakur, Sanyika Shakur, Sanyika (1963–)

Further Reading

Brown, E.G., A.L. Alarcon, and F.M. Cooper. 1983. "Death Penalty—The Caryl Chessman Case-Irreversible Error." *San Fernando Valley Law Review* 11: 21–42.

Chessman, Caryl. 1955. *Trial by Ordeal*. Upper Saddle River, NJ: Prentice-Hall.

Chessman, Caryl. 1957. *The Face of Justice*. Upper Saddle River, NJ: Prentice-Hall.

Chessman, Caryl. 2009. *Cell 2455, Death Row: A Condemned Man's Own Story*. New York: Da Capo Press.

Chessman v. Teets, 354 U.S. 156 (June 10, 1957).

Hamm, Theodore. 2001. *Rebel and a Cause: Caryl Chessman and the Politics of the Death Penalty in Postwar California, 1948–1979*. Berkeley: University of California Press.

Parker, Frank J. 1975. *Caryl Chessman, the Red Light Bandit*. Chicago: Nelson-Hall.

People v. Chessman, 38 Cal. 2d 166 (1951).

People v. Chessman, 52 Cal. 2d 467 (1959).

Chicago Race Riot (1919). *See* East St. Louis Race Riot (1917) and Chicago Race Riot (1919)

Chicago Seven (1968)

The Chicago Seven refers to the individuals who faced federal charges following a three-day antiwar protest that led to a violent clash between demonstrators and police at the 1968 Democratic National Convention in Chicago, Illinois. The trial of the Chicago Seven was highlighted by outlandish behavior by the defendants and questionable judicial rulings. Most of the convictions on multiple charges and court contempt charges were ultimately reversed by an appellate court.

The defendants known as the Chicago Seven were from different walks of life and only loosely connected to one another. Abbie Hoffman and Jerry Rubin were founding members of the Youth International Party (Yippies), a group that promoted unconventional lifestyles and values. David Dellinger and Rennie Davis were members of the

National Mobilization to End the War in Vietnam (MOBE), and argued for a peaceful conclusion to the Vietnam War. Tom Hayden and John Froines were members of the Students for a Democratic Society (SDS), a militant group fighting against racism and other forms of oppression. Lee Weiner was an academic, completing a doctoral degree and working as a teaching assistant. Cofounder of the Black Panther Party, Bobby Seale, was originally charged with the Chicago Seven but was tried separately after a mistrial was granted.

The 1960s are remembered as a time of conflict among Americans. Concerns about Vietnam, civil rights, and defendants' rights resulted in frequent protests and demonstrations that became increasingly hostile. The Democratic National Convention of 1968 provided a national media stage for individuals representing various interests to protest.

Abbie Hoffman and Jerry Rubin, along with Tom Hayden and Rennie Davis, began planning a festival to take place in Chicago at the same time as the Democratic National Convention. The Festival of Life was organized to unite antiwar demonstrators to protest and to react to the perceived unresponsiveness to this issue from the Democratic Party. The organizers planned for attendees to camp out in Chicago's Lincoln Park, and applied for the appropriate permit to avoid illegally trespassing. Mayor Richard J. Daley and other city officials denied the permit application and communication between the city and the protestors broke down. A curfew was also instituted in city parks, closing them at 11:00 p.m. nightly. Approximately 5,000 protestors arrived at Lincoln Park for the Festival of Life on August 25, 1968. The gathering remained peaceful until 20,000 Chicago police officers and National Guard troops entered the park to enforce the 11:00 p.m. curfew (Tracy 1996, 147). When demonstrators refused to vacate the park, officers released tear gas and swung their nightsticks at the protestors. Reports vary on who initiated the violence, but it seems that some of the protestors antagonized police by throwing rocks and smashing car windows. The violent riots continued for four days. Police officers were criticized by the media for their indiscriminate and unrestrained violence against protestors (Kaul 1997, 149).

Indictments against the eight defendants were issued on March 20, 1969, accusing them of conspiring to travel across state lines with the intent of inciting a riot. The defendants were believed to have encouraged other protestors to retaliate against police. Lee Weiner and John Froines were also charged with teaching others how to make a bomb, purportedly to be detonated at an underground parking garage. The defendants vehemently denied the charges, maintaining that conspiracy charges were inappropriate because some of the defendants had not met each other until the arraignment.

The five-month trial began on September 24, 1969, in the courtroom of Judge Julius Hoffman (no relation to defendant Abbie Hoffman). Judge Hoffman was known as a conservative man who strictly adhered to the rules. The case was prosecuted by Thomas Foran and Richard Schultz. The Chicago Seven defendants were represented by attorneys William Kunstler and Leonard Weinglass, who shared with their clients a lack of respect for the judge and courtroom procedure. The eighth defendant, Bobby Seale, insisted on representing himself as his preferred attorney, Charles R. Garry, was unavailable due to a medical condition. This request was denied by Judge Hoffman. The tone of the trial was set on the first day, when defendant Tom Hayden raised a fist to the jury in solidarity and Abbie Hoffman blew a kiss to them.

Seale continued to demand the right to represent himself despite Judge Hoffman's refusal. On October 29, 1969, Judge Hoffman ordered court marshals to remove Seale from the courtroom. Seale returned several minutes later with his ankles shackled to a chair, his arms handcuffed, and a white cloth tied around his mouth. When the cloth was insufficient at muzzling Seale's demands to examine his own witnesses, he was gagged with a piece of adhesive tape. Seale was convicted of 16 counts of contempt of court on November 5, 1969, and Judge Hoffman granted him a mistrial on the conspiracy charges. Because he was retried separately from the other defendants, Bobby Seale is not considered one of the Chicago Seven.

The trial of the Chicago Seven continued with the same outlandish behavior with which it began. The prosecution presented 54 witnesses, including uniformed police officers, undercover officers, and informants, before resting on December 5, 1969. The defendants tried to demonstrate that the police had instigated the violence. Their witnesses consisted of artists and writers testifying that the Festival of Life was not planned with any violent intent. The testimony of these witnesses resulted in what some writers called a transformation of the courtroom into a staged street theater.

The case went to the jury on February 14, 1970. While the jury deliberated on the original charges, Judge Hoffman ruled on the combined 150 instances of contempt of court he had found during the trial. The Chicago Seven and their attorneys received sentences ranging from two months to two years in jail for being in contempt. The jury then returned its verdict on February 18, 1970. All seven defendants were acquitted of the conspiracy charges; Froines and Weiner were also acquitted of bomb charges. Five of the defendants were convicted of promoting a riot: Dellinger, Hayden, Davis, Rubin and Hoffman. The maximum sentence of five years in prison and $5,000 in fines plus the costs of prosecution were imposed by Judge Hoffman.

The convictions and contempt of court sentences were appealed by the defendants, who maintained that Judge Hoffman's actions in the trial constituted judicial error. On November 21, 1972, all convictions were reversed by an appellate court. The appellate court also ordered that the contempt charges be heard by another judge. All but 13 of the original 150 contempt charges were dropped by Judge Edward Gignoux in December 1973, and no fine or sentences were imposed for those that remained.

Since the convictions against his co-conspirators were overturned, Bobby Seale was never retried for his role in the uprising. Eight police officers who were charged with violating the civil rights of demonstrators were eventually acquitted in a separate trial.

SHANNON N. CUNNINGHAM

See also: Bruce, Lenny, Obscenity Trial of (1964)

Further Reading

Alonso, Karen. 2002. *The Chicago Seven Political Protest Trial.* New York: Enslow Publishers, Inc.

Epstein, Jason. 1970. *The Great Conspiracy Trial.* New York: Random House.

Kaul, Arthur J. 1997. "The Case of the Chicago Seven." In Lloyd Chiasson Jr., ed. *The Press on Trial: Crimes and Trials as Media Events.* Westport, CT: Greenwood Press, pp. 147–58.

Levine, Mark L., George C. McNamee, and Daniel Greenberg. 1970. *The Tales of Hoffman.* New York: Bantam Books, Inc.

Tracy, James. 1996. *Direct Action: Radical Pacifism from the Union Eight to the Chicago Seven.* Chicago: The University of Chicago Press.

Chin, Vincent Jen, Murder of (1982)

Vincent Jen Chin (1955–1982) was a Chinese American man, who was brutally attacked by two white men on June 19, 1982. Chin was celebrating his bachelor party with friends when two men, Ronald Ebens and his stepson Michael Nitz, began making racial remarks toward them, blaming them for the downfall of the American auto industry. A fight ensued where Ebens bludgeoned Chin with a baseball bat. This case was crucial to American history because it catalyzed political activity among Asian Americans (Wu 2012). It appeared that Ebens's actions against Chin stemmed from his racial prejudice against Asian Americans. When the conviction against Ebens was overturned on appeal, the Asian American community became outraged at the courts' treatment of this case and spawned a civil rights movement. No incident before this one, and since, involving an Asian American had ever sparked such anger (Wu 2012).

Vincent Chin was adopted from China in 1961 by Hing and Lily Chin who were Chinese immigrants living in the United States (Covert 1983). On June 19, 1982, Chin attended his bachelor party and invited his friends Robert Sirosky and Gary Koivu to meet him at a topless bar (*U.S. v. Ebens* 1986). After an hour there, they headed to the Fancy Pants Lounge, a nude dancing establishment in Highland Park. Koivu picked up one of Chin's friend, Jimmy Choi, to join their group. While inside, Chin and his friends were reported to be laughing and tipping the dancers heavily. During this time, Ronald Ebens and his stepson, Michael Nitz, were sitting directly across the elevated dancing runway from them. Based on the evidence, Ebens started making racial and offensive remarks toward Chin, calling him "Chink" and "Nip," making statements about foreign car imports, and commenting that Chin and his people were putting him out of work. After a further exchange of words, Chin approached Ebens where there was jostling and fighting. The doorman broke them up and took them outside where the fighting resumed. Ebens proceeded to grab a Louisville Slugger baseball bat from Nitz's trunk and upon seeing the bat, Chin fled. Choi went to look for Chin, and upon finding him, they hid at a nearby McDonald's for safety while their friends drove around town to find them and pick them up. At the same time, Ebens and Nitz were also driving around looking for Chin. During their search, they met Jimmy Perry and offered him $20 to help them capture Chin. The final confrontation transpired in the supermarket lot next to McDonald's where Ebens struck Chin several times on the back and head with the bat. Highland Park police officers, who were working as security guards at McDonald's, intervened at this time (*U.S. v. Ebens* 1986).

On the way to Henry Ford Hospital, Chin lost consciousness several times (*U.S. v. Ebens* 1986). Based on medical records, he suffered "two lacerations on the back left side of his head and abrasions on his shoulder, chest and neck" and went into a severe coma. Doctors performed emergency surgery on his brain and it ceased to entirely function. On June 23, 1982, the ventilator that kept him breathing was removed and he was pronounced dead at 9:50 p.m. (*U.S. v. Ebens* 1986). Chin was buried on June 27, 1982, the day of his planned wedding (Covert 1983).

During this time period, the United States was suffering from its highest unemployment rate since World War II and Japan was reviving its steel and automobile manufacturing industries, which led to increased competition for the United States (Reuss 2009). Detroit was a city in crisis and could not compete with Japanese automakers that were able to meet the demands for inexpensive, fuel-efficient cars and whose imports were cheap to buy and run (Zia 2000). Asian Americans became a target.

The climate of hostility worsened when the Vincent Chin story broke out on the news and especially in 1983 when Ebens pled guilty to manslaughter and was given the lenient punishment of three years of probation and a fine of $3,720 (*U.S. v. Ebens* 1986). Chin's story was felt deeply by the Asian American community because if Chin could be brutally beaten to death with his killers freed, nothing would prevent future attacks from happening to them (Zia 2000). Shortly after Ebens's ruling, a small group of Asian Americans gathered for a meeting. Two of the people there, Lisa Chan and Kin Yee, helped push the case forward. Lisa Chan was the only Asian American woman practicing law in Michigan at the time and worked pro bono for Mrs. Chin, Vincent's mother. Kin Yee was president of the Detroit Chinese Welfare Council, which was the public face of local Chinatown organizations.

After further investigation, Chan and Yee realized that the system had failed. Police and court records were incomplete. Police failed to interview numerous key witnesses, such as the dancers at the bar and Jimmy Perry. The first presiding judge had set the initial charges against Ebens at second-degree murder, which legal experts deemed too low. Additionally, when Judge Kaufman rendered his sentence of probation, no prosecutor was present.

Impact of Case on Asian American Community

The Vincent Chin case made a significant impact on the Asian American community. The American Citizens for Justice (ACJ) was created—the first explicitly Asian American grassroots community advocacy effort with a national scope. Asian American organizations like ACJ were formed throughout the United States, providing a social setting to build Asian unity. Furthermore, Asian Americans became more willing to speak out against issues of anti-Asianism, coming together to assert their right to be American.

In June 1984, the federal civil rights trial began in the courtroom of Judge Anna Diggs Taylor. This case posed a significant challenge because of the Constitutional Double Jeopardy clause (Wu 2014). Ebens could not be charged for the same crime twice; thus they had to prove the intent that would make the homicide a civil rights offense, not the act of constituting homicide. Thankfully, a private investigator found proof that Chin's death was a racial incident when Racine Colwell, a dancer at Fancy Pants, admitted that she had overheard Ebens tell Chin, "It's because of you motherfuckers that we're out of work." Her statement was the necessary link to Ebens's racially motivated killing of Chin. The federal jury in Detroit found Ebens guilty of violating Chin's civil rights and was sentenced to 25 years in prison. Nitz was acquitted. A couple of years later in 1986, Ebens won a retrial on appeal because of pretrial publicity and evidentiary errors. The new trial was located in Cincinnati, where the Asian population was almost nonexistent. As a result, the jury was remarkably like Ebens—mostly white, male, and blue collar. Ebens was acquitted at this time, given a no guilty verdict by this jury.

Ebens and Nitz never spent a full day in jail. In 1987, there was a civil suit against Ebens and Nitz to pay a settlement of $1.5 million for the loss of Vincent's life. Ebens stopped making payments toward the judgment in 1989 (Zia 2000).

Lydie R. Loth

See also: *Primary Documents*/Murder of Vincent Chin: Excerpts from *United States v. Ronald Ebens* (1986)

Further Reading

Covert, Colin. 1983. "1983 Flashback: The Ordeal of Vincent Chin's Mother, Lily Chin." *Detroit Free Press*, July 7. http://www.freep.com/article/20120621/NEWS01/120620061/1983-Flashback-The-ordeal-of-Vincent-Chin-s-mother-Lily-Chin-Detro Accessed April 21, 2015.

Reuss, Alejandro. 2009. "What Can the Crisis of U.S. Capitalism in the 1970s Teach Us About the Current Crisis and its Possible

Outcomes?" *Dollars and Sense.* http://www.dollarsandsense
.org/archives/2009/1109reuss.html. Accessed April 21, 2015.

United States v. Ebens, 1986, 800 F.2d 1422 http://www.leagle.com/
decision/19862222800F2d1422_11978.xml/UNITED%20
STATES%20v.%20EBENS. Accessed April 21, 2015.

Wu, Frank H. 2012. "Why Vincent Chin Matters." *The New
York Times.* June 22. http://www.nytimes.com/2012/06/23/
opinion/why-vincent-chin-matters.html?_r=0. Accessed
April 21, 2015.

Wu, Frank H. 2014. "The Case against Vincent Chin." *Huffington
Post Crime Blog Post.* April 30. http://www.huffingtonpost
.com/frank-h-wu/the-case-against-vincent_b_5237359
.html. Accessed April 21, 2015.

Zia, Helen. 2000. *Asian American Dreams: The Emergence of an
American People.* New York: Farrar, Straus, & Giroux.

Chino Hills (CA) Murders (June 4, 1983)

Kevin Cooper (1958–), also known as "The Chino Hills murderer," was arrested on July 30, 1983, for the June 4 murders of Douglas and Peggy Ryen, their 10-year-old daughter, Jessica, their 11-year-old neighbor, Christopher Hughes, and attempted murder of the Ryen's 8-year-old son, Joshua. The murders happened in the Ryen home, while they were sleeping; it is said to be the most gruesome murder scene ever in California. Cooper was convicted of the four murders and attempted murder on February 19, 1985, and sentenced to death on May 15, 1985. California has had a moratorium on execution since 2006. Cooper has exhausted his appeals and is on a list of inmates eligible for immediate execution if California reinstates the death penalty.

Doug and Peggy Ryen, both chiropractors, moved to Chino Hills in 1975, so Peggy could raise Arabian horses and Doug could continue their practice in Santa Ana. On Saturday, June 4, 1983, the Ryen family was at home for the evening after attending a potluck dinner with others who breed Arabian horses, and their son's friend Chris Hughes was spending the night. It was Chris's father who found the victims the next morning when Chris had not returned home to go to church with his family. He came to their home and rang the doorbell. When there was no answer, he walked around the side of the house to peer in the sliding glass doors. He could not believe what he saw, there was blood covering the room and four bodies lying on the floor, and one was his son.

Mr. Hughes could not get in the sliding glass door so he ran to the kitchen door and kicked it in. As he ran down the hallway, he found Jessica Ryen, sprawled across the doorway to the master bedroom with five ax blows and 46 stab wounds. As he entered the master bedroom he found Josh, who was alive but nonresponsive. Next Hughes saw his son, Chris, who had 26 stab wounds and a hatchet wound from his forehead to his nose. Both Mr. and Mrs. Ryen had defensive wounds on their hands and arms. Doug was stabbed 26 times and axed 11 times, while Peggy was stabbed 25 times and axed 7 times. Neither of the Ryen phones worked so Mr. Hughes ran to the neighbor's house to call 911.

Kevin Cooper was born Richard Goodman in Pittsburgh, Pennsylvania, on January 8, 1958. He was placed in an orphanage at two months of age. Four months later Melvin and Esther Cooper adopted him, legally changing his name to Kevin Cooper. The family lived in Homewood-Brushton, Pittsburgh's largest black neighborhood. Kevin says his father began beating him at age five and that is when Kevin started running away. He was arrested several times, and was involved in a serious car accident in a stolen car as he attempted to escape from a juvenile facility. Many note this as a marked time in Kevin's personality transformation. He sustained facial fractures and a brain injury. Cooper dropped out of school and continued in and out of the juvenile system. In 1977, shortly after Cooper turned 17, he began his first adult sentence in state prison for burglary. He escaped, was recaptured, served time, was released, reoffended, reconvicted, re-incarcerated, and was released on a 10-year parole in early 1982. In June 1982, Cooper was arrested for assault on his girlfriend; these charges were later dropped. His final offense in Pennsylvania was a burglary in the summer of 1982. Cooper was awaiting trial in a State Hospital where a mental capacity evaluation was completed. Cooper stole another inmates driver's license and escaped in October, shortly after he was found be to be mentally competent to stand trial. Cooper stole a car and fled, eventually making it to California. Cooper was arrested in 1983 for burglary of two homes in Los Angeles as David Trautman, the name on the driver's license he stole in the State Hospital in Pennsylvania. Cooper landed in the California Institute for Men (CIM), less than five miles from the Ryen's home. Kevin Cooper escaped from CIM two days before the Ryens were murdered. Cooper found a vacant house, only 126 yards from the Ryen's home, convenient as a hideout for a couple of days.

Arrested by police on Santa Cruz Island on July 31, 1983, Kevin Cooper, center, was suspected of the murder of two adults and two children in Chino Hills, California. Here he is escorted by police to a car for transport from Santa Barbara to San Bernardino. (AP Photo)

At trial, the prosecution had a mountain of circumstantial evidence. Kevin Cooper's criminal history, timely escape, and hideout location in the house down the lane looked like perfect circumstances for a conviction. Additionally, the owners of the house Cooper stayed in said a hatchet, two knives, and an ice pick were missing; prison-issued tobacco was found in the Ryen's station wagon; a bloody shoe print matched prison issued shoes; a spot of blood in the hallway of the Ryen's home matched Cooper's blood type; and a button from a prison issued jacket was found in the hideout house with blood on it. Jurors heard testimony from over 140 witnesses and examined nearly 800 pieces of evidence during a three-month trial. The jurors found Kevin Cooper guilty. Kevin Cooper maintained his innocence through the entire process and still, 30 years later, claims he is innocent of the Chino Hills murders.

As much evidence as the prosecution had pointing toward Cooper's guilty, the defense had pointing toward his innocence. The key defense strategy was that Josh Ryen told nurses at the hospital that three white men killed his family; three offenders are more consistent with the amount of weapons used and the fact that the assailant(s) were able to overpower two strong adults in one room—this would have been highly unlikely with one assailant. There was a cluster of blond hairs found clutched in Jessica Ryen's hand that belonged to someone other than her family or Kevin Cooper. Another suspect was not thoroughly followed up on; Lee Furrow, whose girlfriend called the police two days after the murder reporting her boyfriend, showed up in the middle of the night in a strange car with coveralls and no shirt. He came into the house, took off the coveralls, and put on some jeans and a shirt and left. When the girlfriend called the police she reported that she thought her boyfriend was involved in the murders because the coveralls had blood splattered all over them and the T-shirt he had left the house in that day was identical to the one the police found a mile away from the Ryen's home the day after the murders—also splattered with blood. The local police picked up the coveralls, bagged them, took a statement from the girlfriend, and contacted the homicide detective in charge of the case. No one ever came to get the coveralls and after six months in storage, they were destroyed.

Kevin Cooper remains in San Quentin on death row. He has exhausted his appeals, and is awaiting execution.

LISA BELL HOLLERAN

See also: Clutter Family Murders (1959); Duperrault Family Slayings (November 12, 1961); Gilley Family Murders (April 26, 1984); Hudson, Jennifer, Family Murders (October 24, 2008); Wesson Family Massacre (2004)

Further Reading

Blanco, J.I. 2014. "Kevin Cooper." Murderpedia.org. http://murderpedia.org/male.C/c/cooper-kevin.htm. Accessed April 14, 2015.

Fowler, Lori. 2013. "Fate of Convicted Killer Kevin Cooper Unresolved." Daily Bulletin.com. http://www.dailybulletin.com/general-news/20130608/fate-of-convicted-killer-kevin-cooper-unresolved. Accessed April 14, 2015.

O'Connor, J.P. 2012. *Scapegoat: The Chino Hills Murders and the Framing of Kevin Cooper.* Rock Hill, SC: Strategic Media Books.

Christian, Virginia (1895–1912)

Virginia "Gennie" Christian was the first female executed in the state of Virginia. She was also considered a juvenile at the time of her execution because she was 17 years old. Virginia is also the only female juvenile and the last female inmate to be executed by the electric chair in the state of Virginia. Until 2010, Virginia was also the last female to be executed in the state of Virginia. This case is very important in regards to females in the prison system, the punishment of juveniles, and the use of the death penalty.

Virginia Christian was born August 15, 1895. She was an African American maid who worked for a white woman named Ida Virginia Belote, along with her father, Henry. Her mother, Charlotte Christian, was paralyzed and unable to work. Ida often mistreated Virginia and on March 18, 1912, an argument started between the two women. Ida accused Virginia of stealing a locket and a skirt. Ida had told Virginia that she needed to pay $5 for the stolen items.

During the course of the argument, Ida hit Virginia with a spittoon. The argument continued to escalate and both women tried to grab broom handles that were used to prop the windows open. Virginia got to a handle first and she hit Ida in the forehead with it. When Ida began to scream, Virginia grabbed a towel and stuffed it down Ida's throat. Ida died of suffocation due to the towel blocking her airway.

Virginia then left the house taking Ida's purse, some money, and a ring that belonged to one of Ida's daughters. Shortly after Virginia left two of Ida's daughters found her body. It did not take long for the police to suspect Virginia and she was arrested. During the questioning by the police, Virginia admitted to hitting Ida. In her confession, Virginia stated that she was angry at Ida and was trying to hurt her but insisted she had no intentions of killing her. Virginia did not even know Ida was dead until the police told her.

The trial began in April 1912 and lasted only two days. Virginia was convicted of the murder of Ida Belote and the jury took less than an hour to sentence her to death in the electric chair. The trial was a very sensational one and received much attention in the newspapers. Some experts now argue that the trial was unfair because Virginia was not allowed to testify. Virginia's mother and father wrote letters to the Governor William Mann to ask for her sentence to be commuted to life in prison. Ida's brother, Lewter F. Hobbs also wrote to the governor asking that the sentence be carried out. Governor Mann declined to grant clemency to Virginia and her sentence remained death. On August 16, 1912, one day after her 17th birthday, Virginia Christian was executed. Her body was turned over to the state medical school because her parents could not afford to transport her body back to them.

Virginia's case gained renewed interest in 2010 when another convicted female murderer, Teresa Lewis, was executed in Virginia. Virginia and Teresa are the only two women to have been executed in the state of Virginia.

ANGELA M. COLLINS

See also: Buenoano, Judy (1943–1998); Eubanks, Susan (1964–); Lewis, Teresa (1969–2010); Moore, Blanche Taylor (1933–); Puente, Dorothea (1929–2011); Surratt, Mary (1823–1865); Tucker, Karla Faye (1959–1998); *Primary Documents*/Virginia Christian Murder Case: Letter from Defense Attorney George W. Fields to Virginia Governor William H. Mann (1912)

Further Reading

Blanco, Juan Ignacio. "Virginia Christian." Murderpedia. http://murderpedia.org/female.C/c/christian-virginia.htm. Accessed April 14, 2015.

Christman, Roger. 2010. "Virginia Christian: The Last Woman Executed by Virginia?" *Out of the Box: Notes from the Archives @ the Library of Virginia.* September 14. http://www.virginiamemory.com/blogs/out_of_the_box/2010/09/14/virginia-christian-the-last-woman-executed-by-virginia/. Accessed April 14, 2015.

Sinclair, Melissa Scott. 2010. "Blood Sisters." *Style Weekly.* September 15. http://www.styleweekly.com/richmond/blood-sisters/Content?oid=1362230. Accessed April 14, 2015.

Civil War Espionage (1861–1865)

The American Civil War began in 1861. Throughout the war both sides relied on networks of spies to gather information about strategy, troop movement, availability of resources, and strength of the opposition. To a certain extent the civil war provided many unique opportunities for espionage. The first being that since the war was a completely domestic conflict, spies could readily blend in with the general population. Networks of supporters of both sides of the war lived within both Union and Confederate territories. A variety of codes and ciphers were developed during the war along with the use of common household occurrences for passing messages, such as the pattern of clothing on the clothesline or the opening and closing of curtains. Espionage was readily engaged in by women and men, black and white, though more women were involved in espionage during the Civil War than men. Also, while both sides had extensive spy networks, the North's formal espionage force outnumbered that of the South.

The American Civil War lasted from 1861 through 1865 and encompassed some of the bloodiest battles of American military history. The war between the states separated the North (the Union) from the South (the Confederacy) along the lines of states' rights, slavery, economic sufficiency, and political power. From the beginning of the war with the firing on Fort Sumter in South Carolina in April 1861, both sides sought to develop an intelligence network to keep track of the activities, strength and plans, both military and political of the opposition. Sympathizers to the cause of the Union in the Confederacy and to the Confederacy in the Union actively sought one side of the other through the acquisition and provision of intelligence. Sometimes, through involvement in formal and recognized spy networks and at other times, of their own volition, either creating a network unrecognized by the military or political agents of the Union or Confederacy or by working individually. The Civil War created the first official government mandated espionage and intelligence services in America.

Both sides could rely on sympathizers and the general public for a wide range of information. It was very easy for spies to blend in and to join either or both sides, serve in both intelligence services and both militaries. Some female spies even disguised themselves as men to enlist in the military and acquire intelligence, such as Sarah Edmunds, whose abilities with disguise allowed her not only to enlist in the Union army, but to also spy on the confederacy in a variety of male or female personas. The location of the two capitals also benefited the spy networks; the Union in Washington D.C. and the Confederacy in Richmond, Virginia, were only 106 miles apart and the protections between the cities and restrictions on travel between the union and the confederate territories were lax or nonexistent.

The Confederacy created the Signal Bureau of the South first and held the espionage advantage for the first months of the war. The Union's Intelligence Service was formed shortly after the defeat at the Battle of Bull Run, first under the auspices of the State Department and then later under the War Department. Beyond these official new bureaus, both sides had espionage and intelligence services within other branches of their governments and military structures. In both the Confederacy and the Union, generals employed personal spy networks, some, such as Robert E. Lee gathered much of his own intelligence, mostly using a subscription to every Union newspaper in print.

Espionage in the Civil War was assisted by the many newspapers operating in the North and South, which printed a variety of important intelligence nearly unhindered. Newspapers also were given information from various spy networks, which were readily printed. Information was openly available, and many people came into possession of sensitive information. Some saw this as an opportunity for adventure, others for financial gain and still others as a way to support one or both sides of the conflict, especially when military service was not an option.

This was often the case with women. They passed information through a variety of means, sewing it into garments, using codes based on common household items and activities, such as the number of items and the pattern by which they were hung on a clothesline, or the way in which curtains were drawn. Freed and escaped slaves worked in the espionage networks as well, seeing assistance to the Union as a means to protecting themselves and their families. Among them, was Harriet Tubman who used her knowledge of the routes through the South established by the Underground Railroad to gather intelligence and pass information.

Male spies of the civil war included Allan Pinkerton, of the Pinkerton Detective Agency, who turned his investigative network to espionage activity through most of the war for the benefit of the Union and serviced as head of the Union Intelligence Services, a role given to another Union spy after he returned to the private sector, Lafayette Baker, who controlled the Intelligence Service through the assassination of Lincoln and the manhunt for John Wilkes Booth and his conspirators. On the Confederate side, notable spies included Henry Thomas Harrison who worked for General Longstreet and whose intelligence was partly responsible for the convergence of Confederate troops at Gettysburg.

The treatment of a captured or identified spy differed depending on gender and race. Male spies of either Caucasian or African descent were executed by firing squad or hanged. White female spies were threatened or imprisoned or exiled, if caught, while their African counterparts may be imprisoned or hanged. The ways in which spies were detected varied—some were caught with information, while others were identified through anonymous letters or other accusations.

The last known act of the Confederate government before the surrender was the destruction of any existing papers relating to Confederate espionage activities. The Signal Bureau was disbanded as an organization and involvement in espionage networks was not listed on any documentation for military pensions, as Jefferson Davis considered it too great a danger. The various intelligence services created during the Civil War on the Union side slowly morphed into the Secret Service. The legislation for the creation of the Secret Service was enacted in 1865 and was the last presidential act of Abraham Lincoln before his assassination. The Secret Service was first created to control currency counterfeiting rampant after the Civil War and by 1867 its role was expanded to include the investigation of a wide range of activities including land fraud, smuggling, theft of mail and other federal offenses.

CLAIRISSA D. BREEN

See also: Lincoln, Abraham, Assassination of (April 14, 1865); Wirz, Captain Henry (1823–1865)

Further Reading

Brinkley, Howard. 2012. *Spies of the Civil War: The History of Espionage in the Civil War.* CreateSpace Independent Publishing Platform.

CIA, Office of Public Affairs, and Thomas Allen. 2012. *Intelligence in the Civil War.* CreateSpace Independent Publishing Platform.

Markle, Donald E. 2004. *Spies and Spy Masters of the Civil War.* New York: Hippocrene Books.

Stern, Philip Van Doren. 1975. *Secret Missions of the Civil War: First-hand Accounts by Men and Women Who Risked Their Lives in Underground Activities for the North and the South, Woven into a Continuous Narrative.* New York: Praeger.

Winkler, H. Donald. 2010. *Stealing Secrets: How a Few Daring Women Deceived Generals, Impacted Battles, and Altered the Course of the Civil War.* Nashville, TN: Cumberland House.

Clementi, Tyler, Death of (2010)

Tyler Clementi (1991–2010) was 18 years old when he committed suicide by jumping off the George Washington Bridge into the Hudson River on September 22, 2010. At the time of his death, Clementi was a college freshman at Rutgers University in New Jersey, and a skilled violinist, who had recently informed his parents that he was gay (Parker 2012). The events leading up to Clementi's suicide and subsequent criminal proceedings of two Rutgers University students following his death generated a national discussion about the dangers of cyberbullying and victimization of the lesbian, gay, bisexual, and transgender (LGBT) community. Whereas bullying has been associated with outward acts of violence toward others, most notably in the Columbine High School shootings, this case demonstrates another outlet of violence toward self. Clementi's suicide garnered national media attention, generating outcry for strong antibullying legislation and criminal penalties for unauthorized online video footage (Ariosto 2012; Byers 2013; Patterson 2013).

Clementi and Dharun Ravi were roommates at Davidson Residence Hall at Rutgers University, but rarely spent time together socially (Byers 2013; Parker 2012). On September 19, 2010, Clementi asked Ravi if he and his male friend could use the room to be alone for the evening. Ravi, aware of his roommate's homosexuality, set up a secret webcam facing Clementi's bed. Ravi would later claim he set up the webcam out of concern that his personal items may be stolen from Clementi's male friend (Ariosto 2012). Ravi viewed the webcam stream via iChat from his friend Molly Wei's room, which displayed Clementi kissing another male. Both Ravi and Wei also showed the live webcam stream later that evening to four other friends, depicting Clementi engaging in sexual activity with another male. After viewing the video of Clementi, Ravi posted comments on his Twitter account, which were also posted on Facebook stating, "Roommate asked for the room till midnight. I went into molly's room and turned on my webcam. I saw him making out with a dude. Yay" (Kaplan and McClure 2011, 100). Clementi, who followed Ravi on Twitter, discovered the online posts the following day, which included over 100 other followers. Investigators later discovered that Clementi conveyed his resentment about Ravi's actions that day through an online gay forum—*Justusboys* website (Foderaro 2010).

On the night of September 21, Clementi asked Ravi again if he could use the room to be alone with his male friend. After agreeing, Ravi posted to Twitter, "Anyone with iChat, I dare you to video chat me between 9:30 and 12. Yes, it's happening again" (Byers 2013, 253). Clementi viewed the postings prior to his guest's arrival that evening and disconnected the camera. He also reported Ravi to the resident advisor about the online postings and the live video stream his roommate displayed of Clementi engaging in sexual activities with another male (Byers 2013). In turn, Clementi was advised to make a formal complaint in writing and request a room change.

On the evening of September 22, 2010, Clementi left his dorm room to eat dinner and later posted on his Facebook page via his cell phone, "Jumping of the gw bridge sorry" (Byers 2012, 253). Soon after Clementi committed suicide, both Ravi and Wei were charged with various felony counts, specifically invasion of privacy (Byers 2013; Ariosto 2012). Wei accepted a plea agreement, which included three years' probation and 300 hours of community service for testifying against Ravi. Ravi was found guilty and convicted of invasion of privacy, bias intimidation, witness tampering, and other felony counts. Ravi was sentenced to 30 days in prison, three years of probation, 300 hours of community service, counseling, and assessed a $10,000 fine (Koenigs et al. 2012). It was discovered during court proceedings, however, that Ravi made an attempt to apologize to Clementi through text messages the night Clementi committed suicide (Ariosto 2012).

KATHY MARTINEZ-PRATHER

See also: Byrd, James, Jr., Murder of (1998); Columbine High School Shootings (Littleton, CO) (April 20, 1999); Shepard, Matthew, Murder of (1998)

Further Reading

Ariosto, David. 2012. "Guilty Verdict in Rutgers Webcam Spying Case." CNN.com. March 17. http://www.cnn.com/2012/03/16/justice/new-jersey-rutgers-trial. Accessed April 23, 2015.

Byers, David S. 2013. "'Do They See Nothing Wrong With This?'": Bullying Bystander Complicity, and the Role of Homophobic Bias in the Tyler Clementi Case." *Families in Society: The Journal of Contemporary Social Services* 94(4): 251–258.

Crimmins, Danielle M., and Kathryn C. Seigfried-Spellar. 2014. "Peer Attachment, Sexual Experiences, and Risky Online Behaviors as Predictors of Sexting Behaviors among Undergraduate Students." *Computer in Human Behavior* 32: 268–275.

Foderaro, Lisa W. 2010. "Private Moment Made Public, Then a Fatal Jump." *The New York Times.* September 29. http://query.nytimes.com/gst/fullpage.html?res=9B07E6D91638F933A0575AC0A9669D8B63. Accessed April 23, 2015.

Kaplan, Bruce K., and Julia L. McClure. 2011. Brief submitted on behalf of state of New Jersey, *State of New Jersey vs. Dharun Ravi*, Defendant (Superior Court of New Jersey).

Koenigs, Michael, Candace Smith, and Christina Ng. 2012. "Rutgers Trial: Dharun Ravi Sentenced to 30 Days in Jail." *ABC News.* May 21. http://abcnews.go.com/US/rutgers-trial-dharun-ravi-sentenced-30-days-jail/story?id=16394014. Accessed April 23, 2015.

Parker, Ian. 2012. "The Story of a Suicide: Two College Roomates, a Webcam, and a Tragedy." *The New Yorker.* February 6, 36–51.

Patterson, Charlotte J. 2013. "Schooling, Sexual Orientation, Law, and Policy: Making Schools Safe for All Students." *Theory into Practice* 52(3): 190–195.

Star-Ledger Staff. 2011. "New Details Revealed in Rutgers Webcam Suicide Case." *NJ.com.* August 12. http://www.nj.com/news/index.ssf/2011/08/rutgers_suicide_new_details_re.html. Accessed April 23, 2015.

Cleveland Serial Killer. *See* Sowell, Anthony (1959–)

Cleveland Torso Murders (1935–1938)

From September 1935 to August 1938, a series of brutal murders created panic in Cleveland, Ohio. According to the Cleveland Police Department, there were 12 victims, though a few experts and criminologists who have studied the case suggest that the Cleveland torso murders may have been related to similar killings that occurred around

New Castle, Pennsylvania. Eliot Ness, Cleveland's public safety director, directed the investigation, which ultimately focused on two different suspects. The case, however, remains unsolved.

In 1935, Kingsbury Run was a wasteland. A ravine ran along Cleveland's east side, and it was home to discarded garbage, shanties, and drifters living on the fringe during the Great Depression. Two boys playing in an area of Kingsbury Run known as Jackass Hill discovered the first victim on September 23, 1935. The killer had left the naked body—decapitated and emasculated (sexual organs removed)—in a thicket of weeds. Officers arrived at the scene to discover a second body nearby. Police found the second victim, also decapitated and emasculated, wearing only a pair of black socks. Investigators located both heads less than a hundred feet from the bodies. Police identified Edward Andrassy, a hospital orderly, as the second victim.

The coroner examined the bodies and reported that both men had been killed by decapitation—an extremely rare method of murder—and were washed and drained of blood before being left in the open. Rope burns on Andrassy's wrists suggested to police that he had been bound prior to his death. The police initially believed that the men had probably been killed over a woman. The killer had coated the first victim's body in some kind of oil and burned it. The coroner, Arthur Pearce, determined victim one had been killed two or three weeks prior to Andrassy.

A shopkeeper found the dismembered and decapitated body of Florence Polillo, a prostitute, four months later. Wrapped in burlap and left in baskets, Polillo had suffered a fate similar to the previous victims—she had been murdered by decapitation. By some accounts, the police were hesitant to tie the three decapitation murders together (Badal 2001).

Cleveland police find the city's eighth headless body in two and a half years, on February 23, 1937. The decapitated body of a woman was found on the shores of Lake Erie. Here, police carry away the torso. (AP Photo)

Five months later, on June 5, 1936, two boys traversing Kingsbury Run on the way to a fishing spot at the Cuyahoga River pulled a pair of men's jeans out from under some shrubs, and discovered the severed head of the fourth victim. Never identified, John Doe #2 had been decapitated with a sharp instrument, and like the previous victims his body had been washed and drained of blood before being left in Kingsbury Run. Coroner Arthur Pearse noted the similarity in the crimes, but Cleveland Police resisted publicly linking the crimes to one killer. Cleveland was just a few days from hosting the Republican National Convention, and authorities did not want to create a panic.

Given that the four victims had been decapitated while alive, washed, and then carried to the dumping site, Coroner Pearse began to wonder whether those cases were related to the body of a woman found in 1934, washed up at Euclid Beach on the shore of Lake Erie (Bardsley 1998). Though too badly decomposed to know for certain, the "Lady of the Lake," as she was later called, was decapitated, her skin burned like John Doe #1, and body dismembered like Florence Polillo. Officially, she was not considered a victim in the torso murders, but several criminologists nonetheless label her "victim zero" (Badal 2001).

Despite not wanting to draw attention to the killing just days before the Republican National Convention, the press began printing stories of a homicidal maniac. Eliot Ness (1903–1957), who had been hired as public safety director to clean up Cleveland, met with Coroner Pearse, police sergeant James Hogan, and head of the homicide division, David Cowles. Sergeant Hogan felt the murders were not related because the female victims were dismembered and the men were not, and he pointed to the fact that the men were all found in Kingsbury Run and the women were left in other areas of the city. According to Bardsley (1998), Pearse and Cowles disagreed—they both believed it was the work of one offender. Eliot Ness agreed that it was one man, but he left explicit instructions to avoid public panic, ordering them not to suggest to newspapers that Cleveland was looking for one man while the convention was ongoing.

Like the attempts to solve the four prior homicides, the case for John Doe #2 went cold. On July 22, 1936, more than a year later, a teenage girl found the headless corpse of a white man near a hobo camp. The police found him lying on his stomach, nude, but badly decomposed. His head was recovered inside blood-stained clothing. Unlike the previous victims, blood that had dried into the soil indicated that John Doe #3 had been killed on location. Just

two months later, a homeless man tripped over the upper half of a man's torso, and alerted police. They found parts of the John Doe #3 in a filthy nearby pond. In his late 20s, the latest victim died of decapitation like the rest.

Three additional bodies turned up in 1937, including the first African American victim, whose skeletal remains were recovered from a burlap bag. The next year, police discovered the final two victims attributed to the "Mad Butcher" on August 16, 1938. Ironically, the killer left both bodies within view of Eliot Ness's office window.

Other Related Crimes?

Ten years prior to the first torso murders in Cleveland, three headless bodies were discovered in New Castle, Pennsylvania, though they were never officially linked to the Mad Butcher. In 1939, a year after the final victims were found in Cleveland, a headless body was discovered in the swamps near New Castle, followed by three dismembered bodies in boxcars not far from Cleveland. Two more headless corpses were found in Pennsylvania, along with two human legs, which were recovered from a river that ran through Pittsburgh. Though the modus operandi in those cases was similar to that of the torso killings, officially they remain unrelated.

In August 1938, Ness and a group of 35 officers raided the shantytowns in and around Kingsbury Run, rounding up hobos, shipping them off to work camps, and burning their shelters. The raid drew criticism and placed attention squarely on Ness. While the Cleveland Police questioned many people, two men are most frequently associated with the Mad Butcher investigation.

At one point, authorities arrested a bricklayer named Frank Dolezal (Badal 2001). Despite providing a confession before his death in the Cuyahoga Jail, most contemporary researchers dismiss Dolezal as a suspect. Ness and the Cleveland Police turned their attention to the most infamous suspect in the case: Dr. Francis Sweeney (1894–1964).

Born to poor immigrant parents and raised near Kingsbury Run, Sweeney served as a medic in World War I, finished medical school in 1928, and received a residency in Cleveland as a surgeon. At the time of the investigation, his cousin, Martin Sweeney, was a prominent and powerful congressman. Plagued by chronic alcoholism, Dr. Sweeney lost his position with the hospital and saw his marriage dissolve in the months before the Lady of the Lake was killed.

Sweeney was a very tall, very powerful man with a reputation for having an explosive temper. He fitted the profile. Ness interviewed Sweeney personally, and believed that the doctor was responsible for the killings (Badal 2001). Sweeney also failed two rudimentary polygraph exams. Nonetheless, the case against Sweeney was based on weak circumstantial evidence, and with Sweeney's political connections, Ness didn't believe the state could win a conviction. The case went cold. Sweeney voluntarily admitted himself to a mental hospital, and spent the rest of his life moving from one hospital to another. The torso killings remain unsolved.

CHRISTOPHER SHIELDS

See also: Black Dahlia Murder (1947); Dahmer, Jeffrey (1960–1994); Holmes, Dr. H. H. (1861–1896); Sowell, Anthony (1959–)

Further Reading

Badal, James Jenssen. 2001. *In the Wake of the Butcher: Cleveland's Torso Murders.* Kent, OH: Kent State University Press.

Bardsley, Marilyn. 1998. *Eliot Ness: The Man behind the Myth.* Great Falls VA: Dark Horse.

Bardsley, Marilyn. 2013. "The Kingsbury Run Murders or Cleveland Torso Murders." http://web.archive.org/web/2013 1107122643/http://www.trutv.com/library/crime/serial_ killers/unsolved/kingsbury/index_1.html. Accessed April 14, 2015.

Bellamy, John. 1997. *The Maniac in the Bushes.* Cleveland, OH: Gray and Company.

Clinton, Bill, Impeachment Trial of (1999)

Only two presidents in American history, Andrew Johnson and Bill Clinton, have been impeached. Clinton was impeached by the House of Representatives in February 1999 for perjury and obstruction of justice relating to an alleged affair with a White House intern. It will undoubtedly be considered a low point in the nation's history, with the media overscrutinizing every embarrassing fact of the case. Nonetheless, Clinton was acquitted in the Senate and continued his presidency, albeit in the shadow of what amounted to a tabloid scandal. Citizens and scholars will long debate Clinton's impeachment and the presidential missteps and partisan politics that contributed to it.

Clinton's impeachment grew out of an investigation, originally entrusted to Robert Fiske Jr. in 1994 and passed on that same year to attorney Kenneth Starr, into an Arkansas land development deal and banking scandal in which Clinton and his wife, Hillary Rodham Clinton, were allegedly involved. During the investigation, Paula Jones, an Arkansas state employee, sued the president for allegedly making a crude sexual advance toward her in a Little Rock motel while Clinton was governor of Arkansas in 1991. After winning the right in *Clinton v. Jones* (1997) to sue a sitting president in a civil matter related to conduct alleged to have taken place before he took office, Jones's attorneys began interviewing women who might demonstrate that Clinton had harassed other employees.

One of the women deposed by Jones's attorneys was Monica Lewinsky, a 25-year-old White House intern. At about the same time, an adviser of Clinton's, Vernon Jordan, was helping Lewinsky find a job in another city. Moreover, a government employee and friend of Lewinsky, Linda Tripp, approached Starr with tape recordings of conversations in which Lewinsky acknowledged an inappropriate sexual relationship with the president.

As investigators questioned whether the help with employment was in exchange for Lewinsky's testimony denying a sexual relationship with the president, Clinton strongly denied in a public statement having sexual relations with her. The issue was further complicated during a presidential deposition before Jones's attorneys in which the term "sexual relations" was defined in a relatively narrow fashion that may or may not have been understood to include the kind of behavior that Lewinsky, after being given full immunity by Starr, alleged had taken place. A presidential deposition before a grand jury in which the president admitted to engaging in "inappropriate intimate contact" with Lewinsky also demonstrated presidential evasions.

Eventually, Starr presented the House of Representatives with 11 potentially impeachable charges. Most centered around whether the president had committed perjury (lying under oath) in his deposition before Jones's attorneys and/or before the grand jury and whether he had attempted to obstruct justice. Starr further presented a massive report detailing his investigation and containing many salacious details about Clinton's alleged sexual activities with Lewinsky—a report that, like the president's taped grand jury testimony, the House released in full to the public.

Led by Republican Henry Hyde, the House Judiciary Committee eventually presented four articles of impeachment to the full House: perjury before the grand jury, perjury in the Jones case, obstruction of the independent counsel's investigation, and abuse of power. The House voted 228 to 206 to accept the article dealing with perjury before the federal grand jury and 221 to 212 to accept the article dealing with obstruction of justice, but it rejected the other two charges.

Those votes led to a trial in the U.S. Senate presided over by Chief Justice William Rehnquist, under terms of the U.S. Constitution. Hyde and other members of the House Judiciary Committee presented the House side of the case to the Senate, arguing that as the nation's chief law enforcement officer, the president should be held to a high standard. Clinton's attorneys, although acknowledging that the president had behaved evasively and immorally, argued that he had not committed impeachable offenses, debating the meaning of the constitutional phrase "high crimes and misdemeanors." The president's attorneys argued that most of Clinton's denials and equivocations had been designed to protect himself and his family from embarrassment, and that there was no proof that he had obstructed justice by encouraging others to lie or rewarding them for lying. Such actions were largely personal failings rather than the kinds of activities imperiling national institutions for which President Richard Nixon had been charged before his resignation.

On February 12, 1999, the Senate voted on the two articles of impeachment—45 to 55 and 50 to 50, respectively, far short of the two-thirds majorities that would have been needed to convict. Although Clinton was not removed from office, he had undoubtedly been subjected to a humiliating procedure. Moreover, many wondered if the results might have been different if the nation had not been in a period of relative prosperity, or if the Republicans had made substantial gains, rather than suffering losses, in the congressional elections of 1998. Others blamed the trial on the special prosecutor's office and argued that, in the absence of effective limits, the prosecutor had gone beyond the bounds of reasonable investigation.

Even though Clinton was not convicted in the Senate, he was fined more than $90,000 by a district court on July 29, 1999, for giving false testimony to Jones's attorneys. The next day, a Maryland grand jury indicted Tripp for illegally wiretapping her conversations with Lewinsky. Those judgments appeared to end the ordeal, although the media's intense coverage of the impeachment proceedings effectively embedded them into the public consciousness and cast a shadow on Clinton's presidency. Scholars will long debate whether Clinton should have been impeached, how the impeachment will affect his place in history, whether the Senate came to the right conclusion, and whether the special prosecutor law has been ultimately beneficial or harmful.

JOHN R. VILE

See also: Burr, Aaron, Treason Trial of (1807); Johnson, Andrew, Impeachment Trial of (1868); Surratt, Mary (1823–1865)

Further Reading

Aaseng, Nathan. 1999. *Famous Trials: The Impeachment of Bill Clinton*. New York: Lucent Books.

Posner, Richard A. 2000. *An Affair of State: The Investigation, Impeachment and Trial of President Clinton*. Cambridge, MA: Harvard University Press.

Clutter Family Murders (1959)

On November 15, 1959, in Holcomb, Kansas, the Clutter family was brutally murdered by two men in an attempted robbery of their home. The victims were Herbert Clutter (1911–1959), Kenyon Clutter (1944–1959), Bonnie Clutter (1914–1959), and Nancy Clutter (1943–1959). The murderers were Richard Hickock (1931–1965) and Perry Smith (1928–1965), both of whom were sentenced to death and executed in Lansing, Kansas, for their crimes. The two murderers, while incarcerated for prior crimes, received a tip from fellow inmate Floyd Wells that Herbert Clutter kept large amounts of cash in a safe located inside the Clutter farm house. Once the two men were out of custody they devised a plan to rob the Clutters of their money and kill them so that no witnesses remained. The two murderers had planned on using the money to flee to and retire in Mexico. Floyd Wells had previously worked for Herbert Clutter as a farm hand and claimed to have learned of the safe's existence while working for the Clutters. Despite this, the information that Floyd Wells gave to Hickock and Smith was false and in fact there was no safe on the Clutter property and no cash was kept within the home by Herbert Clutter. Once Hickock and Smith found out that there was no money to steal they killed the entire Clutter family and went on the run. The murderers were eventually captured in Nevada and extradited to Kansas where they were convicted, sentenced to death, and executed.

Herbert Clutter was a successful farmer in the southwestern portion of Kansas near the town of Holcomb,

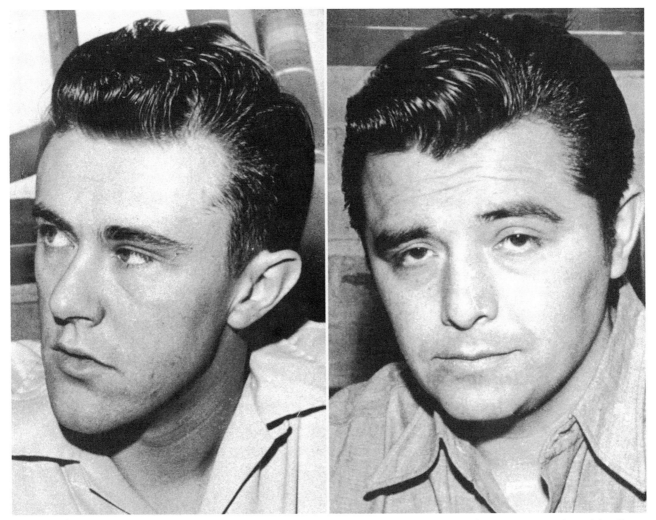

Undated file photos of Richard Hickock, left, and Perry Smith, the two men hanged for the November 15, 1959, murders of the Clutter family in Holcomb, Kansas. Hickock and Smith were executed on April 14, 1965, providing an ending to *In Cold Blood*, the book author Truman Capote was writing about the case. (AP Photo)

Kansas. The Clutter family was active in the nearby town of Holcomb and regularly attended church there. The family farm was known to be a prosperous place that was well respected within the community. Herbert lived with his wife Bonnie Clutter and they raised four children. Two of the Clutter children had since moved on their own when the murders had occurred, but the two teenagers Kenyon and Nancy still lived at home (Smith 2005).

Richard Hickock and Perry Smith were incarcerated when they met Floyd Wells. Wells told the two would be murderers about a large stash of cash at the Clutter family farm in Holcomb. Wells claimed to have seen the cash and the safe it was kept in while working as a farmhand for Mr. Clutter before being incarcerated. Once Hickock and Smith were released from prison, the two men devised a plan to travel to the Clutter family farm and steal the cash while leaving behind no witnesses. The two criminals arrived at the Clutter farm house during the night of November 15, 1959, and entered the house through an unlocked side entrance to the home. The men woke and bound Mr. Clutter to a steam pipe in the basement of the home. Kenyon was bound and lay on a sofa in a room next to the one in which Mr. Clutter was being held. Mrs. Clutter and her daughter Nancy were each bound in separate rooms in the upstairs portion of the home. Once the men discovered that there was no money to steal in the house they killed Mr. Clutter by slitting his throat with a knife and then shooting him in the head at close range with a shotgun. The two criminals then summarily killed the remaining family members by shooting each in the head at pointblank range with the shotgun used to kill Mr. Clutter (Capote 1993).

By the time that Garden City, Kansas police chief Mitchell Geisler and assistant chief Ritch Rohleder discovered the bodies at the Clutter farm house, the killers had already fled and began their trek across the United States and Mexico. The two police officers informed the Kansas Bureau of Investigation (KBI) of the crimes and KBI special agent Alvin Dewey (1912–1987) took over as the lead investigator (Garden City Police Department [GCPD]—Alvin Dewey 2013). After committing the crimes, Hickock and Smith fled first to Kansas City and then to Mexico. After a short stay in Mexico the two murderers traveled to California, Nebraska, Iowa, back to Kansas City, Florida, and finally to Nevada.

It was during this time that Floyd Wells, the inmate who gave the false information about a safe at the Clutter home, contacted prison officials to notify them of his suspicions that Hickock and Smith had committed the murders in exchange for ransom money. On December 31, 1959, the KBI captured Hickock and Smith in Nevada and the two men were extradited back to Kansas to stand trial for their crimes. When Hickock and Smith were captured they were in possession of physical evidence that tied them directly to the murders, including a boot that left a bloody print behind at the murder scene.

The two men initially disputed who had shot which victim and neither man testified at the murder trial. It is still unclear which of the two men shot the victims during the crime. On March 29, 1960, Hickock and Smith were convicted of the murders and received the death penalty for their crimes. They both lived on death row for five years and were executed by hanging in Lansing, Kansas, on April 14, 1965. The two murderers were hung on the same day and died just 38 minutes apart for their crimes.

The murders of the Clutter family were widely publicized by Truman Capote (1924–1984) in his book *In Cold Blood*. Capote traveled to Kansas to research the book from New York. He spent several years researching and writing the book from over 8,000 pages of notes he took from extensive interviews with the surviving family members, their friends, and residents of the Holcomb, Kansas, area (Capote 1993). In addition to Capote, Harper Lee also traveled to Kansas to help him gain the trust of those who Capote would later interview in preparing to write his book about the Clutter family murders. Since the executions of Hickock and Smith, both men were exhumed to obtain DNA samples utilized in the investigation of the murders of the Walker family in Osprey, Florida, on December 18, 2012. During their time on the run, Hickock and Smith

traveled to Florida where the Walker family was murdered. The two men were interrogated about the murders after being arrested for the Clutter family murders, but no conviction was ever obtained. The DNA results from the 2012 reinvestigation of the Walker murders turned out to be inconclusive. Despite this, many believe that Hickock and Smith are responsible for the killing of the Walker family while they were on the run after killing the Clutter family in 1959 (Smith 2005).

DUSTIN EICKE

See also: Duperrault Family Slayings (November 12, 1961); Gilley Family Murders (April 26, 1984); Hudson, Jennifer, Family Murders (October 24, 2008); Wesson Family Massacre (2004)

Further Reading

"Alvin A. Dewey." Garden City Police Department. http://www.gcpolice.org/History/Dewey.html. Accessed April 14, 2015.

Capote, Truman. 1993. *In Cold Blood*. Boston: G.K. Hall.

"Clutter Family Murders." Garden City Police Department. http://www.gcpolice.org/History/Clutter.html. Accessed April 14, 2015.

"Clutter Murders Remembered." 2009. *Wichita Eagle*. http://www.kansas.com/2009/11/11/1050558/clutter-murders-remembered.html. Accessed April 14, 2015.

Smith, Patrick. "Sisters, family: Surviving Clutter daughters hope to preserve their parents' legacy." *Lawrence Journal World*. http://www2.ljworld.com/news/2005/apr/04/sisters_family_surviving/. Accessed April 14, 2015.

Cocoanut Grove Nightclub Fire (Boston) (1942)

In November 1942, Barnet "Barney" Welansky, the owner of the Cocoanut Grove Nightclub in Boston, Massachusetts, and his customers celebrated renewed prosperity among artificial palm trees, creating the exotic atmosphere of some of the tropical islands in the South Pacific where U.S. soldiers were fighting. Weeks later, on November 28, a deadly fire would kill 492 people—32 more than the authorized capacity of the building—and would injure hundreds more. The scope of the tragedy shocked Americans out of their absorption with World War II events, led to reforms of safety standards and codes across America, and brought about major changes in the treatment and rehabilitation of burn victims.

Located in downtown Boston at 17 Piedmont Street near the Park Square theater district, the Cocoanut Grove was built in 1927 and consisted of a single story building with a basement underneath containing a bar called the Melody Lounge and a kitchen, freezers, and storage areas. The first floor featured a large dining room with a retractable roof to roll back during warm weather to dine among the moon and stars. The ballroom contained a bandstand, and several bar areas radiating separately from the ballroom. A revolving door on the Piedmont side of the building served as the Cocoanut Grove's main entrance.

The Cocoanut Grove had been a popular watering hole during Prohibition and after some lean years during the 1930s, patrons again flocked to enjoy its delights during the early World War II years. Owner "Barney" Welansky who had reputed ties with the mafia and shady dealings with some Boston regulatory officials anticipated unlimited patrons and profits.

That evening, some patrons were enjoying dining and dancing, and others were shouting in anticipation of the floor show when at about 10:15 p.m. a bartender ordered a 16-year-old busboy by the name of Stanley F. Tomaszewski to replace a light bulb that had burned out at the top of an artificial palm tree in the corner of the Melody Lounge in the basement. Later, the story surfaced that a patron wanting more privacy with his girlfriend had unscrewed the bulb. The darkness in the area around the palm tree motivated Stanley Tomaszewski to stand on a bench and light a match so he could find the socket for the light bulb. He found the socket and started to screw in the light bulb. According to Stanley, the match fell out of his hand and he thought that it landed on an imitation palm tree under the bench. Later investigators discovered that the palm trees, the draperies, and other items in the Cocoanut Grove were flammable.

Moments later, patrons watched a flicker of flame in the palm trees in the ceiling decorations and soon they watched terrified as the palm tree burst into flames and the bartenders tried to put out the fire with water and seltzer bottles. Quickly the furnishings ignited and a fireball of flame and toxic gas raced across the lounge toward the stairs. People panicked and unsuccessfully attempted to open the emergency exit door at the top of the stairs. The fireball traveled up the stairs to the main entrance. People cried "fire, fire," and stampeded to the revolving door, which quickly jammed. The fireball exploded into the dining room and the panic intensified as customers desperately searched for an exit, many of which were locked, unidentified, or inaccessible. Soon the fire spread through the entire Cocoanut Grove, producing lethal temperatures and equally lethal levels of toxic gas.

Firemen arrived quickly and extinguished the fire within half an hour, but for more than two hours firemen and rescue workers carried out bodies from the smoldering Cocoanut Grove. Many of the Cocoanut Grove customers who had escaped the building collapsed in the street and stacks of living and dead people were piled shoulder high at many of the building exits. Authorities called in Navy, Army, Coast Guard, and National Guard to assist in evacuating and removing injured people to area hospitals, including Boston City Hospital and Massachusetts General Hospital.

Authorities established a temporary morgue in the film distribution garage near the Cocoanut Grove, and medical personnel and volunteers worked to identify them. They had an especially difficult time identifying the female victims because they carried their personal identification in purses or handbags, which they had lost or abandoned in the confusion of the fire.

Three separate investigations of the Cocoanut Grove fire began while the ashes were still warm. The Boston Police Department opened its investigation the day after the fire with the goal of discovering any criminal or corruption activity surrounding the fire. Policemen took statements at Police Department Headquarters, City Hospital, Peter Bent Brigham Hospital, Brighton Marine Hospital, Cambridge City Hospital, and Chelsea Naval Hospitals and conducted 148 interviews. The Police Department recorded testimonies through December 11, 1942, and compiled them in three volumes.

Boston mayor Maurice J. Tobin scheduled an inquest for 3:00 p.m. on November 29, 1942, at the Bristol Street Fire headquarters, placing Boston fire commissioner William Arthur Reilly in charge and naming military officers, FBI agents, and state fire marshal Stephen C. Garrity as observers. The mayor and his colleagues conducted the inquest to discover the fire's cause and to determine if the Boston Fire Department had been negligent. Interviews began immediately and extended through January 30, 1943, totaling 15 sessions in all. Fire commissioner Reilly issued a report of the inquest containing his recommendations, a list of witnesses, and a list of the dead and injured on November 19, 1943. Many witnesses believed that the busboy started the fire, while others thought that electrical problems caused it.

On November 30, 1942, Massachusetts attorney general Robert T. Bushnell and Boston district attorney William J. Foley opened a hearing to fix responsibility for the Cocoanut Grove Fire. Although they called some of the same witnesses as Boston fire commissioner William Reilly, they closed their hearings to the public and the press. For a week, they also called witnesses to shed possible light on corrupt practices, interviewing people and gathering evidence to present to a grand jury. Jury selection began on December 7, 1942, and testimony had been completed by December 29, 1942.

The grand jury indicted 10 people that it considered responsible for the fire. Barnett Welansky, the owner of the Cocoanut Grove, James Welansky, his brother and the person in charge of the club on the night of the fire, and Jacob Goldfine, wine steward, were charged with manslaughter. Fire lieutenant Frank Linney was charged with neglect of duties in inspecting the Cocoanut Grove and Police Captain Buccigross who was on duty at the club the night of the fire was also charged with neglect of duties. Boston building inspector Theodore Eldracher, architect and interior designer Ruben Bodenhorn, contractor Samuel Rudnick, and foreman David Gilbert were charged with conspiracy to violate building codes.

After nearly a month of hearing 130 witnesses and examining 155 exhibits, a jury acquitted James Welansky and Jacob Goldfine, but found Barney Welansky guilty of 19 counts of manslaughter. A judge sentenced him to a 12- to 15-year term in prison, but he was freed in November 1946 because of ill health and died the next spring. The remainder of those indicted were acquitted or given suspended sentences.

KATHY WARNES

See also: Station Nightclub Fire (West Warwick, RI) (February 20, 2003)

Further Reading

Benzaquin, Paul. 1967. *Fire in Boston's Cocoanut Grove: Holocaust!* Boston: Branden Press.

Esposito, John C. 2005. *Fire in the Grove.* Cambridge, MA: Da Capo Press.

Keyes, Edward. 1984. *Cocoanut Grove.* New York: Atheneum.

Reilly, William Arthur, Boston Fire Commissioner. 1944. *Report Concerning the Cocoanut Grove Fire, November 28, 1942.* Boston: City of Boston Printing Department.

Vahey, John P. 1982. *Design for Disaster. Cocoanut Grove Fire, November 28, 1942.* Boston: Boston Sparks Association.

Cole, Tiffany (1981–)

On October 19, 2007, a Florida court convicted Tiffany Ann Cole of two counts each of first-degree murder, robbery, and kidnapping for her role in the July 8, 2005, deaths of Carol (1944–2005) and James Reginald "Reggie" Sumner (1943–2005). Upon her sentencing in March 2008, Cole became the only woman on Florida's death row in Marion County, Florida. Two other participants in the crime, Michael James Jackson (b. 1982) and Alan Lyndell Wade (b. 1987), were also convicted of two counts each of first-degree murder, robbery, and kidnapping. A fourth participant, Bruce Kent Nixon, pled guilty to two counts each of second-degree murder, robbery, and kidnapping.

Prior to their move to Jacksonville, Florida, in February, 2005, the Sumners and Cole were neighbors in Charleston, South Carolina. When the Sumners moved, they sold a car to Cole, who made monthly payments to the Sumners by driving to Florida with Jackson, her then boyfriend. Cole and Jackson also stayed with the Sumners overnight during some of these trips. On one such a visit, Carol Sumner told Cole that the Sumners sold their South Carolina home for a profit of approximately $90,000. The news of the profit from the sold home began the series of events that eventually led to the murders of the Sumners.

According to prosecutors, Tiffany Cole served as the connection between the Sumners and the three other participants. During their trips to Florida, Cole and Jackson spent time with Jackson's friend Wade. Wade's friend Nixon became involved later. According to court records, Cole, Jackson, and Wade began planning to rob the Sumners after the Sumners' Florida home and furnishings, as well as the news of the $90,000 profit from the South Carolina home led Jackson to believe that the Sumners were well off financially.

In the days leading up to the crime, Cole, Jackson, and Wade began purchasing supplies, such as duct tape, rubber gloves, and a toy pellet gun, to carry out the robbery. At some point Wade contacted Nixon about digging a hole for a robbery. Nixon agreed to do so, as he needed drug money. Nixon gathered four shovels, and on the night of July 6, 2005, Cole, Jackson, Wade, and Nixon drove to a remote, wooded area in Charlton County, Georgia, to dig the hole that would serve as the Sumners' grave. Cole held a flashlight for her boyfriend Jackson, Wade, and Nixon while they dug the hole. There is some debate regarding how much Nixon knew about the planned crime at this point. Some testimony indicated that Nixon was only aware of a plan for a robbery, while other testimony indicated that Nixon knew that the intended victims would be killed. What is known, though, is that Jackson agreed to let Nixon participate in the robbery at the request of Wade.

At approximately 10 p.m. on the night of July 8, 2005, Wade and Nixon gained access to the Sumners' home by requesting to use their telephone. Cole and Jackson waited outside the Sumners' home. Nixon used the toy gun purchased by Cole to threaten the Sumners. He and Wade then bound and gagged the Sumners with duct tape. While Nixon kept the Sumners bound in their bedroom, Jackson entered the home, where he and Wade searched for money, property, financial documents, and credit cards. The three men then took the Sumners outside to their car, a Lincoln, and put the couple in the trunk. Wade and Nixon drove the Lincoln to the hole in Charlton County, with Cole and Jackson following in their car, a rented Mazda.

Upon arrival at the Georgia grave location, Jackson joined Wade and Nixon in the Lincoln, while Cole remained parked on the street in the Mazda. Nixon, who drove the Lincoln into the woods, left Jackson, Wade, and the Sumners at the hole that the group had prepared two days prior. Jackson and Wade then buried the Sumners, whose legs, arms, mouths, and eyes were bound with duct tape, while Nixon returned to Cole and the Mazda on the road. After the bodies were discovered, the autopsy revealed that Jackson and Wade buried the Sumners while they were still alive.

When Jackson and Wade returned to the road in the Lincoln, Jackson had a legal pad with the personal identification numbers (PINs) for the Sumners' automated teller machine (ATM) cards. The four then drove to Sanderson, Florida—Nixon and Wade in the Lincoln, and Jackson and Cole in the Mazda. After finding a place to abandon the Sumners' car, they cleaned the vehicle of fingerprints and left the shovels in the trunk. Cole drove Jackson, Wade, and Nixon back to Jacksonville, Florida, where they withdrew money from the Sumners' accounts at an ATM. The groups also returned to the Sumners' home to steal their computer. Starting on July 9, 2005, the day after the Sumners were buried, the group withdrew approximately $5,000 from the Sumners' bank accounts, and Cole pawned Carol Sumner's jewelry. Late on July 9, Nixon returned to his home, while Cole, Jackson, and Wade traveled to Charleston, South Carolina. There, Cole rented two hotel rooms.

On July 10, 2005, Carol Sumner's daughter called the police after being unable to reach her mother. Detectives examined the Sumners' bank records and found that thousands of dollars had been withdrawn. Through tracking the ATM transactions, the police obtained a video of Jackson withdrawing money from the Sumners' accounts. The video also showed the rented Mazda.

On July 12, 2005, an off-duty patrol officer found the Sumners' abandoned Lincoln, which he recognized from a stolen vehicle report. After this development was publicized, Cole and Jackson called the Jacksonville Sheriff's Office, impersonating the Sumners and claiming that their home was burglarized and their car stolen while they were out of town. Investigators did not believe their story, but instead tracked Cole and Jackson's cell phone use. That, combined with global positioning system (GPS) in the Mazda, led law enforcement to the hotel in Charleston, South Carolina, where Cole, Jackson, and Wade were staying. Nixon was later arrested, and he led the police to the gravesite in the woods. On July 15, 2005, the Sumners' burial site was excavated.

On August 18, 2005, a Florida court indicted Tiffany Cole on two counts of first-degree murder, two counts of robbery, and two counts of kidnapping. After only 90 minutes of deliberation, a jury returned a guilty verdict on all counts of the indictment on October 19, 2007. Several months later, on March 6, 2008, a jury recommended a sentence of death by a vote of nine to three. The judge, following the jury's recommendation, sentenced Cole to death for each count of first-degree murder, 15 years for each count of robbery, and life in prison for each count of kidnapping. This sentence of death made Tiffany Cole the only woman on death row in Florida at the time.

Cole filed an appeal with the Florida Supreme Court on March 19, 2008. On March 11, 2010, Cole's appeal was denied, with the Florida Supreme Court affirming her conviction and sentence.

CHERIE M. CARTER

See also: Buenoano, Judy (1943–1998); Eubanks, Susan (1964–); Moore, Blanche Taylor (1933–); Puente, Dorothea (1929–2011); Tucker, Karla Faye (1959–1998); Wuornos, Aileen (1956–2002)

Further Reading

Commission on Capital Cases. 2010. "Alan Lyndell Wade Case Summary." http://www.floridacapitalcases.state.fl.us/case_updates/Htm/J35401.htm. Accessed April 14, 2015.

Commission on Capital Cases. 2010. "Michael James Jackson Case Summary." http://www.floridacapitalcases.state.fl.us/case_updates/Htm/J34141.htm. Accessed April 14, 2015.

Commission on Capital Cases. 2010. "Tiffany Cole Case Summary." http://www.floridacapitalcases.state.fl.us/case_updates/Htm/J35212.htm. Accessed April 14, 2015.

Florida State University College of Law. "Answer Brief of the Appellee, Supreme Court of Florida Case No. SC08–528." http://www.law.fsu.edu/library/flsupct/sc08-528/08-528Ans.pdf. Accessed April 14, 2015.

Florida State University College of Law. "Initial Brief of the Appellant, Supreme Court of Florida Case No. SC08-528." http://www.law.fsu.edu/library/flsupct/sc08-528/08-528ini .pdf. Accessed April 14, 2015.

Coleman, Alton (1955–2002)

During the summer of 1984, Alton Coleman (1955–2002) and his girlfriend, Debra Denise Brown (b. 1962), went on a killing spree across several Midwestern states. At the time of their apprehension, Coleman was wanted for several assaults and murders. Coleman and Brown were both convicted of two murders in Ohio. Coleman was also convicted of murders in Illinois and Indiana. Because of the convictions in multiple states, Coleman was the only person in the United States to have death sentences in three states at the time of his execution in 2002.

Born on November 6, 1955, Coleman was raised by his grandmother and, occasionally, his mother in Waukegan,

Spree killers, Alton Coleman, left, and Debra Brown, both from Waukegan, Illinois, stand before the bench during their arraignment in Cincinnati, Ohio, on January 10, 1985. Convicted of murder in three different states, Coleman was executed in Ohio on April 26, 2002. Brown is currently serving a life sentence. (AP Photo/Al Behrman)

Illinois. His criminal career began early, with frequent run-ins with law enforcement due to petty offenses. As Coleman aged, though, his offenses became much more serious. Between 1973 and 1983, Coleman was charged with six separate sex offenses. Of the six cases, two were dismissed. Coleman pled guilty to lesser offenses in two other cases, and was acquitted in the other two cases. One of the dismissed charges stemmed from a report filed by Coleman's sister in 1983. She reported to the police that Coleman had attempted to rape her daughter, who was eight years old at the time. She later dropped the charges. The dropped charges were indicative of Coleman's manipulation of the criminal justice system. He was known by law enforcement to be skilled at manipulating juries and intimidating witnesses.

Another of the cases involved the 1973 kidnapping, robbery, and rape of an elderly woman. Coleman was convicted of the robbery, but the woman refused to testify about the rape. Coleman served two years in prison for the robbery, but was arrested for another rape shortly after he was released. He was acquitted of that rape, but convicted on lesser charges. He served four years in prison. A year after his release, Coleman was again arrested for attempted rape. That charge was dismissed.

In 1983, Coleman was charged for the rape and murder of a 14-year-old girl who was the daughter of a friend. He was indicted on these charges in early 1984. The indictment initiated Coleman and Brown's multistate killing spree; when Coleman discovered that he was wanted for the crime, he and Brown left Illinois in early May 1984. They first went to Kenosha, Wisconsin, which is less than 20 miles north of Coleman's hometown of Waukegan, Illinois. In Kenosha, Coleman and Brown met Juanita Wheat, Wheat's nine-year-old daughter, Vernita, and her seven-year-old son. Coleman abducted Vernita Wheat on May 29, 1984, after which he and Brown took Vernita back to Waukegan. On June 19, 1984, Vernita's body was found four blocks from Coleman's grandmother's home. She had been strangled.

On June 1, 1984, Coleman and Brown drove to Gary, Indiana, in a car they stole in Waukegan, Illinois. The pair encountered two young girls: Annie, who was nine years old, and Tamika Turks, who was seven years old. Coleman and Brown took the girls into the woods, where they bound and gagged them both. Tamika's crying annoyed Coleman and Brown, so Brown smothered her while Coleman stomped on her chest. Both adults then assaulted Annie, who survived the attack. Like Vernita, though, Tamika's body was found on June 19, 1984, and the cause of her death was determined to be strangulation.

On the same day, June 19, 1984, Donna Williams disappeared from Gary, Indiana. Like Coleman and Brown's previous victims, Williams was also strangled. Her body was found in Detroit on July 11, 1984.

After killing Donna Williams, Coleman and Brown traveled to Dearborn Heights, Michigan. The pair committed a home invasion at the home of Mr. and Mrs. Palmer Jones. The couple were attacked, and Coleman and Brown stole money and the Jones' car. A week later, on July 5, 1984, Coleman and Brown arrived in Toledo, Ohio. There they met Virginia Temple and her nine-year-old daughter Rachelle. Virginia and Rachelle's bodies were later found in a crawl space in their home; Coleman and Brown had strangled them both. On the same day, Coleman and Brown committed a home invasion at the home of Frank and Dorothy Duvendack. The Duvendacks were bound, and like at the Jones' home, Coleman and Brown stole money and the Duvendacks' car. That evening, Coleman and Brown met a reverend, Millard Gay, and his wife in Dayton, Ohio. On July 10, 1984, the Gays brought Coleman and Brown to Cincinnati, Ohio.

In Cincinnati, 15-year-old Tonnie Storey disappeared on July 11, 1984, and her body was found on July 19, 1984. She had been strangled. On July 13, Coleman and Brown went to Norwood, Ohio. In Norwood, they attacked Harry and Marlene Walters in their home and stole the Walters' car, money, and jewelry. Marlene Walters died as a result of the attack, and Harry Walters suffered brain damage from a blow to head with a wooden candlestick. The Walters' car was found abandoned in Lexington, Kentucky.

In Kentucky, Coleman and Brown kidnapped a Williamsburg college professor, Oline Carmical Jr. They drove to Dayton, Ohio, in Carmical's car with Carmical bound in the trunk. On July 17, 1984, Coleman and Brown abandoned Carmical's car with Carmical still in the trunk. Carmical survived, as the authorities found him in his vehicle.

By this time Coleman and Brown had been identified, and a nationwide search for them was underway. The Federal Bureau of Investigation (FBI) was added to the Ten Most Wanted list. Because of the media coverage, Coleman and Brown were recognized by the Reverend Gay and his wife when they returned to the Gays' home in Dayton, Ohio. The pair threatened the Gays with guns and stole their car. They began traveling to Evanston, Illinois. They

stopped in Indianapolis, Indiana, to steal another car. In doing so, they killed the owner of the vehicle, Eugene Scott.

Coleman and Brown arrived in Evanston on July 20, 1984. While crossing the street, Coleman was recognized by a former neighbor. Knowing that Coleman and Brown were wanted, he contacted the police. The police found Coleman and Brown in a nearby park. Both were arrested.

Because Coleman and Brown's crimes were committed across several states, law enforcement officers from six states—Wisconsin, Illinois, Indiana, Michigan, Ohio, and Kentucky—met to determine a strategy for prosecuting the pair. Ohio was chosen as the jurisdiction that would have the first chance at prosecuting and executing Coleman and Brown. In addition to various lesser crimes, both were convicted for the aggravated murders of Tonnie Storey and Marlene Walters. Both were sentenced to be executed. Coleman was also tried and convicted in Indiana for the murder of Tamika Turks, and in Wisconsin for the murder of Vernita Wheat.

After Coleman was sentenced to be executed, he filed multiple appeals alleging violations of constitutional rights. Various appellate courts affirmed his conviction and sentence. Coleman was executed by lethal injection on April 26, 2002, at the Southern Ohio Correctional Facility in Lucasville, Ohio. He was pronounced dead at 10:23 a.m. Coleman's execution was the fourth execution to take place in Ohio since 1999, when the 36-year moratorium ended.

CHERIE M. CARTER

See also: Gaskins, Donald "Pee Wee" (1933–1991); Harp Boys (1770s–1800s); Smith, Lemuel (1941–)

Further Reading

Enstad, Robert. 1987. "Coleman Found Guilty of 4th Murder." *Chicago Tribune.* January 20. http://articles.chicagotribune.com/1987-01-20/news/8701050844_1_4th-murder-guilty-jurors. Accessed November 1, 2014.

O'Brien, John. 1986. "Child-Slayer Coleman Gets 3d Death Sentence." *Chicago Tribune.* May 3. http://articles.chicagotribune.com/1986-05-03/news/8602010088_1_alton-coleman-penalty-sentenced. Accessed November 1, 2014.

Tribune News Services. 1998. "Death Row Appeal Denied for Killer, Molester Coleman." *Chicago Tribune.* December 30. http://articles.chicagotribune.com/1998-12-30/news/9812300242_1_indiana-supreme-court-death-row-alton-coleman. Accessed November 1, 2014.

Wilkinson, Howard. 2002. "Alton Coleman Finally Faces Justice." *The Cincinnati Inquirer.* April 24. http://www.enquirer.com/editions/2002/04/24/loc_alton_coleman.html. Accessed November 1, 2014.

Colosimo, James "Big Jim," Mob Murder of (May 11, 1920)

James Colosimo (1878–1920), often attributed as the first "big-time" mob boss in the Chicago Outfit, was also a notorious kingpin of prostitution and slavery. Having made a huge success in the business of prostitution, Colosimo dismissed the idea of taking part in bootlegging alcohol when the Prohibition began. Starting to view Colosimo as a lazy boss and fearing that they would lose out on a profitable market, Johnny Torrio (JT; 1882–1957) and Alphonse "Al" Capone (AC; 1899–1947), with the assistance of Frankie Uale "Yale" (FY; 1893–1928), arranged and executed a hit on Colosimo. Although Yale became the prime suspect in the murder, a retracted testimony against him has left this mob murder unsolved.

Often referred to as "Diamond Jim" or "Big Jim," Giacomo "James" Colosimo was born February 16, 1878, in Calabria, Italy. Colosimo immigrated to Chicago, Illinois, from Italy in the 1890s at the age of 10 with his parents. Throughout his teens and early 20s, Colosimo worked legitimately shining shoes, selling newspapers, and sweeping the street. However, he began supplementing his income as a Black Hand extortionist (i.e., sending threatening letters to wealthy targets demanding money to prevent the threatened harm), pickpocketing, and pimping (i.e., recruiting and selling) prostitutes. Two aldermen of Chicago's First Ward, Michael "Hinky Dink" Kenna (MK; 1858–1949) and John "Bathhouse" Coughlin (JC; 1860–1938), took notice of Colosimo and recruited him to be their precinct captain and bagman (i.e., collects dirty "protection" money from pimps for the corrupt officials). Then in 1902, at the age of 24, Colosimo married Victoria Moresco (VM; n.d.), a well-established and successful madame of her own brothel (i.e., a prostitution house), whom he met through his bagman position. Together they developed a brothel enterprise throughout the Levee "red-light" district—which was located within the First Ward and protected by corrupt officials such as Kenna and Coughlin. Their enterprise included nearly two hundred brothels and involved various criminal activities such as gambling, extortion, and eventually slavery—the Colosimo's cofounded the Midwest's White Slave Ring with Maurice and Julia Van Beaver (Curtis 2006).

Colosimo's political connections and immensely successful brothels aided in his rise as Chicago's first "big-time" gang boss and his enterprise later became known as "the Outfit." His success did not go unnoticed from the Black Hand extortionists and in 1909 he received his first extortion letter, similar to the ones he used to send to other wealthy victims. To solve the problem, he recruited Victoria's nephew and Brooklyn mobster, Johnny Torrio—also known as "Papa Johnny" or "The Fox"—to come and end the threat. Torrio decided to remain in Chicago after helping his uncle and became Colosimo's right-hand man within the Outfit. A year later, they opened a successful elite society restaurant known as Colosimo's Café. Several years later, in 1919, they opened another brothel down the street from Colosimo's Café at 2222 S. Wabash in which they called the Four Deuces. Torrio brought in Al Capone, a longtime friend and former gang member from Brooklyn, to work as a bouncer and bartender at the Four Deuces. Then, Prohibition took effect in January 1920, not even a year after the Four Deuces opened.

Despite the vast amount of money made at Colosimo's Café and the Four Deuces through smuggled alcohol, Torrio grew tired of buying from middlemen and wished for the Outfit to bootleg their own alcohol and smuggle whiskey directly from Canada. However, Colosimo resisted the opportunity to begin bootlegging alcohol because he did not want the added attention from Prohibition agents, and he was content with being the kingpin of prostitution and slavery. It was also during this time that Colosimo decided to divorce Victoria and marry Dale Winter (DW; 1893–1985), a 19 year-old singer at Colosimo's Café who wanted nothing to do with the Outfit. Since Colosimo began spending all of his time with Dale and refused to start bootlegging, Torrio began to view Colosimo as lazy and undeserving of his role as the boss of the Outfit. Fearing that they would lose out on the profitable market of bootlegging alcohol, Torrio and Capone sent for another former gang member from Brooklyn, Frankie Yale to assist with their hit on Colosimo (Keefe 2005; Schoenberg 1993).

Within a week of Colosimo and Dale's return to Chicago from their honeymoon in Indiana, the planned hit went into action. On Tuesday May 11, 1920, Torrio called Colosimo and informed him that a few bootleggers were coming to Colosimo Café at 4 p.m. to deliver a shipment of whiskey, and they wished to have Colosimo present at the time of delivery. After his bookkeeper, Frank Camilla, and the bartender, "Big Jim" O'Leary, informed him that no whisky deliveries were scheduled to arrive that day Colosimo became worried that he had been set up. When he failed to get his lawyer Rocco De Stefano on the phone,

Colosimo walked out of the back entrance to get in his car and leave. However, as soon as he stepped outside a man who was hiding in the coatroom shot Colosimo twice in the back of the head with a .38 caliber revolver (Keefe 2005).

It was a waiter at the restaurant, Joseph Gabriola, who provided the police with their only description of the suspect; however, the police were unable to discover who exactly arranged the hit. The initial suspect was Dale since they were newlyweds and then police turned to Victoria and her brother, Joe Moresco, thinking it was due to revenge for the divorce. Finally, after interviewing many people—including Capone and Torrio who made a huge ordeal and denying his involvement—police had a break in the case. Gabriola, the waiter who previously provided police with a description of the suspect, picked Yale out from a mugshot that was sent over by New York police. However, by the time Gabriola arrived in New York for a police lineup to confirm it was Yale he had become so terrified that he decided to retract his statement and not testify (Keefe 2005). Reportedly, Capone later confessed to the murder during a conversation with a journalist, Charles Mac Arthur, but this alleged confession was never confirmed. Thus, Yale was never convicted and no one was ever charged in the murder of Giacomo "Big Jim" Colosimo, the king of prostitution and first mob boss of the Chicago Outfit.

Jennifer A. Haegele

See also: Capone, Al (1899–1947); Torrio, Johnny "the Fox" (1882–1957); Yale, Frankie (1893–1928)

Further Reading

Abbott, Karen. 2007. *Sin in the Second City: Madams, Ministers, Playboys, and the Battle for America's Soul*. New York: Random House.

Bilek, Arthur. 2008. *The First Vice Lord: Big Jim Colosimo and the Ladies of the Levee*. Nashville: Cumberland House Publishing.

Binder, John. 2013. *Images of America: The Chicago Outfit*. Chicago: Arcadia.

Curtis, Keith. 2006. *Pimpin Ain't Easy: An Education on the Life*. Lakewood, OH: Condos on the Moon Publishing.

Keefe, Rose. 2005. *The Man Who Got Away: The Bugs Moran Story: A Biography*. Nashville, FL: Cumberland House.

Russo, Gus. 2001. *The Outfit: The Role of Chicago's Underworld in the Shaping of Modern America*. New York: Bloomsbury.

Schoenberg, Robert. 1993. *Mr. Capone: The Real—and Complete—Story of Al Capone*. New York: HarperCollins.

Wendt, Lloyd, Herman Kogan, and Bette Jore. 2005. *Lords of the Levee: The Story of Bathhouse John and Hinky Dink*. Evanston, IL: Northwestern University Press.

Columbine High School Shootings (Littleton, CO) (April 20, 1999)

On April 20, 1999, Columbine High School in Littleton, Colorado, became the scene of what remains the nation's most infamous school shooting. After nearly two years of planning, seniors Eric Harris (1981–1999) and Dylan Klebold (1981–1999) descended on their school, ready to cause mass carnage. Their arsenal included a 9mm carbine rifle, an IntraTec TEC-DC9 semiautomatic pistol, two sawed-off shotguns, multiple knives, and nearly 100 improvised explosive devices (IEDs), such as Molotov cocktails, pipe bombs, and CO_2 bombs. During the 46-minute massacre, nearly 200 rounds of ammunition were fired, and 30 of the IEDs were detonated. By the time the shots had subsided, 12 students and one teacher had been killed. Harris and Klebold then committed suicide in the school's library. An additional 24 students were wounded in the attack.

On the morning of the shootings, Harris and Klebold arrived at the school at 11:10 a.m., parking their cars in the southwest parking lot. The cars each were filled with explosive devices set to detonate when they entered the school. The pair entered the cafeteria and planted two 20-pound propane tank bombs in large duffle bags. The timers on the bombs had been set for 11:17 a.m., the time at which, according to the pair's meticulous reconnaissance, the presence of students would be the highest (nearly 500 students). They returned to their cars and waited for the bombs to explode. They had planned to shoot any fleeing survivors after the bombs had detonated. When the bombs failed to detonate, however, Harris and Klebold decided to change their plan to shoot as many people as possible at the school. A bomb also had gone off in neighboring Clement Park, which had been planted to create a diversion for the shooters.

As they approached the school, firing at random, they encountered students Richard Castaldo and Rachel Scott, who had been eating their lunch on the grass near the school's upper west entrance. Both students were shot—Scott was shot multiple times and killed. Castaldo, also wounded several times, survived but was left permanently paralyzed. As students exited the cafeteria, Harris and Klebold continued to fire their weapons, killing Daniel Rohrbough and wounding seven other students. Around 11:24 a.m., teacher Dave Sanders entered the cafeteria, warning students who had taken refuge under the tables to flee to safety. Moments later, Harris and Klebold entered the school, tossing IEDs along the way. The school's resource officer, Neil Gardner, who also was the first responder, arrived at the south lot of the school at this time.

Upon entering the school, Harris and Klebold continued to shoot at people fleeing, also tossing a number of IEDs on the upper and lower levels of the school. As they made their way down the hallway, they encountered Dave Sanders as he raced up from the cafeteria. Sanders was shot twice in the back as he tried to flee. Students who were hiding in a neighboring science room pulled him to safety once Harris and Klebold had moved into another area of the school, where they tended to his wounds while waiting for first responders. Sanders, however, would later die before help arrived three hours later.

Harris and Klebold then made their way to the school's library, where 56 students, two teachers, and two library employees were hiding. Teacher Patti Nielsen, who had come face to face earlier with the shooters as they entered from the parking lot, had placed a call to 911 and the line remained open during the duration of Harris and Klebold's time in the library. As they made their way toward the library's west windows, they shot and killed Kyle Velasquez, who had been sitting at one of the computer stations, and proceeded to shoot outside at fleeing students and arriving law enforcement officers.

Then, over the next seven-and-a-half minutes, the shooters taunted those hiding, at times demanding that everyone stand up, while at other times singling out athletes wearing white hats. Steven Curnow was killed by a single gunshot from Harris while hiding under a computer table at the south end of the library. Harris then shot and killed Cassie Bernall, Kelly Fleming, and Lauren Townsend. At a neighboring table, Klebold shot and killed Isaiah Shoels and Matthew Kechter, both of whom were athletes at Columbine. He then shot and killed John Tomlin. The last two victims killed in the library were Daniel Mauser and Corey DePooter, though it was unclear which shooter had fired the fatal shots. In addition to those killed in the library, another 12 students were wounded. One student, John Savage, was spared when he came face to face with Klebold, with whom he was acquainted.

The Cultural Impact of Columbine

Though the Columbine High School shootings lasted less than one hour, the impact the event has had on U.S. culture has been far more longstanding.

Though not the first of its kind, Columbine set the precedent for how we think about mass violence in schools. The shooting served as a "call to arms" for changes in school security. Following the shootings, schools across the nation were equipped with metal detectors, armed resource officers, mandatory identification cards, and zero-tolerance policies. Columbine also ignited a heated discourse about gun control, when it was revealed that the killers were able to acquire their guns through straw purchases at local gun shows. Over 800 pieces of legislation nationwide were introduced in the first year after Columbine, with many pieces aimed at closing this "gun show loophole." Though the school would reopen, the memory of April 20, 1999, lingers.

The shooters then left the library, first exchanging fire with the school resource office and arriving law enforcement through the west doors, and then wandering through the school's hallways igniting pipe bombs. They returned to the cafeteria around 11:44 a.m., at which time Harris attempted to detonate the propane tank bombs by shooting at them. When that did not work, Klebold threw a pipe bomb toward the larger device, though that also failed to detonate the propane tanks. Several other devices were ignited, setting off the school's fire alarms and sprinklers. Their actions in the cafeteria were captured on surveillance cameras, footage from which was later released.

Harris and Klebold then left the cafeteria, wandering the school for several minutes, before returning back to the cafeteria around noon. They then headed back upstairs to the library, where they engaged in a shootout with law enforcement officers who were providing cover for paramedics. After several minutes, Harris and Klebold retreated to an area of the library away from their earlier killings. Around 12:08 p.m., the pair committed suicide with gunshots to the head.

A lengthy investigation into the shootings revealed that Harris and Klebold had meticulously planned the attack. Documents left behind by the shooters, including Web postings, personal journals, and video diaries, indicated that the pair also had intended not only on a much higher death toll, but also had written about hijacking a plane and crashing it into the skyline in New York City. Since 2001, an extensive amount of information related to the investigation, including over 26,000 pages of documents, has been released by the Jefferson County Sheriff's Office. Other critical pieces of information, including the Basement Tapes, said to be Harris and Klebold's call to arms for other school shooters, remain sealed.

JACLYN SCHILDKRAUT

See also: Aurora (CO) Movie Theater Shooting (July 20, 2012); Lanza, Adam Peter (1992–2012); Virginia Tech Massacre (April 16, 2007); Weise, Jeffrey (1988–2005); *Primary Documents*/Columbine High School Shootings: Excerpts from the Report of the Governor's Review Commission (2001)

Further Reading

Columbine Review Commission. 2001. "The Report of Governor Bill Owens' Columbine Review Commission." Denver, CO: State of Colorado.

Cullen, Dave. 2009. *Columbine*. New York: Hachette.

Jefferson County Sheriff's Office. 2000. Columbine High School Shootings, April 20, 1999. *The Jefferson County Sheriff's Office Report* [CD-ROM].

Larkin, Ralph W. 2007. *Comprehending Columbine*. Philadelphia, PA: Temple University Press.

Coo, Eva (1889–1935)

Eva Coo was the fifth woman to be executed in New York State for first-degree murder of her 52-year-old handy man, Harry "Gimpy" Wright. Eva Curry was born January 17, 1889, in Halliburton, Ontario, to father Albert Paterson Curry and Margaret McDonald Watt. She was married to a railroad worker, William Coo, but separated from him when she moved to New York in 1921. From 1928 to 1934 she had owned a road stand in Collierville Oneonta, New York, that was called "Little Eva's Place." During Prohibition, this small bar was a speakeasy, serving alcohol and allegedly providing female services to the people who frequented the place. In 1931 Harry "Gimpy" Wright moved into Little Eva's Place when his mother passed away. Eva let him move in after he gave her some of his mother inheritance (approximately $2,000). He worked as a handy man around the bar but also had a tendency to drink too much and walk down Route 7 until other staff and customer would find him and bring him back.

In 1933 Martha Clift, originally from Pennsylvania, went to work in Little Eva's Place and became friends with Eva even though she was close to 10 years younger than her. In June 1934 Coo reported Wright missing from the bar. Police found him dead by the highway around half a mile away from Little Eva's Place. This led the investigators to believe he was hit and killed by a driver.

However, the next day Coo went to Met Life Insurance Company in Oneonta to cash out on an insurance policy on Wright's life. It was later found that Eva had a total of 16 insurance policies on Wright ($7,000–12,000). The insurance company did process the claim, but then reported their suspicions to the police. Along with the allegations that Coo and Clift were trespassing on Crumhorn Mountain, there was enough evidence to open an investigation.

On June 21, 1934, Coo and Clift were brought in for questioning by District Attorney Donald Grant and the local police. Both women accused each other. Coo verbally accused Clift with running over Wright and Clift physically signing a document accusing Coo. The police focused more on Coo due to the fact that she was the beneficiary of Wright's life insurance. In Clift's first statement, Coo hit Wright with the car while Clift and Wright were out of the car and Wright had his back to the car. During her interrogation, it is alleged that the police brought both women to the scene of the crime at Crumhorn Mountain and exhumed Wright's corpse to be a prop in the interrogations. In addition, the police searched Coo's house without a warrant to discover that she had taken out more life insurance policies on friends and staff (crimelibrary.com).

On June 24, 2014, Clift changed her story to incorporate the mallet, the symbol of the trial for the media. She stated that Coo first hit Wright with a mallet and then Clift ran him over with the car. Both women collaborated this story, but Coo said there was no premeditation, while Clift signed saying there was. Clift also explained that she was an accomplice for $200 and that they spent two to three months planning this murder.

The trial began in August 1934 in Cooperstown, New York. The trial was a large media hit with people selling souvenirs. The trial was three weeks (17 days) and 16 defense witnesses testified (*New York Times*, September 6, 1934) and 74 state witnesses (wegoback.wordpress.com). The trial involved many of Eva's staff boarders testifying, with one testifying that the two women were at Crumhorn Mountain, another testifying about Clift's discussion about the car. Wright's body was again exhumed for police to study his wounds. The autopsy proved that the story both women stated could not be entirely true. The autopsy showed that Wright was crushed between two objects with strange markings on his neck. His wounds did not lead the doctor to believe he was run over or smashed by a mallet. However, no other story came to light to explain these and so the trial went forth with the second story Clift told as the correct one. For Clift to testify against Coo, she was granted prison time for second-degree murder. Coo was found guilty, and sentenced to death for first-degree murder on September 10, 1935.

Her defense lawyers put in a notice of appeal that did successfully postpone the execution from October 15, 1934, to June 27, 1935 because Coo was not informed of her right to counsel during her interrogations. Clift was sentenced to 20 years at Bedford Reformatory, but was released after 13 years and returned to her two children.

Eva Coo was executed at Sing Sing at 11:00 p.m. on June 27, 2014. Executioner Robert G. Elliot wrote this notation for her death "New York June 27–1935–11 P.M. 9 Amp. Eva Coo #89508–42 years" (Elliot p., 279). Her last words were to the matrons who walked her to the electric chair "Good bye Darlings," which became iconic words for future writings, plays, and words about Coo.

A few believed her trial was a farce that disregarded most of her rights as a defendant. In one quote from Warden Lewis E. Lane, he stated, "I don't know if she was innocent or guilty. But I do know that she got a rotten deal all around, rotten . . . And I'm not defending her-she may be guilty as well, but she got a raw deal. Her trial attorneys—do you know what they did to help her lately? Know what? One of them wrote to me, saying he'd like four invitations to her execution. That's the kind of defense she had" (Nash 1981, 96). Her family did not recover the body and she was buried in a potter's field.

ELIZABETH BUSH

See also: Allen, Wanda Jean (1959–2001); Barfield, Velma (1932–1984); Buenoano, Judy (1943–1998); Lewis, Teresa (1969–2010); Riggs, Christina (1971–2000); Tucker, Karla Faye (1959–1998); Wuornos, Aileen (1956–2002)

Further Reading

Gado, Mark. 2008. *Death Row Women: Murder, Justice, and the New York Press*. Westport, CT: Greenwood Publishing.
Nash, Robert. 1981. *Look for the Woman*. New York: M. Evans and Co.
"Two Women Held in Auto Slaying." 1934. *New York Times*. June 21: 48.
"Women Ran Over Man in Death Plot." 1934. *New York Times*. June 24: 13.

Cooney, Celia (1904–1992)

Celia Roth Cooney, the so-called Bobbed Haired Bandit, the gun-wielding outlaw went on a crime spree throughout New York in 1924. The 1920s are often historically known for the Harlem Renaissance, the jazz age, and the flapper daughters of upper-class society. Flappers were known for their disdain of conventional behavioral standards and their bobbed hairstyles. The account of a witness to a crime committed by Celia Cooney sealed her media and literary fate when he described a female offender with bobbed hair. It would not be long before New York and all of America would be calling Celia Cooney the Bobbed Haired Bandit.

Celia Cooney and her husband Edward were a young couple from Brooklyn that shared great aspirations for a better life. Their aspirations became intensified when they learned that she was pregnant. Early in 1924 on a Saturday, Cooney officially began her criminal career by robbing a local grocery store. Her reputation as a female serial robber was established when she committed more robberies over the next two weeks. Arguably, economics and financial profit were the primary motivations for Celia

Celia Cooney and Edward Cooney pose for the camera after pleading guilty to various crimes in 1924. The couple was sentenced to 10 years in prison. (Library of Congress)

Cooney's crime spree. That being said, newspapers and other journalists twisted the facts to fit whatever narrative they were trying to push to the public. Newspapers and the public became fascinated with the bobbed haired and gun-wielding female robber. Simultaneously, the New York Police Department and the mayor of New York City, John Hylan, tried to downplay the circumstances and details of the robberies. However, the newspapers of New York City continued to sensationalize the actions of Cooney.

Early into Cooney's crime spree the police arrested a young female named Helen Quigley, claiming that she was the bobbed haired bandit. Police specifically identified her as the "feminine gun terror" of New York. Shortly thereafter, Cooney made headlines by robbing a drugstore of $50. Furthermore, casting much doubt on the authenticity of Helen Quigley as the bobbed haired bandit, Cooney left a derisive message for the New York Police. Cooney addressed the police as "dirty fish peddling bums" and provocatively taunted, "Leave this innocent girl alone and get the right ones which is nobody else but us" (Duncombe and Mattson 2006, 42–43).

Initially, officials did not think that a woman was capable of committing the robberies. In fact, multiple transgendered individuals were brought in to be questioned by police. Then, possibly due to the awareness of the public and the apparent need for a visible response to the bobbed haired bandit, law enforcement officials began questioning any female with bobbed hair found to be involved in crime. Any woman alleged to have committed a crime during Cooney's crime spree made newspaper headlines as suspicion concerning the identity of the bobbed haired bandit intensified. To make matters worse for New York law enforcement officials, Cooney's crime spree took place during the height of an early 1920s crime wave that had swept through the region. Thus, she was not the only bandit, or even the only female, committing crimes in Brooklyn and the other boroughs.

On April 1, 1924, Cooney and her husband attempted a daring broad daylight robbery of the National Biscuit Company payroll office. This heist ended with Edward Cooney shooting and injuring a cashier and Celia somehow dropping an incriminating notebook while fleeing. Witnesses from the National Biscuit Company further confirmed what newspapers had already suggested: the bobbed haired bandit was pregnant.

It did not take long for law enforcement officers to catch up with Cooney after she and her husband had fled south to Florida. She was apprehended and brought into official custody on April 21, 1924. Two days later, thousands of people would crowd the Pennsylvania Station in New York for a chance to see the notorious bobbed haired bandit when she arrived. Noticeably not present when she arrived was the characteristic bobbed hair or a baby. She explained that she had let her hair grow out after her first haircut. Her baby had been born and died while they were fleeing and hiding from law enforcement authorities.

The Bobbed Haired Bandit's narrative is completely dependent on the perspective of whoever is telling it. To some, Celia Cooney was a victim of circumstances or a starlet in some kind of 1920s reality-based romantic tragedy. To others, she was a bandit gungirl that was a menace to society. The newspapers spun their stories of Celia Cooney as a tragic romance, a feminist hero, and even a female Robin Hood. However, Cooney would later explain that poverty and her personal aspirations to provide a better life for her child provided more than enough motivation for her actions. In fact, the money she stole in her first robbery was allegedly used to get a new apartment and better furniture. Newspapers had benefitted greatly from the headlines of the bobbed haired bandit despite Cooney's rather mundane version of events and lack of bobbed hair.

There was not a happy conclusion to the story of Celia Cooney as the bobbed haired bandit. She and her husband were sentenced to 10 years in prison for their crimes. Cooney and her husband were released from prison in November 1931 after serving seven years. The couple were reunited and would soon have two sons. However, Edward Cooney had lost one of his hands in prison and been battling tuberculosis. He would die in 1936, leaving Celia to raise her two sons as a single mother. Celia Cooney hid her legacy as the Bobbed Haired Bandit from her sons until her final days. Shortly before her death in 1992 she confessed to her sons that she had once been the most notorious female criminal in New York during the 1920s.

Cooney came of age during the Roaring Twenties and the era of the New York "newspaper wars." A crime story was big news in the 1920s and helped sell a lot of newspapers. Furthermore, the story of the "Bobbed Haired Bandit" was touted by some papers as a story of a rebellious and attractive female criminal, which only helped to fuel the intrigue of the public. Her crime spree, without the media's coverage, could be interpreted as rather predictable, at times mundane, and fairly routine. That being said, she was a 1920s media darling comparable to contemporary female offenders such as Jodi Arias, Casey Anthony, and Debra LaFave. All of these female offenders, including

Celia Cooney, committed crimes that may have never received media coverage, or received the extreme amount of coverage that they did, had it not been for them being female. Thus, the story of Celia Cooney is not just a story of one of the most notorious crime sprees of the last century, but it is also a story of newspapers and a police department's response to media scrutiny and journalism. Additionally, Celia Cooney serves as a perfect example of a woman that clashed with society's conventional views of appearance, behavior, gender, and crime.

DANIEL RYAN KAVISH

See also: Anthony, Casey, Murder Trial of (May 24–July 5, 2011); Arias, Jodi (1980–); Parker, Bonnie (1910–1934) and Clyde Barrow (1909–1934)

Further Reading

Barbas, Samantha. 2006. "Book Review of the Bobbed Haired Bandit: A True Story of Crime and Celebrity in 1920s New York." *The Journal of American History* 93: 919.

Duncombe, Stephen, and Andrew Mattson. 2006. *The Bobbed Haired Bandit: A True Story of Crime and Celebrity in 1920s New York*. New York: New York University Press.

Miller, April. 2011. "Bloody Blondes and Bobbed-Haired Bandits: The Execution of Justice and the Construction of the Celebrity Criminal in the 1920s Popular Press." In Su Holmes and Diane Negra (eds.). *In the Limelight and Under the Microscope Forms and Functions of Female Celebrity*. New York: Continuum International Publishing Group.

Cooper, D. B., Airplane Hijacking (November 24, 1971)

On November 24, 1971, Northwest Orient Airlines flight 305 was hijacked by a man known only by his alias of D. B. Cooper. The hijacker bought his ticket under the name of Dan Cooper, but a reporter misunderstood the name, causing initial media reports to misidentify him as D. B. After receiving $200,000 in cash, Cooper parachuted from the airplane over the state of Washington. Despite investigating more than 1,000 suspects, the incident still remains an unsolved skyjacking. The identity of D. B. Cooper has never been discovered.

A man identifying himself as Dan Cooper purchased a one-way ticket from Portland to Seattle in November 1971. The employee who sold him the ticket did not recall Cooper exhibiting any nervous behavior. He was described by witnesses as appearing businesslike. Dressed in a dark rain coat, dark suit, and black tie, Cooper carried an attaché case as he boarded the flight. He took the center seat in row 18, the last row of the aircraft, lit a cigarette, and ordered a bourbon and soda. There were 36 passengers and 6 crew members on board.

Shortly after the airplane began taxiing along the runway, Cooper handed a note to flight attendant Florence Schaffner. Schaffner put the note in her purse without looking at it. Cooper told Schaffner that she should look at the note, which she did. Written in black ink, the note read, "MISS, I have a bomb here and I would like you to sit by me" (Gray 2011, 25). Cooper then opened the bag, exposing wire, a battery, and six red sticks. Schaffner showed the note to another flight attendant, Tina Mucklow, who notified the cockpit that the flight had been hijacked. The plane was already in the air.

Upon Cooper's request, Schaffner dictated his instructions as he told them to her. "I want two hundred grand by 5:00 p.m. In cash. Put in a knapsack. I want two back parachutes and two front parachutes. When we land, I want a fuel truck ready to refuel. No funny stuff or I'll do the job. No fuss" (Gray 2011, 39). Schaffner delivered this note to the pilot; upon her return, Cooper was wearing dark sunglasses. He further instructed the pilots not to alert the other passengers to the situation. Because Cooper did not want the plane to land until the money and parachutes were ready at the airport, the pilot told the passengers that they had to circle Seattle due to a minor mechanical issue.

When the plane landed, flight attendant Tina Mucklow exited first and retrieved the $200,000 from law enforcement waiting on the tarmac. The bag of $20 bills weighed 21 pounds. The serial numbers on the bills had been recorded but no ink pack or other device was put into the bag. The flight attendant returned to the plane and gave the bag to Cooper. Cooper then told Mucklow to allow the other passengers to exit the plane.

After all of the passengers had left, Cooper ordered the pilot to fly to Mexico City. He specified that the plane maintain an altitude of no more than 10,000 feet and a relatively slow speed. After the plane took off, Cooper ordered the flight attendants to turn off the cabin lights and go to the cockpit, leaving him alone at the back of the plane. As flight attendant Tina Mucklow closed the curtain to first class, she saw Cooper tying the money bag to his person using rope from one of the parachutes. This is the last time anyone saw the man known as D. B. Cooper.

While in flight, instrumentation in the cockpit indicated that the plane's aft stairs had been released. Mucklow called back into the cabin to advise Cooper that the plane had to land to refuel, but received no response. Upon landing, Cooper was nowhere to be found. It is believed that he opened the aft stairs and parachuted from the airplane with the money.

The fate of D.B. Cooper remains unknown. Some people believe that he must have died during his jump from the plane. He parachuted at nighttime into an area of rugged terrain consisting of forests, canyons, and lakes, in addition to wild animals. The weather conditions at the time were not conducive to parachuting due to wind and stormy weather. Others believe that he survived the fall and got away with the $200,000.

Who Was D. B. Cooper?

Though no one was ever charged for the November 1971 hijacking of Northwest Orient Airlines flight 305, a few individuals have raised suspicion. Barb Dayton, a former pilot, reportedly confessed to her friends. Dayton died in 2002, and the FBI has never officially commented on her. Duane Weber confessed to his wife on his deathbed that he was Dan Cooper. Weber was ruled out as a suspect after his DNA and fingerprints failed to match those recovered from the plane. William Wolfgang Gossett, a former army paratrooper, fell under suspicion after his sons indicated he had confessed before his death in 2003. Gossett fit the physical description of D.B. Cooper, and served in the Korean and Vietnam Wars. Finally, Richard McCoy became a suspect after committing a similar hijacking four months after the Cooper event. He had an alibi for the time of the hijacking.

The identity of D.B. Cooper remains as much of a mystery as his fate. Some believe that Cooper was an employee of the airline, based on his knowledge of airline protocol and of the plane itself. They believe that the plane was chosen because it had the aft stairs necessary for Cooper's escape. This position was refuted by Northwest Orient employees, who indicated that they would have recognized him if he was an employee. Another theory hypothesizes that Cooper was a member of the military, specifically from a paratroopers unit. The parachute used by Cooper is one associated with military use rather than civilian use, and was more difficult to maneuver. Some believe that he

lived in the Washington area, based on his ability to identify the Tacoma area to a flight attendant while in the air.

In 1980, an eight-year-old boy found $5,800 in twenties buried in a bag near the Columbia River. The boy had been enjoying a picnic with his family on Tena Bar, a sand bar that runs along the river's north shore, when he came across the money while looking for firewood. The family notified authorities, who used the serial numbers to confirm that this money matched that which had been given to Cooper. The money was found about 40 miles south of where federal agents predicted Cooper had jumped from the aircraft.

As a result of the hijacking, airplanes were redesigned and security procedures were enhanced to prevent similar crimes. Two years after the incident, the Federal Aviation Agency (FAA) began requiring screenings of passengers and luggage. A device known as the Cooper vane was developed to prevent the aft stairs from being released during flight. Many airlines simply sealed the deployable staircases on their planes.

The true identity of the hijacker of Northwest Orient Airline flight 305 remains a mystery. Tips are still being sent to investigators by people who claim that their family member or friend committed the hijacking; however, none of these tips have resulted in an arrest. Public interest and speculation in the case continues.

SHANNON N. CUNNINGHAM

See also: Cassidy, Butch (1866–1908); O'Connell, John, Jr., Kidnapping of (1933); Sinatra, Frank, Jr., Kidnapping of (1963)

Further Reading

Gray, Geoffrey. 2011. *Skyjack: The Hunt for D.B. Cooper*. New York: Crown Publishers.

Rhodes, Bernie, and Russell Calame. 1991. *D.B. Cooper: The Real McCoy*. Salt Lake City, UT: University of Utah Press.

Cooper, Kevin. *See* Chino Hills (CA) Murders (June 4, 1983)

Copeland, Fay. *See* Copeland, Ray (1914–1993) and Faye Copeland (1921–2003)

Copeland, Ray (1914–1993) and Faye Copeland (1921–2003)

Ray and Faye Copeland, also known as the American Gothic Killers, became the oldest couple ever sentenced to death in the United States; Ray Copeland was 76 at the time of his sentencing and Faye Copeland was 69 at the time of her sentencing. Faye was the oldest woman on death row until her sentence was commuted to life in prison in 1999. Ray and Faye Copeland were charged with the murders of Paul Jason Cowart, John W. Freeman, Jimmie Dale Harvey, Wayne Warner, and Dennis Murphy, all drifters who had worked for the Copelands during the 1980s. It is suggested that the Copelands may have killed at least seven more drifters, although bodies have never been recovered. This case has been documented in an episode of *Forensic Files* and in an episode of *Wicked Attraction*, called *Murder at Twilight*. Additionally, a play written by David Wiltse that appeared off Broadway in 2004, called *Temporary Help*, was also based on this case.

Ray Copeland was born in Oklahoma on December 30, 1914, to Jess and Laney Copeland. His family moved around a lot, eventually settling in Ozark Hills, Arkansas. He had a hard childhood and dropped out of school in the fourth grade to help his family with their farm. Ray was rumored to be a spoiled child; even though he came from a poor family, if he wanted something, his parents would get it for him through whatever means necessary. Ray began stealing during the Great Depression, when he was about 20 years old. He was arrested two years later for forgery. He went on to have a long history of crimes that ranged from petty theft to grand larceny. He was convicted of writing bad checks on numerous occasions.

Faye Copeland was born on August 4, 1921, in Harrison, Arkansas, to Rufus and Gladys Wilson. She and Ray started dating and six months later they were married. Within a year, the couple had their first child, Everett. Two years later they had another son, Billy Ray. In 1944, the Copeland's moved to Fresno County, California. Faye had a baby girl, Betty Lou, the following year. Two years later, a son, Alvia, was born and two years after that, in 1949, their last son, William Wayne, was born. In 1949, after the birth of their last child, Ray was accused of stealing horses. No charges were filed, but his reputation in Fresno County was ruined, so Ray moved his family back to Arkansas. Once back in Arkansas, Ray was quickly arrested for cattle theft, found guilty, and sentenced to a year in jail. Once he finished his sentence, Ray moved his family to Rocky Comfort, Missouri, where he was arrested for cattle theft again and sentenced to manual labor at the judge's farm. Beginning in 1953, the Copelands moved around a lot and Ray was arrested at least five more times for writing bad checks. Finally, during the summer of 1966, the Copelands moved back to Missouri where they bought a small 40-acre farm in Mooresville.

Ray Copeland's reputation in Mooresville was not a good one. Residents viewed Ray as a menace who was abusive toward his wife and children. He was rude to waitresses and many residents noted that they had seen him intentionally run over dogs. For three years, local authorities had been tracking bad checks passed by transients who worked for the Copelands. Ray Copeland and his hired man attended cattle auctions where they would bid well out of their price range. Once they won the auction, the hired man would write a bad check and the twosome would leave with the cattle. The cattle were sold and the hired man would be gone by the time it was clear that the check had bounced. From 1986 to the summer of 1989, at least 12 men had worked with Copeland and $32,000 had been stolen. When questioned, Copeland stated that he did not know what became of the workers and told authorities that they had also written him bad checks.

In September 1989, Jack McCormick, one of Copeland's former hired men, was tracked down by police in Oregon. McCormick offered police details of Copeland's cattle auction scheme. According to McCormick, the two would go to cattle auctions where McCormick would bid on the cattle that Copeland wanted and McCormick would write the checks. McCormick fled when Copeland allegedly pointed a .22 rifle to his head. Ray and Faye Copeland were eventually caught and charged with murder when an anonymous drifter told police that he saw human remains on the Copelands' property. Some reports state that bodies of the murdered men were found buried in shallow graves around the Copelands' farm, but other reports state that the bodies were found 12 miles away on a farm in Ludlow, Missouri, where Copeland would sometimes work. Autopsy reports determined that each man had been shot in the back of the head with a .22 rifle. According to reports, Faye apparently made a handmade quilt out of the dead men's clothing.

On November 1, 1990, Faye Copeland, who was 69 years old at the time, went on trial for the murders of five drifters. Ray Copeland had allegedly concocted a scheme where he would hire drifters, have them pay for cattle with bad checks, and then the drifters would be killed when they were no longer useful. According to the defense and to Faye Copeland, she had no knowledge of the murders and she stuck to this story even after being offered a deal for lesser charges in exchange for information about the remaining missing men. The defense also argued that she suffered from battered woman syndrome. Although it was clear that Faye Copeland was a victim of domestic violence, she was convicted on four counts of murder and one of manslaughter and she was sentenced to death by lethal injection on April 27, 1991. According to the prosecution, Faye had written a list of the names of drifters and each of the murdered drifters had an X next to his name.

On August 10, 2002, while in prison, Faye Copeland suffered a stroke from which she was partially paralyzed and rendered unable to speak. In September 2002, Governor Holden granted medical parole for Faye and she was paroled to a nursing home. On December 30, 2003, Faye Copeland, who was 82 years old, died at the Morning Center nursing home in Chillicothe, Missouri, from natural causes. She was survived by five children, 17 grandchildren, and approximately 25 great-grandchildren.

On March 1, 1991, when Ray Copeland went to trial, he first tried to plea insanity but he eventually gave up. He then tried to work out a plea agreement with the prosecution, but the prosecution was not interested. As such, Ray Copeland was also sentenced to death, but he died in prison of natural causes on October 19, 1993.

SARA B. SIMMONS

See also: Bundy, Ted (1946–1989); Holmes, Dr. H.H. (1861–1896); Ridgway, Gary Leon (1949–)

Further Reading

Flowers, R. Barri, and H. Loraine Flowers. 2001. *Murders in the United States: Crimes, Killers, and Victims of the Twentieth Century.* Jefferson, NC: McFarland and Company.

Greig, Charlotte. 2012. *Serial Killers: Horrifying True-Life Cases of Pure Evil.* London: Arcturus Publishing.

Miller, Tom. 1993. *The Copeland Killings: The Bizarre True Account of Ray and Faye Copeland, The Oldest Couple Ever Sentenced to Death in America.* New York: Pinnacle Books.

Corona, Juan (1934–)

Juan Vallejo Corona, a native of Mexico, came to the United States as a teenager and a couple of decades later he would be convicted of more killings than any other murderer at the time of his conviction. "The Machete Murderer" committed at least 25 murders in California before being apprehended on May 26, 1971. His victims were drifters and migrant field workers with very little ties to the local community. Their bodies, found hacked to pieces by a machete, were discovered in graves that had been dug on the properties of local landowners. Corona's killing spree took place around the same time that usage of the term "serial killer" in America became prevalent. No man would be convicted of more murders than Corona until 1980 when John Wayne Gacy was convicted of killing 33 individuals. In fact, more murders have been attributed to Corona than have been attributed to Charles Manson and The Boston Strangler combined.

Corona entered the United States in 1950 at the age of 16 and worked in the farming region of Imperial Valley as a fieldworker picking produce such as carrots and melons. From there he moved to the Sacramento Valley before settling in the Yuba City area early in the summer of 1953. He started as a simple fieldworker, and in time, became a labor contractor in charge of hiring other fieldworkers for the local farms. Corona married Gloria Moreno in 1959, and they had four daughters together. He had achieved occupational success and effectively provided for his family despite having been diagnosed with schizophrenia early in 1956. The DeWitt State Hospital treated him with over two dozen electroconvulsive shock treatments. Early in 1970 Corona was again committed to DeWitt State Hospital for schizophrenic and paranoid behavior. The bodies of his victims were discovered a little over a year after this second hospital commitment.

Corona's job provided him with a plethora of potential victims. The fieldworkers that he encountered on a daily basis generally lived migrant lifestyles, had few ties to the local community, had no family, or were alcoholics. He would find the migrant fieldworkers housing on Sullivan ranch. It was not uncommon for individuals to vanish without others taking notice or being concerned. In fact, these incidences were common enough that there was no reason to report them to authorities. Corona's victims were discovered by police because local ranchers had reported finding holes freshly dug on their properties. The first body discovered was that of Kenneth Whitacre. The property owner reported discovering a freshly dug hole the day prior. He became suspicious and called law enforcement when he returned to find the hole filled. Shortly thereafter, another fresh grave and victim was discovered. In time, law enforcement officials would discover a total of 25 victims in nearby graves. Whitacre had been stabbed and his head torn apart by a machete. The second victim discovered, Charles Fleming, was found sodomized and also severely disfigured by a machete.

Corona dug the makeshift graves prior to selecting and killing his victims. He sexually assaulted and stabbed those he attacked. His aggression and violence sometimes escalated to include further acts such as possibly shooting his victims and slashing the back of their heads. He sometimes pulled their shirts over their faces or removed their pants in addition to the acts of violence he perpetrated. For the most part, there was a pattern to his killings. First, he dug the graves. Then, he selected his victims and brutally murdered them. Finally, he would bury them in the hole. Some authors have noted that Corona's serial killings could have carried on for a longer time had it not been for the original farmers who had been suspicious of the strange fresh holes on their property.

The trail of evidence was traced directly back to Juan Corona because some of the victims' bodies had been discovered along with receipts signed by Corona and bank documents labeled with his name and address. Also, witnesses reported last seeing some of the victims riding in Corona's truck. Finally, Corona was apprehended and a search warrant executed on his home in Yuba City. Seized from his home during the search were knives, clothing, a wooden club, a meat cleaver, and a machete, some of which were stained with blood. Also seized during the search was what some authors have referred to as a "kill list." Contrary to the menacing nickname applied to this piece of evidence, this was merely a ledger for work that listed the names of 34 individuals. Seven of the individuals listed on the work ledger had been Corona's victims.

Corona's first attorney was a court-appointed public defender named Roy Van den Heuvel. Within a month Van den Heuvel was replaced as Corona's attorney with a private defense attorney named Richard Hawk. In exchange for his representing Corona, Hawk was granted exclusive rights to Corona's life's story. He put forth a standard not guilty defense for Corona and did not attempt to argue insanity or call any psychiatrists for the defense. The trial lasted roughly three months, and the jury deliberated for about 45 hours. Corona was found guilty of all 25 counts of first-degree murder on January 18, 1973. The death sentence was not available at that time, so Judge Richard Patton sentenced Corona to 25 life imprisonment terms without the possibility of parole.

In 1973, Corona was attacked by other inmates while in prison and was stabbed many times. His wife, Gloria, divorced him in 1974. Almost four years later, in May 1978,

Corona's murder convictions were overturned by the California Court of Appeals. The court concluded that Corona's legal defense during the first trial had been incompetent. He received a new trial because his defense in the first trial did not attempt the insanity defense or argue that Corona's schizophrenia was a mitigating factor. Corona's second trial took place in 1982, this time he was represented by Terence Hallinan. Hallinan put forth a much more thorough defense of Corona. The trial lasted about twice as long as the first trial as Hallinan called many witnesses for Corona's defense, including calling Corona himself to the stand. However, Hallinan's thorough defense of Corona failed to produce a different outcome than the original trial. Juan Corona, once again, was found guilty of all 25 counts of first-degree murder. He was returned to prison to serve the remainder of his sentence. Due to correctional reforms, and despite the terms of his imprisonment being stipulated to be served consecutively, Corona has actually been eligible for parole hearings on six separate occasions. Corona has been denied parole each time.

Juan Corona, "The Machete Murderer," was convicted of more killings than any other murderer had been at the time of his conviction. He committed at least 25 murders in California before being arrested, but it is possible there were more victims that went undiscovered. It is possible because his victims were drifters and very little is known about his life in Mexico prior to coming to the United States of America. His infamy continues to be discussed by scholars not only because of the amount of murders he committed, but also because of the brutality of his crimes.

DANIEL RYAN KAVISH

See also: Boston Strangler Murders (1962–1964); Dahmer, Jeffrey (1960–1994); Gacy, John Wayne (1942–1994); Manson, Charles (1934–)

Further Reading

Cray, Ed. 1973. *Burden of Proof: The Case of Juan Corona.* New York: Macmillan.
Kidder, Tracy. 1974. *The Road to Yuba City: A Journey into the Juan Corona Murders.* New York: Doubleday.

Costello, Frank (1891–1973)

Frank Costello, the "Prime Minister of the Underworld," was a powerful and influential mobster who headed the Genovese crime family in New York from 1937 to 1957. Costello, born Francesco Castiglia in Lauropoli, Calabria,

Italy, in 1891, immigrated to New York in 1900. He became involved in neighborhood gang activities. While working for the Morello gang, Costello met Charlie "Lucky" Luciano. They became friends and business associates, forming partnerships with Italian American mobsters like Vito Genovese and Joe Adonis, but also Jewish ones like Meyer Lansky and Benjamin "Bugsy" Siegel. Costello became known as a "thinking man's criminal," preferring to use brains, rather than brawn, to generate business.

Costello and his cohorts, with Jewish mobster Arnold Rothstein's backing, turned toward bootlegging after Prohibition passed in 1920. Breaking the traditions of "Moustache Petes," Old World mafiosi who disdained alliances with non-Italians (and even non-Sicilians), they partnered with criminals regardless of ethnic background. After "Big Bill" Dwyer went to prison in 1926, Costello, with Owney "the Killer" Madden, took over Dwyer's rumrunning operations. Vannie Higgins, Dwyer's associate, contested Costello's involvement, thereby igniting the Manhattan beer wars. Arthur "Dutch Schultz" Flegenheimer supported Costello after Higgins assisted Schultz's rivals, Jack "Legs" Diamond and Vincent "Mad Dog" Coll. In 1927, Costello, Luciano, and Chicago mobster Johnny Torrio organized multiple East Coast rumrunners into one operation. Two years later, they and New Jersey mobster Enoch "Nucky" Johnson hosted an Atlantic City convention uniting underworld figures and make steps toward broader cooperation.

In New York, Salvatore Maranzano challenged Giuseppe Masseria's mafia supremacy. A gang war, known as the Castellammarese War (since Maranzano and his

New York gangster and mob boss Frank Costello is called as a witness in the Senate hearing investigating crime committee's hearing in the U.S. courthouse, Foley Square. An uncooperative witness, Costello refused to be televised, or to answer questions about his finances. (Photo by NY Daily News Archive/Getty Images)

Sicilian faction originated from Castellammare del Golfo), erupted in 1929. Costello was among Masseria's faction, but he and allies on both sides sought peace; internal fighting was ruining business. Costello, Luciano, and their allies betrayed Masseria to Maranzano; Masseria was murdered in April 1931. Maranzano, "boss of all bosses," divided New York's mafia into five families. Costello became consigliere, or adviser, within Luciano's family. Costello and his associates then maneuvered against Maranzano, who was murdered in September 1931. Luciano assumed control of the Commission, a governing body of mafia bosses.

During the 1930s, Costello controlled slot machine and bookmaking operations. In 1934, Mayor Fiorello LaGuardia confiscated many of Costello's New York City slot machines. Costello successfully sued to get his money back from these machines, although the Internal Revenue Service (IRS) took much of it in taxes. Costello then negotiated a deal with Louisiana governor Huey Long to place his machines throughout Louisiana. New Orleans mafioso Carlos Marcello assisted Costello's efforts. In 1936, Luciano, imprisoned for running a prostitution ring, used Costello and Lansky to run his criminal organization. He eventually appointed Genovese the acting boss, but Genovese fled to Italy in 1937 to avoid murder charges. Consequently, Costello became the acting boss.

Costello invested widely in nightclubs and casinos, like the Piping Rock in Saratoga Springs, and discouraged drug trafficking. In 1940, Costello became a partner in the Copacabana, a famous New York City nightclub, with Monte Poser. Costello appointed Jules Podell to oversee his interests; Podell eventually became the club's official owner. The Latin-themed Copa became known for its chorus girls, who wore fruited turbans. The era's top entertainers, including Frank Sinatra, Sammy Davis Jr., and Dean Martin, performed there. Helping launch the Las Vegas strip, Costello was among the chief financiers in Siegel's constantly overbudget Las Vegas casino, the Flamingo, an undertaking that prompted Siegel's 1947 murder. Costello was also involved in the mafia's gambling and casino operations in Florida and Cuba, which stemmed from an agreement with the Cuban government that ended after Fidel Castro's Communist takeover. Costello continued to invest in legitimate businesses, including real estate, stocks, a television company, and meat supply firms.

Costello, consolidating his power in the 1940s, achieved a unique underworld status. He consorted with politicians, police brass, bankers, and judges. He allegedly reached an agreement with FBI director J. Edgar Hoover to ignore mafia activities. This cultivation of associations earned him the nickname "Prime Minister" in a 1947 *Collier's* article by Herbert Asbury, famed underworld chronicler whose works included *The Gangs of New York* (1928). With Luciano's 1946 deportation to Italy, Costello became America's top mafia figure. Genovese's murder charge, however, was dismissed. He immediately began plotting for Costello's position.

Costello in Mob Films

The Vito Corleone character in *The Godfather* book and 1972 film is a composite of various mafia figures, including Costello. The raspy voice that actor Marlon Brando used for Corleone in the film was patterned on Costello's voice, the result of a botched operation in his youth to singe polyps from his throat in which the doctor accidentally burned some vocal cords. Costello has also appeared as a character in many films, including *Mobsters* (1991). Further, his club, the Copa, inspired a 1978 Barry Manilow song and served as a setting in such mob films as *Goodfellas* (1991) and *Carlito's Way* (1993).

In 1950–1951, the U.S. Senate conducted an investigation of organized crime in interstate commerce. Known as the Kefauver Hearings, after the special committee's chairman, over 600 individuals testified before Congress; these testimonies were broadcast on television. Costello, casting off his street-crime origins, still hoped to attain legitimate respectability and status. To his chagrin, he emerged as the hearings' star attraction, billed as America's top mobster and de facto leader of New York's Tammany Hall. Costello did not invoke his Fifth Amendment rights, like most did, although he requested that his face not be televised. Consequently, only his hands were filmed. Costello skirted many questions, but when asked, "What have you done for your country?" he gave the famous reply, "Paid my tax!" He ultimately walked out on the hearings.

Such attention made him a law enforcement and media target; this proved to be his downfall. In 1952, Costello, convicted on contempt for walking out on the hearings, received an 18-month prison sentence. In 1954, he was convicted of tax evasion and received a five-year sentence that was overturned on appeal. In 1956, Adonis, Costello's ally, chose deportation to Italy over prison. In 1957, after Costello was again convicted, sentenced to prison, and released on appeal, Genovese made his move. Costello's remaining ally, Albert Anastasia, had assumed control of the family previously headed by Vincent Mangano. Genovese convinced Carlo Gambino, Anastasia's underboss, to conspire with him against Costello and Anastasia. Genovese's driver, Vincent Gigante, shot Costello in the head; Costello survived. Genovese called a meeting of Luciano family (now the Genovese family) members for them to show their support for his leadership. Anastasia was also murdered in 1957; Gambino took over the family and a Commission seat.

Costello made peace with Genovese and retired. Costello maintained most of his gambling operations and served as an unofficial underworld advisor. He died in 1973 and was interred at Saint Michael's Cemetery in East Elmhurst, New York. Carmine Galante, one of Costello's enemies, blasted his mausoleum's doors off after exiting prison in 1974.

Eric Martone

See also: Gigante, Vincent "the Chin" (1928–2005); Luciano, Charles "Lucky" (1897–1962); Schultz, Dutch (1901–1935)

Further Reading

Davis, John. 1994. *Mafia Dynasty*. New York: Harper Paperbacks.

Katz, Leonard. 1973. *Uncle Frank: The Biography of Frank Costello*. New York: Drake Publishers.

Wolf, George, with Joseph DiMona. 1974. *Frank Costello: Prime Minister of the Underworld*. New York: William Morrow.

Cotton, Ronald (1962–)

Ronald Cotton is a victim of mistaken identity. Cotton was convicted of rape and burglary charges, and spent over 10 years in prison. The primary evidence used against Cotton was eyewitness identification. The victim in the case, Jennifer Thompson, identified Ronald Cotton in a photo lineup and a live lineup, and he was subsequently charged and convicted. It was discovered later that the victim mistakenly identified Cotton, and, on June 30, 1995, he was officially cleared of all charges and released from prison. This case is celebrated for two important reasons. First, it is one of many examples that question the accuracy of eyewitness testimony. Second, the crime also provides a valuable lesson in forgiveness, as both Cotton and Thompson are friends and devoted to a common cause—raising

public awareness about the limits of eyewitness testimony (Thompson-Cannino 2004).

Thompson was raped in her home on July 27, 1984. Instead of trying to fight off her attacker, she decided to focus on gathering information about her attacker—she describes how she studied his face so she would be able to identify him (Thompson-Cannino 2004). She escaped out of the house, ran to a neighbor's home, and called the police. She was questioned about the attack, and taken to a local hospital, where a rape-kit was performed.

In the days following her attack, Jennifer Thompson consulted with a sketch artist to form a composite of her attacker. Ronald Cotton became a suspect when his coworker at a local restaurant contacted the police, suggesting that Cotton resembled the sketch of Thompson's attacker (Thompson-Cannino, Cotton, and Torneo 2009). Later, in both a photo and live lineup, she identified Ronald Cotton as her rapist.

Ronald Cotton was arrested and charged with multiple counts of rape and burglary. Bail was set high because of the seriousness of the allegations, and he remained in jail. He pled not guilty to all charges in November 1984, and his case went to trial in early January 1985. Jennifer Thompson's identification was the state's strongest evidence. Ronald Cotton's defense argued that there was little physical evidence, a suggestion that led to the conclusion that Cotton was not there. The defense suggested that the state's evidence was purely circumstantial and that it was a case of "mistaken identity." The defense suggested that Jennifer Thompson was "too stressed" to properly identify her attacker, but the defense was not allowed to introduce expert testimony about the problems with the identification (Thompson-Cannino, Cotton, and Torneo 2009). After four hours of deliberation, the jury returned with a guilty verdict. Ronald Cotton was sentenced to life in prison plus 50 years on January 18, 1985.

In 1985, Ronald Cotton was imprisoned outside Raleigh, North Carolina. He began writing letters to legal groups, TV stations, newspapers, and Phil Mosely, his attorney, claiming his innocence. He also heard rumors inside that the person who committed the rape was incarcerated with him. At the beginning of Cotton's second year in prison, he received news that the Supreme Court of North Carolina overturned his conviction because the court refused to allow evidence that the victim had picked another man in the lineup (Innocence Project 2013). He would again be tried for Jennifer Thompson's rape and the rape of another woman, who also had identified Cotton as her rapist (Innocence Project 2013). Prior to the beginning of Cotton's second trial, Bobby Poole disclosed to another inmate that he was the true perpetrator behind the crimes in question.

Ronald Cotton's new trial began in November 1987 with an all-white jury and white alternate jurors. Ronald Cotton was again found guilty of Thompson's rape and found guilty of the additional rape. In 1992, Cotton's appellate defender, Malcolm Hunter Jr. contacted Cotton, advising him that Richard Rosen had agreed to look into Cotton's case. Richard Rosen, an attorney and law professor, decided to handle Cotton's appeals and claims of innocence. Rosen spent years working the case, and after he analyzed the case materials, he had serious questions about the evidence, the trial proceedings, and the identification. Almost seven years after being found guilty at his second trial, the chief appellate defender filed an appropriate relief on the basis of inadequate counsel and also filed a motion for DNA testing of the original semen sample (Innocence Project 2013). The DNA did not match Ronald Cotton; it matched another known felon—Bobby Poole, the man Cotton had met in prison. On June 30, 1995, Cotton was officially cleared of all charges and released. One month later, the governor of North Carolina pardoned Cotton.

Ronald Cotton spent 11 years in prison for crimes he did not commit. The mistaken identification in this case raised serious questions about the reliability of eyewitness testimony. In addition, nearly two years after Cotton's release, Jennifer Thompson asked to meet Ronald Cotton because she felt extremely guilty about sending him to prison. It was an emotional meeting, and a special bond was soon formed between them (Thompson-Cannino, Cotton, and Torneo 2009). They also work together to raise awareness about mistaken identification and campaign for the rights of exonerees. Ronald Cotton was eligible to receive only $5,000 compensation from the state of North Carolina in exchange for his 11 years of imprisonment (Innocence Project 2013). Over the years, Cotton and Thompson have worked to increase compensation for exonerees in North Carolina, ultimately raising the amount to $20,000 per year (Innocence Project 2013). Ronald Cotton has since married, had children, and showed the extraordinary potential that those who knew him expected to see. Ronald Cotton and Jennifer Thompson are now close friends and are strong voices in the innocence movement. Bobby Poole died in prison.

KELSEY S. HENDERSON

See also: Adams, Randall Dale (1948–2010); Carter, Rubin "Hurricane" (1937–2014); Central Park Jogger Case (1989)

Further Reading

Innocence Project. 2013. http://www.innocenceproject.org/Content/Ronald_Cotton.php. Accessed April 14, 2015.

Public Broadcasting Service. 2013. "Interview of Richard Rosen." http://www.pbs.org/wgbh//pages/frontline//shows/dna/interviews/scheck.html. Accessed April 14, 2015.

Thompson-Cannino, Jennifer. 2004. "Reforming Eyewitness Identification: Convicting the Guilty, Protecting the Innocent." Symposium speech presented at the Benjamin N. Cardozo School of Law, New York, New York, September 12–13.

Thompson-Cannino, Jennifer, Ronald Cotton, and Erin Torneo. 2009. *Picking Cotton: Our Memoir of Injustice and Redemption.* New York: St. Martin's Press.

Countrywide Financial Mortgage Fraud. *See* Mozilo, Angelo (1938–)

Crafts, Helle, Murder of (1986)

On January 13, 1987, Richard Crafts was charged with killing his wife, Helle Crafts (1947–1986), and disposing of her remains using a chainsaw to dismember her body and a wood chipper to destroy and disperse her corpse. The case would become high profile and culturally significant owing to the gruesome details surrounding the homicide and the groundbreaking techniques used by the prosecution during the trial (Altimari 2014). Mere ounces of Helle Crafts's remains, consisting of hair, tissue, tooth fragments, and a painted toenail, were recovered (Altimari 2014). The trial of Richard Crafts is the first in Connecticut's history where a person was tried and subsequently found guilty of murder without the presence of a body (Zaretsky 1990).

The relationship between Richard and Helle Crafts began when the couple met in May 1969. At the time, Richard Crafts was an Eastern Airlines pilot, and Helle Crafts, originally from Denmark, was training to work as a flight attendant for Pan American. The pair was married on November 29, 1975. At his trial, Richard Crafts indicated that their marriage was somewhat obligatory as Helle was pregnant and "was too far along to have an abortion" (Tancrell 1988b p. 1). The two remained married for the next 10 years, had three children, and resided in Newtown, Connecticut. In the summer of 1986, Helle Crafts began to suspect that her husband might be engaging in extramarital affairs and questioned him about several long-distance phone calls that appeared on their phone bill. Richard Crafts forcefully ripped the bill out of hand. She then contacted Keith Mayo, a private detective, and requested that he uncover the origin of a New Jersey phone number.

Mayo traced the source of the phone number to a condominium located in Middletown, New Jersey, that belonged to an Eastern Airline flight attendant. During the trial, Mayo observed that Richard Crafts, on two separate occasions, spent the night (or nights) there with Nancy Dodd. Mayo obtained photographic evidence of Richard Craft embracing and kissing Dodd. He testified that when he presented Helle Crafts with these pictures, she cried uncontrollably (Tancrell 1988c). Within weeks, Helle Crafts filed for divorce. Richard Crafts testified that following her filing for divorce, Helle Crafts was "unhappy with my behavior" and that his wife told him "we didn't communicate enough to be married" (Tancrell 1988b p 1).

Helle Crafts was last seen on November 18, 1986. Upon her return from working on a flight, she was dropped off at her home by a friend and coworker. Richard Crafts would later tell police that following the morning after her return, Helle Crafts awoke early, got dressed, and simply informed him that she was leaving. On December 1, 1986, after being contacted by Anderson, Mayo called the Newtown Police to report Helle Crafts missing. According to Mayo, the police initially dismissed his assertion that Helle Crafts was missing, and responded that eventually she would return home to her husband. Helle Crafts, however, never returned home.

Upon the insistence of Mayo and Helle Crafts's friends and family, the state police launched an investigation and subsequently made a series of discoveries. One such revelation was that Richard Crafts spent $967.50 to rent a wood chipper from November 18 to 21. Richard Crafts had also purchased a new Ford pickup truck and had requested that it be equipped with a commercial grade hitch. An electrical fire on the inside of Richard Crafts's newly purchased pickup delayed the installation of the hitch, so the dealer made arrangements to allow Richard to use a U Haul truck that was equipped with a similar hitch.

Dr. Henry Lee

The Helle Crafts case is attributed with being pivotal for the career of the now-famous forensic scientist, Dr. Henry Lee. At the time of the investigation, Dr. Lee was well on his way in establishing a reputable forensics lab in Connecticut, but his assistance in linking key blood and trace evidence in the Crafts case brought him into the international spotlight. The work conducted by Dr. Lee during the Crafts investigation introduced the important role of science in criminal investigations. Since his work on the Crafts case, Dr. Lee has consulted on many high-profile criminal cases, including those involving, O. J. Simpson, JonBenét Ramsey, Scott Peterson, and the Washington Snipers (John Allen Mohammed and Lee Boyd Malvo). Dr. Lee is currently retired from state service, but still provides consulting on criminal investigations. He is employed by the University of New Haven in the university's Forensic Institute.

In the early morning hours of November 20, 1986, Joseph Hine, a local employee of the public works department, observed a man shredding something with a wood chipper along the side of the road. Hine was able to recall the incident vividly due to the peculiarity of the event. Hine remembered that the wood chipper was attached to a box truck, and that it was approximately 3:30 a.m. Upon being contacted by police, Hine was able to bring the investigators to the exact location. Police were able to recover shredded mail belonging to Helle Crafts along with minuscule pieces of human remains, including a tooth with an unusual crown, bone chips, and more than 2,600 bleached blond human hairs (Altimari 2014). Police also recovered a chain saw belonging to Richard Crafts, which also contained traces of blood, tissue, and hair. The discovery led the medical examiner's office to conclude that Helle Crafts was deceased. Shortly thereafter, Richard Crafts was arrested and charged in the death of Helle Crafts.

Richard Crafts was tried twice for the murder of his wife. The first trial lasted over three months and was declared a mistrial in July 1988 when a lone juror refused to convict and the jury remained deadlocked following 17 days of deliberation (Farrell 1989). Richard Crafts was found guilty at the close of a second trial. At the trials, testimony was given by Dawn Thomas, Crafts's live-in babysitter, who told the jury that in the days following Helle Crafts's disappearance, Richard Crafts removed his bedroom carpet and also replaced their upright freezer. A number of key experts also testified on behalf of the prosecution. Dr. C.P. Karazulas, a forensic odontologist, testified that a capped tooth and partial gold crown found by state police definitely belonged to Helle Crafts. Dr. Henry Lee, who was at the time an up-and-coming forensic expert, attempted to use a new technique known as DNA testing to determine if the human tissue belonged to Helle Crafts. Although the sample was too degraded for such testing, Dr. Lee was able to conclude that the blood type of the tissue remains was the same as Helle Crafts's and that the blood belonged to a female (Altimari 2014). Richard Crafts also took the stand in his defense and denied having anything to do with the disappearance of his wife (Tancrell 1988b).

At sentencing, Judge Martin Nigro noted that Richard Crafts showed no remorse, and stated that he believed the murder was intentional if not premeditated (Zaretsky 1990). He was sentenced to 50 years in prison, and is currently imprisoned in MacDougall-Walker Correction Institution in Suffield, Connecticut (Shugarts 2006). It is anticipated he will be released in December 2021, on his 84th birthday (Shugarts 2006).

ELIZABETH GILMORE

See also: Levin, Jennifer, Murder of (August 26, 1986); Levy, Chandra Levy, Disappearance of (2001–2002); Peterson, Laci, Murder of (2002–2004); Von Bulow, Claus (1926–)

Further Reading

Altimari, Dave. 2014. "Connecticut's Legendary Expert on Evidence—Unraveling Crime, Henry Lee Transformed Art of Forensic Science." *Hartford Courant*, April 27. Newsbank. Accessed September 24, 2014.

Farrell, John. 1989. "Sensational Case in Spotlight Again—Second 'Wood Chipper Murder' Trial Scheduled This Month." *Boston Globe*. September, 3.

Shugarts, Jonathan. 2006. "Few Can Ever Forget the Woodchipper Case." *Republican American*. December 5.

Tancrell, Paula. 1988a. "Expert Matches Tooth, Crown to Dental X-Ray of Helle Crafts." *New Haven Register*. May 13.

Tancrell, Paula. 1988b. "Crafts Testifies, Denies He Killed Wife." *New Haven Register*. June 17.

Tancrell, Paula. 1988c. "Investigator Testifies on Crafts' Affair." *New Haven Register*. April 8.

Tancrell, Paula. 1988d. "Baby Sitter Testifies in Chipper Case." *New Haven Register*. April 13.

Zaretsky, Mark. 1990. "'Wood Chipper' Killer Gets 50 Years." *New Haven Register*. January 9.

Craigslist Killer. *See* Markoff, Philip (1986–2010)

Crane, Bob, Murder of (1978)

Born in 1928, Robert Edward "Bob" Crane was murdered on June 29, 1978, at age 49, in Scottsdale, Arizona, at the Winfield Place Apartments. At the time of his death, he was best known for his role as "Colonel Robert Hogan" on *Hogan's Heroes*. The investigation into his death brought his numerous sexual escapades to light in what was previously known only among the Hollywood elite. The police began to collect evidence and focused their investigation on Crane's longtime friend John Henry Carpenter. Evidence collected, during the 1978 investigation, focused on blood smears on Carpenter's rental car, and numerous photos of the crime scene. Carpenter, a photographer, also became a suspect because the police believed the murder weapon was a camera tripod, which has never been found. Due to limitations in scientific testing in 1978 blood smears found on the rental car of Carpenter could only be type-matched to Crane. Based on the lack of evidence the Maricopa County attorney declined to press changes. This case would go cold for 12 years until 1990 when the county attorney would reopen the case in an effort to clear cold cases. Evidence collected in 1978 was reexamined and tested and resulted in murder charges against John Carpenter in 1992. The trial of Carpenter took place in 1994 and resulted in an acquittal. While found not guilty, suspicion followed Carpenter until his death in 1998. Crane's murder is still, to this day, listed as unsolved.

After *Hogan's Heroes*, Bob Crane found it somewhat difficult to find success in acting on the scale of his role as Colonel Hogan. It is believed this is in part due to him being typecast and because of his known sexual escapades by numerous Hollywood elite. In 1978, Crane took part in dinner theater shows for the Windmill Dinner Theater in Scottsdale, Arizona. The theater rented apartments for its actors at the Winfield Place Apartments, and this would be the scene of Crane's murder. In the early hours of June 29, 1978, it is believed that Bob Crane was bludgeoned to death while sleeping. Victoria Ann Berry, Crane's costar at the dinner theater, found the actor's badly beaten lifeless body, with trauma focused on his head, in his apartment after he failed to show up for a scheduled luncheon.

During the investigation into Crane's death, videotapes and photos of Crane's various sexual escapades with numerous women were discovered. Police believed that Crane was killed via blunt force trauma to the head and by an electrical cord tied around his neck. The suspected murder weapon was deemed to be a missing camera tripod. From very early on, police focused on Crane's longtime friend and associate in his various sexual escapades, John Carpenter. Numerous photos were taken of the crime scene and show that Crane was killed in his bed. Scottsdale Police photographed and searched the rental car of Carpenter and found blood smears. Since DNA testing was not yet available, the blood smears could only be type-matched and were found to match Crane's blood type. The evidence they had at the time of the investigation was circumstantial and flimsy at best and coupled with the lack of a murder weapon, the Maricopa County attorney declined to file charges.

In 1990, as part of a broader attempt to clear cold cases, Maricopa County Attorney Richard Romely reopened the Crane case to reexamine and retest evidence obtained during the original 1978 investigation. Now that DNA testing was available, the blood found on Carpenter's rental car was tested, but the results were inconclusive. While reexamining photographic evidence of the car, detective Jim Raines, discovered that a photo of the car's interior showed what seemed to be a piece of brain tissue. This tissue sample was lost sometime between the original investigation and the 1990 reinvestigation. With only the newly rediscovered photo evidence, showing what was believed to be brain tissue in Carpenter's car, the original blood type match, and the theory that Crane was killed using a tripod, Carpenter was charged in 1992 with the murder of Bob Crane.

At trial Crane's oldest sons testified that his father was about to end the longtime friendship with Carpenter and went on to testify that his father had called Carpenter the night before his death to end their longtime friendship. Since the case itself was based on what amounted to speculation and circumstantial evidence, concerning what the object was in the photo, prosecutors insisted it was brain tissue and the defense called this mere speculation, and with the lack of a murder weapon, Carpenter was acquitted of the charges in 1994. With the acquittal, speculation still followed Carpenter who insisted he was innocent until his death in 1998. Numerous theories exist that perhaps one of Crane's sex partners or their significant other could have been involved in his murder. While alive, Crane had maintained that those in the photos and videos had consented to acts and the filming and photos, many stated they first

heard of their existence during the initial police investigation. With the 1994 acquittal of Carpenter this more or less ended the active legal saga of this case. As of today, this case is still listed as officially unsolved.

The lasting effects of the Crane murder focus on the notion that murder is one of the few crimes without a statute of limitations. While this case remains officially unsolved, the officials in Maricopa County feel that Carpenter got away with murder. Another issue that could have emerged with this case is that of double jeopardy. If new evidence had turned up that would have pointed to Carpenter he could not have been retried due to his acquittal in 1994. The only way for this case to be closed would be for additional evidence to point toward Carpenter that would clearly point to his guilt, the murder weapon, or for a new suspect to emerge and be brought to justice. Since the end of the trial in 1994, no additional steps have been taken to actively end this case one way or another. Furthermore, now when people conduct Internet searches for Bob Crane not only do they see him as an actor, but they also find information about his various sexual exploits. At the time of his murder, these types of public outing of an actor could tarnish a reputation, while now they seem commonplace and helpful to a career.

MARK C. SABER

See also: Blake, Robert, Murder Trial of (2005); Cunanan, Andrew; Fleiss, Heidi (1965–); Mineo, Sal, Murder of (1976); Spector, Phillip "Phil" Harvey (1939–); Stompanato, Johnny, Death of (1958)

Further Reading

Associated Press. 1978. "TV, Film Star Bob Crane Found Beaten to Death." *Youngstown Vindicator*. June 30. http://news.google.com/newspapers?id=OKpJAAAAIBAJ&sjid=WYQMAAAAIBAJ&pg=3541,5676842&dq=bob+crane+sigrid+valdis&hl=en. Accessed January 22, 2015.

Associated Press. 1993. "Crane Case to Go Forward." *The Bulletin*. March 12. http://news.google.com/newspapers?id=e45TAAAAIBAJ&sjid=doYDAAAAIBAJ&pg=3759,5008597&dq=bob+crane+john+henry+carpenter+sex&hl=en. Accessed January 22, 2015.

Associated Press. 1994. "Bob Crane's Son Testifies in Trial." *The Telegraph*. October 4. http://news.google.com/newspapers?id=XqJdAAAAIBAJ&sjid=7VwNAAAAIBAJ&pg=2022,5749978&dq=bob+crane+john+henry+carpenter+son&hl=en. Accessed January 23, 2015.

Kim, Eun-Kyung. 1994. "Crane's Friend Acquitted." *Pittsburgh Post-Gazette*. November 1. http://news.google.com/newspapers?id=XLJRAAAAIBAJ&sjid=AnADAAAAIBAJ&pg=6925,36069&dq=bob+crane+carpenter+friendship&hl=en. Accessed January 22, 2015.

United Press International. 1978. "Actor Bob Crane Beaten to Death." *The Milwaukee Sentinel*. June 30. http://news.google.com/newspapers?id=TAQkAAA AIBAJ &sjid=6BEEAAAA IBAJ&pg=6456,6334771&dq=bob+crane+death&hl=en. Accessed January 22, 2015.

Crimmins, Alice, Murder Trials of (1968, 1971)

The Alice Crimmins murder trials exemplify the problems of tunnel vision and confirmation bias as well as the importance, yet lack of reliability, of eyewitness testimony. In the United States, a person is innocent until proven guilty; though this is not how Alice Crimmins (1939–) was treated. Detective Jerry Piering thought Alice Crimmins was guilty from the start of the investigation and testified

On September 4, 1968, Alice Crimmins waits in a car to be returned to prison after a bail reduction hearing in the Brooklyn Supreme Court in New York. The bail reduction was granted pending her appeal of her manslaughter conviction for strangling her four-year-old daughter. (AP Photo)

to things not included in the official police report. Additionally, in both trials eyewitness testimony played a large role, specifically the eyewitness testimony given by Sophie Earominski. Earominski likely mistook another man, Marvin Weinstein, and his wife as Crimmins's and a supposed "criminal companion" on the night of the children's disappearance, leading to Crimmins's first conviction. After this conviction was overturned, Crimmins was again convicted primarily because of an illegal statement made by the prosecutor. Crimmins was convicted of murder twice, but on both occasions the verdict was overturned. She did, however, serve time in prison for a manslaughter conviction. Despite the upheld conviction, the question remains: Did Alice Crimmins murder her children?

On July 14, 1965, separated husband and wife Eddie and Alice Crimmins reported their children missing. Alice Crimmins had been caring for the children, Eddie Jr., age five, and Alice "Missy", age four, the night before and could not find them in the morning. The children slept in a room with a hook and eye latch on the outside of the door, supposedly to keep Eddie Jr. from raiding the refrigerator in the middle of the night. When Alice Crimmins undid the latch in the morning, the children's window was open and the children were gone. Missy's body was found in a vacant lot a few hours after a search began; Eddie's body was not found for five more days, until it was located badly decomposed near Van Wyck Expressway, close to where the family lived.

The detective assigned to the case, Jerry Piering, immediately believed Alice to be guilty of murdering her children. Alice Crimmins lived a promiscuous life style, had an upcoming custody hearing for the children, and did not burst into tears when she was told her daughter's body was found. Piering took all these as signs of guilt. Detective Piering was also not fond of the fact Alice Crimmins had four times as many men in her address book as women.

Importance of Eyewitness Testimony

Crimmins's conviction weighed heavily on eyewitness testimony, specifically that of Sophie Earominski. Trials often rely heavily on eyewitness testimony, which is often flawed. Event factors such as lighting, duration, colors, and violence need to be taken into account as well as witness factors. Witness factors include stress and fear, weapons focus, expectations, gender, and drugs. Earominski's head injury, the short duration, and poor lighting made her a less than ideal witness.

Alice Crimmins claimed the night the children vanished she had taken them to Kissena Park between 2:30 and 4:30 p.m. for a picnic, then picked up veal, green beans, and soda from Server's Deli for dinner. She then called her custody attorney, Michael LaPenna, because she was concerned about accusations from a former housekeeper, Evelyn Linder, who claimed Crimmins owed her $600 and if Crimmins did not pay, Linder would testify against her at the custody hearing. After dinner, she claimed she took the children for a ride to Main Street to pass Eddie Crimmins's new apartment in hopes of finding him living with another woman, which she could use against him at the custody hearing. While Alice was preparing the children for bed she went to replace the screen in their window, which was torn, but the new screen had been soiled by the family dog, so she placed the old screen in the window but failed to latch it. She put the children to bed at 9 p.m., which was confirmed by a former babysitter who was passing by their window at that time.

Alice and Eddie Crimmins had discord in their marriage. After Eddie Jr. was born, Alice Crimmins began taking birth control, which went against their religion. The two separated and Alice took on a string of lovers. This information helped to bias Detective Piering against Alice Crimmins. Eddie Crimmins was interested in technology and placed bugs in Alice's phone. The police hoped to hear a confession on one of these bugs; however, Alice Crimmins was aware of the bugs and often starting speaking saying, "I hope you're listening you bastards!"

Alice Crimmins first trial began May 9, 1968. In this trial she was tried only for Missy's death since Edddie Jr.'s body was too decomposed to say he was murdered. The press called Crimmins a "Modern day Medea" and clung to the theory that she had killed her children to keep them from her husband. This was fueled by her lover, Joseph Rorech, who testified she had told him that she would rather see the children dead than with her husband and that she had confessed to him and asked for his forgiveness. Upon this statement, Alice Crimmins stood up and exclaimed "Joseph! How could you do this? This is not true!" There was no way to rebut this statement on cross-examination.

Another key witness in the case was Sophie Earominski who testified that she saw Alice Crimmins with a man, little boy, and dog walking around with a bundle in her arms around 2 a.m. the night the children disappeared. The jury relied heavily on Earominski's testimony. The defense had tried to damage Earominski's credibility as she had permanent brain damage from a prior incident. The judge concluded this was beyond the scope of the trial and the jury never heard this important fact.

Other Explanations

At the first trial, a medical examiner stated Missy's last meal was markedly different from what Alice fed the children that night. Crimmins had fed the children veal, green beans, and soda. Missy's stomach contents contained manicotti that the medical examiner testified had been eaten within two hours of her death. Det. Piering claims to have seen manicotti leftovers in the refrigerator and a box of it in Crimmins's trash; however, neither of these pieces of evidence was recorded or photographed and Piering only mentioned them after the medical examiner spoke of Missy's stomach contents. Another man, F. Suterhland Maclem, who was not called for either trial, claimed he saw two children fitting the description of the Crimmins's children hitchhiking in Queens on the morning of July 14, 1965. Simultaneously, there were also reports of a prowler trying to lure young boys out of their homes near where the Crimmins family resided.

On May 27, 1968, a jury of 12 men found Alice Crimmins guilty of manslaughter in the first degree; she was sentenced to 5–20 years. In December 1969, the Appellate Division of the New York Supreme Court granted Alice Crimmins a new trial because three of the jurors went to Sophie Earominski's apartment to see the view for themselves. The Supreme Court ruled that by doing this the jurors made themselves secret, untested witnesses not subject to cross-examination and stated unauthorized visits were prejudicial. Additionally, the court did not feel the prosecution had proved the case beyond a reasonable doubt. Crimmins's conviction was overturned.

Alice Crimmins went on trial again on March 15, 1971. Eddie Jr.'s death could now be considered murder because it could be "inferred" from his sister's murder. At this trial, a man named Marvin Weinstein testified in rebuttal to Sophie Earominski. He stated that he, his wife, infant daughter, young son, and dog had been out for a walk the night the Crimmins children went missing. His wife came to the trial and it was noted that she strongly resembled Alice Crimmins. Another witness, Tina Devita, gave testimony to corroborate Sophie Earominski. On April 23, 1971, Alice Crimmins was found guilty of murder in the first degree in the death of Eddie Jr., and manslaughter in the first degree in the death of Alice "Missy" Crimmins. She was remanded to Bedford Hills Prison on May 13, 1971, with a sentence of life for Eddie Jr.'s murder plus 5–20 years for Missy's death.

In May 1973, the Appellate Division of the New York Supreme Court ruled that the prosecution did not prove beyond reasonable doubt that Eddie Crimmins Jr.'s death was the result of murder. In February 1975 the Court of Appeals dismissed this murder conviction, but upheld the manslaughter charge. Alice Crimmins served 30 months in prison and nine months on work release before being granted parole on September 7, 1977.

COURTNEY D'ALLURA

See also: Anthony, Casey, Murder Trial of (May 24–July 5, 2011); Downs, Elizabeth Diane Frederickson (1955–); Lindbergh Kidnapping Case (1932); Smith, Susan (1971–); Yates, Andrea (1964–)

Further Reading

Borowitz, Albert. 2000. *The Medea of Kew Gardens. The Mammoth Book of Murder and Science.* Edited by Roger Wilkes. New York: Carroll & Graf Publishers, Inc.

Gross, Kenneth. 1975. *The Alice Crimmins Case.* New York: Alfred A. Knopf, Inc.

Smith, Thomas C. 1994. *Great American Trials: From Salem Witchcraft to Rodney King.* Edited by Edward W. Knappman. Detroit: Visible Ink.

Crow Dog. See *Ex parte Crow Dog* (1883)

Crowley, Francis "Two Gun" (1912–1932)

Francis Crowley was a 20th-century outlaw who terrorized New York City. His criminal career began with auto theft and escalated to murder. In a shoot-out at an American Legion, Francis earned the nickname "Two Gun" because he carried two pistols. Francis "Two Gun" Crowley became one of New York's most notorious killers primarily because of his dramatic capture that resulted in a two-hour shoot-out with the police. Crowley's crime spree and dramatic capture were a media sensation that characterized Crowley as a "mad Irish gunman" with "the face of an altar boy" (English 2005, 480). This characterization became a common stereotype of the time period, the reckless Irish gangster. He was portrayed a heartless and ruthless killer (Radelet 1990). Crowley was tried, convicted, and sentenced to death for the murder of a Long Island patrolman. He served his time at Sing Sing Prison and was one of the youngest convicts on death row until the day of his execution by electric chair on January 21, 1932. Crowley and his crimes are hardly remembered today, but his story has been immortalized in the film *White Heat* by Raoul Walsh (Mayo 2008).

Born the second son of an unwed mother, Crowley was put up for adoption. As a young man Crowley developed a deep hatred for police officers, which was exacerbated in 1925 when his adoptive brother, John, was killed during a confrontation with police (Newton 2002). Crowley's first run-in with the law occurred on May 3, 1929. Although he was arrested for stealing a car, the grand jury did not indict (officially charge) him for the crime. He was arrested for auto theft again on July 4, October 21, and November 16, but he was never charged for these crimes.

Crowley's criminal career seemed to end when he met Helen Walsh, but she did not approve of his "hoodlum pals." When she rejected his marriage proposal in 1930, Crowley began to drink and went back to his gang (Downey 2008). Crowley's next crime was when he went to a dance at an American Legion with two other youths. Several of the Legion's members tried to throw Crowley and other youth out, but before he exited Crowley drew two guns and wounded two of the Legions members: an act that earned him his nickname "Two Gun" Crowley. After this incident, Crowley's criminal career took off.

Now wanted for attempted murder, Crowley was under the watchful eye of Detective George Schaedel. Detective Schaedel was determined to catch Crowley and bring him to trial for attempted murder so he periodically stopped where Crowley worked (Downey 2008). In March, he evaded the detective by wounding him and held up a bank two days later. Crowley's crime streak continued to escalate as he invaded the West 90th Street flat of a real-estate broker, Rudolph Adler, in April. Adler tried to resist, in response Crowley drew his pistols and shot Adler five times. Crowley left the flat empty handed when Trixie, Adler's dog, chased him and his accomplices, an act that likely saved Adler's life.

Twelve days after shooting Adler, Crowley and his partner in crime, Rudolph "Fats" Duringer (December 10, 1905—December 11, 1931), went for a joyride with a dance-hall hostess, Virginia Brannen (Newton 2002). When Duringer began making sexual advances toward Brannen she resisted; Duringer responded by shooting Brannen in Crowley's car. Crowley and Duringer dumped Brannen's body over a stone wall in Yonkers while she was still alive. Brannen died before her body was found, an action that fueled the police department's efforts to locate Crowley. At the end of April police received a tip that Crowley was spotted driving in the Bronx; this information led to a police pursuit, but Crowley escaped after engaging the police in a gun battle.

On May 6, 1931 two patrolmen, Frederick Hirsch and Peter Yodice, found Crowley parked with his 16-year-old girlfriend, Helen Walsh, in Long Island (Downey 2008). As the patrolmen approached his car and asked to see his license Crowley pulled a gun while pretending to reach for his wallet. Patrolman Hirsch pulled the trigger on his gun, but it misfired twice; Crowley began shooting. The confrontation ended with Crowley killing Hirsch, wounding Yodice, and escaping. The hunt for Crowley was intensified by the murder of Patrolman Hirsch and the incorrect assumption that Crowley also murdered Walsh. To escape the manhunt Crowley began hiding out at an ex-girlfriend's apartment on West 90th Street, on May 7, 1931, with Walsh and Duringer. Crowley's ex-girlfriend notified police that Crowley was in her apartment after seeing him with a different woman.

Police officers surrounded the apartment armed with rifles, submachine guns, and canisters of tear gas (Newton 2002). Around 15,000 citizens watched as Crowley and the officers engaged in a shoot-out. During the shoot-out, the police began tossing tear gas canisters into the apartment, but Crowley threw the tear-gas canisters back out of the apartment and into the street. Crowley, who was wounded four times and bleeding profusely, surrendered as police officers broke down the door two hours later; this event became known as "The Siege on West Ninetieth Street." Some accounts suggest that Crowley was wounded three times, but all accounts indicate that the wounds were in his extremities. Crowley said he threw their guns out the window, but when the arresting officers patted him down they found two pistols strapped to Crowley's legs. After being checked out at Bellevue Hospital, it was determined that Crowley's wounds were not life threatening. He was transferred to a hospital in Long Island where he was arraigned for the murder of Patrolman Hirsch.

On May 29, 1931, Crowley was convicted for this and was sentenced to death on June 1; the jury only deliberated for 25 minutes. Crowley asked his lawyer if he could take the rap for Brannen's murder, but Duringer was convicted and sentenced to death instead.

Crowley was confined to death row at Sing Sing Prison in Ossing, New York, but he continued causing trouble. While incarcerated, Crowley stuffed his clothing down the toilet, assaulted guards, and made homemade weapons. This destructive behavior continued, until his execution drew near. At this time, he adopted and fed a starling (a small to medium-sized bird) that flew into his cell. On January 21, 1932, Crowley was put to death by electric chair, officially ending his criminal career.

Michelle Harner

See also: Adams, Randall Dale (1948–2010); Coleman, Alton (1955–2002); Gillis, Lester Joseph "Baby Face Nelson" (1908–1934); Graham, Barbara (1923–1955); O'Banion, Dion, Mob Murder of (November 10, 1924)

Further Reading

Blumenthal, Ralph. 2004. *Miracle at Sing Sing.* New York: St. Martin's Press.

Downey, Patrick. 2008. *Bad Seeds in the Big Apple: Bandits, Killers, and Chaos in New York City, 1920–1940.* Nashville, TN: Cumberland House Publishing.

English, T. J. 2005. *Paddy Whacked: The Untold Story of the Irish American Gangster.* New York: HarperCollins.

Helmer, William J., and Rick Mattix. 2007. *The Complete Public Enemy Almanac.* Nashville, TN: Cumberland House Publishing.

Mayo, Mike. 2008. *American Murder: Criminals, Crimes, and the Media.* Canton, MI: Visible Ink Press.

Newton, Michael. 2002. *The Encyclopedia of Robberies, Heists, and Capers.* New York: Facts on File, Inc.

Radelet, Michael. 1990. *Facing the Death Penalty: Essays on a Cruel and Unusual Punishment.* Philadelphia, PA: Temple University Press.

Cullen, Charles (1960–)

Charles Cullen is an American serial killer who committed murders in New Jersey and Pennsylvania between

1988 and 2003. Cullen was a male nurse who murdered patients at the hospitals where he was employed. During his 19-year nursing career, Cullen worked at 10 different hospitals and may have committed murders at each one. His style of killing earned him the moniker "The Angel of Death." Charles Cullen confessed and pled guilty to the murder of 22 people. On March 20, 2006, he was sentenced in New Jersey to multiple life terms. His crimes led to sweeping new legislation that changed many reporting requirements for hospitals.

Charles Cullen was born February 22, 1960. His father died seven months after his birth, and he was raised in a family with eight older siblings. They survived largely on church charity and disability income. Cullen described his home life as miserable. He stated that his siblings often engaged in drug use and prostitution. He expressed deep affection for his mother, who was killed during his senior year of high school (Graeber 2013, 5). Cullen tried to commit suicide at least 20 times throughout his life, including soon after his mother died. He enlisted in the navy in 1978 but was discharged in 1984 after another failed suicide attempt. In March 1984, he enrolled in the Mountainside Hospital School of Nursing in Montclair, New Jersey. By all accounts, he was an excellent student and was even elected to be the class president. While in nursing school, he met and later married Adrianne Baum (pseudonym). His first

Serial-killer nurse Charles Cullen sits alone in court during his sentencing in Somerville, New Jersey, on March 2, 2006. The nurse who admitted to killing as many as 40 patients, received 11 consecutive life terms in prison, making him ineligible for parole for nearly 400 years. (AP Photo/Mike Derer)

nursing job was at the burn ward at St. Barnabas Medical Center in Livingston, New Jersey.

Cullen committed his first murder here on June 11, 1988. John W. Yengo Sr. was being treated for an allergic reaction to blood-thinning medication. Cullen administered a lethal dose of insulin, which would become one of his preferred weapons of choice (Assad 2004). He also frequently used digoxin. During his career, Cullen may have also tampered with intravenous (IV) bags that were later administered to patients. It is unknown how many of these bags Cullen tampered with or how many deaths may be attributed to tainted IV fluids. In 1992, while St. Barnabas began investigating the tampered IV bags, Cullen quit and began working at the Warren Hospital in Phillipsburg, New Jersey. The next year, Adrienne filed for divorce.

In 1994, Cullen became a licensed nurse in the state of Pennsylvania and worked at 10 different hospitals over 16 years. It is impossible to know exactly how many people Charles Cullen killed, but there is no doubt that he committed homicides at every hospital where he worked. One of the difficulties in establishing a specific number of victims, and perhaps his crimes went undetected for so long, is that many of his victims were already in the process of dying. These were typically elderly patients, or critically wounded individuals, and doctors and family members were not necessarily surprised by death. Few death investigations were launched. Some hospital records had been destroyed by the time Cullen was arrested in 2003. Cullen confessed that his motivation for killing came from a desire to give mercy to individuals who were suffering and waiting for death.

A few death investigations were performed. Some investigations found amounts of controlled medications in the victim's system that were not prescribed to them. This could be accounted for by several explanations, including error in distributing medications or perhaps the medications themselves were corrupt. Due to a lack of adequate computerized controls, no hospital that Cullen worked was able to link tampered medication to him. Suspicions were raised several times in his career, but often Cullen would simply resign or be forced to resign. He was never terminated and no hospital ever handed case information over to the police. By all accounts he was a well-trained, experienced trauma nurse. He worked diligently, was an ideal employee, and never had trouble finding another place of employment.

It is shocking that none of Cullen's employers were aware of his previous issues. It is perhaps more disconcerting

that none of his employers were ever made aware of his deteriorating mental state. He was checked into mental health facilities numerous times, usually after failed suicide attempts. While employed at the Warren Hospital in April 1993, for example, Cullen had made yet another failed attempt to commit suicide by taking a large amount of an antianxiety medication. He was taken by ambulance to the New Jersey State Lunatic Asylum where he underwent several days of counseling and therapy. This stay ended when the Warren Hospital called the facility to ask Charles Cullen to come back to work.

In the summer of 2003, Charles Cullen was employed at the Somerset Medical Center in New Jersey. That year the hospital recognized several patients who died under suspicious circumstances. Two patients overdosed on Digoxin in less than one month, neither of them was prescribed this medication. The hospital reported these incidents to the New Jersey Poison Control Center and Dr. Steven Marcus was assigned to investigate. Dr. Marcus quickly came to the conclusion that the suspicious deaths were most likely attributed to criminal acts. He urged Somerset Medical Center to notify authorities, but they waited approximately three months before the police were brought in to investigate. During this time, Cullen killed five more people.

Worst Serial Killer Ever?

Due to a lack of record-keeping, controls, reporting laws, and privacy laws, Charles Cullen was able to go on killing in hospitals for over 10 years. It was impossible to go back and investigate every patient who died under his care. Some had concluded that he may have killed over 300 victims but no one will ever know for sure. If true, however, Charles Cullen could be the worst serial killer in American history.

Police investigators did not receive full cooperation from the hospital as they only received information from the hospital when ordered to do by a judge. There were two elements to their investigation. First, they examined printouts from a computerized drug dispensing machine called "Pyxis." The patterns of Cullen's access to the system raised detectives' suspicions but it was not proof beyond a reasonable doubt. Second, primarily because the hospital refused to cooperate, the detectives worked with fellow nurse Amy Ridgeway who agreed to participate in a sting operation. Ridgeway translated Pyxis printouts, recorded phone calls, and ultimately secured Cullen's initial confession. She wore a wire when she went to meet him at a restaurant. During that conversation, she told Cullen that police were investigating her for murder and that she knew he was responsible. She managed to get Cullen to make incriminating statements. Once he left, the police took him into custody. Cullen then gave a full confession that lasted nearly seven hours.

The Cullen case significantly impacted hospital record-keeping. In 2004, the New Jersey State Legislature passed The Patient Safety Act and an Enhancement Act that require hospitals to report suspicious events to the Department of Health and certain information about their employees to the Division of Consumer Affairs. In the wake of Cullen's arrest, 35 states other than Pennsylvania and New Jersey also passed laws that protect employers who provide truthful but possibly damaging information about their employees.

CHARLES GIBERTI

See also: Dahmer, Jeffrey (1960–1994); Holmes, Dr. H.H. (1861–1896); Kevorkian, Jack (1928–2011); Toppan, Jane (1854–1938)

Further Reading

Assad, Matthew. 2004. *Former Judge Was First Cullen Victim.* The Morning Call. http://articles.mcall.com/2004-12-01/news/3569887_1_municipal-court-judge-electric-chair-new-jersey-supreme-court. Accessed April 15, 2015.

"Charles Cullen." University of South Florida. http://myweb.usf.edu/~agraff/index.html. Accessed April 15, 2015.

Graebner, Charles. 2013. *The Good Nurse: A Story of Medicine, Madness, and Murder.* New York: Twelve Hachette Book Group.

Messick, Graham. 2013. "Angel of Death." *Sixty Minutes.* CBS.

Cunanan, Andrew (1969–1997)

Andrew Cunanan was a spree killer that murdered victims in multiple states in the late 1990s. His killing spree started in Minnesota and ended three months later when he was discovered dead in a houseboat in Miami. His final victim was the famed designer Gianni Versace. His killing spree received an incredible amount of attention in the news because of the number of victims he murdered, the celebrity of Versace, and because of the struggles law enforcement had in bringing him to justice.

Andrew Cunanan was born in California. He was identified as being a creative liar, making up intricate stories about his life. His mother did not approve of him being gay, which led to him moving out of the house at 19. He attempted to get a college education but eventually dropped out and moved to San Francisco where he allegedly became a prostitute. Andrew also had an obsession with celebrities. He went to numerous events that celebrities attended. Many of his encounters with these celebrities did not end well as he frequently became angry. He also had problems with drugs and alcohol (Orth 1999).

On April 26, 1997, Andrew Cunanan started his killing spree. His first victims were Jeff Trail and David Madson, both previous lovers of Cunanan. Andrew called David and Jeff and told them that he wanted to see them and that he was coming to Minnesota for a visit. David picked up Andrew at the Minneapolis airport and let him stay at his apartment. Andrew told David that he had "business" to discuss with Jeff. Jeff reluctantly agreed and meet him at David's apartment. When Jeff arrived to the apartment Andrew went downstairs to let him in. No one knows what transpired between the two but their conversation was very brief and aggressive. Andrew went into the kitchen and grabbed a hammer from the dining room table and started bludgeoning Jeff in the face, head, and upper torso. There were a total of 27 fatal blows to Jeff's body. It is not certain whether David was present during this attack or if he was out walking his dog, like he did most nights around that time, but either way Andrew threatened or manipulated David in to helping him clean up the mess. They rolled Jeff's body into a rug and cleaned up some of the blood. Soon after, they left in David's jeep. On May 3, in Chisago County Minnesota, David Madson's body was found shot twice in the back and once through the eye, the bullets were from Jeff Trail's stolen gun (Orth 1999).

About a week later Cunanan ended up in Chicago, where he killed his third victim, Lee Miglin. Nobody really knows if Lee and Cunanan had ever met before the night of May 3, 1997, but Lee's body was found with his hands and face bound with tape, feet tied together with an extension cord, brutally beaten, stabbed in the chest repeatedly, and throat slit severely with a bow saw. He also had two bags of cement thrown on top of him. Cunanan stole numerous items from Miglin's home and drove off in his Lexus.

After the discovery of this crime, Andrew Cunanan was added to the FBI's top 10 most wanted list. He knew that he needed to find a remote place that he could hide where no one would look for him. He chose the Finns Point National Cemetery. Here he murdered his fourth victim. William Reese was the cemetery groundskeeper and was reading the Bible when Andrew entered through the side door. Cunanan pulled out his gun and demanded that Reese give him his truck keys. He reached in his pocket but that is when Cunanan shot Reese at point-blank range (Orth 1999).

Andrew headed south to Miami in William Reese's pickup truck with a stolen South Carolina license plate. When he arrived, he paid cash for a room that he stayed in for about two months. He was recognized as the guy from America's Most Wanted by a waiter who contacted the police, but he was able to escape before he was apprehended.

His next and final victim was Italian fashion designer Gianni Versace. Gianni Versace started his international fashion house, Versace, at the age of 25 in Milan, and was known for creating famous costume designs for theater and films. As his innovative designs and never-before-seen fashions became popular and sought after by fashion lovers all over the world, Versace decided to expand his boutiques to Paris, the United States, Russia, Japan, and several other countries. Celebrities started wearing Versace fashions, including Princess Diana, Cher, Madonna, Elton John, and various other fashion icons. Versace was also famous for his personal life. He was openly gay and known for falling in love with a model named Antonio D'Amico. They remained happy partners until he was murdered by Andrew Cunanan. Friends stated that Andrew was jealous of the lifestyle that Versace lived. He wanted more than ever to be rich and famous, and live the good life. He resented that Versace came from nothing and was now a big icon in the gay community. It is quoted that Andrew said that Versace was "the worst designer ever" and was "pretentious, pompous, and ostentatious." Versace's life was the life that Andrew had yearned for so badly his entire life (Orth 1999).

Largest Failed Manhunt Ever?

To some the Andrew Cunanan manhunt was the "largest failed manhunt in U.S. history." Since these crimes were committed in different states it was hard for law enforcement to figure out who had

jurisdiction to work the case. So, Cunanan was able to escape while law enforcement was figuring out this jurisdictional squabbles. Also, the media leak that Andrew was being tracked by the police was a significant mistake and led to Andrew disappearing again. Finally, homosexuality seemed to play a role in Andrew's motive and the victims he chose but law enforcement tried to ignore this fact because, at that time, there was an unease when it came to law enforcement dealing with homosexuality in their cases. This case showed some of the weaknesses in law enforcement communication that have since been addressed.

Gianni Versace and Andrew Cunanan's paths crossed on July 15, 1997. Versace had numerous houses all over the world but one of his favorites was in Miami. Cunanan shot him twice in front of his home. A witness started to pursue Cunanan but he got away. His partner D'Amico heard the commotion and went outside and found Versace covered in blood on the steps (Orth 1999).

Cunanan reportedly went back to the stolen pickup truck, changed clothes, and then ran away on foot. He was found on July 23, 1997, eight days after Versace's murder, on a private houseboat on the Indian Creek Canal. The owner of the houseboat was on vacation and had one of his employees check on the boat to make sure everything was okay while he was gone. The employee noticed the door to the boat was ajar so decided to check it out. He found that someone had been sleeping there. As he went to get a closer look he heard a shot above him on the second floor. Frightened he made a run for it and contacted the police. The police surrounded the houseboat and tried to contact the man inside but got no response. The SWAT team entered the houseboat and found Andrew Cunanan on the bedroom floor with a self-inflicted gunshot wound to his head.

One of the biggest mysteries of this case was his motive. In 1997 Cunanan was convinced that he had contracted the acquired immunodeficiency disease (AIDS) virus, which then triggered his killing spree. Some believe he targeted Versace because he rejected him at a party. Since he committed suicide, however, we will never truly know his motive.

STEPHANIE A. NELSON

Cunanan, Andrew (1969–1997)   207

See also: Bundy, Ted (1946–1989); Starkweather, Charles and Caril Ann Fugate, Murder Spree of (1957)

Lacayo, Richard. 1997. "Tagged for Murder." *Time*. http://content.time.com/time/magazine/article/0,9171,138062,00.html. Accessed April 11, 2015.

Orth, Maureen. 1999. *Vulgar Favors: Andrew Cunanan, Gianni Versace, and the Largest Failed Manhunt in the U.S. History.* New York: Delacorte.

Versace. (2010). "Corporate History". http://www.versace.com/en/history. Accessed April 11, 2015.

Czolgosz, Leon. *See* McKinley, William, Assassination of (September 6, 1901)

D

Dahmer, Jeffrey (1960–1994)

On July 22, 1991, in a West Side Milwaukee neighborhood, police officers encountered a man claiming to have been handcuffed and threatened with a knife inside another man's apartment. The ensuing investigation led officers to the residence of Jeffrey Dahmer, who allowed them to enter his apartment. Upon entering Dahmer's bedroom, officers noticed photographs of numerous young men in sexually explicit poses. Many of these photos involved corpses displayed in various positions and were taken in Dahmer's apartment. Officers continued to search the house, discovering a severed head in the refrigerator, human remains in the freezer, seven human skulls, a 57-gallon drum filled with human torsos, and numerous other body parts scattered about. Further investigation revealed that Dahmer had killed and dismembered 17 young males. The shocking and gruesome nature of the crimes led to national media attention, and Dahmer eventually discussed his crimes on nationally aired interviews. His candor combined with the gruesome nature of the crimes caused people to focus more on why he did it rather than if he did it. His trial focused on whether his actions were caused by insanity. The jury found him sane, and he was sentenced to 957 years in prison.

Jeffrey Dahmer's first murder occurred in 1978 a few weeks after his high school graduation. Following years of violent sexual fantasies, fixations on animal dismemberment, and excessive drinking, he acted on his desires by picking up a hitchhiker in Bath, Ohio, bringing him back to his childhood home, and killing him. With his recently divorced parents both living elsewhere, Dahmer dissected the body in the ensuing weeks and disposed of it in nearby woods. Dahmer abstained from further violence while briefly attending college and then spending two years in the military. In December 1981 Dahmer moved to Milwaukee to live with his grandmother. He drank excessively and frequented bathhouses, pornography shops, and gay bars where he began to live out his fantasies. He met men, took them to hotels or his grandmother's home, drugged them, and had sex with them according to his preferences and not theirs. He murdered again in November 1987. He followed his normal routine of drugging a sexual partner, but Dahmer claims to have unconsciously killed the man in the middle of the night. He took the body to his grandmother's house where he dismembered and disposed of it. This incident caused Dahmer to stop resisting his fantasies, and his murder spree began.

Between January 1988 and July 1991, Dahmer killed 15 more young men. He lured physically attractive targets to his home with the promise of sex or money and then drugged them, had sex with them, strangled them, performed sexual acts with their bodies, and dismembered the corpses. He ate or kept parts of the bodies and began building a temple adorned with human skulls and skeletons. His routine deviated only in that he attempted to keep the last few victims alive and in a zombie-like state by

In a Wisconsin courtroom, serial killer Jeffrey Dahmer faces eight additional charges of first-degree murder. Charged with 15 homicides, Dahmer was sentenced to 15 consecutive life terms. He was killed in prison by another inmate in November 1994. (AP Photo/Allan Y. Scott)

drilling holes in their skulls and inserting acid or boiling water into their brain with a baster. He did make a few mistakes. At the beginning of his killing spree, he pled guilty to fondling a 13-year-old boy and was placed on probation. Two other victims escaped, but police did not follow up on their complaints. His 13th victim, a 13-year-old boy and the brother of the boy that Dahmer was convicted of molesting, escaped and was found by local residents sitting naked and dazed on a street curb. Dahmer, a skilled liar, invited officers into his home and convinced them that the incidence was merely a domestic dispute. His final mistake brought police into his apartment on July 22, 1991, where they discovered the evidence of his crimes.

Jeffrey Dahmer confessed to his crimes, and so his trial focused on his mental state at the time of the murders. According to Wisconsin law, Dahmer was not guilty by reason of insanity if he suffered from a mental disease or defect that caused him to not appreciate the wrongfulness of his conduct or did not allow him to conform his conduct to the requirements of the law (Drukteinis 1992). Experts found him competent to stand trial; he reasoned logically, was capable of problem solving, and could delay gratification. Court experts agreed that Dahmer suffered from alcoholism, paraphilia (sexual deviance), and various personality disorders. They disagreed about how much control he had over his actions. The defense argued that

Dahmer was plagued by necrophilia, which produced irresistible urges to kill and have sex with dead bodies (Ewing and McCann 2006). Experts also testified that the coexistence of murder, necrophilia, and a desire for comatose victims is truly unique in the annals of abnormal psychology. Such abnormality must mean insanity.

Prosecutors argued that Dahmer had a mental disease, but it did not inhibit his ability to follow the law or recognize that his actions were wrong. Dahmer's paraphilia controlled the focus of his sexual arousal, yet he could control his response to those impulses. One expert said that his sexual urges were not as strong as those commonly experienced by teenagers in the backseats of cars. Moreover, Dahmer behaved in a calculated manner during the act of killing. He used condoms, concealed his actions, and destroyed evidence to prevent detection. Even Dahmer's most bizarre behaviors were rational responses to his underlying desire to control and be close to his victims. Dahmer desired a fully submissive and continuous sexual partner. Drugging and then killing a victim provided a short-term partner, but bodies decompose. His treatment of corpses prolonged the closeness that Dahmer experienced with his victims, and cannibalism allowed Dahmer to feel like his victims were a part of him. The prosecution argued that Dahmer's efforts to create a sex zombie were practical and reasonable attempts to achieve a goal. Dahmer could not find live persons that fulfilled his desires, and dead victims only provided temporary solutions. He started to experiment with live victims, hoping that they would not die (Ewing and McCann 2006). After the trial, during an interview with Stone Phillips on MSNBC, Dahmer supported the prosecution's theory by saying, "The only motive that there ever was was to completely control a person, a person that I found physically attractive and keep them with me as long as possible, even if it meant just keeping a part."

On February 15, 1992, the jury agreed with the prosecution, and the judge sentenced Jeffrey Dahmer to 957 years in prison. By all accounts he was a model inmate and claimed to experience a religious conversion in prison. He was, however, targeted by other inmates. On November 28, 1994, another inmate bludgeoned Jeffery Dahmer to death as they were cleaning a prison bathroom. Dahmer's crimes continue to foster both debate and the search for plausible explanations of his pathology and motivation (see Silva, Ferrari, and Leong 2002).

TIMOTHY LAUGER

See also: Bundy, Ted (1946–1989); Gacy, John Wayne (1942–1994); Holmes, Dr. H.H. (1861–1896); Sowell, Anthony (1959–)

Further Reading

Drukteinis, Albert M. 1992. "Serial Murder—The Heart of Darkness." *Psychiatric Annals* 22(10): 532–538.

Ewing, Charles P., and Joesph T. McCann. 2006. *Minds on Trial: Great Cases in Law and Psychology.* New York: Oxford University Press.

Silva, J. Arturo, Michelle M. Ferrari, and Gregory B. Long. 2002. "The Case of Jeffrey Dahmer: Sexual Serial Homicide from a Neuropsychiatric Developmental Perspective." *Journal of Forensic Science* 47(6): 1–13.

Dakota Conflict Trials (1862)

While the mass execution of 38 Dakota prisoners on December 26, 1862, was the largest in U.S. history, fewer than 13 percent of the original 303 condemned were hanged. The Dakota conflict trials, which tried 393 prisoners over the course of six weeks in front of a military commission and without the benefit of legal counsel, have often been called into question. The actions taken by the Dakota during the course of the conflict were not treated as war crimes, but rather as the actions of common criminals; this should have entitled them to due process, but did not. Those overseeing the trials saw them as a necessary measure to avoid vigilante action by civilian mobs, which concern was borne out when settlers attacked the prisoners on multiple occasions. President Abraham Lincoln, however, risked the rising tempers of the Minnesota settlers and personally reviewed all of the trial transcripts before commuting the vast majority. The attention paid to justice, rather than public opinion, created a legal standard for dealing with future uprisings.

Historically, the Sioux were a nation of seven separate subnations that held councils every summer at an assembly called the Seven Council Fires. The last such assembly was held in 1850, as the next year six of the seven subnations—who together formed the Dakota people—ceded much of their territory in exchange for 240 square miles of reservation land along the Minnesota River and more than a million dollars to be paid over the course of the next 50 years. Approximately 7,000 Dakota moved to the new reservations in the summer of 1851. In 1858, the Dakota ceded a portion of their reservation back to the United States in exchange for an increase in their annuity payments.

In the summer of 1862, the annuity payments were coming late and the Civil War threatened the supply of gold in which the Dakota were paid. There were conflicts between the Dakota and the traders who transported the funds, leading the traders to refuse to provide provisions on credit, even though the Dakota were suffering from hunger and the traders had sufficient supplies warehoused nearby. While the annuity payments were en route, Dakota was unaware and the funds would not arrive until after the first steps were taken toward war.

On Sunday, August 17, 1862, four young Dakota men stole eggs from a settler's home, and exhorted one another to further action until one challenged the others to join him in killing the owners of the home. Three men, one woman, and a teenage girl were killed. When the young men returned to camp and told what they had done, the Dakota council had to choose between attempting to reconcile with the whites or treating the unprompted attack as the opening declaration of war. While many members of the Dakota were initially reluctant to make such a move, warmongers swung the vote of the council and the movement rapidly gained momentum.

In the first day of fighting, 44 Americans were killed and 10 were captured. Attacks in and around New Ulm over the next week resulted in over one hundred fatalities, and ultimately the town's evacuation. When Dakota troops lay siege to Fort Ridgley, one of the last populations of whites in the immediate area, Colonel Henry Sibley was appointed to command the American volunteer forces intended to suppress the uprising. He led 1,400 soldiers to Fort Ridgley and succeeded in ending the siege on August 21, changing the nature of the conflict from Dakota attacks against settlers and small groups of soldiers to a series of battles between Dakota and American troops.

In early September, Major General John Pope was appointed the commander of U.S. troops in the Northwest and charged with suppressing the Dakota uprising, while Little Crow, the de facto general of the warring Dakota, led attacks against military targets. By September 23, when the Battle of Wood Lake resulted in heavy casualties for the Dakota, those Dakota who had initially been opposed to the idea of war were gaining ground. These "friendlies" were able to take control of and release 269 white prisoners into American hands; between Dakota losses and the actions of the friendlies, hundreds of warriors were convinced to surrender. Over the course of the 37 days of fighting, approximately 500 whites and 100 Dakota were killed.

On September 28, 1862, Colonel Sibley appointed a five-member military commission to try the captured Dakota for "murder and other outrages," rather than war crimes (Berg 2013, 166). The Reverend Stephen Riggs, who spoke Dakota, gathered evidence and witnesses on behalf of the Dakota, and urged along with Bishop Whipple that the commission grant clemency for Dakota involved in battles and execute only those who committed rape or killed women or children. The commission determined that simply firing shots, however, constituted participation in battle and was grounds for the death penalty. Over the next six weeks, 393 of the Dakota prisoners were tried and 323 were convicted. Of those, 303 were to be executed, and the majority of those acquitted were still incarcerated.

President Abraham Lincoln met with his cabinet in mid-October to review the proceedings, and on October 17 he sent General Pope with a message for Colonel Sibley, that "no executions be made without his sanction" (Berg 2013, 37). When the trials were finished in early November, the 303 condemned Dakota were moved through New Ulm to be housed at Camp Lincoln. While in New Ulm, the captives were attacked by angry civilians. General Pope urged President Lincoln to be hasty in reviewing the trial records, warning that mob violence would only continue if the executions were put off for too long. This was reinforced in early December, when civilians attacked the camp where the condemned were held.

President Lincoln, having met with Bishop Whipple, determined that only two Dakota had been convicted of raping women or children, and 37 had been convicted of participating in the massacres of settlers. Those 39 were condemned by executive order on December 6, 1862. One man was exonerated between then and the date of execution, but the other 38 were hanged in Mankato, Minnesota, on December 26, 1862.

In April 1863, Congress enacted a law providing for the removal of Dakota bands from Minnesota to South Dakota, while those prisoners convicted but not executed were moved to Camp McClellan in Iowa. On March 22, 1866, the 177 surviving prisoners were released on President Andrew Johnson's order and removed to a reservation in Nebraska.

The Sioux uprising did not officially end until December 29, 1890, with the battle of Wounded Knee in South Dakota.

BERNADETTE STEWART

See also: Peltier, Leonard (1944–); Sand Creek (CO) Massacre (November 29, 1864); Wounded Knee Incident (SD) (February 27–May 8, 1973); Wounded Knee Massacre (SD) (December 29, 1890)

Further Reading

Anderson, Gary C., and Alan R. Woolworth, eds. 1988. *Through Dakota Eyes: Narrative Accounts of the Minnesota Indian War of 1862.* Minneapolis: Minnesota Historical Society Press.

Berg, Scott W. 2013. *38 Nooses: Lincoln, Little Crow, and the Beginning of the Frontier's End.* New York: Pantheon Books.

Danziger Bridge Shootings (New Orleans, LA) (September 4, 2005)

On August 29, 2005, Hurricane Katrina devastated New Orleans and the surrounding regions of the Gulf of Mexico. Hurricane Katrina broke levies within New Orleans and led to mass flooding. The resulting devastation attributed to widespread looting within the city and stretched the capabilities of the police department. The police department attempted to stop the lawlessness being experienced. Unfortunately, there were reported instances of misconduct by a small number of law enforcement officers during this time. One such instance that received national attention occurred on the Danziger Bridge six days after Hurricane Katrina made a landfall. This event left two citizens dead and four more wounded. The resulting trial rocked not only the city of New Orleans but the nation as a whole.

On September 4, 2005, police responded to the Danziger Bridge for a shots fired call. Police Sergeant Kenneth Bowen, Sergeant Robert Gisevius, Officer Anthony Villavaso, and Officer Robert Faulcon responded to the call. Upon arrival the officers opened fire on the Bartholomew family with assault rifles and a shotgun. The Bartholomews were walking to a grocery store and were forced to shelter behind a concrete barrier when the officers started to fire. One member of the group, James Brissette, was killed and four wounded at his position. Two other members of the group fled the scene and were subsequently pursued by Gisevius and Faulcon in an unmarked police vehicle. Faulcon shot one of the men, Ronald Madison, with a shotgun from the moving vehicle. This man later died from his wounds. The other man was taken into custody and charged with attempted murder of police officers. Surprisingly, no weapons were recovered from the scene. It was later found that the reported shots came from trapped residents attempting to get the attention of rescuers.

The initial investigation resulted in an attempted cover-up by law enforcement. The four responding officers reported they had been fired upon and were forced to return fire. The lead investigator, Detective Arthur Kaufman, concealed evidence in an attempt to make the shootings appear justified. Furthermore, New Orleans Police Department Lieutenant Michael Lohman supported false testimony from the officers and suggested that a firearm be planted near the scene.

The four officers were indicted for murder and attempted murder and subsequently taken into custody on January 2, 2007. Gisevius, Bowen, and Villavaso were charged for the murder of Brissette. Faulcon was charged with the murder of Madison. Just over one year later, on August 13, 2008, the indictments were dismissed by the district judge under the ruse of prosecutorial misconduct. However, the investigation was not over. Two weeks later the Department of Justice and the FBI took over the investigation. The federal government lacks jurisdiction to file murder charges in such as this. However, the government was able to file charges under the federal civil rights statute of the Fourteenth Amendment. Specifically, under the "Deprivation of Rights Under Color of Law" subsection, anyone who acts under the color of law to unlawfully deprive a citizen of their right to life may be sentenced to death. It was this subsection of the law that allowed the federal government to continue the investigation legally.

The cover-up charges were solved via guilty pleas by those involved in 2010. Lieutenant Lohman pled guilty to obstruction of justice. Other patrol officers privy to the orchestrated cover-up pled guilty for failing to report the cover-up to the proper authorities. On July 13, 2010, a federal grand jury indicted Bowen, Gisevius, Faulcon, and Villavaso for both the shootings and cover-up. One year later, on August 5, 2011, guilty verdicts were handed down for the shootings and the cover-up by the lead investigator, Detective Kaufman. Gisevius and Villavaso were both found guilty of five counts of deprivation of rights under color of law, two counts of using a weapon during commission of a crime of violence, as well as conspiracy, obstruction of justice, and civil rights conspiracy. Bowen and Faulcon were found guilty of six counts of deprivation of rights under color of law as well as using a weapon during the commission of a crime, conspiracy, obstruction of justice, and civil rights conspiracy. Kaufman was found guilty of 10 crimes relating to the cover-up of the shootings.

Sentencing was held on April 4, 2012. Faulcon was sentenced to 65 years, Bowen and Gisevius both received 40 years, Villavaso was sentenced to 38 years, and Kaufman received 6 years. Not unlike normal proceedings, the convicted officers appealed their convictions a month later. The five officers argued that federal prosecutors had engaged in a public relations campaign by posting anonymous comments on the website of the local New Orleans newspaper. The same district judge who had sentenced the men conducted a year-long examination into their appeal. On September 17, 2013, the district judge vacated the five officers' convictions and ordered a new trial. The judge stated the prosecutors engaged in leaking information to certain media outlets and posting comments to online forums. The judge ruled that these actions tainted the trial by influencing public opinion. He further asserted that the retrial was a small price to pay to protect the validity of the verdict in the case, the integrity of his court, and the criminal justice system as a whole.

While the convictions were overturned and a new trial ordered, the district judge was not able to point to specific instances of the jury being tainted. The retrial is yet to take place, but the Department of Justice is moving forward with plans to retry the case. In fact, in November 2014, the Department of Justice requested a new judge be assigned for the retrial. The four officers convicted in the shooting remain incarcerated while the government appeals the vacated convictions.

The Danziger Bridge shootings were tragic for the families involved, the city of New Orleans, and the nation as a whole. The police are meant to protect the civilian population, and the gross misconduct exhibited by the officers involved in the shooting and subsequent cover-up hurt community–law enforcement relationships. Furthermore, the legal proceedings have yet to be concluded with the overturned convictions and impending retrial.

M. Hunter Martaindale

See also: East St. Louis Race Riot (1917) and Chicago Race Riot (1919); King, Rodney, Beating of (1991); Martin, Trayvon, Death of (February 26, 2012)

Further Reading

Mustian, Jim. 2014. "Justice Department Blasts Kurt Engelhardt in Danziger Appeal, Requests New Judge in the Event of Retrial." November 30. http://www.theneworleansadvocate.com/news/crime/10935166-123/justice-department-blasts-engelhardt-in. Accessed January 28, 2015.

Thompson, A.C. 2013. "Danziger Bridge Convictions Overturned." September 17. http://www.propublica.org/nola/story/danziger-bridge-convictions-overturned. Accessed January 27, 2015.

Dartmouth College Murders (January 27, 2001)

Robert Tulloch, born in May 1983, and James Parker, born in May 1984, were only teenagers when they murdered Half and Susanne Zantop on January 27, 2001. The significance of this case lies in its inexplicability, in regards to both the victims and the killers. The Zantops were well-respected and well-liked professors at Dartmouth College. Why would anyone want to kill them? Early in the investigation, authorities had trouble developing suspects and finding leads, until they were able to track evidence left at the crime scene to Parker. However, when Tulloch and Parker were labeled as suspects, people in the boys' hometown who knew them had a difficult time believing that either boy could have committed such a heinous crime. The subsequent investigation revealed the boys had simply become bored with life in Chelsea and wanted to "escape." Their attempts to get money culminated with the murders of Susanne and Half Zantop.

When Tulloch and Parker were named as suspects in the murders of Half and Susanne Zantop, the residents of the small town of Chelsea, Vermont, were stunned. Tulloch's teachers considered him smart and by his junior year of high school, he was the president of student council (Francis 2002). Similarly, Parker was a likeable boy who was known as the class clown (Zuckoff and Lehr 2003). Throughout their schooling, Tulloch and Parker became best friends, with Tulloch emerging as the leader. The two eventually decided they were bored living in Chelsea and wanted to get out. Their destination was Australia, and they determined they would need $10,000 to move there.

Since neither had financial resources, they turned to various criminal activities to obtain the cash they needed. Tulloch and Parker first considered relatively minor crimes, including searching through mail in an attempt to find credit cards to steal and use, which ultimately failed. Tulloch eventually suggested the best option would be to jump people and kill them to steal their bankcards. After two failed attempts of burglarizing and murder, Tulloch and Parker turned their attention to Hanover, New Hampshire, where they believed they would have better luck of finding wealthier targets.

On the morning of January 27, 2001, a family friend confirmed with Susanne Zantop that she was having dinner at the Zantop's house in Etna, New Hampshire, at

6:30 p.m. (Francis 2002). Sometime between that phone call and 6:30 p.m., Tulloch and Parker murdered the Zantops. To gain entry into the house, the boys pretended to be students from a nearby school conducting an environmental survey. After Mr. Zantop invited the boys into his study and talked with them, he suggested they get in contact with a friend of his. When Mr. Zantop went to his wallet to look for his friend's phone number, Tulloch saw money and began stabbing him. Mrs. Zantop came in from the kitchen when she heard her husband scream, and Parker slit her throat on command from Tulloch. After the Zantops were dead, Tulloch then slit Mr. Zantop's throat and stabbed Mrs. Zantop in the head several times (Zuckoff and Lehr 2003).

When the family friend arrived, she found the Zantops dead in the study, both stabbed at least half a dozen times. Investigators spent four days processing the inside of the house. The key pieces of evidence found by them were two sheaths used for SOG Navy Seal 2000 Combat Knives. Since there were two sheaths, investigators began considering the possibility that there were two killers. However, investigators were unable to make progress. The Zantops were well known and well liked, but the extreme violence of the crime indicated the killers may have known the Zantops. Also, if the Zantops' deaths were the result of a robbery, there were thousands of dollars of valuables the killers missed.

When the knife sheaths were tracked back to Parker through online sales records, the investigators finally had a lead. After investigators went to question the boys in February 2001, Tulloch and Parker fled to a truck stop in Sturbridge, Massachusetts, where they were able to hitchhike with a trucker. Sergeant Bill Ward happened to be watching the news when he saw a story explaining that Tulloch and Parker were believed to be hitchhiking across the country. Later, he pretended to be a trucker when he heard on the radio that another trucker was looking for someone to take two boys he had with him. Tulloch and Parker were then dropped off at the Flying J Travel Plaza in Spiceland, Indiana. The boys were arrested, taken to the Henry County Jail in New Castle, Indiana, and flown back to New Hampshire.

While in custody, Tulloch talked to his cellmates about the murders. One of these cellmates then recounted to authorities what Tulloch had told him. According to this cellmate, Tulloch claimed that "he wanted to kill somebody" at the house he and Parker chose to burglarize (Zuckoff and Lehr 2003, 301). Authorities had finally determined a motive for the Zantop murders—to kill and rob for money. The physical evidence investigators had against the boys to help make the case even stronger included the bloody knives, Parker's fingerprints, the Zantops' blood on the floor mat of Parker's mother's car, and Tulloch's bloody footprint.

In December 2001, Parker confessed to the murders after he discovered that he would not be able to be prosecuted in the juvenile system and therefore faced much stiffer sentences if he was found guilty. Parker ultimately pled guilty to being an accomplice to second-degree murder and agreed to cooperate fully, in addition to testifying against Tulloch at trial. In exchange for his cooperation, Parker was sentenced to 25 years to life. In April 2002, Tulloch, against the advice of his defenders, also pled guilty. He was sentenced to a mandatory life sentence without parole. At their trial, the boys' personality differences became obvious. Tulloch was not remorseful, while Parker struggled to control his emotions as he issued an apology to the daughters of the Zantops.

As of the date of this publication, Parker and Tulloch are being held in separate prisons in New Hampshire. However, in a 5-to-4 ruling by the Supreme Court in June 2013, *Miller v. Alabama* established that mandatory life sentences without parole for individuals under 18 years old are unconstitutional. Because Tulloch was 17 at the time of his sentencing, a judge has ordered that Tulloch receive a new sentencing hearing (Associated Press, 2013).

VICTORIA CLAUSEN

See also: Gallaudet University Murders (2000–2001); Leopold, Nathan (1904–1971) and Richard Loeb (1905–1936); Schwartz, Robert, Murder of (December 8, 2001); Virginia Tech Massacre (April 16, 2007)

Further Reading

Associated Press. 2013. "Tulloch, Vermont Teen Convicted in Dartmouth Professor Murders, Gets New Sentencing." *Burlington Free Press*. July 29. http://www.burlington freepress.com/viewart/20130729/NEWS07/307290029/. Accessed January 5, 2015.

Butterfield, Fox. 2002. "Teenagers Are Sentenced for Killing Two Professors." *The New York Times*. April 5. http://www .nytimes.com/2002/04/05/us/teenagers-are-sentenced-for-killing-two-professors.html. Accessed January 10, 2015.

Francis, Eric. 2002. *The Dartmouth Murders*. New York: St. Martin's Press.

Zuckoff, Mitchell, and Dick Lehr. 2003. *Judgment Ridge: The True Story behind the Dartmouth Murders*. New York: HarperCollins.

Dating Game Killer. *See* Alcala, Rodney (1943–)

Davis, Angela, Trial of (1972)

Born on January 6, 1944, Angela Davis is a political activist who was prosecuted on charges of conspiracy, aggravated kidnapping, and first-degree murder stemming from the August 7, 1970, courtroom abductions in San Rafael, California. Although Davis was not present during the events that ultimately led to the deaths of Judge Harold Haley, inmates James McClain, William Christmas, and the perpetrator, Jonathan Jackson, she was indicted for the crimes under California law, which treated all persons involved in a crime, whether directly committing it or not, as principals. Davis initially fled California becoming a fugitive and the third woman to ever be listed on the Federal Bureau of Investigation's (FBI) 10 most wanted list. Davis was arrested in New York City on October 13, 1970, and returned to California for prosecution. From the beginning, Davis asserted her innocence claiming she was being prosecuted for her political affiliations. She was initially denied bail and was detained for six months before a judge considered whether there was sufficient evidence to proceed in her case. As a result of the political frenzy surrounding her prosecution, several organizations nationally and internationally actively worked toward her "liberation." At trial, the prosecution presented a circumstantial case, which focused primarily on her fleeing after the events occurred. Davis's legal team presented a strong defense, and she was acquitted of all charges. After the trial, Davis remained politically active twice running for vice president on the Communist Party USA ticket. She also resumed her career as a professor researching, among other things, prisons and prisoners' rights.

On August 7, 1970, Jonathan Jackson entered the courtroom of Judge Harold Haley. James McClain, an inmate at San Quentin Prison, was on trial for assaulting a prison guard. Another inmate, Ruchell Magee, was being examined by the assistant district attorney, Gary Thomas. During the examination, Jackson stood up brandishing a gun. Jackson retrieved another gun from his satchel and handed it to McClain. Together, the two men freed a third inmate, William Christmas, who was in court to testify. The three men took the judge, the assistant district attorney,

Political activist Angela Davis seen on April 3, 1973, in the offices of the New York Committee to Free Angela Davis on Fifth Avenue. She had been acquitted of all charges against her in June 1972. (AP Photo)

and three female jurors as hostages and left the building. The hostages were loaded into a rented van parked nearby. The men attempted to exit the parking lot in the van, but two cars from San Quentin prison blocked the exit. The van came to a stop, and a gunfight broke out. In the aftermath, McClain, Christmas, Jackson, and the judge were all dead. Thomas, Magee, and one of the jurors were wounded.

Jackson's actions were believed to be in response to charges levied against the Soledad Brothers, three African American inmates who were charged with the murder of a white prison guard, John Mills, at California's Soledad Prison on January 16, 1970. The Soledad Brothers— Fleeta Drumgoole, John Clutchette, and George Jackson (Jonathan Jackson's older brother)—were accused of murdering Mills in retaliation for the shootings of three other black inmates three days earlier by Opie Miller, another white guard. Davis was a leader of the Soledad Brothers Defense Committee, a group that attempted to raise funds for the three men's defense and to raise public awareness about the case.

Davis was implicated as an accomplice in Jonathan Jackson's crimes partly due to her connection with the

Soledad Brothers. In addition, Davis had purchased the guns that Jonathan Jackson used. Although Davis had purchased three of the firearms over the previous year, the fact that she purchased the shotgun that Jackson used to kill Judge Haley only two days prior was a substantial focus in the case. Davis admitting to purchasing the shotgun and giving it to Jackson; however, she insisted that it had been given to him for the protection of the Soledad House. Davis claimed that Jackson must have stolen the other weapons from her.

The remaining evidence in the case was circumstantial. Several witnesses testified that they had seen Davis and Jackson together in the days prior to the event placing them together at the courthouse, at San Quentin Prison, at a nearby gas station, and in the vicinity of the U.S.–Mexico border. Davis insisted that she had hired Jackson as a bodyguard after her firing from University of California at Los Angeles (UCLA) as protection from extremists. Although forensics inspected the van used in the escape, Davis's fingerprints were not found in the van itself. Two books in Jackson's satchel, *The Politics of Violence in the Modern World* and *Violence and Social Change* (both inscribed "Angela Davis") did bear her fingerprints. Additionally, Davis's fingerprints were found on two pamphlets in the van, an M-1 carbine manual and a copy of *The Mini-Manual of the Urban Guerrilla*.

Davis's legal team, Leo Branton and Howard Moore, requested that the trial be moved to San Francisco, but the request was denied. A change of venue moving the trial from Marin County to Santa Clara County was granted citing the inability to find an impartial judge in the county where the crimes had taken place. Ultimately, Judge Richard Arnason presided over the trial. During opening remarks, Davis spoke for 80 minutes, outlining her version of events and characterizing her desire to free George Jackson as part of her greater political agenda. She also spoke about the impact of her political alignment with the Communist Party USA and the Black Panther Party. During the trial, Davis chose to not take the stand. Although Davis later refused to answer questions about why she did not testify, her attorneys insisted that she had been prepared to and the decision not to put her on the stand was made only as the defense began its case.

Davis's legal team employed what was at the time a revolutionary strategy; they hired psychologists to help determine which members of the jury pool might favor their arguments. Despite these efforts, the jury deliberated for three days, and reports that the jury might be deadlocked circulated. However, on the third day, after 13 total hours of deliberation, the all-white jury returned a verdict of not guilty. The jury decided that the fact that Davis owned the guns was not sufficient to establish her involvement.

Davis's political activism, a defining aspect of her trial, began long before the abductions. In the 1960s, as a leader within the Communist Party USA, Davis emerged nationally as a radical activist. Through her involvement in the civil rights movement, Davis also had relations with the Black Panther Party although she was never a member. In 1969, Davis, an assistant professor at the UCLA at the time, voiced opposition to several prominent issues including the Vietnam War, racism, sexism, and the prison-industrial complex. The Board of Regents of the University of California, urged by Governor Ronald Reagan, fired Davis for her affiliation with the Communist Party. Davis sued, and the court ordered her reappointment. The board was later successful in firing Davis by citing inflammatory utterances from various speeches including her referring to the police as pigs. After her acquittal, Davis was later employed as a professor in ethnic studies at San Francisco State University and the University of California, Santa Cruz, where she was the director of the university's Feminist Studies program.

Anne Li Kringen

See also: Attica Prison Riot (1971); Hampton, Fred, Shooting of (December 3, 1969); Jackson, George, Death of (1971); *Primary Documents*/Angela Davis Case: National United Committee to Free Angela Davis "People's Suit" Cover (1971)

Further Reading

Aptheker, Bettina. 1999. *The Morning Break: The Trial of Angela Davis.* Ithaca, NY: Cornell University Press.

Cotj, Lawrence. 1972. "The Facts behind the Angela Davis Case." *Human Events.* June 17.

Davis, Angela. 1974. *Angela Davis: An Autobiography.* New York: International Publishers.

DeSalvo, Albert. *See* Boston Strangler Murders (1962–1964)

Detroit Halloween Fires (1972–)

For many the Detroit Devil's Night Fires are a cultural phenomenon that defies explanation. Since the early

1970s, Detroit becomes an arsonist's playground on October 30. Despite a downturn in the number of fires in the mid-1990s, the tradition continues and occasionally spreads into the outlying suburbs with over a dozen fires reported annually. Devil's Night has also produced record numbers of fires, between 200 and 300 in a single night, as well as the occasional spree wherein the entire month of October has seen a spike in arsons to over 800. In response, starting in 1995, the city of Detroit has instituted Angel Nights from October 29 through the 31 to increase community involvement in nonviolent and nonflammable activities, as well as in protecting neighborhoods and property.

The city of Detroit has been plagued with civil unrest for decades. The first major race riots took place in Detroit in 1863 after the trial of an African American man for the rape of a white woman; this riot resulted in one homicide and multiple arsons, with property destroyed in 30 locations. Tension continued through World War I, though no riots followed. The next major riots took place in 1943, a great embarrassment to the city as the United States was fighting in World War II and domestic unrest was considered very unpatriotic. Nine whites and 25 African Americans were killed and property damage was valued in the millions. In 1967, racial tension boiled over again and a five-day riot began after a police raid at an afterhours night club where 82 people were celebrating the return of two soldiers from Vietnam. The riot resulted in the death of 43, thousands of injuries and arrests, and untold property damage with fires and looting spreading through the city; the National Guard was required to assist local law enforcement in ending the riot.

After the riots, curfews were established, but tensions remained. Overcrowding, poverty, and a vast racial divide remained. "Devil's Night," originally called "Mischief Night," was an annual Halloween Eve (October 30) event in Detroit and other cities. Since the 1940s, it had been common for teenagers and young adults to engage in acts of minor vandalism such as toilet-papering houses and egging or soaping windows. In most cases this behavior was tolerated as juvenile pranks and was limited in scope. Rarely did these mischief makers engage in serious property damage or violence. This changed in Detroit in the early 1970s. On October 30, 1972, arson fire began to replace toilet paper, soap, and eggs.

The fires were seen by some as an extension of the race riots of 1967, that even though the violence in the streets had stopped, the causes and concerns remained and the fires were a way to let those tensions reach the surface. For the most part, the fires typically target abandoned or unoccupied buildings, either residential or nonresidential properties, such as abandoned warehouses or closed shops. The fires in the early years were predominately localized to the same neighborhoods in the inner city that were most affected by the race riots of the prior decades. However, over time the fires spread through the entire city and into the suburbs.

The fires at the beginning were set only after dark and only on October 30. However, by the early 1980s, reaching their peak in 1984, the fires started on October 27 and could be set at any time. In 1984, more than 800 fires were set during that three-day period leading up to Halloween and throughout the rest of the 1980s it was not uncommon for fires to number between 500 and 800. People would stand on their front porches and stoops or in front of their businesses with weaponry to protect their property from vandals and arsonists. The fires took on an almost carnival atmosphere with people coming from neighboring communities to watch the buildings burn. Suburbanites and tourists mixed with concerned neighbors as they watched the fires burn. In many cases the fire departments were overwhelmed by the number of fires and some isolated abandoned buildings would be allowed to burn down, with firefighters watching to prevent only the spread of the fire. Crowds would gather to watch and share food and discussions of previous fires.

Informal groups of young people and formal groups established by community organizations and churches would patrol the area to attempt to prevent new fires. Firefighters from all over the country would come to Detroit to watch fires or lend a hand to the overworked local departments. It was not until the early 1990s that the city itself decided on a formal response to the Devil's Night tradition of arson. In 1994, the city of Detroit saw the worst spread of arson since the 1980s and the Mayor, Dennis Archer promised residents that the city would take action.

After the 1994 fires, the city itself began Angel Nights to counteract the Devil's Night mayhem. A tradition that continues to this day, calling for property owners and concerned citizens to adopt abandoned buildings in their neighborhood to protect them from arson, and to provide activities for young people to prevent them from participating in the vandalism. As a response to the institution of Angel Nights from October 29 through October 30, the fires dropped to a more manageable level for the rest of the decade. Angel Nights include a curfew for all young people and require chaperones for young people who are traveling after 6 p.m. or before 6 a.m., as well as a city ordinance that prohibits the sale of fuel in portable containers starting on October 27. In the 2000s the fires spiked again, but have remained between 80 and 175 each year.

The Detroit fires have been blamed on young people as well as adults. The fires have been considered an extension of the earlier race riots, as well as an opportunity for insurance fraud, revenge, or mean-spirited mischief. In reality, they probably have as many motivations as the variety of people who have set them over the decades. Despite concentrated efforts, very few people have been arrested for arson associated with Devil's Night, and the majority of arrests are for curfew violations. The fires have become part of popular culture, being mentioned in films, such as *The Crow*, *Grosse Pointe Blank*, and *8 Mile*. They have been used as plot devices in television shows, such as *Criminal Minds*, as well as in songs and rap.

CLAIRISSA D. BREEN

See also: Detroit Riot (1943); Detroit Riot (1967)

Further Reading

Capeci, Dominic J. 1991. *Layered Violence: The Detroit Rioters of 1943*. Jackson: University Press of Mississippi.

Chafets, Ze'ev. 1990. *Devil's Night and Other True Tales of Detroit*. New York: Random House.

City of Detroit. 2014. Angels Night Information. http://www.detroitmi.gov/How-Do-I/Volunteer/Angels-Night-Information. Accessed April 15, 2015.

Fine, Sidney. 1989. *Violence in the Model City: The Cavanagh Administration, Race Relations, and the Detroit Riot of 1967*. Ann Arbor: University of Michigan Press.

Sauter, Van Gordon, and Burleigh Hines. 1968. *Nightmare in Detroit: A Rebellion and Its Victims*. Chicago: Regnery Publishers.

Schneider, John C. 1980. *Detroit and the Problem of Order, 1830–1880: A Geography of Crime, Riot, and Policing*. Lincoln: University of Nebraska Press.

Sugrue, Thomas. 1996. *The Origins of the Urban Crisis: Race and Inequality in Post-War Detroit*. Princeton, NJ: Princeton University Press.

Detroit Riot (1943)

As Detroit experienced a boom of higher-paying jobs during the expansion of manufacturing for the war effort, recruiters worked hard to draw new residents from across America to fill these new jobs. A large number of both white and black workers were recruited from the American Deep South and Appalachia. These workers were promised higher-paying jobs and a future with more opportunity. The resulting influx of factory workers meant that available housing was sparse. In response, the federal government undertook efforts to develop housing for both black and white families. The government constructed separate housing for blacks and whites in Detroit. The black housing complex was constructed in an all-white neighborhood which set off strong resistance and protest from white residents who did not believe that blacks should be allowed to live in their neighborhoods. After trying to relocate black families, the federal government decided to allow the black families to move into the newly constructed housing. Whites protested violently and refused to allow the black families into their new homes. The Detroit mayor at the time, Edward Jeffries (1900–1950), ordered the state police and Michigan state troops to ensure the safety of the black families. After the families were moved into their new homes, the Packard manufacturing plant decided to promote two black workers to work alongside white workers. The result was a massive protest wherein 25,000 workers walked out. Shortly thereafter, several rumors circulated through Detroit that whites had attacked a black mother and her child, ultimately killing them and throwing them in the Detroit River. Similar rumors were circulated about blacks attacking white women. The result was a bloody riot that lasted three days and required federal troops to quell.

The riots themselves started when a black man was accused of insulting a white sailor's girlfriend while they were at Belle Island, a popular park near the Detroit River. The insult that the black man was accused of resulted in a brawl between blacks and whites that would escalate into the riot. More accusation of violence between blacks and whites circulated throughout the city, but much of the information was false. Large white mobs began to attack black citizens as they traveled to and from work on street cars. These attacks escalated into large-scale fighting between various black and white mobs in Detroit. The fighting was focused in predominantly black neighborhoods as whites sought out blacks to seek revenge for the atrocities described in the false rumors that were circulating around Detroit at the time. As the mobs grew in size, the fighting escalated into the destruction of property. Cars and businesses were burned in and around the black neighborhood known as Paradise Valley. The fighting then turned to citizens that were not involved in the mobs. Many pedestrians and motorist traveling through the area were attacked and beaten. Mayor Jeffries then asked President Roosevelt (1882–1945) to intervene with federal troops to end the

Passengers climb from the rear of a streetcar stopped by a mob during race riots in Detroit, June 22, 1943. (Rear of "a" streetcar)

riot. The three-day riot resulted in 34 dead, 25 of whom were black citizens, and over 600 injured. There were over 1,800 people arrested as a result of the riot. Of those black citizens killed, 17 were killed by police officers. Of those injured during the rioting, 75 percent were blacks. Furthermore; out of the 1,600 arrestees, 85 percent were black citizens. Many citizens claimed that the disproportionate number of blacks hurt, and arrested, represented further discrimination by the government and white elite.

In the aftermath of the riots, people were looking for explanations and to assign blame for the costly property damages, over $2 million, and loss of life. Many of the city officials in Detroit blamed blacks for the violence, and openly voiced their opinion claiming that young black men acted to inflame tensions between black and white residents. Mayor Jeffries joined those who voiced blame toward young black men for the violence. Other officials blamed black organizations, such as the NAACP, for instigating the violence in an attempt to further their agenda in the city and to take control of the local government to serve their own ends. Many white citizens claimed that the large number of blacks arrested is an indication of who should be blamed for the riots. However, the vast majority of those injured were black citizens that were attacked as they attempted to move through the city on their way to work.

Other leaders, including Thurgood Marshall who was a leader with the NAACP at the time, blamed the deaths of the 25 dead black citizens on the lack of police support during the riots. These sentiments were also reflected by leaders of the Axis nations who encouraged blacks to not fight on behalf of the Allied powers. These leaders of the Axis nations wanted to point out that the riots were a reflection of the weakness and disorganization in America. Marshall claimed that the Detroit police were targeting blacks for social unrest and placed a disproportionate amount of pressure on black citizens while doing little if anything to intervene when white citizens rioted and harmed black citizens and businesses. He pointed out that 85 percent of those arrested were black citizens, while large white mobs were allowed to burn cars and loot businesses with immunity. Some wild claims were made by Martin Dies, who was a representative from Texas during the riots, that Japanese Americans had infiltrated Detroit in an attempt to subvert war efforts by flaming hatred between black and white citizens.

The governor of Michigan at the time, Harry Kelly, commissioned an investigation of the events that led up to the riots. This commission was criticized for their quick investigation that was not seen as being thorough. The conclusion of the investigative commission appointed by Kelly determined that black youth were to blame for the riots by instigating violence against white citizens. Many of those young black men who went on trial in the aftermath of the riot faced all-white juries who had already seen the commissions claim that these young black men were responsible for the riots. The result was an unfair trial for many of these young black men who were subsequently convicted. Roosevelt also failed to address the riots publicly for fear of protest by his financial supporters in the South. His only acknowledgment of the riots and the resulting destruction came in the form of a letter he wrote to a New York congressman. After the Detroit Riots of 1943, subsequent rioting took place in the New York neighborhood Harlem. There were no long-standing political or legal changes made in Detroit to address the riots or their cause. Detroit would again experience rioting during the civil rights movement in 1967.

DUSTIN EICKE

See also: Detroit Halloween Fires (1972–); Detroit Riot (1967); Harlem Riot (March 19–20, 1935); Harlem Riot (August 1–2, 1943)

Further Reading

"American Experience: TV's Most-Watched History Series." PBS. http://www.pbs.org/wgbh/americanexperience/features/general-article/eleanor-riots. Accessed April 15, 2015.

Johnson, Marilynn. 1998. "Gender, Race, and Rumors: Re-examining the 1943 Race Riots." *Gender & History* 10 (2): 252–277.

Lee, Alfred McClung, and Norman Daymond Humphrey. 1968. *Race Riot, Detroit 1943*. New York: Octagon Books.

Detroit Riot (1967)

The start to the 1967 Detroit Riot was a routine enforcement raid of a known speakeasy in the predominantly black 12th Street area of the city. Forty-three citizens were killed. Perhaps one of the most shocking statistics is the fact that there were 7,231 arrests during, and following, the riot. The level of property damage was just as staggering, with over 2,500 buildings partially or completely destroyed, and many families were rendered homeless. Many local business were also destroyed, and would never return. While the exact economic costs of the riot are disputed, the estimates of these costs range from $40 to $45 million. The social implications for black and white relationships was just as perilous. After the riot, many blacks in Detroit supported complete social separation from whites. The social and economic scars would haunt Detroit for decades in the forms of lost taxation dollar, crippled tourism markets,

and loss of jobs and migration away from the city. Trust of the Detroit Police Department was further eroded by the riot, and many black communities began to see the predominantly white police force as oppressors. This lack of trust in the criminal justice system within Detroit would further hamper efforts to improve community relations within the city. Following the riot, the 12th Street area of Detroit suffered from poor housing conditions and was rife with allegations of police brutality.

The lead-up to the riot was the result of a police raid of a popular black speakeasy, also known as a blind pig. Following Prohibition, many of these illegally operating businesses became an important, and engrained, part of the culture in Detroit. The particular establishment that sparked the 1967 Detroit Riot occupied the top floor of a printing business and was also the office of the United Community League for Civil Action in Detroit. At night, the club was a bustling center of activity that included illegal alcohol sales and unlicensed gambling. It was for these reasons that the Detroit police would raid the establishment during the predawn hours of Sunday, July 23, 1967. Once the raid began, the police quickly realized that they had far underestimated the number of patrons that would be present at the club. The large crowd included 82 people that were celebrating the return of two U.S. servicemen from the Vietnam War.

The police were quickly overran by the large and densely populated community. An initial breakout of violence directed at the police officers quickly erupted into full-scale looting of nearby businesses. To further complicate matters, police were hampered by the fact that it was very early Sunday morning, and the mobilization of backup officers was a slow process. The rioting began to spread to adjacent neighborhoods and the Wayne County sheriff's office, Michigan State Police, and the Michigan National Guard were all mobilized by then governor George Romney. This was done after Governor Romney contacted Attorney General Ramsey Clark who in turn contacted President Lyndon Johnson. The first fire was set on Sunday July 23, and firefighters were prevented from entering. As the first day of rioting came to a close, several business had been completely looted or destroyed.

On the July 24, reinforcements from the Michigan National Guard, Michigan State Police, and the Wayne County Sheriff's office began to reach the riot. Due to the large number of looters, police were still not able to effectively slow the progress of the riot. By the end of the second day of rioting, almost 500 fires had been started and thousands of firearms began to proliferate the streets after being looted from local businesses. Firefighters came under attack from the looters, and were unable to adequately perform their duties. The result was hundreds of businesses, both black and white owned, were left burning and were completely destroyed. The quickly deteriorating situation in Detroit led President Johnson to authorize federal troops to enter Detroit using a law designed to quell insurrection against the government. This included nearly 5,000 soldiers from the 82nd Airborne.

By the time that federal troops entered Detroit, the situation had further escalated as police officers began to resort to brutality as a response to the rioting. Many citizens were reportedly abused while in custody of the Detroit Police, including women that were sexually assaulted by officers. In the aftermath, it was discovered that some officers went as far as to commit execution-style murder of black men. Many of the atrocities committed by the Detroit Police were documented in photographs taken by both the citizens of Detroit and the police themselves. The infusion of troops, and the State Police, eventually led to the de-escalation of violence on the streets of Detroit. By the July 29, all federal and state soldiers had been removed from Detroit.

After the rioting ended, by July 28, much of the blame for what had taken place was attributed to the inclusion of state and federal troops. Black leaders within the Detroit community would later point to the way the Detroit police attempted to arrest those citizens at the speakeasy where the rioting began. The distrust sowed within the community would lead to deep distrust between both black and white citizens. Many leaders, in both black and white political circles, who were considered moderate before the rioting, moved to more extremist positions. Many blacks would call for a complete separation from whites, both politically and socially. The breakdown of political and social relations among the races was met with serious economic losses resulting from the rioting. These included the loss of further economic investment and development in the black communities of Detroit, much of which is still present. Late into the 1990s, much of the burned structures was either left vacant, or was reduced to empty lots overgrown with weeds and littered with trash.

During the riots, the loss of life was disproportional among black and white citizens. Of the 43 people killed during the violence, nearly 77 percent of them were black. In comparison, 10 whites lost their lives during the five-day ordeal. Nearly 500 injuries were reported, of which, only 38 percent were reported to be citizens. The vast majority of recorded injuries were those of officers and soldiers. These disparities further drove the divide between the black and white communities. In the end, much of Detroit still suffers from the economic and social losses after the rioting.

DUSTIN EICKE

See also: Detroit Halloween Fires; Detroit Riot (1943); Harlem Riot (March 19–20, 1935); Harlem Riot (August 1–2, 1943)

Further Reading

Fine, Sidney. 1987. "Rioters and Judges: The Response of the Criminal Justice System to the Detroit Riot of 1967." *Wayne Law Review* 33(5): 1723–1763.

Meredith, Robin. 1997. "5 Days in 1967 Still Shake Detroit." *The New York Times.* July 22. http://www.nytimes.com/ 1997/07/23/us/5-days-in-1967-still-shake-detroit.html. Accessed April 9, 2015.

Vance, Cyrus. 2008. *Final Report of Cyrus R. Vance, Special Assistant to the Secretary of Defense, Concerning the Detroit Riots, July 23 through August 2, 1967.* October 1. http://www.lbjlib.utexas.edu/johnson/archives.hom/oral history.hom/vance-c/detroitreport.asp. Accessed April 9, 2015.

Diallo, Amadou, Shooting of (1999)

The shooting of Amadou Diallo (1975–1999) is a case of police brutality, excessive force, zero tolerance policing, and racial profiling that has refueled distrust between police and ethnic minorities in the United States. The incident centers around the dubious circumstances that caused four white plainclothed police officers from New York Police Department's (NYPD) now-defunct Street Crimes Unit to shoot a barrage of semiautomatic firepower at an unarmed African immigrant who had no criminal record. During the investigation into the shooting, the four officers were placed on administrative leave until the NYPD concluded that their conduct was justified according to the department's use of force policy. The investigation's results prompted massive protests by both the African American and Latino communities. A grand jury finally indicted the officers for second-degree murder and reckless endangerment, but an appellate court granted a change of venue to Albany, New York, due to a concern over having a fair trial in the Bronx. Approximately a year after the shooting a jury acquitted the four officers of all charges, accepting the defense's narrative that the shooting was an unfortunate but reasonable misunderstanding given the conditions and circumstances. The verdict sparked demonstrations and the media generated a national discussion and examination of the social, political, and legal causes of police violence. The Amadou Diallo shooting has become a criminal justice cause célèbre concerning police brutality and race relations in the United States.

On February 4, 1999, Amadou Bailo Diallo, a 23-year-old immigrant from Guinea, was shot and killed by officers Kenneth Boss, Sean Carroll, Edward McMellin, and Richard Murphy from NYPD's Street Crimes Unit right outside the door of his building in the Bronx. The elite anticrime unit that operated under the motto "we own the night" was well known for its aggressive tactics and undercover work. Diallo had no criminal record and was known as a devout Muslim who made a living as a street vendor. The exact circumstances surrounding the shooting remain ambiguous. At around midnight, the four officers drove around in a Ford Taurus when they spotted and approached Diallo, suspecting that he was the armed serial rapist that they had been searching for. After they identified themselves, the officers claim that Diallo moved away from them toward his front door to reach for an item in his pocket, disregarding their pleas to put his hands up. Assuming that it was a gun, all four officers fired 41 shots with 19 hitting Diallo. The post-shooting investigation revealed that Diallo was unarmed. The item that he pulled out of his pocket was his wallet, possibly presuming that the four plainclothed armed men that approached him were looking to rob him.

While placing the officers on administrative leave, the NYPD continued their investigation and ruled that the officers used deadly force appropriately. Many citizens were outright skeptical of the NYPD's findings given that at least two out of the four officers were previously involved in a police shooting. Demonstrations erupted immediately over Diallo's death and the NYPD's findings, with a number of protestors demanding the officers' arrests. In the following weeks, an organized campaign of civil disobedience headed by the Reverend Al Sharpton and other well-known community leaders and political activists kept pressure on the NYPD and made Diallo's shooting the top headline in national news. Eventually a variety of groups from all multicultural backgrounds and sections of society got involved in the protests. As the media attention intensified, many famous celebrities also joined the protests and sit-ins. Several celebrities were even arrested, which include New York City's first and only African American mayor David Dinkins, actress Susan Sarandon, and civil rights activist Jesse Jackson. After more than 12,000 arrests

during close to a month of protests, the Bronx prosecutor finally decided to indict the four officers for second-degree murder and reckless endangerment.

Although the officers were indicted, their defense attorneys were able to change the venue by arguing that their clients would not get a fair trial anywhere in New York City. The trial was moved from the Bronx, one of the most diverse boroughs in New York City, to Albany, the state's capital city where whites make up the majority. During the trial, the jury had to depend largely on the testimony of the officers themselves to understand what exactly happened in the moments that led up to the shooting. Despite Diallo's violent death, the prosecution knew they would not get the convictions that they argued for. Any jury would be horrified by Diallo's violent death, but when considering the circumstances, the shooting appeared to be an unfortunate encounter with an unintended outcome. Some legal analysts covering the trial blamed the prosecution for not going after the NYPD and the obvious issues surrounding the case that include the department's history of excessive force, racial profiling, and other controversial policies. A strategy that involves these issues might have convinced the jury to convict the officers for the homicide at a lesser degree of guilt. In the end, the racially mixed jury found all four officers not guilty of any of the charges.

When all four police officers were acquitted, protests resumed. Activists claimed that the Amadou Diallo shooting case was one of injustice that started with his homicide, amalgamated by the results of the police investigation and the change of venue, and sealed by the police officers' not guilty verdict. The Justice Department refused to file civil rights charges as protestors now demanded, since there was no evidence of the officers' intent. As time passed, Amadou Diallo's death became the standard case of police brutality, zero tolerance policing, and racial profiling during the Giuliani years that continued to strain the relationship between the NYPD and the city's immigrant and minority communities. In spite of the negative attention the Amadou Diallo case brought to the NYPD, other comparable victims of police abuse of force continued to emerge that include the homicide of Patrick Dorismond by plainclothed officers less than a month after the acquittal of the four officers in the Diallo case, the homicide of Ousmane Zongo in 2003 while unarmed in a warehouse raid, the unarmed 19-year-old Timothy Stansbury in 2004, as well as Sean Bell on the morning before his wedding in 2006. The elements in each of these incidents were reminiscent of the Amadou Diallo case in that each victim was black and confronted by overly aggressive police officers. The improvement of the quality of life and the decrease of crime in New York City were commendable during those years but the strategies used were disproportionately aimed at minorities and progress was achieved at a heavy price that cost many including Amadou Diallo their lives.

NABIL OUASSINI

See also: King, Rodney, Beating of (1991); Los Angeles Riots (1992); Serpico, Frank (1936–)

Further Reading

Diallo, Kadiatou, and Craig Wolff. 2009. *My Heart Will Cross This Ocean: My Story, My Son, Amadou.* New York: Random House Digital, Inc.

Roy, Beth. 2009. *41 Shots and Counting: What Amadou Diallo's Story Teaches Us about Policing, Race, and Justice.* Syracuse, NY: Syracuse University Press.

Diamond, Jack "Legs" (1897–1931)

Known to the world as "the gangster who couldn't be killed" and the "Clay Pigeon," Jack "Legs" Diamond was one of the most prominent bootleggers during the Prohibition era. Notoriously known as a ruthless and loyal, but double-crossing, Irish gangster, Diamond was involved in illegal alcohol sales, mayhem, kidnappings, as well as shooting and killing several men inside his New York speakeasies. By the mid-1920s, Diamond worked for Arnold "The Brain" Rothstein (1882–1928), first as his bodyguard and then as his partner in heroin sales. Despite the lucrative capacity of the heroin business with Rothstein, Diamond wanted more and decided to pick up the hobby of hijacking other bootleggers' liquor trucks in his spare time. This was a hobby that made Diamond an unwelcome person in the gangster world and made him fair game to anyone who could eliminate him from the bootlegging market. Although he miraculously survived at least three attempts on his life, two hitmen brought an end to his career with three bullets to his head in 1931.

Born July 10, 1897, in Philadelphia, Pennsylvania, to Irish immigrant parents, Jack Diamond was commonly known to the world as "Legs" or "Gentleman Jack," and often went by the alias "Jack Moran." When he was a small child, Diamond's mother Sara suffered from various health issues and upon her death in 1913 from a viral infection his father John moved Diamond and his younger brother Eddie (n.d.) to Brooklyn, New York. Diamond often struggled throughout grade school and due to his family's impoverished status Diamond and Eddie turned to a life of violence and theft with a local street gang known as "the Moyer Street Gang" or "the Boiler Gang." In February 1914, at the age of 16, Diamond's first burglary arrest occurred when he broke into a jewelry store. He was also arrested more than a dozen more times throughout his life for several robberies, burglaries, and mayhem. In 1917, at the age of 20, Diamond married a girl by the name of Florence Williams, but they divorced within a few short months. It is not clear when or how Diamond earned his nickname "Legs," but it is speculated that it stems primarily from his ability to run from the scene of a crime with superior swiftness and secondarily from his exceptional dancing skills.

During one of his many trips to a juvenile penitentiary, Diamond was drafted into the U.S. Army after spending only a few months in detention. After serving less than a year during World War I, army life did not suit well for Diamond, and he decided to go absent without leave (AWOL). However, he was caught shortly after, convicted for desertion, and sentenced to serve three to five years at the Federal Penitentiary in Fort Leavenworth, Kansas. It was during this prison stay that the Eighteenth Amendment of the Constitution went into effect on January 17, 1920, banning alcohol in the United States, which gave rise to Diamond's illicit liquor empire. Therefore, when released from prison in 1921, Diamond and Eddie relocated to Manhattan's Lower East Side where Diamond thought they could make their fortune in the profitable underworld enterprise of smuggling alcohol during the Prohibition.

It was in New York City that Diamond organized liquor truck heists to supply his speakeasies and quickly became known in the bootlegging world as an extremely violent and murderous gangster. By 1923, Diamond was also working various jobs with fellow prominent gangsters and racketeers such as Charles "Lucky" Luciano (1897–1962) the first mob boss of the Genovese crime family, Charles "Vannie" Higgins (1897–1932) a prominent bootlegger, Jacob "Little Augie" Orgen (1893–1927) a bootlegger and labor racketeer, and Arnold "The Brain" Rothstein (1882–1928) a well-known racketeer, businessman, and gambler. In 1923, Orgen placed a hit on labor racketeer Nathan "Kid Dropper" Kaplan (1891–1923) to gain control of his territory. Although it is clear that Diamond played a part in the murder of Kaplan, there is debate on what his role specifically entailed such as whether he only hired hitman Louis "Kerzner" Cohen (1904–1939) for the job, was the mastermind behind the hit, or if he had plans to double-cross Orgen once the hit was carried out and take over Kaplan's territory himself.

It was Diamond's relationship with Rothstein that was the financial break he was waiting for to take his criminal career to the next level. Starting out as Rothstein's bodyguard, Diamond quickly became a partner in Rothstein's lucrative heroin business. During this time, Diamond married his second wife Alice Kenny (n.d.–1933) in 1926 but continued his relationship with mistress Marion "Kiki Roberts" Strasmick and several other women on the side. Once Diamond felt that he had profited enough money through Rothstein's business, he decided that it was time he and Eddie to branch out on their own hijacking and bootlegging alcohol. Unfortunately, Diamond's hobby did not sit well with the other bootleggers in the area; thus, several bootleggers issued a mutual hit, making him fair game to anyone who could eliminate him from the bootlegging market. As a result, the first of many attempts on his life was in 1927 when he and Orgen were walking down a Lower East Side street in Manhattan the day he substituted for Eddie as Orgen's bodyguard. Three men approached the two and began shooting, fatally wounding Orgen and hitting Diamond two times below the heart. Initially, police suspected Diamond as an accomplice to the murder, but the charges were eventually dropped.

Wanted in 1930 for the murder of roadhouse owner Harry Western—who contributed heavily to the bootlegging market—Diamond fled to Europe where he also attempted to procure liquor illegally from Germany. Shortly after he was caught and deported back to the United States, another attempt on his life was made while he was staying in the Hotel Monticello where he was shot five times. Then in 1931, while waiting on a call from his lawyer at the Aratoga Inn to discuss the charges he faced for the kidnapping and torture of applejack liquor truck driver Grover Parks, Diamond was shot three times with a shotgun and survived yet again. When the kidnapping and torture case against Diamond finally went to court later that year, he was acquitted after his first appeal on December 17, 1931. On December 18, 1931, while celebrating his acquittal, two hit men pinned him down and put three bullets in his head bringing an end to his criminal career. However, the individual responsible for Diamond's death is still unknown. Over the years speculation has been placed on several individuals such as the Oley Brothers, Dutch Schultz, and even the Albany Police Department after allegedly receiving an order from political leader Dan O'Connell.

JENNIFER A. HAEGELE

See also: Capone, Al (1899–1947); Luciano, Charles "Lucky" (1897–1962); Schultz, Dutch (1901–1935)

Further Reading

Bruno, Joe. 2014. *Mobsters, Gangs, Crooks and Other Creeps: Volume 1—New York City*. n.p.: Joe Bruno, printed by Createspace Independent Publishing Platform.

Downey, Patrick. 2011. *Legs Diamond: Gangster*. n.p.: Patrick Downey, printed by Createspace Independent Publishing Platform.

Levine, Gary. 1979. *Anatomy of a Gangster: Jack "Legs" Diamond*. Fleischmanns, NY: Purple Mountain Press.

Dillinger, John (1903–1934)

John Dillinger, a notorious 1930s bank robber, was part of the Great Depression era crime wave that included Bonnie and Clyde, "Pretty Boy" Floyd, and Ma Barker and the Barker Boys. Dillinger's daring escapades made him a celebrity criminal and media sensation. Named "Public Enemy No. 1," he was ultimately gunned down by federal agents after a two-year crime spree.

Dillinger was born in Indianapolis, Indiana, in 1903. His mother died when he was three years old, leaving him with his father, a strict disciplinarian. While young, Dillinger, a school dropout, was involved in mischief with his neighborhood gang, "the Dirty Dozen." In 1920, Dillinger's father sold his grocery store to settle on a farm in Mooresville, Indiana. Dillinger, however, remained working at an Indianapolis machine shop and engaged in late-night carousing. In 1923, he stole a car to impress a girl and joined the U.S. Navy to avoid police capture. Dillinger went through basic training, but then jumped ship; he was dishonorably discharged.

In 1924, Dillinger married 16-year-old Beryl Ethel Hovious. They settled in his father's farmhouse. Struggling to survive financially, Dillinger stole some chickens. His father negotiated a deal to keep the case out of court. Nevertheless, it escalated tensions between the two. Dillinger and his wife moved out. Later that year, with the disreputable Edgar Singleton, Dillinger robbed a grocery store. He was caught and, without a lawyer, sentenced to 10 to 20 years in prison.

Dillinger was sent to the Indiana State Reformatory in Pendleton. His personality earned him friends there, including Harry Pierpont and Homer Van Meter. In 1929, Beryl divorced him. Shortly thereafter, he was denied parole. He requested a transfer to the Indiana State Prison in Michigan City. There, reunited with Pierpont and Van Meter, Dillinger learned the skills to become a professional and more dangerous criminal. He became friends with other prisoners, like Walter Dietrich, a protégé of infamous bank robber Hermann Lamm.

Pierpont and Van Meter hatched an escape plan involving robberies to finance a prison break. Dillinger, due to be freed first, was brought into the fold and coached how to proceed once released. They gave him lists of targets, accomplices, and fences. In May 1933, Dillinger was paroled to be with his dying stepmother. He then staged several robberies, executing his friends' scheme, and arranged for guns to be smuggled inside the prison. After he helped them escape in September, they went to Hamilton, Ohio. Meanwhile, Dillinger had visited a female friend in Dayton. Police, who had been watching Dillinger, received a tip from his landlady. Police arrested Dillinger, who was then incarcerated in a jail in Lima. Pierpont and his gang raided the jail to free Dillinger, in the process murdering the sheriff.

Dillinger and his gang went to Chicago, orchestrating a series of organized, daring—and deadly—bank robberies. To support their efforts, they raided a police arsenal. The gang received sensationalist press coverage, which called them either the Dillinger or Pierpont Gang. Over three months, they robbed banks throughout Illinois, Indiana, and Wisconsin. The heists often demonstrated a taste for the theatrical. For example, the gang once pretended to be a film crew shooting a crime film to pull the heist off. A popular story emerged—fueling a Robin Hood image—that Dillinger told a man making a deposit during a robbery to keep his money; the only money he wanted was "the banks."

In December 1933, the gang vacationed in Florida. Before leaving, one of them shot a police officer at a repair shop. The Chicago Police Department formed a "Dillinger Squad" to take the gang down. Early in 1934, Pierpont suggested they head for Arizona. On his way, Dillinger, along with girlfriend Billy Freshette and Red Hamilton, robbed the First National Bank in Gary, Indiana. During the robbery, Hamilton was wounded; Dillinger shot a police officer. Meanwhile, the rest of the gang reached Tucson. A hotel fire tipped police off to their whereabouts and they rounded the gang up. Dillinger and Freschette, who arrived after the fire, were caught at a nearby motel. Midwest authorities negotiated for the prisoners' extradition. Each state claimed supreme jurisdiction; eventually, different gang members were sent to different states for trial.

Dillinger, with escort Police Captain Matt Leach, went to Indiana.

Dillinger was brought to the Lake County sheriff's office, which was mobbed with reporters and photographers. Dillinger stayed at Crown Point Prison, known for being inescapable, while awaiting trial. In March 1934, however, Dillinger escaped without firing a shot. According to tradition, he used a wooden gun blackened with shoe polish. Dillinger stole a police car and drove to Illinois. By crossing state lines in a stolen vehicle, he came under the jurisdiction of the Federal Bureau of Investigation (FBI). The FBI had not been involved previously because bank robberies were not yet considered a federal crime. This changed later that year, partially in response to Dillinger's actions.

In Chicago, Dillinger formed a new gang that included Van Meter and the notorious Lester Gillis, known as "Baby Face Nelson." They relocated to Minnesota, igniting a crime spree through four states. During a bank robbery in Iowa, Dillinger and another gang member were wounded; consequently, they hid in Wisconsin while recovering in a lodge known as "Little Bohemia." The lodge's owner, recognizing Dillinger, informed the U.S. attorney general. Local FBI agent Melvin Purvis was contacted shortly thereafter. In April 1934, FBI agents raided the lodge. During the ensuing gunfight, Dillinger and his gang escaped through the woods.

Dillinger went into hiding. The FBI named him "Public Enemy No. 1" and placed a bounty on him. Meanwhile, Dillinger underwent crude plastic surgery and began using an alias. In June 1934, he committed his last bank heist at Merchant's National Bank in South Bend, Indiana. Baby Face Nelson opened fire, drawing attention and police. During a gun battle, several police officers, hostages, and pedestrians were killed or wounded. Van Meter was also killed.

Meanwhile, Purvis began negotiating with Anna Sage, a Romanian immigrant. How Dillinger exactly knew Sage, a former prostitute who then ran a Chicago brothel, is unknown. Some suggest that Dillinger met her through his girlfriend, Polly Hamilton, who worked for Sage. Sage had informed a police detective with whom she was involved about her immigration difficulties; he in turn introduced her to Purvis. She agreed to help the FBI capture Dillinger in exchange for Purvis's efforts to prevent her deportation.

On July 22, 1934, Sage informed the FBI that Dillinger intended to see a movie at the Biograph or Marboro Theater. Agents staked out both locations; Purvis positioned himself at the Biograph. As Dillinger exited the Biograph and passed Purvis, Purvis lit a cigar to alert agents to Dillinger's identity. Purvis pulled his gun and asked Dillinger to surrender. Dillinger began to run, reaching for a hidden gun. He was gunned down in the street. Crowds formed around his body; onlookers attempted to grab souvenirs. Police had to be called to help the FBI to secure the area and remove Dillinger's body. He was buried at Indianapolis's Crown Hill Cemetery.

ERIC MARTONE

See also: Barker, Kate "Ma" (1873–1935); Floyd, Charles Arthur "Pretty Boy" (1904–1934); Gillis, Lester Joseph "Baby Face Nelson" (1908–1934); Parker, Bonnie (1910–1934) and Clyde Barrow (1909–1934); *Primary Documents*/Excerpts from John Dillinger's Autopsy Report (July 23, 1934)

Further Reading

Burrough, Bryan. 2004. *Public Enemies: America's Greatest Crime Wave and the Birth of the FBI, 1933–34*. New York: Penguin.

Girardin, G. Russell, and William Helmer. 2009. *Dillinger: The Untold Story*. Bloomington: Indiana University Press.

Matera, Dary. 2005. *John Dillinger: The Life and Death of America's First Celebrity Criminal*. New York: Da Capo Press.

Dorner, Christopher (1979–2013)

Christopher Dorner was a former Los Angeles police officer who was responsible for a series of shootings from February 3 to 12, 2013, killing four people, including three and wounding six law enforcement officers. Dorner died from a self-inflicted gunshot wound while engaging in a shootout on February 12, 2013, following a weeklong manhunt. In the early days of his shooting spree, Dorner allegedly authored a manifesto exacting revenge on the Los Angeles Police Department (LAPD) for spoiling his good name and unjustifiably firing him. As an African American, Dorner felt the LAPD's motives for his termination were racist and believed the shooting spree would bring attention to the corruption of the LAPD.

Dorner was raised in Los Angeles County, California, and graduated from Cypress High School in 1997. He graduated from Southern Utah University in 2001. In 2002, Dorner commissioned as a reserve officer in the U.S. Navy. In 2005, Dorner was hired with the LAPD. Dorner was married less than one month to April Carter in 2007.

In August 2007, Dorner claimed to have observed his Field Training Officer Teresa Evans kick a handcuffed mentally disturbed man twice in the face. Dorner subsequently filed a formal complaint against Evans alleging excessive force. The LAPD's internal affairs divisions investigated Dorner's allegations, and it was determined that Dorner lied about the incident. During his internal review board hearing, Dorner was represented by Randal Quan, an attorney for the city of Los Angeles and former LAPD captain. In September 2008, Dorner was terminated by the LAPD due to filing what was believed to be a false report against his training officer. In 2010, Dorner appealed the LAPD's decision to terminate him, but a Los Angeles County Superior Court judge upheld the LAPD's decision and his appeal was rejected. At the time of his termination, Dorner continued to work as a navy reserve officer, but was honorably discharged on February 1, 2013. Dorner blamed the LAPD for ending his career as a navy officer.

Two days later, on the evening of February 3, 2013, the bodies of Monica Quan, the daughter of Randal Quan, and her fiancé, Keith Lawrence, a public safety officer at the University of Southern California, were found inside Monica Quan's parked car in the parking lot of her condominium complex in Irvine, California.

On February 4, 2013 at 1:15 a.m., Dorner checked into a San Diego, California, hotel room and allegedly posted a "manifesto" on his Facebook page. The nearly 11,000-word document began by saying, "I know most of you who personally know me are in disbelief to hear from media reports that I am suspected of committing such horrendous murders and have taken drastic and shocking actions in the last couple of days . . . Unfortunately, this is a necessary evil that I do not enjoy but must partake and complete for substantial change to occur within the LAPD and reclaim my name." The manifesto outlines Dorner's witnessing and subsequent reporting of his training officer's excessive use of force, followed by the accusation that Dorner lied, unsuccessful Board of Rights hearing, and subsequent termination of employment. The manifesto goes into great detail with names and dates of incidents of perceived racism, injustice, and abuse of power in the LAPD. Dorner warns, "The Violence of action will be HIGH . . . I will bring unconventional and asymmetrical warfare to those in LAPD uniform whether on or off duty" (see McNary, Bergman, and Peterson 2013). Dorner also mentions all of the tactics, training, and arsenal of weapons he intends to use against LAPD officers; specifically those who he felt did some sort of injustice against him, their families, and any other law enforcement officers. Dorner discusses his intent to die as a result of his actions. Immediately following the posting of Dorner's manifesto on Facebook, over 50 families had to be protected by LAPD officers round the clock due to being mentioned and targeted in Dorner's manifesto.

On February 6, 2013, in Riverside, California, a Riverside Police car occupied by Officer Michael Crain and his trainee, Officer Andrew Tachias, was stopped at a red light when Dorner's Nissan pickup truck drove through the red light and pulled up alongside Crain and Tachias's patrol car. Dorner fired multiple rounds from an assault rifle, killing Crain and critically wounding Tachias.

On Thursday, April 7, 2013, Dorner's Nissan Titan was found burnt along a snowy road in the mountains of Big Bear, California, and a team of multiple southern California law enforcement agencies and U.S. marshals responded to the area in an attempt to locate Dorner in the snowy mountains for nearly five days, with no sign of Dorner.

On Tuesday, February 12, 2013, Jim and Karen Reynolds, a couple who own the Mountain Vista Resort in Big Bear Lake, California, went into one of their rental cabins to clean and found Dorner inside. Dorner proceeded to zip tie the couple's hands and feet before stealing the couple's Nissan Rogue and fleeing. The Reynolds were able to free themselves, and contact law enforcement and inform them that Dorner was in the area.

Dorner was able to evade police who spotted him driving and hid in an unoccupied cabin. Deputy Jeremiah McKay and Detective Alex Collins of the Bernadino County Sheriff's Office were two of the officers who responded to the area and began to look for Dorner on foot near the cabin. From inside the cabin Dorner fired multiple rounds, striking Collins and McKay, severely wounding Collins and killing McKay.

Several law enforcement officers responded to the scene and began firing multiple rounds into the cabin occupied by Dorner. Officers ordered Dorner to surrender and informed him that he was surrounded, but Dorner refused. Officers threw a canister of pepper spray into the cabin, but Dorner did not emerge. Officers then drove an armored tractor with an extendable claw toward the cabin and tore down the cabin's east wall, but Dorner still failed to emerge. Officers then deployed several canisters of CS gas in the cabin, which caused the cabin to set on fire. The cabin burned for approximately 10 minutes before officers heard a single gunshot from inside the cabin.

On February 13, 2013, Dorner's charred remains were located in the debris of the burnt cabin. An autopsy confirmed that Dorner had died from a self-inflicted gunshot wound to the head. Following Dorner's death, the shoot-out in Big Bear, California, was highly criticized, citing that Dorner had not been given an opportunity to surrender and that law enforcement officials had intentionally burned down the cabin to prevent Dorner from unveiling scandals in the LAPD. While many people viewed Dorner as a murderer who had killed innocent people in cold blood, others viewed him as somewhat of a folk hero who fought against oppression and shed light on the corruptions of the LAPD.

Shortly after Dorner's death, Los Angeles police chief Charlie Beck reopened Dorner's termination case in an effort to ensure public confidence in the LAPD. Chief Beck determined that his termination had been justified and handled appropriately.

CAITLIN G. LYNCH

See also: Rudolph, Eric (1966–); Serpico, Frank (1936–)

Further Reading

Abdollah, Tami. 2013. "Chris Dorner Review Finds that Firing was Justified, Says His Allegations of Racism were Unfounded." June 4. http://www.huffingtonpost.com/2013/06/04/chris-dorner-review-finds_n_3386228.html. Accessed April 15, 2015.

Goffard, Christopher, Joel Rubin, and Kurt Streeter. 2013. "The Manhunt for Christopher Dorner." December 8. http://graphics.latimes.com/christopher-dorner-manhunt/. Accessed April 15, 2015.

McNary, Sharon, Ben Bergman, and Molly Peterson. 2013. "LAPD Manhunt: Christopher Dorner's Promising Career Ended with Angry Manifesto, Fugitive Status." February 8. http://www.scpr.org/news/2013/02/08/35876/lapd-manhunt-racism-fuels-christopher-dorner-ex-la/. Accessed April 15, 2015.

Downs, Elizabeth Diane Frederickson (1955–)

Elizabeth Diane Frederickson was born on August 7, 1955, in Phoenix, Arizona, to Wes and Willadene Frederickson. On May 19, 1983 she loaded her three children, ages four, eight and nine, into her car, drove to a rural spot, shot all three and herself, and then slowly drove to the local hospital. Upon arriving she claimed a "bushy-haired" man flagged her down, and it was him who shot them. Diane is currently serving life plus 50 years in prison for her acts, but still refuses to take responsibility.

Elizabeth Frederickson was the eldest of four children. During her early childhood the family moved about a good deal (Rule 2006). However, when the U.S. Postal Service

During an interview on March 12, 1989, Diane Downs talks about her conviction for the murder of her seven-year-old daughter and attempted murders of her two other children, ages Three and Eight. In 1984, she was sentenced to life in prison plus 55 years. (AP Photo/Peter Cannata)

hired her father, Wes, they were able to settle in one place. Elizabeth was 11 years old. Upon turning 14, Elizabeth started to use her middle name Diane, and became very defiant of her parents. She cut and bleached her hair, and wore provocative clothing. At age 16 she met a boy, Steven Downs, who lived across the street, and developed a relationship with him. The Fredericksons did not approve of the relationship, but Diane did not care.

After graduating high school her boyfriend joined the navy, and Diane attended Pacific Coast Bible College. She was expelled after the first year due to promiscuity. In 1973, she and Steven Downs married. Almost immediately they fought a good deal, mostly over money, infidelity, and their marriage became a revolving door with one or the other leaving for periods of time.

In 1973, Diane became pregnant with her first child Christie. Six months after she gave birth she joined the navy, but was sent home after three weeks. She and Steven

continued their rocky relationship, and Diane thought about becoming a surrogate mother (Rule 2006). She had enjoyed being pregnant with Christie and thought it a great way to make money. However, she could not pass the psychological tests, and one of the psychologists noted that although she seemed quite intelligent, she was also psychotic.

Diane had her second child, Cheryl Lynn, in 1975. It was at this point Steven decided he did not want to father more children, and he had a vasectomy. Diane began to have affairs with other men. She became pregnant, and in 1979 gave birth to Stephen Daniel. Diane and Steven divorced in 1980. The three children would stay with Diane's parents, Danny's father, or often she would leave six-year-old Christie to watch over the others. While Christie was in all-day school, and Danny was at a local day care, Cheryl would come home to an empty house to wait for her mother to get off work. Neighbors expressed concern about the general neglect of the children, especially when they were left on their own. Diane had dreams of starting a surrogate clinic of her own, and did have one child for which she was paid $10,000.

Diane had struck up a relationship with a married fellow postal worker, Robert Knickerbocker. Diane saw Nick as "the man of her dreams" (crime.about.com), and became obsessed about wanting to be with him. However, Nick was not interested in taking on a woman and three children, and he said he felt confined by Diane and was still in love with his wife. Diane decided to move back to Oregon, but continued to write to Nick and visited him in Arizona one final time in April 1983. Nick completely rejected Diane during the visit, again telling her he did not want to take care of her children.

On May 19, 1983, Diane took her children over to friend's house, and then took a longer route home along back roads. At one point she pulled off the road onto the shoulder, got out of the car, produced a handgun, and reaching inside the car shot each of her children at point-blank range. She then shot her own left arm, disposed of the gun, and slowly drove to a local hospital. When she arrived, she claimed a "bushy-haired" strange man had flagged her down on the rural road, and then demanded her car. When she refused, he pulled a gun and started shooting into the car. She said she was so shocked at what happened, she did not see where he ran after the shooting.

Cheryl Lynn was pronounced dead at the emergency room, but both Danny and Christie were still alive. However, Christie experienced a stroke due to shock, and was in critical condition, unable to talk, for several weeks. Danny was paralyzed from the chest down, and would be confined to a wheelchair for the rest of his life. Diane treated each of her visits to the hospital as a media event, and seemed to relish the attention.

During the police investigation several forensic issues arose. The blood spatter in the car did not match up to the story Diane told detectives about what occurred. Blood spatter can show where the shooter is standing in relationship to the victim, and if anything or anyone is in between them. Diane's story kept changing as to the series of details, and she would go days without visiting her children in the hospital (Rule 2006). When interviewed by the media, her comments all focused on herself, and not on the condition of her children. The hospital staff taking care of the children found this behavior very odd in comparison to other parents whose children had been critically injured.

Police detectives spent eight months putting together a case to charge Diane with murder and attempted murder. Diane did not admit she owned a .22 caliber pistol, which was the type of gun used in the shooting. Detectives traveled to Arizona and a home Diane had once lived in, to find a bullet lodged in the floor of the house that matched the ones used to shoot the children. They also found Diane's diary, in which she wrote obsessively about her relationship with Nick, along with lots of passages about the issue of Nick not wanting to be around her children. A witness finally came forward saying he was behind Diane's car the night of the shooting, and saw her driving very slowly. This observation was of Diane's driving after the shooting, and it was different from her claims that she sped to the hospital for help.

While investigators were looking for other evidence, Christie and Danny were recuperating at the hospital. When Christie was able to answer questions, she identified the shooter as her own mother. She repeated this statement in court during her mother's trial. A jury found Diane Downs guilty for the murder of Cheryl Lynn, and the attempted murders of Christie and Danny. On June 17, 1984, Diane was sentenced to life in prison plus 50 years.

At the time of Diane's conviction for shooting her own children she was again pregnant, and delivered the child while in jail. The child was then taken by child protective services and placed for adoption. The prosecuting attorney and his wife adopted and continued to care for both Christie and Danny. In 1987, Diane escaped from prison, but was shortly recaptured, and sentenced to additional time. She has been up for parole twice, the most recent in 2010, but

was denied parole due to her refusal to take responsibility for what she did. She maintains that someone else shot her children. She will not come up for parole again until 2020.

Trisha M. King Stargel

See also: Routier, Darlie Lynn (1970–); Smith, Susan (1971–); Tinning, Marybeth (1942–); Yates, Andrea (1964–)

Further Reading

Montaldo, Charles. "Diane Downs: Guilty of Shooting Her Three Children." About Crime. http://crime.about.com/od/female_offenders/a/Diane0Downs.htm. Accessed April 15, 2015.

Rule, Ann. 2006. *Small Sacrifices: A True Story of Passion and Murder*. Boston, MA: Sphere.

Dred Scott Decision (1857)

The Dred Scott decision, *Dred Scott v. Sandford*, was the landmark decision of the U.S. Supreme Court on slavery. It also foreclosed the possibility of the federal government regulating slavery in the expanding western territories of the United States, meaning that slaveowners could bring their slaves into any territory owned by the federal government. Also, in Justice Roger Taney's majority opinion, the Court ruled that persons of African descent could not ever be citizens of the United States, and did not have standing to sue in her courts. Dred Scott represented the most aggressively proslavery opinion ever issued by the highest court in the land, hailing slavery as a permanent and laudable institution in America. From the moment it was handed down the decision was heavily criticized for its flawed legal reasoning, misuse of prior precedents, and ignoring a large body of statutory and common law that proved many of the Court's statements to be factually incorrect. It is now recognized almost universally as the worst decision ever handed down by the Supreme Court. The decision was a watershed moment, further driving a wedge between slave and free states, accidentally paved the way for a Republican president, and yet another incident that propelled the United States toward a bloody civil war.

Despite being the catalyst for one of the most infamous legal decisions in American history, little is known of Dred Scott. Dred Scott was born a slave in Virginia in 1795. In 1820, his master, Peter Blow, took him to Missouri. It was in Missouri that Dr. John Emerson, a U.S. arm surgeon, purchased Scott. Emerson took Scott to posts in the Wisconsin Territory, Illinois, and eventually back to Missouri. Eventually, Emerson died, and his widow inherited Scott.

Scott attempted to purchase his freedom, but she refused. Scott then sought his freedom through the courts.

In essence, Scott's arguments rested on certain aspects of the Missouri Compromise of 1820, where it was agreed that slavery would not exist above the 36'30" parallel in the United States. By taking Scott into Illinois and the Wisconsin Territory, Scott argued that he was free by virtue of being taken to a place where slavery did not exist. Missouri's courts had long held that Scott's argument was sound, and that those slaves taken into the territories or free states could no longer be held as slaves. In 1850 a Missouri court, following clear precedents on the issue, found Scott to be a free man. Emerson's widow appealed, though this time she had transferred ownership to her brother, John Sandford. In 1852, the Missouri Supreme Court overturned the trial court, erasing nearly three decades of clear precedent on the matter. In doing so, Justice William Scott of the Missouri Supreme Court ominously wrote the following:

> Times are not now as they were when the former decisions on this subject were made. Since then not only individuals but States have been possessed with a dark and fell spirit in relation to slavery, whose gratification is sought in the pursuit of measures, whose inevitable consequences must be the overthrow and destruction of our government. Under such circumstances it does not behoove the State of Missouri to show the least countenance to any measure which might gratify this spirit. She is willing to assume her full responsibility for the existence of slavery within her limits, nor does she seek to share or divide it with others (*Scott v. Emerson*, 15 Mo. 576, 586 (1852))

Slaveowners had long believed slavery to be under attack from the North. This was making slave states and proslavery advocates more aggressive in asserting slavery's place in America. Justice Scott's opinion reflects this.

In 1853, Scott sued for his freedom again, but this time in a federal court. The Federal District Court of Missouri followed the Missouri Supreme Court's ruling, and held that Scott was not free. Eventually, Scott's case wound up in front of the U.S. Supreme Court.

Justice Taney, writing for a 7-to-2 majority, upheld the ruling of the lower courts holding that Scott was a slave. But they went further. The Court also ruled that, as a person of African descent, Scott did not even have the ability to sue in a court of law. The Court also ruled that the federal government did not have the authority to ban slavery in the territories. The Court ruled that it would violate the Fifth Amendment due process clause if the federal government were to free slaves brought into federal territory, as it would deprive the slaveowners of their property rights. In a shocking turn, the Court also ruled that African Americans could not be citizens of the United States. This deprived freed slaves of their right to vote, hold property, exercise free speech, and all of the other rights attendant with being an American citizen.

The case represented a titanic shift in American jurisprudence. For years, freed slaves had been able to be become citizens of several states. At the time of independence, African Americans could become citizens of 5 of the 13 colonies. Dred Scott stripped all African Americans, free or slave of essentially all of their rights.

However, in taking such a proslavery position, the Supreme Court may have accidentally doomed the practice. The Democratic Party, ostensibly the proslavery party, held sway both in Northern and Southern states. Stephen Douglas, from Illinois, was the favorite for the 1860 presidential nomination for the Democrats. But Dred Scott presented a massive problem. Northern Democrats had long tolerated slavery so long as it remained in the South. Dred Scott implied the practice could extend across the United States. This was unacceptable. Douglas advanced what was known as the Freeport Doctrine, essentially arguing that, despite the ruling of the Supreme Court, a state could choose to keep slavery at bay by refusing to positively protect the practice. This, in turn, angered Southern Democrats, who wanted positive protections for slavery in all new territories. Slavery was the lynchpin issue in the 1860 presidential election.

The result was that the Democratic Party nominated two different candidates for the presidency in 1860. The Northern Democrats nominated Stephen Douglass, and the Southerners nominated John C. Breckinridge, then vice president of the United States. This split the Democrat votes. Further confounding the election was the breakoff of the Constitutional Union party from the old Whig party, who sought to avoid the slavery issue altogether. Only Republicans, behind Abraham Lincoln, were united.

The result was that Lincoln won the presidency. The South seceded, in large part, due to their perception that Lincoln's election was tantamount to a declaration of war on the practice of slavery. In Confederate vice president Alexander Stephens stated that the new Confederate nation "rest[ed] upon the great truth that the negro is not equal to the white man; that slavery—subordination to the superior race—is his natural and normal condition. This, our new government, is the first, in the history of the world, based upon this great physical, philosophical, and moral truth." The same basis for the Dred Scott decision was now the basis of the American Civil War.

JOHN FRIEND

See also: *Amistad* Slave Ship Case (1839); Harpers Ferry (VA), Raid on (October 17, 1859); *Primary Documents*/Report of the Decision of the U.S. Supreme Court in the Case of *Dred Scott v. John F.A. Sandford* by Benjamin C. Howard (1857)

Further Reading

Delombard, Jeannine Marie. 2007. *Slavery on Trial: Law, Abolitionism, and Print Culture.* Chapel Hill: University of North Carolina Press.

Fehrenbacher, Don E. 1979. *The Dred Scott Case: Its Significance in American Law and Politics.* Oxford: Oxford University Press.

Friedman, Lawrence. 2005. *A History of American Law: Third Edition.* New York: Touchstone.

McPherson, James. 2009. *This Mighty Scourge: Perspectives on the Civil War.* Oxford: Oxford University Press.

Scott v. Emerson, 15 Mo. 576, 586 (1852).

Du Pont, John (1938–2010)

John Eleuthere du Pont was known as the "wealthiest murder defendant" in America. He was brought to trial and found guilty for the 1996 murder of U.S. Olympic wrestling hopeful, David Schultz, who was living and training on du Pont's 800-acre Foxcatcher Estate. This matter garnered national attention on the issues of mental illness and treatment of the wealthy in the U.S. criminal justice system. Ultimately, du Pont was found guilty, but mentally ill. His multimillion dollar defense team presented an unprecedented 24-hour mental competency hearing that included a 13-hour Saturday session. At least six psychiatrists agreed that du Pont suffered from some form of mental illness, but was he so mentally ill that he couldn't understand that he had committed murder? Many people, including the judge overseeing the mental competency hearing, prison staff, and courtroom observers, wondered if du Pont was truly mentally ill, or crazy like a Foxcatcher.

Du Pont's relationship with his victim started idyllically. Du Pont, a multimillionaire heir to the du Pont chemical company fortune, was an avid wrestling fan. In 1986, he started a wrestling program at Villanova University and hired Shultz as a coach. Du Pont made donations to the U.S. Olympic team and eventually provided training facilities and housing for Team Foxcatcher on his Pennsylvania estate. Schultz moved with his wife and two children to the 800-acre Olympic-caliber training facility and lived there for years.

Over time, Du Pont's mental health began to decline and he became paranoid, erratic, and verbally abusive. He chased guests out of his home, but would then send them checks for $10,000. By 1995 he was calling himself the Dalai Lama of North America and believed that he was controlling worldwide events. As du Pont's paranoia increased, he installed extreme security measures around the estate. This included erecting a fence topped with razor wire to foil the Russian Army's attempt to invade his estate. Eventually, he became afraid of the color black and ordered everything of that color removed from his estate, including the African American wrestlers on his team.

On January 26, 1996, Schultz was working on his car outside of his Foxcatcher residence. His wife was making her way outside to join him when she heard a gunshot, then a scream. She saw her husband lying on the ground drenched in blood and watched du Pont, seated behind the wheel of his silver Lincoln Town car, fire his weapon once again at Schultz's prone body. Du Pont simply drove away and remained holed up in his Foxcatcher mansion for the next 50 hours.

Over the course of the next two days, du Pont issued demands to law enforcement officers who had encircled his home. Strategically, the police disconnected the boilers providing heat to the mansion. Apparently cold due to the frigid January weather, du Pont nonchalantly walked outside to fix the boilers where he was apprehended.

Immediately, du Pont's mental health was questioned. At his preliminary hearing, du Pont, dressed in a blue sweatshirt, told his attorneys that he didn't understand the purpose of the hearing. Du Pont was ordered to stand trial for the murder and undergo a mental competency hearing. Du Pont and his legal team argued that his mental state did not allow him to assist in his defense, nor did he understand the charges or the court proceedings.

The prosecution argued that du Pont's actions, even while in solitary confinement, showed that he was keenly aware of the reason for his incarceration. For example, from prison, du Pont hired a company to erect a "Foxcatcher Prison Farm" sign on his property. Further, the prosecution pointed out, du Pont received hundreds of visits from his attorneys. Clearly, the prosecution argued, du Pont must be talking about his case with his legal team.

"What are they discussing, the menu?" the prosecutor quipped at one hearing.

A hearing was held to decide whether du Pont was sane enough to stand trial. His team presented many witnesses to describe du Pont's strange behavior, including former attorneys fired by du Pont because he believed that they were a part of a CIA conspiracy against him. On the other hand, the prosecution presented testimony from the staff at Foxcatcher that du Pont was still running the estate and prison handlers who believed that du Pont had been coached by his legal team to fake his mental illness.

The psychiatric evaluations were also conflicting. Psychiatrists for the defense opined that du Pont was a paranoid schizophrenic. Doctors for the prosecution testified that du Pont was mentally ill, but accused him of faking his behavior to make it appear that he was more ill. The court-appointed psychiatrists determined that he was mentally ill.

On September 24, 1996, despite grave misgivings by Judge Patricia Jenkins, who indicated that she believed that she had witnessed du Pont's legal team coaching him to say "I don't understand," found du Pont mentally ill and unable to stand trial. Judge Jenkins said that the scales of justice tipped ever so slightly in du Pont's favor. She ordered that he be committed to a state mental health facility and medicated involuntarily.

Mental Competency

It is a tenet of the American justice system that a defendant must have the mental capacity to be able to assist in his or her own defense. The defendant must be able to talk to and understand lawyerly advice or give lawyers information that they can use to mount a defense. The defendant must also understand the proceedings. If it is unclear whether a defendant can assist in his or her own defense, he or she must undergo a mental competency hearing. If the court finds that the defendant is competent, then the trial can go forward.

Nonetheless, a person can be deemed mentally competent enough to go to trial, but still plead insanity. The insanity plea claims that a person was insane during the commission of the crime. However, proving insanity is difficult. The defense team must show that the defendant could not appreciate the nature of his or her actions at the time of the incident.

In this case, the defense had to show that du Pont either didn't understand, know or realize that he was shooting Schultz or that du Pont didn't realize that shooting Schultz was wrong.

After a few months of treatment, Judge Jenkins held a hearing to determine if du Pont had gained competency. On December 9, 1996, the judge found du Pont fit to stand trial. Instantly, du Pont's legal team filed notice that it intended to pursue an insanity defense. The defense argued that du Pont had intense, yet irrational fears for his safety. One psychiatrist testified that du Pont believed that Schultz was a terrorist sent to assassinate him. In another scenario, the doctors opined that du Pont had blamed a slip and fall that occurred at Schultz's house as an act committed by a Russian soldier.

The prosecution, on the other hand, countered with evidence of du Pont's sanity such as his multiple requests to speak to his attorneys after the shooting. The prosecution also noted that du Pont reloaded the gun used to kill Schultz and appeared to have stocked an arsenal of weaponry to defend himself against the police.

On February 25, 1997, a jury determined that du Pont was guilty of third-degree murder, but mentally insane. The verdict required that du Pont remain incarcerated, either in the state mental institution or, once deemed no longer mentally ill, in prison, for the length of his sentence. Du Pont was sentenced to 13–30 years in prison for the murder of David Schultz. John du Pont died in prison on December 9, 2010, at age 72.

CHARLISA HOLLOWAY EDELIN AND JOHN JACKSON

See also: Fish, Albert (1870–1936); Hinckley, John, Jr. (1955–)

Further Reading

Ordine, Bill, and Ralph Vigoda. 1996a. "Judge Finds du Pont Unfit to Stand Trial." *The Philadelphia Inquirer.* September 25, A1.

Ordine, Bill, and Ralph Vigoda. 1996b. "Prosecutors: du Pont Still Runs Things—Lawyers Argue About his Competence." *The Philadelphia Inquirer.* July 21, B01.

Ordine, Bill, and Ralph Vigoda. 1998. *Fatal Match inside the Mind of Killer Millionaire John du Pont.* New York: Avon Books, Inc.

Turkington, Carol. 1996. *No Holds Barred the Strange Life of John E. du Pont.* Atlanta: Turner Publishing, Inc.

Dugard, Jaycee, Kidnapping of (1991)

In 1991, Phillip and Nancy Garrido kidnapped 11-year-old Jaycee Lee Dugard. She was held in captivity for 18 years and was repeatedly raped during that time period. Ms. Dugard was discovered and released in 2009. Phillip Garrido was on parole after serving 11 years of a 50-year federal sentence for kidnapping and rape. From 1988 to 1999 he was under the supervision of federal parole agents; from 1999 to his arrest in 2009, the California Department of Corrections and Rehabilitation (CDCR) supervised Mr. Garrido. The kidnapping and long-term captivity of Jaycee Lee Dugard led to criticism of the parole system. The primary area of focus for this criticism was the quality of parole supervision, especially for high-risk offenders.

On June 10, 1991, Phillip Craig Garrido and his wife Nancy kidnapped 11-year-old Jaycee Lee Dugard from near her home in South Lake Tahoe, California. Jaycee was taken to the Garridos's home in Antioch, California, 170 miles away, and held captive for the next 18 years.

A family handout photo of the released kidnap victim. Jaycee Dugard on her way to the Rose Parade before her ordeal. Following Jaycee's liberation from her captors in August 2009, a family spokesperson said that the family was spending time "reconnecting .. sharing stories," and that Jaycee, now 29 years old, was getting to know a sister of hers who was just a baby when she was abducted by convicted rapist Phillip Garrido from outside her home in 1991. Garrido fathered two children with Jaycee during her captivity in a hidden backyard at his home in Antioch, California. (Photo by Mark Ralston/Getty Images)

According to Ms. Dugard's account of her experience, Mr. Garrido first sexually assaulted her approximately a week into her captivity and continued doing so regularly for the next 18 years (Dugard 2012). The Garridos lived in a neighborhood on a one-half acre lot surrounded by other homes. Their backyard was divided into two parts by fences: one part looked like any normal backyard; the other part was a concealed compound, a "secret backyard" (Dugard 2012). This is where Ms. Dugard primarily lived during her captivity, in a series of tents and buildings. Jaycee gave birth to two daughters during her captivity, both fathered by Phillip Garrido. The first daughter was born on August 18, 1994, when Jaycee was 14 years old. The second daughter was born on November 13, 1997, when Jaycee was 17 years old. Jaycee was renamed "Alyssa" by the Garridos, and during their captivity the children were told that "Alyssa" was their sister.

In 2009, Mr. Garrido started a church called God's Desire and went to the campus of the University of California, Berkeley to distribute fliers; Jaycee and her two daughters (then aged 11 and 15) were with him. Campus security officers asked for information to register his organization with campus authorities. When they conducted a background check they discovered his past and contacted his parole officer because he had young children with him and he was a registered sex offender. The parole office did not have any record of him having children. Upon further investigation, Jaycee admitted to the officers that she was a kidnap victim. The authorities were contacted, and on August 26, 2009, both Phillip and Nancy Garrido were arrested.

On August 28, 2009, the Garridos were charged with 29 felonies, including: kidnapping someone under 14 years of age, kidnapping for sexual purposes, multiple counts of forcible rape, multiple counts of forcible lewd act upon a child, and false imprisonment by violence. Phillip Garrido pled guilty on June 2, 2011, was sentenced to 431 years. Nancy Garrido pled guilty to two charges and was sentenced to 36 years to life.

During the investigation after Ms. Dugard's existence was revealed, numerous facts came to light that led to criticism about the parole system. In 1977, a Nevada court gave Mr. Garrido a five-years-to-life sentence for forcible rape and he was given 50-year federal sentence for kidnapping. He was released on federal parole in Nevada in January 1988 after serving 11 years in prison, and was supervised by federal parole authorities from 1988 to 1999. In March 1999, Mr. Garrido was discharged from federal parole and he was transferred to the Nevada state parole system; in June 1999 his state parole was transferred to CDCR authorities. Federal and state parole agents visited Garrido's home on several occasions during Ms. Dugard's imprisonment. For example, in 1993 Phillip Garrido went back to prison for a month for federal parole violations after drugs and a pipe were found in the main house (Dugard 2012). Mr. Garrido was released with an electronic monitor and remained on electronic monitoring (including passive GPS monitoring starting in April 2008) until he was arrested in 2009.

In November 2009, California inspector general David Shaw conducted a special investigation of the CDCR's supervision of Phillip Garrido. The report released by the Special Investigations Unit included an assessment by a CDCR administrator, who found only 12 months of satisfactory supervision out of the total 123 months Garrido was under CDCR parole supervision ("Special Report" 2009, 16). Seven specific deficiencies were indicated in the report: (1) department failure to properly classify Phillip Garrido; (2) supervisor failure to detect inadequate oversight of Garrido; (3) department failure to provide timely mental health assessment of Phillip Garrido; (4) departmental recommendations (four) to discharge Garrido from parole supervision; (5) departmental failure to provide GPS supervision policy; (6) failure to adequately train parole agents; (7) several missed opportunities by the CDCR to discovery the existence of Jaycee and her daughters, including failure to "investigate clearly visible utility wires running from the Garrido's house towards the concealed compound," failure to "investigate the presence of a 12-year-old female during a home visit," failure to "talk to neighbors of local public safety agencies," and failure to "act on information clearly demonstrating that Garrido had violated his parole terms" (2009 Annual Report, 2009, 8).

Cases Impact on Parole System

The Jaycee Dugard case significantly impacted the parole system in California. Specifically, the inspector general made 14 recommendations to improve the deficiencies that CDCR exhibited in the parole supervision of Phillip Garrido. In response to the special investigation report, Governor Schwarzenegger's office announced a number of parole reforms that would take place beginning in March 2010. These included risk assessments of all parolees, targeting resources (including closer supervision) toward more dangerous offenders, reducing caseloads, and improving GPS policies and training (including periodic review of all GPS tracks).

Jaycee Dugard filed four claims with the California Victim Compensation and Government Claims Board for herself and her two daughters. The CDCR mediated the case in June 2010 and, through the Department of Justice, agreed to settle the claims for the total sum of $20 million (AB 1714 2010). In the bill, it was noted that the CDCR has immunity, but because of the "unique and tragic character" of the case, the damages that might be awarded by a jury "could be extremely high" (AB 1714 2010). Ms. Dugard also filed a complaint in 2011 against the federal government for not adequately monitoring Phillip Garrido while he was under federal parole supervision. Ms. Dugard states that any money received from the federal suit would go to the JAYC Foundation, a nonprofit organization she founded to help children and families "recovering from abduction and the aftermath of other traumatic experiences" (JAYC 2014). The foundation is involved in reunification efforts and counseling, has developed curriculum for school-based life skills workshops, and provides workshops for law enforcement officers, including probation and parole officers.

Since her release and subsequent court hearings, Ms. Dugard has chosen to live secluded, along with her daughters. She has stated that she wants them to be able to live normal lives and not be in the public eye.

Lynn M. Greenwood

See also: Hagerman, Amber, Kidnapping and Murder of (1996); Ramsey, JonBenét, Murder of (1996); Smart, Elizabeth, Kidnapping of (2002); Walsh, Adam, Kidnapping and Murder of (1981)

Further Reading

"California Assembly Bill AB1714." 2010. June 30. http://www.leginfo.ca.gov/pub/09-10/bill/asm/ab_1701–1750/ab_1714_cfa_20100701_112156_asm_floor.html. Accessed April 15, 2015.

Dugard, Jaycee. L. 2012. *A Stolen Life: A Memoir.* New York: Simon & Schuster.

"Jaycee Dugard Kidnap: US Couple Plead Guilty." 2011. *BBC News.* April 28. http://www.bbc.co.uk/news/world-us-canada-13233396. Accessed April 15, 2015.

JAYC Foundation, Inc. 2014. "About Us." http://thejaycfounda tion.org/. Accessed April 15, 2015.

"Kidnap Victim Jaycee Dugard Talks About Her 18 Years of Terror." 2011. *CNN.com.* July 12. http://www.cnn.com/2011/ US/07/10/dugard.abc.interview/. Accessed April 15, 2015.

"Special Report: The California Department of Corrections and Rehabilitation's Supervision of Parolee Phillip Garrido." 2009. Officer of the Inspector General: State of California. http:// www.oig.ca.gov/media/reports/ARCHIVE/BOI/Special%20 Report%20on%20CDCRs%20Supervision%20of%20Pa rolee%20Phillip%20Garrido.pdf. Accessed April 15, 2015.

The People of the State of California vs. Phillip Greg Garrido and Nancy Garrido, Superior Court of California, County of El Dorado. Case No: P10CRF0364.

"Timeline: Jaycee Lee Dugard Case." 2011. *BBC News.* June 2. http://news.bbc.co.uk/2/hi/americas/8226715.stm. Accessed April 15, 2015.

"2009 Annual Report: Office of the Inspector General." 2009. Office of the Inspector General: State of California. http://www .oig.ca.gov/media/reports/Reports/annual/archive/2009%20 OIG%20Annual%20Report.pdf. Accessed April 15, 2015.

Duperrault Family Slayings (November 12, 1961)

In November 1961, the Duperrault family went on a sailing vacation in the Bahamas to escape from the harsh Wisconsin winter. Arthur and Jean Duperrault had three children, Brian (14), Terry Jo (11), and Rene (7). Arthur was a successful optometrist that wanted his family to experience the Bahaman waters he sailed during World War II. As such, the Duperrault family planned on spending at least a week chartering a yacht. They rented the *Bluebelle* in Fort Lauderdale, Florida and hired a former Air Force fighter pilot and experienced sailor named Julian Harvey to captain the *Bluebelle*. While the family expected to be at sea for a week, there was no way they could have prepared themselves for the horror that awaited them. The chartered trip would be remembered as nothing less than a tragedy.

The vacation started off like a dream. The family spent four days bouncing from island to island. They snorkeled and experienced everything the Bahaman Islands had to offer. Harvey's wife, Dene, joined them during the week. On November 12, 1961, Harvey began the voyage back to Florida. Dene Harvey prepared dinner for what would, ultimately, be the last meal served on the *Bluebelle*. Early that evening, around 9 p.m., Terry Jo went below deck to go to sleep while the rest of her family remained above

deck. In the middle of the night Terry Jo was awakened by her brother's screams. Confused, Terry Jo slowly made her way out of her cabin and up the stairs. Once she made it to the main cabin she saw her mother and brother laying in a pool of blood. Terry Jo continued up the stairs before she encountered Captain Harvey. Harvey yelled at her to stay down there. Terry Jo returned to her cabin frightened. After a few minutes she noticed the *Bluebelle* was starting to take on water. She could see water fill the cabin and hear the water slapping the side of the ship.

Terry Jo went topside again. Once she arrived on the deck she saw the *Bluebelle*'s dinghy and life raft were floating beside the ship. After asking if the ship was sinking, Harvey handed her the line holding the dinghy and told her to hold on to it. In a state of shock, Terry Jo let the line slip from her grasp. As the dinghy started to move away from the *Bluebelle* Harvey jumped in the water and swam after it. Luckily, Terry Jo remembered there was a life float in the main cabin. She was able to launch the life float just as the ship sank into the ocean. Terry Jo had the presence of mind to stay low in the float. She thought the captain was responsible for the murders and wanted to make sure he didn't find her. One thing Terry Jo could not shake from her mind was where were her father and sister? She had seen her mother and brother dead, but she never did see the rest of her family or Harvey's wife, Dene.

Terry Jo floated aimlessly in the ocean. She had no food or water. Furthermore, the only clothing she had was a shirt and pants. These events occurred on Sunday night. Monday morning was her first full day in the raft. While the night had been frigid, the day was hot and she was fully exposed to the sun. While she floated, fish nibbled at her feet and she became more dehydrated. On Tuesday she saw a small plane flying overhead. She tried to gain the pilot's attention, but she was too small and blended into the whitecaps of the ocean. After surviving another hot day, Terry Jo was relieved to experience the lower temperatures of Tuesday night. On Wednesday she began to hallucinate as she neared death from the elements. Miraculously she survived the night. It was now Thursday, her fourth day floating alone in the ocean. Terry Jo was falling in and out of consciousness. However, in the middle of the morning the unthinkable happened. She was spotted by a passing ship. She awoke to sounds of voices and then felt her body raised to the ship. She was rescued.

While Terry Jo had been alone in the ocean, Captain Harvey had been rescued on Monday by an oil tanker. Harvey was sent to Miami where he told the Coast Guard that he was the sole survivor of a terrible accident. He told the authorities the *Bluebelle* was damaged in a sudden squall on Sunday night. He said the masts and rigging collapsed and injured Dene and the Duperrault family. It was at this point that the ship caught fire and sank. According to Harvey, it was a miracle that he was able to save himself from the sinking ship. On Thursday, Harvey heard that Terry Jo had survived the ordeal. A maid at the hotel found bloody sheets in his room. When she couldn't open the bathroom door she called police. The authorities found Harvey's body on the floor. He had committed suicide.

Terry Jo was sent to a hospital in Miami to recover. After a week authorities questioned her about the events of November 12, 1961. Terry Jo recounted the events of that night. In doing so, she disproved all of Harvey's story. The authorities now knew that he had murdered his wife, Dene, and the rest of the Duperrault family. The authorities believe that he killed Dene to collect money from her life insurance policy. It is speculated that Arthur Duperrault caught Harvey in the act. This theory speculates that Harvey was forced to commit the other murders in an attempt to cover up the death of Dene. It is theorized that Harvey didn't murder Terry Jo because he didn't believe she would be able to survive. He may have believed that she would have gone down with the ship.

Terry Jo's determination and will to live brought clarity to a tragic event that would have been remembered as an accident. Terry Jo returned to Wisconsin to live with her aunt and cousins. She subsequently changed her name to Tere. In 2010, Tere Duperrault-Fassbender released a book recounting the fateful night on the *Bluebelle*.

M. HUNTER MARTAINDALE

See also: Clutter Family Murders (1959); Gilley Family Murders (April 26, 1984); Wesson Family Massacre (2004)

Further Reading

Logan, Richard D., Tere Duperrault Fassbender, Jo Anna Perrin, and Les Stroud. 2010. *Alone: Orphaned on the Ocean*. Old Saybrook, CT: Tantor Media.

Dyer, Mary Barrett, Execution of (1660)

Mary Barrett Dyer converted from being an English Puritan to following the "inner light" of Quakerism and paid for her conversion by being one of the four Quakers known as the Boston martyrs executed on June 1, 1660, in Massachusetts. After embracing Quakerism and repeatedly defying a Puritan law banning Quakers from Massachusetts Bay Colony, she engaged the learned elders of Massachusetts Bay Colony in theological argument and stood by her principles as they led her to the gallows.

There is little concrete documentary evidence and much speculation about Mary Barrett's early life, including the unproven theory that she was the daughter of Lady Arabella Stuart from a secret marriage with her cousin Sir William Seymour. Born in England about 1611, and described as "fair and comely," Mary Barrett married William Dyer, a milliner and a Puritan, at St. Martin-in-the-Fields in London on October 27, 1633. By 1635, the Dyers had immigrated to Massachusetts and were admitted to the Boston church on December 13, 1635. Since they were educated and cultured, the Dyers were considered to be among the most intelligent citizens, and William advanced in public esteem. On March 3, 1635, William became a freeman of the Massachusetts Bay Colony, a distinction awarded to an established member of a colony not under legal restraint. In 1638 his fellow citizens elected him clerk and he received a land grant at Rumney Marsh on December 14, 1635 and January 16, 1637.

By 1637, William and Mary Dyer openly supported Anne Hutchinson who preached that God speaks to people directly instead of only through ministers or antinomianism, a belief that the Puritans of the theocratic state of the Massachusetts Bay Colony considered heresy. Mary Dyer and Anne Hutchinson were such close friends that when Mary gave premature birth to a stillborn daughter on October 17, 1637, Anne assisted in the birth along with midwife Jane Hawkins and an unidentified woman who later gave testimony about the baby's deformity and the manner of her burial that the Puritans used against Mary Dyer.

In November 1637, Massachusetts Bay Colony disenfranchised and disarmed William Dyer and dozens of other followers of Anne Hutchinson, and when the church excommunicated Anne Hutchinson on March 22, 1638, Mary Dyer walked out of the church with her. Mary and William Dyer followed Anne Hutchinson to the Colony of Rhode Island and Providence Plantations. In 1652, William and Mary Dyer traveled to England on a political mission with Roger Williams and John Clarke. During Mary's five year stay in England, she became a follower of George Fox, founder of the Society of Friends or Quakers, whose idea of the Inner Light resembled Anne Hutchinson's Antinomianism.

When Mary Dyer returned to New England in 1657, she discovered that John Endicott had succeeded John Winthrop as governor and that Governor Endicott opposed religious diversity, fearing that allowing Quakers to practice their beliefs in Massachusetts Bay Colony would cause the entire church-state structure to collapse. Governor Endicott used his influence and when the Massachusetts General Court met in in mid-October 1656, it passed several laws against "the cursed sect of heretics … commonly called Quakers."

After Mary's ship arrived in Boston, the Massachusetts Bay authorities immediately arrested her and her friend Anne Burden and held them isolated in darkened jail cells for three months, burning Mary's books and Quaker papers. Finally Mary managed to smuggle a letter through a crack to a friend outside the jail, but it took several weeks to reach William Dyer in Newport. William barged into Governor Endicott's home, demanding Mary's release. The Boston authorities respected William's position in Rhode Island, so Governor Endicott released Mary on the condition that she never return to Massachusetts.

Mary Dyer continued to travel throughout New England preaching Quakerism, and in 1658, New Haven, Connecticut, authorities arrested and expelled her for preaching Inner Light and expressing that idea that men and women ranked equally in church worship and organization. In the summer of 1659, Mary illegally returned to Massachusetts to visit two English Quaker friends William Robinson and Marmaduke Stephenson and the Massachusetts authorities imprisoned her.

Again William Dyer interceded for his wife. In a letter dated August 30, 1659, he castigated the magistrate for putting his wife in prison without evidence or legal authority. He pointed out that she had just come to visit her friends in prison and not to preach or stir up trouble and that she intended to return to her family in Rhode Island. On September 12, 1659, Massachusetts authorities released the Quakers from prison and banished them from Massachusetts Bay Colony, threatening them with execution if they returned. Nicholas Davis and Mary Dyer obeyed the law, but William Robinson and Marmaduke Stephenson felt it their duty to continue their ministry in Massachusetts. Within a month they were rearrested and Mary Dyer, Hope Clifton and Marry Scott, a niece of Anne Hutchinson trudged from Providence to Boston to plead for the release of Christopher Holder and the other Quakers. The authorities arrested Mary Dyer as she spoke to Christopher Holder through prison bars.

Mary Dyer, Martyr

The deaths of Mary Dyer and countless other Quakers defeated the heavy-handed and illegal efforts of the Boston magistrates to eliminate the Quaker challenge. Gradually people viewed Mary's death as martyrdom and in Massachusetts her death contributed to the elimination of anti-Quaker laws. In 1959, the Massachusetts General Court, which had sentenced her to death 300 years before, authorized a bronze statue built in her memory to be placed on the grounds of the State House in Boston, with a statue of her friend Anne Hutchinson standing in front at the other wing. Her words written from her cell in the Boston jail are engraved beneath Mary Dyer's statue: "My life not availeth me in comparison to the liberty of the truth."

The actions of Mary and her Quaker friends challenged the legal right of Massachusetts Bay governor John Endicott to put Quakers to death. Following the example of their fellow Quakers in England, they returned to their ministry as soon as they were released from prison, practicing passive resistance. On October 19, 1659, Mary Dyer, William Robinson, and Marmaduke Stephenson were tried before the Massachusetts Bay Colony General Court and Governor John Endicott pronounced the death sentence for all three of them. On October 27, they were led through the streets of Boston to the gallows. William Robinson and Marmaduke Stephenson were hanged. With the hangman's noose around her neck, Mary received a last-minute reprieve because of the intercession of Governor John Winthrop, Jr. of Connecticut, Governor Thomas Temple of Nova Scotia and her son William Dyer, Jr. The Massachusetts Bay authorities ordered her to leave and never return.

After being escorted back to Rhode Island, Mary Dyer still burned with the fervor of her mission. In April 1660, obeying her conscience, defying Massachusetts law, and not telling her husband, she returned to Boston once again. The General Court summoned Mary to appear before it on May 31, 1660. Mary upheld her Quaker beliefs and Governor Endicott reimposed her death sentence to be carried out at 9 a.m. on June 1, 1660.

KATHY WARNES

See also: Hutchinson, Anne, Trial of (1637–1638); Rogers, Mary, Murder of (1841)

Further Reading

Burgess, Robert S. 2000. *To Try the Bloody Law: The Story of Mary Dyer*. Burnsville, NC: Celo Valley Books.

Plimpton, Ruth Talbot. 1999. *Mary Dyer: Biography of a Rebel Quaker*. Bloomington: Indiana University Press.

Rogers, Horatio. 2009. *Mary Dyer of Rhode Island: The Quaker Martyr That Was Hanged on Boston Common*, June 1, 1660. n.p.: BiblioLife.

E

East St. Louis Race Riot (1917) and Chicago Race Riot (1919)

From 1916 to 1970, six million black Americans moved from the rural areas in the South to the urban areas in the North, Midwest, and West. This phenomenon was brought about by the culture in the South post–Civil War. In the South, white supremacy had increased and the segregation policies established by the Jim Crow laws in the South were making black American lives more difficult. Although the Ku Klux Khan (KKK) dissolved in 1869, there was a growing underground movement that continued to violate black American Families.

With the new form of discontent in the South paired with unsatisfactory economic opportunities, the Southern black population became interested in moving North to large cities. Many urban businesses recruited this population due to the need for laborers.

With the large population of black Americans moving, all new and old residents had to handle the increased competition for living space and livelihood. The tension between races resulted in horrifying massacres and riots. These instances became constant enough that the summer of 1919 was called the "Red Summer."

East St. Louis Riot of 1917

East St. Louis was one of the cities that had taken in 10,000–12,000 black Southern Americans. The events leading to the riot can be traced back to an Aluminum Ore Company's strike. In February 1917, 470 black Americans were hired to replace white American workers who were on strike from the company. Many started to blame the migratory workers for the poor working conditions not improving (blackpast.org).

On May 28, 1917, white American workers attended the city council meeting and voiced a formal complaint against the migrating black Americans to the mayor of East St. Louis. This same day there was news of a black man attempting to rob a white man. The white mobs formed and began beating all the black Americans they came across. They stopped trolleys and street cars and pulled individuals off to beat them. The Illinois governor Frank O'Lowden called the National Guard to stop the violence. No additional precautions were taken and the National Guard left on June 10, 1917 (blackpast.org).

The violence began again July 2, 1917. Along with the continuing beatings the mobs set fire to the homes of many black Americans. This caused the residents to either stay in the house to die or to run out in the streets to be beaten. Some parts of the city had started to lynch the East St. Louis black population. The violence did not stop until the National Guard came back to set everything to order. The riot ended with $400,000 in property damage, 6,000 homeless black Americans, eight white American deaths, and 40 black American deaths.

Chicago Riot of 1919

With the Great Migration, Chicago watched its black American population increase from 44,000 in 1910 to 109,000 in 1920. With the movement much of the struggle came with the industrial labor competition, overcrowding in urban ghettos, and the fact that both white and black Americans now had military training after the Civil War. Chicago found both sides unable to fulfill housing needs. Two years prior to the 1919 riot, 27 black Americans were killed for moving into white neighborhoods. Many vigilante groups of white men would kill any black men who passed into the "white" neighborhoods.

The event that triggered the violence was on July 27, 1919. An 18-year-old boy named Eugene Williams was swimming on the 29th street beach on the south side of Chicago. The boy was stoned to death for swimming on the "white" beach by a white American named George Stauber. Though the police officer, Daniel Callahan, witnessed the violence, he did not arrest Stauber. Black Americans began to organize and attacked Callahan for not intervening while Stauber would be arrested by two other police officers later.

When the news of Williams's death spread, that night white gangs and black gangs began to attack each other. Black Americans were reported as derailing trolley cars and turning over automobiles to beat up white American passengers. That night 500 patrolmen had to occupy black districts to calm the violence.

The next day (July 28, 1919) white gangs attacked black stockyards workers as they were traveling home after work (Givan 1919). White Americans raided black neighborhoods and set fire to the homes of black residents.

On July 29, 1919, the rioting had moved up North to what residents of Chicago called "the loop." There white rioters raided black shops and homes. They also had drive-by-shootings through black neighborhoods.

It was seven days of shootings, arsons, and beatings. The rioting lasted until August 3, 1919, when Mayor Bill Thompson requested militia intervention. The rioting did decease, but the damage had been done. By then, 23 black Americans and 15 white Americans were killed (Essig 2005). For other damage, 342 black Americans and 195 white Americans sustained significant injuries (Essig 2005).

ELIZABETH BUSH

See also: Detroit Halloween Fires (1972–); Detroit Riot (1943); Detroit Riot (1967); Harlem Riot (March 19–20, 1935); Harlem Riot (Augsut 1–2, 1943)

Further Reading

Blackpast.org. "East St. Louis Race Riot: July 2, 1917. The Black Past: Remembered and Reclaimed." Blackpast.org. http://www.blackpast.org/aah/east-st-louis-race-riot-july-2-1917. Accessed April 22, 2015.

Essig, Steven. 2005. "Race Riots." Chicago Historical Society. http://www.encyclopedia.chicagohistory.org/pages/1032.html. Accessed April 22, 2015.

Givan, Becky. "Global Mappings: Chicago Race Riot of 1919." *Global Mappings: Chicago Race Riot of 1919.* http://diaspora.northwestern.edu/mbin/WebObjects/DiasporaX.woa/wa/displayArticle?atomid=602. Accessed April 22, 2015.

"People & Events: The East St. Louis Riot." PBS. http://www.pbs.org/wgbh/amex/garvey/peopleevents/e_estlouis.html. Accessed April 22, 2015.

East Village (NY) Groovy Murders (1967)

The East Village Groovy murders were important for a myriad of reasons, mainly because of their signification as the end of the hippie movement (O'Neill 2011) and the increased attention they brought to the structural conditions of poverty and related social problems that plagued the East Village of New York City and other large U.S. cities in the 1960s (Mele 2000, 178). This increased attention to economic and social problems (such as drug use) existed against the social backdrop of the conflict that marked the civil rights movement and brought increased conflict between police and the hippies of the East Village (Mele 2000, 178). The deaths of James Leroy "Groovy" Hutchinson (1943–1967) and Linda Rae Fitzpatrick (1949–1967) were the catalyst for this massive social change and were used by the mass media to change societal perceptions about hippies, from relative acceptance to social disgust (O'Neill 2011). Previous mass media accounts of the hippie movement showed hippies to be harmless people, but the brutal deaths of these two prominent figures (as a result of media spin) led the mass media to describe the hippie movement and its prescribed lifestyle of love, drugs, and multiple sex partners as a dangerous lifestyle that could result in sickness or even death (Porter 2012). The Groovy murders are perhaps most important because, as many contend, they exposed the hippie movement for what it really was, while exposing racial and police tensions with the hippie movement, coupled with urban decline (Mele 2000, 176).

James "Groovy" Hutchinson and his girlfriend Linda Fitzpatrick were murdered in the East Village of New York

City either late in the night on October 7, 1967, or early in the morning on October 8, 1967, at 169 Avenue B. in the boiler room. Both Hutchinson and Fitzpatrick had their skulls smashed with a brick, and Fitzpatrick was raped in the process (O'Neill 2011). Having last been seen high on the sidewalk at 165 Avenue A, the Psychedelicatessen, police believed the victims had been lured to the boiler room in the basement of the structure to buy LSD (Dunn and Hood 2004, 247).

Hutchinson was sort of a hippie community organizer within the East Village who let others frequently use his apartment as a crash pad for other drifters (McCabe 2013). Coming from a broken home himself, this crash pad was a place where homeless drug addicts could recover (MacDonald 1975). Because the lifestyle of those involved in the hippie movement was still something of an enigma to the media, Hutchinson became a popular media figure (McCabe 2013). Linda Fitzgerald enjoyed a background completely different from that of Hutchinson, as she grew up in the wealthy area of Greenwich, Connecticut. She attended Greenwich Country Day School where she excelled in athletics and went on frequent vacations with her family on expensive trips to destinations like Bermuda (where she also used LSD and smoked marijuana). Linda frequently took trips to the East Village over the course of several weekends and eventually moved there, convincing her parents she was going there to pursue a career as an artist. After arriving, Linda told her parents she had secured a stable living arrangement, but instead was living at The Village Plaza, a hippie crash pad far from that envisioned by her parents. She continued to use illegal drugs, first experimenting with LSD, and eventually using speed (amphetamine).

After the Groovy murders police arrested four suspects on charges related to the murders (*The Times-News* 1967, 10), all of which were young and poor black males from the ghettos that were in such conflict with the well-to-do white youths that "invaded" the East Village (Mele 2000). The four suspects included Donald Ramsey, a former convict and member of the West African Yoruba religion, charged with homicide and rape; Thomas Dennis, a drifter charged with homicide and rape; and Fred Wright, the janitor of the building where the murders took place, charged with raping and robbing a separate victim hours before (police originally thought this crime was connected to the Groovy murders); and a fourth unnamed suspect who was charged with rape and murder directly in connection to the Groovy murders. It is important to note that Ramsey and Wright were also charged in raping the woman victimized

earlier in the evening (The Associated Press 1967, 3; *The Times-News* 1967, 10). Ultimately Ramsey and Dennis were arrested, confessed, and convicted of the murders, but they had no explanation as to what their motives were (Fletcher 2009, 261; Dunn and Hood 2004, 247). Police believed the offenders, like the victims, were also on an LSD trip (*The Times-News* 1967, 10). Most sources show only Ramsey and Dennis were convicted of the Groovy murders (and not on rape charges); however, little information exists on the sentences received by the convicted felons.

American perceptions of crime and criminal justice often focus on individual criminality. Therefore, it is interesting to note how the reading related to the Groovy murders chooses not to focus on the outcomes related to the trial/sentencing of Ramsey and Dennis (or other aspects of the criminal justice process), but instead on the social and cultural impact of the murders themselves. Prior to the Groovy murders hippies were in conflict with the police in several ways: the police frequently cracked down on drug related behaviors (Mele 2000, 175), the hippies created a communal bail fund for when the police cracked down harder on their drug behaviors, and protested various police behaviors related to drug busts, drug laws, and the Vietnam War, among other protested social issues (Hinckley 1998). The conflict between hippies and the police was just one of many conflicts that existed in the East Village. Other conflicts existed between hippies and local East Villagers and hippies and the tourists that came to see the "freak show" that was the hippie culture (Mele 2000, 175). The murders of Hutchinson and Fitzpatrick helped change the way people thought about the hippie movement because Hutchinson had been so positively portrayed by the media and the public became shocked to know that a young woman like Fitzpatrick could become such a tragic victim after coming from such a prominent family and well-to-do background (Fletcher 2009, 261–262).

Free Love

Hutchinson and Fitzpatrick were just two of many that flocked to the East Village to enjoy in the free-love, drug-use, peace-promoting culture, as 1967 was the Summer of Love. The hippies were attracted to the East Village because of its racial and ethnic diversity, but ultimately left for the same reasons (Mele 2000). Editor of the *East Village Other*, Alan

Katzman, described the racial tensions that existed between the hippies that settled in the East Village and locals by stating, "They resent it when they find the hippies, kids from middle-class backgrounds, are rejecting television and cars and suburban homes, the very things the people in the ghetto want. It's like an insult" (Maeder 2001, n.p.).

After the Groovy murders the police and the hippies were able to reconcile their differences for a short while, as the New York Police Department (NYPD) formed a unit tasked with the responsibility of protecting defenseless hippies (Hinckley 1998). This period of peace, however, was short-lived because as the public became more aware of the social problems experienced in the East Village the prescribed solution to the village problems increasingly favored police action and the village youth pushed back against law enforcement actions, such as narcotics crackdowns (Mele 2000, 178). Overall, the Groovy murders significantly contributed to the end of a national movement, public fear, community disinvestment, and the East Village community decline that followed (O'Neill 2011; Mele 2000, 179).

ALLEN COPENHAVER

See also: Altamont Free Concert (Alameda County, CA) (December 6, 1969); Atlanta Race Riots (1906); Chicago Seven (1968); King, Martin Luther, Jr., Assassination of (April 4, 1968); Malcolm X, Assassination of (February 21, 1965); Stonewall Riots (New York City) (June 28–July 1, 1969)

Further Reading

The Associated Press. 1967. "Two Indicted in Hippieland Double Killing." *The Kane Republican (Kane, PA)*. November 2.

Dunn, Brad and Daniel Hood. 2004. *New York: The Unknown City*. Vancouver, B.C.: Arsenal Pulp Press, 247.

Fletcher, T. 2009. *All Hopped Up and Ready to Go: Music from the Streets of New York 1927–77*. New York: W.W. Norton & Company.

Hinckley, David. "Groovy: The Summer of Love, 1967." *Daily News*, last modified October 15, 1998. http://www.nydaily news.com/archives/news/groovy-summer-love-1967-article-1.806459?pgno=1.

Lukas, J. Anthony. 1967. "The Two Worlds of Linda Fitzpatrick." *The New York Times*. Last modified 1967. http://www.nytimes.com/books/97/10/26/home/luckas-fitzpatrick.html.

MacDonald, Ross. "Don't Shoot—We Are Your Children!." *New York Times*. Last modified 1975. http://www.nytimes.com/books/97/10/26/home/lukas-shoot.html.

Maeder, Jay. "Lambs to the Slaughter: Horror in Hippieland, October 1967 Chapter 355." *Daily News*. Last modified May 22, 2001, http://www.nydailynews.com/archives/news/lambs-slaughter-horror-hippieland-october-1967-chapter-355-article-1.935950.

McCabe, Scott. 2013. "Crime History, Oct. 8, 1967: 'The Groovy Murders' A Wake Up Call for Suburban America." D.C. Crime Stories (blog), October 13. http://dccrimestories.com/crime-history-oct-8-1967-the-groovy-murders-a-wake-up-call-to-middle-america/.

Mele, C. 2000. *Selling the Lower East Side: Culture, Real Estate, and Resistance in New York City*. Minneapolis: University of Minnesota Press.

O'Neill, W.L. 2011. *Dawning of the Counter-Culture: The 1960s*. Venice: Now and Then Reader.

Porter, Bruce. "Lost and Found." *Columbia Journalism Review*. Last modified November/December 2012. http://www.cjr.org/feature/lost_and_found.php.

The Times-News. 1967. "Arrest Murder Suspect." http://news.google.com/newspapers?nid=1665&dat=19671010&id=t6RPAAAAIBAJ&sjid=hCQEAAAAIBAJ&pg=3847,776536. Accessed January 3, 2015.

Eastern Air Lines Hijacking (1970)

The hijacking of Eastern Air Lines Flight 1320 took place on March 17, 1970, during a regularly scheduled shuttle flight between Newark International Airport in Newark, New Jersey, and Logan International Airport in Boston, Massachusetts. John Divivo, 27, forced his way into the cockpit midway through the flight and instructed the pilots to fly east until the airplane ran out of fuel. When the pilots insisted that they be able to turn the plane toward Logan Airport to refuel, Divivo panicked and opened fire, killing the copilot and injuring the pilot. However, before he died, the copilot was able to use Divivo's own gun to shoot and injure him. The pilot was then able to subdue Divivo and land the plane safely while bleeding from two gunshot wounds. The incident is famous because it resulted in the first death from air piracy in U.S. history (Russell 2013).

Divivo had a tumultuous upbringing before he committed the hijacking. He dropped out of high school in the ninth grade and used a gun to attempt suicide at age 16 (Newton 2002). Doctors were unable to remove the bullet from his head, which later led reporters to speculate that this may have contributed to his deteriorated mental state (*The Spokesman Review* 1970). Newton (2002) also noted that the gunshot wound may have affected Divivo's personality and caused him to have violent mood swings. At the time of the hijacking, Divivo lived in a tenement with his mother, two brothers, and sister and was employed by the Palisades Amusement Park (*The Norwalk Hour* 1970). He had formerly been a short-order cook (*The Day* 1970).

On March 17, 1970 Eastern Air Lines departed as normal from Newark with 73 passengers on board (*Ludington Daily News* 1970). Approximately 30 miles from Logan Airport, as was the custom, the stewardess began to collect the $15.75 fare requisite for the shuttle service. Divivo told the stewardess that he did not have enough money, brandished a .38 caliber revolver at the stewardess, and ordered her to take him into the cockpit. When the stewardess, Christine Peterson, knocked on the cockpit door and said that a man wanted to meet with the captain, Captain Robert Wilbur Jr. initially told her that he was busy. However, after Peterson told him that the man was armed, Wilbur allowed the man inside the cockpit and told her to return to the main cabin and alleviate any potential fears the passengers were having (*The Evening News* 1970). Once inside the cockpit, Divivo made it clear he was hijacking the airplane. Captain Robert Wilbur Junior assumed he wanted asylum in Cuba because that was the prevailing trend of hijackers at the time (Walker 2009). However, Divivo then told Wilbur "Fly east. I don't have any place to go. Just fly east until the plane runs out of gas" (Newton 2002). However, Captain Wilbur appealed to Divivo to allow the plane to land at Logan Airport because it was low on fuel. Divivo appeared to accede to the plea; however, when Wilbur made the necessary bank, Divivo opened fire (*The Spokesman-Review* 1970). As Divivo opened fire, First Officer James Hartley Jr. lunged for the gun. Divivo shot Hartley once in the chest, mortally wounding him. However, before he died, Hartley Jr. was able to wrestle the gun away from Divivo and shoot him twice, including at least once in the chest. As a result, Divivo temporarily lost consciousness. When he revived, Captain Wilbur used Divivo's pistol to knock him unconscious (Walker 2009). During the gunfire, Divivo had shot Wilbur twice, once in each arm. However, Wilbur was still conscious and recognized the need to land the plane immediately. Wilbur did not tell anyone in the control tower of his injuries and followed every protocol as if it was a normal landing. At first, passengers in the cabin were only vaguely aware anything was wrong with the airplane. However, passengers would later recall that, in the final moments of the flight, the plane descended very rapidly over Back Bay, causing them to think that the aircraft was about to crash-land in the water below. Other passengers

also recalled that when the plane sharply banked before its descent someone shouted to ask if anyone was flying the plane. A passenger seated toward the cockpit answered in the affirmative (*Montreal Gazette* 1970). Wilbur was able to land the airplane safely. As he taxied toward the terminal Wilbur radioed the control tower and said "My copilot is shot, where the hell do you want me to put this thing!" (*Norwalk Hour* 1970).

Upon arrival at the terminal, Wilbur collapsed from shock and blood loss (Newton 2002). Five police officers arrived and hauled Divivo off the plane. Both Wilbur and Divivo were transported to Massachusetts General Hospital where doctors operated on them for their bullet wounds (*Ludington Daily News* 1970). On March 24, 1970, the U.S. Senate passed a resolution honoring Wilbur and Hartley for acts of heroism. On March 26, 1970, Secretary of Transportation John A. Volpe presented Wilbur with a Federal Aviation Administration (FAA) award commending his extraordinary efforts (*The Tuscaloosa News* 1970).

East Boston District Court charged Divivo with murder in an "aircraft in flight over the United States" as part of a recently created statute meant to more harshly punish hijackers. On April 9, 1970, John Divivo pled not guilty to the charges filed against him (*The Virgin Islands Daily News* 1970). The presiding judge, Wilfred Paquet, remanded Divivo to Bridgewater State Hospital, where he was to be held without bond for 35 days for a mental evaluation. After the evaluation was completed, Divivo was relocated to Suffolk County Jail to await trial. At 3:00 a.m. on October 31, 1970, Divivo tied a neckerchief to one of the bars in his jail cell and strangled himself to death.

AARON SAFER-LICHTENSTEIN

See also: Cooper, D.B., Airline Hijacking (November 24, 1971); September 11 Terrorist Attacks (2001)

Further Reading

"Assailant Stopped by Dying Co-Pilot." 1970. *The Montreal Gazette.* March 19, p. 25.

"Award for Hero Pilot." 1970. *The Tuscaloosa News.* March 27, p. 14.

"Copilot Is Killed in Airliner Shooting." 1970. *The Day.* March 18, p. 1.

"Copilot Sacrificed His Life." 1970. *The Spokesman-Review.* March 19, p. 1.

"Divivo Pleads Innocent." 1970. *The Virgin Islands Daily News.* April 10, p. 2.

Newton, M. 2002. *The Encyclopedia of Kidnappings.* New York: Infobase Publishing.

"Pilot Shot, Lands Jet OK with 73 Aboard." 1970. *The Evening News.* March 18, p. 1.

Russell, David Lee. 2013. *Eastern Air Lines: A History, 1926–1991.* Jefferson, NC: McFarland & Company Inc.

"Shot in Arms, Pilot Lands OK." 1970. *The Norwalk Hour.* March 18, p. 1.

Walker, Adrian. 2009. "Friends in High Places." *Boston Globe.* March 20. www.bostonglobe.com. Accessed April 15, 2015.

"Wounded Pilot Lands Jetliner with Slain Copilot Beside Him." 1970. *Ludington Daily News.* March 18, p. 1.

Edwards, Edward Wayne (1933–2011)

Edward Wayne Edwards, also known as the "Sweetheart Killer," murdered five individuals between 1977 and 1996. Though Edwards was questioned as a suspect in three separate investigations, police were unable to connect him to the murders until 2009, after DNA analysis linked him to a reopened cold case in Wisconsin. During police interrogations, Edwards waved his right to remain silent and confessed to the murders of Judith Straub (1959–1977) and Bill Lavaco (1956–1977) in Ohio, Timothy Hack (1961–1980) and Kelly Drew (1961–1980) in Wisconsin, and Dannie Boy Edwards (1971–1996). He received multiple life sentences in Ohio and Wisconsin for the murder of two couples and received the death penalty for the murder of his foster son in 1996. Through careful planning, Edwards manipulated the judicial system in Ohio and Wisconsin to obtain the death penalty. In Wisconsin, Edwards pled guilty to only the murders in 1980 and received two consecutive life sentences to be served after his prison time in Ohio. He did not receive the death penalty for the 1977 murders in Ohio because a Supreme Court ruling disavowed state executions as a legal form of justice in Ohio during five years in the 1970s. However, during his 2010 trial in Ohio, Edwards pled guilty to murdering his foster son in 1996, during which time the death penalty was legal, and ensured his death sentence. Overruling his multiple life sentences in two states, he was sentenced to death by lethal injection on August 31, 2011, but died of natural causes on April 7, 2011.

Edwards had a long criminal career. His book *Metamorphosis of a Criminal* depicts his turbulent childhood and crimes throughout the 1950s and 1960s. He spent his early years in an orphanage where he was physically abused by nuns, deciding to never again submit to mistreatment and proclaiming his new life dream of being a good criminal. Edwards drifted across multiple states throughout his life, scamming women and robbing banks and stores. He spent five years in prison where he allegedly transformed his life; after his parole, he published his book and became an inspirational speaker to criminals, encouraging them to renounce their life of crime. However, his new life was short-lived as he was arrested several times, charged with criminal activities, spent more time in jail, escaped prison, was added to the FBI's 10 most wanted fugitives list in 1961, and became a famous serial killer.

In 1977, Edwards murdered Judith Straub, 18, and Bill Lavaco, 21, in Ohio. Their bodies were found at Silver Creek Metropolitan Park in Norton, Ohio, shortly after their murders. Both were shot in the neck at point-blank range with a shotgun. Edwards's motives for killing the couple are unclear; however, prior to their deaths, he lived in the same neighborhood as them. He was never a suspect in their murder investigation. In 1980, Edwards murdered Tim Hack, 19, and Kelly Drew, 19. They disappeared from a wedding reception and were found two months later. Their decomposed remains were located several miles from the dance hall; Drew was discovered in the woods, strangled to death, and Hack was found in a nearby cornfield, stabbed to death. Edwards worked as a handyman at the campground adjacent to the dance hall and remained a suspect in the investigation. After police questioning, Edwards abruptly left Wisconsin. In 1996, Edwards murdered his foster son Dannie Boy Edwards, 25. Dannie changed his name in the mid-1990s from Dannie Law Gloeckner to Dannie Boy Edwards to display his love for his foster family. Edwards convinced Dannie to take out a $250,000 life insurance policy and premeditated his murder for a year prior to killing Dannie. Edwards convinced Dannie to go absent without leave (AWOL) from the army, and under the disguise of discussing ways to elude the army, lured him into the woods behind the Edwards's home. Edwards shot Dannie twice in the face at point-blank range with a shotgun and buried him in a shallow grave behind a cemetery where he was found a few months later. Edwards stated his motive for killing Dannie as greed for his insurance money.

In early 2000, Wisconsin cold case division received extra funding to reopen several cold cases, one of which was the Hack–Drew murder. They extracted DNA samples from semen found on Drew's pants during the investigation but were unable to link the samples to a specific killer. The division aired a news story on the murders in 2009, which was seen by one of Edwards's children. The child called the division and tipped the police on Edwards as a suspected killer, recalling Edwards working near the scene of the murders and their abrupt move after the start of the school year and directly after the discovery of Hack and Drew's remains. The police matched Edwards's DNA with the DNA found at the crime scene and linked him to the murders. During his interrogations, Edwards denied that he had ever gone deer hunting, refuting a statement he had made in 1980 during the original murder investigation. This discrepancy in Edwards's testimony strengthened the case against him and confirmed police suspicions. Edwards ultimately admitted to having sex with Drew in a field outside the dance hall and watched as several boys trampled Hack and Drew to death.

While under investigation of the Hack–Drew murders, Edwards confessed to killing Straub and Lavaco in 1977, a crime in which he was never a suspect. After pleading guilty to murders of Hack and Drew, Edwards agreed to plead guilty to murdering Straub and Lavaco. During his trial in Ohio, Edwards testified to killing Dannie Boy Edwards in 1996 in hope of receiving the death penalty. After multiple life sentences, a jury conceded to the death penalty by lethal injection and honored Edwards's request of jailing him in Ohio. At the age of 77 Edwards died on death row of natural causes.

While Edwards testified to killing five people, it is widely speculated that he killed many more. The most notable murders linked to Edwards include Larry Peyton and Beverly Allen, murdered in 1960 in Portland, and Mary Leonard and Ricky Beard, murdered after leaving a drive-in theater in Akron in 1979. Both couples were young and involved knife and gunshot wounds with rape and strangulation, all pertinent in Edwards known as "Sweetheart Murders." However, three young men were arrested in the 1960s for the Peyton–Allen murders, but the Leonard–Beard murders currently remain open. Edwards admitted to only committing five murders, and no DNA or witnesses link him to any other murders; therefore, his part in other deaths remains highly speculative.

Lauren Parker

See also: Bundy, Ted (1946–1989); Franklin, Joseph Paul (1950–2013); Zodiac Killer (1960s–)

Further Reading

Andreadis, Cleopatra. 2010. "Elderly Conman Confesses He Killed 4 During Career as Motivational Speaker." *ABC News*. June 10.

Brueck, Dana. 2012. "Tim Hack and Kelly Drew Case; Program to Feature Investigation." *MWTV*. July 12.

"Edward Wayne Edwards: A Timeline of His Life." 2010. *Wisconsin State Journal*. June 9.

Edwards, Ed. 1972. *Metamorphosis of a Criminal*. New York: Hart Publishing Company.

"The Final 'Con'? A Convicted Killer's Jailhouse Confession." 2010. WKCY. June 18.

"Hack-Drew Suspect Denies '80 Murders." 2009. *Daily Union*. August 27.

John, Finn J.D. 2013. "Did Oregon miss chance to stop a serial killer?" *News-Register*. May 14.

Lea, Jason. 2010. "(VIDEO) Former Troy man Pleads Guilty in '96 Death of Foster Son." *The News-Herald*. August 26.

Simms, Patricia. 2010. "Serial Killer Edwards Pleads Guilty in Sweetheart Slayings, Heads to Ohio." *Wisconsin State Journal*. June 10.

Einhorn, Ira (1940–)

Ira Einhorn was convicted and sentenced to life in prison in 2002 for the 1977 murder of his ex-girlfriend, Holly Maddux. Einhorn was an American environmentalist who called himself the Unicorn because his surname had the same German Jewish meaning. Maddux and Einhorn were in a romantic relationship for almost five years when she ended their relationship and moved to New York City. She

Convicted in absentia of murder, Ira Einhorn is shown in this 1979 photo with a Philadelphia sheriff's deputy. On June 16, 1997, the FBI reported that Einhorn had been arrested by French authorities. (AP Photo/Temple Univ. Archives)

began dating someone else which made Einhorn very unhappy and caused him to develop a plan to get her to return to Philadelphia to pick up her things. Maddux reluctantly agreed and no one saw her alive again. During the initial police investigation, Einhorn told police that Maddux left to go to the store and never returned. Einhorn beat Maddux to death and then stored her body in a locked trunk in his apartment for almost a year and a half before her body was discovered by the police. Eighteen months later Einhorn's neighbors reported an unpleasant smell in his apartment and when police investigated, they discovered the deteriorating corpse of Maddux. After his arrest for the death of his ex-girlfriend, Einhorn was granted bail and fled to Europe for 17 years before his extradition, trial, and conviction for her murder.

Einhorn, 37, and Maddux, 25, started dating in 1972 and began sharing an apartment in Philadelphia shortly thereafter. Maddux was the oldest of five siblings who grew up in Texas. She was a petite mild-mannered former cheerleader, but Einhorn was quite the opposite in size, dress, and demeanor. Einhorn was outspoken about his political views and as a result made acquaintance with a number of highly eccentric, influential, and wealthy individuals who shared similar views. While Maddux's family outwardly supported their daughter in her relationship, they quietly expressed their concerns after seeing the way Einhorn treated her in public, which appeared disrespectful and sometimes controlling. News reports released following the disappearance of Maddux suggested that Einhorn had a history of overpowering and violent encounters with women in his previous relationships. There was also speculation that Maddux would have ended the relationship much sooner but she may have been afraid of Einhorn's reaction. While she had expressed a desire to end the relationship to family members, Maddux had to build the courage to end her relationship. When she finally had the nerve to call things off, Maddux left Philadelphia for New York City where she started a relationship with Saul Lapidus. She later called Einhorn to let him know she would not be coming back to him. Einhorn, angered by the thought of her with another man and no possibility of restoring their relationship, insisted that she return to Philadelphia to retrieve her things right away or he would get rid of them. Maddux returned to their apartment for her belongings, and no one ever heard from her again.

Maddux's family and friends questioned Einhorn's story from the beginning. He told investigators that Maddux had indeed returned to Philadelphia but that after leaving for the store had never returned and that he did not know where she was. However, when no one heard from her, the family hired their own investigators after the local police were not persistent in following up with the case. As stories circulated that Maddux had previously tried to leave the relationship, combined with Einhorn's lack of cooperation with investigators, a foul smell and brown liquid coming through the ceiling in the apartment below, and Einhorn's refusal to allow anyone from the apartment staff to investigate the odor, law enforcement eventually obtained evidence needed to justify the issuance of a search warrant of Einhorn's apartment in March 1979. After an extensive search of the apartment, investigators found Maddux's body stuffed in a trunk in a closet providing law enforcement the proof they needed to finally make an arrest.

There was no shortage of character witnesses to testify on Einhorn's behalf at his bail hearing. Einhorn was well connected and had a well-known reputation for his environmental activism demonstrated by his active involvement in the first Earth Day celebration. Einhorn was also known to have a distrust of the government actively questioning U.S. policies. The idea that someone with such a high reputation could be responsible for the brutal death of someone close to him, they argued, was unimaginable, and supporters further argued he was too smart to have committed a crime of this magnitude all while hiding the evidence in his home. His status was a contributing factor to the delay in the investigation and after his arrest. Einhorn argued that he was being framed and spewed conspiracy theories to whomever would listen. Despite the seriousness and heinousness of the offense for which he was charged, Einhorn's attorney, Arlen Specter, secured his pretrial release when bail ($40,000) was granted and he posted a $4,000 bond. Einhorn didn't wait around to see how the case would progress.

Before his trial began in January 1981, Einhorn fled the United States for Europe. For the next 17 years, American law enforcement would track Einhorn and attempt to intercept him several times in multiple European countries but were always two steps behind him. In 1993, Pennsylvania prosecutors conducted a jury trial for Einhorn and convicted him of Maddux's murder. By 1997, authorities finally tracked Einhorn to France where he was living lavishly in France with a wealthy Swedish wife, Anika Flodin, under an assumed name. It appeared as though Einhorn's luck had finally run out; however, Einhorn won an early victory when the French government refused his extradition, citing French law that did not recognize the ruling of a court's decision when the defendant was not present to present their defense. After several more failed attempts at extraditing Einhorn, the American courts agreed to grant Einhorn a new trial. Einhorn was finally extradited in July 2001 and went to trial the following year. The state presented witnesses who testified to Maddux's suspected physical abuse by Einhorn during their relationship and argued that Einhorn killed her out of jealousy over her new relationship and that he tried to cover up the crime by hiding her body in a small trunk. Einhorn took the stand in his own defense testifying that the American government had framed him for Maddux's murder because of his criticism and investigation into their policies in the 1960s. The prosecution's arguments combined with the presentation of physical evidence linking Einhorn to the murder were enough to secure a first-degree murder conviction after a jury trial in late 2002. While neither of Maddux's parents was living by the time the case went to trial, her siblings received closure as a result of Einhorn's conviction. Upon conviction, Einhorn was sentenced to life in prison without the possibility of parole. He is currently housed in the Pennsylvania Department of Corrections Houtzdale Institution.

BROOKE MILLER

See also: Levy, Chandra, Disappearance of (2001–2002); Peterson, Laci, Murder of (2002–2004); Simpson, O.J. (1947–); Von Bulow, Claus (1926–)

Further Reading

Anderson, Kevin, Tom Skerritt, and William A. Graham. *The Hunt for the Unicorn Killer.* DVD. 1999. Studio Works.

Dwyer, Kevin, and Jure Fiorillo. 2006. *True Stories of Law & Order: The Real Crimes Behind the Best Episodes of the Hit TV Show.* New York: Berkley Trade.

Geringer, Joseph. "Ira Einhorn: The Unicorn Killer." crimelibrary.com 2006. http://www.crimelibrary.com/notorious_murders/famous/einhorn/index_1.html. Accessed April 16, 2015.

Levy, Steven. 1990. *The Unicorn's Secret.* n.p.: Onyx.

Ellsberg, Daniel. *See* Pentagon Papers Leak (1971)

Enron Case (1985–2001)

The failure of Enron is widely recognized as one of the largest corporate scandals in U.S. history. Enron was an energy supply company that became involved in unregulated energy sources by trading supply contracts. The company was once well respected, having been named the most innovative company in America six years in a row by *Fortune.* This reputation turned to one of crime and greed after Enron collapsed amid accusations of securities fraud and inside trading. The fraud began when executives became primarily concerned with increasing stock prices to attract investors. To do this, Enron relied heavily on accounting manipulations instead of furthering legitimate business ventures. Losses were widely disguised as profits and losing ventures spun off into shell companies, offering an inaccurate appearance of steady growth. Enron illustrates the dangers of both organizational deviance through deception and manipulation of financial markets and the increased complication of corporate finance, making it difficult to discern the true health and viability of companies. Along with similar cases, Enron was responsible for the passage of the Sarbanes–Oxley Act of 2002, which aimed to increase accountability for executives, accountants, and securities analysts. Enron is often cited as a symbolic illustration of corporate greed in the early 21st century.

Enron began in 1985 as the first interconnected national gas pipeline in the United States under the leadership of economist Kenneth Lay (1942–2006), who became the company's first chief executive officer (CEO) and chairman. By taking advantage of energy deregulation and increasing control over the distribution through energy trading, Enron's leaders were able to siphon off energy and offer long-term contracts at higher rates than competitors. Many consider these tactics to be a major contributor to California's energy crisis in the late 1990s. Under the direction of chief operating officer (COO) Jeffery Skilling (1953–), they bought other energy companies, pipelines, broadband fiber optic cables, and electricity plants to control energy distribution. Their increasingly complex business structure was also problematic due to the use of mark-to-market accounting, carried out by chief financial officer (CFO) Andrew Fastow (1961–). Using this method, transactions were recorded based on projected future earnings instead of actual income, allowing substantial profits to be recorded with little or no evidence of accuracy. To hide spending and losses misspecified as profits, hundreds of special-purpose vehicles (SPVs), also known as shell corporations, were created to remove debt from Enron's balance sheets. This gave the appearance of strong financial performance, which artificially inflated the company's stock price. This stock manipulation was further exacerbated by executive compensation offered in the form of stock options. By attracting talent through these options, executives were incentivized to increase the stock price with the goal of generating personal wealth when the options were exercised.

The crimes at Enron were facilitated by an environment centered on concentration of corporate power, deregulation of the energy markets, and limited resources for regulators, which permitted Enron's excessive trading of energy contracts with limited government oversight. By donating to political campaigns and arguing for energy and financial market deregulation, lobbyists were gradually able to limit the authority of existing regulators such as the Securities and Exchange Commission (SEC), as well as liability for accounting fraud. Enron pushed heavily for relaxed regulations on energy trading.

Fraudulent activities at Enron were not uncovered by various securities regulators. Complete financial statements reflecting the actual condition of the company were not provided to investors, fraudulently influencing them to continue investing in Enron. Financial analysts and credit rating agencies relied on these erroneous statements to make recommendations, with rating agencies continuously giving Enron healthy ratings and analysts issuing strong buy recommendations. Having received millions of dollars in fees from Enron, auditors at accounting firm Arthur Anderson and analysts at Lehman Brothers and Merrill Lynch were incentivized to ignore irregularities. Having signed off on Enron's use of accounting methods, the SEC failed to recognize these false transactions and inadvertently legitimized the speculative projections. This lack of accountability enabled the misrepresentations at Enron for many years.

The true nature of Enron's dealings became known in 2001 when they could no longer rely on new projects to provide the appearance of growth. In 2000, Enron's stock price had peaked and began to steadily decline. Failed ventures into broadband and weather trading contributed to the decline. Skilling replaced Lay as CEO in February 2001, only to resign six months later. Skilling and other executives began cashing in their stock options. This was considered a red flag to investors who also decided to sell, further driving down the stock value. As the price sharply dropped in October 2001, retirement accounts of line-level employees were frozen, many of whom had been strongly encouraged to place their entire life savings with Enron. When Enron's earnings were restated, money formerly allocated as profits was reclassified as losses. In early December 2001, Enron filed for bankruptcy at less than one dollar per share, having been downgraded by credit rating agencies to junk status. Tens of thousands of employees lost their jobs, with many losing everything they had invested.

Enron remained defunct after bankruptcy and was turned into a recovery company, selling its assets and paying back creditors and investors. Federal prosecutors criminally pursued Enron executives and many were found guilty of securities fraud, money laundering, and insider trading. Skilling was sentenced to 24 years in prison in 2006 (later reduced to 14 years in 2013) for insider trading and securities fraud and Fastow pled guilty in 2004 to wire and securities fraud, receiving a six-year sentence. Lay was found guilty of securities fraud, but died of a heart attack prior to sentencing. Numerous other executives were also convicted. Accounting firm Arthur Anderson was found guilty of obstruction for shredding thousands of Enron documents. The firm itself collapsed in 2002.

The subsequent Sarbanes–Oxley legislation was touted as fundamental reform of corporate governance designed to hold companies and executives accountable for fraudulent financial statements. Several fundamental problems contributing to Enron's collapse were addressed, including shareholder and board independence, auditor conflicts of interest, and statement certification by CEOs and CFOs. However, these provisions were cited by many as inadequate and have been watered down over time. The law failed to address other issues, such as conflicts of interest with securities analysts and rating agencies, executive compensation through stock options, concentration of corporate power in the financial and energy sectors, and criminogenic corporate cultures. These issues persisted beyond Enron and throughout the 2000s with countless other corporate scandals, such as WorldCom, Adelphia, Tyco, Fannie Mae, HealthSouth, Global Crossing, Bear Stearns, Washington Mutual, Lehman Brothers, and American International Group (AIG). Enron continues to be cited as an example of the downside of unrestrained free market capitalism and the dangers of the unchecked drive toward quick and easy money at the expense of sound business practices.

Brandon A. Sullivan

See also: *Exxon Valdez* Oil Spill (1989); Madoff, Bernard (1938–); Stewart, Martha, Insider Trading Case (2001–2004); *Primary Documents*/Enron Case: Excerpt from Sarbanes–Oxley Act (2002)

Further Reading

Coffee, John C. 2003. "What Caused Enron? A Capsule Social and Economic History of the 1990s." *Cornell Law Review* 89: 269–309.

Giroux, Gary. 2008. "What Went Wrong? Accounting Fraud and Lessons from the Recent Scandals." *Social Research* 75 (4): 1205–38.

Healy, Paul M., and Krishna G. Palepu. 2003. "The Fall of Enron." *Journal of Economic Perspectives* 17 (2): 3–26.

McLean, Bethany, and Peter Elkind. 2003. *The Smartest Guys in the Room: The Amazing Rise and Scandalous Fall of Enron.* New York: Portfolio.

Sullivan, Brandon A. 2015. "Corporate-Financial Crime Scandals: A Comparative Analysis of the Collapses of Insull and Enron." In Gregg Barak, ed. *International Handbook on the Crimes of the Powerful.* New York: Routledge.

Essex, Mark James Robert (1949–1973)

Notoriously known as the spree shooter responsible for the Howard Johnson Tragedy of January 7, 1973, Mark Essex waged war on New Orleans, Louisiana, resulting in a total of 9 dead and 12 seriously injured over a week-long period. Essex, a 23-year-old former dental assistant for the U.S. Navy, was exposed to Black Panther and Muslim ideologies, developing an extreme hatred for white people. The first conflict began on December 31, 1972, when Essex went to the New Orleans Police Department (NOPD) headquarters to seek revenge for the death of two black protesters on November 16, 1972. Essex used a Ruger carbine .44 Magnum to kill two officers and escaped to Gert Town a few miles away. After a week of avoiding law enforcement Essex began another set of attacks on January 7, 1973. Choosing the Howard Johnson Hotel because of the location, Essex shot people in the hotel and started fires, intending to draw out the NOPD so he could kill as many officers as possible. After 11 hours of confusion and fighting, Essex was killed on the roof of the Downtown Howard Johnson Hotel by a CH-46 Marine helicopter carrying police sharp shooters. As a result of Essex's massacre, the NOPD changed their procedure for responding to 911 calls and many experts believe the tragedy became a blueprint for future shooters.

Mark James Robert Essex was born in Emporia, Kansas, on August 12, 1949. Beginning in 1969, Essex was motivated by Black Panther politics while serving in the U.S. Navy as a dental assistant. Developing his hatred toward

Photo of Mark Essex while in the U.S. Navy. Essex committed numerous homicides of police officers in New Orleans before eventually being killed atop a Howard Johnson Motor Lodge. (Mark Meyer/The LIFE Images Collection/Getty Images)

white people from the alleged racial abuse he endured from white sailors; Essex was discharged on February 10, 1971 for going AWOL (absent without leave) and telling the court about his hatred toward white people. Within the next several years, Essex would first spend some time in New York City engaging in Black Panthers politics. In August 1972, Essex moved to New Orleans to live with an old friend from the navy. Essex's hatred for law enforcement officers developed after he witnessed the death of two black demonstrators shot by the local police in Baton Rouge on November 16, 1972. In late December 1972, Essex sent a letter to WWL, a New Orleans television station, explaining in detail his reason for declaring war against the police and his plans for the events on January 7.

At approximately 11:00 p.m. on December 3, 1972, Essex made his first attack, on the NOPD's headquarters. Planning to attack during the shift change, Essex used a Colt .38-caliber revolver and a Ruger .44 Magnum carbine rifle that resulted in the death of one police officer. After firing four shots Essex ran from NOPD's headquarters and came across two unsuspecting officers 15 minutes later. Taking cover in the Burkart business office across the street, Essex fired at the officers less than 40 feet away. One of the officers was shot in the back and died two months later from his injuries. Essex, however, was able to escape and hid inside Saint Mark Baptist Church.

The NOPD officers searched for Essex and followed the trail of bullet cartridges to where Essex was hiding. However, Chief of Police Clarence Giarrusso had to make the tough decision of calling off the search. After receiving complaints from locals about the officers obtrusive search tactics, Essex was able to get away for a third time.

On January 7, 1973, Essex made his final stand at the Howard Johnson's Hotel. A 17-story building, the hotel is separated from the New Orleans City Hall and the Louisiana Supreme Court by a park. The NOPD headquarters is a few blocks from City Hall. Essex made his way to the hotel using the car that he stole and climbed to the 18th floor. Passing three black maids in the hallway, Essex told them not to worry, that he is only there to kill whites. Wanting to lure the NOPD to the hotel, Essex killed a married couple and set their room on fire. Moving down to the 11th floor, Essex killed the assistant manager and continued to set rooms on fire. Essex moved to the 10th floor where the general manager was killed. Essex also shot another hotel guest as firemen and police arrived at the scene. Essex shot at them, successfully hitting a fireman in the arm.

Essex battled officers from NOPD, and killed two more officers before heading to the roof. In the hotel lobby, Chief of Police Clarence Giarrusso established the command post, forcing officers to run through the gun fire to get either in or out. The Deputy Police Chief Louis Sirgo attempted to rescue officers with a team composed of volunteers and got killed by Essex in the process. Uncertain of the information being transmitted, Giarrusso sent officers up to handle the possible scenario of three gunmen with hostages. As officers stormed the roof, Essex was able to shoot more officers from a safe location behind a cinderblock wall.

As all this was occurring, the media was airing footage live. Chuck Pitman, a Marine Corps Lieutenant Colonel, watched the officers storm the roof from his television. A former helicopter pilot, Pitman contacted the NOPD to offer his expertise and gained approval to report to the hotel. Pitman arrived in the CH-46 Marine helicopter and Giarrusso was able to get four police officers who agreed

to shoot from the helicopter. After several attempts to find Essex's hiding spot, hours passed before the officers were finally able to lead Essex out. At that point, Essex was hit by over 200 bullets from the officers on the roof and helicopter.

This mass casualty attack by Essex significantly impacted the New Orleans community. It also forced the NOPD to revise how they responded to such situations. These attacks impact both how police officers are trained to respond to such situation and the strategies used when arriving at the scene. In addition, Essex's affiliation with the Blank Panther Party contributed to a crackdown on the organization and other members. As a result of the Howard Johnson Tragedy, some experts argue that Essex's actions became a leading example for future criminals, including the Washington DC Beltway Sniper John Allen Muhammad (Hustmyre n.d.).

CHELSEY R. BELL

See also: Kennedy, John F., Assassination of (November 22, 1963); Texas Bell Tower Shootings (August 1, 1966); Washington, D.C., Area Snipers (October 2–24, 2002)

Further Reading

Hustmyre, Chuck. n.d. "Mark Essex, the Howard Johnson Hotel Sniper." http://web.archive.org/web/20130607143306/http://www.trutv.com/library/crime/notorious_murders/mass/mark_essex/index.html. Accessed April 16, 2015.

Eubanks, Susan (1964–)

Since the modern death penalty era began some 40 years ago, 178 women have been sentenced to death in the United States (Streib 2013). Susan Diane Eubanks is one of them. The 33-year-old mother of four committed the rare crime of filicide against her own children. This was a horrific crime that shook up even the most experienced police officers who responded to the scene. Experts agree that mothers and fathers who kill their children have different motives—mothers tend to kill out of desperation, while fathers tend to kill out of anger. Eubanks claimed to have killed her sons in an act of love to save them while she was in a diminished state of mind from drinking all day and taking prescription drugs. Prosecutors in the case, however, claimed she killed her children as a final act of rage and revenge against the men in her life who had left her. A jury and judge agreed, and Susan Eubanks was handed down a rare death sentence for the murder of her sons. She is one of 20 women on death row in California, which hasn't executed a woman since 1962 (Streib 2013). The actual execution of women on death row throughout the United States is rare.

Women on Death Row

The 178 death sentences for women in the United States amount to only 2.1 percent of all death sentences imposed since 1973. While women represent a relatively small number of homicide offenders (11% according to the FBI's Uniform Crime Report on homicide from 2011), they represent a much smaller portion of offenders sentenced to death. Certain crimes are designated as death penalty eligible, referred to as capital murders. "Domestic homicide—the killing of relatives and sexual intimates—appears to be discounted in perceived seriousness and punishability, at least as compared to homicides by and against strangers. In contrast, the most common crimes committed by those on death row today are felony murders, homicides committed during a dangerous felony such as robbery or rape" (Streib 2005, 11). Women mostly kill an intimate partner or family member (60%), and rarely kill strangers (10%). Men kill acquaintances (50%) and strangers (29%) more than family members (20%) (UCR 2011).

On October 26, 1997, Susan Eubanks shot and killed her four sons in their San Marcos, California, home. The oldest, Brandon Armstrong, was 14 years old. Austin, Brigham, and Matthew Eubanks were seven, six, and four, respectively. Eubanks left all of her children home alone that afternoon while she drank and watched football at a local bar with her boyfriend, Rene Dodson. The couple began arguing at the bar, and the fight continued as they arrived back at the house. Eubanks refused to let Dodson leave when he threatened to end the relationship. She purportedly slashed his tires, damaged his windshield, and even dumped sugar in the gas tank of his vehicle. After fleeing to a nearby gas station by foot, Dodson called police to escort him to the house so that he could grab his belongings. Brandon also ran to a payphone during the fight to call his best friend's mother, Kathy Goohs. He asked her to come get him and his brothers away from the fighting. Soon after, Eubanks called Goohs and begged her to come

and get the boys. Goohs testified at trial that she did not have enough seat belts in her car to pick up all of the boys, and feared it would cause her a problem if police were still present at the house.

Susan's estranged husband, Eric Eubanks, showed up at the house around the same time, though it is not clear why. Susan Eubanks became really furious once Rene Dodson gathered his belongings and left with Eric. The two men drove together back to the bar. Susan, Eric, and Rene were all regulars at the local bar, so Susan's estranged husband and new boyfriend hanging around each other wasn't as strange as it seems. As they drove, Rene Dodson told Eric Eubanks that Susan had said she was going to kill the boys and herself. Susan called Brandon's father, John Armstrong, in a rage to tell him the police had been to the house and she was afraid the children would be taken away. She also called Eric Eubanks, while he was at the bar drinking with Rene Dodson. After receiving an alert on his pager and a disturbing voicemail from Susan, Eric Eubanks called 911 to request a welfare check on her and the children. Once deputies arrived back at the house, they heard Susan crying for help and found her in the master bedroom with a self-inflicted gunshot wound to the abdomen. Upon checking the rest of the residence, police found Austin and Brigham dead in a bedroom with gunshot wounds to their heads. Matthew was in the same room and had also been shot, but was still breathing. He passed away shortly after being flown to a children's hospital. Brandon's body was found in the living room. He had also suffered a gunshot wound to the head. Susan Eubanks's six-year-old nephew was found unharmed in the house. Susan was in critical condition and underwent emergency surgery before being arraigned from her hospital bed.

Prosecutors in the case alleged that Susan Eubanks killed her four children in a fit of rage and anger brought on by her many failed relationships. Court documents detail five separate suicide notes discovered in the home. In the letter to Eric Eubanks, Susan accused him of betraying her and stated it was time for him to lose everyone he loved like she had. She was apologetic in her letter to Brandon's father, John Armstrong, maintaining that she couldn't let Brandon live without his younger brothers. There was also a letter for Susan's boyfriend, Rene Dodson, her niece, and her sister. Prosecutors also contended that Eubanks had been abusing prescription drugs and alcohol in the time leading up to the murders. The defense sought to prove that she was incapable of premeditation (a necessary condition for first-degree murder) in the crime because of her intoxication. After just two hours of deliberation, a jury found Susan Eubanks guilty on four counts of first-degree murder.

During the penalty phase of her trial, relatives discussed incidents of previous abuse of the boys by Susan Eubanks. Other relatives testified that she was a loving mother, but had suffered a traumatic childhood herself. The defense insisted that Susan Eubanks was raised by alcoholic parents who frequently fought. Susan lived between family members since the age of eight, when her mother died in a house fire. She also allegedly suffered abuse at the hands of her estranged husband, Eric Eubanks, having received two restraining orders against him. Both Susan and Eric Eubanks had well-documented legal problems because of their heavy drinking. The jury weighed the circumstances and decided that Susan Eubanks would receive the death penalty for killing her sons. Judge Joan Weber referred to the murders the single most horrific episode in the history of this county, and upheld the sentence. Very few homicides occured in San Marcos, California, and the murders especially affected the community because of the wide age range of the boys—from elementary to high school. An automatic appeal of the death sentence was rejected by the state's highest court, and Susan Eubanks remains on death row awaiting execution.

Nicole LaRosa

See also: Barfield, Velma (1932–1984); Riggs, Christina (1971–2000); Tucker, Karla Faye (1959–1998)

Further Reading

Perry, Tony. 1997. "4 Boys Killed: Wounded Mother Is Suspect." *Los Angeles Times*. October 28. http://articles.latimes.com/1997/oct/28/news/mn-47522. Accessed February 3, 2015.

Streib, Victor. 2005. "Rare and Inconsistent: The Death Penalty for Women." *Fordham Urban Law Journal* 33: 609.

Streib, Victor. 2013. *Death Penalty for Female Offenders: January 1, 1973, through December 31, 2012*, Issue # 67. http://www.deathpenaltyinfo.org/documents/FemDeathDec2012.pdf. Accessed April 16, 2015.

United States Department of Justice, Federal Bureau of Investigation. 2012. *Crime in the United States, 2011*. September. https://www.fbi.gov/about-us/cjis/ucr/crime-in-the-u.s/2011/crime-in-the-u.s.-2011. Accessed April 16, 2015.

Eugene, Rudy (1981–2012)

Rudy Eugene, known as the "Miami Cannibal," may be considered an instigator of the panic regarding a zombie apocalypse; his was one of a rash of crimes that contributed to the craze of "zombified" behaviors. This craze was attributed to a type of drug, known as bath salts, as well as synthetic marijuana. Bath salts are a type of designer drug that contains synthetic chemicals that are similar to amphetamines. Bath salts commonly use Mephedrone, methylenedioxypyrovalerone (MDPV), or methylone. Although no link was found between the Miami Cannibal and bath salts or synthetic marijuana, it is still a widespread belief that there was something in the attacker's system that went undetected in toxicology reports. After the attack, a Miami police union official suggested that the attacker was under the influence of bath salts and this belief perpetuated throughout the nation. In this specific incident, Rudy Eugene attacked Ronald Poppo, a homeless man, who lost his nose, both eyes, and 80 percent of his face in the attack. A Miami police officer shot and killed the unarmed, naked attacker in what has been considered a justified killing. The ultimate cause of Eugene's behavior remains unknown. Eugene has been dubbed the "Miami Cannibal," the "Miami Zombie," and the "Causeway Cannibal" as a result of his crime. The attack and the ensuing panic prompted the Centers for Disease Control and Prevention (CDC) to release a statement noting that there is no virus or condition that reanimates the dead nor is there one that presents zombie-like symptoms.

Born on February 4, 1981, Rudy Eugene was a 31-year-old black man of Haitian descent. Eugene's parents divorced just a few months after his birth and he never had contact with his father, who died when he was six years old. Eugene was a divorced, former North Miami High School football player, who was employed at a car wash at the time of the crime. He had a criminal record with a number of petty crimes ranging from trespassing to marijuana possession from when he was 16 years old until 2009. Although after the attack on Poppo, Eugene's friends and family stated Eugene was a religious, introspective, and private man, who did not exhibit any violent behavior or obvious signs of mental illness prior to this incident, there are differing reports from his mother and ex-wife. In 2004, Eugene's mother called the police during a fight with her son in which he beat her up and threatened to kill her. He became the first person tasered by the North Miami Police Department; the Taser was used on him three times before he was subdued. Ultimately, the charges for battery were dropped and he pled guilty to resisting arrest and was sentenced to probation. In 2007, Eugene and Jenny Ductant ended their 18-month marriage due to his steadily increasing violence toward her. Friends and family of Eugene also said Eugene was not known to drink or do any drugs harder than marijuana. There is some disagreement as to whether or not Eugene and Poppo met prior to the attack. According to some sources, they had met before when Eugene volunteered with Miami's homeless community and he had served food to Poppo. Poppo, however, does not recall ever meeting Eugene before the attack.

The victim, Ronald Poppo (May 17, 1947–) grew up in Brooklyn, New York, and attended Manhattan's Stuyvesant High School. Poppo enrolled, but subsequently dropped out of City College. He became homeless in 1976. Poppo was an alcoholic who had numerous criminal charges. At the time of the attack, his family, including his daughter, had not heard from him in over 30 years. They assumed he had committed suicide many years prior. After the attack, Poppo was admitted to the Jackson Memorial Hospital, where a fund was started to help with his medical expenses.

On May 26, 2012, Eugene attacked Ronald Poppo, a 65-year-old homeless man, on the MacArthur Causeway. When Eugene left his house early that morning, he drove to South Beach for Urban Beach Weekend, where he parked his purple Chevrolet Caprice near Tenth and Alton Road. When he could not get his car to restart, he walked over to MacArthur Causeway carrying his Bible. On his way, he removed his clothes, leaving them in the street. Reports suggest that Eugene knocked Poppo unconscious, stripped him of his pants, and then proceeded to bite off most of Poppo's face above his beard, including his left eye. Poppo was left blind in both eyes. A witness called 911 and police arrived shortly. Based on security footage from a camera on the *Miami Herald* building, the attack lasted 18 minutes before police arrived. Ultimately, the first police officer on the scene, Jose Rivera, shot Eugene once and Eugene stopped only to growl at the officer and then he resumed his attack of Poppo. Rivera shot Eugene three more times, killing him. Poppo survived the attack.

After the incident, it was speculated that what caused Eugene's zombie-like behavior was the use of bath salts. Toxicology reports uncovered only trace amounts of marijuana. This incident sparked a media-fueled panic about an ensuing zombie apocalypse having linked Eugene to the use of bath salts and synthetic cannabis, as well as the rash of "zombie" behaviors that followed. Additionally, no flesh was found in Eugene's digestive system. When police located his car, they found a copy of the Koran and five, recently purchased, water bottles. The water bottles helped perpetuate the conclusion of drug use because it was assumed that he was thirsty due to his use of drugs, particularly the use of Ecstasy, which is known to increase thirst.

After the attack, many South Florida cities began enacting laws aimed at eradicating the use of synthetic drugs. The publicity garnered from the Miami cannibal incident, as well as other incidents that occurred around the country following Eugene's attack on Poppo, helped push forward these laws. Many cities in Florida have succeeded in banning bath salts and many more cities are attempting to ban both bath salts and synthetic marijuana.

SARA B. SIMMONS

See also: Fish, Albert (1870–1936); Holmes, Dr. H.H. (1861–1896)

Further Reading
Balaji, Murali, ed. 2013. *Thinking Dead: What the Zombie Apocalypse Means.* Lanham, MD: Lexington Books.
Temple, Davis L., Jr. 2013. *Secret Keeper: Pursuit of the Cannibals.* Tucson, AZ: Wheatmark.

Evers, Medgar, Assassination of (June 12, 1963)

In June 1963, Medgar Evers (1925–1963), Mississippi's first field secretary for the National Association for the Advancement of Colored People (NAACP), was murdered in Jackson, Mississippi, by Byron De La Beckwith, a white supremacist. Beckwith stood trial twice in the years that followed, but each trial resulted in a hung jury consisting entirely of white male jurors. Beckwith remained a free man until 1994, when he was again tried, this time by a jury that included eight African Americans. At the trial in 1994, Beckwith was found guilty of the murder of Medgar Evers and he received a sentence of life without parole.

Medgar Evers grew up in the Jim Crow culture of the South. He dropped out of high school to join the military and served overseas in World War II. While in Europe, he noticed a distinct difference in the treatment he received. While at home in Mississippi, Evers and other African Americans experienced constant racism. In Europe, though, Evers was treated with respect; whites treated Evers and other blacks as equals. However, he did notice parallels between the Jim Crow South and Hitler's Nazi regime. Upon returning to the United States, Evers was inspired to work to improve the treatment of African Americans in the South. After graduating from Alcorn Agricultural and

On June 12, 1963, Medgar Evers, the Mississippi field secretary for the National Association for the Advancement of Colored People, was shot down outside his home. Thirty-seven years old, Evers was a husband and father of three. (AP Photo)

Mechanical College (a state school for blacks where he met his future wife, Myrlie Beasley) in 1952, Evers applied to the University of Mississippi law school in the wake of the *Brown v. Board of Education* ruling (1954), in an attempt to desegregate the university. His admission was denied but the attempt to integrate the university caught the attention of the NAACP's national office. He had already been working with the local NAACP office, and in 1954 he was offered the position of field secretary for the Mississippi NAACP. His work took him all over the state, and he made a name for himself as a civil rights activist in Mississippi. One notable activity he undertook was an investigation of Emmett Till's murder in 1955. His activism was often controversial in the Jim Crow culture, and he was repeatedly targeted by white supremacists because of his work. For example, he suffered a beating, his house was firebombed, and white men threatened him with firearms in an attempt to prevent Evers (and other blacks) from voting.

In the early morning hours of June 12, 1963, Medgar Evers returned home from a long day working for the NAACP. Earlier in the evening, President John F. Kennedy had delivered a televised speech in which he stated that although Abraham Lincoln had issued the Emancipation Proclamation to free slaves 100 years prior, African Americans still did not have freedom in the United States. As if to drive home the point that racism still flourished, Byron De La Beckwith chose that night to murder Medgar Evers because of his race and his civil rights activism. Beckwith was a member of the White Citizens' Council as well as the Ku Klux Klan (KKK), two white supremacist groups. When Evers arrived home, Beckwith was lying in wait nearby with a rifle. Beckwith fired a single shot, which struck Evers in the back as he was walking into his home. He staggered several feet before collapsing by the front door. His wife Myrlie and their three young children heard the gunshot and ran outside as Evers died.

Beckwith's rifle was found near the scene of the murder, and witnesses told investigators that they had seen him in the vicinity of the Evers home shortly before the crime took place. Beckwith was arrested and stood trial for the assassination two separate times in 1964. White supremacist groups funded Beckwith's legal defense and bail in large part to show their support of his actions. All of the jurors in both trials were white males, and each of the trials ended in a hung jury.

For years, Medgar's widow, Myrlie, fought for justice for her husband's death but was unsuccessful until the 1990s, when the district attorney reopened the case. Beckwith was ultimately found guilty. Prosecutors in the third trial presented no new physical evidence, but did introduce new testimony by witnesses who claimed that over the years, Beckwith had boasted about committing the murder, including doing so at a KKK rally. During the third trial, the jury was more representative of Mississippi's population, including African American and female jurors. On February 5, 1994, Beckwith was convicted of first-degree murder. He was sentenced to life in prison without the possibility of parole. Beckwith appealed the conviction but was unsuccessful. In January 2001, Beckwith died at the age of 80.

Although some people did not see the purpose of prosecuting an elderly man for a crime he had committed decades earlier, proponents of civil rights were pleased to see that justice was finally served. Also, the conviction of Beckwith set a precedent for moving forth with investigations and trials for other cold cases that may not have seen justice during the period of civil rights turmoil.

Although the assassination of Medgar Evers is today not as well known as those of Martin Luther King Jr. or Malcolm X, Evers's death did impact the civil rights movement. Due to his high profile as a civil rights activist in Mississippi, the federal government began to increase its involvement in investigating hate crimes. The Federal Bureau of Investigation (FBI) arrested Beckwith, although he was not prosecuted in federal court.

Jim Crow Culture

After the abolishment of slavery in the United States, Southerners found other ways to discriminate against African Americans. Jim Crow laws can be summed up by the phrase "separate but equal"—that is, as long as African Americans had their own facilities such as restrooms and water fountains, they could be barred from using facilities marked "whites only." Unfortunately, the accommodations for people of color were not of "equal" quality. Being forced to use a separate restroom or give up one's seat on a bus for a white patron ingrained in many black children the feeling that they were in some way inferior to their white peers. Resistance to these Jim Crow laws was often met with retaliation by whites in the form of harassment, criminal charges, and even lynching.

The prosecutor in the 1994 trial, Robert DeLaughter, went on to author a book about his experience with the Beckwith trial. A 1996 film titled *Ghosts of Mississippi* (based on the book by Maryanne Vollers) starring Alec Baldwin, James Woods, and Whoopi Goldberg depicted the events of Evers's assassination and the final trial. Myrlie Evers-Williams later became a chair of the NAACP herself, and there is now a foundation named after the Everses (the Evers Institute).

In addition to its importance to civil rights and legal proceedings, Evers's assassination became a notable event in popular culture. In addition to the 1996 film, Evers's death was memorialized in songs by Bob Dylan, Nina Simone, and Phil Ochs. Dylan performed his song ("Only a Pawn in Their Game") to remember Evers at the March on Washington in 1963, during which Martin Luther King Jr. delivered his celebrated "I Have a Dream" speech.

ARNA L. CARLOCK

See also: King, Martin Luther, Jr., Assassination of (April 4, 1968); Ku Klux Klan (1866–); Malcolm X, Assassination of (February 21, 1965); Stephenson, David Curtiss (1891–1966); Till, Emmett, Murder of (1955)

Further Reading

DeLaughter, Bobby. 2001. *Never Too Late: A Prosecutor's Story of Justice in the Medgar Evers Case.* New York: Scribner.

Evers, Medgar Wiley. 2005. *The Autobiography of Medgar Evers: A Hero's Life and Legacy Revealed Through His Writings, Letters, and Speeches.* Edited by Myrlie Evers-Williams and Manning Marable. New York: Basic Civitas Books.

Nossiter, Adam. 2002. *Of Long Memory: Mississippi and the Murder of Medgar Evers.* New York: Da Capo Press.

Ribeiro, Myra. 2002. *The Assassination of Medgar Evers.* New York: The Rosen Publishing Group.

Vollers, Maryanne. 1995. *Ghosts of Mississippi: The Murder of Medgar Evers, the Trials of Byron De La Beckwith, and the Haunting of the New South.* New York: Little, Brown.

Ex parte Crow Dog (1883)

The 1883 *Ex parte Crow Dog* Supreme Court case revealed the stark differences between the white and Native American legal ideas and systems, the differences between Native Americans themselves and continued the sovereignty issues of the Cherokee cases of 1831 and 1832. Like the Cherokee cases, *Ex parte Crow Dog* had far-reaching effects on the U.S. government and the U.S. legal system and underscored the impact of the Bureau of Indian Affairs on Indian life.

Created in 1824 as a continuation of federal government efforts to deal with Indian tribes, the Bureau of Indian Affairs (BIA) in the 1800s embraced the idea of assimilating Indians into the dominant American culture, which included criminal jurisdiction over Indian affairs. BIA agents actively worked to implement this policy within a divided group of native traditionalists who adhered to the old customs and those who accommodated and cooperated with the white man. These opposing forces came to a head in the U.S. Supreme Court case *Ex Parte Crow Dog*.

On August 5, 1881, Crow Dog, a Brule Sioux sub chief, a traditionalist, and a tribal police force captain shot and killed a principal chief called Spotted Tail. The BIA considered Sioux Chief Spotted Tail a great peace chief who accommodated and cooperated with the white man's agenda and gave him a two story house on the Rosebud Creek reservation in what is now the state of South Dakota. According to various accounts, the feud between Crow Dog and

Spotted Tail involved reservation politics, a power struggle, and the charge that Spotted Tail, "the white man's chief" had taken a member of Crow Dog's family, Light in the Lodge, as an unwilling second wife.

Both Crow Dog and Spotted Tail were from the same tribe and the killing happened on reservation land so acting Indian agent John Lelar allowed the Sioux Tribe to handle the case according to its traditions. The Sioux Tribe ordered Crow Dog to pay Spotted Tail's family a payment of $600, eight horses, and one blanket, which amounted to a significant payment for the time. As far as the Sioux Tribe was concerned, the case was closed, but whispers and rumors still circulated through the community. The official account had it that Eagle Hawk, the head of the Indian police, had not dared arrest Crow Dog and a story in the *Black Hills Daily Times* kept the rumors alive. Although Indian agent John Lelar appeared to be satisfied with the tribal jurisdiction, he yielded to a telegram from the BIA.

Hugh Campbell, U.S. attorney in Deadwood, sent Agent Lelar a telegram dated August 15, which expressed the desire of the Indian Department that Crow Dog should be criminally prosecuted for the murder of Spotted Tail. Agreeing with the Interior Department, Attorney General Campbell based his interpretation on a clause in the first part of the 1868 treaty with various tribes of the Sioux Indians that said if "bad men" among the Indians committed a crime against anyone subject to U.S. authority, they could be tried by the United States and punished according to the laws of the United States. The actions of Hugh Campbell and John Lelar and the BIA directly contradicted one hundred years of treaty law.

Based on this interpretation, Crow Dog and Black Crow, a son-in-law of Spotted Tail, thought to be in collusion with Crow Dog, were arrested and sent to Fort Niobara, Nebraska, until their trial, with only Crow Dog held on a murder charge. The trial took place in March 1882 in the territorial court of Deadwood, South Dakota, the first time in U.S. history that an Indian was tried for the murder of another Indian.

Crow Dog's attorney, A.D. Plowman, argued that the court had no jurisdiction over the Brule Sioux, but he lost the jurisdictional argument. The jury found Crow Dog guilty and the Court sentenced him to hang for the murder of Spotted Tail on January 14, 1884. Crow Dog convinced the federal marshal to let him go home to Rosebud to prepare his death song and his white buckskin death suit. A blizzard covered Deadwood the day that Crow Dog was scheduled to turn himself in to the federal marshal, and

everyone bet that he wouldn't appear. After he walked into the federal marshal's office on schedule, newspapers reported Crow Dog's honorable return and attorneys volunteered to file a writ of habeas corpus for him at the Supreme Court of the United States.

In November 1883, Crow Dog's lawyers presented arguments to the U.S. Supreme Court in *Ex parte Crow Dog*, contending that the federal court lacked jurisdiction and citing an 1834 act specifically excluding crimes committed by one Native Americans on another from federal jurisdiction.

The U.S. government argued that the 1868 Treaty of Fort Laramie with the Sioux requiring the tribe to surrender criminals to the United States superseded the earlier law.

On December 17, 1883, Chief Justice Stanley Matthews announced the unanimous decision of the U.S. Supreme Court that the Dakota Territorial Court had no jurisdiction over the Rosebud reservation and that the conviction of Crow Dog was overturned. The Court cited a previous Supreme Court ruling in *Worcester v. Georgia*, an 1832 case brought by the Cherokee tribe against the state of Georgia, where the Court ruled that Native Americans were entitled to federal protection from state government actions infringing on the sovereignty of the tribe.

Justice Matthews rejected the U.S. argument that the 1868 Treaty of Fort Laramie by implication repealed the prosecution exceptions. He said that the law had not been amended or changed and that a repeal required "a clear expression of the intention of Congress," which was not present in the Crow Dog case. Justice Matthews also noted that under *Cherokee Nation v. Georgia* (1831) the Brule tribe had a right to its own law in Indian country. The Court based part of its ruling on the U.S. Constitutional tradition at the time that Indians were not U.S. citizens and didn't participate in selecting representatives and making laws. The Court's decision maintained the sovereignty of Indian tribes. The writ of habeas corpus was issued and Crow Dog was released.

The BIA and outraged private citizens protested the *Ex parte Crow Dog* Supreme Court decision loudly and persistently to Congress and insisted that it outlaw the "heathenish" "laws and customs of the Indians. In an amendment to the Appropriation Act of March 3, 1885, Congress included a section called The Major Crimes Act, which placed seven major crimes—murder, kidnapping, rape, assault, incest, arson, and burglary—under federal jurisdiction if they occurred on Indian territory, even if both the perpetrator and victim were Indians. By limiting Indian court jurisdiction, the Major Crimes Act eroded tribal sovereignty and solidified the legal standing of Indian tribes as wards of the federal government. In 1886, two Hoopa Indians were convicted of committing a murder on a California reservation and the Supreme Court upheld their convictions.

KATHY WARNES

See also: *Cherokee Nation v. Georgia*, Forced Removal of Indian Tribes (1831); Wounded Knee Incident (SD) (February 27–May 8, 1973); Wounded Knee Massacre (SD) (December 29, 1890); *Primary Documents*/Crow Dog Case: Major Crimes Act (1885)

Further Reading

Brown, Dee. 2007. *Bury My Heart at Wound Knee: An Indian History of the American West*. New York: Holt.

Calloway, Colin G. 2011. *First Peoples: A Documentary Survey of American Indian History*. 4th ed. New York: Bedford/St. Martin's Press.

Deloria, Vine, Jr., and Clifford M. Lytle. 1983. *American Indians, American Justice*. Austin: University of Texas Press.

Harring, Sidney L. 1994. *Crow Dog's Case: American Indian Sovereignty, Tribal Law, and United States Law in the Nineteenth Century*. Studies in North American Indian History. Cambridge: Cambridge University Press.

Prucha, Francis Paul. 1986. *The Great Father: The United States Government and the American Indians*. Abridged ed. Lincoln: University of Nebraska Press.

Exxon Valdez Oil Spill (1989)

On March 24, 1989 at 12:04 a.m., the *Exxon Valdez* oil tanker bound for Long Beach, California, ran aground on the Bligh Reef in Prince William Sound, Alaska, causing hundreds of thousands of barrels of crude oil to spill into the icy waters. At the time, the oil spill was the largest spill in U.S. history, recently eclipsed by the 2010 *Deepwater Horizon* oil spill in the Gulf of Mexico. Today, the *Exxon Valdez* oil spill remains one of the most devastating environmental disasters of all time as 11 million gallons of oil covered 1,300 miles of coastline and 11,000 square miles of ocean, killing millions of fish and wildlife in one of the world's most pristine natural environments. The immediate effects of the oil spill included the deaths of hundreds of thousands of seabirds, close to 3,000 otters, 300 harbor seals, 247 bald eagles, 22 orcas, and millions of salmon and herring. The long-term consequences of this environmental crime continue to impact this area.

The *Exxon Valdez* was traveling outside of normal shipping lanes to avoid icebergs. However, after leaving the shipping lanes to avoid the ice, the vessel did not return to the shipping lanes. Within six hours of the spill, 11 million gallons of the 53 million gallons aboard spread into the ocean, the equivalent of 17 Olympic-size swimming pools. Within a week, the oil spill extended 90 miles from the origin of the spill, eventually covering 1,300 miles of shoreline, including the Kenai Peninsula, Cook Inlet, and Kodiak Island. The remoteness of the location made it challenging for quick and efficient clean-up efforts. Regardless, Exxon was widely criticized for the slow response to clean up the spill although the company eventually committed over $2 billion to clean-up efforts. Over 11,000 personnel, 1,400 vessels, and 85 aircraft were involved in the clean-up efforts. Media images of heavily oiled shorelines and dead and dying wildlife were broadcast around the world. Clean-up efforts continued into summer of 1990 and 1991. Even though many clean-up techniques were utilized including hot water treatment, cold water treatment, mechanical clean-up, bioremediation, and solvents/chemical agents, the waves created during winter storms appeared to trump all man-made clean-up efforts.

The National Transportation Safety Board (NTSB) determined that there were five main causes of the *Exxon Valdez* oil spill. The Exxon Shipping Company failed to supervise the master and ensure an adequate and rested crew. The third mate failed to properly maneuver the oil tanker, possibly due to fatigue and excessive workload. The Exxon Shipping Company failed to maintain radar equipment and Exxon management knew about the faulty radar equipment for over a year prior to the disaster. Captain James Hazelwood was reported to have been drinking heavily prior to the spill although he was not at the controls when the tanker ran aground. The NTSB investigation found that the captain failed to adequately supervise his crew. Exxon blamed the captain for the disaster even though the company was aware of Hazelwood's battle with alcoholism and despite his relapse from sobriety. The NTSB also blamed the Coast Guard for failing to provide an effective vessel traffic system.

Criminal and civil cases ensued in 1991. In the criminal case, Exxon was charged with numerous environmental crimes and later pled guilty to one count each of violating the Clean Water Act, the Refuse Act, and the Migratory Bird Treaty Act. As the result of the plea negotiation, Exxon was fined $150 million but the Court forgave $125 million in recognition that Exxon had cooperated in cleaning up the spill and had paid private claims. Restitution in the amount of $100 million was paid to federal and state governments.

In the 1994 civil case representing a consolidated class membership of over 32,000 victims (primarily commercial fisheries and subsistent fishers and hunters), *Baker v. Exxon*, the victims detailed extensive economic loss and emotional devastation. An Anchorage jury found Exxon liable for $287 million in compensatory damages and $5 billion for punitive damages, an enormous sum of money but equal to about one year of profits for the most profitable publicly traded company in the world. At the time, $5 billion was the largest punitive damages award in U.S. history.

Exxon appealed the case and in 2001, the Ninth Circuit Court of Appeals ordered the lower court to reduce punitive damages. Judge Holland reduced punitive damages to $4 billion in 2002 but Exxon appealed again. In 2003, the appellate court ordered Judge Holland to reconsider the punitive damages once again. Judge Holland actually increased the award to $4.5 billion in 2004, leading to another appeal to the Ninth Circuit. In 2006, the punitive damages were reduced to $2.5 billion. Unsatisfied, Exxon again appealed to the Ninth Circuit but the appellate court declined to hear the case, paving the way for the case to be heard by the U.S. Supreme Court. On February 27, 2008, the Supreme Court heard oral arguments for 90 minutes and then proceeded to vacate the $2.5 billion award, stating that the amount of damages was excessive with respect to maritime common law. Exxon was subsequently ordered to pay $507.5 million in punitive damages. Almost 25 years later, the litigation still has not been fully settled.

The state of Alaska charged Captain Hazelwood with operating a vessel under the influence of alcohol. An Alaskan jury found him not guilty of the operating a vessel under the influence but found him guilty of negligent discharge of oil, a misdemeanor. Hazelwood was fined $50,000 and ordered to perform 1,000 hours of community service.

In response to the *Exxon Valdez* oil spill, Congress passed the Oil Pollution Act of 1990 (OPA). Studies conducted by the state of Alaska found short-term and long-term environmental and economic consequences including the loss of wildlife and the pristine environment, recreational fishing losses, and tourism losses. Habitats and wildlife have not fully recovered and some habitats and wildlife are not recovering at all. Oil is still found on beaches today in Alaska. On the 20th anniversary of the oil spill in 2009, the *Exxon Valdez* Oil Spill Trustee Council reported that some areas are still as toxic today as they were weeks after the spill in 1989 and that it will take decades or longer for the remaining oil, estimated at 20,000 gallons, to dissipate completely.

Melissa L. Jarrell

See also: Enron Case (1985–2001)

Further Reading

Cruciotti, T., and R.A. Matthews. 2006. "The Exxon Valdez Oil Spill." In R.J. Michalowski and R.C. Kramer, eds. *State-Corporate Crime: Wrongdoing at the Intersection of Business and Government*. New Brunswick, NJ: Rutgers University Press.

Exxon Valdez Oil Spill Trustee Council. 2013. www.evostc.state.ak.us. Accessed April 16, 2015.

Ott, Riki. 2008. *Not One Drop: Betrayal and Courage in the Wake of the Exxon Valdez Oil Spill*. Burlington, VT: Chelsea Green Publishing.

F

Feldman, Dora (1872–1930)

Like the second trial of Harry K. Thaw for the murder of architect Stanford White, the trial of Dora Feldman Barkley McDonald for the murder of her lover Webster Guerin took place in January 1908. The parallels between the two cases also include histories of mental illness in the lives of both Harry K. Thaw and Dora Feldman. A jury found Harry K. Thaw not guilty by reason of insanity and another jury acquitted Dora McDonald because of her mental problems, which stretched back into her childhood.

Dora Feldman, the daughter of Prussian Jewish immigrants Rabbi Fogel "Frank" Feldman and Frances Shaffner Feldman, was born about 1872 in Memphis, Tennessee. Dora suffered several psychotic episodes as a child that modern psychiatrists term borderline personality disorder, which her parents hoped that she would outgrow. They relocated to Chicago's Westside in the Jewish quarter on Peoria Street and eventually moved to 406 Ashland Boulevard, directly across the street from the mansion of gambler and Chicago Democratic boss, Michael McDonald. Dora played with Michael McDonald's adopted son Harley and Michael McDonald often brought home fistfuls of candy for the children. As time passed, the hopes and prayers of Rabbi Feldman and his wife for Dora's future seemed to be realized for as their daughter grew older, her erratic behavior diminished.

When she was 18, Dora Feldman met baseball player Samuel W. Barkley in Chicago and they married and moved to Pittsburgh and eventually to Chicago where Samuel opened a tavern at 292 West Madison Street. He and Dora had a son, Harold, born around 1895.

Samuel Barkley had opened a new tavern at 15 North Clark Street which acquired a shady reputation that dismayed the social climbing Dora. As her interest in her marriage to Samuel Barkley diminished, Dora developed her stage career. Quick witted, rebellious, and imperious, Dora carved out a minor career for herself on stage, playing in such shows as Aladdin Jr. and other amateur theatricals under the name of Madame Alberta. She had a talent for whistling light opera arias and Irish folk tunes, with double-tongued whistling as her specialty. She began to believe that Sam could never provide her with the mansion with servants that she deserved and an assured future for her son Harold and that Michael McDonald could and would.

Dora and Samuel Barkley were divorced and she married Michael McDonald in 1898 when she was 26 and he 59. Michael McDonald catered to Dora's every whim, adopting her son Harold and accommodating her family, even providing a home and burial for Rabbi Feldman after his death. Michael McDonald gave Dora the life of glitter and glamor that she had craved and missed with her first husband Sam Barkley, sacrificing his relationship with his sons by his first marriage, Cassius and Guy.

In 1899, Michael McDonald celebrated his 60th birthday and by 1903, after only five years of marriage and despite his unstinting efforts to please his wife and keep up with her, Michael experienced the pangs of aging and jealousy as Dora's glances rested more frequently on 13-year-old Webster Guerin who lived across the street from the McDonalds.

Over the following months and years the relationship between Dora McDonald and Webster Guerin developed into a torrid, tangled affair, complicating the lives of the two families. Dora gave Webster Guerin money for years and set him up in a portrait and framing business in a downtown office. Several people reported that she was paranoid about Guerin's attentions to other women and his attempts to free himself from their relationship. On February 21, 1907, Dora McDonald went to Webster Guerin's studio in a Loop office Building, and they quarreled. Dora shot him with the .38 caliber pearl handled revolver that he had given her for Christmas just a month earlier.

Dora told her husband that Webster Guerin had been blackmailing her. After she shot her lover and the police arrested her, she had what appeared to be a nervous breakdown. Michael McDonald used his influence to delay his wife's trial and had her put in a private sanitarium. He established a $25,000 defense fund for Dora's trial and she hired several of Chicago's finest attorneys, including J. Hamilton Lewis, later a U.S. senator from Illinois, and her uncle Benjamin Schaffner. Alfred Trude, the lawyer who had defended Michael McDonald's wife Mary against a charge of attempted murder, led Dora's defense team.

In the days after her arrest Mike McDonald never left his wife's side, giving her the benefit of the doubt. He didn't learn until the inquest that shortly before she shot him, she had told Webster Guerin that she was through with Mike and was going to New York or somewhere else. She also told Guerin that if she decided to kill herself she would take him with her.

The shock of his wife's betrayal and her act of shooting of her lover proved to be too much for Mike McDonald, already in his 60s and in poor health. He suffered a heart attack and before he died he returned to the Catholic Church, renouncing his marriage to Dora. He died on August 9, 1907, with his first wife Mary at his side and $2 million in assets that Dora and his other heirs would fight over for decades.

One of the most popular and controversial trials in Chicago history, the murder trial of Dora McDonald began on January 20, 1908, in the courtroom of Judge Theodore Brentano, and lasted for three weeks. The litigants agreed that no Jews would serve on the jury, but welcomed the national press to report and sometimes sensationalize the proceedings. Attorney J. Hamilton Lewis read a prepared statement that contended that Mrs. McDonald suffered from a severe case of neurodementia, which made it impossible for her to think or speak coherently. Judge Brentano agreed to allow Dora McDonald's nurse Amanda K. Beck and her attending physical Dr. James Whitney Hall to sit beside her during the entire trial.

The three-week trial featured almost nonstop drama. Assistant state attorneys Edward S. Day and William A. Rittenhouse, heading the prosecution, charged that jurors and leading witnesses were being offered bribes by Dora's brother Emil Feldman and detectives and other members of the Chicago Police Department, perhaps evidence of the continuing influence of Michael McDonald, even from the grave. Dora herself provided much of the excitement, fainting away several times, and shouting and crying and then sleeping peacefully when Webster Guerin's brother Archie testified. The defense argued that Dora might die from the stress of the trial before it concluded. The court heard closing arguments on February 10, 1908, and despite the irrefutable evidence of her guilt, it took the jury five hours to acquit her.

After her acquittal, Dora McDonald remained in Chicago for the next 18 years, battling Mike McDonald's first wife Mary and her two sons for a larger share of Mike's estate. After many lawsuits against Michael McDonald's estate and nuisance suits against city entities, Dora McDonald left Chicago for good in 1925. She settled in Los Angeles, and married Dr. Carmen A. Newcomb. She died on July 1, 1930, at age 60, and was buried in a mausoleum in Hollywood Forever Cemetery.

Kathy Warnes

See also: Hinckley, John, Jr. (1955–); White, Stanford, Murder of (1907–1908)

Further Reading

Enright, Laura L. 2005. *Chicago's Most Wanted: The Top 10 Book of Murderous Mobsters, Midway Monsters, and Windy City Oddities.* Washington, DC: Potomac Books, Inc.

Lindberg, Richard C. 2009. *The Gambler King of Clark Street: Michael C. McDonald and the Rise of Chicago's Democratic Machine.* Carbondale: Southern Illinois University Press.

Roth, Walter. 2005. *Looking Backward: True Stories from Chicago's Jewish Past.* Chicago: Academy Chicago Review Press.

Ferguson v. City of Charleston (2001)

In *Ferguson v. City of Charleston*, 10 women who had received prenatal care at the Medical University of South

Carolina (MUSC) were arrested under a policy devised by the MUSC and law enforcement to use the urine test collected at prenatal visits to determine cocaine use at differing stages of pregnancy. Consent was not given to use the urine tests in this manner and the validity of the policy was challenged under the Fourth Amendment protection from unreasonable searches. The respondent claimed consent was given, and that searches were reasonable based on special purposes. The jury was instructed that they were to rule in favor of the petitioners unless they found consent. The jury found for the respondents even after the judge's instructions speaking to the fact that no search warrants were issued and that these searches were basically unreasonable. Upon this decision the petitioners appealed based on insufficient evidence and the Court of Appeals for the Fourth District affirmed, but did not make a decision on the issue of consent. The majority in this decision gave the terminology of "special needs" as their reason for the decision stating that the hospital's interest in reducing medical costs and helping the mother and their unborn children was paramount to the need for consent. Certiorari was granted by the U.S. Supreme Court for the purpose of reviewing the previously defined "special needs" doctrine of the Fourth Amendment. The case was argued on October 4, 2000, and the decision was handed down on March 21, 2001.

The MUSC became concerned about an increase in "crack babies" and expectant mothers using cocaine while making use of MUSC's prenatal services. It initially started a program to use urine screens to check for cocaine use and refer those who tested positive to counseling. The results were not very beneficial, so a new program was begun in conjunction with the hospital staff and the Charleston Police Department.

This new collaborative policy set up nine criteria to determine, which women would be subject to urine screens for cocaine. The new program essentially used the threat of arrest as a motivating factor in getting these women into treatment. Based on the criteria and directives of the new policy, 10 women who received prenatal care from the MUSC were arrested. These 10 women filed a lawsuit with the contention that these drug screens were unconstitutional because no warrants were issued, nor was consent given. The respondents countered that "as a matter of fact" petitioners did consent, and that by law, the searches were reasonable; meaning that they knew they were giving urine for the prenatal exam, so they had given consent.

The district court denied the reasonable search defense because the searches were not done for independent reasons. The jury was instructed that no warrants were issued and they should find for the petitioners unless the defendants had shown that the petitioners had consented to the taking and testing of the urine with knowledge of possible dissemination of results to police. The jury found for the defendants. The women appealed, claiming insufficient evidence to decide the case. The Court of Appeals for the Fourth District affirmed, but did not answer the question of consent. The dissent in the Court of Appeals concluded that the "special needs" clause as set forth by the Supreme Court did not apply to this case.

The U.S. Supreme Court granted certiorari. The Court concluded that the ruling of the U.S. Court of Appeals for the Fourth District should be reversed and remanded for a decision on the issue of consent. The majority opinion was delivered by Justice Stevens, and he was joined by O'Connor, Souter, Ginsburg and Breyer, and Justice Kennedy offered a concurring opinion. Stevens stated in the majority decision that the primary concern in this case was the issue of "special needs," and that it is assumed that consent was not given for purposes of their decision. He clarified that because the hospital was state operated, those employees work for the government, and therefore fall under the obligations of the Fourth Amendment. Stevens also stated that in all previous cases involving special needs, urine screens had been classified as searches, even when not handed over to police.

Justice Stevens additionally pointed out that this case was much different from any other "special needs" case that the Court had heard previously. He contended that the Court found this intrusion of privacy much more severe since the results were handed over to a third party, rather than used by the agency that collected the evidence. Stevens added that the expectation of privacy is great when undergoing tests in a hospital. In stating the Court's reasoning further, Stevens stated that based on precedents, if the purpose was governmental in nature, but not law enforcement related, there was a "special need" and this could be argued based on the interest of the government and the privacy of the individual under the Fourth Amendment. However, in this case, with law enforcement being involved from the inception, the "special needs" clause did not apply.

Stevens then covered the contention by the respondents that the policy was an issue with being concerned with the health of the mother and the child. He pointed out that nowhere in the policy is there any clause to this claim. The purpose of the policy from the directives involved clearly pointed to a policing role. The entire policy seemed to be to arrest expectant mothers who use drugs. While the ultimate goal may have been to get these expectant mothers into treatment, the immediate objective was to use the searches to gain evidence for law enforcement.

Those in the dissent were represented by Justice Scalia, who was joined by Rehnquist and Thomas. Scalia stated that the social judgment in this case was not for the Supreme Court to rule on; that this was supposed to be done by the elected officials of Charleston. He contended that the main issue in the case was whether the conduct by the police involved unreasonable searches and seizures under the Fourth Amendment, and he believed it did not. Scalia did not see urine as property, concluding that this is waste that is discarded like trash, and trash left on the street shows the owner no longer wants it and it is free for whoever wants it. Scalia saw the urine sample as given with consent because the patients were not forced to give a sample.

Scalia also cited *Miranda v. Arizona* and the "standard of knowing waiver," stating that "using lawfully (but deceivingly) obtained material for purposes other than those represented, and giving that material or information derived from it to the police, is not unconstitutional" (*Miranda v. Arizona*, 1966). Scalia also felt that the Court made a decision without even discussing all of the components that were important to the case. He felt the ruling overstepped boundaries and created unanswered questions for law enforcement.

NICK HARPSTER

See also: Miranda, Ernesto (1941–1976)

Further Reading

Chandler v. Miller, 520 U.S. 305, 137 L. Ed. 2d 513, 117 S. Ct. 1295 (1997).

Ferguson v. City of Charleston 532 U.S. 67 (2001), 121 S. Ct. 1281.

Miranda v. Arizona, 384 U.S. 436, 86 S. Ct. 1602, 16L.Ed.2d 694 (1966).

Skinner v. Railway Labor Executives' Assn., 489 U.S. 602, 617, 103 L. Ed. 2d 639, 109 S.Ct.1402 (1989).

Treasury Employees v. Von Raab, 489 U.S. 656, 103 L. Ed. 2d 685, 109 S. Ct. 1384 (1989).

Vernonia School Dist. 47J v. Acton, 515 U.S. 646, 132 L. Ed. 2d 564,115 S. Ct. 2386 (1995).

Fernandez, Raymond. *See* Lonely Hearts Killers (1947–1949)

Fish, Albert (1870–1936)

Albert Fish (born Hamilton Howard Fish) was a serial killer active in the New York City area between 1910 and 1935. In 1935 he was tried for the kidnapping and murder of 10-year-old Grace Budd, who he confessed to strangling, dismembering, and eating. Fish was executed via the electric chair at Sing Sing Prison in 1936. His criminal career was characterized by extreme sexual perversion, including self-mutilation by inserting metal pins into his pelvic region and sexually torturing his child victims before killing them. His discovery and trial were important for two primary reasons. First, his trial demonstrated flaws in the M'Naghten insanity defense. Attempting to have him committed to a psychiatric hospital instead of being executed, Fish's defense utilized psychiatric testimony to demonstrate that he was medically insane. However, his defense was unable to meet the legal definition of insanity, drawing attention to conflict between medical and legal definitions of the term. Second, the Fish trial received heavy media attention, increasing the public's awareness of sexual deviance and its connection to crime. Due to his long period of criminal activity prior to detection, the Fish case was used by politicians and the media to suggest that there were more serial killers like Fish active in the community, stalking and murdering children. The case was a prelude to the passage of sexual psychopath legislation, which allowed criminal justice authorities the indefinite psychiatric commitment of those convicted of minor sexual offenses (Freedman 1987; Jenkins 1998).

When he was discovered by the authorities, a case with Fish's combination of sexual perversion, serial murder of children, and cannibalism had never been documented in the American criminal justice system before. At the time of his psychiatric examination, which is described in *The Show of Violence* (1949), Dr. Wertham claimed that "Fish's sexual life was of unparalleled perversity. I did research in the psychiatric and criminological literature and found no published case that would even nearly compare with this" (1949, 72). Fish claimed that he was driven to sexually mutilate children by an extreme religious psychosis, in which he felt that he needed to torture and sacrifice his victims

Two guards escort Albert Fish from the White Plains, New York, courthouse after he is convicted of the first-degree murder of Grace Budd. Fish was executed at Sing Sing prison in January 1936. (New York Daily New Archive/Getty Images)

to God as a form of atonement for sins. He suffered from hallucinations in which he would hear voices and see bodies being tortured. Most notably among his paraphilias, Fish would insert needles into the region near his genitals and underneath his fingernails. At his trial X-ray images revealed 27 needles embedded within his pelvic region.

By the time he was arrested for the murder of Grace Budd in 1934, Albert Fish had been actively stalking, molesting, torturing, and murdering children for a period of some 20 years. Describing his modus operandi to Wertham, Fish explained that he would seduce or bribe children and lead them to secluded areas to sexually torture them. He would typically change addresses following an offense, never returning to the same area. Fish routinely targeted poor, African American children since they did not garner much attention from the criminal justice system when they went missing. The total number of Fish's victims is unknown. Despite claiming to have victimized approximately 100 children, it was unclear to Wertham

(1949) whether he had molested or killed that many. He was only a formal suspect in five murders.

Fish was finally apprehended by the criminal justice system due to his role in the death of Grace Budd. In June 1928, the Budd family placed a newspaper advertisement seeking employment for their son Edward. Using the alias of Frank Howard, Fish responded to the ad with the intention of killing Edward. Instead, he claimed that upon seeing Grace Budd he decided that he would eat her (Wertham 1949). Fish offered to take Grace to a birthday party for his sister's children and return her that evening, an offer which her parents accepted. At that point, Fish led Grace away from her parents and they did not hear from either of them for nearly six years, until Fish sent an anonymous letter to Grace's mother in November 1934. In the letter he described bringing Grace to an empty house in Westchester, New York, where he strangled her before dismembering and eating her over the course of nine days. The envelope of the letter Fish sent to Mrs. Budd provided detectives with a clue that led to his apprehension. The envelope was the official stationary of a benevolent association in New York City and was traced to an employee who had left it in his former lodgings; the same room in a boarding house on 52nd Street, which Fish had only just recently vacated.

At his murder trial, the legal question was not whether Fish had killed Grace Budd—when he was arrested Fish confessed to the murder no less than six times and brought the authorities to the house where the crime took place to point out Grace's bones. Rather, the question at trial was of Fish's sanity. The prosecution sought to establish Fish's legal sanity, which would allow the state to execute him, while his defense argued for his legal insanity, which would result in his commitment to a psychiatric hospital. Governed by the M'Naghten rule, the consideration at trial was whether Fish understood his actions, and whether he recognized his actions as legally right or wrong. Fish's defense relied on the psychiatric testimony of Dr. Frederic Wertham to establish insanity. Through his interviews with the defendant, Wertham described that while Fish deliberately planned his crimes and knew that the actions were legally wrong, he had a distorted notion of what it meant for an action to be morally right or wrong. For instance, Fish identified himself with the biblical Abraham, believing that if his murders were wrong then an angel would have stopped him from committing them. While Fish's condition suggested that he was insane by medical standards, the prosecution called four psychiatrists to attest to his legal sanity. Ultimately, the court found him to be legally sane. In January 1936 Albert Fish was executed via the electric chair at Sing Sing prison. Wertham (1949) observed that Fish welcomed his death, believing that he was atoning for his sins. After the trial one of the jurors commented that most of the jury felt that Fish was insane, but believed that he should be executed anyway (Wertham 1949).

Origins of the Insanity Defense

At the time of Albert Fish's trial, the U.S. court system used an insanity test that originated in the United Kingdom, called the M'Naghten Rule. The test arose from the case of *Queen v. M'Naghten* (8 Eng. Rep. 718 [1843]). Daniel M'Naghten, who suffered from delusions and believed the government was trying to have him killed, was charged with murder of civil servant Edward Drummond, whom he had mistaken for Prime Minister Sir Robert Peel. The jury ruled that he was not guilty because of insanity. This case resulted in the creation of the M'Naghten rule, which stated that "to establish a defense on the ground of insanity, it must be clearly proved that, at the time of the committing of the act, the party accused was laboring under such a defect of reason, from disease of the mind, as not to know the nature and quality of the act he was doing; or, if he did know it, that he did not know he was doing what was wrong."

The trial of Albert Fish demonstrated faults in the strict M'Naghten test of legal insanity. The uniqueness of the case drew attention to the incompatibility between the legal definition of insanity in the M'Naghten test, and new medical understandings of insanity, which was a subject of debate in psychiatric circles for some time following the trial. The details of the Fish case were sensationalized in the media, portraying Fish as the prototypical sex offender, and suggesting that minor sexual offenders would eventually escalate to Fish's level of deviance (Jenkins 1998). In this sense, the Fish case was a prelude to the passage of sexual psychopath laws, which allowed authorities to indefinitely confine, examine, and treat sex offenders in psychiatric facilities. These laws were predicated on the notion that even minor sexual offenders may suffer from a mental

disorder which could lead to more serious offenses. The Fish case was an important factor that contributed to the climate which developed that legislation.

JASON RYDBERG

See also: Holmes, Dr. H.H. (1861–1896); Toppan, Jane (1854–1938)

Further Reading

Davidson, Henry A. 1950. "The Psychiatrist's Role in the Administration of Criminal Justice." *Rutgers Law Review* 4: 578–96.

Freedman, Estelle B. 1987. "Uncontrolled Desires: The Response to the Sexual Psychopath, 1920–1960." *The Journal of American History* 74: 83–106.

Jenkins, Philip. 1989. "Serial Murder in the United States 1900–1940: A Historical Perspective." *Journal of Criminal Justice* 17: 377–92.

Jenkins, Philip. 1998. *Moral Panic: Changing Concepts of the Child Molester in Modern America.* New Haven, CT: Yale University Press.

Wertham, Frederic. 1949. *The Show of Violence.* New York: Doubleday.

Fisher, Amy (1974–)

A young lover is scorned and takes revenge in the form of an attempted murder. This is not a description from a Hollywood blockbuster movie but rather a true event that took place in New York in 1992. The perpetrator of the crime is a 17-year-old young woman named Amy Fisher. The media would dub her "Lethal" or "Lolita," but the most common alliteration associated with Fisher would be the "Long Island Lolita." This entry devotes discussion to the crime Fisher committed, her trial, the media fascination with her, and the significance of the case to the criminal justice field.

Amy Elizabeth Fisher was born in 1974 in Long Island, New York. During Fisher's childhood and early teenage years, several traumatic events occurred in her life including sexual abuse by a family member and being raped at age 13 by a contractor working in the family home. In her mid-teens, Fisher had numerous casual dating relationships, one of which led to a pregnancy but ended in an abortion. However, a chance meeting of a man in 1990 altered the course of her life and resulted in her becoming a household name. In December 1990, Fisher went with her father to a body shop called Complete Auto Body & Fender Inc. The owner of the shop was Joey Buttafuoco, a onetime weightlifting and arm-wrestling champion.

Enamored with Buttafuoco, Fisher would find numerous reasons to bring her car to his shop so she could see him. In the summer of 1991, Buttafuoco, 35 years old, and Fisher, 16 years old, began an intimate love affair. Despite the fact Fisher knew Buttafuoco was married and had two children, she would meet him to have sex on a regular basis at motels, her home, in his shop, and on his boat. According to Fisher, during this time together, Buttafuoco not only began to reveal that he was unhappy with his marriage, but also dropped hints about getting Mary Jo "out of the picture." In late 1991, at the alleged suggestion of Buttafuoco, Fisher began working as an escort to be able to make ends meet. As time passed, Fisher's feelings for Buttafuoco only intensified and by November 1991, she asked him to choose between her and his wife. It came as a shock to Fisher when Buttafuoco chose his wife. Enraged yet undeterred by his answer, Fisher decided the best way to solve her "problem" would be to kill her. According to Fisher, she told Buttafuoco of her intentions to kill his wife and, in turn, he responded by telling her how best to accomplish it. On May 19, 1992, Fisher decided to carry out her plan by going to his house in Massapequa, New York. She rang the doorbell to his house and upon seeing Mary Jo answer the door, attempted to start a conversation with her. When Mary Jo tried to end the conversation, Fisher pulled out a .25 caliber pistol and shot Mary Jo in the head (Fisher and Weller 1994). Miraculously Mary Jo, although severely injured, survived the attack and described her attacker as a petite teenager with brunette hair. Buttafuoco stated he knew the girl she described and identified the assailant as Amy Fisher, then a 17-year-old high school senior.

At Fisher's arraignment in June 1992, her bail was set at $2 million. Fisher's family was unable to afford the bail, but her attorney appealed to Hollywood by offering to sell her life story to a publisher or movie company to acquire enough money to bail her out. KLM Productions bought Fisher's story for $80,000 and with her family selling everything they owned Fisher was released a few months later. In September 1992, Fisher pled guilty to one count of aggravated assault. She was later sentenced to up to 15 years in prison at the Albion Correctional Facility in New York. However, Fisher would serve a total of seven years in prison and remained on parole until 2003 (Fisher and Woliver 2004). As for Buttafuoco, during the entire court proceedings he profusely proclaimed his innocence and claimed that Fisher was a delusional liar when she implicated him. While Buttafuoco was never charged for his alleged role in the attempted murder, the district attorney's office investigated him on statutory rape charges. With evidence mounting against him, Buttafuoco pled guilty to one count of statutory rape and served six months in jail.

The media's reaction to the crime Amy Fisher committed, from the time the story first broke to current day, can best be described as a "feeding frenzy." The public hungered to learn everything there was to know about Fisher, referring to her as the "Long Island Lolita," who turned to violence to get the man she loved and desired; they didn't have to wait long as the media promptly satisfied their cravings with a vengeance. Her crime spurred three television movies, an interview by Oprah, the publication of countless books, numerous newspaper and magazine covers, endless tabloid alliterations, fueled monologues featured in the popular late-night television shows, a musical, and even a comic book with a pinup drawing of Fisher holding a pistol. The media reaction to Fisher's case enforced the notion that if a crime is interesting enough, you'll become famous.

When it comes to the crime Fisher committed at the young age of 17, there is no doubt that the attempted murder of Mary Jo Buttafuoco was shocking and controversial. However, when it comes to the motivations behind why Amy Fisher committed this act of violence, there are many unanswered questions concerning the role that Joey Buttafuoco played and why Fisher thought violence was the answer to her love triangle. Research has demonstrated that: (1) women tend to act in aggression, and even violence, to satisfy internal emotional expressive needs; (2) victimization experienced in childhood increases the risk for violent and delinquent behavior in both males and females, and (3) that males are more likely to have a stronger influence on females' involvement in delinquency and even acts of violence, especially when the female and male are romantically involved (Belknap 2007; Chesney-Lind 1989). This does not mean every child and adolescent who has a history of being physically and/or sexually abused means that they will turn to delinquent behavior or violence. However, Fisher was sexually abused as a child, raped at the age of 13, and was at an impressionable age when she became sexually involved with Buttafuoco and these events provide some understanding behind the motivations of her violent actions. Overall, the significance of the case, at the time and even today, points to the fact that there is still a need of academic research on the exact triggers of violent behavior in adolescent girls and what role manipulation and coercion plays in fostering their criminal behavior.

Fisher continues to remain in the public spotlight by participating in numerous media outlets including mainstream radio and television shows and pornographic movies. The crime was shocking for many reasons, but one of the main reasons why her crime was given so much attention is the fact that violent behavior exhibited by girls or women is often sensationalized by the media.

JANE POORE AND ELAINE GUNNISON

See also: Knox, Amanda, Murder Trials of (2009–2015); Longet, Claudine (1942–); Tucker, Karla Faye (1959–1998); Zamora, Diane (1978–) and David Graham (1977–)

Further Reading

Belknap, Joanne. 2007. *The Invisible Woman.* Belmont, CA: Thomson, Wadsworth.

Chesney-Lind, Meda. 1989. "Girl's Crime and Woman's Place: Toward a Feminist Model of Female Delinquency." *Crime and Delinquency* 35(1): 8–10.

Fisher, Amy, and Sheila Weller. 1994. *Amy Fisher: My Story.* New York: Pocket Publishers.

Fisher, Amy, and Robbie Woliver. 2004. *If I Knew Then. . . .* n.p.:. iUniverse Publishers.

Fleiss, Heidi (1965–)

Heidi Fleiss is best known for starting a high-end prostitution business. Her business flourished as she was able to obtain and sustain a clientele full of wealthy and well-established individuals. She even had international clients willing to pay upward of a million dollars for her prostitutes. Fleiss also did well with her employees. She claimed to have to turn women down because she had so many coming to her for a position. While it seemed to be going well, others in the area who also were in the prostitution business were not happy with her success. They contacted the local police and they set up a sting. They were able to arrest some of her prostitutes and Fleiss herself. Fleiss was charged and convicted at both the state and federal levels. She served three years in prison and is currently out and, at the time of this publication, living in Nevada.

On December 30, 1965, Heidi Fleiss was born to pediatrician Dr. Paul Fleiss and schoolteacher Elissa Fleiss in Los Angeles, California. Heidi was raised in a large family with three sisters and two brothers. Her childhood is one that most would describe as normal. She had a happy childhood and a good relationship with her parents and siblings. The family would go on vacations over the summer where they would spend time together hiking and camping throughout the United States. She also started

babysitting around the age of 12 for neighborhood families. This became her first venture into the business world, as she became in such high demand that she began a babysitting service and employed her friends. Fleiss was not as successful in academia. She began to worry that failing grades would hurt her chance of getting into college and began paying others for answers. She would skip school to go to the beach or other places she enjoyed. Eventually, she ended up dropping out of high school when she was in 10th grade. Fleiss held many small jobs such as waitressing and being a salesperson until she was 19. At this point in Fleiss's life, she attended a party where she was introduced to Bernie Cornfeld. Cornfeld hired Fleiss as his personal secretary. They eventually started a relationship, but it did not last and she moved back to Los Angeles, California, where she obtained her real estate license.

At the age of 22, Fleiss began dating Ivan Nagy, a filmmaker, who introduced her to Elizabeth Adams. Adams was a 60-year-old women who ran one of the most prosperous prostitution services in Los Angeles, California. She

Heidi Fleiss poses in the pressroom during Comedy Central's First Ever Awards Show *The Commies* at Sony Pictures Studios in Culver City, California. Fleiss ran a profitable prostitution business before being arrested, charged, and convicted of pandering. She spent three years in prison. (Photo by Fredrick M. Brown/Getty Images)

was nicknamed Madam Alex and she was looking for an individual to take over her business for her. Madam Alex began grooming Fleiss to take over her business. This meant that Fleiss had to learn the business of prostitution, and in attempt to learn it became a prostitute. This stint did not last long though as Madam Alex quickly promoted her to assistant madam. Fleiss's first task was to hire young and attractive women. Fleiss proved successful at this task by employing word-of-mouth recruiting tactics. Many of the new recruits were acquaintances of Fleiss and took the position in hopes of meeting wealthy men. In addition, Madam Alex and Fleiss grew their clientele and began servicing some of Hollywood's top producers, directors, movie stars, royal figures, businessmen, heads of state, and other wealthy individuals. It is suggested that with these new hires and clientele, profits increased, however Fleiss did not see much of the profit and decided she would leave Madam Alex and venture out on her own.

In her new business adventure, Fleiss had the same task of recruiting. Again, she proved successful and ended up hiring many young, attractive, and ambitious individuals. Her new hires consisted of aspiring actresses, university students, and business women. Eventually, she no longer needed to recruit as she continuously had women approaching her. The prostitutes working for her received 40 percent of the profits they made plus their tips. Fleiss grew her clientele and her successful business practices even gained her international attention. She would often send her girls overseas to service wealthy customers. She had successfully secured a high-end clientele and was earning millions.

On June 9, 1993, police arrested Fleiss. The day before, the local police had set up a sting operation. An undercover officer called Fleiss and arranged for her to send some of her prostitutes to a local hotel. Four women were sent to the hotel with 13 grams of cocaine.

Upon arrival, the undercover officers acted as interested clients and engaged the women in small talk. Eventually, the women indicated that they were willing to engage in sexual activity. Once this verbal agreement was secured and caught on tape, officers from the adjoining room entered and arrested the women. Fleiss was arrested the following day outside of her home in Beverly Hills. She was charged with five counts of pandering and one count of possession of narcotics. Fleiss's defense lawyer presented the argument that the police entrapped her. Deliberation lasted for four days and on December 2, 1994, the jury found her guilty on three of the five pandering counts. She was eventually sentenced to three years in prison and fined

$1,500. When the defense discovered that some jurors had traded votes, an appeal was filed. In addition, Fleiss also was charged at the federal level and in August 1995, a federal jury convicted her on eight counts of conspiracy, tax evasion, and money laundering. One of the main media attractions of the trial was the hope that Fleiss would release the names of her clients. As previously discussed, her clients were wealthy and many were famous. She never revealed the identity of any of her clients. However, two men did come forward during the trial phase and admitted to using her service: actor, Charlie Sheen and a Texas billionaire business man, Robert T. Crow.

Fleiss spent three years in a federal penitentiary in Dublin, California, and was released in September 1999. After release, she remained on federal probation, state parole, and was expected to perform 300 hours of community service. Shortly after release, she filed for bankruptcy. In 2001 she began dating Tom Sizemore. They seemed to have a happy relationship for a while, but it began to deteriorate and in 2003 Fleiss filled charges against Sizemore for domestic abuse. He was found guilty in August 2003. Fleiss published a biography titled *Pandering* in 2003. She has also been in drug rehabilitation centers a few times since her release. Fleiss has held several jobs since her release: a talk show host, sex tip advisor, and actress are a few.

MELISSA J. TETZLAFF-BEMILLER

See also: Adler, "Polly" Pearl (1900–1962); Bickford, Maria, Murder of (1845); Jewett, Helen, Murder of (1836)

Further Reading

Bell, Rachael. N.D. "Heidi Fleiss: The Million Dollar Madam." http://www.trutv.com/library/crime/notorious_murders/celebrity/heidi_fleiss/index.html. Accessed April 16, 2015.

Fleiss, Heidi. 2003. *Pandering*. 1 Hour Entertainment, LLC. Los Angeles, CA.

Florida A&M Hazing Death (November 19, 2011)

Robert Champion (1985–2011) was a 26-year-old drum major and student at Florida Agricultural and Mechanical University (FAMU). On November 19, 2011, Champion was found unresponsive on a charter bus in a hotel parking lot after the Florida Football Classic in Orlando, Florida. The investigation discovered that his death was a result of a hazing ritual where Champion had to walk backward from the front to the back of the bus while being beaten by fellow band members. Fifteen band members have been charged with hazing and manslaughter as of January 2014. Seven were sentenced to combinations of probation and community service, two have pleaded no contest to manslaughter and are awaiting sentencing, and six are slated to go to trial in 2014. In addition to the charges filed against participants, the investigation revealed a culture of hazing within the band at FAMU. This led to personnel and policy changes, as well as a year-long suspension of the band.

Champion was a 26-year-old college student at FAMU when he was killed during a hazing ritual. Champion lived in Decatur, Georgia, before moving to Tallahassee, Florida, to pursue his education at FAMU where he was majoring in music. Champion was part of FAMU's famed marching band, the Marching 100, which had performed at Super Bowls and presidential inaugurations.

Champion had traveled with other band members to Orlando, Florida, on November 19, 2011. FAMU's football team was to play their rivals, Bethune-Cookman University, and the band was to perform during halftime. The hazing occurred after the game was lost and the band returned to their hotel. There, Champion was beaten on the bus. Champion was found unresponsive on the bus and was transported to Doctor Phillips Hospital where he was pronounced dead. The investigation indicated that hazing was involved and the death was ruled a homicide. According to Florida law, any death resulting from hazing is a third-degree felony. The hazing incident that took place was termed Crossing Bus C, by those questioned by authorities. During this ritual, a pledge, the person being hazed, walks backward from the front of the bus to the back of the bus while being slapped, kicked, punched, and hit. A pledge who falls is stomped on and dragged to the front of the bus to attempt the crossing again.

Champion was found with bruises to his chest, arms, shoulders, and back. He reportedly suffered bleeding from soft tissues, which caused him to go into shock. Champion's autopsy "was performed by Associate Medical Examiner Sara H. Irrgang of Florida's District 9 Medical Examiner's Office in Orlando, with oversight from Chief Medical Examiner Jan C. Garavaglia" (Martinez 2011). The autopsy results state that there were "extensive contusion of his chest, arms, shoulder, and back," and that he died from "hemorrhagic shock—the result of excessive internal bleeding—due to soft tissue hemorrhage, due to blunt force trauma sustained during a hazing incident" (Martinez 2011). Further, it was found that Champion died within an hour of the incident. Despite the beating that Champion suffered, he did not have any internal injuries or bone fractures. There was also no evidence of drugs or alcohol in his system.

Shortly after the death of Champion, four fellow band members were expelled from FAMU for suspected involvement in hazing, however, they were reinstated after police asked the school to stop disciplinary action until the investigation was complete. Initially, ten band members were charged with felony hazing in 2012, but the charges were upped to manslaughter in 2013. Fifteen former band members were charged with manslaughter and hazing in Champion's death. Eight defendants accepted deals, one pleaded no contest. Of the fifteen defendants, two were charged with misdemeanors, while the others were charged with felonies. While most were sentenced to probation and/or community service, both Jessie Baskin and Dante Martin were sentenced to jail time. Jessie Baskin was sentenced to nearly a year in jail, but has since been released. Dante Martin was sentenced to six years in prison for manslaughter, felony hazing and two counts of misdemeanor hazing related to two other band members. The prosecution has completed its case against all students involved.

In addition to criminal charges for members of the band, Champion's parents have filed wrongful-death lawsuits against the company that owns the bus and FAMU. Champion's parents filed the lawsuit against the bus company because they say that the bus driver stood outside the bus and allowed the hazing to happen. The company responded to the accusation by stating that the driver was helping band members outside the bus with their equipment. The lawsuit was brought against FAMU after an unsuccessful mediation session between attorneys for both sides. FAMU offered to pay $300,000 dollars to the family, but the settlement was rejected. In September 2015, a $1.1 million settlement was reached. The agreement included $300,000 that FAMU will pay through the state Department of Financial Services and an insurance payout from the Rosen Plaza hotel where the death occurred.

Hazing Research

According to a study on hazing from the University of Maine, 55 percent of college students who are involved in extracurricular activity are involved in hazing (University of Maine, Hazing Research Files). While one out of five have witnessed hazing taking place, in 95 percent of the cases, it was not reported to campus officials. The most common forms of hazing involve humiliation, alcohol consumption, sexual acts, or isolation. However, as of February 10, 2012, 96 individuals have died as a result of hazing.

The investigation into his death not only revealed that hazing was involved with his death, but it was also a prevalent factor within the band. In fact, many have termed it a culture of hazing. This so-called culture of hazing led to some changes within FAMU. Soon after the Champion's death, the now-former president, James Ammons, suspended the band. According to Ammons, the band was to be suspended out of respect for Champion and to give officials time to restructure the band. Prior to the band's suspension, other hazing incidents were discovered to have taken place. There have been charges filed in some of these other hazing incidents. In addition, it was revealed that many band members were not actually enrolled at FAMU. The suspension was lifted for the 2013 school year. However, the band returned with fewer participants. The band's 145 members are less than half of the 420 it had before the November 2011 suspension. FAMU initiated changes to the student code of conduct. Further changes to FAMU included changes in personnel with the departure of the band director, and the resignation of two faculty members and the university's president.

It is also important to note that some people believe that Champion may have been a victim of hazing just because he was a pledge. There is speculation that he was hazed due to his sexual orientation. His parents and friends have alluded to the idea that he may have been beaten so severely because he was gay. His parents also indicated that Champion had been bullied because of sexual preference. However, there have not been any charges to suggest that this was a reason for the beating. In addition to homosexuality, other reasons surfaced for the beatings. Some alleged the hazing was due to his candidacy for chief drum major, while others suggest it was because of his disdain for the band's culture of hazing. Regardless of which, if any, of these suggested reasons are found to be true, Champion lost his life due to the beatings he sustained during a hazing ritual.

MELISSA J. TETZLAFF-BEMILLER

See also: Genovese, Catherine Susan "Kitty," Murder of (1964); Virginia Tech Massacre (April 16, 2007); *Primary Documents/Florida A & M Hazing Death: Florida A & M Anti-Hazing Regulation (2012)*

Further Reading

Allan, Elizabeth, and Mary Madden. 2008. "Hazing in View: College Students at Risk." http://umaine.edu/hazingresearch/files/2012/10/hazing_in_view_web1.pdf. Accessed January 28, 2015.

Brown, Robbie. 2012. "Criminal Charges for 13 in Florida A&M Hazing Death." *New York Times.* May 2. http://www.nytimes.com/2012/05/03/us/13-charged-in-hazing-death-at-florida-am.html?_r=0. Accessed April 16, 2015.

Johnson, Jason. 2012. "Hazing Is a Lazy Excuse for Robert Champion's Death." *Politic365.* May 3. http://politic365.com/2012/05/03/hazing-is-a-lazy-excuse-for-robert-champions-death/. Accessed January 12, 2015.

Levs, Josh. 2011. "Florida A&M Band Suspended after Suspected Hazing Death." *CNN.* November 23. http://www.cnn.com/2011/11/22/justice/florida-possible-hazing-death/index.html?iref=allsearch. Accessed April 16, 2015.

Martinez, Michael. 2011. "Expert: Autopsy of Florida A&M Drum Major Shows Badly Beaten Muscles." CNN. December 22. http://www.cnn.com/2011/12/21/justice/florida-am-investigation/index.html?hpt=hp_t1. Accessed April 16, 2015.

Stop Hazing: Educating to Eliminate Hazing. 2010. http://www.stophazing.org/. Accessed April 16, 2015.

"The 2013 Florida Statutes: Hazing Prohibited." Online Sunshine. http://www.leg.state.fl.us/Statutes/index.cfm?App_mode=Display_Statute&Search_String=&URL=1000–1099/1006/Sections/1006.63.html. Accessed April 16, 2015.

University of Maine. Hazing Research Files. http://umaine.edu/hazingresearch/files/2012/10/National_Agenda_Hazing_Prevention.pdf. Accessed April 28, 2015.

Floyd, Charles Arthur "Pretty Boy" (1904–1934)

"Pretty Boy" Floyd was a notorious American gunman, bank robber, and murderer throughout the late 1920s and early 1930s. Despite numerous accusations of robbery and murder, Floyd was rarely convicted of his crimes and only charged with the murder of ATF Special Agent Curtis C. Burke in 1931. During his short-lived career as a criminal, he became known as one of the nation's most feared bank robbers. He was particularly known for entering and robbing banks during daylight hours, immaculately dressed, wielding a submachine gun, and without a mask to hide his identity, all while remaining a gentleman to his victims. For this, Floyd briefly gained the status of "Public Enemy No. 1" on the FBI's most wanted list. In October 1934, nearly two years after his participation in the infamous June 1933 Kansas City Massacre, Floyd's life ended within minutes of a standoff with FBI officials and local police officers on a farm in Ohio.

Known to the world as "Pretty Boy" Floyd—often going by the aliases of "Jack Hamilton," "Frank Mitchell," or

"George Sanders"—Charles Arthur Floyd was born on February 3, 1904, in Bartow County, Georgia. Very little is known about Floyd's childhood years other than the fact that his parents relocated to Oklahoma in 1911 where his father was a farmer and alcohol bootlegger. In 1924, at the age of 20, Floyd married 16-year-old Wilma "Ruby" Hargrove and worked as a sharecropper (i.e., farm crop harvester) in eastern Oklahoma. Prior to their marriage, Wilma became pregnant with their only son Jack Dempsey Floyd.

Since the economy was tough during that time, Floyd felt the pressing need to turn to a life of crime to support his small family. Despite a few accusations, his first known criminal offense was in 1925 when he committed a $5,000 payroll robbery at a Kroger store-warehouse in St. Louis, Missouri. He was convicted of the robbery and during his stay at the Missouri State Penitentiary, Wilma filed for divorce in 1929. It was also in 1929 that Floyd was paroled and released back to Oklahoma after serving only three years of his five-year sentence. While on his return home, Floyd learned that Jim Mills killed his father in relation to a generations-long blood feud, but he was not convicted because he claimed self-defense for the murder. Soon after this discovery, Mills disappeared, and Floyd fled Oklahoma for Kansas City, Missouri.

Along the way, Floyd connected with several individuals who would become accomplices in various robberies throughout Missouri, Ohio, and Oklahoma such as Alfred "Red" Lovett, James "Jim" Bradley, Jack Atkins, William "Billy the Killer" Miller, and George Birdwell, a church deacon-turned outlaw. It was also during this time that Floyd began using a submachine gun during robberies, a trademark in which he became known for. In 1930, Floyd, Bradley, and Atkins robbed a bank in Sylvania, Ohio, and during the subsequent pursuit Bradley killed motorcycle officer Harlan Manes. Police were able to apprehend all three of the men when Atkins crashed their getaway car into a telephone pole. Despite receiving a 10- to 25-year sentence for the bank robbery, Floyd escaped during transport to the Ohio State Penitentiary; Atkins was sentenced to a life sentence while Bradley was sentenced to the electric chair. After he escaped, Floyd fled to Toledo, Ohio, where he met up with Miller.

While working with Miller, Floyd gained the status of "Public Enemy No. 1" on the FBI's most wanted list. Although the two already had enough money to retire, they often traveled to Michigan to execute several robberies of small farmers, gas stations, and banks while taking refuge

in a Kansas City brothel (i.e., whorehouse), where it is claimed that he first received his nickname "Pretty Boy." Throughout 1931 and 1932, Floyd accumulated a list of officer killings such as Patrolman Ralph H. Castner and Chief of Police Carl M. "Shorty" Galliher, Bureau of Alcohol, Tobacco, Firearms (ATF) special agent Curtis C. Burke, and former sheriff turned bounty hunter Erv A. Kelley. It was after the 1931 murder of Chief of Police Galliher—during a shootout with officers, Floyd, Miller, and two gun molls (i.e., female professional criminal), sisters Rose Ash and Beulah Bird—that Floyd hooked up with Birdwell and executed several more bank robberies. However, Birdwell was killed a year later, in late 1932, during a bank robbery in which Floyd had not participated.

After the death of Birdwell, Floyd joined forces with Adam Richetti, George "Baby Face" Nelson, and John Dillinger and his gang in Kansas City. It was through this connection that Floyd became one of the hired hands in what became infamously known as the 1933 "Kansas City Massacre," and ultimately led to his death in 1934. The Kansas

Mugshot of bank robber Charles "Pretty Boy" Floyd wanted in connection with the killing of one policeman and the wounding of another during the holdup of the Rensselaer County Bank in Rensselaer, New York. (Bettmann/Corbis)

City Massacre occurred outside the east entrance of Union Station on the morning of June 17, 1933, in an attempt to rescue escaped federal prisoner Frank "Gentleman" or "Jelly" Nash—a notorious underworld figure and considered the most successful bank robber in U.S. history—who was in custody for transportation to serve his 25-year sentence for the assault of a mail custodian. Floyd, Richetti, and Vernon Miller—a freelance gunman and good friend of Nash—discharged their submachine guns at the five officers who had just loaded Nash into a vehicle to return him to the Leavenworth penitentiary.

The rescue attempt was botched, however, when the trio killed not only Police Chief Otto H. Reed and FBI special agent Raymond J. Caffrey, but also Nash himself. Standing near the front of the car was special agent in charge Reed E. Vetterli, who escaped with a minor flesh wound, while the two agents inside the car survived by slumping forward in their seats, and an agent who responded from inside the station remained unharmed as well. Their escape from the scene led to a massive manhunt, which began with the evidence first pointing to Miller as their primary suspect. However, after tracing him to Chicago, officers found Miller dead in a ditch near Detroit, Michigan. Upon this discovery, agents turned their attention to Floyd and Richetti, who had made their way to Ohio after the massacre—both were identified in the Kansas City Massacre by fingerprints. Nevertheless, Floyd denied having any involvement in the incident, a claim that he maintained until his death.

Agents learned of the two men's whereabouts in late 1934 when local police spotted them after they crashed their car, which resulted in a gunfight and the capture of Richetti. Then, on October 22, 1934 four FBI agents, led by agent Melvin H. Purvis, and the local Ohio police finally caught up with Floyd on a farm near Clarkson, Ohio. While attempting to obtain a ride to the local bus station from the farm owners, officer Chester Smith spotted Floyd getting into the car and shot him in the arm when he jumped from the car to flee. Continuing in his effort to dart for cover and flee into the nearby wooded, all of the agents and local police began firing their weapons, and Floyd fell to the ground. Although he was still alive when the officers first recovered him, he died at the scene within minutes.

JENNIFER A. HAEGELE

See also: Capone, Al (1899–1947); Dillinger, John (1903–1934); Gillis, Lester Joseph "Baby Face Nelson" (1908–1934); Parker, Bonnie (1910–1934) and Clyde Barrow (1909–1934)

Further Reading

King, Jeffery. 1999. *Life and death of Pretty Boy Floyd.* Kent, OH: Kent State University Press.
Wallis, Michael. 2011. *Pretty Boy: The Life and Times of Charles Arthur Floyd.* New York: W.W. Norton & Co.

Ford, Gerald, Assassination Attempts on (1975)

In September 1975, two separate assassination attempts were made upon President Gerald Ford (July 14, 1913–December 26, 2006). Neither attempt was successful and both were unique in that they were perpetrated by women with connections to radical antigovernment groups of the era.

In 1969, Charles Manson (November 12, 1934–) and five of his followers were convicted of the murder of actress Sharon Tate (January 24, 1943–August 8, 1969). While Manson did not directly play a part in her murder, he did recruit and motivate the cult members who perpetrated that heinous crime, however not all of his followers were imprisoned after his conviction.

Lynette Fromme (October 22, 1948–) was the prototypical recruit for the Manson cult. She was involved with drugs and alcohol as early as junior high school. While she did eventually graduate, she left home and stayed with various friends for long stretches of time. She became more and more dependent on drugs like LSD, the drug Manson used as a brainwashing tool. Fromme's home life ended for good when she moved out for the last time while attending junior college. She wound up in Venice Beach, California, where she met Charles Manson when she was only 18. They took a liking to each other immediately and Manson offered to let Fromme travel the country with Mary Brunner and himself.

The Manson family moved onto the estate of George Spahn, an 80-year-old man who was the caretaker of the property. Spahn was blind and Manson assigned Fromme the duty of taking care of the aging man. She allegedly earned the nick name "Squeaky" because of the noise she made when Spahn ran his hand up her thigh. It is rumored that her duties included maintaining a sexual relationship with Mr. Spahn. Later, Manson renamed her "Red" because it was her assignment to save the Redwood trees.

When Manson was arrested for the murder of Sharon Tate, Fromme became the leader of the gang and was arrested several times for protest style antics during the trial. Unlike many of his followers, Fromme never stopped trying to earn Manson's favor. On September 5, 1975, she attempted to do so one more time.

She pushed her way through a crowd outside of the State of California Capitol, pointed a .45 caliber handgun at President Gerald Ford, and from a distance of less than five feet she pulled the trigger. The shot would have been difficult to miss and the injury would have been difficult to survive, but Ms. Fromme forgot to chamber a round before the attack. Instead of firing, the gun made an empty "Click" and Fromme was taken to the ground by secret service agents.

Seventeen days after Fromme's attempt, Sarah Jane Moore (February 15, 1930–) went to the St. Francis Hotel in San Francisco and successfully fired a round at Ford from about 40 feet away. She shot while Ford was exiting his vehicle and missed his head by several feet. A bystander, former marine Oliver Sipple, wrestled her to the ground before Secret Service agents could get to her. Moore had several fringe associations with radical groups that were very active at the time. Because of her involvement, the FBI had actually recruited her to become an informant before the attempt on Ford's life. Fromme stated that she believed that the assassination of the president would trigger a violent revolution throughout the country. After the attempt, a calm President Ford continued to the stage where he delivered a speech on crime.

In many ways, Moore's background is in sharp contrast with Fromme's. She had relationship issues early in life and suffered through five divorces. A mother of four and a bookkeeper for a charitable organization, no one would have suspected that she would attempt to assassinate the president. She had attempted to complete nursing school but her involvement in radical politics quickly became her true passion. While she never fell in line with a group similar to Manson's she did exhibit erratic and unpredictable behavior according to her coworkers.

Lynette Fromme's trial was particularly unique. Consistent with Manson's own defense style, Fromme represented herself. She did not introduce relevant testimony but instead used the attention as a platform to spread her political agenda. During the course of the trial, she was forcefully removed from the court several times and even threw an apple at a prosecutor's head.

Sarah Moore was paroled in December 2007 after 32 years in prison. Lynette Fromme was released from prison in 2009 also after a 30-year stay. Both women were actually successful in escaping from prison during their detainment. Fromme escaped in 1987 from a low-security prison in Alderson, West Virginia. She was recaptured two days later. Fromme stated that she escaped in an attempt to be closer to Manson who is being held in California. Moore escaped in 1979 but was captured only a few hours later.

In the aftermath of both assassinations, California governor Edmund G. Brown Jr signed two new gun laws into effect. The first enacted mandatory sentencing for offenders who used guns during the commission of serious crimes. The second extended the current waiting period for the purchase of a firearm from five to 15 days. The laws governing how private collectors can deliver firearms also changed. Moore had purchased two pistols from a private collector, Mark Fernwood, the day before her assassination attempt. Today, private party transfers of firearms are illegal in the state of California.

After the assassination of President John F. Kennedy in 1963, the Secret Service was expanded to provide more manpower. These additions did little to prevent the attacks on Ford and later President Reagan. These attacks led to further changes in policy, technology, and techniques used in protecting the president. Gone are the days where crowds can provide cover for a lone gunman to approach the president with a weapon drawn. Instead, barricades, metal detectors, and vehicles funnel crowds into precise locations and give the president a wide protection.

CHARLES GIBERTI

See also: Cermak, Anton Joseph, Assassination of (February 15, 1933); Fromme, Lynette "Squeaky" (1948–); Lincoln, Abraham, Assassination of (April 14, 1865); Manson, Charles (1934–); Wallace, George, Attempted Assassination of (May 15, 1972)

Further Reading

Farabaugh, Kane 2013. "Agents Say JFK Assassination Transformed Secret Service." *Voice of America.* November 19. http://www.voanews.com/content/agents-say-jfk-assassination-transformed-secret-service/1793565.html. Accessed April 13, 2015.

"Gov. Brown Signs Bills Tightening 2 Gun Laws." 1975. *The New York Times.* September 24. http://query.nytimes.com/mem/archive/pdf?res=F40F1EFF3B5D137B93C6AB1782D85F418785F9. Accessed April 13, 2015.

McKinley, J.C. 2009. "Woman Who Tried to Kill Ford in '75 Is Paroled." *The New York Times.* August 4. http://www.nytimes.com/2009/08/15/us/15release.html. Accessed April 13, 2015.

Seelye, Katharine Q. 2009. "One of Two Women Who Tried to Kill Gerald Ford Explains Why." *The New York Times.* March 28. http://thelede.blogs.nytimes.com/2009/05/28/one-of-two-women-who-tried-to-kill-gerald-ford-explains-why/. Accessed April 13, 2015.

Fort Hood Shooting (2009). *See* Hasan, Nidal Malik (1970–)

Foster, Vince, Death of (1993)

The death of deputy White House counsel Vince Foster in 1993 shocked many inside Washington, D.C. and sparked scores of conspiracy theories regarding the cause of his death and the involvement of President Clinton and First Lady Hillary Rodham Clinton. Numerous investigations followed, including ones by the U.S. Park Police, the Federal Bureau of Investigation (FBI), both houses of Congress, and two different independent counsels, and each investigation concluded that Foster had committed suicide after suffering from intense stress and depression. Foster had been a lifelong friend of Bill Clinton and was the former law partner of Hillary Rodham Clinton. He had followed the Clintons to the nation's capital following President Clinton's 1992 election but within months, Foster's body was found in a suburban Virginia park with a gunshot to his head.

Born on January 15, 1945, Vince Walker Foster Jr. was in the same kindergarten class as Bill Clinton and future White House chief of staff Mack McLarty. Foster attended Hope High School and Davidson College where he obtained a B.S. in psychology. Foster then attended Vanderbilt Law School but soon joined the Arkansas National Guard during the Vietnam War and transferred to the University of Arkansas Law School so that he could continue his National Guard training. Foster was a standout in law school and served as the managing editor of *The Arkansas Law Review* and graduated first in his class. Following graduation, Foster obtained the highest score on the Arkansas bar exam.

Foster joined the Rose Law Firm, and was named a partner in the firm after just three years. Foster met Hillary Rodham Clinton, who had just married Bill Clinton. At Foster's suggestion, the Rose Law Firm hired Hillary Rodham Clinton and Foster and the future first lady, senator, and secretary of state became fast friends.

Following Bill Clinton's election to the presidency in 1992, Foster was asked to join the administration as a deputy White House counsel. Foster's responsibilities included assisting in the selection and vetting for the president's nominees for attorney general of the United States and justices to the U.S. Supreme Court. Foster and the White House ran into early trouble with several nominees, including two proposed attorney generals, when it was discovered that they had hired undocumented aliens as house workers. Controversy continued for Foster and the White House after seven staffers in the White House Travel Office were fired. Critics claimed that the firings were executed for purpose of making room for friends and confidants of the Clintons.

Foster was also responsible for managing the White House response to the emerging Whitewater scandal, which included an investigation into a failed savings and loan bank in Little Rock, Arkansas, that had been operated by James and Susan McDougal, friends of the Clintons. Foster was personally cited and attacked by the press for his role in these scandals.

Following his death, a note was found in Foster's briefcase, which read, "I was not meant for the job or the spotlight of public life in Washington. Here ruining people is considered sport" (Hamilton 2007, 153). In the same note, Foster wrote: "The WSJ editors lie without consequence" (Hamilton 2007, 153).

In the days before his death, Foster had placed a call to his sister and confessed that he was depressed. After she provided him with the names of three psychiatrists, Foster contacted a family doctor and sought and obtained a prescription for depression.

On July 20, 1993—which was precisely six months after Clinton's inauguration—Foster's body was found by a private citizen around 6:00 p.m. in dense foliage in Fort Marcy Park in nearby Virginia. The private citizen who had found Foster's body reported that he had not seen a gun in Foster's hand but several of the initial responders stated that Foster was found with a .38 caliber pistol in his right hand and his right thumb was trapped in the trigger guard. Investigation later revealed gunshot residue-like material on Foster's right hand. There were no eye witnesses to Foster's death and Foster left no suicide note. Investigators determined that there were no signs of a struggle. Investigators determined that Foster had suffered a gunshot wound through the back of his mouth that exited through the back of his head. Despite numerous searches, the fatal gun could not be found and investigators could not locate any fingerprints on the gun. Investigators concluded that the gun used by Foster had originally belonged to Foster's father and had been passed down to Foster by Foster's mother. Foster's wife and children, in addition to one of Foster's sisters, had difficulty positively identifying the weapon. There were conflicting reports regarding whether a briefcase was inside Foster's car at the scene of his death.

Foster's death spurred numerous rumors and conspiracy theories, many of which were reported upon and investigated by the national and local press. Foremost among the claims was the suggestion that Foster had been murdered and his body had been moved to the park. These theories were premised on the notion that Foster was engaged in an affair with Hillary Rodham Clinton or that his death was part of an effort to cover up aspects of the Whitewater investigation. These suspicions gained steam after numerous Whitewater documents—which had been in the possession of the U.S. Department of Justice—were found in Foster's White House office following his death.

The "Whitewater" Tangle

"Whitewater," as it became known, was a controversy involving the Clintons and their prior real-estate dealings in Arkansas. In 1978, the Clintons joined their friends, Jim and Susan McDougal, in a real-estate endeavor, and, after combining to borrow a little over $200,000, the group formed the Whitewater Development Corporation, and purchased 230 acres of land. The venture was ultimately unsuccessful and the Clintons lost tens of thousands of dollars in the investment. More importantly, Jim McDougal became entrenched in a subsequent fraudulent real-estate venture and used Hillary Rodham-Clinton's law firm for legal advice. This investment ultimately cost the United States $73 million. Years of investigation followed, ultimately resulting in 15 convictions, the McDougals' imprisonment, the investigation of the president by Kenneth Starr, and Clinton's eventual impeachment by the House of Representatives.

There were numerous investigations of Foster's death. The U.S. Park Police (with the FBI's assistance) initially investigated the death. The Department of Justice opened its own investigation after the discovery of the note in Foster's briefcase. On August 10, 1993, the DOJ, FBI, and the Park Police jointly announced that they had concluded that Foster had committed suicide.

Due to growing calls for an independent investigation, President Clinton asked Attorney General Janet Reno to appoint an independent counsel. On January 20, 1994, Reno appointed Robert B. Fiske Jr. to conduct an investigation. In June 1994, Fiske concluded that the "overwhelming weight of the evidence compels the conclusion . . . that Vincent Foster committed suicide" (Foster Report, Part II (B)).

Congressional Republicans similarly began their own investigations, in both the Senate and the House of Representatives but again reached the same conclusion, with a House committee stating that the facts led to the "undeniable conclusion" that Foster's death had been a suicide (Foster Report, Part 2 (C), 1997).

Despite these findings, Kenneth Starr was appointed as another independent counsel in August 1994 and was tasked with examining, among other things, the Whitewater deal and Foster's death. Starr retained and utilized a number of experts, including a forensic pathologist, an expert in physical evidence, and a suicideologist, each of which concluded that Foster had committed suicide. Starr's team noted in its final report that the absence of a suicide note was not unusual and that the lack of fingerprints on the gun was not extraordinary given the texture of the gun handle. Despite the consistent findings of investigators, critics of the Clintons and conspiracy theorists maintained the belief that Foster's death was due to foul play. At the very least, Foster's death represented one of the low points of the Clinton presidency.

MICHELE BISACCIA MEITL

See also: Clinton, Bill, Impeachment Trial of (1999); Levy, Chandra, Disappearance of (2001–2002); Watergate Scandal (1972–1974)

Further Reading

Boyer, Peter J. 1995. "Life after Vince." *The New Yorker*. September 11, pp. 54–59.

Hamilton, N. 2007. *Bill Clinton: Mastering the Presidency*. New York: Public Affairs.

Labaton, Stephen. 1997. "A Report on His Suicide Portrays A Deeply Troubled Vince Foster." *New York Times*. http://www.nytimes.com/1997/10/11/us/a-report-on-his-suicide-portrays-a-deeply-troubled-vince-foster.html. Accessed January 20, 2015.

Office of the Independent Counsel. 1997. "Report on the Death of Vincent W. Foster, Jr." (Foster Report). *Washington Post*. October 11.

Frank, Leo (1884–1915)

Leo Frank was born on April 17, 1884, in Cuero, Texas. Soon after his birth, his parents relocated to Brooklyn,

New York. Leo Frank attended New York Public Schools for much of his life before graduating from the Pratt Institute in 1902. He went on to receive a degree in mechanical engineering from Cornell University. After graduation, Frank was invited to Atlanta to interview for a position with the National Pencil Company, in which his uncle was a major shareholder. Frank was offered the job, but before starting his employment at the National Pencil Company, Frank traveled to Germany to study pencil manufacturing. In 1908, Frank completed his nine-month apprenticeship, and returned to the United States to begin his career. Less than a month later, Leo Frank was named the superintendent of the factory.

Living in Atlanta, Frank became very involved in his Jewish faith. At the time, Georgia had the largest Jewish population of all the Southern states. In 1912, Frank was elected president of a local Jewish fraternal organization. Frank also married Lucille Selig, who came from a prominent Jewish family in the Atlanta area. Together, they enjoyed a rather upscale lifestyle.

Portrait of Leo Frank from about 1910. Frank was convicted of murder and later killed by a lynch mob. (Library of Congress)

On April 26, 1913, Mary Phagan (1899–1913) went to the National Pencil Company factory to pick up her pay from Frank. Phagan had been laid off earlier that week due to a shortage of supplies needed to do her job. In the early morning hours of April 27, the night watchman, Newt Lee, made his way down to the basement to use the bathroom. When Lee arrived in the basement, he discovered the body of a young girl. The girl was found in the basement next to an incinerator with her dress at her waist, a part of her coat wrapped around her neck, and visible bruises and scratches on her face, head, and neck. Police later identified the dead girl as Mary Phagan.

Upon further investigation, police found bloody fingerprints on the basement door and a pipe just outside the door that they believed was used to break into the building. Additionally, police found two notes next to Phagan's body. The evidence led police to their first suspect—Newt Lee. The police arrested both Lee and a friend of Phagan's for her murder. When questioned, Lee told police that he attempted to call Frank after he found the body in the basement, but he did not answer. As police gathered additional evidence from the crime scene, and spoke with both suspects, they soon determined that Lee and Phagan's friend were not the murderers.

Acting on a tip from E.F. Holloway, the factory day watchman, in which he claimed to have witnessed Jim Conley, the janitor at the factory, washing a shirt that was covered in blood, police arrested Conley for the murder of Phagan. Conley told police that he was out drinking and gambling the day of the murder. Further, Conley told police that he could not read or write, suggesting that he could not have written the letters left at the crime scene. Subsequently, police found that he could read and write, and was asked to write a portion of the letter. There were clear similarities between the letter found at the crime scene and those written by Conley. He later told police that he met with Leo Frank that day and was told to write the letters.

In late May, Conley changed his story, telling police that he did not meet with Frank the day of the murder, but rather the day after. Additionally, he told police that Frank dictated what to write in the letters. Police arranged a meeting between Frank and Conley in an effort to determine the truth. Frank declined to meet because his attorney was out of town. The next day, Conley made yet another statement to police. He told them that Frank stated he had picked up the girl and she fell and hit her head. Further, Conley said they took the girl to the basement using the elevator and then returned to Frank's office where he dictated the letters. He also stated that Frank promised him $200 on Monday if he was not caught.

Later that month, a grand jury returned an indictment against Frank and the trial began soon after. Hundreds of spectators filled the court room, with hundreds more outside the courthouse. The prosecution team presented a case based on Conley's last statement, which was that Frank murdered Phagan, and told Conley what to write in the letters. Conversely, the defense team stated that Conley was the murderer, wrote the notes himself, and fabricated evidence to frame Frank. On August 25, 1913, Frank was convicted of murder. Crowds that had gathered at the courthouse began to chant "hang the Jew." Frank appealed the verdict to the Georgia Supreme Court, but it was denied. He also sought a writ of habeas corpus to the U.S. Supreme Court and was again denied.

The following year, Conley's attorney publicly stated that he believed his client to be the real murderer. Frank's lawyers filed a writ of error, which allowed Frank to again appeal his case to the U.S. Supreme Court. The Court agreed to hear the case, and ruled 7-to-2 in favor of the state. Having exhausted all of his appeals, Frank requested that the Georgia State Prison Commission commute his sentence to life in prison. The commission voted 2-to-1 denying Frank's petition. The commission's report was submitted to Governor John Slaton. Slaton reviewed all of the documentation from the trial, as well as new evidence that had been discovered after the trial, and in June 1915, five days before Slaton was to leave office, and one day before Frank would have been executed, commuted his sentence to life in prison.

Frank was taken to a medium-security work farm to serve his life sentence. Within a few days, an inmate attempted to slash Frank's throat, but was unsuccessful. It was not long after this attempted murder that a group of prominent men, known as the Knights of Mary Phagan, publicly stated that they planned to kidnap Frank from prison. On August 16, the group traveled to the facility and kidnapped Frank. He was taken to a site not far from where Phagan lived, and was lynched. Hundreds of people gathered at the site to take pictures and collect souvenirs. After the lynching, approximately 1,500 Jewish Americans left the Atlanta area.

Almost 70 years later, Alonzo Mann, Frank's office boy at the time of the murder, told a journalist that he had seen Conley in the factory the night of the murder alone carrying Phagan's body toward the basement. Mann's statement

was the basis for a petition to the Georgia State Board of Pardons and Paroles to exonerate Frank. After reviewing the case, the board ruled that there was not sufficient evidence to pardon Frank. A second petition was submitted in 1986, in which the board recognized the state's culpability in Frank's death, but did not indicate Frank's innocence.

JOSEPH M. McKENNA

See also: Jena Six (Jena, LA) (2006); Sheppard, Sam (1923–1970)

Further Reading

Alphin, Elaine. 2010. *An Unspeakable Crime: The Prosecution and Persecution of Leo Frank*. Minneapolis, MN: Lerner Publishing Group.

Dinnerstein, Leonard. 2008. *The Leo Frank Case*. Athens: University of Georgia Press.

Oney, Steve. *And The Dead Shall Rise: The Murder of Mary Phagan and the Lynching of Leo Frank*. New York: Pantheon Books.

Franklin, Joseph Paul (1950–2013)

Joseph Paul Franklin was an American serial killer who was convicted of eight murders and confessed to several more. Dr. Dorothy Lewis, a New York psychiatrist and one of the country's foremost experts on the murderous mind, recently diagnosed Franklin as "a chronically paranoid schizophrenic person who suffers psychotic behaviors such as blasphemous thoughts, auditory hallucinations, and delusional beliefs (such as the belief that he is a Nazi and a Jew)" (Terry, November 19, 2013). Experts speculate that his actions stemmed from his early childhood, books, and white supremacist organizations. Franklin's father constantly beat him as a young boy, and his mother verbally and physically abused him. The abuse stunted Franklin's social growth and mental development by 10 to 15 years. He lived in Mobile, Alabama, during the 1950s and 1960s where the Southern perception of African Americans permeated his thought process; coupled with pictures of his mom's family in Germany during World War II bearing swastikas and involved in Hitler's youth movement, Franklin conformed to the notion of white supremacy over blacks and Jews. After reading *Mein Kampf*, he became obsessed with Hitler and declared himself as a racist and anti-Semite targeting Jews, blacks, and interracial couples. As a young adult, he joined the American Nazi Party, the National States Rights Party, and the Ku Klux Klan but became an extremist individual force due to his desire for physical action against "subhumans," not just derogatory thought and speeches. His killing spree lasted from 1977 to 1980 and spanned multiple counties. He was convicted of killing eight people but claimed responsibility for 20 murders. He was executed by lethal injection on November 20, 2013 in Missouri after conflicts involving an appropriate lethal drug.

In 1976, Franklin changed his name from James Clayton Vaughn Jr. to Joseph Paul Franklin after Paul Joseph, Hitler's minister of propaganda, and Benjamin Franklin. He heard inner thoughts and dreams ordering him to kill Jews and African Americans. In 1977, Franklin bombed the home of Morris Amitay, a Jewish lobbyist, in Maryland and the Beth Sholom synagogue in Chattanooga, Tennessee. In Madison, Wisconsin, while waiting for an opportune time to kill Judge Archie Simonson, Franklin encountered an interracial couple in a mall parking lot; after a heated argument, Franklin killed Alphonse Manning Jr., a 23-year-old black, and Toni Schwenn, a 23-year-old white. In Richmond Heights, Montana, Franklin fired five shots into a parking lot at the Brith Sholom Kneseth Israel congregation synagogue. He killed Gerald Gordon, 42, and wounded two others. In 1978, Franklin killed Johnny Brookshire, a 23-year-old black, and wounded his wife Joy Williams, a 23-year-old white, in Atlanta, Georgia. In Lawrenceville, Georgia, Franklin shot Larry Flynt, the publisher of "Hustler" magazine, after he published a photo shoot featuring a black man and white woman together. Flynt survived the shot but was paralyzed from the waist down. In Chattanooga, Tennessee, Franklin shot at an interracial couple in a parking lot, killing William Bryant Tatum, a black man, and wounding his white girlfriend Nancy Hilton, 18. In 1979, Franklin shot Harol McIver, a 29-year-old black, in Georgia; Raymond Taylor, a 28-year-old black, in Virginia; Jesse E. Taylor, a 42-year-old black, and Marion Bresette, a 31-year-old white, in Oklahoma City; and Mercedes Lynn Master, a 15-year-old prostitute who serviced black men. In 1980, Franklin shot Lawrence E. Reese and Leo Thomas, both African Americans, in Indianapolis; and Rebecca Bergstrom, a 20-year-old white, in Wisconsin. He targeted Reverend Jesse Jackson in Chicago but was spooked away by the police; he immediately drove to Fort Wayne, Indiana, and wounded Vernon E. Jordan Jr., president of the National Urban League and advisor to President Bill Clinton, to gain national fame. In Cincinnati, Ohio, Franklin shot Darrell Lane, 14, and Dante Evans Brown, 13, two black cousins. In Johnstown, Pennsylvania, Arthur Smothers, a 22-year-old black, and Kathleen Mikula, a 16-year-old white, were fatally shot; in Virginia,

Nancy Santomero, a 19-year-old white, and Vickie Durian, a 26-year-old white, were also fatally shot after one admitted to having a black boyfriend. In Salt Lake City, Utah, Franklin noticed two black men, Ted Fields and David Martin, running with two white teenage girls, Terry Elrod and Karma Ingersoll; he hid in a vacant lot and fatally shot Martin and Fields. On September 25, 1980, Franklin was arrested for car theft in Kentucky but escaped from jail five hours later. His escape started a nationwide manhunt and forced state agencies to collaborate on high-profile sniper shootings.

In October 1980, Franklin was caught by the FBI and indicted by a federal jury for violating the civil rights of Fields and Martin. In early November, the jury charged Franklin for first-degree murder in the deaths of Fields and Martin. In March 1980, Franklin was charged with murder in Oklahoma, Indiana, and Utah and received multiple life sentences. Three days after arriving in federal prison in Marion, Illinois, black inmates stabbed Franklin 15 times; he was permanently placed in solitary confinement. In 1984, Franklin confessed to his synagogue bombings in Tennessee to be transported to another federal prison. In 1995, Franklin confessed to his murders in Chattanooga, Tennessee, and Richmond Height, Virginia, claiming a dream told him to confess to these murders. On February 27, 1997, Franklin received the death penalty in Missouri for killing Gerald Gordon. Franklin was convicted of only eight murders: Manning and Schwenn in Wisconsin, Tatum in Tennessee, Lane and Brown in Ohio, Fields and Martin in Utah, and Gordon in Missouri. He received life sentences for seven convictions and the death penalty in Missouri. He was charged for several other murders and attempted murders but was either acquitted of these murders or the cases against him were dropped.

In past lethal injections, Missouri used a three-drug injection method in executions but was forced to change methods when drug makers stopped selling the drugs to correction institutions and prisons. Missouri switched its execution drug to propofol; however, Governor Jay Nixon eventually banned its use in capital punishment cases due to public outcry. The corrections department chose pentobarbital as its form of lethal injection in executions shortly before Franklin's execution date. This decision led to three separate appeals by Franklin's lawyer: Franklin is mentally ill and his life should be spared, claiming faulty instruction by the jury regarding the death penalty, and concerns about Missouri's first use of pentobarbital. Flynt publicly spoke against capital punishment as a form of justice and collaborated with the American Civil Liberties Union in court to stop Franklin's execution. Two district judges granted Franklin two separate stays of execution regarding the risk of using pentobarbital, which were appealed by the state of Missouri to the 8th U.S. Circuit Court of Appeals. The court overturned the granted stays, leading Franklin to appeal to the Supreme Court. The Supreme Court refused to hear Franklin's claims, sealing his fate. After a six-hour delay, Franklin was executed on November 20, 2013.

LAUREN PARKER

See also: Byrd, James, Jr., Murder of (1998); Ku Klux Klan (1866–); Till, Emmet, Murder of (1955); Washington, D.C., Area Snipers (October 2–24, 2002)

Further Reading

Adams, Brooke. 2013. "Joseph Paul Franklin Timeline." *The Salt Lake Tribune.* November 20.

Ayton, Mel. 2011. *Dark Soul of the South: The Life and Crimes of Racist Killer Joseph Paul Franklin.* Washington, DC: Potomac Books Inc.

Ayton, Mel. 2011. "How Hate Groups Influenced Racist Killer Joseph Paul Franklin." *History News Network.* http://historynewsnetwork.org/article/139368. Accessed April 16, 2015.

Jett, Tyler. 2013. "Interview with a Serial Killer: Joseph Paul Franklin." *Times Free Press.* November 19.

"Joseph Paul Franklin a/k/a James Clayton Vaughn, Jr." 2013. *Clark Prosecutor.* November 20.

Terry, Don. 2013a. "As Execution Approaches, Racist Serial Killer Joseph Franklin is Philosophical." *Southern Poverty Law Center.* November 19.

Terry, Don. 2013b. "Hatewatch Exclusive: Racist Serial Killer, Facing Death, Recants." *Southern Poverty Law Center.* October 17.

Fromme, Lynette "Squeaky" (1948–)

As a devoted member to the Manson Family, Lynette (known as "Squeaky" due to her voice) Fromme continued to memorialize her undying love to Charlie while he was in prison. Squeaky set out in an attempt to assassinate President Ford on September 5, 1975, showing allegiance to Manson. Fromme's case is significant because the power of mind control over an individual provided motive for criminal behavior and the constant aim to please Manson after his conviction. After imprisonment in various federal correctional facilities and one federal medical center, Squeaky was released on parole in August 2009. Reports indicated she moved to Marcy, New York. According to the U.S. Parole Commission, Fromme was to have supervised release

for two years and required to meet with her parole officer on a regular basis. Local residents of Marcy interviewed about the possibility of Fromme living in their community did not show signs of fear as most recognized her crime was 34 years prior. While Marcy, New York, was mentioned, Fromme's exact whereabouts are unknown today.

Fromme was born on October 22, 1948, in Santa Monica, California, to William, an aeronautical engineer, and Helen, a homemaker. Involved in dancing as a child, she appeared to have what is typically viewed as a normal family life. In 1963, her family moved to Redondo Beach, California, where in high school, Fromme began drinking and taking drugs, yet graduated from Redondo Union High School in 1966. During a brief attendance at El Camino Junior College, an argument with her father led to leaving her home and moving to Venice Beach, California, in 1967. Meeting Manson along with intrigue from his philosophies, they became friends and Fromme moved to Spahn Ranch where the Manson Family was born.

As a disciple of Manson's teachings, Fromme and other family followers attended the trials of Manson, Susan Atkins, Patricia Krenwinkel, Leslie Van Houten, and Charles "Tex" Watson. Squeaky was never implicated in the murders of Sharon Tate and her houseguests or the La Biancas. Carving an X in her forehead and preaching Manson's apocalyptic philosophies to the media, Fromme was convicted of attempt to prevent imprisoned followers from testifying as well as contempt of court for refusal to testify in the trials. Short jail sentences were served for both offenses and Squeaky moved to Sacramento, California, with another follower Sandra Good to be closer to Manson who was serving time in Folsom prison; however, little did they know Manson was soon to be transferred to San Quentin.

On the morning of September 5, 1975, dressed in a red robe and armed with a .45-caliber pistol, Fromme pushed through a crowd toward President Gerald Ford who was greeting individuals before walking into the California State Capitol building in Sacramento. President Ford noticed the colorful outfit and assumed the young woman wanted to shake his hand like other well-wishers. As President Ford turned toward Squeaky, she grabbed the gun in her thigh holster and aimed at him. Fromme was immediately grabbed and wrestled to the ground by Secret Service agents who removed the gun from her hand. President Ford was not harmed. As she was being taken into custody, Fromme complained about her gun not firing and also asked the Secret Service agent who tackled her down why he was protecting someone who was not a public

Escorted by a U.S. Marshal, Lynette "Squeaky" Fromme returned to federal court in Sacramento, California, on October 16, 1975, for a closed-door hearing. The hearing was to determine whether a movie showing Fromme discussing the use of firearms could be used as evidence in her trial for the attempted assassination of President Gerald Ford. (AP Photo/Walt Zeboski)

servant. After a search of Fromme's house and an interview with Sandra who claimed no knowledge of the assassination attempt, authorities found this was supposed to be a "wake-up" call about pollution. According to Fromme, she knew President Ford was in town and wanted to speak with him then realized he would not talk to her; therefore, she decided to take the gun. Squeaky never thought she would end up in prison; however, Fromme mentioned she never had any regrets about the incident.

Stop the Presses! A Change in Legislation

In 1984, the Sentencing Reform Act was passed changing legislation for federal criminals with charges ranging from murder to attempted assassination of a president. The legislation was developed as a way to provide a new sentencing structure for individuals found guilty of a federal offense. This legislation abolished parole for a federal crime, although individuals may petition for a reduction in sentence. There must be an extraordinary circumstance in order to examine such petitions and a reduction in sentence may be applied. The court is allowed to include a period of supervised release if deemed necessary. For each case, federal judges are urged to consider the nature of the offense as well as criminal history, appropriate sanctions for those convicted of violent or more serious offenses, and any alternatives to imprisonment. This act, however, was not retroactive; thus Squeaky was able to make parole.

During Fromme's trial, she refused to attend most days and when she was present, frequent outbursts would occur.

John Virga, appointed to defend Fromme, argued her intent was not to shoot President Ford but to raise awareness to environmental issues and Manson's case. After examination of the gun, a few bullets were found, but not located in the chamber. Squeaky, however, was convicted of life imprisonment under the 1965 Federal Act created after President Kennedy's assassination. This act made attempted presidential assassinations a federal crime where sanctions involved a maximum sentence of life in a prison. Thirty years was considered a life sentence and prisoners could be paroled after they have served this time as long as a record of good behavior was proven.

Fromme was originally sentenced to Federal Prison Camp Alderson in West Virginia. After prison officials declared her as a model inmate, Squeaky was transferred to Federal Correctional Institution, Dublin in California in 1978. In 1979, Squeaky and another inmate were tending a garden on prison grounds. Fromme attacked the other inmate with a hammer and was transferred back to Federal Prison Camp Alderson in West Virginia. On December 23, 1987, Squeaky escaped from Federal Prison Camp Alderson in West Virginia after hearing Manson had testicular cancer, a claim that was later refuted. Fromme was captured on December 25, 1987, and moved to facilities in Kentucky and Florida before landing at Federal Medical Center, Carswell in Fort Worth, Texas, in 1998 to serve out her sentence. This facility was designed to provide medical and mental health services to female inmates. Maximum- and minimum-security units, as well as a unit for low-security inmates, are all located in this institution. It is unclear whether Fromme was deemed as an inmate needing the special services. In past press releases, the public was informed that Squeaky was placed in the maximum-security unit reserved for inmates involved in assaults or who have escaped previously.

In July 2008, Lynette Squeaky Fromme was granted parole for good time, but was not released from the Federal Medical Center, Carswell, until August 2009. This was due to additional time for the prison escape in 1987. Although her whereabouts are unknown and her name has not been in the press since her release, one question remains: Is Squeaky Fromme still a devout follower of Charles Manson and his philosophies? If the answer is yes, we may not have seen the last of Lynette Squeaky Fromme.

STACIE MERKEN

See also: Ford, Gerald, Assassination Attempts on (1975); Kennedy, John F., Assassination of (November 22, 1963); Kennedy,

Robert F. "Bobby," Assassination of (1968); King, Martin Luther, Jr., Assassination of (April 4, 1968); Manson, Charles (1934–)

Further Reading

Brown, Angela K. 2009. "Squeaky Fromme, Would-Be Ford Assassin, Released From Prison." *The Huffington Post.* August 14. http://www.huffingtonpost.com/2009/08/14/squeaky-fromme-would-be-f_n_259681.html. Accessed April 14, 2015.

Guinn, Jeff. 2013. *Manson: The Life and Times of Charles Manson.* New York: Simon & Schuster.

Hayes, Ashley. 2009. "After 34 Years, Lynette 'Squeaky' Fromme to Be Released." CNN. August 5. http://www.cnn.com/2009/CRIME/08/05/squeaky.fromme.release/. Accessed April 15, 2015.

Internet Archive Wayback Machine. 2000. "Lynette "Squeaky" Fromme." http://web.archive.org/web/20060708104703/http://www.squeakyfromme.org/index.html. Accessed April 13, 2015.

"Manson Follower 'Squeaky' Moving to Upstate NY." 2009. *The Huffington Post.* http://www.huffingtonpost.com/huff-wires/20090915/us-manson-follower-ford/. Accessed April 14, 2015.

Fugate, Caril Ann. *See* Starkweather, Charles, and Caril Ann Fugate, Murder Spree of (1957)

Fugitive Slave Laws (1793, 1850)

One of the inherent difficulties in the practice of slavery in America was the fact that not every state was a slave state. Slaves would often flee from slave states in the South to free states in the North. Often, Northern states were hesitant to send slaves back into bondage, preferring instead to give them shelter. This created significant tension. In an attempt to deal with this issue, Congress passed a series of fugitive slave acts; the first in 1793, the second, and more significant, in 1850. In response, free states passed a series of "Personal Liberty" laws to make it more difficult for anyone to actually enforce these fugitive slave laws. The Fugitive Slave Act of 1850 in particular made nonslave states feel more and more as though the power of slavery was growing. The Dred Scott decision handed down only a few years later reinforced this fear. The Fugitive Slave Act of 1850 become a touchstone that called into question the

Supremacy Clause of the Constitution, the ability of Congress to dictate legal process to the states, and, ultimately, was yet another grievance between slave and free states that led to the Civil War.

Fugitive slave laws in the United States have their roots in the 1600s. In 1643, the short-lived alliance between Massachusetts, Plymouth, New Haven, and Connecticut known as the "New England Confederation" passed a law providing for the return of slaves among those colonies. However, it was not until well over 100 years later that fugitive slave laws would become a major issue in America. And the reason it became an issue was a ruling by an English court.

In 1772, Lord Mansfield heard the case of *Somerset v. Stewart,* wherein a slave brought to England from Virginia sued for his freedom. Lord Mansfield ordered that this slave, Somerset, was a free man the moment he stepped onto English soil. Avid legal readers, American colonists were well aware of the ruling. But its effect on America was not entirely clear.

After the United States won its independence from Britain, Southern slaveowners demanded protections from the results of the *Somerset* decision. The result was the so-called fugitive slave clause of Article IV, Section 2, in the U.S. Constitution, which states that "[n]o person held to service or labour in one state, under the laws thereof, escaping into another, shall, in consequence of any law or regulation therein, be discharged from such service or labour, but shall be delivered up on claim of the party to whom such service or labour may be due."

In 1793, Congress passed the first Fugitive Slave Act. Section 3 stated that a person accused of being a slave could be brought into court and, "upon proof … before any Judge," would be sent back to their master. An inherent problem noted by contemporary attorneys was the fact that "upon proof" does not establish what the burden of proof on the person seeking to have another person declared a slave was. Read literally, it seemed to indicate that only "proof" was required. Because of this, courts went on to hold that only the testimony of a witness was required; this is a very low burden of proof. The act also made it a crime to help a runaway slave. States fought back almost immediately.

Free states began passing Personal Liberty laws to fight back against the Fugitive Slave Act of 1793. The purpose of these laws was not to attempt to nullify the Fugitive Slave Act; a state cannot pass a law that nullifies a federal law. However, these laws instead attempted to make enforcement of the Fugitive Slave Act such a practical hassle that law enforcement would simply refuse to get involved.

A good example is the Pennsylvania Personal Liberty Law of 1826. For starters, this law made it a felony to seize an African by force. This carried a fine of up to $2,000 and a prison sentence of at least seven years. To reclaim a runaway slave in Pennsylvania, the slaveowner had to apply for a warrant from a state official who would then authorize the local sheriff to seize the slave. The warrant itself could be obtained only if the owner provided a sworn affidavit authenticated by a judge in the state where the owner and the slave in question were from. Once seized by the sheriff, the owner had to prove to court that the owner was actually a slave belonging to the owner under the laws of the state from which the slave fled. Critically, to ensure jury trials for the accused slave, the Pennsylvania law specifically removed jurisdiction from aldermen and justices of the peace. Only a jury could declare someone a fugitive slave.

Of course, the result of these laws was a steep decline in enforcement. Slave states complained bitterly that free states were not executing the laws. Eventually, the Supreme Court got involved in the case of *Prigg v. Pennsylvania,* decided in 1842. In *Prigg,* the Court overturned the Pennsylvania Personal Liberty Law as unconstitutional, ruling that the states could not do what amounted to adding extra regulations to a federal law. However, Justice Story also stated in the opinion that "the states cannot be compelled to enforce [the Fugitive Slave Act of 1793]; and it might well be deemed an unconstitutional exercise of the power of interpretation, to insist that the states are bound to provide means to carry into effect the duties of the national government." This yielded an interesting result: free states could now simply cease lending any support to slaveowners attempting to track down runaways and have them returned.

The response was predictable. Many free states passed laws forbidding state officials from aiding in the enforcement of the Fugitive Slave Act. An 1843 Massachusetts law provided that "no judge of any court of record of Massachusetts, and no justice of the peace, shall hereafter take cognizance or grant a certificate" in and fugitive slave case, and that "no sheriff, deputy-sheriff . . . or other officer of Massachusetts, shall hereafter arrest or detain, or aid in the arrest or detention or imprisonment in any jail . . . of any person for the reason that he is claimed as a fugitive slave." Connecticut, Massachusetts, Ohio, Pennsylvania, Rhode Island, and Vermont quickly followed suit, passing laws forbidding state officials from aiding in the return of any fugitive slave. Accused fugitive slaves could not even be held in state owned jails.

This made the act, once again, practically unenforceable. In response, Congress, with a coalition of Southerners and Northern Democrats, passed the Fugitive Slave Act of 1850, as part of the Compromise of 1850. This act greatly strengthened the ability of a slave owner to reclaim a slave. This act provided for several grossly offensive measures to the citizens of free states. For example, "commissioners" were appointed to deal with slave act cases. These commissioners would function as judge and jury. The accused fugitive slave was also not allowed to testify. Of 332 accused slaves brought before these commissioners, only 11 were declared free (Campbell 1970). But of all the provisions of the 1850 act, the one that drew the most virulent anger from free states was the provision requiring all citizens to aid in the capture of a fugitive slave. Failure to do so could result in criminal charges.

Ultimately, the Fugitive Slave Act of 1850 backfired tremendously against the slave states. Northern citizens were enraged at the notion that refusal to join in a posse to hunt down a runaway slave could result in criminal process against them. Abolitionists were infuriated by the fact that an accused could not even testify solely because of their skin color. The act only galvanized those who were again slavery in the convictions that slavery was an abhorrent practice that needed to be stamped out.

JOHN FRIEND

See also: *Amistad* Slave Ship Case (1839); Dred Scott Decision (1857); Harpers Ferry (VA), Raid on (October 17, 1859); *Primary Documents*/Excerpts from Gerrit Smith's Arguments against the Constitutionality of the Fugitive Slave Law during the Trial of Marshal Henry W. Allen (1852)

Further Reading

Campbell, Stanley W. 1970. *The Slave Catchers: Enforcement of the Fugitive Slave Law 1850–1860.* Chapel Hill: The University of North Carolina Press.

Dattel, Gene. 2009. *Cotton and Race in the Making of America: The Human Costs of Economic Power.* Chicago: Ivan R. Dee.

Delombard, Jeannine Marie. 2007. *Slavery on Trial: Law, Abolitionism, and Print Culture.* Chapel Hill: The University of North Carolina Press.

Prigg v. Pennsylvania, 41 U.S. 539 (U.S. 1842).

G

Gacy, John Wayne (1942–1994)

On December 21, 1978, residents of Des Plaines, Illinois, a middle-class suburb of Chicago, became aware that a serial killer lived among them. After investigating a missing person's report, police searched the home of local businessman and political leader John Wayne Gacy and found human remains in the crawlspace under the house. Later that night Gacy confessed to killing many young men. In the ensuing days, local residents and media watched as police officers carried bags of human remains from the house and waited for the Cook County medical examiner to announce the daily body count. In total, police found the bodies of 27 young men under the house, 2 in other parts of the property, and 4 more along the Des Plaines River. From 1972 to 1978 Gacy murdered 33 known victims. Although the gravity of the offenses and the location of bodies shocked the public, Gacy's double life was equally disturbing. Those who knew Gacy described him as engaging and affable. He was an active volunteer in the community, entertained children by performing as a clown, and hosted large dinner parties in his home. How could a seemingly normal person be one of the worst serial killers in American history? Facing overwhelming evidence of his guilt, Gacy pled not guilty by reason of insanity. The jury found him guilty and sentenced him to death. He was executed in May 1994.

During the days leading to his arrest, John Wayne Gacy confessed to his lawyer and close associates that he killed over 30 people. He was equally talkative with police and even drew a diagram of where to find the bodies under the house. Gacy admitted to targeting attractive young males and luring them into the house with either the promise of a job or money in exchange for sex. He sometimes posed as a police officer or forced victims into his car at gunpoint. At his home Gacy tricked victims into wearing handcuffs. He then raped and gagged them before strangling them with a rope and tourniquet knot (*People v Gacy* 1984). He also targeted individuals with a history of problems, which caused police to assume that missing person reports were runaway rather than murder cases. However, his last victim, age 15, was an honor student and boy scout who had a good relationship with his family. Police instigated a full investigation after discovering that Gacy had been the last to see him alive. They arrested Gacy 10 days later.

Police learned more about Gacy's methods from individuals who survived assaults and could recount how he coerced them into sexual situations. In 1967 and 1968 Gacy spent 18 months in prison for sodomizing a teenage boy in Waterloo, Iowa. He lured the teenager into home, showed him pornographic films, got him drunk, and then engaged in oral sex with the boy. His pattern of behavior escalated after prison. He handcuffed, choked, and/or threatened to molest numerous individuals before and during his killing spree. One victim recalled being raped, strangled, immersed under water, urinated on, and having items inserted into his rectum. The victim passed out multiple times and awoke to Gacy repeating the abuse. Gacy then placed a gun to the man's head and played "Russian roulette," pulling the trigger many times before the gun went off; it fired a blank (*People vs. Gacy* 1984). Gacy eventually released the victim. There is no way to tell if all his murder victims suffered the same abuses, but such horror stories revealed much about Gacy during his crimes.

The contrast between Gacy's crimes and his normal public persona confused and disturbed the general public. National media interviewed Gacy's stunned friends and family who reported that he was ambitious, hardworking, likable, and even a loving father (see Kneeland 1979). Years after his trial, during a radio interview on *Chicago Live*, Gacy's attorney said, "The scariest thing about John Gacy was that he wasn't scary at all." The effort to reconcile this contradiction in Gacy's life led to a question that became the focus of Gacy's trial: Is he crazy or evil?

John Wayne Gacy pled not guilty by reason of insanity. During his trial, the defense relied on four psychiatrists and two psychologists to demonstrate that Gacy was insane at the time of his murders. They argued he suffered from "pseudo-neurotic paranoid schizophrenia," an illness that caused temporary psychosis so that Gacy had no awareness of or control over his actions. Although he was sane most of the time, stress triggered episodes in which Gacy projected how he felt about himself on his victims (*People v. Gacy* 1984). The boys represented what Gacy could never achieve in life (health and physical attractiveness), or he projected himself onto them and became his raging father during the murders. He was punishing himself when he abused and killed his victims. To support this theory, the defense provided evidence that Gacy's father publicly belittled and physically abused his son. Gacy's imprisonment for sodomy verified his status as a failure and made his efforts to please his father, who died while Gacy was in prison, impossible. The impossibility of redemption produced a mental state that allowed episodes of insanity to occur (*People v. Gacy* 1984).

Experts for the prosecution diagnosed Gacy as a narcissist with antisocial personality disorder; he demonstrated a lack of concern for others while pursuing power, control, and purely selfish endeavors. They argued he could function normally when it benefitted his business and social standing, but he was also capable of raping, torturing, and killing without concern for the victim if it pleased him. Gacy was a habitual liar and manipulator who took pleasure in tricking victims into handcuffs and enjoyed the power that followed. Prosecutors also noted

that Gacy's methods were well planned, thoughtful, and required a rational mind to complete. Victims who survived Gacy's attacks also described him as being calculating, in control, and aware of his actions during the abuse. The prosecution undermined defense experts' diagnoses as being heavily influenced by the assumptions of psychoanalytical theory and suitable as a method of treatment but not for diagnosis. The psychiatric community did not widely recognize "pseudo-neurotic paranoid schizophrenia" as a valid illness. Some of Gacy's behavior also did not fit with a diagnosis of schizophrenia. His general level of functioning was too high in his public and work life. He also lied on psychological tests to appear worse than what he actually was. This was more typical of a narcissist who is aware of and in control of his behavior (*People v. Gacy* 1984).

On May 12, 1980, after deliberating for less than two hours, the jury agreed with the prosecution and found John Wayne Gacy guilty on 33 murder charges. They sentenced him to death the following day. While on death row, Gacy agreed to television interviews whereby he maintained his innocence, blatantly lied about case facts, showed interviewers how to tie tourniquet knots, and insulted victims and their families. He was executed on May 9, 1994, by lethal injection. That night a large crowd gathered outside Stateville prison in Illinois. Most people had come to celebrate his execution.

TIMOTHY LAUGER

See also: Bundy, Ted (1946–1989); Dahmer, Jeffrey (1960–1994); Sowell, Anthony (1959–)

Further Reading

Kneeland, Douglas E. 1979. "Suspect in Mass Deaths Is Puzzle to All." *New York Times*. January 10, p. A-14.
People v. Gacy (1984). 103 Ill. 2d 1.

Gallaudet University Murders (2000–2001)

The Gallaudet University murders were the two murders that occurred on September 28, 2000, and February 4, 2001, in Cogswell Hall dorm rooms on the campus of Gallaudet University, a school traditionally attended by the deaf and hearing impaired, in Washington, D.C. On February 13, 2001, Joseph Mesa Jr., a fellow student who lived across the hall from the first victim, was arrested in connection with the murders. The crimes shocked the

Gallaudet community, who could not believe that one of their members committed the crimes.

On September 28, 2000, Eric Plunkett, 19, uncharacteristically did not show up for dinner. The resident living across the hall, Joseph Mesa Jr., told the resident assistant (RA) that Plunkett had not shown up for math class and that there was a strange smell emanating from the room (Fernandez 2001). Upon opening the door, the RA discovered that Plunkett had been beaten and killed. From the bruises on his neck, police determined that he had been beaten to death with a chair. Police later discovered that Plunkett had been placed in a chokehold and kicked several times in the head before being fatally assaulted (Tucker and Abraham 2002). Police initially investigated the crime as a possible hate crime because Plunkett was the secretary of a club for the gay community and had told other students he was gay (Fernandez 2001).

On Tuesday, October 3, 2000, police brought in Thomas Minch, 18, for questioning related to the murder. Minch, 18, a friend of Plunkett, admitted to arguing with Plunkett and physically striking him. At that point, the interrogator, Kyle Cimiotti, stopped the interview and arrested Minch for Plunkett's murder. However, Minch was released less than 24 hours later due to a lack of evidence. Even so, police continued to investigate Minch as the prime suspect in the case until the murder of Benjamin Varner in February. Minch was suspended from school and barred from returning while under suspicion. On February 2, 2001, Minch appeared before a grand jury to submit DNA and handwriting samples.

On February 3, 2001, a RA responding to a fire alarm going off found the body of Benjamin Varner, 19, stabbed to death and covered in blood in his dorm room in Cogswell Hall. Police would later determine that Varner had been stabbed at least 16 times, mainly in the face and throat. Officers determined that Varner had likely been dead for at least a day. At the scene, police found blood left by the killer in the struggle as well as bloody shoe prints. Just outside the hall, police found a bloody jacket and knife in a trash can. Crucially, the police officers also noticed that Varner's checkbook was missing. They obtained a bank's security video of an individual cashing a check for $650 using one of Varner's checks. The check had been made out to Joseph Mesa Jr. Police also searched Mesa's dorm room and discovered a pair of bloody shoes that matched the shoeprints found at the second murder scene. On February 13, 2001, Mesa walked into a campus security building and confessed to officers his involvement in both murders.

Mesa Jr., the only deaf member of his family, was born in San Francisco while his father lived in the military, and moved to Guam when he was two. Mesa was athletic while growing up, becoming the first deaf player in his football league and wrestling in high school. However, despite being generally well liked, he had an extensive history of thievery. As a sophomore in high school, Mesa stole $45 from the wallet of another student (Fernandez 2001). As a student in the college preparatory program run at Gallaudet University, Mesa stole an automated teller machine (ATM) card from his roommate and used it to steal $3,000 (Van Biema 2001). As a result, Mesa was suspended from school for a year and forced to pay back the money. When Mesa had alerted the RA of an unusual odor, leading to the discovery of Plunkett, police had failed to investigate his background or the fact that no unusual odor actually existed in Plunkett's room (*Mesa v. United States* 2005). Furthermore, for several weeks, police had failed to notice that Plunkett's wallet and credit cards were missing at the scene of the first murder. This fact may have implicated Mesa before the death of Varner (*Varner v. District of Columbia* 2006).

During Mesa's trial, the prosecution argued that he had methodically planned and conducted surveillance before each murder. By contrast, Mesa's attorney, Ferris R. Bond, pursued a mental illness defense. While Mesa had confessed to the murders in his February 13 police interview, Bond alleged that Mesa was driven to murder, not by voices in his head but by a pair of black-gloved hands that were directing Mesa to kill. Mesa described the visions as over-sized hands wearing black leather gloves, but otherwise unattached to any part of the body. The hands often held weapons and made either slashing or strangling motions, directing Mesa to kill people, including a vision that directed him to kill the lead prosecutor in the case. Mesa said the hands had been in his brain since he was 10 years old, which resulted in him slaughtering 10 cats at his home in Guam while the rest of his family was asleep. Finally, Mesa argued that he knew he was mentally ill and therefore tried to leave police officers clues to catch him. Mesa used this argument to explain why he had bought gifts for his family using the credit cards stolen from the Plunkett murder and why he had hidden his jacket and knife in such a conspicuous location after the Varner murder (Santana 2002).

On May 21, 2001, after only three hours of deliberation, the jury found Mesa Jr. guilty on two counts of first-degree murder and 13 other felony-related counts. Judge Robert

Richter sentenced Mesa to two life-without-parole prison terms. While Mesa Jr. expressed remorse for his crimes, psychiatrists who testified at the sentencing hearing declared that Mesa enjoyed the murders and exhibited a psychological profile similar to that of serial killers examined in an FBI study (Tucker and Ibrahim 2002). Mesa remains in prison to this day.

AARON SAFER-LICHTENSTEIN

See also: Dartmouth College Murders (January 27, 2001); Jovin, Suzanne, Murder of (1998); Le, Annie, Murder of (2009); Schwartz, Robert, Murder of (December 8, 2001)

Further Reading

Fernandez, Manny. 2001. "Four Lives Cross Tragically; Different Paths, One Bond Led Students to Gallaudet." *Washington Post.* March 4, p. A01.

Mesa v. United States, Supreme Court of the District of Columbia (2005).

Santana, Arthur. 2002. "Gallaudet Suspect Tormented by Visions; Mesa Tells of Hands Wearing Black Gloves That Twice Ordered Him to Kill." *Washington Post.* May 15, p. B02.

Santana, Arthur. 2002. "Jury Sees Confession in Gallaudet Slaying; Mesa Describes Stabbing in Police Video." *Washington Post.* May 7, p. B02.

Thompson, Cheryl W., and Manny Fernandez. 2001. "Clues Missed in 1st Slaying at Gallaudet; Missteps Took D.C. Police Further From Defendant." *Washington Post.* April 22, p. A01.

Tucker, Neely, and Alia Ibrahim. 2002. "Mesa Gets Life Terms in Gallaudet Slayings; No Parole in Two Students' Deaths, Judge Decides." *Washington Post.* July 11, p. B01.

Van Biema, David. 2001. "Murder in a Silent Place." *Time.* June 25, p. 157.

Varner v. District of Columbia, D.C. Appellate Court (2006).

Watson, Traci. 2001. "Gallaudet Reels at Arrest of 'One of Our Own' in Killings." *USA Today.* June 15, p. 4A.

Gamsky, Joe. *See* Hunt, Joe (1959–)

Garfield, James, Assassination of (July 2, 1881)

President James Garfield (1831–1881) was shot on July 2, 1881, but did not die for over two full months after being shot. The loss of a second commander in chief in just 16 years was something that held the United States in a two-month stasis. The killing of James A. Garfield was something atypical for murders of this high a profile. The

James A. Garfield, 20th president of the United States. Garfield only served seven months of his term before he was assassinated on July 2, 1881. He would die two months later on September 19. (Library of Congress)

instrument of death, Charles Guiteau (1841–1882), did not seek to reignite a war or topple some inconceivably large political engine. Instead of striving toward some perceived or imagined greater good, Guiteau felt wrongfully ignored for what he held to be a significant contribution to the election of Garfield to the office of the president (Clark 1993).

After a few short months into his presidency it seemed as though the country had chosen an effective, dedicated, and assertive man to lead. President Garfield appointed several African American candidates to federal positions, breaking barriers that had been holding the country back from some semblance of equality, he appointed a chief justice to the Supreme Court (Stanley Matthews), he fought to root out corruption in one of the largest government organizations at that time (The U.S. Post Office) and he pushed for improvements to the provision of civil rights and universal education to all Americans (Thayer 1881). He felt strongly that Southern resistance to the incorporation of freed slaves into American culture was entrenched in the systematic proliferation of illiteracy and exclusion from governmental operations.

Additionally, President Garfield laid the seeds for positive relations of American foreign policy, and aided in the formation of plans to improve and modernize the American Navy (though it was not until after his death that the real effect of his works could be reaped) (Thayer 1881). He did all of these things in a few short months in office. During this time he balanced his dedication to his office and the obligation he had to care for his ailing wife. Lucretia Garfield fought illness throughout the time, leading up to the shooting of the president. To aid in her care and condition she was moved out of the city of Washington D.C. (Clark 1993).

On June 18, 1881, the Garfields left Washington by way of train. Unbeknownst to the president, Guiteau was at the station that day with pistol in hand, but chose to abandon his efforts that day due to what he would later claim was the condition of Mrs. Garfield (Clark 1993). Guiteau had been stalking the president for some time before this incident, and when the president returned to Washington nine days later he was again under the stalking eye of Charles Guiteau. He would be shot at the Sixth Street train station five days later.

Charles Guiteau was born to a respectable family, one that he oftentimes exploited for financial or lodging services (Clark 1993). He squandered monetary windfalls that he received in failed attempts at starting a business and through association with a secular communal group. One thing that drew Guiteau to this group was its prescription to what could be called today "free-love." Still, in a community of open sexuality, Guiteau was rejected and spurned (Clark 1993). In a letter to his father the communal leader described Charles as not fitting in and being possibly unstable (Clark 1993).

Still feeling wronged from his past endeavors, Charles Guiteau then threw himself into a devotion to the Republican Party. He expected to be rewarded by the spoils system because he felt he contributed to the election of Garfield. This is ironic because of Garfield's disdain for all things nepotistic or spoils based (Thayer 1881). Not finding his reward at the party headquarters in New York, Guiteau made his way to Washington just after the inauguration of the president. He spent the next few months trying to gain an audience with the president, all the while leaving copies of a rambling speech at the White House and the State Department (Clark 1993).

After a series of unsuccessful attempts to obtain a position or compensation that he felt he was owed, eventually he was barred from the White House waiting room. The continued fixation with the president, combined with the general mental instability of Guiteau, drove him to morph his efforts from persistent and annoying to pervasive and violent. Following a particularly ineffective encounter with the secretary of state, James Blaine, Guiteau sent out final warning to the White House calling for the removal of Blaine (Thayer 1881; Clark 1993). Like the rest of his messages, both in person and written, he was ignored.

The Transfer of Presidential Power

The period of time in 1881 from July, when the president was shot, until his death in September was one of great uncertainty for the country. While the first half of the year was marked by all manner of governmental progress, the state of the president brought the government to a standstill. Chester Arthur, the vice president, was unsure of how to proceed with the succession of power while the president was alive. With a lack of legal specification for the transference of power during times of presidential incapacitation, Vice President Arthur did not want to seem to be racing toward the seat of high power. It was made clearer after President Garfield's death how this process would be carried out in the future, but it would not be for over 80 years, until the passage of the Twenty-Fifth Amendment to the Constitution, that the modern succession line was established.

Guiteau purchased a .44 caliber revolver with money that he borrowed, never to pay back like the majority of his debts (Clark 1993). He wrote letters to government officials with both blatant and cryptic illusions to his actions to come (Clark 1993). He spent the entire month of June following the president around Washington. Having decided to execute his plan, he went to the train depot on June 18, 1881, but changed his mind when he found the president in the company of his infirmed wife (Clark 1993). His first attempt at assassination had ended like everything else in Guiteau's life—impotent failure.

On the morning of July 2, 1881, President Garfield was on his was to Williams College, his alma mater, to deliver a speech. He was accompanied by two of his sons, Secretary of State Blaine and Secretary of War Robert Todd Lincoln. Guiteau approached the president from behind at the station and fired at point-blank range. The first bullet only grazed the president, but made everyone aware of what was happening. Guiteau fired a second shot into the abdomen of the president; this would ultimately be the fatal wound. Guiteau was apprehended on his way out of the station (Clark 1993).

The president was grievously injured, but it is widely held that without the constant exploration of the doctors over the course of the next two months that the president could have survived the shooting (Clark 1993). As such, after 70 days of constant pain and suffering he died on September 19, 1881, with his wife at his side. His body was returned to Washington to lie in state for two days before being taken to Cleveland, Ohio. President Garfield was buried on September 26, 1881.

After the death of the president, Guiteau was tried and convicted of murder. He remained defiant to the end that his actions were just and even intended to go on a lecture tour following his acquittal, with further grandiose plans to run for president in 1884 (Clark 1993). His trial was something of a media spectacle based on the nature of the offense and uncommon behavior on the part of Guiteau during the trial. Guiteau was found guilty on January 25, 1882, and after appeals he was hanged on June 30, 1882; just two days short of the one year anniversary of his crime.

CHARLES HOGAN

See also: Hinckley, John, Jr. (1955–); Ford, Gerald, Assassination Attempts on (1975); Kennedy, John F., Assassination of (November 22, 1963); McKinley, William, Assassination of (September 6, 1901); *Primary Documents*/Assassination of President James Garfield: His Chief Doctor's Account of His Death (September 19, 1881)

Further Reading

Clark, J.C. 1993. *The Murder of James A. Garfield: The President's Last Days and the Trial and Execution of His Assassin.* Jefferson, NC: McFarland & Company Inc.

Thayer, W.T. 1881. *From Log Cabin to White House.* Boston: James H. Earle, Publisher.

Gaskins, Donald "Pee Wee" (1933–1991)

Donald Gaskins "Pee Wee" is the most successful serial killer in South Carolina. In attempt to show himself as bigger than his small nickname, he killed, raped, tortured, and committed cannibalism. He succeeded in cementing

himself and his nickname in history. He gained other nicknames including "Meanest Man in America" (Documentary 2013) and "Junior Parrott" (Profile n.d.); however, the name that stuck is the one he tried his entire life to get rid himself of.

Pee Wee's murder-related fame also stems from his success in pulling off what appeared to be nearly impossible—committing a murder while in a maximum-security prison. Pee Wee murdered another prisoner on death row by crafting a bomb using tools he had access to as a maintenance man in the prison and disguising the bomb as a communication device. This trick placed Gaskins himself on death row: Pee Wee was executed in the electric chair.

Gaskins spent the last months of his life detailing his killings to Wilton Earl, a journalist. The result was *Final Truth*, which describes the "bothersome feelings" he experienced and the "special mind" he had that allowed him to have "permission to kill" (crimeandinvest n.d.). Pee Wee takes credit for having killed over 100 people; however, the bodies have not been found and thus his claims go unconfirmed. Pee Wee's final body count remains unknown (crimemuseum n.d.).

Donald Henry Gaskins Jr. was born March 13, 1933, in South Carolina. His mother had a series of boyfriends who physically abused Gaskins. When his mother married his stepfather, Gaskins was subjected to further physical abuse (crimeandinvest n.d.). The physical abuse continued at school where Gaskins frequently fought with schoolmates. Gaskins dropped out of school when he was 11 and began working in a car garage. He became friends with two boys and formed "The Trouble Trio." The Trouble Trio committed burglaries, hired prostitutes, and raped younger boys (crimemuseum n.d.). The trio split after they gang-raped one of the boy's younger sisters. Gaskins continued to commit crimes by himself. Gaskins burglarized a home and was caught by one of the children who lived there in 1964. Gaskins hit the girl with an axe. The girl survived, and Gaskins was placed in the South Carolina Industrial School for Boys until he was a legal adult. Gaskins escaped from the school on multiple occasions, but he returned to finish his sentence.

When Gaskins turned 18, he married and had a daughter, Shirley (Documentary 2013). Gaskins obtained a job on a tobacco farm and began partaking in insurance fraud by charging farmers to burn down their barns, so the farmers could collect the insurance money. When a farmer's daughter accused him of this fraud, Gaskins beat her with a hammer. Gaskins was given a five-year sentence. While serving his sentence, Gaskins killed his first victim in hopes of making himself a "Power Man" and avoiding being a sex slave. Power men are the most feared and ruthless inmates. After he was released from prison in August 1961, he continued to commit crimes. He was arrested in 1962 for statutory rape. Gaskins fled to North Carolina where he married a 17-year-old. His wife finally reported him to the police citing statutory rape charges. Gaskins was sentenced to six years in Columbia Penitentiary for his crime. He was paroled in November 1968 and vowed never to return to prison (crimemuseum n.d.).

Gaskins frequently referred to "them aggravated and bothersome feelings" that could only be relieved by seeing blood (Documentary 2013). As his daughter says, her daddy often referred to himself as a vampire (Documentary 2013). In the fall of 1969 Gaskins gave a ride to a female hitchhiker. Gaskins flirted with his passenger who responded by laughing at him: Gaskins beat, raped, sodomized, and tortured her. He then took her to a swamp and dumped her in, alive. The female hitchhiker was his first "Coastal Kills" (Profile n.d.). Gaskins defined his "Coastal Kills" as the killing of random people. Gaskins perfected the technique of torture, fine-tuning his ability to torture his victims and keep them alive for days while occasionally forcing them to eat their own flesh or forcing them to watch him eat it. No specific type of person was singled out for "Coastal Kills." "Coastal Kills" to Gaskins were "weekend recreation" (crimemuseum n.d.). Gaskins said he had killed about 90 people in "Coastal Kills" (crimeandinvest n.d.). Gaskins also committed what he termed "serious murders." These types of murders were murders of people Gaskins knew including his niece Janice Kirby and Patricia Alsobrook, a friend of his niece's (Profile n.d.). "Serious murders" were quick slayings (crimeandinvest n.d.).

In 1973, Pee Wee bought a car, a hearse with a sign on the back stating, "I hold dead bodies" (Documentary 2013). People joked about his car. The same year Gaskins killed pregnant Doreen Dempsey and her two-year-old because Doreen agreed to have sex with Gaskins but refused to allow Gaskins to have sex with her daughter (Profile n.d.). Both mother and daughter were raped, sodomized, killed, and buried (crimemuseum n.d.).

Gaskins became a hit man. He was hired by a woman to kill her ex-boyfriend. A group of buddies helped Gaskins lure the man from his house and watched while Gaskins killed him. Two of the partners later tried to blackmail Gaskins and ask for hush money. Pee Wee killed them both

(Profile n.d.). Gaskins continued his deadly streak, making a significant error in confessing to Walter Neely, an ex-con. Gaskins asked him to help hide some of the bodies. Neely turned Gaskins in when he was questioned by police. Gaskins was arrested and charged with eight counts of murder (crimemuseum n.d.). On May 24, 1976, Gaskins was charged and sentenced to the death penalty. To avoid this punishment, Gaskins confessed to seven additional murders. Fortunately for Gaskins, in November 1976 the Supreme Court concluded that the death penalty violated the Constitution, and thus Gaskin's sentence was changed to seven consecutive life sentences (cimemuseum n.d.). Of little consequence to Gaskins at the time was the fact that the death penalty was deemed constitutional again in 1978 (crimemuseum n.d.).

While in prison, Gaskins committed his last murder. Tony Cimo, the son of Bill and Myrtle Moon, hired Gaskins to kill Rudolph Tyner, another inmate. Tyner robbed the Moons's convenience store and killed both Bill and Myrtle (crimeandinvest n.d.). Tyner was on death row for his crimes but had avoided it for years due to procedural problems, and Cimo had waited long enough (Documentary 2013). Cimo hired Gaskins to kill his parents' murderer. Gaskins constructed a home-made bomb, disguised it as a communication device, and created a similar one for his cell. Gaskins explained to Tyner that they would be able to talk to each other while in their cells using his device. The pair picked a time to talk and when Tyner turned on his communication device, it exploded. Pee Wee exclaimed, "The last thing he heard was me laughing" (Profile n.d.). Gaskins was sentenced to death for this murder (Profile n.d.).

During his time on death row, Gaskins talked to journalist Wilton Earle and told the story of his life. In his book *Final Truth*, Gaskins confessed to close to 200 murders, including the daughter of James Cuttion Jr., the South Carolina senator (Profile n.d.). Gaskins was executed via the electric chair on September 6, 1991. The total number of people Gaskins murdered is unknown because his claims cannot be verified (crimemuseum n.d.).

Emily C. Smedley

See also: Bundy, Ted (1946–1989); Dahmer, Jeffrey (1960–1994); Gacy, John Wayne (1942–1994)

Further Reading

"Donald 'Pee Wee' Gaskins." http://www.crimeandinvestigation.co.uk/crime-files/donald-pee-wee-gaskins. Accessed April 16, 2015.

"Donald 'Pee Wee' Gaskins." http://www.crimemuseum.org/crime-library/donald-pee-wee-gaskins. Accessed April 16. 2015.

"Donald Pee Wee Gaskins in the Meanest Man in American (Documentary)." 2013. www.youtube.com. Accessed April 16, 2015.

Gaskins, Donald H. and Wilton Earle. 1992. *Final Truth: The Autobiography of a Serial Killer*. Hartwick, GA: Adept.

"Profile of an American Serial Killer: Pee Wee Gaskins." http://prolifickillers.wordpress.com. Accessed April 16, 2015.

"South Carolina's Worst Killer Remembered on Anniversary of His Execution." http://www.carolinalive.com/news/story.aspx?id=660119#.VcphF_lG0T8. Accessed April 16, 2015.

Gates, Wyley (1969–)

The outcome of many criminal cases depends on the careful collection of forensic evidence in addition to the representation of facts attorneys depict for the jury. When physical evidence is lacking, the determination of guilt rests heavily on the statements of both the attorneys and the witnesses, and the jury must interpret these arguments through the law as instructed by the judge. This was the dilemma the jury faced in the 1986 case of Wyley Gates, a 17-year-old high school student charged with murdering four family members. Wyley Gates confessed to both planning the murders and shooting his four family members at their home within hours of the crime. Despite a seemingly straightforward case, the jury struggled with a lack of physical evidence and inconsistencies in testimonies, which would lead to an outcome that would change the small town of East Chatham, New York, for years to come.

Wyley Gates was a quiet, intellectual boy who believed he was destined for great things. He was preoccupied with computer games, money and escape from his life. Despite coming from a family who cherished a small town environment, Wyley wanted to leave East Chatham and pursue college elsewhere. He idealized his biological mother, who lived in California, and he shared similar personality traits with her. However, Wyley felt tension between himself and the members of the extended family with whom he lived, including his father, Robert Gates Sr., brother, Robert Gates Jr., father's girlfriend, Cheryl Brahm, and young cousin, Jason Gates. Wyley Gates found refuge through his friendship with several boys in the town, Damian Rossney, Miles McDonald, and John Bailey. Wyley and Damian particularly formed a close bond and, according to testimony, pursued antisocial activities together including burglarizing their school along with other homes in the town.

In addition, they educated themselves about firearms and practiced shooting guns.

On December 13, 1986, Wyley Gates walked to his grandmother's house and told her that he had found his whole family dead in their home. Police arrived at the scene and found all four family members shot to death. Robert Gates Sr. was found reaching for a phone that was off the hook. Cheryl Brahm was shot to death and appeared to have been in a physical altercation with the perpetrator because her blouse was torn. Robert Gates Jr. was found next to his drum set with a live round near the body. Three-year-old Jason Gates was shot in front of the television. The investigating police officers decided to speak with Wyley Gates regarding the murders because he had been the one to find the bodies. Investigators Walter Shook and John Cozzolino questioned Wyley outside of his grandmother's home, and Wyley was read his Miranda rights in their patrol car. They then asked him if he would take a polygraph to which Wyley agreed. Wyley's grandmother, Vivian Gates, arranged for a local civil attorney they had worked with, Richard Hogle, to attend the polygraph with Wyley, but he ended up not being present when the examination occurred. During this time, the polygraph examiner, Thomas Francis Salmon, explained the examination and attached the machine to Wyley to calibrate it. He then removed all of the attachments except for the cardio cuff on Wyley's arm, and continued to explain how the testing works. According to the polygraph examiner, Wyley confessed right before the exam began that he had both planned the murders and killed his family.

At that time he allegedly outlined the events of the murder, including practicing shooting the gun. He had originally planned to only kill his father and brother. Wyley waited until his father ended his phone call and then entered the rec room where his father, father's girlfriend, and cousin were sitting. He shot his father first, who tried to reach for the phone. He said he then shot Cheryl. He listened for his brother who was still in another room over the garage playing drums and had not noticed the gunshots. He realized Cheryl was still alive and trying to move toward the stairs so he shot her another time. His next victim was his brother, Robert Gates Jr. who was shot two times before the gun jammed. Wyley explained that he cleared the gun and shot his brother once or twice more. Wyley claimed to then shoot Jason because the young boy would have been able to identify Wyley as the shooter. After the murders were committed, Wyley explained that he drove to Damian's house and confessed to his friend, leaving the gun in Damian's possession. After this detailed confession, the examiner asked Wyley if he would be willing to answer questions concerning the murders during an actual polygraph examination. Wyley did not take the test and asked Thomas Salmon to tell his attorney that he had confessed. The police had a detailed confession from Wyley himself witnessed by not only Thomas Salmon but also state trooper Bernard Keller and Walter Shook who were watching in an observation room.

Detecting Guilty Minds

The polygraph examination, known as the lie detector test, is widely used for testing deception. The polygraph measures physiological responses associated with deception such as increased heart rate and respiration. In theory, when the examinee conceals knowledge of information relevant to the questions being asked, he or she will have an autonomic biological response. The validity of the polygraph is highly debated. Anxious innocent people may produce increased physiological responses. Also, guilty people may suppress physiological responses using countermeasures. In criminal cases, innocent people may have knowledge of the crime due to contaminating interaction with police officers or media accounts, leading them to test positive for some questions. Despite the controversies regarding the polygraph examination, it continues to be a powerful aid to investigators.

Some people infer that this confession may have influenced the amount of evidence that was collected. During the investigation of the murders, the gun was not fingerprinted, Wyley's clothes were not tested for gunpowder residue, and the blood on the gun was not tested. All of this forensic evidence could have solidified a case against Wyley Gates or possibly eliminated him as a suspect and implicated someone else in the crime. Unfortunately, the most solid evidence against the defendant was oral testimony. Therefore, his trial hinged on the confession—the confession that was not taped, written, or signed by Wyley. Wyley Gates was charged with eight counts of second-degree murder, two for each victim, in addition to second-degree criminal possession of a weapon, and second-degree conspiracy. Wyley's defense attorney, Charles Wilcox, argued that there was significant reasonable doubt in this case

as there was not enough forensic evidence to incriminate Wyley, and the confession was given under extreme stress without the presence of Wyley's attorney. According to Charles Wilcox, Wyley's psychologist found him to be a mentally disturbed young man who confessed to cover for the real murderer, one of his friends. The prosecuting attorney, Eugene Keeler, questioned multiple witnesses who produced testimony stating that they had heard either Wyley confess or heard that Wyley was planning the murders.

At the conclusion of the trial, the judge instructed the jury to use the facts of the case to weigh the credibility of the witnesses as well as the confession. He reminded the jury that criminal defendants are presumed innocent until it can be proved beyond a reasonable doubt that they are guilty. To find Wyley Gates guilty of the murder charges, the jury must be convinced beyond a reasonable doubt that he was the one who caused the deaths, that he had the intent to shoot and kill the four family members, and that the shooting is what caused the deaths. Between the dates of October 1, 1987 and October 6, 1987, the jury endured a painstaking deliberation but finally agreed on a verdict. Wyley Gates was found not guilty on all charges except for the charge of second-degree conspiracy. He was sentenced to not less than eight and one third and not more than 25 years in a state prison. He was released from prison in August 2003 under parole supervision.

MARY FISHEL

See also: Clutter Family Murders (1959); Duperrault Family Slayings (November 12, 1961); Wesson Family Massacre (2004); Yates, Andrea (1964–)

Further Reading
Gelb, Alan. 1990. *Most Likely to Succeed: A True Crime Story, Multiple Murder and the Elusive Search for Justice in an American Town.* New York: Penguin.

Gburek, Otillie. *See* Klimek, Tillie (1876–1936)

Gein, Ed (1906–1984)

Following an investigation that began November 1957, at the small town of Plainfield, Wisconsin, the nation was shocked by the events that had transpired. Operating with an annual budget of $11,500, a new sheriff, and only two full-time deputies, Waushara County was largely ill prepared for the assortment of human remains that would be found on the remote Gein farm (Schechter 1989). Ed Gein's horrific murders and necrophilia quickly granted him national infamy. His bizarre crimes and behavior presented an issue to the criminal justice system as his legal sanity and competency to stand trial were questioned. Gein has been cited as the source of "all modern American horror" as his extreme deviant behavior inspired characters such as Norman Bates in *Psycho*, "Leatherface" in *The Texas Chainsaw Massacre*, and Buffalo Bill in *The Silence of the Lambs* (Schechter 2008, 549).

Edward Theodore Gein (pronounced "geen") was born August 27, 1906, in La Crosse County, Wisconsin. He was the second and final child to parents George (1873–1940) and Augusta (1878–1945). Augusta was a meticulous and domineering mother who sought to instill Puritanical religious beliefs into her sons. She preached of the world's immoralities, including the evils of women and drinking. Augusta also despised her husband for his alcoholism and inability to hold a job. In 1914 the family moved to a remote farm in Plainfield, Wisconsin. At the time when land was typically male-owned, the farm was unsurprisingly deeded to Augusta (Schechter 1989). Ed was a shy, timid child with strong feelings of idolization toward his mother. He developed poor social skills and was bullied by his classmates who considered him strange with his awkward mannerisms, seemingly random laughter, and weak demeanor.

In 1940, Ed's father George died of heart failure related to alcoholism. In their 30s at the time, Ed and his older brother Henry (1901–1944) began picking up odd jobs around the community to help support the family. By locals, both men were considered to be decent and reliable individuals. Ed often worked as a handyman and babysitter, as he seemed to easily relate with youth. On May 16, 1944, Ed and Henry were involved in a vegetation fire that spiraled out of control. It is a source of contention whether or not the fire was started intentionally. After Ed reported his brother missing, a search party found Henry dead, lying face down with no sign of injury caused by the flames. Schechter (1989) suggested Henry had bruising on his head. Any notion of foul play was dismissed by law enforcement and asphyxiation was listed as the cause of death.

The family now consisted of only Ed and his mother. Shortly after Henry's death Augusta suffered a stroke. Ed devotedly became her sole care provider until 1945, when she died at age 67. His mother's death left him devastated and virtually alone in the world. Ed boarded up the rooms in the farmhouse his mother had once used, leaving himself a small living space, which like the rest of the farm deteriorated rapidly. When asked later why he boarded up the rooms, Ed suggested he closed off the house because it was too large to heat (Morrison and Goldberg 2004). It has commonly been suggested, however, that this was Gein's way of ensuring his shrine to his mother remained pristine.

On November 16, 1957, Bernice Worden (1899–1957), a local hardware store owner, was reported missing by her son, Frank Worden. When police arrived on scene, there was blood in the store and the cash register was missing. Frank immediately highlighted Ed Gein as a suspect, stating he had been hanging around the store and had stopped by the previous evening to inquire about antifreeze. Upon further probing, the most recent sales receipt for the purchase of antifreeze was located, written in Bernice's handwriting.

The police acted quickly, heading to Gein's farm in an effort to find Mrs. Worden. What they found when searching the property was unforeseen. The body of Bernice Worden was discovered in the shed hanging upside-down by the ankles from a wooden crossbar. She was decapitated and her torso had been cut open and dressed out like a deer. These mutilations were postmortem (occurring after death). The cause of death was a .22 caliber gunshot to the back of the head—a gunshot that in the future, Gein would always claim to be accidental (Schechter 1989).

With continued search of the house, authorities discovered a horrifying assortment of human remains, some of which had been fashioned into furniture or clothing. Among the findings were skulls decorating bedposts and made into soup bowls, four noses, bones and fragments, four chairs upholstered with skin, lips attached to the drawstring of window shades, lampshades of skin, nine female genitalia in a shoebox, a belt of human nipples, and wastebasket, hunting knife sheath, lampshade, bracelet, vest, leggings, and masks of human skin (Schechter 1989). Schechter (1989, 2008) noted that there were human remains found from 15 different women. Among the remains was the head of Bernice Worden in a seed sack. Within a paper bag was the face of Mary Hogan, the owner of the Pine Grove Tavern who had been missing since 1954.

Through questioning, Gein eventually confessed to the murders of Mary Hogan and Bernice Worden. When asked about the other remains, Gein explained that in a dazed state he had gone to graveyards and exhumed bodies of recently deceased women he had read about in the obituaries. Gein said he had visited about 40 graves, but often had awoken from his dazed state and went home. He admitted however to unearthing somewhere around 9 (Schechter 1989) to 11 (Odell and Gregg 2006) graves. Investigators were skeptical and looked into the possibility that the female remains found in Gein's home were truly missing persons from the area that Gein had murdered. In an effort to substantiate Gein's graveyard story, he was given a series of lie detector tests and a limited number of graves were exhumed, all of which seemed to validate Gein's claims.

Ed was arraigned for armed robbery related to the stolen cash register and one count of first-degree murder for the death of Bernice Worden. After medical evaluation it was determined that Gein was not competent to stand trial. He was then sent to Central State Hospital for the Criminally Insane from 1957 to 1968. In 1968 Gein's doctors determined his mental state had improved and he was competent to stand trial. The trial lasted one week, after which Gein was ultimately found to be not guilty by reason of insanity and was sent back to Central State Hospital. Overtime he was transferred to Mendota Mental Health Institute where at 77 years old, he died of respiratory failure. Gein was buried in Plainfield Cemetery next to his mother.

CHAE M. MAMAYEK

See also: Bundy, Ted (1946–1989); Dahmer, Jeffrey (1960–1994); Holmes, Dr. H. H. (1861–1896)

Further Reading

Fox, James Alan, and Jack Levin. 2005. *Extreme Killing: Understanding Serial and Mass Murder.* Thousand Oaks, CA: Sage Publications.

Morrison, Helen, and Harold Goldberg. 2004. *My Life among the Serial Killers: Inside the Minds of the World's Most Notorious Murderers.* New York: William Morrow.

Odell, Robin, and Wilfred Gregg. 2006. *Murderers' Row: An International Murderers' Who's Who.* Stroud, UK: Sutton.

Schechter, Harold. 1989. *Deviant: The Shocking True Story of Ed Gein, The Original Psycho.* New York: Pocket Books.

Schechter, Harold. 2008. *True Crime: An American Anthology.* New York: Library of America.

Genovese, Catherine Susan "Kitty," Murder of (1964)

Catherine Susan Genovese (1935–1964), better known as Kitty, was born and raised in the New York City area. At age

Catherine "Kitty" Genovese, posing for a portrait while working in a bar. Bystanders ignored Kitty's cries for help as she was knifed on Austin Street in Kew Gardens. (New York Daily News Archive/Getty Images)

19, Genovese decided to stay close to New York City when her parents and siblings moved to Connecticut. A few years later she moved to an apartment building with her friend. On March 13, 1964, Genovese arrived home from her job at approximately 3:15 a.m. and was approached by a man as she walked to her door. This man, later identified as Winston Moseley, stabbed Genovese multiple times. A witness, hearing Genovese's cries for help, called out the window for Moseley to stop and he ran away. Minutes later he returned, continuing to stab Genovese as well as rape and rob her. *The New York Times* reported that 38 individuals observed Genovese's attack and only one made an attempt to call the police. Though this number was overestimated, Genovese's murder had a significant impact because it called attention to what would later become known as the "bystander effect." According to the bystander effect, the more individuals who observe an incident, the less likely they will be to report the incident. This is due, in part, to the diffusion of responsibility. Individuals believe that someone else will report the incident so they feel less inclined to do so themselves.

Catherine Susan Genovese was born on July 7, 1935. Soon after her birth, she became known as Kitty. Genovese, born in New York City, was the oldest daughter of Rachel and Vincent Andronelle Genovese. Due to increased violence in the city, Genovese's family decided to move to Connecticut in 1954. Nineteen at the time, Genovese decided to stay closer to New York City. For the next nine years, Genovese worked various jobs and continued to live her life in the city. She would often visit her family in Connecticut on the weekends and spend time with her four siblings. In 1963, Genovese moved in with her friend Mary Ann Zielonko. The two lived in an apartment building on Austin Street in Queens, close to Ev's Eleventh Hour Sports Bar, where Genovese had recently begun working as a manager.

On March 13, 1964, Genovese arrived home from her job at approximately 3:15 a.m. She parked her car in the Long Island Rail Road parking lot close to her apartment's door. This parking lot was situated at the back of Genovese's building. She was approached by a man, later identified as Winston Moseley, as she was walking toward the door of her apartment building. Realizing that she was being followed, Genovese began to run toward the front of her building where there was a police call box. Moseley was quickly able to catch up to Genovese and stabbed her twice in the back. After being stabbed, Genovese began to scream for help. Several of her neighbors reportedly heard her screams; however, only a few of them realized that something was wrong. One neighbor, Robert Mozer, claimed that he shouted for the attacked to stop. After hearing Mozer's shout, Moseley ran away from Genovese. After Moseley retreated, Genovese began attempting to get to the door of her apartment building. Genovese eventually made it through a door and into the hallway of her apartment building.

Several witnesses observed Moseley leaving in his car after initially attacking Genovese. These witnesses also reported seeing Moseley return to the apartment building approximately 10 minutes later. Moseley found Genovese inside the hallway of her apartment building. Genovese, badly hurt and barely conscious, was unable to make it through the last locked door into the safety of her building. Moseley continued his attack on Genovese and stabbed her multiple times. After stabbing Genovese, Moseley raped her and stole the money out of her purse. Both attacks occurred during a half-hour time period.

After the second attack, the first person to call the police was Karl Ross. According to records, Ross's call was received at approximately 3:50 a.m. After receiving Ross's call, police arrived on the scene to find Genovese, barely conscious and lying in the hallway. On the way to the

hospital, Genovese died. Her time of death was approximated at 4:15 a.m. Genovese was buried in her family plot at Lakeview Cemetery in Connecticut.

Moseley was arrested six days after murdering Genovese during an attempted house burglary. He confessed to killing Genovese while being interviewed by the police. Along with Genovese's murder, Moseley also confessed to murdering two other women in the area and committing approximately 30 burglaries. According to Moseley, he did not intend to specifically kill Genovese the night of the murder, he only knew that he wanted to kill a woman. He saw Genovese walking to her apartment building from the parking lot and decided that she would be his victim. Moseley noted that women were easier to kill because they put up less of a fight. Moseley was found guilty on June 11, 1964. He was sentenced to death on June 15, 1964. After an appeal regarding Moseley's sanity, his sentence was reduced to life plus two 15-year sentences. He was most recently denied parole for the 15th time on November 7, 2011. Genovese's siblings have reported that they will do everything necessary to ensure that Moseley is not released from prison.

Initially, Genovese's murder received little media attention. Ten days after Genovese's death, the metropolitan editor of *The New York Times*, Abraham Rosenthal, became aware of the story and assigned a reporter to the case. *The New York Times* reported that 38 witnesses had observed the attack and failed to report it to the police. This number was later criticized for being inaccurate, the more realistic number being closer to one dozen individuals. According to reports, many of the witnesses were not even aware that the disturbance they heard was a woman being stabbed. The neighborhood in which Genovese lived was not considered a crime-prone area; however, hearing noise in the street at night was not uncommon. Because of this, Genovese's neighbors had no reason to believe that a violent attack was occurring. Also, the layout of Genovese's apartment building made it difficult for any neighbors to actually observe any activity in the areas that Genovese was attacked.

Genovese's death has had a much greater impact than anyone could have imagined, the effect on the fields of psychology, sociology, and, most importantly, criminology. The term "bystander effect" was associated with witnesses not intervening in a situation depending on actual number of them present. If a large number of individuals witness an event, they will be less likely to intervene because they are able to diffuse the responsibility of taking action. In Genovese's case, it is hypothesized that more neighbors did not call the police because they assumed other people would and they did not want to get involved.

After Genovese's death, the New York City Police Department made changes in their telephone crime reporting system. These changes made the system much more user friendly in the hopes that individuals would be more likely to call when crimes were occurring. Also, many neighborhoods in New York City began to develop neighborhood watch programs to assist with any crimes that might be taking place.

Darla D. Darno

See also: Central Park Jogger Case (1989)

Further Reading

Krajicek, David. 2011. "The killing of Kitty Genovese: 47 Years Later, Still Holds Sway over New Yorkers." http://www.nydailynews.com/news/crime/killing-kitty-genovese-47-years-holds-sway-new-yorkers-article-1.123912. Accessed April 16, 2015.

"No Parole for Kitty Genovese Killer; '64 Slaying Shocked New York." 2011. http://latimesblogs.latimes.com/nationnow/2011/11/kitty-genovese-killer-denied-parole.html. Accessed April 16, 2015.

Rosenthal, Abraham. 1964. *Thirty-Eight Witnesses: The Kitty Genovese Case*. Berkeley: University of California Press.

Genovese, Vito (1897–1969)

Vito Genovese was an Italian-born mobster who led New York's Genovese crime family and became the "boss of bosses" of the American mafia in the 1950s. Genovese was born in Tufino, in the Italian region of Campania, in 1897. He immigrated to America as a teenager. He began his criminal career in New York, robbing vendors and performing mob errands. Members of Genovese's family followed his path; two of his brother s would join his criminal organization and his cousin became a Pittsburgh mob boss.

Genovese became an associate of rising Italian American gang leader Charlie "Lucky" Luciano. During the 1920s, Genovese began working for mafia boss Giuseppe Masseria. Involved in the extortion and bootlegging operations that followed the passage of Prohibition, Genovese also served as one of Masseria's enforcers. In 1930, he allegedly murdered Gaetano Reina, a powerful mobster whom Masseria suspected of conspiring with his rival, Salvatore Maranzano.

By 1931, the Castellammarese War, a feud between Masseria and Maranzano over control of New York's mafia, was hurting business. To end this conflict, Luciano and his associates, including Genovese and Frank Costello, betrayed Masseria to Maranzano. In April 1931, four gunmen (Genovese, Albert Anastasia, Joe Adonis, and Benjamin "Bugsy" Siegel) murdered Masseria at a Coney Island restaurant. Maranzano organized New York's mafia groups into five families, one of which was led by Luciano; Genovese became Luciano's underboss. In September 1931, Luciano and his cohorts maneuvered against Maranzano. Maranzano was murdered by gunmen (possibly Jewish mobsters Bo Weinberg and Red Levine) posing as federal Internal Revenue Service (IRS) agents.

In 1931, Genovese's first wife died. He sought to marry Anna Petrillo; however, she was already married. In March 1932, her husband was found mysteriously murdered. Shortly thereafter, she married Genovese.

In 1936, Luciano, convicted of running a prostitution ring, was sentenced to prison. He soon appointed Genovese as acting boss. Genovese became a naturalized U.S. citizen at this time (he was denaturalized in the 1950s). In 1937, however, he fled to Italy to avoid prosecution for mobster Ferdinand Boccia's murder. Three years earlier, Genovese allegedly murdered Boccia in a dispute over shares of a gambling swindle. Genovese settled near Naples, while Costello became acting boss; Willie Moretti became underboss.

Genovese became a prominent mobster in Italy. He was involved in narcotics trafficking and organized a black market operation with influential Sicilian Mafioso Calogero Vizzini. After a large "donation" to the Italian government, Genovese became acquainted with fascist dictator Benito Mussolini and received Italy's highest civilian medal. In 1943, Genovese allegedly ordered the murder of an Italian publisher of an anarchist newspaper in New York, possibly carried out by Carmine Galante, as a favor for Mussolini. When Allied forces invaded Italy in 1943 to help win World War II, Genovese offered his services to the U.S. Army. He became an interpreter/liaison officer in Naples.

Military police in Italy arrested Genovese upon investigating his black market activities. He was eventually shipped to New York as a fugitive to face trial. Mobster Ernest Rupolo had implicated Genovese in Boccia's murder. However, two further witnesses for the prosecution were murdered. Without corroboration of Rupolo's testimony, charges were dismissed in 1946. Rupolo was eventually murdered.

Genovese returned to his New York crime family as a caporegime, or captain in charge of a crew of soldiers, in Greenwich Village. Genovese, previously underboss and acting boss, considered this a demotion. Meanwhile, he learned that his wife had been unfaithful while he had been away. The man responsible was murdered and mutilated.

During the Kefauver Hearings, a congressional committee investigated organized crime in interstate commerce. Mobsters were called to testify; the testimonies were broadcasted on television. The Commission, an underworld governing board Luciano established comprised of mafia bosses, was displeased with Moretti's testimony; he was murdered in 1951. The increased media and law enforcement attention Costello received due to the hearings led to his downfall. He was constantly engaged in legal proceedings during the 1950s. Genovese, now underboss, plotted against Costello. Genovese neutralized Costello's ally, Anastasia, through an alliance with Anastasia's underboss, Carlo Gambino. In 1957, Genovese ordered Costello's murder. Costello survived the attempt, but he retired. Genovese become boss. Later that year, Anastasia was murdered in a barber shop; Gambino became boss of his crime family.

Vito Genovese and Joseph Valachi

In the early 1960s, while in prison, Genovese suspected mobster Joseph Valachi of being an informant. Valachi, who feared being murdered, killed another inmate after taking him for a mafia hit man. After receiving a life sentence for the murder, Valachi became a government witness, providing Americans with a firsthand account of mafia (or Cosa Nostra) activities in America. The U.S. Department of Justice encouraged Valachi to compose a memoir about his life in the Genovese crime family. Eventually, a journalist's interviews with Valachi formed the basis of a book, *The Valachi Papers* (1968), which was adapted into a 1972 film.

In November 1957, Genovese called a meeting of the Commission and leading Mafiosi in America to attend a meeting to affirm his new status as boss of the Genovese crime family and head of the Commission. The conference was scheduled to be held at mobster Joseph Barbara's farm in Apalachin, New York. State police, however, noticed an increase in activity at the farm and went to investigate. The attendees fled the location in a panic, some on foot through the woods. Genovese was stopped while driving away from the farm; the police let him go after questioning him. Caporegime Anthony Carfano refused to attend the conference; he was murdered in 1959.

During the late 1950s, Senator John McClellan helped form and chaired the Select Committee on Improper Activities in Labor and Management to investigate organized crime's influence in labor unions. In 1958, Genovese testified under subpoena. However, he cited his Fifth Amendment rights to avoid answering questions. Shortly thereafter, Genovese was indicted and convicted on narcotics trafficking charges. He received a 15-year prison sentence. Some speculated that Genovese and his supporters, including future Bonanno family boss Galante, were framed by Costello's powerful friends, Luciano and Meyer Lansky, as revenge. In 1962, Genovese ordered mobster Anthony Strollo's murder on suspicion that he helped plot to put him in prison.

Genovese's sycophants—Tommy Eboli, Gerardo Catena, Mike Miranda, and Philip Lombardo—controlled the organization on his behalf during his years in prison. Genovese died in 1969 in prison custody. Shortly thereafter, Lombardo took control of the crime family, which he led until 1981, using "front bosses" as decoys to confuse law enforcement.

ERIC MARTONE

See also: Costello, Frank (1891–1973); Luciano, Charles "Lucky" (1897–1962)

Further Reading

Maas, Peter. 2003. *The Valachi Papers*. Reprint ed. New York: William Morrow.
Raab, Selwyn. 2006. *Five Families: The Rise, Decline, and Resurgence of America's Most Powerful Mafia Empires*. New York: St. Martin's Press.
Reppetto, Thomas. 2004. *American Mafia: A History of Its Rise to Power*. New York: MJF Books.

Gerhartsreiter, Christian Karl. *See* Rockefeller, Clark (1961–)

Getty, John Paul, III, Kidnapping of (1973)

John Paul Getty III was grandson to one of the wealthiest men in the world, John Paul Getty Senior, the founder of Getty Oil Company. As the grandson of an oil tycoon, John Paul Getty III would become an ideal target for kidnapping to obtain a large ransom due to his family's wealth. As it turned out, the young Paul would be abducted at the age of 16. He was held captive for five months before his grandfather decided to provide over $2 million for ransom. Unfortunately, by the time the ransom was given, Paul had been beaten, lost an ear, and suffered from infection and massive blood loss. Despite these injuries, Paul still survived and was left on a hillside on December 15, 1973, to find his way home (Weber 2011). Within a few years after the traumatic experience, John Paul overdosed, leaving him paralyzed, mute, and almost completely blind (Fryer 2011).

On November 4, 1956, John Paul Getty III was born into one of the wealthiest families in the world. Getty did not have an easy childhood, with his parents getting divorced at an early age and his father having a heavy addiction to drugs. Young Getty was given drugs by his father's mistress at an early age and by the time he was 15, he had been kicked out of school. His father abandoned him, and so Getty was left on his own in Rome and began to sell drugs to get by. He enjoyed the nightclub scene and was often found drunk and partying on the streets. On the night of July 10, 1973, Getty got extremely drunk and wandered the streets when a car pulled up next to him and several men got out and grabbed him; Getty was abducted. He reported later that he was only given whisky to drink through the entire car ride, leaving him completely drunk and unable to stay awake (Fox 2013).

At first, Getty's own family and the police refused to believe that the teenager was actually abducted. Getty had previously stated that he would fake his own kidnapping just to get his frugal grandfather to give him money. His grandfather believed that if this kidnapping were real and he did pay, then what was to keep his other grandchildren from getting kidnapped. While his family would not address the kidnappers or pay the ransom, Getty was kept in various locations from caves to makeshift huts by a group of Calabrian gangsters. A few days after the kidnapping, Getty was forced to write a letter to his mother explaining that the kidnappers had threatened to cut off body parts unless they were paid $18 million. John Getty Senior offered his son money to pay the ransom under the conditions that it would be taken out of his inheritance, but John Getty II never accepted the offer and so his son remained in captivity (Fox 2013).

A while after the first letter, another one was sent to Getty's parents pleading for the ransom and his freedom. This time, the kidnappers reduced the ransom to $5.5 million. Unfortunately for Getty, his family only offered $500,000; soon after another letter came, with further threat of dismemberment. Still, the family did not respond and Getty continued to get moved around to various caves and hideout spots. All the time Getty was in captivity, he was given little food, beaten, and kept from ever seeing the faces of his captors. Finally, Getty was forced to write another letter, this time giving his family 15 days to provide the ransom or else they would receive Getty's ear and a lock of his hair.

On October 21, 1973, the kidnappers woke Getty and told him it was the day they would have to cut off his ear. They blindfolded him and gave him something to bite down on before lowering his head to a chopping block. With a razor, one man cut off Getty's ear. Getty bled profusely for over 36 hours with no antiseptic or pain killers. As blood flowed from Getty's body, he became more and more delirious and believed death would be inevitable. The kidnappers mailed the preserved ear and hair, but it did not reach the family for 28 days due to a mail strike. The Getty men refused to believe it was really his ear at first, but eventually they believed that young Getty was actually in trouble after Getty's mother sent them enlarged pictures of the ear. Not long after the letter was received, John Paul Getty Senior offered the kidnappers over $2 million in ransom (Fox 2013).

On December 15, 1973, John Paul Getty III was left on a hill in the freezing cold, weak from blood loss, and with an infection growing in his ear. He made his way to the nearest populated area and was ignored by many people, likely scared of his deteriorated condition. Finally, a truck driver called the police who eventually picked Getty up and brought him to safety. In the end, nine men were arrested, although only two received prison sentences. It turns out that a Calabrian mafia was behind Getty's abduction (Weber 2011).

Only a few years after his abduction, Getty, 24, overdosed on drugs and alcohol leading to a stroke that paralyzed him for the remaining 30 years of his life. It is believed that Getty suffered some form of posttraumatic stress after the kidnapping, but his father refused to help with medical bills, and believed Getty was responsible for his own addiction after being released by his captors. Getty died at the age of 54, never able to enjoy his life after the age of 16, when he was first abducted.

Getty was one of the more well-known kidnappings in the 1970s in Italy. During this era, Italy experienced an epidemic of kidnappings where more than 80 individuals, typically from wealthy families, were taken for ransom. To combat this problem, police created a policy that would freeze the bank accounts and all assets of these wealthy families so they could not pay the kidnappers. They also passed laws that prevented these families from raising money to pay the ransom. Getty was lucky enough that his family was able to pay and he was set free; unfortunately for many of those kidnapped, they were never seen again (Popham 2004). The Italian criminal justice system also reacted by increasing prison terms for kidnapping and punishing anyone who withholds information. They also added increased sentences for any cruel treatment of captives, such as was the case of John Paul Getty III, who had his ear removed. These methods were intended to reduce the profitability of kidnapping and potentially deter would-be offenders from kidnapping (Haberman 1990). Ultimately, the police crackdown did foster a decline in kidnappings over time, although there seems to be a recent increase in kidnappings in the early 2000s, according to Popham (2004).

KATHLEEN FREY

See also: Lindbergh Kidnapping Case (1932); Ross, Charley, Kidnapping of (1870); Sinatra, Frank, Jr., Kidnapping of (1963)

Further Reading

Fox, Charles. 2013. *Uncommon Youth: The Gilded Life and Tragic Times of J. Paul Getty III.* New York: St. Martin's Press.

Fryer, Jane. 2011. "Proof that Money Can't Buy Happiness: John Paul Getty III Destroyed by His Family's Billions." *Mail Online.* February 7. http://www.dailymail.co.uk/news/article-1354365/John-Paul-Getty-III-destroyed-familys-billions.html. Accessed April 16, 2015.

Haberman, Clyde. 1990. "Italy Sets Hard Line on Kidnappers and Ransom." *The New York Times.* February 18. http://www.nytimes.com/1990/02/18/world/italy-sets-hard-line-on-kidnappers-and-on-ransom.html. Accessed April 16, 2015.

Popham, Peter. 2004. "Nightmare of Kidnapping Returns to Italy as Millionaire's Wife is Held." *The Independent.* June 22. http://www.independent.co.uk/news/world/europe/nightmare-of-kidnapping-returns-to-italy-as-millionaires-wife-is-held-6166970.html. Accessed April 16, 2015.

Weber, Bruce. 2011. "J. Paul Getty III, 4, Dies: Had Ear Cut Off by Captors." *The New York Times.* February 7. http://www.nytimes.com/2011/02/08/world/europe/08gettyobit.html?_r=0. Accessed April 16, 2015.

Giancana, Sam (1908–1975)

Sam "Mooney" Giancana was a Chicago crime boss in mid-20th-century America. Conspiracy theorists have linked him to the assassinations of U.S. president John Kennedy and entertainment personality Marilyn Monroe.

Giancana, born to Sicilian immigrant parents in 1908, grew up in Chicago. As a youth, he became involved with local gangs, most prominently the Forty-Two Gang. He attracted the attention of Capone's criminal syndicate, known as the Outfit, in the 1920s. He served as a "wheelman" and then a "triggerman."

During the 1930s, while climbing the Outfit's ranks, he married Angeline DeTolve; they had three daughters. During the 1940s, after a stint in federal prison, Giancana established hegemony over Chicago's illegal gambling operations, in the process taking over Chicago's African American "policy" (lottery) payout system. The extensive revenue these operations brought in facilitated Giancana's ascendency as boss in the mid-1950s, replacing Tony Accardo.

Accardo had assumed control of the Outfit in the 1940s. Capone nicknamed him "Joe Batters" after he beat Outfit turncoats to death at a dinner with a baseball bat. Around this time, the Outfit expanded into slot and vending machines, counterfeit liquor and tax stamps, and drug trafficking. The Outfit further branched out into other cities across the United States, especially in Florida, California, Nevada, and several Midwestern states (like Kansas, Oklahoma, and Wisconsin). Wrestling control of gaming in Las Vegas from the mafia crime families based in New York, the Outfit dominated organized crime in the western United States.

Although Giancana became boss around 1957, Accardo and Paul Ricca, who had first wrangled supreme power in the 1930s, still wielded substantial influence. Other prominent Outfit members included political "greasers" Murray Humphries and Gus Alex, and enforcer Charles Nicoletti. In 1957, Giancana attended Vito Genovese's infamous mafia meeting in Apalachin, New York, which was raided by police. In 1959, the FBI planted a wire in Giancana's headquarters at the Armory Lounge, secretly gathering intelligence for several years.

After Angeline died in 1954, Giancana became notorious for his flashy social life and womanizing. He frequently associated with singer/actor Frank Sinatra and dated famous entertainers, including Phyllis McGuire (of the singing group the McGuire Sisters). Giancana even appeared in the 1965 film *Peep Show.* He spent a night with Marilyn Monroe shortly before she died in 1962. Some speculate that he was involved with her death. Another of Giancana's mistresses, actress Judith Campbell, had an affair with U.S. president John Kennedy. Some speculate that she delivered messages between the two regarding Cuban dictator Fidel Castro.

The exact nature of Giancana's ties with the Kennedys has been debated. The president's brother, Attorney

General Robert Kennedy, increased pressure on the mafia as part of a war on crime. However, ballot-stuffing in Chicago during John Kennedy's presidential campaign helped ensure his victory; Giancana and the Outfit were quick to claim responsibility for such tampering and that the Kennedys "owed" them. Consequently, conspiracy theorists speculate that the mafia and/or Giancana had a hand in President Kennedy's 1963 assassination.

Both the U.S. government and Outfit perceived Castro as an enemy; the former perceived him as a threat to U.S. security, while the latter lost substantial money after he took over Cuba and the mafia's extensive gambling rackets there (which the previous government had encouraged). Consequently, the Central Intelligence Agency (CIA) felt that the mafia might have incentive for removing Castro. In 1960, the CIA contacted the mafia via "Handsome" Johnny Roselli, an influential mobster who helped the Outfit control Hollywood and Las Vegas. Roselli brought in his alleged boss, Giancana, and Florida crime boss Santo Trafficante Jr. who had been incarcerated in Cuba for nine months following Castro's 1959 takeover. They refused the $150,000 fee the CIA authorized for the service. Trafficante recruited a Cuban exile who arranged for a CIA-supplied poison pill to be slipped into Castro's food. His attempts, however, were unsuccessful. Meanwhile, Giancana suspected his mistress, Phyllis McGuire, of having an affair with comedian Dan Rowan. The CIA, to ensure Giancana's support against Castro, arranged for surveillance. Local authorities caught and arrested the agent sent to do the wire-tapping. Danger of revealing the CIA's plot for Castro's removal and its connections with mafia figures caused the agency to intervene, forcing the charges to be dropped in the interest of national security. Kennedy's administration attempted Castro's overthrow in the botched 1961 Bay of Pigs invasion. It subsequently initiated Operation Mongoose, a covert operation to facilitate Castro's removal.

In the mid-1960s, Giancana refused to testify before a grand jury and was sentenced to one year in prison. Giancana subsequently stepped down as boss in 1966, retiring to Mexico. He continued to make money through international gambling operations in Iran and Central America, but refused to share this money with the Outfit.

In 1974, Giancana, extradited to testify before another grand jury, began cooperating with federal authorities. He was subsequently called to testify before a Senate Committee regarding mafia involvement in a CIA plot to kill Castro, but was killed before testifying. In 1975, he was shot while cooking in his home. No one was arrested for the murder; suspects include former mistresses, nervous CIA operatives, and various rival mafia figures. Roselli did testify before the committee about mafia involvement in the CIA plot against Castro; his mutilated body was found in a steel fuel drum floating near Miami in 1976.

Aiuppa became the Outfit's prominent figurehead after Giancana. During the 1970s and 1980s, Tony "the Ant" Spilotro replaced Marshall Caifano as the Outfit's Las Vegas representative. Charged with protecting the Outfit's illegal casino profits, Spilotro worked with his friend, Frank "Lefty" Rosenthal, who managed several Outfit-backed casinos, like the Stardust. Spilotro became involved in other criminal enterprises, like fencing, burglary, and loan-sharking that attracted authorities' attention. In 1986, as part of authorities' efforts to clean up Las Vegas, Aiuppa and other mafia leaders were convicted of illegally skimming money from Las Vegas casinos. Aiuppa was sentenced to 25 years in prison. That year, Spilotro and his brother were brutally beaten and buried in an Indiana cornfield, possibly because Aiuppa blamed them for his conviction.

Giancana's daughter, Antoinette, wrote a tell-all entitled *Mafia Princess*, which was adapted into a 1986 television miniseries starring actor Tony Curtis as Giancana. Giancana has been featured as a character in films, most detailing the lives of the entertainment personalities with whom he associated, including *Sinatra* (1992), *Sugartime* (1995), and *The Rat Pack* (1998). Giancana also inspired the character Joseph Palmi, played by Joe Pesci, in *The Good Shepherd* (2006). Giancana has been featured in works of fiction by authors like Norman Mailer, Max Allen Collins, and James Ellroy.

Eric Martone

See also: Capone, Al (1899–1947); Genovese, Vito (1897–1969); Kennedy, John F., Assassination of (November 22, 1963); Monroe, Marilyn, Death of (1962); Nitti, Frank "the Enforcer" (1888–1943)

Further Reading

Earman, J. S. 1996. *CIA Targets Fidel: The Secret Assassination Report.* Melbourne, Australia: Ocean Press.

Farrell, Ronald, and Carole Case. 1995. *The Black Book and the Mob: The Untold Story of the Control of Nevada's Casinos.* Madison: University of Wisconsin Press.

Giancana, Sam, and Chuck Giancana. 1992. *Double Cross: The Explosive, Inside Story of the Mobster Who Controlled America.* New York: Warner Books.

Roemer, William, Jr. 1996. *Accardo: The Genuine Godfather.* New York: Ivy Books.

Russo, Gus. 2001. *The Outfit: The Role of Chicago's Underworld in the Shaping of Modern America.* New York: Bloomsbury.

Giffords, Gabrielle "Gabby," Shooting of. *See* Loughner, Jared Lee (1988–)

Gigante, Vincent "the Chin" (1928–2005)

Vincent "the Chin" Gigante, a powerful Italian American mobster, led New York's Genovese crime family from 1981 to 2005. His ploy of feigning mental illness to avoid criminal prosecution earned him the media nickname "the Oddfather."

Gigante was born in Manhattan in 1928 to Italian immigrants from Campania. His nickname "the Chin" stemmed from his mother's Italian pronunciation of his name, Vincenzo. In his youth, Gigante fought as a professional boxer and was a sparring partner of future mafioso Dominick Cirillo. Gigante soon became a mafia enforcer for what became the Genovese crime family. Three of his four brothers followed him; one, however, became a priest. In 1957, Gigante was tasked with murdering Frank Costello as part of Vito Genovese's plot to become boss. Although Costello survived a shot to the head, he retired, refused to identify his shooter, and made peace with Genovese.

During his early criminal career, Gigante became Genovese's and future boss Philip Lombardo's protégée. In 1959, Gigante was convicted with Genovese for drug trafficking. He received a seven-year prison sentence. After his release, Gigante became a caporegime, a street boss in charge of a crew, within the Genovese family. He and his crew controlled most of the organized crime activities in downtown Manhattan and developed connections extending into the Bronx and Westchester County. Capitalizing on his pug-nosed ex-boxer appearance, Gigante cultivated a façade of stupidity that made people underestimate him. The act, which helped him survive the turmoil following Genovese's death in 1969, would be supported by doctors over the years who claimed Gigante suffered from disorders like schizophrenia, dementia, and psychosis.

Lombardo retired as boss in 1981. Gigante became the de facto boss, although Anthony "Fat Tony" Salerno officially occupied the position. Salerno received a 100-year prison sentence after his 1986 conviction on murder and racketeering charges. His conviction was part of the Mafia Commission Trial, which had indicted New York's five mafia family bosses and six other leading mafia figures on

Bathrobe-clad Vincent (The Chin) Gigante is placed under arrest. For decades the mobster headed one of the most powerful New York families. He was charged with various crimes, but tried to avoid prosecution by pretending to be criminally insane. (New York Daily News Archive/Getty Images)

charges under the Racketeer Influenced and Corrupt Organization Act (RICO). Initial defendants included bosses Paul Castellano (Gambino family), Salerno (Genovese family), Carmine Persico (Colombo family), Anthony "Tony Ducks" Corallo (Lucchese family), and Philip Rastelli (Bonanno family). However, Rastelli received a separate trial and Castellano was murdered during the trial as part of John Gotti's seizure of power within the Gambino family. Persico decided to defend himself at the trial, which marked the first successful large-scale use of RICO against the Mafia. The trial resulted in the end of the Commission, a mafia governing board, and helped propel U.S. attorney Rudolph Giuliani's bid for New York City mayor. At this time, mob informant Vincent Cafaro revealed that Salerno was a figurehead; Gigante was the actual Genovese family's boss.

As boss, Gigante increased Genovese control over many of New York's lucrative criminal operations. He maintained an elusive leadership style that contrasted sharply with his flamboyant contemporary Gotti, whom the media dubbed the "Dapper Don." Gigante delivered instructions through trusted associates, like Cirillo, to insulate himself from other bosses and lower-ranking mafia members. He also courted practices that made him seem, on appearance, uninvolved. At meetings, for example, Gigante often outwardly distanced himself by playing cards. When he needed to communicate orders, he did so in whispers to avoid being recorded by a wiretap. Nevertheless, Gigante was not afraid to authorize violence to assert his control. Meanwhile, Gigante furthered the appearance of mental illness. Aware of FBI surveillance, he strolled around neighborhoods in a bathrobe muttering to himself. Once, when FBI agents served him a subpoena, he walked into the shower with an umbrella. Such unique habits helped Gigante retain power longer than his contemporaries.

Although the Commission had approved Gotti's disposal of Castellano, Gigante feared Gotti's ambition. The Genovese and Gambino families began competing over certain criminal activities, particularly in the area of construction. The Gambino family also began increasing its operations in New Jersey, a state in which the Genovese family had a strong presence, through an alliance with mafia figures in Philadelphia. After a Gambino encroachment on Genovese territory in New Jersey soon after Gotti assumed power, Gigante plotted to murder Gotti and his brother, Gene. The FBI, which had bugged the restaurant at which the murders were discussed, felt compelled to warn Gotti. In turn, unable to murder Gigante due to increased security, the Gambino family arranged the murder of Genovese underboss Vincent Rotondo. Although a mob war was averted, Gotti remained Gigante's nemesis.

Gigante and Popular Culture

Gigante has become part of popular culture. He has appeared as a character in films on John Gotti, including *Witness to the Mob* (1998). The character of Junior Soprano in the HBO television mafia series *The Sopranos* used an insanity defense similar to Gigante's. Similarly, fictional mafia boss Paul Vitti, portrayed by Robert De Niro, feigns insanity to secure an early prison release in the mob comedy *Analyze That* (2002).

During his adult life, Gigante maintained a residence in northern New Jersey with his wife, whom he married in 1950, and a residence in Manhattan with his mistress. However, he also frequented his mother's home in Greenwich Village, the base of his criminal activities.

Gigante, charged with racketeering and murder in 1990, eventually went to trial in 1997. After John Gotti's 1992 conviction, Gigante had become the most powerful mafia boss in America. His lawyers produced witnesses to testify to his mental illness and that he was unfit to stand trial, but a turnover of high-ranking mafia figures turned the tide against him. Salvatore "Sammy the Bull" Gravano, former Gambino underboss and star witness in the successful trial against Gotti, and former acting Lucchese boss Al D'Arco testified that Gigante was neither insane nor incompetent. Philadelphia mafioso Phil Leonetti implicated Gigante in several 1980s murders of Philadelphia mafia figures. Finally, Anthony "Gaspipe" Casso, former Lucchesse underboss, implicated Gigante in an attempted murder on Gotti. Gigante, convicted on racketeering and conspiracy charges, received a 12-year prison sentence.

In 2003, the aging Gigante pled guilty to obstruction of justice, admitting that his "insanity" was a ploy to evade prosecution, as part of a deal to avoid another lengthy trial on new charges. He died in prison custody in 2005.

ERIC MARTONE

See also: Costello, Frank (1891–1973); Genovese, Vito (1897–1969); Gotti, John (1940–2002)

Further Reading
Blum, Howard. 1993. *Gangland: How the FBI Broke the Mob*. New York: Simon & Schuster.
Cummings, John, and Ernest Volkman. 1992. *Goombata: The Improbable Rise and Fall of John Gotti and His Gang*. New York: Avon.
Gigante, Rita, with Natasha Stoynoff. 2012. *The Godfather's Daughter: An Unlikely Story of Love, Healing, and Redemption*. New York: Hay House.
The Gotti Tapes. 1992. New York: Times Books.

Gilley Family Murders (April 26, 1984)

Billy Gilley Jr. was born into a family where physical abuse was commonplace. As a child, he and his sisters, Jody and Becky, also dealt with an alcoholic father. Billy started committing delinquent acts early in life, with a criminal record that included burglary and arson by age 15. Late in the night of April 26, 1984, Billy beat his mother and father to death with a baseball bat. Hearing the noise, his younger sister, Becky, entered the room and was beaten as well. She would later die at the hospital due to head trauma. Jody Gilley was in her bedroom at the time of the murders. After killing his family, Billy entered Jody's bedroom and told her they needed to get out of the house. Soon after, Jody called the police to report the crime. Billy was arrested and charged with three counts of aggravated murder. He was originally sentenced to three life terms; however, due to discrepancies in his representation at trial, his sentence was overturned. Billy currently resides in Oregon Correctional Facility with a new sentence of at least 36 years.

Linda and Billy Gilley Sr. were farm workers who married young. Billy Sr. had drinking problems, which led to fights within the home. These fights did not improve after the births of their three children, Billy Jr., Jody, and Becky. By the time Billy was in second grade, he was having trouble in school. Billy reports that there was physical abuse in the home and that the children were often beaten with a garden hose if they displeased their father. He also claims to have called child protective services multiple times to try to get help for the children. Billy started shoplifting at an early age and by age 15 had been arrested for burglary and arson. Billy dropped out of high school in the ninth grade after being held back multiple times. He was diagnosed with learning disabilities and borderline personality disorder. Billy's sister, Jody, reports that she was sexually abused at a young age by her brother. She claims to have told her parents; however, they did not believe her.

On April 26, 1984, Jody Gilley skipped her high school classes. This led to an argument with her mother when she returned home later that day. After the argument, her brother stated that he was mad at their parents for arguing with Jody. That evening after Jody had gone to bed, Billy brought their younger sister, Becky, to Jody's room. He informed Jody that he wanted her to keep Becky in the room with her for a while. Jody, who had been sleeping and was disoriented, did not follow Billy Jr.'s instructions and allowed Becky to follow Billy out of the room. Later that night, Billy murdered his mother and father by bludgeoning them with a baseball bat. His younger sister, Becky, heard the noise and ran into the room. Billy then beat her severely as well.

While Billy was clubbing his mother, father, and sister to death, Jody Gilley prepared herself to die next. When Billy entered her room, he did not have his baseball bat in his hand and kept repeating the phrase, "We're free." Billy told his sister that they needed to leave the house and went to

change his clothes. The two then went to a friend's house where Billy hoped to play cards and socialize. When they arrived at the friend's house, Billy left to buy cigarettes. This gave Jody an opportunity to tell someone what her brother had done and she called the police.

Billy was arrested in the early morning hours of April 27, 1984, by Oregon State Police troopers. He was arraigned that afternoon. The next day, Jody Gilley sought legal advice and attempted to obtain a legal guardian to assist her. Since she had not been killed, rumors were being spread that she was in on the murders. On April 29, 1984, Billy Jr.'s sister, Becky, died in the hospital due to the head trauma she suffered. Billy was indicted on May 2, 1984, on three counts of aggravated murder. On May 31, 1984, he pled not guilty after having a psychological evaluation. Billy attempted suicide on September 18, 1984, while in jail. This led to further psychological examinations and delayed his trial, which was originally set for September 25, 1984.

Billy Jr.'s trial began on November 14, 1984. On November 15, 1985, Billy Jr.'s sister, Jody, testified against him. Billy Jr.'s attorney, Stephen Pickens, did not call a single defense witness to the stand. No evidence was given to mitigate the facts presented by the prosecution. Pickens claimed that Billy did not want to testify; however, Billy now claims that he did want to testify. On November 16, 1984, jurors returned a guilty verdict on all three counts of aggravated murder. Billy was sentenced to three consecutive life terms on December 27, 1984. In January 1985, Billy filed an appeal claiming lack of effective representation. This appeal was denied by the court. Billy spent the next few years serving his sentence. He filed a civil suit seeking postconviction relief to potentially change his sentence on October 12, 1994. On July 8, 1998, the postconviction relief was denied as well.

Billy filed a petition for a writ of habeas corpus on July 14, 1998. This would appeal his conviction and his sentence. He maintained that he was not adequately represented during his trial and that this impacted his conviction and sentence. On December 30, 2004, Billy's representation during trial was found to be below the standard for reasonable performance. His lawyers stated that information on his past abuse should have been presented during his initial trial. This added information led to Billy being granted a new trial. On March 16, 2005, the Oregon Department of Justice determined that the new evidence provided did not present enough information to grant a new trial. The state was then asked to overrule the previous finding. On November 9, 2005, the U.S. District Judge called for a new trial for Billy. The state appealed the case and it was sent to the 9th United States Circuit Court of Appeals on December 7, 2005. On August 31, 2007, the Court of Appeals affirmed the opinion that Billy had inadequate representation during his trial. They determined that the conviction should stand; however, the life sentences he had been given were overturned.

In December 2008, the judge heard testimony from Jody Gilley, neighbors of the Gilley family, and psychologists. The court also saw a video of 18-year-old Billy confessing to the murders. The judge determined that Billy would serve at least an additional 36 years. Since receiving this new sentence, Billy has been serving his time at Oregon State Penitentiary. Billy's sister, Jody, has since changed her name to Jody Arlington. She has written about her experience growing up in the Gilley family and surviving the murders and has also assisted with other projects detailing the Gilley family's story. One such book, *While They Slept: An Inquiry into the Murder of a Family* written by Kathryn Harrison in 2009, provides information from Jody as well as interviews with Billy.

DARLA D. DARNO

See also: Clutter Family Murders (1959); Duperrault Family Slayings (November 12, 1961); Gates, Wylie (1969–); Wesson Family Massacre (2004); Yates, Andrea (1964–)

Further Reading

Arlington, Jody. 2005. "After the Horror." WashingtonPost.com. http://www.washingtonpost.com/wp-dyn-content/article/2005/06/11/AR2005061100177.html. Accessed April 16, 2015.

Harrison, Kathryn. 2009. *While They Slept: An Inquiry into the Murder of a Family.* New York: Ballantine Books.

Lemon, Sarah. 2007. "Murderer's Life Sentence Overturned." MailTribune.com. http://www.mailtribune.com/apps/pbcs.dll/article?AID=/20070908/NEWS/709080323/-1/SPECIAL30. Accessed April 16, 2015.

Gillis, Lester Joseph "Baby Face Nelson" (1908–1934)

Baby Face Nelson (1908–1934) was notoriously noted as one of the most dangerous, violent, and volatile bank robbers in the United States throughout the late 1920s and early 1930s. Upon the death of a fellow gangster John Dillinger in 1934, Nelson moved into the rankings of "Public Enemy No. 1" on the Federal Bureau of Investigation's (FBI) most wanted list. However, Nelson's life as "Public Enemy No. 1" was short-lived. In November 1934, Nelson's life as the nation's most callous bank robber ended shortly after a standoff with two FBI officials. Despite a successful getaway from the scene, Nelson succumbed to his injuries at the age of 26 that evening. FBI agents found Nelson the next day after receiving an anonymous telephone call that a body had been dumped near a cemetery in Illinois.

Known to the world as "Baby Face Nelson," Lester Joseph Gillis was born on December 6, 1908, in Chicago, Illinois. After his parents emigrated from Belgium, his father Joseph Gillis began working in the United States as a leather tanner; very little is known about his mother Mary Gillis. Throughout his early childhood, Nelson had a reputation for a short temper that often resulted in fights with his classmates, and by the time he was 13 years old he had already begun a life of crime that landed him in the St. Charles School for Boys. Over the next few years, he joined a gang of juvenile hoodlums in Chicago and spent much of his time in and out of juvenile facilities for his criminal activities such as petty theft, bootlegging, auto theft, and armed robbery.

It was in 1922, at the age of 14, that he was nicknamed "Baby Face" by his fellow gang members due to his juvenile appearance, shorter stature, and lower body weight as compared to the others. During this time, Nelson's father also committed suicide. Then, in 1928, 20-year-old Nelson met 16-year-old Helen Wawzynak (1912–1987) and the two got married. Throughout their marriage, Helen retained her husband's given name Gillis even after he adopted the last name Nelson. Within the first few years of their marriage, Helen and Nelson had their only two children, a son whom they named Ronald (1930–n.d.) and a daughter whom they named Darlene (1932–n.d.). After robbing a Chicago bank in 1931 Nelson was sentenced to a year at the Illinois State Penitentiary in Joliet, Illinois. However, after only serving a year in confinement, he escaped from custody during his return transport from Wheaton, Illinois, where he stood trial for another bank robbery charge.

Over the course of his criminal career, Nelson had teamed up with various gangsters and mobsters such as Charles "Pretty Boy" Floyd (1904–1934), Fatso Negri, Al Capone (1899–1947), and Roger "The Terrible" Touhy (1898–1959). However, it was while he was on the run that Nelson became particularly involved with John Paul Chase (1901–1973)—who was involved in liquor smuggling operations. Over the next few years, Nelson and

Chase engaged in numerous criminal activities together and in 1934, the pair joined up with legendary bank robber John Dillinger (1903–1934)—who at the time was considered "Public Enemy No. 1." Shortly after, Nelson and his family were hiding out at the Little Bohemia Lodge in northern Wisconsin with Dillinger and his gang when Nelson was nearly caught by FBI agents who had learned of his whereabouts. However, dogs alerted the gang to the FBI's arrival allowing Nelson, Dillinger, and the other gang members to escape in the dark to a nearby home and force their way in with two hostages.

Nevertheless, Special Agents J. C. Newman and W. Carter Baum along with the local Constable Carl Christensen followed the gang to their new location. When they arrived at the home, Nelson rushed to the car before they could get out and shot at all three men, killing Special Agent Baum instantly. As a result, Attorney General Homer S. Cummings issued a reward for capture or information leading to the arrest of Nelson. In June 1934, Nelson, Dillinger, and Homer Van Meter (1905–1934) executed a robbery of the Merchants National Bank in South Bend, Indiana, where they also shot and killed a police officer who was on duty at the time. Following the robbery, the trio fled back to Chicago and when Nelson arrived at the arranged meeting place two police officers were approaching the location triggering Nelson to open fire on them, killing both officers at the scene.

On July 22, 1934, Dillinger was ambushed outside the Chicago Biograph Theater in Lincoln Park by FBI agents and killed. Dillinger's death bumped Nelson into the "Public Enemy No. 1" position, which was announced the very next day by FBI director J. Edgar Hoover. Although he fled Chicago for California and managed to evade capture for several months, the FBI finally caught up with him during one of his many trips back to Chicago and Wisconsin. In November 1934, two FBI agents alerted Inspector Samuel P. Cowley of the FBI's Chicago Office—who had been assigned to search for Nelson—to a sighting of Nelson driving in a stolen car along with Helen and Chase near Barrington, Illinois. Nelson, having noticed the two agents, pulled up behind their vehicle so Chase could fire his automatic rifle into the agents' car; however, one of the agents was able to return fire and one of the bullets pierced the radiator of Nelson's car.

Meanwhile, Inspector Cowley and Special Agent Herman Edward Hollis arrived at the scene and began pursuing Nelson, Chase, and Helen in a car chase, which resulted in Nelson veering off the highway because of the punctured radiator. Nelson and Chase immediately got out of the vehicle and before Cowley and Hollis had time to react, or even get out of their vehicle, Nelson and Chase began firing their automatic rifles into the agents' car. During the short-lived standoff, Chase and Helen were not harmed, Agent Hollis was killed at the scene, and Inspector Cowley—who died the next morning—and Nelson were both mortally wounded. After the standoff, Chase helped Nelson—who was hit by 17 bullets—into the agents' car and Helen—who had been in the field nearby—jumped into the vehicle as Chase drove off. Despite their getaway, Nelson succumbed to his injuries and died that evening at the age of 26. FBI agents found his body the next day dumped near a cemetery in Illinois after receiving an anonymous telephone call directing them there.

JENNIFER A. HAEGELE

See also: Barker, Kate "Ma" (1873–1935); Capone, Al (1899–1947); Dillinger, John (1903–1934); Floyd, Charles Arthur "Pretty Boy" (1904–1934)

Further Reading

Burrough, Bryan. 2004. *Public Enemies: America's Greatest Crime Wave and the Birth of the FBI, 1933–34.* New York: The Penguin Press.

Charles River Editors. 2013. *American Outlaws: The Life and Legacy of Baby Face Nelson.* Boston: Charles River Editors LLC.

Nickel, Steven, and William Helmer. 2002. *Baby Face Nelson.* Nashville: Cumberland House.

Gilmore, Gary (1940–1977)

Gary Gilmore's criminal case is important because it intersected debates about the death penalty. In the 1960s capital punishment was ruled "cruel and unusual," which made it unconstitutional under the Eighth Amendment. Because capital punishment was viewed that way, the death penalty was suspended in the United States while guidelines and circumstances were discussed in regards to the justification of implementing such an extreme punishment. The decade-long hibernation of capital punishment on U.S. soil was brought to an end with the execution of an American spree killer, Gary Gilmore (Anderson 2010). Being the first person in the United States to be executed since the reinstatement of the death penalty, Gilmore's execution received an extraordinary amount of cultural and media attention.

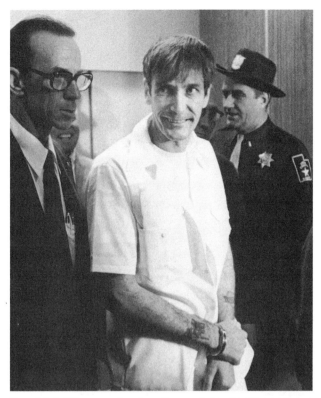

Gary Mark Gilmore arrives heavily guarded to 4th District Court in Provo, Utah, on December 1, 1976. Gilmore was executed by firing squad in 1977. (AP Photo/Ron Barker)

Gary Mark Gilmore was born Faye Robert Coffman, on December 4, 1940, in McCamey, Texas. His mother changed his name only a few weeks after his birth because Coffman was an alias his father was using at the time to hide from the law (Ramsland 2013). His family moved frequently while Gilmore was younger, from Texas to Oregon down to Salt Lake City, Utah, and back up to Oregon again. Gilmore's father was an abusive alcoholic and Gary was his favorite target for the physical and emotional abuse. Gilmore eventually became an American spree murderer who had spent more than half of his life in and out of jails and prisons (Gilmore 1995). From a young age Gilmore had many run-ins with the law, mostly small time or auto thefts, which ended with the culmination of him murdering two innocent people in Utah, in cold blood. Although many murderers have acquired body counts much greater in number than Gilmore's, few of them have had quite as substantial an impact as Gilmore and his trial had on the country.

On the night of July 19, 1976, Gary Gilmore and his girlfriend, Nicole, had an intense argument, resulting in him and his girlfriend breaking up, which ended up leaving Gilmore in an unstable mind-set and emotional state.

After this fight took place, Gilmore went for a drive and ended up at a Sinclair gas station in Orem, Utah. It was at this gas station where he forced the attendant, Max Jensen, to lay face down on the floor and shot him execution style. Gilmore testified that he shot Jensen twice, before the first shot was fired he said "This one's for me" and before the second shot he stated "This one's for Nicole" (Ramsland 2013). On the very next evening, July 20, 1976, Gilmore murdered another young man, Bennie Bushnell, who was the manager at the local motel in Provo, Utah. Immediately after Bushnell was shot, Bushnell's wife entered the room, spooking Gilmore and made him take off running. Knowing that he was in trouble, Gilmore then decided to dispose of the gun. While throwing the gun into a nearby bush, it went off and sent a bullet through Gilmore's right hand (A&E 2000). Needing medical attention for his injury, Gilmore called his cousin Brenda, whom he had been staying with in Utah. After hearing what had happened, Brenda reported him to the police shortly after she hung up the phone with Gilmore. Gilmore was apprehended shortly by Utah State police right outside of Provo, Utah, and surrendered without any problems or altercations (Ramsland 2013).

Gilmore went to trial on October 5, 1976, with a plea of not guilty. The entire court process took two days from beginning to the end. On the second day, the jury took only a few hours to deliberate and reached a unanimous verdict. Because of the brutal and heinous nature of these crimes, Gilmore was ultimately found guilty and sentenced to death. Gilmore was given the option of being executed by hanging or firing squad to which he chose the latter because he believed more things could go wrong with a hanging (Ramsland 2013).

At first, Gilmore tried to claim that he was dissociated at the time of the crimes and therefore is not guilty by reason of insanity. Gilmore mentioned how drugs, alcohol, and mental stress had played a big part on his actions, therefore making him disassociated and legally insane at the time of the crimes. The court disagreed with Gilmore on this account and ruled against the claim stating that he knew what he had done was wrong and did not fit the legal criteria for the insanity plea (A&E 2000). After learning of this, Gilmore retracted his request and seemed to give up all hope. Gilmore accepted the penalty of death and did not use any of his appeals or file for any stays of execution. Despite his acceptance of his sentence, Gilmore was granted several stays of execution through the efforts put forward by the American Civil Liberties Union (*Times* 1977).

Gilmore's trial received a lot of media attention, causing Americans to divide into those who believed the death penalty was too extreme of a punishment, even for cases as despicable as Gilmore's, and those who believed criminals like Gary Gilmore deserved to pay the ultimate price, their life. In the state of Utah, where the trial was held, the majority believed the capital punishment was unconstitutional and should stay in hibernation within the U.S. criminal justice system like it had done for the past 10 years. On July 2, 1976, the state laws were revised and the Supreme Court ruled that for certain types of murder, the death penalty could be carried out (*Time*, 1977). This ruling took place 17 days before Gilmore committed his murder spree, making him eligible for execution.

Methods of Execution

In the United States, there have been five methods of execution: lethal injection, electrocution, gas chamber, hanging, and firing squad that have been historically used. Prior to 1890, the most frequent method was hanging, but many variables could affect that execution style, making it less than efficient and not desirable. Although Gilmore was given the option, inmates today aren't usually given a choice. Today only Utah and Oklahoma recognize the firing squad. In Utah, only prisoners who have elected to be executed by firing squad prior to 2004, when it was eliminated, can be executed in that manner. In Oklahoma, it's only an option if lethal injection is ruled unconstitutional (Robillard 2010).

The American public was affected by Gary Gilmore in more than just a political manner. The crimes, trial, sentencing, and execution of Gilmore had a cultural impact on the general public when actors, authors, and even musicians incorporated the events into their art forms. In 1977, songs such as "Gary Gilmore's Eyes" by The Adverts and "Gary Gilmore and the Island of Dr. Moreau" by the punk band Chain Gang, were released. In 1979, The Police wrote a song titled "Bring on the Night," which went into the mind of Gary Gilmore the night before his execution (Sutcliffe and Fielder, 1981). Books such as the Pulitzer Prize-winning *The Executioner's Song* by Norman Mailer (1979) began to surface. In 1982, Mailer's book was then turned into a television movie where Tommy Lee jones played Gary Gilmore.

Even to this day, the debate of whether or not the death penalty is unconstitutional is a prevalent and frequently discussed topic. Gilmore's trial is an interesting example of a death penalty case because the opposition to the death penalty in this situation did not come from the defendant, but rather the defense team, outside groups, and people who were not involved directly with the case itself. It was also a unique case because of the fact that Gilmore was the first to be executed in the United States in a decade, bringing back capital punishment in U.S. prisons.

JOHN F. GONSLER

See also: Barfield, Velma (1932–1984); Starkweather, Charles and Caril Ann Fugate, Murder Spree of (1957); *Primary Documents*/Gary Gilmore Murder Case: Excerpts from *Gilmore v. Utah* (December 13, 1976)

Further Reading

"After Gilmore, Who's Next to Die?" 1977. *Time*. January 31.

"An American Punishment Again." 1977. *New York Times*. January 18.

Anderson, Aly. 2010. "The 1977 Execution of Gary Gilmore." *Utah Communication History Encyclopedia*. May 4.

Center, Death Penalty Information. 2014. "Part 1: History of the Death Penalty." *Introduction to the Death Penalty*. http://www.deathpenaltyinfo.org/part-i-history-death-penalty. Accessed January 15, 2015.

Gilmore, Mikal. 1995. *Shot in the Heart*. New York: Anchor Books.

Ramsland, Katherine. 2013. "Gary Gilmore." *Crime Library: Criminal Minds & Methods.* http://web.archive.org/web/20131211025958/http://www.trutv.com/library/crime/notorious_murders/mass/gilmore/index_1.html. Accessed April 16, 2015.

Robillard, Kevin P. 2010. "Making a Killing: A History of Execution Methods in the United States." *Newsweek*. June 16.

Sutcliffe, Phil, and Hugh Fielder. 1981. *L' Historia Bandido*. New York: Proteus.

Glen Ridge (NJ) Rape Case (March 1, 1989)

On March 1, 1989, a 17-year-old mentally handicapped female was raped by members of the local high-school football team in Glen Ridge, New Jersey. Reports suggest that her IQ was 64, but some places report it as low as 42. This IQ and her reading comprehension placed her at the level of an eight-year-old child. She was convinced to go to a local house where she was sexually assaulted by multiple men. Once the four offenders were arrested and the trial began, defense attorneys painted a picture of a promiscuous deviant female who seduced the men. The jury, however, found the men guilty.

On March 1, 1989, the female victim, referred to as M.G. to protect her identity, ventured out to the local park where she encountered fellow students. One of the males at the park asked her if she would like to attend a party at a near-by house. Initially, the female refused, but eventually agreed to go when she was promised a date with her crush, Paul Archer. She was accompanied into a basement where other male members of athletic teams from the high school were. According to reports, 12 males were in the basement when she arrived, 13 if you include the one that escorted her. A short time later, six males left the basement and seven remained. The seven males were all on the football team. Six of the males were seniors and one was a junior. The seven who remained were Chris Archer, 17; Kevin Scherzer, 18; Kyle Scherzer, 18; Bryant Grober, 17; Paul Archer, 18; Peter Quigley, 18; and Richard Timothy Corcoran Jr., 18.

While in the basement, the female was vaginally and orally raped by more than one individual. The men penetrated the female with a broom handle and baseball; some reports also include a stick. The broom handle and baseball bat were covered with a plastic bag, which was coated with Vaseline. Once the sexual assault culminated, a sort of pact was made in which the victim agreed to not tell anybody about what happened in the basement. Eventually, she did tell a female student and her swim instructor, but retracted it when she was told the men would get in trouble. A few other teachers were told of the events as well. Three weeks passed before the assault was brought to the attention of others and eventually the police.

The first arrests in this case happened nearly three months after the rape took place. Some of the charges included one count of conspiracy, four counts of aggravated sexual assault, and four counts of aggravated sexual contact. Four of the males were arrested: Paul Archer, Bryant Grober, and Kevin and Kyle Scherzer. All of these men had participated in the rape. The other three men who were present were not arrested. Police investigation determined that while they were present and either verbally encouraged the acts or did nothing to stop it, they did not physically partake in the rape.

The trial began September 21, 1992, and continued for nearly six months. Defense attorneys portrayed the female victim as a dangerous and sinister temptress. They suggested that her mental handicap made her obsessed with sex and that she was willing, able, and anxious to engage in sexual acts with the men. The defense dug into all aspects of the victim's life in an attempt to portray her as a person who was a troublemaker that had previously been involved in deviant acts. This was done in an attempt to make the jury believe that she was not the innocent victim that the prosecution said she was. The defense even questioned individuals concerning the victim's past sexual history. The victim had been previously sexually assaulted at age 12. The defense did not discuss the assault; just that she had been sexually active since age 12. The victim was also using birth control. The victim's mother later testified that victim did not know about the birth control, but she felt it necessary after realizing her daughter's vulnerability for sexual assault. In addition, the defense played up the notion that boys will be boys and that the young men were just engaging in normal sexual male behavior for their age. The defense pushed the idea that they were athletes and good boys.

Before the trial ended, the victim took the stand and testified. By this time the jury had heard several testimonies from teachers, family members, experts, and others concerning her mental capabilities. In fact, the victim blamed herself for the trouble the offenders were in. She felt that it was her fault because she broke the promise of not telling anybody what happened in the basement. The victim even considered these young men to be her friends and even told the court room that she still cared about the men.

On March 4, 1993, the seven women, five men, racially mixed jury began their eight-day deliberation. The central question was whether the victim was capable of consenting to the sexual acts. Defense lawyers argued that she was and the prosecution argued that she was not. Jury members suggested that it was evident that the victim was unable to comprehend the entire situation and therefore could not give consent. The issue ended up being whether the offenders knew that she was unable to give consent. The jury convicted Chris Archer and Kevin Scherzer with a second-degree count of conspiracy and two first-degree counts of sexual assault: one for assault against a mentally defective woman, and one for use of force and coercion. Kyle Scherzer was found guilty of second-degree conspiracy, first-degree aggravated sexual assault by use of force or coercion, and second-degree attempted aggravated sexual assault. Bryant Grober was only convicted of a third-degree conspiracy charge. After the convictions were read, the prosecution attempted to get the judge to revoke bail, but the request was denied and the convicted were allowed to remain free until their sentencing date. Chris Archer and Kevin Scherzer were sentenced to serve 15-year terms, while Kyle Scherzer was sentenced to serve seven years. The three men were given indeterminate sentences not to exceed 15 years in a Youth Correctional Facility. Bryant Grober was sentenced to 200 hours of community service and three years of probation. The case was appealed and the men were allowed to remain free until the decision in 1997. The convictions for aggravated sexual assault through force and coercion were dismissed, but the others were upheld and the men spent their first night locked up. They have all since served their sentences.

MELISSA J. TETZLAFF-BEMILLER

See also: Big Dan Gang Rape Case (1983–1984); Bryant, Kobe, Rape Accusation against (June 30, 2003); Steubenville (OH) Rape Case (August 12, 2012)

Further Reading

Hanley, Robert. 1993. "Verdict in Glen Ridge; Four are Convicted in Sexual Abuse of Retarded New Jersey Woman." *The New York Times.* March 17. 1993. http://www.nytimes.com/1993/03/17/nyregion/verdict-glen-ridge-4-are-convicted-sexual-abuse-retarded-new-jersey-woman.html. Accessed February 25, 2015.

Lefkowitz, Bernard. 1997. *Our Guys: The Glen Ridge Rape and the Secret Life of the Perfect Suburb.* Berkeley: University of California Press.

McGoey, Christine. S. 1993. "When 'Regular Guys' Rape, the Trial of the Glen Ridge Four." *On the Issue Magazine: A Magazine of Feminist, Progressive Thinking.* http://www.ontheissuesmagazine.com/1993fall/Fall1993_McGoey.php. Accessed February 25, 2015.

Goetz, Bernhard (1947–)

In the 1980s, New York City witnessed extraordinary rates of crime—with murders averaging almost 2,000 a year. The case of Bernhard Goetz, best known by his moniker "the Subway Vigilante," became a flashpoint for the rising crime and racial tensions in New York City in the 1980s. Goetz, who was born in 1947 in Queens, New York, was an electrical engineer who owned a small business and was active in local affairs, with an emphasis on cleaning up the city and getting rid it of the crime that plagued the metropolis. In January 1981, Goetz was assaulted by three teenagers in a New York subway station and suffered a permanent injury as a result of the attack. After authorities failed to catch or prosecute his attackers, Goetz took matters into his own

hands and applied for a gun permit (which was denied), but he eventually purchased a .38 caliber firearm, which he carried daily. Then, just three years later, in the week before Christmas in 1984, Goetz entered another New York subway train and was encountered by four unarmed teenagers (Troy Canty, Barry Allen, Darrell Cabey, and James Ramseur) who asked for or demanded money from Goetz. Goetz later claimed that he had anticipated that he was about to be mugged and fired his gun at all four teens, wounding each of them and paralyzing one—Cabey. Goetz fled the scene following the incident but turned himself days later. After a grand jury initially refused to indict Goetz for the shootings, he was indicted on four counts of attempted murder and illegal possession of a firearm. After a six-month trial, Goetz was acquitted of the murder charges but was found guilty on the gun counts. Goetz ultimately served eight months in prison. A civil jury later found Goetz liable for $43 million.

During the 1984 incident, the four teens had first entered the train in the early afternoon. They were traveling to a video arcade where they admittedly hoped to steal quarters using screwdrivers that they had bought with them. The teens were loud and disruptive on the train. Goetz, who was then 37 years old and appeared meek given his glasses and windbreaker, however, sat near the teens when he boarded the train at the Fourteenth Street station. Goetz, as was his custom, was carrying his gun filled with hollow-point bullets (designed to maximize damage) in his waistband. Two of the teens, Canty and Allen, approached Goetz and, depending on which account was to be believed, either asked for or demanded $5 from Goetz. Goetz asked Canty to repeat the demand/request and subsequently began firing at the teens. Canty was struck first, with a wound to his chest, followed by a shot in Allen's back. The third bullet traveled through Ramseur's arm and into his side. Goetz missed with his fourth shot, which had been aimed at Cabey. Goetz then approached Cabey, and again, depending on which version of events is to be believed, told Cabey that "you don't look so bad, here's another" (Fuchs 2013) and fired a round that pierced Cabey's spinal cord or fired the round prior to making such a statement. After brief questioning by the train conductor, Goetz fled the scene, hid out in the state of Vermont for nine days, and disposed of the gun and clothes he had worn during the incident before turning himself in on New Year's Eve. Goetz gave two confessions—first to New Hampshire police (where he had turned himself in) and then to New York Police Department detectives.

Following the incident, Goetz was catapulted to hero status in the New York, and was labeled the Subway

Bernard Goetz, right, dubbed the "subway hero" for his defensive attack on four youths in a New York subway, receives the Good Samaritans award from Frank Borzellieri, president of the Queens Good Samaritans Committee at a New York State Rifle and Pistol Clubs annual luncheon in New York, on April 24, 1988. Goetz delivered a speech to raise money for his legal defense fund. He was convicted of firearms charges, but was acquitted of the more serious crimes of murder and assault. (AP Photo/David Bookstaver)

Vigilante by an adoring public. Notably, then-Mayor Ed Koch was not supportive of Goetz's actions and derided the vigilante nature of the incident. Nonetheless, and at least initially, Goetz received encouragement from celebrities such as Joan Rivers and was hailed in public opinion polls. After the public became aware of the statements Goetz had made to Cabey and other statements Goetz had made in regards to racial issues, public opinion became more divided and the case became a symbol of the city's tensions between crime-fighting and race relations.

Goetz's trial began on December 12, 1986, with jury selection under the guidance of Judge Stephen Crane. After four months, a jury was selected and the district's attorney's office, led by lead prosecutor Gregory Waples, opened

the prosecution by arguing that Goetz had shot one of the teens in the back as he was trying to flee and had shot another teen while he was seated. The defense, led by attorney Barry Slotnick, attacked the teens, labeling them "thugs" and "savages." One of teens, Canty, testified and admitted to his drug use, prior criminal history, and intention of the teens, on the day of the shooting, to have robbed the video arcade. Both the prosecution and defense focused on whether the teens had asked or demanded money from Goetz. Two of the other teens effectively refused to testify. Several other first responders, medical personnel, and eye-witnesses were called to the stand with their testimony focusing on the actions and statements purportedly made by Goetz and the teens.

During the trial, Goetz's taped confessions were played for the jury, including Goetz's admission that he had approached the seated Cabey and stated "you seem to be all right, here's another" as he fired another round of ammunition at Cabey. Other witnesses' accounts, however, suggested that the shots had come rapidly, without time to make this statement. Nonetheless, jurors later admitted that the confessions were crucial pieces of evidence that changed their opinion of Goetz from that of a meek-looking, mild-mannered individual to that of a dangerous individual. Psychologists were also called by the defense to explain Goetz's actions as nothing more than an adrenaline response. Finally, the jury also was taken to a nearly identical subway car for inspection of what would have been the crime scene. Court watchers believed that the witnesses for the state were ineffective and often damaged the prosecution's theory of the case. After four days of deliberations, on June 16, 1987, the jury convicted Goetz of the firearm charges but acquitted Goetz on the four counts of attempted murder and criminal assault. Goetz ultimately served eight months for his conviction.

Goetz was later sued civilly by the teens. Notably, in these proceedings, which did not begin until the mid-1990s and amid a radically different climate in New York City, Goetz claimed that he shot at the teens not because they had demanded money from him but, rather, because of the facial expressions and demeanor of the teens. Goetz also argued that society would have been better off if Cabey's mother had had an abortion. After five hours of deliberations, and without Goetz in the courtroom, the jury found Goetz liable and ordered him to pay $43 million in damages. Goetz declared bankruptcy. In 2001, Goetz ran unsuccessfully for mayor of New York. In 2013, Goetz was arrested on drug charges in an undercover operation.

Michele Bisaccia Meitl

See also: Central Park Jogger Case (1989); *Primary Documents/ Excerpts from The People of the State of New York v. Bernhard Goetz* (1986)

Further Reading

Fletcher, George P. June 1990. *A Crime of Self-Defense: Bernhard Goetz and the Law on Trial*. Chicago: University of Chicago Press.

Fuchs, Erin. 2013. "1980s 'Subway Vigilante' Shot Four Black Teens Who Asked Him For $5, And He Got Off, Too." *Business Insider*. July 15. http://www.businessinsider.com/is-george-zimmerman-like-bernhard-goetz-2013-7. Accessed April 16, 2015.

Johnson, Kirk. 1987. "Goetz Is Cleared in Subway Attack; Gun Count Upheld; Acquittal Won in Shooting of 4 Youths—Prison Term Possible On Weapon Charge." *The New York Times*. June 17. http://www.nytimes.com/1987/06/17/nyregion/goets-cleared-subway-attack-gun-count-upheld-acquittal-won-shooting-4-youths.html?pagewanted=all&src=pm. Accessed April 16, 2015.

Goldman, Emma, and Alexander Berkman, Trial of (1917)

Emma Goldman and Alexander Berkman were long familiar with the American political and legal systems before they were arrested on June 15, 1917, under the Espionage Act and tried and sentenced on July 9, 1917. This conviction paved the way for their deportation.

The road from immigration to deportation proved to be a straight ideological one for Emma Goldman and Alexander Berkman. Born on June 27, 1869, in Kovno, Russia, Emma Goldman immigrated to the United States in 1884 to live with her sister in Rochester, New York. Family financial hardships forced Emma to leave school and work as a seamstress in a clothing factory. As she and her family struggled for physical survival, Emma shaped her political persona through the filter of her hands-on experience with miserable working conditions and what she considered to be government oppression of workers.

The Haymarket Riot in Chicago in 1886 solidified Emma Goldman's anarchist beliefs, and joined by anarchist writer Alexander Berkman, her lifelong friend and lover, she began writing and lecturing vehemently advocating free speech, women's rights, and social concerns. In 1892, Emma Goldman and Alexander Berkman, who immigrated to the United States from Russia in 1888, planned the assassination of industrialist and financier Henry Clay Frick. Although Frick survived the assassination attempt, authorities sentenced Alexander Berkman to 22 years in prison, but released him on May 18, 1906, after he had served 14 years of his sentence.

In the years that followed, Emma Goldman herself served multiple prison sentences for inciting to riot and illegally distributing birth control information. From 1906 to 1917, she and Alexander Berkman edited and published the anarchist journal *Mother Earth* and Berkman established his own journal, *The Blast*, in 1917. Emma Goldman wrote five books.

Congress passed the Selective Service Act of 1917, requiring all males age 21–30 to register for the draft.

Emma Goldman saw these actions as exercises in capitalist militarist aggression and she declared in *Mother Earth* that she intended to resist conscription and to oppose American involvement in World War I. Emma Goldman and Alexander Berkman organized the No Conscription League of New York which became the center of activism against the draft, with chapters springing up in other cities.

On June 15, 1917, the police raided the offices of the No Conscription League of New York, confiscating anarchist records and propaganda and arresting Emma Goldman and Alexander Berkman. Back by the newly enacted Espionage Act, the authorities charged them with conspiracy "to induce persons not to register," and set bail at $25,000 each.

The arresting officials whisked Alexander Berkman and Emma Goldman away to the New York City Prison, or the Tombs II, where they were held nearly incommunicado until their friends could raise bail. A federal grand jury had issued a formal indictment.

On June 27, 1917, the trial began in front of Judge Julius Mayer. Emma Goldman and Alexander Berkman represented themselves. The defendants requested a postponement, citing the fact that they had quite recently been released from prison and had no time to summon witnesses or prepare their case. They also cited Alexander Berkman's physical condition, pointing out that before his arrest he had sprained his leg and appeared in court on crutches. Judge Mayer denied both requests, insisting upon an immediate trial.

Prosecutor Harold Content opened his case on Monday, July 2, 1917. Characterizing the two defendants as "disturbers of law and order," he asserted that he would show that in their writings and public addresses both defendants had tried to influence the ignorant in the men of military age not to register. He presented newspaper reporters, printers, binders, and other witnesses who testified about the contents, printing and binding of Mother Earth, The Blast, and No-Conscription literature. The defendants admitted the authorship of the writings, but they argued that the testimonies were superfluous.

Prosecutor Content called a police stenographer as a witness and she testified that in a speech given at Harlem River Casino on May 18, Emma Goldman had advocating using violence. Emma Goldman denied saying such a thing and called many witnesses who corroborated her denial. A lengthy discussion about the question of violence and using violent methods to advance

Anarchist propaganda followed. The Prosecution called the proprietor of the Harlem River Casino, who testified that the May 18 meeting had been orderly despite the efforts of a group of flag-carrying soldiers who attempted to challenge the speakers. Magazine writers John Reed and Lincoln Steffens testified that they had known Emma Goldman and Alexander Berkman for many years and that they didn't regard either of them as violent. Others testified that Emma Goldman had not urged violence at the Harlem River Casino meeting.

Alexander Berkman and Emma Goldman outlined the case of the defendants, arguing that the First Amendment to the Constitution gave them the right of free speech and speaking out against the draft and questioning and criticizing the government was not an illegal activity. Emma Goldman asked how the government could claim to fight for democracy abroad while suppressing free speech at home.

After eight days, the trial ended on Monday, July 9, 1916. In the closing statements, Alexander Berkman spoke for two hours, Emma Goldman for over an hour, and Harold Content's summation for the government lasted about an hour. The jury deliberated for 39 minutes. The jury found the defendants guilty.

Emma Goldman immediately arose and moved that the verdict be set aside as absolutely contrary to the evidence. Judge Mayer denied her motion. Next, Emma asked that the sentence be deferred for a few days and that bail be continued in the sum already fixed in the case. Again, Judge Mayer denied her motion.

Judge Mayer imposed a sentence of two years in prison for Alexander Berkman and Emma Goldman and fined each of them $10,000. He instructed Prosecutor Content to send the record of the convictions to the immigration authorities so they could take such action as they considered suitable when the prisoners had served their terms. Under the new federal law, the government could deport an alien who had been convicted of a crime twice to the country of his or her origin.

Midnight trains spirited the prisoners away. Alexander Berkman went to Atlanta, Georgia, and Emma Goldman went to Missouri State Penitentiary, now Jefferson City Correctional Center. Both spent 22 months behind bars and both spent much of their time following the events in Russia. When they were released from prison in 1919, they were arrested with hundreds of other people deemed dangerous to America and deported to Russia.

KATHY WARNES

See also: Haymarket Square Riot/Bombing (Chicago) (1886); Rosenberg, Julius and Ethel Rosenberg Espionage Case (1950–1953)

Further Reading

Avrich, Paul, and Avrich, Karen. 2012. *Sasha and Emma: The Anarchist Odyssey of Alexander Berkman and Emma Goldman.* Cambridge, MA: Harvard University Press.

Berkman, Alexander. 1992. *Life of an Anarchist: The Alexander Berkman Reader.* New York: Four Walls Eight Windows Press.

Berkman, Alexander, and Goldman, Emma. 2012. *Trial and Speeches of Alexander Berkman and Emma Goldman in the United States District Court, in the City of New York, July, 1917.* Detroit: Gale.

Falk, Candace. 1990. *Love, Anarchy, & Emma Goldman: A Biography.* New Brunswick, NJ: Rutgers University Press

Moritz, Theresa. 2001. *The World's Most Dangerous Woman: A New Biography of Emma Goldman.* Vancouver: Subway Books, 2001.

Wexler, Alice. 1984. *Emma Goldman: An Intimate Life.* New York: Pantheon Books.

Wexler, Alice. 1989. *Emma Goldman in Exile: From the Russian Revolution to the Spanish Civil War.* Boston: Beacon Press.

Gonzales, Julio (1954–)

On March 25, 1990, Julio Gonzales argued with his ex-girlfriend at the Happy Land nightclub. He caused a scene, threatening violence, and the bouncer at the door evicted Gonzales from the premises. Gonzales walked away from the club and sought out a means of revenge against the bouncer and his ex-girlfriend. He returned to the club with gasoline. He threw the gasoline at the club and lit a match. In the ensuing fire and panic, 87 people were killed, most due to smoke inhalation and an inability to leave the club due to blocked exits. Gonzales's ex-girlfriend was one of a handful of people who escaped.

Julio Gonzales was born in 1954. A native of Cuba he had spent much of his life in trouble. In Cuba he was imprisoned as an army deserter in 1974 and in 1980 he claimed that he was a drug dealer so that he could participate in what came to be known as the freedom flotilla. On May 15, 1980, Cuba emptied many of the cells of its overflowing prison and loaded prisoners onto boats that were cast off to the sea. The occupants were thieves, rapists, murders, drug dealers, and political prisoners, male and female, young and old. They reached Key West, Florida, a few weeks later on May 31 and were accepted by the Carter administration as refugees.

Gonzales held no formal education and once in the United States he made his way to the Tremont neighborhood of the Bronx, where others from the flotilla had settled. There he was sponsored by the American Council for Nationalities that helped him adapt to American culture and find several low-paying labor jobs. It was while he was living in Tremont that he met Lydia Feliciano in 1984 and moved into her apartment as her boyfriend soon after. The relationship was a rocky one. The two broke up many times over the six years they knew each other. The two were separated again by March 1990 and Feliciano had no intention of resuming the relationship. Feliciano worked at the Happy Land social club. The Happy Land was one of over a hundred and fifty illegal ethnic social clubs operating without a license in the neighborhood in the 1980s and 1990s. These clubs did not have operating or liquor licenses and as such would be shut down immediately when they were found. Most of these clubs were in buildings that were in disrepair. In the Happy Land, the dance floor would shake under the feet of revelers and the city had ordered it shut down due to the presence of only a partial sprinkler system as its only mitigation strategy against fire.

March 25, 1990, was the weekend of the Punta Carnivale, a Honduran festival and the club was packed with revelers. Feliciano and Gonzales were both there. Gonzales had recently lost his job and was hustling in the streets to attempt to pay rent. He hoped to convince Feliciano to take him back. The two argued and when Feliciano attempted to leave their table, Gonzales grabbed her. A bouncer intervened and removed Gonzales from the club. Gonzales threatened the bouncer and told him that he would return and shut the club down. Walking away from the club, Gonzales found a discarded gallon container and went to a local gas station to fill it. The clerk originally refused, but Gonzales and another patron convinced him to let Gonzales purchase a dollar worth of gas, about ¾ of a gallon at the time.

He returned to the club around 3 a.m. and, finding no one outside the club, threw the gasoline into the door way. He lit the gasoline and stood across the street in front of the club to watch it burn. When first responders arrived he walked to the bus stop and took the bus home. The fire remained in the doorway until the first individuals escaped, opening doors that allowed for additional oxygen to join the fire and it rose to the second floor. The disc jockey attempted to warn the patrons on the dance floor when he noticed the fire, turning on the house lights and shouting at the crowd. Panic ensued, a few people escaped, including the disc jockey who was badly burned. The rest, 87 people, were killed mostly by smoke inhalation carbon monoxide mixed with cyanide and other poisonous gases released by the burning of the substandard building materials that made the club structure. People were overcome so quickly, that some were found dead still on their bar stools or at their tables with drinks in hand. Thirteen firefighters were injured trying to bring the blaze under control. As firefighters entered the building, they were met by piles of the dead, in stairwells, doorways, and on the dance floor, but very few were actually burned. Burns were superficial since everyone died either due to smoke inhalation or trampling. It was considered the worst fire in New York City since the Triangle Shirt Factory fire, ironically having occurred on March 25, 1911.

The club had no fire exits, no alarms, and only a partial sprinkler system. These factors had resulted in an order for the club to be shut down weeks before the fire. The owners had disregarded the order. By 4 p.m., the police had found Linda Feliciano, who had been one of the first and few who escaped the fire. She told investigators about the argument with her boyfriend and they sought Gonzales out at home for questioning. When he answered the door he smelled of gasoline and went quietly with the police. He was Mirandized, but quickly admitted to setting the fire as revenge against Feliciano. He told officers that the devil had entered into him. At 2 a.m., he was arraigned for 87 counts of homicide and remanded without bail to a psychiatric ward for evaluation and observation. The trial took place in the summer of 1991 and by August 19 he was found guilty of arson and two counts of homicide per victim, for a total of 174 counts. He was sentenced to 25 years to life for each count, but would be eligible for parole after 25 years, but his parole is unlikely. A stone memorial marks the site of the fire in the Bronx.

CLAIRISSA D. BREEN

See also: Cocoanut Grove Nightclub Fire (Boston) (1942); Station Nightclub Fire (West Warwick, RI) (February 20, 2003); Triangle Shirtwaist Factory Fire (1911)

Further Reading

Angier, Natalie. 1990. "Death in Seconds: Toxins or a Searing Flashover Suspected." *New York Times*. March 27.

Bukowski, Richard. 1992. "Analysis of the Happyland Social Club Fire with Hazard." *Fire and Arson Investigator* 42 (3) (March): 36–47. http://www.fire.nist.gov/bfrlpubs/fire92/PDF/f92041.pdf. Accessed April 16, 2015.

Koleniak, Mike, and Andrea Peyser. 1990. "Fire Hardened Vets Shaken by the Piles of Bodies." *New York Post*. March 26.

Oliver, Chris. 1990. "He Sold Gas—Now Their Pain Is His." *New York Post*. March 27, p. 9.

Magnuson, Ed. 1990. "The Devil Made Him Do It." *Time* Magazine. April 9, p. 38.

Parascandola, Rocco. 1990. "Cries Begin to Fade on Street of Tears." *New York Post*. March 28.

Parascandola, Rocco, and Andrea Peyser. 1990. "Festive Mood Turned to Mourning." *New York Post*. March 26.

Gotti, John (1940–2002)

John Gotti was the notorious Gambino family Don (boss), one of the youngest Dons in mafia history. Gotti became one of the most infamous criminals of his time due to his ability to elude prosecution. However, his ability to avoid prosecution ended in 1992 when the Department of Justice (DOJ) secured the testimony of Gotti's right-hand man Salvatore "Sammy the Bull" Gravano (1945–). With this testimony, John Gotti became one of the first individuals prosecuted under the Racketeer Influenced and Corrupt Organizations (RICO) statute. The trial inevitably ended Gotti's reign in the mafia by sentencing him to live the remainder of his life in a maximum-security federal prison, where he eventually died in 2002 from throat cancer (Mustain and Capeci 2002).

Often referred to as "Teflon Don" or "Dapper Don," John Joseph Gotti was born on October 27, 1940, in the Bronx, New York, and named after his father, a construction worker. When he was 12 years old, his family moved to Brooklyn, New York—an area already thriving with mafia activity. Already having a reputation in the streets as a tough fighter who could "hold his own" against the neighborhood thugs, Gotti became involved in petty street crime and running errands for the neighborhood mobsters. When he was 16, Gotti dropped out of high school and joined a local teenage gang known as the Fulton-Rockaway Boys, where he quickly became the leader. Gotti was arrested several times for petty crimes between 1957 and 1960, but every charge either received a reduced sentence or was dismissed.

In the early 1960s, Gotti married Victoria DiGiorgio (1962–), with whom he had five children. During this time, Gotti attempted to make a life for his family with legitimate employment, but nothing stuck. Still struggling for money, Gotti began working as a gambling bookie and took part in several small-scale larcenies, some of which he served a couple short stints in jail. During this time, Gotti also became involved with brothers, Carmine and Daniel Fatico, who ran a mafia crew under Aniello Dellacroce (1914–1985), the Gambino underboss. After serving a one-year stint in jail for attempted burglary in 1965,

Gotti was arrested, convicted, and sentenced to three years in prison in 1969 for hijacking a warehouse at the John F. Kennedy airport in New York in 1967 (Mustain and Capeci 2002). Gotti's actions made an impression on the Gambino crime family, and shortly after his release, he was asked to participate in the 1973 murder of James McBratney—who was suspected of killing Don Carlo Gambino's (1902–1976) nephew. Gotti was indicted for and pled guilty to the murder of McBratney in 1975. After serving only two years of the prison sentence, he was paroled.

Upon his release from prison, Gotti was "made" into the Gambino family (i.e., a formally initiated member) and became "acting captain" to the Bergin crew, though continuing to report to Dellacroce. A year later, Gambino passed away from a heart attack, and Paul Castellano (1915–1985) became the new don of the Gambino crime family, despite the fact that Dellacroce was next in line to succeed as family Don. Although Dellacroce remained the underboss of the Gambino crime family, Gotti was angered that Dellacroce did not receive the position.

In 1980, Frank Gotti, John Gotti's 12-year-old son, was accidently killed by John Favara (1929–1980), a neighbor and family friend of the Gotti's, when Frank rode his motorbike into the street and in front of Favara's oncoming car. Several months after the police ruled the death an accident, Favara began receiving threats on his life and decided to move his family out of town, but disappeared before he could do so. Favara's disappearance has been a topic of debate, where some people suspect Gotti was responsible for the apparent murder while others concluded that Gotti did not give blessing for the kidnapping and that it was done to win his approval. Nevertheless, the police were never able to link Gotti to Favara's disappearance, discover what became of his body, and no one was ever charged.

Throughout the late 1970s and early 1980s, the Federal Bureau of Investigation (FBI) agents began heavy surveillance on Gotti. It was also during this time that Gotti began developing his crew into a strong and independent organization, taking part of crimes without approval from Castellano. In December 1985 Dellacroce passed away from cancer. Upon Dellacroce's death, Castellano appointed his bodyguard Thomas Bilotti (1940–1985) as his new underboss, despite the fact that Gotti was next in line to succeed as the family underboss. Again, Gotti was outraged that the Gambino crime family would allow the rightful successor for the open position to be passed over for a second time. Without Dellacroce there to keep him in check, Gotti decided that that was also the last time it was going

to happen. Therefore, with a significant amount of help from Gravano, Gotti and his crew began devising a plan to end Castellano and Bilotti's reign. Within two weeks, Castellano and Bilotti were ambushed and gunned down outside of Sparks Steak House in Manhattan, New York. No charges were ever brought in the murders and their deaths led to Gotti taking the position of Don, and Frank DeCicco (1935–1986) taking the position of underboss in the Gambino crime family.

Gotti was on the U.S. most wanted list by the late 1980s. Authorities made several attempts at prosecuting Gotti for various charges, but each time the charges would not stick; which is how Gotti earned the name "Teflon Don." For instance, in 1987 Gotti was facing the possibility of an extended jail term for charges of racketeering but was acquitted after the jury concluded that there was not enough evidence to convict him. This verdict was imposed despite the testimony of 90 witnesses arguing against Gotti (Blum 2009). Despite U.S. attorney Andrew Maloney telling the press, "The jury has spoken. Obviously they perceived there was something wrong with the evidence," many officials, such as FBI agents Bruce Mouw and George Gabriel, believed that Gotti tampered with the jury through bribery or threats (Blum 2009, 198–199).

Then, in 1992 the reign of Gotti "The Teflon Don" came to an end. The surveillance compiled on Gotti by FBI agents and the testimony of Salvatore Gravano provided enough evidence for the Department of Justice (DOJ) to file new charges against Gotti for racketeering and murder. This time the charges stuck making John Gotti one of the first individuals prosecuted under the RICO statute (Gotti and Gravano, 1992). The trial inevitably ended Gotti's reign in the Mafia, and he was sentenced to live the remainder of his life in a maximum-security federal prison in Marion, Illinois, without the possibility of parole. In 2002, after spending 10 years in prison, Gotti died from throat cancer (Mustain and Capeci 2002).

Jennifer A. Haegele

See also: Capone, Al (1899–1947); Gravano, Salvatore "Sammy the Bull" (1945–); Luciano, Charles "Lucky" (1897–1962)

Further Reading
Blum, Howard. 2009. *Gangland: How The FBI Broke the Mob*. New York: Simon & Schuster.
Capeci, Jerry, and Gene Mustain. 1996. *Gotti: Rise and Fall*. New York: Onyx.
Cummings, John, and Ernest Volkman. 1992. *Goombata: The Improbable Rise and Fall of John Gotti and His Gang*. New York: Avon

Davis, John. 1993. *Mafia Dynasty: The Rise and Fall of the Gambino Crime Family*. New York: Harper Torch.

Gotti, John, and Salvatore Gravano. 1992. *The Gotti Tapes: Including the Testimony of Salvatore (Sammy the Bull) Gravano*. New York: Times Books.

Mustain, Gene, and Jerry Capeci. 2002. *Mob Star: The Story of John Gotti*. Indianapolis: Alpha Books.

Goudeau, Mark (1964–)

Mark Goudeau was charged and found guilty for the heinous acts of serial rape, murder, and robbery in Phoenix, Arizona, which landed him the name as the Baseline Killer or Baseline Rapist. This serial spree occurred between 2005 and 2006, and Goudeau is now incarcerated on death row. The atrocious events had Phoenix, Arizona, in a public frenzy due to the high rates of crime and the unknown suspect at large for a lengthy period of time. To this day, Goudeau and his family claim his innocence and deny any affiliation with the Baseline crimes. His supporters argue he was arrested only because of racial discrimination and think that he was arrested only because he was an African American male with a police record who was just in the wrong place at the wrong time.

Goudeau was born September 6, 1964, in Phoenix, Arizona. He is the son of Willie and Alberta, who later divorced, and has 13 siblings, with Goudeau being the second youngest. Goudeau has a history of family troubles including drug and alcohol abuse. Alberta passed away when Goudeau was 12 years old. He attended Corona del Sol High School in Tempe, Arizona, where he participated in sports, such as football, but lacked enough credits to graduate high school.

After dropping out of high school, Goudeau's life took a downhill turn. In 1989, his brother and he were arrested for raping a woman but were not charged. Goudeau then got in trouble for trespassing in 1987 and driving under the influence in 1988. In 1989, he was sentenced to 15 years in a prison for abducting, assaulting, and raping a woman. Goudeau served 13 years and was paroled in 2004. He moved with his wife, Wendy Carr, to a house where he got a job as a construction worker.

The crimes began a year later in 2005. The first reported crime took place on August 6 when the offender molested two sisters. It is believed that the first murder took place only a month after the sexual assaults. Unfortunately, the DNA evidence gathered from the crime was mishandled, and the one swab of DNA was never tested. Multiple robberies, sexual assaults, and murders occurred between 2005 and 2006. All crimes were linked together through ballistic evidence.

The Phoenix Police Department continued to work the case by following up on tips and looking for leads, as well as offering a $100,000 reward for information leading to the arrest of the Baseline Killer. Police reports suspected a light-skinned black male as the offender. Once the public received sketches of the suspect, the parole officers at the Northeast Parole Office with Arizona Department of Corrections recognized a possible match. Goudeau was under their supervision at the time and in August, 2006, the parole officers informed the Phoenix Police Department of the possible match based upon the sketches. While on a home visit, the parole officers found a ski mask and a toy gun in Goudeau's residence, which allowed the police to use this information for a search warrant. The police then searched the house and found supplementary items to link Goudeau to the crimes such as victims' jewelry and traces of blood. The offender was labeled as the Baseline Killer and Baseline Rapist because some crimes took place near Baseline Road in South Phoenix, Arizona.

The police also associated the serial spree with the crimes against the two sisters in 2005. The second DNA swab was tested once revealed it was never analyzed for the original crimes. After approximately a year of investigation, the police were able to scientifically link Goudeau to the crimes based upon the DNA taken from the swab.

On September 4, 2006, police arrested Goudeau as a suspect for a double rape and sexual assault of the two sisters in 2005. He was found guilty on September 7, 2007, and sentenced to prison for 438 years on charges related to the double rape. Goudeau was also linked to the Baseline Killer crimes with the help of DNA evidence. He was found guilty of all Baseline Killer crimes, except for three counts of robbery and one of kidnapping that was originally believed to be linked to the serial crimes. Goudeau was linked to 9 counts of first-degree murder, 15 sexual assaults, 11 accounts of kidnapping, and multiple armed robberies according to reports. On December 14, 2007, Goudeau was sentenced to death and is presently being held at Arizona State Prison Complex Eyman. Despite being found guilty and sitting on death row, Goudeau continues to be defended by his family and friends with a belief that he did not commit the crimes and the police framed him. His supporters argue he was arrested because he was an African American male with a police record who was just in the wrong place at the wrong time, which suggested a racial discrimination concern with Goudeau's conviction.

All victims were women, despite one male who is believed to be murdered on accident. Goudeau disguised himself with masks, hats, and portrayed himself as being lost, homeless, or a drug addict to get close to the victims. The women were usually abducted from the street corner and taken to a secluded environment where they were shot in the head. Only one female victim failed to follow the routine and was killed at her home. Reports state there was no motive for the brutal crimes, which included shooting all victims in the head with the same gun.

KADEE L. BRINSER

See also: Bundy, Ted (1946–1989); Dahmer, Jeffrey (1960–1994); Gein, Ed (1906–1984); Manson, Charles (1934–); Sowell, Anthony (1959–)

Further Reading

Alfano, Sean. 2007. "Trial of Alleged Baseline Killer Begins." CBS News, July 23. http://www.cbsnews.com/stories/2007/07/23/national/main3087799.shtml?tag=contentMain;content Body. Accessed April 16, 2015.

Hogan, Shanna. 2009. "Unreasonable Doubt?" *Times*, June 9. http://shannahogan.com/unreasonable-doubt-times-publications-june-2009/. Accessed April 16, 2015.

Kreiser, John. 2006. "Arrest in Phoenix 'Baseline Killer' Probe." CBS News, September 7. http://www.cbsnews.com/stories/2006/09/07/national/main1982348.shtml?tag=content Main;contentBody. Accessed April 16, 2015.

"Wife of Suspect in 'Baseline Killer' Case Stands by Him." 2007. ABC News. July 5. http://abcnews.go.com/GMA/story?id=3347852&page=1. Accessed April 16, 2015.

Graham, Barbara (1923–1955)

Barbara Graham was a 20th-century murderess who became the third female to be legally executed in California and the 37th woman executed in the United States. She was put to death in San Quentin Prison's gas chamber for murdering Mabel Monahan, an elderly widow in Burbank, California. She was executed on the same day as her two accomplices, Emmett Perkins and Jack Santo. Though there were three defendants on trial, the press focused on Graham who they labeled as the femme fatale. As police ran their investigation and identified the suspects, two of them immediately cooperated with the police; however, the first was kidnapped and murdered to prevent his testimony. The other suspect testified that

Graham "pistol-whipped the victim into a bloody heap" (Headsman 2011). Graham's case is used as an example for antideath penalty activists to argue that the death penalty should be abolished, but her case could be used as an example for both sides (Linn 2013). Graham's crime was not sensational, but the trial and her execution were and have been immortalized in the film *I Want to Live!* by Robert Wise (Cairns 2013).

Barbara was given the nickname "Bloody Babs" and "Iceberg Blonde" by the press. Born in Oakland, California, in 1923 to an unwed teenage mother, Hortense Wood, her childhood was spent in reformatories. By age 27, Barbara had three ex-husbands and two baby boys. Additionally, she had been arrested for petty crimes as well as prostitution, perjury, and vagrancy. In 1950, Barbara met Henry Graham. Henry would become her fourth husband and the father of her third son. It was soon after this she became addicted to heroin and was convicted of committing murder.

Mabel Monahan was the former mother-in-law of a gambler Tutor Scherer. Mable lived in a house Tutor had owned and it was rumored that Scherer left a safe with $100,000 in the house. Armed with this knowledge, Perkins put together a team of five people for a heist, including himself: Perkins, Baxter Shorter, Jack Santo, John True, and Barbara Graham. Police arrested Shorter for an unrelated crime and he began talking to police about Monahan's murder.

The day after Shorter's apprehension was announced, he was abducted from his home at gunpoint and was never seen again. His wife, Olivia Shorter, identified her husband's abductor as Perkins and described the getaway car to police and reporters as a 1951 Plymouth or Dodge, which linked Santo to the kidnapping. When this information became public, True followed in Shorter's footsteps and began talking about the murder in exchange for immunity.

According to True, Graham's roll was to ring Monahan's doorbell and say she had car trouble. Graham was then to ask if she could use the phone, which was how the four men planned on gaining entry to the house. However, Monahan began yelling and would not stop so Graham responded by hitting her repeatedly in the face with the butt of a pistol to shut her up. Before they left the house, Graham put a pillowcase over Monahan's head and Santo wrapped a piece of cloth around Monahan's neck. Though Monahan had several large, gaping wounds in her head, the blows did not kill her; instead police investigators determined a

Barbara Graham is pictured here as she entered the San Quentin Prison gates. With two male accomplices, Graham was convicted of the 1953 murder of Mabel Monahan of Burbank, California. All three were executed in the gas chamber. (Bettmann/Corbis)

cloth tied around her neck strangled her. The five intruders never found the safe and left Monahan's things alone, despite the fact that Monahan had several pieces of expensive jewelry on and her purse having almost $500. The criminals still left empty handed.

Graham denied participating in Monahan's murder and the evidence against her was circumstantial. There were no fingerprints, weapons, or other physical evidence to link Graham to the murder scene besides True's testimony. However, True had an extraordinarily strong incentive to place Graham at the murder scene since prosecutors offered him immunity if he testified; the district attorney dismissed the charges against True. While in jail awaiting trial, she had an affair with a fellow inmate, Donna Prow, who offered to have a friend, Sam Sirianni, say he was with Graham the night of the murder. The caveat to this agreement was that Graham had to confess to

Sirianni so he would provide the alibi. However, unknown to Graham, Sirianni was an undercover police officer. Jack Hardy, Graham's attorney, as well as Graham felt that he was to blame for seeking out an alibi because he continuously told her that she would be sentenced to death if she could not remember what she did that night. The jury deliberated for less than seven hours before notifying the court that they reached a verdict; Graham, Perkins, and Santo were all found guilty of first-degree murder, but did not offer a recommendation on sentencing. In the early 1950s this meant one thing: death in San Quentin's gas chamber.

While incarcerated, Graham was a sought-after interviewee and one of the country's most glamorous death-row inmates. She received Bibles, versus from scripture, and hundreds of letters, and was interviewed by several reporters. As they interviewed her, several reporters became convinced that Graham was innocent and began working to get her a stay of execution and a new trial. Before the execution occurred, Graham was granted a total of three stays; one on November 26, 1954, which extended the date of execution from December 3.

In March, the U.S. Supreme Court denied Graham's petition and lifted the stay, which allowed the Superior Court judge to set a new execution date of June 3, 1955. Graham was scheduled to go first at 10:00 a.m. and her accomplices, Perkins and Santo, were scheduled to be executed together at 1:00 p.m. the same day. A little after 9:00 a.m. on June 3, the governor ordered Graham's second stay of execution to hear a petition by Al Matthews, Graham's appellate attorney; this led to the execution being rescheduled for 10:45 a.m. At 10:25 a.m. the court turned down Matthews's appeal and the execution was back on. As Graham prepared to leave the holding cell the telephone rang again; the governor agreed to a third stay of execution. At 11:15 a.m. the court denied this appeal and the execution was rescheduled again for 11:30 a.m.; Graham left her holding cell and was led to the gas chamber. Graham's death was not quick or easy; she repeatedly gasped and flung her head back and forth. The door to the gas chamber closed at 11:34 a.m. and Graham was pronounced dead at 11:42 a.m. by the state of California.

MICHELLE HARNER

See also: Baker, Lena (1900–1945); Barfield, Velma (1932–1984); Eubanks, Susan (1964–); Gunness, Belle (1859–c. 1908); Lewis, Teresa (1969–2010); Moore, Blanche Taylor (1933–); Tucker, Karla Faye (1959–1998); *Primary Documents*/Barbara Graham Murder Case: Excerpts from *People v. Santo* (1954)

Further Reading

Bovsun, Mara. 2010. *Mother from Hell, Hortense Wood, Led to Rise of Barbara "Bloody Babs" Graham.* http://www.nydailynews.com/news/crime/mother-hell-hortense-wood-led-rise-barbara-bloody-babs-graham-article-1.446937. Accessed April 17, 2015.

Cairns, Kathleen. 2013. *Proof of Guilt: Barbara Graham and the Politics of Executing Women in America.* Lincoln: University of Nebraska Press.

Gillespie, Kay. 2000. *Dancehall Ladies: Executed Women of the 20th Century.* Lanham, MD: University Press of America, Inc.

Headsman. 2011. *1955: Barbara Graham, of "I Want to Live" Fame.* http://www.executedtoday.com/2011/06/03/1955-barbara-graham-i-want-to-live/. Accessed April 17, 2015.

Linn, Sarah. 2013. *Proof of Guilt: The Tragic Life and Public Death of Barbara Graham.* http://www.kcet.org/arts/artbound/counties/san-luis-obispo/proof-of-guilt-barbara-graham.html. Accessed April 17, 2015.

Graham, David. *See* Zamora, Diane (1978–) and David Graham (1977–)

Gravano, Salvatore "Sammy the Bull" (1945–)

Salvatore "Sammy the Bull" Gravano is one of history's most famous underbosses of the century. Enraged by a recorded conversation between John Gotti (1940–2002) and Frank Locascio (1933–), and feeling as though he was being set up, Gravano provided the testimony that ended Gotti's reign as the Gambino crime family boss. His testimony also contributed to the conviction of at least a dozen other crime family members, capos, associates, and informants. Most of what is known of Gravano's life prior to the testimony comes from his interview for the 1996 book *Underboss: Sammy the Bull Gravano's Story of Life in the Mafia*, written by Peter Maas.

Salvatore Gravano was born on March 12, 1945, in Brooklyn, New York, to Italian immigrants from Sicily. While in school, children often made fun of Gravano because of a learning disorder (dyslexia). Eventually, Gravano had enough of the harassment and began fighting anyone who offended him. Although his family gave him the nickname "Sammy" because he looked like his Uncle Sammy, around the age of 10 he received the remainder of his nickname "the Bull" after he was involved in a fight. The fight, which took place in front of a local mafia hangout, was in response to some older kids stealing his bicycle. A wiseguy (a fully initiated member or associate of the mafia) who helped break up the fight exclaimed, "he's like a little bull, Sammy the Bull." By his 16th birthday, Gravano dropped out of high school, started spending all of his time with the Rampers street gang, and began running errands for the local wiseguys. Most of Gravano's crimes with the Rampers included stealing cars for parts and commercial property burglaries.

In the early 1960s, Gravano was arrested twice—first for assaulting a police officer and then for a burglary—before he was drafted into the army. However, after basic training he became involved in gambling and loansharking while stationed in Indiana. After serving two years in the army, Gravano received an honorable discharge and went back to his life with the Rampers. In 1968, Gravano was invited to become an associate in the Colombo crime family and assigned to capo (i.e., high-ranking full member of a crime family) Thomas "Shorty" Spero's (1923–1980) crew. Shortly after, Gravano added murder to his already-long list of crimes, admitting to participating in at least 19 since the early 1970s. However, Gravano claims that his first assignment, the murder of Joe Colucci in 1970, was the only murder in which he actually pulled the trigger.

In 1971, Gravano married 17-year-old Deborah Scibetta, with whom he had a daughter and a son. Shortly after the wedding, Gravano partnered with Tommy Spero—nephew of capo Shorty Spero and former fellow member in the Rampers—to open a shop named "The Hole in the Wall." Together Gravano and Spero sold merchandise they claimed was "hot" (i.e., stolen), but were actually only slightly damaged products that department stores would not purchase for resale. Soon after they let Ralph Spero —Tommy's father and brother of capo Shorty Spero—in on the business, Gravano discovered that he was only there to steal the profits. Despite Gravano selling his half of the store, tension remained between him and the Spero family. It was known that the Gambino crime family wished to take Gravano in, so to resolve the conflict Shorty Spero allowed Gravano to transfer from the Colombos to the Gambinos. With the Gambinos, Gravano was assigned as an associate under capo Salvatore "Toddo" Aurello.

In 1975, with the Gambino crime family under the reign of new Don Paul Castellano (1915–1985), Gravano was "made" (i.e., a formally initiated member) into the family (Maas 1996; Raab 2005). In the late 1970s Gravano and his brother-in-law, Edward Garafola, went into business together for plumbing and drywall. Castellano, having a great interest in the construction industry, took a great liking to Gravano and not only relied on Gravano to fix problems at his home (often referred to as the White House), but also invested in his and Garafola's company. Under Castellano's guidance Gravano opened the Plaza Suite, an afterhours club that doubled as his construction headquarters.

In 1985, the Gambino underboss and John Gotti's mentor, Aniello Dellacroce (1914–1985), passed away from cancer. Despite the fact that Gotti was next to succeed as underboss, Castellano appointed his bodyguard Thomas Bilotti (1940–1985) for the position. Outraged, Gotti ordered a hit on both Castellano and Bilotti, recruiting Frank DeCicco (1935–1986) and Gravano for the job. Gravano hoped that DeCicco would become the new boss, so he agreed to the hit. Upon Castellano and Bilotti's murder, Gotti took the position of Don and DeCicco underboss in the Gambino crime family. It was also during this time that the government began surveillance on Gotti.

In the summer of 1990, the Gambino crime family realized that the government was planning another indictment for Gotti over the Castellano/Bilotti murders. By fall, although Joseph Armone was current underboss (DeCicco died in 1986 car bombing), Gotti appointed Gravano the official underboss knowing that he could be incarcerated for more than a year, even if acquitted. In 1990, police swarmed the Ravenite club and arrested Gotti, Gravano, and Frank Locascio. At Gravano's bail hearing, police played surveillance recordings of a conversation between Gotti and Locascio depicting Gravano as a crazed killer. Enraged, and feeling as though Gotti was setting him up to take the fall for everything, Gravano prepared a deal with the government. Despite having the surveillance recordings, prosecutor John Gleeson knew the Castellano–Bilotti murders were the weakest part of the case; thus, having Gravano as a witness would place Gotti at the scene and solidify the case. Gravano's testimony did just that; the jury returned with a guilty verdict in 1992.

Gravano also gave testimony against George Pape (a bribed juror), a New York Police Department employee (informant for the Gambino family), Genovese Don Vincent "Chin" Gigante (1928–2005), Joseph "Joe the German" Watts, and several capos of the Gambino, Colombo, Genovese, and DeCavalcante crime families. In 1994, because of his cooperation, Judge Glasser sentenced Gravano to only five years in prison and three years of supervision upon his release despite his participation in numerous crimes, including murder. After his release, several of Gravano's victim's families filed a civil suit against Gravano, Peter Maas (*Underboss* author), HarperCollins publishing, International Creative Management, and 20th Century Fox under the New York State "Son of Sam" statute because of the royalties he received for the book and movie. The Son of Sam statute in New York prevents convicted felons from profiting on their crimes. However, in 1998 the New York Supreme Court dismissed the case basing the decision on the fact that Gravano was convicted of federal, not state, crimes. The state appellate court upheld the decision in 2000. After authorities entered Gravano into the Witness Protection Program, he turned to a life of selling drugs in Arizona. In 2000, Gravano and his family (wife and both children) all pled guilty to masterminding an ecstasy drug ring that operated from Arizona to New York. Gravano is still alive at the time of this writing and serving his prison sentence (a maximum of 23 years).

JENNIFER A. HAEGELE

See also: Costello, Frank (1891–1973); Genovese, Vito (1897–1969); Gigante, Vincent "the Chin" (1928–2005); Gotti, John (1940–2002); Luciano, Charles "Lucky" (1897–1962)

Further Reading

Gotti, John, and Salvatore Gravano. 1992. *The Gotti Tapes: Including the Testimony of Salvatore (Sammy the Bull) Gravano.* New York: Times Books.

Maas, Peter. 1996. *Underboss: Sammy the Bull Gravano's Story of Life in the Mafia.* New York City: HarperCollins.

Raab, Selwyn. 2005. *Five Families. The Rise, Decline, and Resurgence of America's Most Powerful Mafia Empires.* New York: St. Martin's Press.

Great Brink's Robbery (1950)

On a January 17, 1950, 11 men robbed the Brink's Armored Car Depot in Boston, Massachusetts, getting away with an astonishing $2.7 million—the largest heist in the U.S. history at that point. The crime had been meticulously researched, choreographed, and executed leaving behind virtually no evidence. It was proclaimed by the media as "the near-perfect crime" and by the FBI as "the crime of the century." After six years of extensive investigation and thousands of leads, costing the FBI nearly $29 million, the case was finally solved. The nine surviving criminals were charged just days before the statute of limitations ran out. This case gained national attention, spawned numerous books and movies, and helped affirm the FBI as a premiere law enforcement agency.

The mastermind of the robbery was Anthony (Tony) Pino, a professional thief and safecracker. Pino with the assistance of Joseph "Big Joe" McGinnis, Joseph "Specs" O'Keefe and Stanley "Gus" Gusciora observed the daily operations of the building, including staffing and armored truck routes. Pino was eventually able to identify the activity inside the building based on which lights were on. During this time, Pino entered the building on several occasions wearing various disguises and under false pretenses to learn the layout of the facility and steal keys.

Approximately two years prior to the robbery, Pino began to recruit several criminal associates who had the skills necessary to complete the crime, including Vincent Costa, Michael Vincent Geagan, Adolph "Jazz" Maffie, Thomas Francis Richardson, Henry Baker, James "Jimma" Faherty, and Joseph "Barney" Banfield. Together, they began routinely and surreptitiously entering the Brink's building after employees had left for the day. The gang discovered security at the facility was severely lacking. The gang continued to enter the building, memorized the floor layout, examined internal records revealing when the most cash was on hand and removing door locks to duplicate keys. These activities continued for two years without detection. By the time of the actual robbery, the gang had held several rehearsals of the heist and aborted six previous attempts before deciding the conditions were favorable.

On January 17, 1950, shortly before 7:00 p.m., seven men entered the Brink's Armored Car Depot at 169 Prince Street in Northern Boston. The men were dressed similarly to Brink's employees, wore gloves to avoid leaving fingerprints, rubber-soled shoes to reduce noise, and Halloween-type masks to conceal their identity. They moved through the building to the second floor with methodical precision, just as they had rehearsed. When they arrived at the cash sorting room, the robbers forced the staff to lie on the ground, bound them with ropes, covered their mouths with tape, and took four revolvers from them.

In less than 30 minutes, the robbers exited the building with $1,218,211 in cash and $1,557,184 in checks, money orders, and other securities weighing nearly half a ton. They joined two others in a stolen pickup truck and fled to a nearby house. Once they arrived, they quickly counted and distributed a small portion of the money. They agreed not to use the remainder of the money until the statute of limitations had expired, in six years' time. After the hasty meeting, each man scattered to establish an alibi and dispose of any evidence.

Shortly after the men had made their escape the Brink's employees managed to free themselves and reported the robbery. The Boston Police Department responded immediately and began to search for evidence, interview witnesses, and question suspects. The only evidence discovered was the tape and rope used to constrain the workers, a chauffeur's cap, and a witness who observed a truck leaving the area. The next morning local newspaper reporters clamored at the crime scene and published headlines describing the heist as, "Biggest Robbery in U.S. History," "The Perfect Crime," and "The Great Brink's Robbery." Millions of Americans across the country were captivated by the crime as perhaps no other crime during the 1950s. The media attention also captured the interest of the Federal Bureau of Investigations. Within days, the FBI claimed the robbery was a federal crime (due to the federal security notes stolen) and took the lead on the investigation billing it "the crime of the century."

Due to a lack of evidence, the investigation floundered from the beginning. The only additional evidence recovered was the recovery of several of the stolen revolvers and the suspected getaway vehicle, which had been cut into small pieces and placed in a junk yard. Yet the investigators relentlessly followed up on thousands of leads, conducting dragnets of potential suspects and accomplices throughout the underworld of Boston and of infamous criminals nationwide.

Over time, the Boston community began to find the investigation amusing and idealized the robbery suspects as a type of American heroes. Many comedians, including Ed Sullivan and Fred Allen, mocked the case on national television and radio programs. The FBI, however, believed they knew who committed the crime and began grand jury hearings on 10 of the 11 men involved. However, the evidence presented was based solely on suspicion and entirely circumstantial. Therefore, a Boston grand jury returned a no true bill (refusing to indict due to lack of evidence). The investigation continued to languish for years with few new leads.

However, there was an internal falling-out developing among the gang members. Several, including Specs O'Keefe, were arrested on unrelated charges. After he was released and returned to Boston in 1954, he began to badger the other gang members for his share of the money. Eventually, three separate assassination attempts on O'Keefe occurred before he was arrested again on unrelated charges. On January 6, 1956, after repeated aggressive visits by the FBI, a disgruntled O'Keefe admitted his involvement in the Brink's robbery. O'Keefe agreed to testify on behalf of the prosecution for a reduced sentence.

On January 11, 1956, charges were filed against all 11 involved in the robbery. The charges came just six days before the statute of limitations would expire. Within a few weeks, all the suspects were in custody and later that year eight of the men faced trial for robbery and other charges. Despite pleading innocent (except for O'Keefe), all the men were found guilty and sentenced to life in prison. Two other men (Gusciora and Banfield) had died prior to the trial, and O'Keefe had turned state's evidence against the others involved. O'Keefe was in prison for only four years and upon release coauthored a book about the robbery. The others served an average of 15 years of a life sentence.

The investigation of "the crime of the century" lasted six years, becoming one of the more famous FBI investigations and costing the agency $29 million to complete. Despite the massive expenditure of time and effort, only $51,906 was recovered. Several books have been written about the crime and four movies have been produced based on the incident. Even after decades, The Great Brink's Robbery remains one of the largest thefts in the U.S. history. Given the lack of evidence left behind and the difficulty of the investigation, it almost was the perfect crime.

BENJAMIN F. STICKLE

See also: James, Jesse (1847–1882); Quantrill's Raiders (1861–1865); Purple Gang (Detroit); Ray Allen Gang (1974–1980)

Further Reading

Behn, Noel. 1977. *Big Stick-up at Brink's!*. New York: Putnam.

The Brink's Job. 1978. DVD. Directed by William Freidkin. Hollywood, CA: Universal Studios, 2011.

"Famous Cases & Criminals: The Brinks Robbery." FBI. http://www.fbi.gov/about-us/history/famous-cases/brinks-robbery. Accessed March 1, 2015.

Keefe, Joseph James, and Bob Considine. 1961. *The Men Who Robbed Brink's: The Inside Story of One of the Most Famous Holdups in the History of Crime*. New York: Random House.

Schorow, Stephanie. 2008. *The Crime of the Century: How the Brink's Robbers Stole Millions and the Hearts of Boston*. Beverly, MA: Commonwealth Editions.

Great Migration. *See* East St. Louis Race Riot (1917) and Chicago Race Riot (1919)

Green, Debora (1951–)

Debora Green was a successful physician and mother of three who had achieved an enviable life before she set a fire that killed two of her children and she attempted to poison her husband to death. Green's was a sensational case covered scrupulously by the media that spurred a *New York Times* #1 best-selling novel by true-crime author Ann Rule. *Deadly Women*, a true-crime documentary series on Investigation Discovery also included the case in a 2010 episode. After an extensive investigation, Debora Green was charged with two counts of murder in the first degree, two counts of attempted murder, and aggravated arson. Her $3,000,000 bail was the highest ever ordered at that time in Johnson County, Kansas. Debora eventually pled no contest to the charges against her, denying any memory of what happened the night of the fire. She submitted a request for a new trial on the foundation of having been left incompetent by the psychiatric medications she was taking, but withdrew it to avoid the death penalty. A second request was denied in 2005, and Debora continues to serve two concurrent 40-year prison sentences. It seems that despite her intelligence and attainment, Debora's lack of self-control and her need to punish her husband exceeded her love for her children.

Debora Green thrived in school, graduating as co-valedictorian of her high school. She graduated college in 1972 and went on to study emergency medicine. It was then that she met Duane Green, her first husband. The marriage was short-lived, but ended cordially. Debora Green soon met Michael Farrar, a medical student, and they married in 1979. They were living in Ohio when their first child, Timothy, was born. Kate was born two years later. Both Debora and Michael joined established medical practices near Kansas City, Missouri. Debora started her own oncology practice soon after, but took time off for the birth of the couple's third child, Kelly. The Farrar children were enrolled in an exclusive private school, and Debora had achieved a desirable life complete with her own medical practice and an attractive, successful husband. In 1992, Debora gave up her practice and became a homemaker, working part-time from the house processing medical peer reviews and Medicaid applications. Those who worked with her at this time described Debora as withdrawn and callous, having displayed obsessive resentful demeanors toward her husband.

By the early 1990s, Michael Farrar was working long hours to avoid the turmoil at home, while Debora escorted the children to their numerous activities. There is speculation that Debora began involving the children in the marital problems, causing them to resent and defy their father. Timothy and Michael Farrar were especially argumentative with each other. Michael asked Debora for a divorce in 1994 and moved out of the family home. The separation only encouraged a reconciliation, and the couple eventually purchased a luxurious home in the elite Kansas City neighborhood of Prairie Village. Debora and Michael Farrar put effort into making their marriage

work once the family moved into the new house, but the improvements did not last long. Michael decided to delay suggesting divorce again, however, as not to ruin a trip the family had planned to Peru. During the trip in the summer of 1995, Michael met Margaret Hacker, a registered nurse also unhappy in her marriage. The two began a physical affair after the trip, and Michael soon asked Debora for a divorce.

In the early hours of October 24, 1995, Michael Farrar received a phone call about a fire at the Prairie Village home where Debora still lived with the children. When firefighters arrived, Debora and 10-year-old Kate were outside the blazing home. Debora seemingly stared at the fire quietly, while Kate begged the responders to help her brother and sister who were still inside. Despite two search attempts, the house quickly became consumed by flames. Thirteen-year-old Timothy and six-year-old Kelly died in the fire. Noting the swift destruction of the house, authorities considered the fire suspicious and an investigation ensued. The family members were taken for questioning by the police. Debora told police she woke up to the fire alarm, and opened her bedroom door to find the hallway full of smoke. She escaped the house via the deck attached to her bedroom. Timothy was calling for her on the intercom system, asking what he should do. Debora explained that she instructed Timothy to stay in the house and wait to be rescued. She then went to a neighbor's house to summon 911. Meanwhile, Kate had climbed out onto the roof of the house and jumped to safety. During the interview, detectives noted that Debora remained calm and did not appear to have been crying. Debora was released from questioning.

Michael Farrar was also questioned by police. He told them about health problems he had been experiencing for two months. Shortly after returning from the trip to Peru, Michael had become ill with vomiting, nausea, and diarrhea. Michael attributed the illness to his travels and soon recovered. His health worsened again the next week, however; and he was hospitalized with a serious fever and dehydration. Doctors were unable to pinpoint the source of his problems, and Michael also contracted sepsis. He recovered again, only to suffer from a third bout of symptoms after eating dinner that Debora had prepared. Michael's girlfriend, Margaret Hacker, suggested Debora was poisoning him. Once he discovered castor beans and empty vials of potassium chloride in Debora's purse, he contacted police in an attempt to get Debora into psychiatric care. She was diagnosed with bipolar disorder and suicidal impulses during her four days in the hospital. Michael researched castor beans in the meantime, and concluded that Debora had been poisoning him with the ricin in the beans. It was then that he moved out of the family home, about a month before the deadly fire. Michael recounted to police that he had confronted Debora the night before the fire, saying that he knew she had poisoned him and he would protect the children if she could not get her life in order.

The arson investigation revealed that a flammable liquid had been poured throughout the house, stopping at the door of the master bedroom. Though Debora denied ever being close to the flames, her hair samples and bathrobe showed evidence of singeing. Neighbors reported that her hair was wet when she came calling for help. Detectives continued to investigate the fire and deaths, now alerted to the possible attempted murder of Michael Farrar through poisoning. Debora Green (who reverted to her former last name after the divorce) was arrested on November 22, 1995. Her defense team claimed that the fire had been set by her son, Timothy Green. They also accused him of poisoning his father, Michael Farrar. The defense even argued that Debora's psychiatric medications were responsible for her lack of emotion following the fire. Faced with the death penalty and overwhelming evidence against her, Debora Green agreed to an Alford plea of no contest to the five charges. She acknowledged setting the fire, but denied any recollection of it. She maintained her claim that Timothy was the one who poisoned Michael. The judge accepted Debora's plea, and subsequent motions to withdraw it have been unsuccessful. She continues to serve two 40-year sentences at the Topeka Correctional Facility.

NICOLE LAROSA

See also: Barfield, Velma (1932–1984); Eubanks, Susan (1964–); Riggs, Christina (1971–2000)

Further Reading

"Kansas Doctor Is Accused in Fire That Killed 2 of Her Children." 1995. *The New York Times.* November 24. http://www.nytimes.com/1995/11/24/us/kansas-doctor-is-accused-in-fire-that-killed-2-of-her-children.html. Accessed April 17, 2015.

Knox, J., director. 2010. In Luscombe, J., executive producer. *Deadly Women: The Sacred Bond (II).* Investigation Discovery. Video.

Rule, Ann. 1997. *Bitter Harvest: A Woman's Fury, a Mother's Sacrifice.* New York: Pocket Books.

Green, Erica Michelle Marie. *See* "Precious Doe" (2001)

Green River Killer. *See* Ridgway, Gary Leon (1949–)

Grimes Sisters, Murder of (1956)

The murder of the Grimes sisters remains one of the United States' most famous unsolved murder mysteries. On Friday, December 28, 1956, 15-year-old Barbara Jeanne Grimes and 13-year-old Patricia Kathleen Grimes disappeared after having gone to Brighton Theater in Chicago to see the Elvis Presley film, *Love Me Tender.* The girls were two of six children to Joseph and Loretta Grimes, a truck driver and an office clerk, respectively. They left home at 7:30 p.m. They had been seen by friends at the theater at about 9:30 p.m., and one school friend said that she sat next to them during the movie. The girls lived at a walking distance from the theater and were expected home before midnight. Sometime after 2:00 a.m. their mother, Loretta Grimes, reported them missing.

Initially, the police had hoped that the case was one of mere runaways, especially as reports of sightings poured in. A bus driver thought he dropped them off after 11:00 p.m. A security guard thought he gave them directions thereafter. A school mate thought she saw Patricia the next day. As late as January 9, persons reported seeing them in various business establishments—at a hotel and at a music counter. On January 14, the parents of a classmate of Patricia reported getting two mysterious telephone calls from a frightened girl whom they believed was Patricia asking for their daughter, but the person hung up abruptly each time. There was even a fake ransom demand from a mental patient and a report of a sighting of the girls in Nashville fueling speculation that they had run off to meet Elvis. Some reports of seeing the girls in a car consistently referred to a Mercury model vehicle. The girls' mother, however, asserted consistently that it was not like her daughters to run away, leaving clothing, supplies, and Christmas presents behind. As time passed, concerns grew. The eventual extensive search for the Grimes sisters included officers from neighboring towns such as Willow Springs, Bedford Park, Bridgeview, La Grange, Summit, Justice, and the Cook County Forest Reserve. The detectives on the case were Ernest Spiotto, Neal Carr, Sheldon Teller, Richard Austin, James Micus, and Albert Parks. In 1974, Spiotto, the only one left on the case from the original investigation reported that they had no credible suspects.

Their bodies were found January 22, 1957, along German Church Road, a highway southwest of Chicago, in the suburbs of Willow Spring. The girls' frozen bodies were naked with ice pick-like wounds on Barbara's chest and other bruises on Patricia. The cause of death was recorded as exposure to severe cold. The person who found them, Leonard Prescott, thought that he was looking at mannequins as he drove home. He then returned to the sight with his wife when he realized that he was looking at actual bodies and he contacted the police. The girls were believed to have been there for about two weeks. Some of the bruises on the body were attributed to animals, likely rodents. The girls had apparently died within 12 hours of going missing because they had their December 28 dinner still in their stomachs. The search for evidence was further hindered by the weather. The funeral for the girls was donated and the service was attended by the likes of Chicago's mayor Richard Daley. The story remained front-page news in Chicago for some time.

Thousands of persons were interviewed. By January 27, 1957, a 21-year-old dishwasher named Edward Lee "Dennis" Bedwell was charged with murdering the two sisters after a confession. He claimed that he and a companion named Frank held the girls captive for seven days before beating them and leaving them by the road. Bedwell was eventually cleared of all charges when it was determined that he was mentally retarded and had been coerced by police into a false confession after being held for four days. His friend Frank, actually William Willingham, a habitual drunk familiar to the police, denied any involvement. Bedwell's reports did not match the physical evidence from the bodies. His claims of meals with the girls did not match their stomach contents. The sheriff at the time however, Joseph Lohman, reportedly died in 1969 believing that Bedwell was the Grimes sisters' killer.

A lesser known suspect in the case was Walter Krantz, a self-proclaimed psychic. On January 15, Krantz called the police saying that he saw where the Grimes sisters' bodies were in a dream. He became a suspect when it turned out that he was less than two miles off from the actual location.

A man familiar with the investigation claimed that the police heard that the girls drank with adult men at bars (a point that virtually everyone who knew the girls well denied) and that their dead bodies showed signs of sexual assault but that these details were not made public to avoid sullying their memory.

Related Murders

There were several major cases that occurred at about the same time in around Chicago, and there was some speculation that the cases may be related in some way. Three Chicago school boys of similar ages (Robert Peterson, 13, and brothers John and Anton Schuessler, 13 and 11, respectively) went missing in October 1955. Their bodies were found in a forest reserve. The boys had all been strangled. A third murder of a child that shocked Chicago was that of Judith Mae Anderson, age 15, on August 17, 1957. Her dismembered corpse was found in containers in Montrose Harbor. She had been shot. A massive law enforcement campaign followed these events to teach children to be wary of strangers.

A more recent clue in the story of the Grimes sisters case is that Loretta Grimes, who died in 1989, reported having received a telephone call after another 15-year-old girl's nude body was found, Bonnie Leigh Scott. The person boasted about having gotten away with both sets of murders, Scott and the Grimes. He mentioned details about her daughters that had not been made public, but the caller has not been identified.

Camille Gibson

See also: Dugard, Jaycee, Kidnapping of (1991); Kanka, Megan, Murder of (1994); Ramsey, JonBenét, Murder of (1996); Walsh, Adam, Kidnapping and Murder of (1981)

Further Reading
"Bodies of 2 Sisters Found Near Chicago." 1957. *New York Times*. January 23, p. 16.
Griffin, W. 1974. "Probe Turns Up Few Clues: Grimes Killing Still Baffling Police." *Chicago Tribune*. December 26, p. 4.
"Hunt 4 Men Named Trudy in Grimes Murders Probe." 1957. *Chicago Tribune*. February 9, p. 2.
"Man Held in Chicago as Killer of 2 Girls." 1957. *New York Times*. January 28, p. 46.
Shaffer, T. 1997. "Death and the Maidens." *Chicago Reader*, March 20.

Grossberg, Amy (1978–) and Brian Peterson (1978–)

Amy Grossberg and Brian Peterson, two upper-class white college kids, were charged with murder in the first degree of their newborn baby on November 12, 1996, in Newark, Delaware. This particular crime, neonaticide, the killing of a newborn in the first 24 hours of life, is usually committed by mothers who are unwed, poor, uneducated. This case grabbed the attention of the media and the country because both parents participated in the murder, and the couple was not poor and uneducated.

Grossberg and Peterson grew up in the suburb of Wyckoff, New Jersey, and started dating at Ramapo High school. Both were raised in an image-conscious family where the teenagers' status symbolized the parents' image in the community. The per capita income in Wyckoff was almost twice the national average. Teens from Wyckoff were groomed for college and were expected to excel professionally and personally.

Amy and Brian followed the dreams of their community and matriculated to the University of Delaware and Gettysburg College, respectively. What they didn't know, or let anyone else know, is their baby was matriculating as well. While in college, Amy concealed her pregnancy from everyone, even when she visited her mom two weeks prior to her delivery.

Amy Grossberg, left, and Brian Peterson appear at the "Holiday Ball" in this 1996 Ramapo, New Jersey, High School yearbook photo. The two college freshmen from the New York City suburbs of Bergen County, New Jersey, were accused of murder in the death of their baby whose body was found in a garbage bin. (AP Photo/Ramapo High School Yearbook)

On November 12, 1996, in room 220 at the local Comfort Inn, Amy gave birth to a baby boy. Brian was the only person by her side. Brian picked up the baby with a towel to slide him into a bag. This movement tore the umbilical cord causing blood to splatter on the bed sheets. With Amy in a hysterical state, Brian threw the baby in a dumpster behind the motel.

However, their naiveté caught up with them. They failed to wait for Amy to expel the placenta, so a few hours later, Amy started having seizures and had to be rushed to the hospital. Doctors, recognizing the evidence of after-birth, became suspicious when Amy denied that she had been pregnant. Brian finally admitted to the police that he put what he thought was a stillborn child in the dumpster behind the hotel. Delaware's attorney general charged the couple with first-degree murder with the possibility of a death sentence. Interestingly, the charges were criticized as too harsh as many pundits believed that this couple was young and they simply panicked. What many critics did not know was that in typical neonaticide cases, that involve poor, uneducated women, capital murder is almost always charged. It seemed as if law enforcement and prosecutors were being criticized for treating this upper middle class couple the same as others who commit the same crime.

Ultimately, Amy and Brian pled guilty for killing their newborn son. Expert testimony proved that, contrary to Amy and Brian's contention that the boy was stillborn, the child was alive and that the cause of death was multiple skull fractures. The fractures were likely caused when the baby was thrown into the trash bin.

On March 9, 1998, Brian pled guilty to manslaughter in exchange to testify against Amy. This testimony was damning to Amy. Brian claimed that Amy refused to get an abortion and after the delivery she demanded that he discard the child.

Ultimately, on April 22, Amy also pled guilty to manslaughter. Amy was sentenced to two and half years at a Women's Correctional Institute, while Brian was sentenced to two years of incarceration. After they were released, both Amy and Brian went their separate ways and moved on with their lives. Amy started her own business with her parents and stayed in New Jersey and Brian moved to Florida where he lives with his wife.

Charlisa Holloway Edelin and Sherleen Sabin

See also: Downs, Elizabeth Diane Frederickson (1955–); Smith, Susan (1971–); Tinning, Marybeth (1942–); Yates, Andrea (1964–)

Further Reading

Most, Doug. 1999. *Always in Our Hearts: The Story of Amy Grossberg, Brian Peterson, and the Baby They Didn't Want.* Hackensack, NJ: Record.

Shelton, Joy, et al. 2011. "Neonaticide: A Comprehensive Review of Investigative and Pathologic Aspects of 55 Cases." *Journal of Family Violence* 26 (4): 263–276.

"Teen Pleads Guilty in Death of Newborn Left in Trash Bin." 1998. CNN. April 22. http://www.photius.com/dumpster.html. Accessed April 17, 2015.

Guiteau, Charles. *See* Garfield, James, Assassination of (July 2, 1881)

Gunness, Belle (1859–c. 1908)

Norwegian born Brynhild Paulsdatter Størseth immigrated to the United States in 1881, assuming a more American-style name that would eventually coin her as Belle Gunness—a lonely-hearts killer who is widely considered to be one of America's first female serial killers. Between 1884 and 1908, Gunness reportedly murdered more than 40 people, including husbands, suitors, and her own children. While most of the deaths occurred through poisoning, either by chloroform or by strychnine, the most notable signature of Gunness was the disposal of her victims inside of her farm's hog pen. Gunness collected insurance payments from her victims, or (in the case of her suitors) advised them to bring money with them for various reasons. She allegedly accumulated more than $250,000, equivalent to approximately $6.3 million today. Originally thought to have perished in a fire that destroyed her home and killed her children, there is evidence to suggest that the scene was planned and Gunness escaped. For decades later, sightings of Gunness poured in from major cities across the United States, though no concrete evidence has been found that confirms or denies that she survived.

After moving to Chicago in 1884, Gunness married Albert Sorenson and had four children (Caroline, Axel, Myrtle, and Lucy). Caroline and Axel allegedly died of acute colitis as infants, though some hold the opinion that they were Gunness's first victims—the symptoms of acute colitis are very similar to poisoning, and both children were reported to have life insurance policies that were paid after their demise. Many, however, consider her husband to be the first victim, Sorenson, died on July 30, 1900; while the first doctor to see him suspected strychnine poisoning, the family doctor had been treating him for an enlarged heart, causing the coroner to officially list heart failure as the cause of death. Gunness applied for insurance payouts on two separate policies one day after the funeral, policies that happened to overlap only on the day of her husband's death. Once the insurance had paid out, Gunness purchased a farm on the outskirts of La Porte, Indiana, in 1901. On April 1, 1902, she married Norwegian-born Peter Gunness, and eight months later Peter died from a "tragic accident" involving scalding hot brine and a traumatic head injury from a sausage-grinding machine. Once again a hefty life insurance policy was paid out, causing suspicion amongst the people of La Porte. Shortly thereafter, in May 1903, Gunness gave birth to her fifth child, Phillip.

Belle Gunness employed farm hand Ray Lamphere in 1907. She then began advertising in matrimonial columns of the Chicago newspapers, with several middle-aged men responding. Suitors would arrive carrying large amounts of cash, and would disappear a few days later. This continued steadily for close to a year. Supposedly, Lamphere fell in love with Gunness, and was willing to assist in the disposal of the bodies. However, he started causing issues whenever the suitors came around, and Gunness fired him in February 1908.

Asle Helgelien began to worry that his brother had not returned home, and reached out to Belle. Based on Helgelien's suspicion and insistency to visit, Gunness now viewed Lamphere as a significant liability. She informed a lawyer in La Porte that she feared for her and her children's lives due to death threats from Lamphere. Gunness had the lawyer draw up a will in case the threats were carried out, leaving her entire estate to her children; afterward, she paid off her mortgage for the farm and withdrew almost everything from her accounts. As she never reported the threats to the police, it is speculated that Gunness was actually planning an arson.

In April 1908, Joe Maxson (Lamphere's replacement) awoke from smelling smoke in his room on the second floor of the Gunness residence, and was barely able to escape. Four bodies were discovered inside—the children and (supposedly) Gunness. However, the female remains could not immediately be identified, as the head was missing. While the corpse stood 5'3" and approximately 150 pounds, Gunness was reportedly taller than 5'8" and weighed between 180 and 200 pounds. However, a piece

of bridgework was found at the scene after authorities began sifting the remains. Gunness's dentist identified them as belonging to her, leading Coroner Charles Mack to conclude that the body was indeed the remains of Belle Gunness. County sheriff Smutzer had been aware of Gunness's claims of threats by Lamphere, causing Lamphere to be arrested and charged with murder and arson.

Around this time, Asle Helgelien appeared in La Porte and discussed his suspicions with Sheriff Smutzer. Joe Maxson then came forward with information pertaining to large loads of dirt ordered to the hog pen by Gunness, subsequently leading to plans regarding excavation of the hog pen. On May 3, 1908, the first set of remains were unearthed. While the exact number of individuals uncovered from the property cannot be determined due to poor recovery methods, the widely accepted approximation stands at 12. Several of these individuals could not be positively identified due to the condition of the remains.

On May 22, 1908, Ray Lamphere was tried for murder and arson. Lamphere's lawyer was able to utilize testimony from a local jeweler and local doctors showing that the bridgework used for Gunness's identification must have been planted there after the fire due to lack of evident damage. Therefore, while Lamphere was found guilty of arson, he was acquitted of murder, and was sentenced to 20 years in state prison. In January 1910, the Reverend E.A. Schell revealed a confession made by Ray Lamphere as he was dying. Lamphere claimed that Gunness was a murderess, and was still alive. He detailed her methods of killing, including drugging victims before splitting their heads with a meat chopper, using chloroform when the victim was sleeping, or poisoning the victim's coffee with strychnine. She varied her disposal methods as well, performing dissections before bundling the remains and disposing of them in the hog pen, dissolving the remains in the hog-scalding vat with quicklime, or feeding the remains to the hogs. Lamphere also stated that the headless female misidentified as Gunness was lured from Chicago, on the premise of gaining employment as a housekeeper. Gunness allegedly drugged the woman before bashing in her head and decapitating the body; she then disposed of the head in a swamp. Afterward, she used chloroform on her children, smothered them, and dragged them and the headless victim to the basement before setting the house ablaze. Lamphere did admit to helping Gunness, though he claimed she did not meet up with him as planned, and instead escaped into the woods. His final revelation was that Gunness had murdered approximately 42 men by his count, and had allegedly accumulated more than $250,000—a fortune in those days, equal to around $6.3 million in present day. Gunness was allegedly sighted in cities and towns across the United States for decades after her crimes. No concrete evidence exists to explain the fate of Belle Gunness after the fiery destruction of the La Porte farm.

CASSANDRA RAUSCH

See also: Lonely Hearts Killers (1947–1949); Markoff, Philip (1986–2010); Toppan, Jane (1854–1938); Wuornos, Aileen (1956–2002)

Further Reading

Chronicling America: Historic American Newspapers. 1908. The Library of Congress. *The Times Dispatch.* (Richmond, VA). http://chroniclingamerica.loc.gov/lccn/sn 85038615/1908-06-01/ed-1/seq-3/. Accessed April 17, 2015.

De La Torre, Lillian. 1955. *The Truth about Belle Gunness.* New York: Gold Medal Books.

Duke, Thomas Samuel. 1910. *Celebrated Criminal Cases of America.* San Francisco: The James H. Barry Company.

Langlois, Janet. 1978. "Belle Gunness, the Lady Bluebeard: Community Legend as Metaphor." *Journal of the Folklore Institute* 15:147–160.